BEGINNINGS OF CIVILIZATION

Japan c. 3000 B.C.

Shang China c. 1600 B.C.

Vietnam c. 8000 B.C.

China c. 4000 B.C.

Indus Valley c. 3000 B.C.

Indus Valley c. 3000 B.C.

Middle East c. 8000 B.C.

Sumer c. 4000 B.C.

Kush c. 1000 B.C.

Egypt c. 3100 B.C.

Hittites c. 1300 B.C.

Central Africa c. 3000 B.C.

Greece c. 4000 B.C.

Greece c. 1300 B.C.

Nile Valley c. 5000 B.C.

Chavín c. 900 B.C.

Olmecs c. 1200 B.C.

Peru c. 4000 B.C.

Mesoamerica c. 5000 B.C.

PACIFIC OCEAN

INDIAN OCEAN

ATLANTIC OCEAN

PACIFIC OCEAN

N
W — E
S

Early Agricultural Communities

Early Civilization

Africa

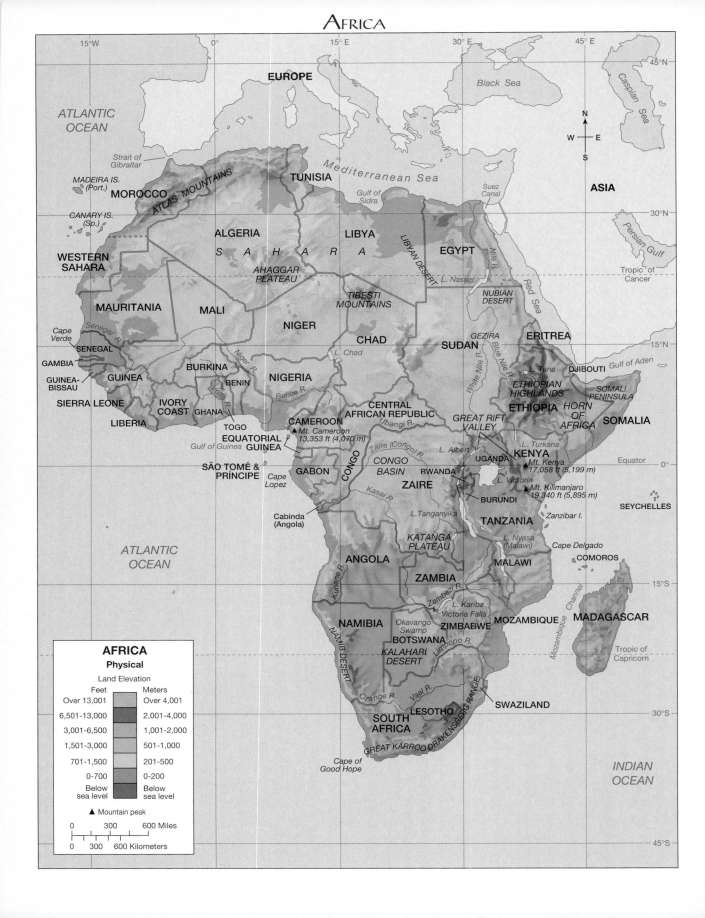

EUROPE

ASIA

ATLANTIC OCEAN

Black Sea

Caspian Sea

Strait of Gibraltar

MADEIRA IS. (Port.)

MOROCCO

TUNISIA

Mediterranean Sea

Gulf of Sidra

Suez Canal

CANARY IS. (Sp.)

ALGERIA

LIBYA

EGYPT

WESTERN SAHARA

S A H A R A

LIBYAN DESERT

Tropic of Cancer

AHAGGAR PLATEAU

L. Nasser

Nile R.

Red Sea

Persian Gulf

MAURITANIA

MALI

TIBESTI MOUNTAINS

NIGER

CHAD

NUBIAN DESERT

SUDAN

ERITREA

Cape Verde

SENEGAL

Senegal R.

Niger R.

L. Chad

GEZIRA

Blue Nile R.

DJIBOUTI

Gulf of Aden

GAMBIA

BURKINA

L. Tana

White Nile R.

GUINEA-BISSAU

GUINEA

BENIN

ETHIOPIAN HIGHLANDS

SOMALI PENINSULA

SIERRA LEONE

IVORY COAST

GHANA

NIGERIA

Benue R.

CENTRAL AFRICAN REPUBLIC

ETHIOPIA

HORN OF AFRICA

SOMALIA

LIBERIA

TOGO

CAMEROON

GREAT RIFT VALLEY

▲ *Mt. Cameroon 13,353 ft (4,070 m)*

Ubangi R.

EQUATORIAL GUINEA

Gulf of Guinea

Zaire (Congo) R.

L. Albert

UGANDA

KENYA

▲ *Mt. Kenya 17,058 ft (5,199 m)*

Equator

SÃO TOMÉ & PRÍNCIPE

GABON

Cape Lopez

CONGO

CONGO BASIN

ZAIRE

RWANDA

L. Victoria

BURUNDI

▲ *Mt. Kilimanjaro 19,340 ft (5,895 m)*

SEYCHELLES

Kasai R.

L. Tanganyika

TANZANIA

Zanzibar I.

Cabinda (Angola)

ATLANTIC OCEAN

KATANGA PLATEAU

L. Nyasa (Malawi)

Cape Delgado

COMOROS

ANGOLA

ZAMBIA

MALAWI

Kunene R.

Zambezi R.

MOZAMBIQUE

Mozambique Channel

MADAGASCAR

L. Kariba

Victoria Falls

NAMIBIA

Okavango Swamp

ZIMBABWE

Tropic of Capricorn

BOTSWANA

Limpopo R.

NAMIB DESERT

KALAHARI DESERT

Orange R.

Vaal R.

SWAZILAND

DRAKENSBERG RANGE

SOUTH AFRICA

LESOTHO

GREAT KARROO

Cape of Good Hope

INDIAN OCEAN

AFRICA
Physical

Land Elevation

Feet		Meters
Over 13,001		Over 4,001
6,501–13,000		2,001–4,000
3,001–6,500		1,001–2,000
1,501–3,000		501–1,000
701–1,500		201–500
0–700		0–200
Below sea level		Below sea level

▲ Mountain peak

0	300	600 Miles

0	300	600 Kilometers

15°W   0°   15° E   30° E   45° E

45°N

30°N

15°N

0°

15°S

30°S

45°S

Asia

ASIA
Physical

Land Elevation

Feet	Meters
Over 13,001	Over 4,001
6,501-13,000	2,001-4,000
3,001-6,500	1,001-2,000
1,501-3,000	501-1,000
701-1,500	201-500
0-700	0-200
Below sea level	Below sea level

▲ Mountain peak

0   400   800 Miles
0   400   800 Kilometers

PACIFIC OCEAN

EUROPE

AFRICA

AUSTRALIA

NEW GUINEA

ARCTIC OCEAN

North Pole

FRANZ JOSEF LAND

SEVERNAYA ZEMLYA

NEW SIBERIAN IS.

EAST SIBERIAN SEA

LAPTEV SEA

KARA SEA

BARENTS SEA

Novaya Zemlya

BERING SEA

KAMCHATKA PENINSULA

SEA OF OKHOTSK

SAKHALIN

KURIL IS.

HOKKAIDO

HONSHU

JAPAN

SEA OF JAPAN

SHIKOKU

KYUSHU

NORTH KOREA

SOUTH KOREA

KOREA PEN.

YELLOW SEA

EAST CHINA SEA

RYUKYU IS.

TAIWAN

SIBERIA

RUSSIA

URAL MOUNTAINS

Ob R.

Irtysh R.

Yenisey R.

Lena R.

Amur R.

L. Baikal

SAYAN MTS.

ALTAI MTS.

MONGOLIA

MONGOLIAN PLATEAU

GOBI (DESERT)

DA HINGGAN MTS.

CHINA

Huang He (Yellow R.)

SICHUAN BASIN

Chang Jiang (Yangtze R.)

SLN MTS.

Xi Jiang (West R.)

HAINAN

SOUTH CHINA SEA

PHILIPPINE SEA

PHILIPPINES

LUZON

VISAYAS

MINDANAO

CELEBES SEA

CELEBES

MOLUCCAS

BANDA SEA

ARAFURA SEA

TIMOR

FLORES

LESSER SUNDA ISLANDS

JAVA SEA

JAVA

GREATER SUNDA IS.

BORNEO

INDONESIA

BRUNEI

MALAYSIA

MALAY PENINSULA

SUMATRA

Strait of Malacca

Gulf of Thailand

THAILAND

CAMBODIA

LAOS

VIETNAM

INDOCHINA PENINSULA

Mekong R.

MYANMAR (BURMA)

Irrawaddy R.

Salween R.

BAY OF BENGAL

ANDAMAN IS.

NICOBAR IS.

BANGLADESH

BHUTAN

NEPAL

Mt. Everest

HIMALAYAS

Ganges R.

Brahmaputra R.

PLATEAU OF TIBET

TIBET

KUNLUN MTS.

TAKLIMAKAN (DESERT)

TARIM R.

JUNGGAR BASIN

TIAN SHAN

KYRGYZSTAN

L. Balqash

Aral Sea

KAZAKHSTAN

PAMIR MTS.

HINDU KUSH

KARAKORAM RANGE

TAJIKISTAN

UZBEKISTAN

TURKMENISTAN

AFGHANISTAN

PAKISTAN

Indus R.

THAR DESERT

INDIA

DECCAN PLATEAU

EASTERN GHATS

WESTERN GHATS

INDIAN PENINSULA

SRI LANKA

LACCADIVE IS.

MALDIVES

INDIAN OCEAN

ARABIAN SEA

Gulf of Oman

IRAN

PLATEAU OF IRAN

ELBURZ MTS.

ZAGROS MTS.

CASPIAN SEA

CAUCASUS MTS.

GEORGIA

ARMENIA

AZERBAIJAN

BLACK SEA

TURKEY

ANATOLIAN PLATEAU

CYPRUS

LEBANON

ISRAEL

SYRIA

SYRIAN DESERT

IRAQ

Tigris R.

Euphrates R.

JORDAN

EGYPT

SINAI PENINSULA

MEDITERRANEAN SEA

SAUDI ARABIA

KUWAIT

BAHRAIN

QATAR

UNITED ARAB EMIRATES

Persian Gulf

ARABIAN PENINSULA

OMAN

YEMEN

RED SEA

Gulf of Aden

Don R.

N. Dvina R.

Volga R.

Tropic of Cancer

Arctic Circle

Equator

Luzon Strait

Gulf of Thailand

N   E   S   W

160°W

180°

160°E

120°E

100°E

80°E

60°E

40°E

20°N

20°S

40°N

60°N

80°N

AUSTRALIA AND OCEANIA

AUSTRALIA AND OCEANIA
Physical

Land Elevation

Feet	Meters
Over 13,001	Over 4,001
6,501-13,000	2,001-4,000
3,001-6,500	1,001-2,000
1,501-3,000	501-1,000
701-1,500	201-500
0-700	0-200
Below sea level	Below sea level

▲ Mountain peak

0   400   800 Miles
0   400   800 Kilometers

PACIFIC OCEAN

PACIFIC OCEAN

Tropic of Cancer

Tropic of Capricorn

Equator

International Date Line

N
W — E
S

HAWAIIAN ISLANDS (U.S.)

MIDWAY IS. (U.S.)

WAKE I. (U.S.)

MARQUESAS ISLANDS

TUAMOTU ARCHIPELAGO

FRENCH POLYNESIA (Fr.)

PITCAIRN (U.K.)

LINE ISLANDS

SOCIETY IS.

TAHITI

COOK ISLANDS (N.Z.)

KIRIBATI

TOKELAU (N.Z.)

AMERICAN SAMOA (U.S.)

WESTERN SAMOA

NIUE (N.Z.)

WALLIS AND FUTUNA (Fr.)

TONGA

TUVALU

FIJI

MARSHALL ISLANDS

NAURU

SOLOMON ISLANDS

VANUATU

LOYALTY IS.

NEW CALEDONIA (Fr.)

NORTHERN MARIANA ISLANDS (U.S.)

GUAM (U.S.)

CAROLINE IS.

FEDERATED STATES OF MICRONESIA

PALAU

BISMARCK ARCHIPELAGO

PAPUA NEW GUINEA

New Guinea

Mt. Wilhelm
(14,790 ft.; 4,508 m)

NEW ZEALAND

NORTH ISLAND

SOUTH ISLAND

CHATHAM IS. (N.Z.)

Mt. Cook
(12,349 ft.; 3,764 m)

TASMAN SEA

CORAL SEA

Great Barrier Reef

GREAT DIVIDING RANGE

Mt. Kosciusko
(7,316 ft.; 2,230 m)

AUSTRALIA

GREAT ARTESIAN BASIN

Lake Eyre

Darling R.

Murray R.

TASMANIA

GREAT SANDY DESERT

GIBSON DESERT

GREAT VICTORIA DESERT

Great Australian Bight

TIMOR SEA

PHILIPPINE SEA

ASIA

INDIAN OCEAN

EUROPE

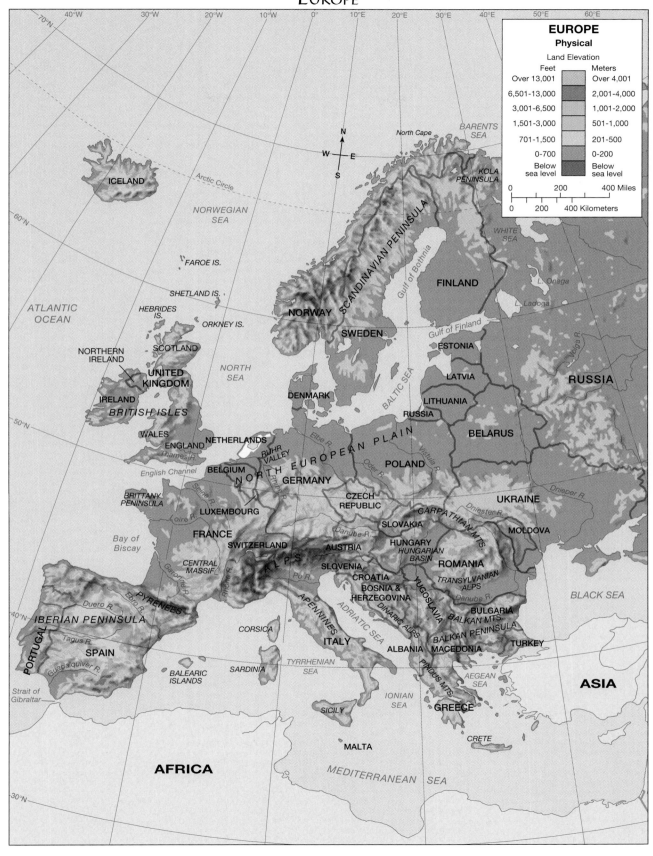

EUROPE
Physical

Land Elevation

Feet	Meters
Over 13,001	Over 4,001
6,501–13,000	2,001–4,000
3,001–6,500	1,001–2,000
1,501–3,000	501–1,000
701–1,500	201–500
0–700	0–200
Below sea level	Below sea level

0   200   400 Miles
0   200   400 Kilometers

ICELAND

ATLANTIC OCEAN

NORWEGIAN SEA

FAROE IS.

SHETLAND IS.

HEBRIDES IS.

ORKNEY IS.

NORTHERN IRELAND

SCOTLAND

UNITED KINGDOM

IRELAND

BRITISH ISLES

NORTH SEA

WALES

ENGLAND

NETHERLANDS

English Channel

Thames R.

BELGIUM

LUXEMBOURG

BRITTANY PENINSULA

FRANCE

Seine R.

Loire R.

Bay of Biscay

CENTRAL MASSIF

Garonne R.

SWITZERLAND

Rhône R.

ALPS

PYRENEES

IBERIAN PENINSULA

Duero R.

Ebro R.

PORTUGAL

Tagus R.

SPAIN

Guadalquiver R.

Strait of Gibraltar

BALEARIC ISLANDS

SARDINIA

CORSICA

ITALY

APENNINES

TYRRHENIAN SEA

SICILY

IONIAN SEA

MALTA

AFRICA

MEDITERRANEAN SEA

SCANDINAVIAN PENINSULA

NORWAY

SWEDEN

Gulf of Bothnia

North Cape

BARENTS SEA

KOLA PENINSULA

WHITE SEA

FINLAND

L. Onega

L. Ladoga

Gulf of Finland

ESTONIA

LATVIA

LITHUANIA

RUSSIA

BALTIC SEA

DENMARK

Volga R.

RUSSIA

BELARUS

NORTH EUROPEAN PLAIN

Elbe R.

RUHR VALLEY

GERMANY

Rhine R.

Oder R.

POLAND

Vistula R.

CZECH REPUBLIC

Danube R.

Dnieper R.

UKRAINE

Dniester R.

SLOVAKIA

CARPATHIAN MTS.

MOLDOVA

AUSTRIA

HUNGARY

HUNGARIAN BASIN

ROMANIA

SLOVENIA

CROATIA

Po R.

BOSNIA & HERZEGOVINA

YUGOSLAVIA

TRANSYLVANIAN ALPS

Danube R.

BULGARIA

BALKAN MTS.

ADRIATIC SEA

DINARIC ALPS

BALKAN PENINSULA

ALBANIA

MACEDONIA

TURKEY

PINDUS MTS.

AEGEAN SEA

GREECE

CRETE

BLACK SEA

ASIA

North America

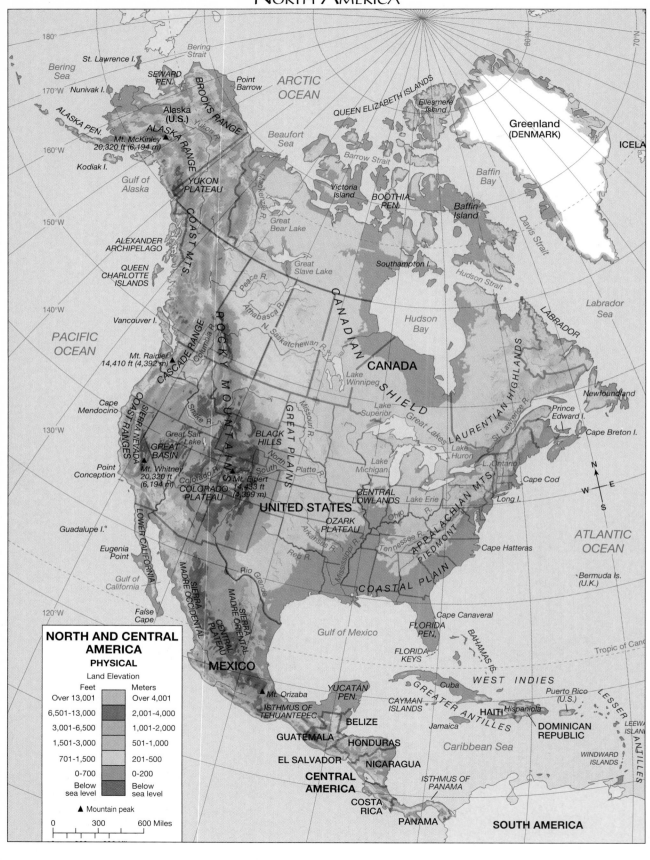

NORTH AND CENTRAL AMERICA

PHYSICAL

Land Elevation

Feet	Meters
Over 13,001	Over 4,001
6,501–13,000	2,001–4,000
3,001–6,500	1,001–2,000
1,501–3,000	501–1,000
701–1,500	201–500
0–700	0–200
Below sea level	Below sea level

▲ Mountain peak

0   300   600 Miles

Bering Sea
St. Lawrence I.
Nunivak I.
ALASKA PEN.
Kodiak I.
Gulf of Alaska
Alaska (U.S.)
SEWARD PEN.
BROOKS RANGE
ALASKA RANGE
Mt. McKinley 20,320 ft (6,194 m)
YUKON PLATEAU
Yukon R.
Point Barrow
Bering Strait
ARCTIC OCEAN
Beaufort Sea
Barrow Strait
QUEEN ELIZABETH ISLANDS
Ellesmere Island
Greenland (DENMARK)
ICELA
Baffin Bay
Victoria Island
BOOTHIA PEN.
Baffin Island
Mackenzie R.
Great Bear Lake
Great Slave Lake
Southampton I.
Davis Strait
Labrador Sea
ALEXANDER ARCHIPELAGO
QUEEN CHARLOTTE ISLANDS
COAST MTS.
Vancouver I.
PACIFIC OCEAN
Cape Mendocino
CASCADE RANGE
COAST RANGES
SIERRA NEVADA
Mt. Rainier 14,410 ft (4,392 m)
ROCKY MOUNTAINS
Peace R.
Athabasca R.
N. Saskatchewan R.
Columbia R.
Snake R.
CANADIAN SHIELD
Hudson Bay
Hudson Strait
LABRADOR
Newfoundland
Prince Edward I.
Cape Breton I.
CANADA
Lake Winnipeg
Lake Superior
Great Lakes
LAURENTIAN HIGHLANDS
St. Lawrence R.
GREAT BASIN
Great Salt Lake
GREAT PLAINS
BLACK HILLS
Missouri R.
Platte R.
North Platte R.
South Platte R.
Lake Michigan
Lake Huron
L. Ontario
Lake Erie
Cape Cod
Long I.
Point Conception
Mt. Whitney 20,320 ft (6,194 m)
COLORADO PLATEAU
Colorado R.
Mt. Elbert 14,433 ft (4,399 m)
UNITED STATES
CENTRAL LOWLANDS
OZARK PLATEAU
Arkansas R.
Ohio R.
Tennessee R.
Mississippi R.
APPALACHIAN MTS.
PIEDMONT
Cape Hatteras
ATLANTIC OCEAN
Guadalupe I.
Eugenia Point
Point Conception
Gulf of California
LOWER CALIFORNIA
Red R.
Rio Grande
SIERRA MADRE OCCIDENTAL
CENTRAL PLATEAU
SIERRA MADRE ORIENTAL
COASTAL PLAIN
Bermuda Is. (U.K.)
Tropic of Canc
False Cape
Gulf of Mexico
Cape Canaveral
FLORIDA PEN.
FLORIDA KEYS
BAHAMAS IS.
WEST INDIES
Puerto Rico (U.S.)
LEEWARD ISLAN
LESSER ANTILLES
MEXICO
Mt. Orizaba
ISTHMUS OF TEHUANTEPEC
YUCATÁN PEN.
BELIZE
GUATEMALA
HONDURAS
EL SALVADOR
NICARAGUA
CENTRAL AMERICA
COSTA RICA
PANAMA
ISTHMUS OF PANAMA
GREATER ANTILLES
Cuba
CAYMAN ISLANDS
Jamaica
HAITI
Hispaniola
DOMINICAN REPUBLIC
Caribbean Sea
WINDWARD ISLANDS
SOUTH AMERICA

SOUTH AMERICA

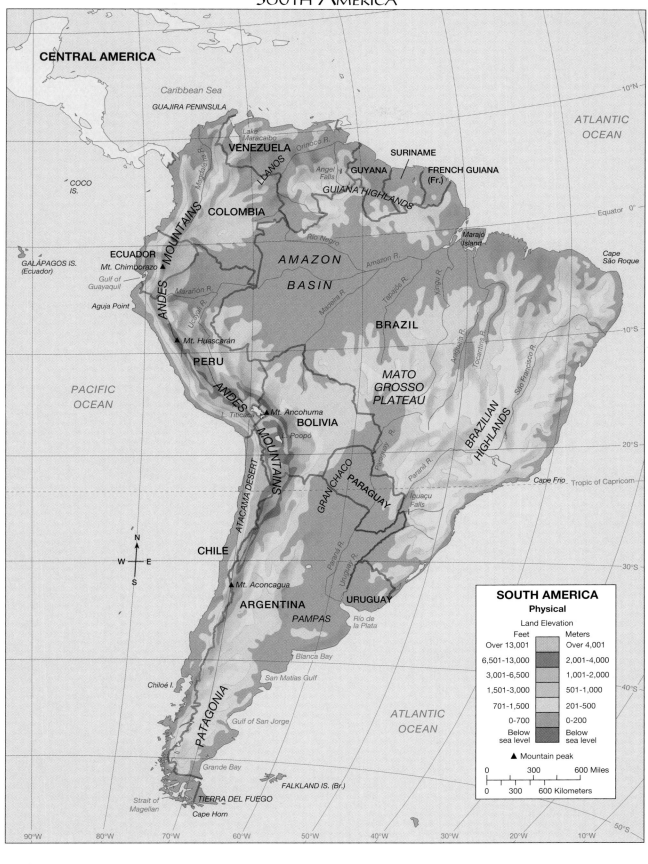

CENTRAL AMERICA

Caribbean Sea

GUAJIRA PENINSULA

10°N

ATLANTIC OCEAN

VENEZUELA
Orinoco R.

SURINAME

Lake Maracaibo

Magdalena R.

LLANOS

Angel Falls

GUYANA

FRENCH GUIANA (Fr.)

ANDES MOUNTAINS

COLOMBIA

GUIANA HIGHLANDS

Equator 0°

COCO IS.

ECUADOR

Rio Negro

Marajó Island

Cape São Roque

GALÁPAGOS IS. (Ecuador)

Mt. Chimborazo ▲

Gulf of Guayaquil

AMAZON BASIN

Amazon R.

Marañón R.

Madeira R.

Tapajós R.

Xingu R.

Aguja Point

Ucayali R.

Araguaia R.

Tocantins R.

São Francisco R.

10°S

▲ Mt. Huascarán

BRAZIL

PERU

PACIFIC OCEAN

ANDES MOUNTAINS

MATO GROSSO PLATEAU

BRAZILIAN HIGHLANDS

L. Titicaca

▲ Mt. Ancohuma

BOLIVIA

Poopó

Paraguay R.

20°S

ATACAMA DESERT

GRAN CHACO

PARAGUAY

Paraná R.

Iguaçu Falls

Cape Frio Tropic of Capricorn

N
W ⊹ E
S

CHILE

Paraná R.

Uruguay R.

30°S

▲ Mt. Aconcagua

URUGUAY

ARGENTINA

PAMPAS

Río de la Plata

Blanca Bay

San Matías Gulf

40°S

Chiloé I.

PATAGONIA

Gulf of San Jorge

ATLANTIC OCEAN

Grande Bay

FALKLAND IS. (Br.)

Strait of Magellan

TIERRA DEL FUEGO

Cape Horn

50°S

90°W   80°W   70°W   60°W   50°W   40°W   30°W   20°W   10°W

SOUTH AMERICA
Physical

Land Elevation

Feet	Meters
Over 13,001	Over 4,001
6,501-13,000	2,001-4,000
3,001-6,500	1,001-2,000
1,501-3,000	501-1,000
701-1,500	201-500
0-700	0-200
Below sea level	Below sea level

▲ Mountain peak

0   300   600 Miles

0   300   600 Kilometers

THE CONTEMPORARY WORLD

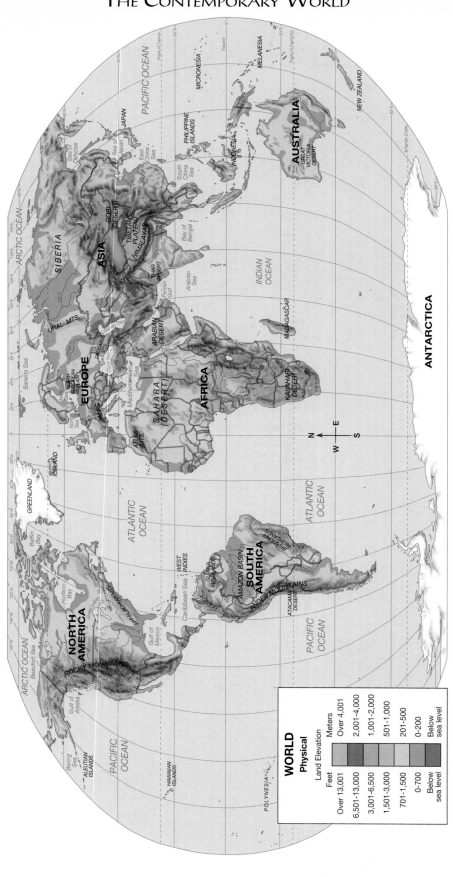

CIVILIZATIONS OF THE WORLD

THE HUMAN ADVENTURE

THIRD EDITION

VOLUME C: FROM 1800

RICHARD L. GREAVES
Florida State University

ROBERT ZALLER
Drexel University

PHILIP V. CANNISTRARO
Queens College, CUNY

RHOADS MURPHEY
University of Michigan

An imprint of Addison Wesley Longman, Inc.

New York • Reading, Massachusetts • Menlo Park, California • Harlow, England
Don Mills, Ontario • Sydney • Mexico City • Madrid • Amsterdam

Executive Editor: Bruce Borland
Director of Development: Betty Slack
Developmental Editor: Judith M. Anderson
Supplements Editor: Jessica Bayne
Project Editor: Dora Rizzuto
Design Manager and Text Designer: Wendy Ann Fredericks
Color Insert Designer: Paul Agresti
Cover Designer: Paul Lacy
Cover Art: Batik with a design of Portuguese in dug-out
    canoes, Indonesia, early 20th century. Private collection,
    Prague, Czech Republic. (Werner Forman Archive/Art
    Resource, New York)
Art Studio: Mapping Specialists Limited
Photo Researcher: Joanne de Simone
Electronic Production Manager: Valerie A. Sawyer
Desktop Administrator: Jim Sullivan
Manufacturing Manager: Helene G. Landers
Electronic Page Makeup: BookMasters, Inc.
Printer and Binder: RR Donnelley & Sons Company
Cover Printer: The Lehigh Press, Inc.
Insert Printer: RR Donnelley & Sons Company

Library of Congress Cataloging-in-Publication Data

Civilizations of the world : the human adventure / Richard L. Greaves
    . . . [et al.]. — 3rd ed.
      p.   cm.
    Includes bibliographical references and index.
    ISBN 0-673-98310-2 (SVE free copy). — ISBN 0-673-98000-6 (single
v. ed.). — ISBN 0-673-98001-4 (v. 1).— ISBN 0-673-98002-2 (v. 2).
— ISBN 0-673-98003-0 (v. A). — ISBN 0-673-98004-9 (v. B). — ISBN
0-673-98005-7 (v. C)
    1. Civilization—History.   I. Greaves, Richard L.
CB69.C576   1997
909—dc20   96-15134
                                                             CIP

ISBN 0-673-98000-6 (single volume)
ISBN 0-673-98310-2 (instructor's edition)
ISBN 0-673-98001-4 (volume one)
ISBN 0-673-98002-2 (volume two)
ISBN 0-673-98003-0 (volume A)
ISBN 0-673-98004-9 (volume B)
ISBN 0-673-98005-7 (volume C)

12345678910—DOW—99989796

Contents

Chronologies and Genealogies

Maps and Graphs

Preface

The demise of the Soviet empire and the subsequent restructuring of international relations underscore the premise of this book: Our ability to relate to other cultures and peoples demands some understanding of their history and values, and without this understanding there can be no responsible citizenship, no informed judgment, and no effective commitment to seek peace and dignity for all. Americans do not live in isolation from people in Asia, Africa, Europe, Latin America, and the Middle East. Our ability to understand and respect one another necessitates an awareness of our historical roots.

Civilizations of the World was from its beginning a *world* history—a conscious effort to broaden the Western cultural background of most students by giving substantial coverage to all the major civilizations and by trying to place historical events, customs, and cultures in a global context. The enthusiastic reception of the first and second editions of *Civilizations of the World: The Human Adventure* has shown the extent to which many of our professional colleagues and their students find this approach meaningful.

Biographical Portraits

World histories sometimes fail to give students a sense of personal intimacy with the subject. Migratory movements, famines and plagues, trading patterns, and imperial conquests are all important in history, but the individual also matters. Scholars used to write about the past in terms of its "great men" (rarely its women). The great figures still appear in our text, of course, as in any broad historical study. But to give a true sense of the diversity of the human achievement, we have included in most chapters biographical portraits of significant personalities from each epoch and region of the globe, not all famous in their own time but each an important reflection of it. Among them are cultural figures, such as the Greek poet Sappho, the Japanese artist Hokusai, and the American dancer Josephine Baker. Others are religious leaders, such as Gautama Buddha; the accomplished musician Hildegard of Bingen; and the Quaker pamphleteer Margaret Fell. Some were prominent in the political world: the rebel Chinese emperor Hung-wu; the South American liberator Simón Bolívar; India's Indira Gandhi; and David Ben-Gurion, a founding father of Israel. Others, such as England's Mary Wollstonecraft and the Soviet feminist Alexandra Kollontai, were especially concerned with women's rights; some, like Isabella Katz, testified to the endurance of the human spirit. All offer special insights into the times of which they were a part. Biographical portraits are marked in the text with this symbol 💃.

Urban Portraits

Civilization begins with the city, and modern society is increasingly urban. We have therefore provided accounts of how cities around the world have developed. Some of the cities—Italy's Pompeii and Mexico's Teotihuacán, for example—are now in ruins, while others—Shanghai, Baghdad, Moscow—are thriving. Jerusalem, Paris, Tokyo (Edo), and Rome are revisited at different periods to give a sense of how they changed over time. Like the biographical portraits, the urban portraits are fully integrated into the narrative and provide instructors with excellent topics for discussion, essay questions, and unusual lecture themes. Students will find them intriguing subjects for term papers. In the text, this symbol ✳ identifies urban portraits.

Women and Minorities

This text continues to focus particularly on women and minorities. The contributions of women to both Western and non-Western societies—whether as rulers, artists and writers, revolutionaries, workers, or wives and mothers—are systematically considered. The biographical portraits are the most obvious illustrations of the attention given to women, but discussions of their contributions are also interwoven throughout the text's narrative. Special consideration is also given to the role of minorities. Four African or African-American figures are highlighted in the portraits: the dancer and social activist Josephine Baker, the African monarch Mansa Musa, Jomo Kenyatta of modern Kenya, and Dr. Martin Luther King, Jr. As one of the founders of Western civilization and a significant force throughout their history, the Jews are covered more fully in this text than in any comparable work. They are followed from their settlement in ancient Palestine to their persecution and exile under the Romans and from their medieval migrations to their return to Palestine and the founding of modern Israel. By recounting the histories of these groups, we hope to make students aware of their achievements.

Social and Cultural Coverage

Recent scholarship has placed considerable emphasis on social and cultural history. That scholarship is reflected throughout this text, but perhaps most clearly in two chapters that are unique among survey texts. Chapter 7, "The Ancient World Religions," offers a comparative overview of the great religions and philosophies of the ancient world, with a discussion of Islam immediately following, in Chapter 8. Chapter 23, "The Societies of the Early Modern World," provides a broad overview of such key aspects of the world's societies in the sixteenth and seventeenth centuries as marriage, the family, sexual customs, education, poverty, and crime. Moreover, at eight different points throughout the text we pause to consider four significant sociocultural themes: writing and communication, the human image, mapping, and the human experience of death. Here again are special opportunities for distinctive lectures, discussions, essay topics, and research papers.

Map Atlas and Full-Color Art Inserts

Two types of special color inserts are featured in the book. The first, included in the front matter, is an eight-page full-color atlas showing the physical characteristics of major areas of the globe. This section is intended as a reference that students can use to improve their knowledge of geography. More than 100 maps appear in the text itself.

In addition to the atlas, the combined volume includes eight full-color inserts titled "The Visual Experience," each insert featuring about eight illustrations—of painting, sculpture, architecture, and *objets d'art*—that are related in a meaningful way to the text's presentation of history. In the split volumes, selected color inserts are included. The text illustrations consist of a separate program of nearly 400 engravings, photographs, and other images chosen for their historical relevance.

Primary Source Documents

To enhance the usefulness of this text, we have provided not only a generous complement of maps and illustrations but also a comprehensive selection of primary sources. By studying these documents—usually four or five per chapter—students can sample the kinds of materials with which historians work. More important, they can engage the sources directly and so participate in the process of historical understanding. To emphasize the sense of history as a living discipline, we survey changing historiographic interpretations of the Renaissance, the French Revolution, imperialism, and fascism.

Reading Lists

The discipline of history goes far beyond merely amassing raw data such as names, places, and dates. Historical study demands analysis, synthesis, and a critical sense of the worth of each source. As a guide to students who wish to hone their historical understanding and analytical skills, an up-to-date reading list is provided at the end of each chapter.

Major Changes in the Third Edition

The most significant change in the third edition is the addition of a chapter on Africa, 1400–1800. Inclusion of this new chapter (Chapter 21) gives added depth to this period of African history; the chapter is enriched with new documents and maps. The discussion of modern Africa in Chapter 42 has also been substantially rewritten, and recent developments in Africa and Latin America are discussed. New biographical portraits featuring Hildegard of Bingen and Christine de Pizan appear in Chapters 14 and 16, respectively. Chapter 39 has been extensively revised to emphasize and consolidate the events occurring during the Cold War. The final chapter, "The Contemporary Age" (Chapter 43), has been updated to reflect the many changes which have occurred as a result of the collapse of the Soviet Union and the emerging republics. New sections on music have been added to Chapters 14 and 16. Other changes appear throughout the text, reflecting both new scholarship and suggestions from readers, and a number of new primary source readings have been added.

In revising this book the authors have benefited from the research of many others, all of whom share our belief in the importance of historical study. To the extent that we have succeeded in introducing students to the rich and varied heritage of the past, we owe that success in a very special way to our fellow historians and to the discipline to which we as colleagues have dedicated our careers.

RICHARD L. GREAVES
ROBERT ZALLER
PHILIP V. CANNISTRARO
RHOADS MURPHEY

Supplements

The following supplements are available for use in conjunction with this book.

For Instructors

- *Instructor's Resource Manual* by Richard L. Greaves and Robert Zaller. Prepared by authors of the text, this instructor's manual includes lecture themes, special lecture topics, topics for class discussion and essays, an extensive film list, identification and map items, and term paper topics. Also included is *Mapping the Human Adventure: A Guide to Historical Geography* by Glee Wilson, Kent State University. This special addition provides over 30 reproducible maps and exercises covering the full scope of world history.

- *Discovering World History Through Maps and Views,* Second Edition, by Gerald Danzer, University of Illinois, Chicago, winner of the AHA's James Harvey Robinson Award for his work in the development of map transparencies. The second edition of this set of 100 four-color transparencies is completely updated and revised to include the newest reference maps and the most useful source materials. The collection includes source and reference maps, views and photos, urban plans, building diagrams, and works of art.

- *Test Bank* by Edward D. Wynot, Florida State University. Approximately 50 multiple-choice and 10 essay questions per chapter. Multiple-choice items are referenced by text page number and type (factual or interpretive).

- *TestMaster Computerized Testing System.* This flexible, easy-to-master test bank includes all of the test items in the printed *Test Bank.* The TestMaster software allows you to edit existing questions and add your own items. Tests can be printed in several different formats and can include figures such as graphs and tables. Available for DOS and Macintosh computers.

- *Text Map Transparencies.* A set of all the maps in the text bound in a three-ring binder with teaching tips.

For Students

- *Study Guide* by Richard L. Greaves and Robert Zaller. Prepared by authors of the text, each chapter contains a chapter overview; map exercises; study questions; a chronology; and identification, completion, short answer, and document exercises, along with a list of term paper topics.

- *SuperShell Computerized Tutorial* by David Mock of Tallahassee Community College. This interactive program for DOS computers helps students learn major facts and concepts through drill and practice exercises and diagnostic feedback. SuperShell provides immediate correct answers and the text page number on which the material is discussed. Missed questions appear with greater frequency; a running score of the student's performance is maintained on the screen throughout the session.

- *World History Map Workbook* in two volumes. Volume I (to 1600) and Volume II (from 1600) by Glee Wilson of Kent State University. Each volume includes over 40 maps accompanied by more than 120 pages of exercises. Each volume is designed to teach the location of various countries and their relationship to one another. There are numerous exercises aimed at enhancing the student's critical thinking abilities.

- *World History Atlas.* This four-color atlas contains a variety of historical maps. Current scholarship and global coverage is reflected in this up-to-date atlas. It is available shrink-wrapped with *Civilizations of the World* at a low cost.

- *TimeLink Computer Atlas of World History* by William Hamblin, Brigham Young University. This Hyper-Card Macintosh program presents three views of the world—Europe/Africa, Asia, and the Americas—on a simulated globe. Students can spin the globe, select a time period, and see a map of the world at that time, including the names of major political units. Special topics such as the conquests of Alexander the Great are shown through animated sequences that depict the dynamic changes in geopolitical history. A comprehensive index and quizzes are also included.

Acknowledgments

The authors are grateful to Bruce Borland, history editor; Judith Anderson, developmental editor; and Dora Rizzuto, project editor. This book could not have been completed without the invaluable assistance of Judith Dieker Greaves, editorial assistant to the authors. The authors wish additionally to thank the following persons for their assistance and support: Lili Bita Zaller, Philip Rethis, Kimon Rethis, Robert B. Radin, Stanley Burnshaw, Julia Southard, Robert S. Browning, Sherry E. Greaves, Stephany L. Greaves, and Professors Eric D. Brose, Peter Garretson, Roger Hackett, Victor Lieberman, Winston Lo, Bawa S. Singh, Donald F. Stevens, Thomas Trautmann, Ralph V. Turner, and Edward D. Wynot, Jr.

The following scholars read the manuscript in whole or in part and offered numerous helpful suggestions:

J. Chris Arndt
James Madison University

James S. Austin, Jr.
Hawaii Pacific University

Roger B. Beck
Eastern Illinois University

Martin Berger
Youngstown State University

Donna Bohanan
Auburn University

Allen Cronenberg
Auburn University

Cecil B. Egerton
Chaffey College

Thomas C. Fiddick
University of Evansville

Mary B. Hagerty
Iona College

Kennell Jackson
Stanford University

Mario D. Mazzarella
Christopher Newport University

Barbara Mitchell
Chaffey College

Dennis J. Mitchell
Jackson State University

David E. Rison
Charleston Southern University

David R. Smith
California State Polytechnic University, Pomona

William A. Sumruld
College of the Southwest

Arlene F. Wolinski
Mesa College

We are also indeted to the reviewers of the first and second editions:

Dorothy Abrahamse
California State University, Long Beach

Winthrop Lindsay Adams
University of Utah

George M. Addy
Brigham Young University

Jay Pascal Anglin
University of Southern Mississippi

Karl Barbir
Siena College

Charmarie J. Blaisdell
Northeastern University

Robert F. Brinson
Santa Fe Community College

William A. Bultmann
Western Washington University

Thomas Callahan, Jr.
Rider College

Miriam Usher Chrisman
University of Massachusetts, Amherst

Jill N. Claster
New York University

Cynthia Schwenk Clemons
Georgia State University

Allen T. Cronenberg
Auburn University

John Dahmus
Stephen F. Austin State University

Elton L. Daniel
University of Hawaii at Manoa

Leslie Derfler
Florida Atlantic University

Joseph M. Dixon
Weber State College

John Patrick Donnelly
Marquette University

Mark U. Edwards, Jr.
Harvard University

Charles A. Endress
Angelo State University

Stephen Englehart
California State Polytechnic University, Pomona

William Wayne Farvis
University of Tennessee

Jonathan Goldstein
West Georgia College

Edwin N. Gorsuch
Georgia State University

Joseph M. Gowaski
Rider College

Tony Grafton
Princeton University

Coburn V. Graves
Kent State University

Janelle Greenberg
University of Pittsburgh

Christopher E. Guthrie
Tarleton State University

Craig Harline
University of Idaho

Udo Heyn
California State University, Los Angeles

Clive Holmes
Cornell University

Leonard A. Humphreys
University of the Pacific

Donald G. Jones
University of Central Arkansas

William R. Jones
University of New Hampshire

Thomas Kaiser
University of Arkansas at Little Rock

Thomas L. Kennedy
Washington State University

Frank Kidner
San Francisco State University

Winston L. Kinsey
Appalachian State University

Thomas Kuehn
Clemson University

George J. Lankevich
Bronx Community College

Richard D. Lewis
Saint Cloud State University

David C. Lukowitz
Hamline University

Thomas J. McPartland
Bellevue Community College

Elizabeth Malloy
Salem State College

John A. Mears
Southern Methodist University

V. Dixon Morris
University of Hawaii at Manoa

Marian Purrier Nelson
University of Nebraska at Omaha

William D. Newell
Laramie County Community College

James Odom
East Tennessee State University

William G. Palmer
Marshall University

William D. Phillips, Jr.
San Diego State University

Paul B. Pixton
Brigham Young University

Ronald R. Rader
University of Georgia

Dennis Reinhartz
University of Texas at Arlington

Leland Sather
Weber State College

Irvin D. Solomon
Edison Community College

Gerald Sorin
State University of New York, New Paltz

Kerry E. Spiers
University of Louisville

Paul Stewart
Southern Connecticut State University

Richard G. Stone
Western Kentucky University

Alexander Sydorenko
Arkansas State University

Teddy Uldricks
University of North Carolina at Asheville

Raymond Van Dam
University of Michigan, Ann Arbor

John Weakland
Ball State University

David L. White
Appalachian State University

Richard S. Williams
Washington State University

Glee E. Wilson
Kent State University

John E. Wood
James Madison University

Edward D. Wynot, Jr.
Florida State University

Martin Yanuck
Spelman College

Donald L. Zelman
Tarleton State University

A Note on the Spelling of Asian Names and Words

Nearly all Asian languages are written with symbols different from our Western alphabet. Chinese, Japanese, and Korean are written with ideographic characters, plus a phonetic syllabary for Japanese and Korean. Most other Asian languages have their own scripts, symbols, diacritical marks, and alphabets, which differ from ours. There can thus be no single "correct spelling" in Western symbols for Asian words or names, including personal names and place names—only established conventions. Unfortunately, conventions in this respect differ widely and in many cases reflect preferences or forms related to different Western languages. The Western spellings used in this book, including its maps, are to some extent a compromise, in an effort to follow the main English-language conventions but also to make pronunciation for English speakers as easy as possible.

Chinese presents the biggest problem since there are a great many different conventions in use and since well-known place names, such as Peking or Canton, are commonly spelled as they are here in most Western writings, even though this spelling is inconsistent with all of the romanization systems in current use and does not accurately represent the Chinese sounds. Most American newspapers and some journals now use the romanization system called *pinyin,* approved by the Chinese government, which renders these two city names, with greater phonetic accuracy, as Beijing and Kwangzhou. However, pinyin presents other problems for most Western readers, and the words are commonly mispronounced.

The usage in this book follows the most commonly used convention for scholarly publication when romanizing Chinese names, the Wade-Giles system, but gives the pinyin equivalents for modern names (if they differ) in parentheses after the first use of a name. Readers will encounter both spellings, plus others, in other books, papers, and journals, and some familiarity with both conventions is thus necessary.

In general, readers should realize and remember that English spellings of names from other languages (such as Munich for München, Vienna for Wien, and Rome for Roma), especially in Asia, can be only approximations and may differ confusingly from one Western source or map to another.

Introduction to Volume C

Human civilizations arose in widely separated parts of the world following the invention of agriculture, which made possible settled communities, trade and barter, and ultimately states and empires. Social organization offered a variety of new pursuits, including specialized crafts, religious divination, and warfare. The need to record transactions prompted the invention of writing. With the development of commerce and of religious and warrior elites, individuals and groups could accumulate wealth and wield power and influence over their fellows.

One of the world's earliest civilizations arose around 3000 B.C. in what is now Pakistan, in the valley drained by the Indus River. Archaeological evidence shows a highly developed culture, with sophisticated technology and art, a system of writing, and forms of worship that anticipated the development of Hinduism. The Indus civilization declined after about 2000 B.C., in part because of soil exhaustion. Although the script of the Indus people has not yet been deciphered, they appear to have been related to the modern population of southern India.

After 1800 B.C. the Aryans, a people from central Asia, migrated into the Indian subcontinent and over several centuries conquered much of the north. Other Aryan tribes apparently migrated westward into Europe. The Aryans spoke an early version of Sanskrit, which became the basis of what is now called the Indo-European language group, including Persian, Greek, Latin, and the languages of modern Europe. They never dominated southern India, which remains culturally and linguistically distinct to the present day.

The Aryans mixed their own tribal gods with those of the Indian subcontinent, and Hinduism, the oldest of the world's great religions, gradually emerged from their sacred texts (c. 1500–600 B.C.). The three chief deities of the Hindu pantheon—Brahma, the creator; Vishnu, the preserver; and Shiva, the destroyer—represent aspects of the universal cycle of existence. The worshipper who faithfully executed his prescribed duties earned rewards in a future life, but he was punished if he failed to perform his duties. Reacting against the priestly control of Hinduism, Gautama Buddha ("The Enlightened One"), whose given name was Siddartha, propounded a new religion in the sixth century B.C. based on the renunciation of personal desire and the observance of proper conduct and respect toward all living things. Buddhism never supplanted Hinduism in India, but it made its way into the rest of east Asia, where it remains the dominant religion.

Indian culture was also characterized by the institution of caste, which divided it into ranked and segregated groups, particularly after the fifth century A.D. Caste may originally have been a mechanism for distinguishing the Aryans from the darker-skinned peoples they had conquered, but it developed into a strict hierarchical system. Members of a given caste were limited to certain occupations, could not marry outside their group, and even avoided sharing their food or water with other castes. Although officially proscribed in modern India, caste distinctions continue to determine much of India's social, economic, and political life.

Civilization began in China about 2000 B.C. and entered recorded history about 1600 B.C. with the rise of the Shang dynasty. The Shang, who excelled in metallurgy and produced magnificent bronze figures, were overthrown by one of their vassal states, the Chou (Zhou), around 1027 B.C. Like the Shang, the Chou lived on the flood plain of the Yellow River of northern China, largely isolated from the ethnically and linguistically distinct regions to the south. The Chou began to break up after 770 B.C. Not until the late third century B.C. was north China unified.

During this unsettled period Confucius (K'ung Fu-tze or Kongfuzi), a contemporary of Gautama Buddha, laid down what remain the basic ethical precepts of Chinese civilization: filial loyalty, respect for superiors, and social benevolence. According to Confucius' and his disciple Mencius, social order depended on government by virtuous men whose task was to set a proper moral example for all those below them. Confucius' contemporary Lao-tze urged a different course. According to Lao-tze, inner harmony was to be achieved by understanding the order of nature and submitting to its immutable patterns. Taoism (Daoism), as Lao-tze's philosophy was called, was mystical and contemplative, whereas Confucianism was rational and activist, but most Chinese combined both philosophies as a code of conduct.

The first Western civilizations—successively those of Sumer, Akkad, Babylon, and Assyria—arose in Mesopotamia about 3500 B.C. They introduced bronze, an alloy of copper and tin; developed complex systems of irrigation; and produced writing systems, law codes, and the first extant works of literature. At about the same time a powerful civilization arose along the Nile delta in Egypt, which maintained a largely unbroken dynastic continuity until its conquest first by Persia and then by Alexander the Great in the first millennium B.C. Like its sister civilizations in Mesopotamia, that of Egypt was based on slavery, a priestly elite, and the cult of a divinized ruler. But it was in Egypt that monotheism arose, the basis of both Hebrew and Persian religion, as it was later of Christianity and Islam.

The Hebrews, a tribe of Semitic origin, founded a kingdom in Palestine about 1000 B.C., only to be overrun by the Assyrians and Babylonians. Even under conquest, however, they remained united in their belief in a single, omnipotent God, as expressed in their sacred book the Torah (Hebrew Bible). Far larger was the empire of the Persians, a people of Aryan descent, which at its height around 500 B.C. dominated all of western Asia from Egypt to the frontiers of India.

The first civilization on European soil was that of Greece, which developed in the third millennium B.C., produced its first great cultures on the island of Crete (Minoan) and the Peloponnesian peninsula (Mycenaean) in the second millennium B.C., and achieved its finest flowering in the city-state of Athens in the first millennium. Though they borrowed freely from the neighboring civilizations of western Asia, the Greeks gave Western culture much of its founding traditions, from tragic drama to science, philosophy, and political democracy. Internecine warfare among the Greek city-states made them vulnerable to the ambitions of a Hellenized neighbor to the north, Macedon, which under Alexander the Great conquered all of western and much of central Asia.

At Alexander's death in 323 B.C. his generals divided his empire. One briefly seized most of western Asia; another founded a new, Hellenized dynasty in Egypt; and a third kept control of Macedonia and Greece proper. These dynasties were in turn conquered by a new power, Rome, which, having unified the Italian peninsula and defeated its great maritime rival, Carthage, extended its control over Alexander's former dominions in the second century B.C. and eventually absorbed most of them as provinces.

Unlike other great ancient empires, Rome was governed not by a monarchy but by an aristocratic republic that gradually incorporated popular elements. As the empire expanded, however, the disparity between rich and poor grew, as did the dependence of the latter on public assistance. When Augustus emerged as the undis-puted ruler of Rome in 27 B.C. after a series of civil wars, an imperial system replaced the republic. Although shorn of power, many of the republic's old legal forms and institutions survived and provided not only continuity but a model for later Western development.

Rome borrowed its philosophy and art from Greece and its gods from western Asia. To Western culture it contributed its jurisprudence, which remains the basis not only of Western and much of Asian, African, and American law today, but also of most international law codes. Rome also provided the setting for the birth of Christianity, based on the teachings of the Jewish prophet Jesus of Nazareth. After Jesus' death in 29 A.D. Paul, a convert from Judaism and Christianity's first theologian, carried the Christian message (the "gospel") to the major cities of the eastern Roman empire. Christianity differed from Judaism in stressing its ethical teachings rather than its ceremonial traditions, in proselytizing among other groups, and in believing in the resurrection of Jesus as the Son of God. The Christian churches gradually codified their own beliefs and sacred texts, including the Hebrew scripture ("The Old Testament"). Christianity thus retained much of Judaism, although its attitude toward Jews was increasingly hostile. By the fourth century Christianity had become the official religion of the Roman Empire. The following century the bishop of Rome, popularly called the pope, claimed power over the entire church.

At the height of Rome's power in the second century A.D. it incorporated all of Europe south of the Rhine and Danube rivers, north Africa, and western Asia as far as the Persian Gulf and the Caspian Sea. By the fifth century, however, it had been forced to abandon most of its western dominions, including the city of Rome itself, and much of Africa and Asia. A successor empire, Byzantium, based in the eastern Roman capital of Constantinople, maintained itself for 1000 years despite threats from Persia, the Arab empire, and the West, until finally it succumbed to the Ottoman Turks in 1453. Byzantium remained faithful to Christianity, but a schism with the Latin church of the West created a breach that continues to the present day.

The last centuries of the first millennium B.C. saw the rise of two other great empires besides that of Rome. In India the Maurya dynasty (322–c. 180 B.C.) united most of the subcontinent, but after a brief, brilliant flowering, it reverted to its tradition of separate principalities and succumbed to successive invasions by central Asian tribes, notably the Kushans, who established a new dynasty in the north around 100 B.C. Northern India enjoyed another golden age under the Gupta dynasty (c.

320–550 A.D.), which, like its Mauryan and Kushan predecessors, made its capital at Pataliputra in the central Ganges valley. However, after its fall the region was again divided and subject to fresh waves of invaders. The subcontinent as a whole was not to be reunified until the seventeenth century A.D.

In China the short-lived Ch'in (Qin) empire united the northern and southern halves of the country for the first time in 221 B.C. and, under its first emperor, Shih Huang Di, built the Great Wall in the north as a barrier to steppe-based nomadic invaders. It was succeeded by the Han dynasty (202 B.C.–220 A.D.), which enlarged the Ch'in empire by conquering northern Korea, northern Vietnam, and Sinkiang (Xinjiang) in the desert northwest, the starting point of the silk route that ran through central Asia and, through intermediary traders, reached as far as Rome. The Han empire was larger and more populous than that of Rome. Its founder, Liu Pang (Liu Bang), was born a peasant and rose through sheer ability, a precedent for later dynasties. The Han recruited able men to serve the state, laying the foundations for a well-organized civil service system based on competitive examinations. Han technology was advanced and included iron suspension bridges, water-powered mills, paper, and an early form of porcelain. The Han also built an extensive network of roads supplemented by canals. Han art in sculpture, in wall paintings, and in palace and temple architecture reflected the vigor and confidence of a great empire, and its commissioned histories display a sense of pride and tradition. Palace intrigues and provincial warlords weakened the empire after the first century A.D., and the last Han emperor abdicated amid general anarchy and decline. No dynasty was to reunify the country for 400 years.

The last of the world's great civilizations to develop was also the only one that grew directly out of a new religion. The prophet Muhammad (c. 570–632), a native of Mecca on the Arabian peninsula, introduced a monotheistic creed known as Islam ("submission") in the early seventh century whose duties and precepts—including prayer, almsgiving, fasting, and pilgrimage—were inscribed in a sacred text, the Koran. The attributes of Allah, the God of Islam, were similar to those of the Jewish and Christian God, and Islam incorporated the Hebrew figures of Moses and David as well as Jesus among the prophets who had preceded Muhammad in revealing the divine will. The followers of Muhammad, called Muslims, had divided into two principal groups by the end of the seventh century: the Shi'ites, who accepted only the laws and beliefs found in the Koran as well as those articulated by a true imam (caliph), and the Sunni, who regard the tradition established by Muhammad and the Koran as complete.

Muhammad's immediate successors had no prophetic status, but they welded the scattered tribes of the Arabian peninsula into a fighting force that spread the new faith by conquest. By midcentury, Islamic armies had overrun a vast territory from Tunisia in central Africa to Afghanistan in central Asia, defeating the Sassanid dynasty in Persia and inflicting heavy losses on the Byzantine Empire. By the early eighth century all of northern Africa was in Muslim hands, and Muslim forces had established themselves on the Iberian peninsula and had briefly penetrated the Frankish kingdoms beyond the Pyrenees. The empire thus created was ruled from Damascus (Syria) by the Umayyad family (661–750) and later from Baghdad (Iraq) by the Abbasids (750–1258). Muslim civilization was commercially active and sophisticated, made significant contributions in science and mathematics, and devised a splendid and distinctive architecture. Like the Byzantines, Muslims accorded women certain property rights, although in neither society did they enjoy equality with males.

The Abbasid dynasty ruled the largest Muslim empire ever created, but by the tenth century its power had ebbed, and after 1055 it gave way in all but name to nomads from central Asia, the Seljuk Turks. The Seljuks drove Byzantium out of Asia Minor, only to be succeeded in turn by another Turkic group, the Ottomans. By the end of the fourteenth century the Ottomans had penetrated deep into southeastern Europe, encircling Byzantium and ensuring its doom. The Ottomans made Byzantium's capital their own, and from that position conquered Syria and Egypt in the early sixteenth century and attacked central Europe. At its height the Ottoman Empire spanned three continents and embraced 50 million people. Although its power waned after the seventeenth century, its final demise did not come until after World War I.

Another spur of Islam established itself in India, which was invaded by Arabs in the eighth century and by Turks in the eleventh and sixteenth centuries. An Islamic sultanate based at Delhi was launched in the early thirteenth century, but not until 1526 did a Muslim dynasty, the Mughal, gain a secure footing. With a western outpost in Kabul it controlled much of central Asia, and under Aurangzeb (1658–1707) it reached almost to India's southern tip, only to succumb to Persian and European invaders in the eighteenth century. The Muslim conquerors at first attempted to impose their faith on the Hindu population but were forced to concede a substantial measure of both religious toleration and self-government. Meanwhile, a third major Islamic empire, the Shi'ite Safavid dynasty, established itself in Persia (1501–1736). In the sixteenth and early seventeenth centuries these empires, though often at odds with one another, constituted the most powerful politico-religious bloc in the world.

After four centuries of disunity, the T'ang dynasty (618–907) reestablished the empire of the Han in China. The T'ang capital at Ch'ang An, the largest city of its time in the world, with a population of 1 million, was the center of a brilliant, cosmopolitan culture that attracted Indian Buddhists, Muslims, Christians, and Jews. At its height the T'ang empire was the largest the world had seen, flourishing for two and a half centuries. It weakened and collapsed under factional strife and was succeeded by another dynasty of great splendor and prosperity, the Sung (960–1279). Despite reduced borders, Sung China too, with its population of 100 million, was incomparably the largest and most powerful state of its time. Nomadic invaders occupied Sung territory north of the Yangtze River in the twelfth century, but only with the arrival of the Mongols, a fierce steppe tribe led by Chinghis (Genghis) Khan, were its inner defenses breached. By Chinghis' death in 1227 the army he molded had conquered all of central Asia, including the proto-Russian state of Kiev, and spurs of it had reached eastern Europe. Chinghis' grandson, Kubilai Khan, completed the conquest of the Sung and inaugurated his own dynasty, the Yuan (1279–1368).

Kubilai's territory (itself only a branch of the far larger Mongol empire that now overspread much of the Eurasian continent) included not only China but Korea and north Vietnam, while south Vietnam, Siam (modern Thailand), Burma, and Tibet were reduced to the status of tributary states. He was able to govern, however, only with the help of Chinese officials, and in less than a century China's independence was restored under a new dynasty, the Ming (1368–1644). The imperial founder, Hung-wu, retained most of the Mongol tributary states and added Japan. His successor, Yung-lo, launched a series of great naval expeditions to India, the Near East, and Africa that displayed Chinese power to the world, although it left no permanent commercial or imperial connections. The Ming dynasty followed the pattern of its predecessors, uniting the country and establishing firm and effective government in its early phases but declining into faction and anarchy at the end. Once again an ethnically foreign dynasty succeeded it, the Ch'ing (Qing) or Manchu (1644–1911). Unlike the Mongols, however, the Manchus were largely Sinified by the time of their conquest, and their rule was in time accepted as legitimate. China resumed its wonted prosperity and dominance in eastern Asia, not to be challenged until the nineteenth century.

Major offshoots of Chinese civilization appeared in Korea and Japan. Korea adopted Confucianism and, under the Yi dynasty (1392–1910), the Chinese civil service system, although its indigenous language and culture remained distinct. The inhabitants of Japan, originally from northeast Asia, settled the islands during the Han period but did not become literate until the eighth century. Thereafter Japanese society, though heavily influenced by China's, developed rapidly. A first imperial capital was founded at Nara, and moved to what is now Kyoto during the Heian period (794–1185), where a refined court culture flourished. Imperial rule was nominal, however, because the Japanese regarded the emperor as divine and hence above politics or administration. Real control was exercised by feudal lords or shoguns. The Kamakura shogunate (1185–1333), based near modern Tokyo, was the major power in the country after the Heian period, but its authority was contested, as was that of its successor, the Ashikaga shogunate (1339–c. 1570). After a period of struggle among ambitious warlords, Tokugawa Ieyasu established Japan's first truly centralized government in 1600. The Tokugawa shogunate ruled Japan until 1868, during which time a modernizing commercial society developed despite the persistence of feudal forms and a policy of isolation from the rest of the world.

Sub-Saharan Africa, the birthplace of the human species, was relatively isolated from the rest of the world until the spread of Islam in the seventh century A.D. Dark-skinned Bantu tribes, originally from west Africa, fanned out in search of arable land during the second millennium B.C., eventually settling most of sub-Saharan Africa and producing a culture notable for its fine work in copper and bronze. On the east coast the powerful kingdom of Kush flourished on the upper Nile and later to the south at Meroë. Kushite culture reflected commercial and military contacts with Egypt (which the Kushites ruled for 60 years in the eighth century B.C.), Greece, Persia, and India; at its peak in the first century A.D., it exchanged ambassadors with Rome. Soil and forest erosion contributed to its decline in the fourth century, but a Christian kingdom, Axum, succeeded it. It established itself along the Red Sea, traded widely, and in the sixth century annexed what is now Yemen on the Arabian peninsula.

Arab invaders brought general literacy and oceanic commerce along a broad belt of central and east Africa, tying the continent to the great Eurasian trading zones and stimulating the development of three regional empires in west Africa: Ghana (c. 700–1203), Mali (c. 1250–c. 1460), and Songhai (c. 1335–c. 1600). All adopted Islam, although native religions continued to flourish in the hinterlands. In addition, a group of prosperous city-states, the Hausa, emerged in west Africa, and another group in the Swahili-speaking territory of the east. The principal such city-state, Kilwa, impressed a fourteenth-century Arab traveler as one of the most beautiful cities in the world. South of the Hausa were the forest states of Ife and Benin, with their splendid carved art, and Great Zimbabwe, possibly south Africa's first state, which built up a large trade based, like that of Mali, on gold and other metals.

Slavery and slave trading had always been a part of African life, but with the coming of Europeans in the sixteenth century the transportation of millions of Africans to the mines and plantations of the Americas began. Most of these slaves were supplied by African factors, although the superior military technology of the Europeans left native states increasingly vulnerable and powerless. It was not until the later nineteenth century, however, that the full-scale European conquest of Africa was undertaken.

The first inhabitants of the Americas crossed the Ice Age land bridge from Siberia to Alaska over what is now the Bering Strait more than 20,000 years ago. Their descendants slowly migrated southward, reaching the tip of South America by 9000 B.C. Agriculture was first developed in Mesoamerica (from central Mexico to Guatemala and Honduras, and on the highlands of the Andes), where the land and climate were suitable for cultivation. Here the major Amerindian civilizations took root: the Olmec (c. 1500 B.C.–c. 100 A.D.), on Mexico's Gulf Coast; the Mayan (c. 100 A.D.–c. 1000), the heart of whose territory was the Yucatan peninsula and Guatemala; the Toltec (c. 750–c. 1150), in central Mexico; the Aztec, founded in the early fourteenth century and embracing much of Mexico; and the Inca, which flourished for only about a century until the Spanish conquest, but, centered in Peru, embraced more than a million square miles of coastal and highland territory.

The civilizations of Central America were highly urbanized. Teotihuacán, the Maya capital, may have had a population of 200,000, as did Aztec Tenochtitlán, on the present site of Mexico City. Like the contemporary African civilizations of the Sudan, they engaged in long-distance trade, constructed colossal temples and pyramids, and produced magnificent carved art. At the same time they practiced human sacrifice and self-mutilation as a way of appeasing sinister gods, and, in the case of the warrior Aztecs, engaged in ritual cannibalism. The Inca, in contrast, developed no great city, in part because of their mountainous terrain, practiced human sacrifice only rarely, and maintained an elaborate program of social welfare. Their most extraordinary achievement was a system of paved roads that spanned 19,000 miles, entirely for foot travel, because the Inca (like other Amerindian peoples) never developed wheeled transport.

Spanish conquerors overran both the Aztec and Inca empires in the early sixteenth century, in part because of internal division and in part because of the Spaniards' superior weapons and mobility. Spain successfully claimed most of the Americas, although vast regions remained unexplored until the nineteenth century, and the Portuguese were awarded title to Brazil. The European conquest was a demographic and cultural disaster for the Amerindians, most of whom perished from European diseases to which they had no resistance. African slaves were imported to work in their stead, a traffic that did not cease until the nineteenth century, although the native population had long since recovered. The Spanish ruled their farflung empire through an elaborate bureaucracy, but Napoleon's conquest of Spain in 1808 quickly ended it; by 1825 all of Central and South America had become independent.

The Amerindian tribes who settled North America did not achieve civilizations on the order of those to the south, but the cultures of the Ohio, Mississippi, and Rio Grande valleys and those of the desert southwest were complex and often impressive. Farther north the population was sparse and continued to subsist as hunter-gatherers. Permanent European settlements arrived shortly after 1600, and for a century and a half England and France fought to control eastern North America. The English prevailed in 1759. Their victory was shortlived; the thirteen colonies of New England and the mid-Atlantic seaboard successfully rebelled, achieving independence in 1783 and founding the United States of America, the world's largest republic.

With the demise of Rome, Europe experienced a difficult period marked by population loss, nomadic invasion, and the collapse of city life and commerce. By the end of the fifth century, however, the Frankish (Germanic) tribes of northern Europe had established new kingdoms and adopted Christianity. A fresh challenge arose in the early eighth century, when the Arabs conquered the Iberian peninsula, but after a few forays into France they retreated behind the Pyrenees.

The high point of Frankish culture was attained in the reign of Charlemagne (768–814), who united most of Europe in a single state and extended his protection to the Roman papacy. Charlemagne's kingdom collapsed shortly after his death, but his vision of a renewed Christian empire was to exert a powerful hold on the European imagination until the sixteenth century.

No strong state emerged again in Europe until the eleventh century, but economic and political life revived under the protection of local lords and their sworn followers or vassals, a regime described by historians as the feudal order. By the fourteenth century Europe's population had doubled to about 75 million. For most of this period the dominant institution in Europe was the papacy, which launched multinational expeditions, known as crusades, for the recovery of the Christian Holy Land in Palestine. The crusades marked the reassertion of Europe's control of the Mediterranean Sea and the revival of its commerce.

Disaster struck the Continent in 1348, when an outbreak of bubonic plague, which had devastated Asia, reduced Europe's population by a third. The so-called Black Death hastened the collapse of feudally based monarchies and ushered in a period of political instability and economic decline. The Catholic church, its assumption of secular powers already under attack, was divided when rival popes contended for its leadership. By the early sixteenth century a German reformer, Martin Luther, had repudiated papal authority. The resulting fissure, the Protestant Reformation, divided western Christendom. At the same time a broadly based revival of Europe's classical heritage, the Renaissance, placed renewed emphasis on secular and humanistic concerns. Even more unsettling to traditional beliefs was the Scientific Revolution, which not only overturned long-cherished notions of humanity's place in the cosmos but propounded a new standard of truth, the scientific method, that challenged all previous assumptions and, ultimately, the authority of biblical revelation itself.

The sixteenth century was a turning point for the West in other respects as well. European explorers discovered a new world in the Western Hemisphere, exploiting its treasure and conquering its peoples. The infusion of new wealth stimulated Europe's economy and swelled its monarchs' coffers. Despite the century of religious wars that accompanied the Reformation and the occupation of much of southeastern Europe by the Ottoman Turks, the West had begun a sustained period of economic growth, technological development, and imperial expansion. By the eighteenth century European merchants had fashioned a global economy, albeit one whose presence in the great trading markets of the east was still at the sufferance of native rulers. With the British conquest of the decadent Mughal dynasty in India, however, begun in the mid-eighteenth century and largely complete by 1815, Western imperialism had a staging point for the domination of east Asia.

While Europeans looked to extend their influence and control over other peoples, they increasingly challenged traditional forms of authority at home. Revolutions in 1640 and 1688 had curbed the power of Britain's monarchy, and the broad eighteenth-century cultural movement known as the Enlightenment demanded that all claims to civil, social, intellectual, moral, and religious authority be submitted to the test of reason. By that standard, many of Europe's institutions were judged wanting. Some rulers, the so-called Enlightened Despots, attempted to place themselves in the vanguard of reform, but when revolution broke out in France in 1789, the Continent united against it.

The energies released by the revolution resisted all efforts to contain them. All legal hierarchies were abolished, and all Frenchmen (though not Frenchwomen) were declared equal in status and rights. By 1793 a republic had been established whose armies in subsequent years overran much of Europe. Under Napoleon Bonaparte, a victorious general who seized dictatorial power and later declared himself emperor, France defeated its continental rivals and established the largest empire on European soil since that of Charlemagne. It was short-lived. A disastrous invasion of Russia, the vast Eurasian state carved out of the former Mongol empire, cost Napoleon most of his army and emboldened a new coalition, led by Britain, to oppose him. By 1814 he had been stripped of his throne and sent into exile, and France returned to its former boundaries. The victorious allies, led by Britain, Russia, Austria, and Prussia, met in Vienna to make a general peace, establish security for the future, and restore the prerevolutionary Old Regime, with its hereditary aristocrats and monarchs. The profound changes wrought by a generation of war and revolution were not, however, so easily overturned.

CIVILIZATIONS
OF THE WORLD

CHAPTER 31

The Industrial Revolution

From the beginning of history to the nineteenth century, all physical labor was accomplished by human or animal muscle or by implements using such muscle. This power was reinforced by levers, pulleys, and weights and supplemented by running water, moving air, or fire. Since then, work has been performed increasingly, and in the more developed regions of the world predominantly, by machines powered by steam, electricity, combustible gases, and the exploding atom. The enormous consequent increase in productive capacity and technical mastery of the resources of the globe has transformed work, society, and the face of the planet itself more than any single development since the introduction of agriculture. This process is still known by the name given to it by the nineteenth-century British historian Arnold Toynbee: the Industrial Revolution.

Background: Population, Energy, and Technology

The Industrial Revolution began in western Europe, particularly in Great Britain. Europe had achieved an aggregate growth of population, commerce, and energy between the fifteenth and eighteenth centuries. Such growth, at an even faster relative rate, had been experienced between the eleventh and thirteenth centuries, only to be succeeded by the demographic catastrophe of the fourteenth. Some observers, such as the Englishman Thomas Robert Malthus (1766–1834), feared at the end of the eighteenth century that Europe was on the brink of such a catastrophe again. In his *Essay on Population* (1798), Malthus noted with alarm the surge in Europe's

The blast furnace: iron and steel manufacture at a plant in Pittsburgh, 1886. The Industrial Revolution called for both an unprecedented outlay of capital and a highly coordinated workforce.

population and calculated that Europeans would soon outstrip their resources. The result would be scarcity, famine, and war.

Had the Industrial Revolution not transformed Europe's productive capacity, Malthus' dire prophecy might have come true. By the end of the eighteenth century, the continent's once abundant forests had been seriously depleted by industrial demand and agricultural clearance. At existing rates of consumption the exhaustion of the continent's major energy source and chief building material seemed inevitable.

The solution was the replacement of wood by coal. Coal had become an important fuel source in the sixteenth century in the Flemish city of Liège, in whose surrounding basin it was mined, and even more so in Newcastle on the Tyne basin in England, where after 1600 it was used extensively in the production of salt, glass, bricks, and tiles. It was used as well in metal and sugar refining, and in baking and brewing. But its more general use was restricted by the difficulty and danger of mining it, the lack of overland transportation to distribute it, and the foul-smelling sulfur released in burning it.

One of the chief hazards of coal mining was subsurface water. At the beginning of the eighteenth century, Thomas Savery, a London inventor, and Thomas Newcomen, a Dartmouth blacksmith, developed a steam-powered pump that Savery called "the Miners' Friend." The efficiency of this pump was increased fourfold when the Scotsman James Watt (1736–1819) developed a condenser that kept the steam from being dissipated into the atmosphere. By 1782 he had converted it into a double-action rotary engine capable of turning heavy machinery. Twenty years later, some 500 such engines were in use in Great Britain.

Just as industrial progress was limited by the use of wood as its primary source of energy, so too was it limited by its dependence on wood and stone as its chief construction materials. Running a poor third to these, though indispensable for everyday domestic products as well as heavy implements such as stoves and weapons, was iron. Smelting iron, which involved separating it from its ore, was a complex, labor-intensive process (60,000 workers were said to be employed in iron manufacture in the Italian city of Brescia in the late fifteenth century), requiring heavy machinery and great amounts of fuel. The product itself, like coal, was difficult to transport, and most iron for domestic use was produced in small quantities on the village level.

Smelting was accomplished by the use of charcoal, which required that all large ironworks be located near forest areas. The search for an alternative fuel as the forests dwindled led to coke, a waste product obtained from coal essentially as charcoal is obtained from wood.

Its high sulfur content resulted in an unacceptably brittle product, however, until the Quaker ironmaster Abraham Darby was able to produce a coke-smelted iron suitable for heavy utensils and military ordnance in 1709. The demand for munitions during the Seven Years' War led to a considerable expansion of coke-fed blast furnaces in Great Britain. But it was not until 1784, when Henry Cort introduced the puddling process for converting crudely cast pig iron into the lighter and more tensile wrought iron necessary for most domestic products, that the iron industry was freed from its dependence on wood.

The result of these technical innovations was that by the 1780s Europe stood on the verge of a great breakthrough in its industrial capacity. The use of steam facilitated the extraction of coal; the use of coal made possible the increased production of iron; and iron (with other metals) was first to supplement and then to replace wood and stone as the prime industrial material. At the same time, transportation was improved by new highways called turnpikes that could bear far heavier loads and by canals that turned Britain's waterways into an integrated transport system. The first phase of the Industrial Revolution culminated in the 1820s in the locomotive, which, made of iron and powered by steam and coal, was to provide industry with an incomparably cheap and efficient method of transportation.

These neatly interlocking developments suggest that the Industrial Revolution was a more or less straightforward consequence of certain technical improvements in mining and metallurgy, prompted by a threatened scarcity of traditional resources. But such an explanation by itself would be misleading. Other societies, including previous European ones, had faced scarcity without finding a key to increased productivity. Other societies had achieved technical levels comparable to those of eighteenth-century Europe without an industrial breakthrough. The Chinese had used coal for domestic heating for several thousand years and for metalworking from about 500 B.C. Their smelting processes were far more sophisticated, and they were able to produce wrought iron and steel of far higher quality. The swords forged with this steel, proceeding westward along the trade routes, had enabled Persian cavalrymen to rout Roman legions in the third century A.D. Western metalworking, despite considerable advances between the eleventh and eighteenth centuries, was still inferior to that of China and India; and when in 1591 the Portuguese captured a cargo of Indian steel, no blacksmith in Lisbon or Spain was able to forge it. Yet at the same time the fine silks and cottons of China and India, so much in demand in eighteenth-century Europe, were woven on looms whose

Malthus on Population

The English clergyman and economist Thomas Malthus, writing at the beginning of the population ex-plosion, concluded that the permanent pressure of population would frustrate all efforts to achieve a more perfect society and that only sexual abstinence could prevent widespread misery.

In plants and irrational animals, the view of the subject is simple. They are all impelled by a powerful instinct to the increase of their species; and this instinct is interrupted by no doubts about providing for their offspring. Wherever therefore there is liberty, the power of increase is exerted; and the superabundant effects are repressed afterwards by want of room and nourishment.

The effects of this check on man are more complicated. Impelled to the increase of his species by an equally powerful instinct, reason interrupts his career, and asks him whether he may not bring beings into the world for whom he cannot provide the means of support. If he attend to this natural suggestion, the restriction too frequently produces vice. If he hear it not, the human race will be constantly endeavoring to increase beyond the means of subsistence. But as, by that law of our nature which makes food necessary to the life of man, population can never actually increase beyond the lowest nourishment capable of supporting it, a strong check on population, from the difficulty of acquiring food, must be constantly in operation. This difficulty must fall somewhere, and must necessarily be severely felt in some or other of the various forms of misery, or the fear of misery, by a large portion of mankind.

That population has this constant tendency to increase beyond the means of subsistence, and that it is kept to its necessary level by these causes, will sufficiently appear from a review of the different states of society in which man has existed. But, before we proceed to this review, the subject will, perhaps, be seen in a clearer light if we endeavor to ascertain what would be the natural increase of population if left to exert itself with perfect freedom; and what might be expected to be the rate of increase in the productions of the earth under the most favorable circumstances of human industry.

It will be allowed that no country has hitherto been known where the manners were so pure and simple, and the means of subsistence so abundant, that no check whatever has existed to early marriages from the difficulty of providing for a family, and that no waste of the human species has been occasioned by vicious customs, by towns, by unhealthy occupations, or too severe labor. Consequently in no state that we have yet known has the power of population been left to exert itself with perfect freedom.

Source: T. Malthus, *An Essay on Population* (London: Dutton, 1914), pp. 6–7. First published in 1798.

crudeness astonished Western visitors. Clearly, the relation between craft and technology was complex, nor do we fully understand the social processes that inhibited technology in China after the thirteenth century at just the moment it had begun to advance in what had only recently been one of the most backward sectors of the globe, western Europe.

The technical breakthrough of eighteenth-century Europe should therefore be seen not as the beginning but as the end product of a complex process of social change.

That process had at least three distinguishable components: commercial, agricultural, and scientific.

Commerce and the Formation of Capitalist Society

Before the term *Industrial Revolution* had been coined, the nineteenth-century social critics Karl Marx (1818–1883) and Friedrich Engels (1820–1895) had

The first railway track was laid inside this circular enclosure near what is now the site of the great Euston train station in London to demonstrate Richard Trevithick's steam locomotive in 1808. The first commercially usable engine was built in the 1820s, and by the 1840s rail networks had begun to span Europe and the United States. The enormous capital outlays forced business, industry, and the state into partnership on an unprecedented scale. The drawing is by Thomas Rowlandson.

identified the banking and commercial classes of Europe—the bourgeoisie—as critical in the development of the new industrial society. "The bourgeoisie," they wrote,

> **has subjected the country to the rule of the towns. It has created enormous cities, . . . agglomerated population, centralized means of production, and has concentrated property in a few hands. . . . [It] has created more massive and more colossal productive forces than have all preceding generations together.[1]**

Marx and Engels saw the bourgeoisie as a group unique to modern Western society, differing from merchant elites in all previous societies in its ability to grasp, organize, and exploit the basic elements of production: capital, land, and labor. Exaggerated though this view may be, it is certainly true that the development of business and commerce had become critical to the prosperity and expansion of Europe.

Commerce becomes a specialized economic function when consumers no longer obtain their goods directly from producers. In commercial economies, producers and consumers typically consummate their exchange through a person appropriately called a middleman, or merchant. By extending the links in this chain—by adding more intermediaries—goods can be shipped around the world, joining producers and consumers who

share no common language or currency or even knowledge of one another's concrete existence.

What expands the number of links, and hence the economy itself, is capital. Capital can be defined in stocks of goods or resources, in warehousing and shipping facilities, in command or control of a labor supply. But its simplest form is money, since money is freely interchangeable into all the other elements. The term *capital* in this sense was first used in the West in the twelfth and thirteenth centuries. A *capitalist,* as the term emerged by about the mid-seventeenth century, was someone who possessed a large stock of money, whether or not he or she chose to invest it. Although the term *capitalism* can be found as early as 1753, it emerged as a description for an entire economic system only in the early twentieth century. Marx himself never used the term.

Capitalist society—the distinctive form of the modern West and increasingly of the world—may then be understood as one in which economic relations are integrated by those who possess, as personal or corporate property, the means of production, through which they command both the labor force and the range of consumer choice. In this sense, capitalism as a fully developed system cannot be said to have existed before the transformation of European society by the Industrial Revolution in the nineteenth century. Yet if the Industrial Revolution made capitalism possible as a distinctive economic system, the capitalist element in the preindustrial economy—the activity of the bourgeois or merchant class—was the most dynamic element in that economy, the activity that enabled it to grow.

Preindustrial capitalism was, in short, commercial capitalism, a capitalism not of producers but of distributors. The two states of eighteenth-century Europe where this capitalism was most advanced were Great Britain and the Netherlands. Dutch prosperity, the envy of Europe in the previous century, was chiefly the result of commercial activity; at its height, Dutch shipping carried half of the world's trade, exclusive of China.

The culture of early modern capitalism was nowhere better displayed than in the Netherlands. Dutch harbors were crammed with the treasures of the Americas and the Indies—sugar, silks, spices, cocoa, tobacco; their shipyards launched 2,000 new seagoing vessels each year. Cloth manufacturing and finishing remained the staple industry, as it had been since the Middle Ages, but there were hundreds of other industries and specialized trades such as diamond cutting, lens grinding, and bookmaking. Business was serviced by a host of bankers, factors, jobbers, and commodity and discount brokers. The great commercial families, the so-called regent class, ruled with all the aplomb of the traditional European aristocracies.

The Dutch had had a miniature Industrial Revolution of their own in the sixteenth and seventeenth centuries. The introduction of a movable cap and a drive shaft crank to the windmill, traditionally an important power source in the Netherlands, enabled the Dutch to hew the giant Baltic timbers they used in shipbuilding with far greater precision and efficiency. By adapting the crank to other kinds of implements—hammers, rams, paddles—they were able to convert the windmill to a host of industrial uses: hulling, oilseed crushing, fulling, boring, and paper and dye preparation, among many others. Even more significant was the development of the water-pumping mill, which enabled the Dutch to

drain lakes and marshes and thus to add significantly to their land-poor country. Such large-scale reclamation projects were financed by groups of wealthy merchants, particularly Amsterdammers; thus once again commercial capital, industrial innovation, and economic development went in tandem.

The British were slower to develop as a commercial power, but during the eighteenth century their growing naval and imperial supremacy, their control of the lucrative slave trade, and the systematic creation of capital and credit through the expansion of the national debt enabled them to outstrip the Dutch. At first much of this expansion was financed by the Dutch themselves, who as

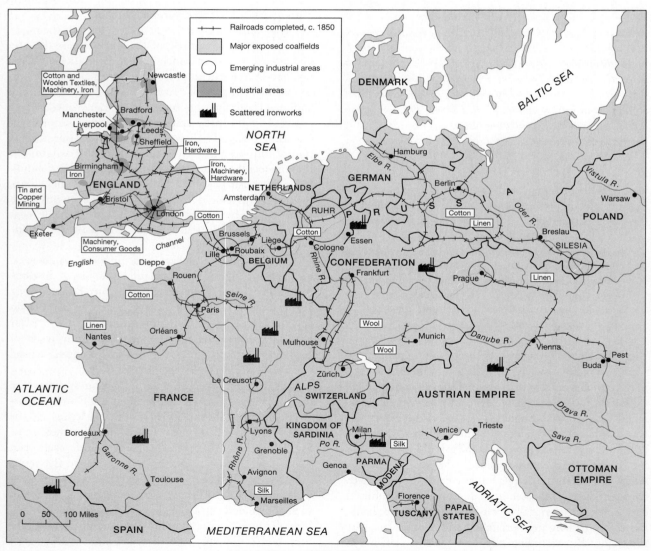

MAP 31.1   EUROPEAN INDUSTRIALIZATION, c. 1850

late as 1776 held 43 percent of the British debt, but this share rapidly declined thereafter. By 1815 it was held almost entirely by the British upper classes themselves: noblemen, gentry, and well-to-do merchants. This oligarchy not only determined the expenditure of the debt through their control of the government but also reaped a direct return through the payment of interest on it, estimated in 1815 at nearly a tenth of the government's revenue. In effect, the British state itself had been converted into a giant corporation paying dividends to its wealthy shareholders. This great capital, the spoil of commercial profit, war, and empire, was a fuel that stoked the engines of the Industrial Revolution no less than coal and steam.

The Agricultural Revolution

The backbone of European society was the traditional peasant village, typically structured around open fields divided into narrow, unfenced strips. These strips were worked by individual peasants, but since they comprised a single large field, the strips were all plowed, sown, and harvested as one. These rhythms enforced the communal cooperation and solidarity that characterized peasant society. The peasants' life was the life of their villages: traditional, conservative, immemorial as the soil and the seasons. But that life was soon not only to change but within a few generations actually to disappear.

The two necessities of the peasant's life were to feed his family and to pay dues and taxes—to the lord, the church, and the state. These two necessities constituted the task of subsistence—survival—since peasants who could not meet their obligations to the lord would lose the use of the land. Subsistence was difficult in the best of times, and only the wealthiest of peasants could think of producing for the market. The majority dared not experiment with new crops or techniques that promised greater productivity. Their existence held no margin for error.

But changes in both demography and the structure of land ownership undermined these traditional patterns. The general surge in population in the sixteenth century had put great pressure on the food supply, driving up land and food prices. This made life harder for the average peasant, whose increased cost for seed was not compensated by higher food prices, since he did not produce for the market and indeed was often a purchaser of food himself. But it opened great opportunities for those able to speculate in land and sell grain. In England this class of substantial landowners, the gentry, had already been enriched by the purchase of church lands at the time of

the Reformation. In the seventeenth and eighteenth centuries they set out to maximize their profits, partly through land acquisition and enclosure (expropriation of communal grazing land) and partly through the importation of new techniques developed by the Dutch and the Flemish.

Most enclosure before the seventeenth century was for the purpose of pasturing sheep, which the gentry raised for market. Thereafter it was increasingly justified as a means of raising agricultural productivity to feed a growing population through the introduction of crops and fertilizers on land that peasants lacked either the means or the desire to "improve." But when the increase in population temporarily leveled off, as it did in the late seventeenth century, the lure of profit did not. Agrarian capitalism—the replacement of small-scale farming for subsistence by large-scale farming for the market—had begun to transform the traditional village; it would end by destroying it.

The improvement of enclosed land involved a variety of new techniques. As in the Low Countries, marshland was extensively drained and filled in. Marl and clay were mixed in sandy soils to make them more productive. Jethro Tull (1674–1741) introduced the planting of seeds in straight, even rows in place of the wasteful old method of sowing them at random (broadcast), while Lord Charles Townshend—"Turnip" Townshend, as he came to be nicknamed—demonstrated that yields could be significantly improved by rotating crops and planting with turnips and clover fields that had previously lain fallow. Both plants replenished the soil and provided winter fodder to sustain animals that would otherwise have been slaughtered for lack of feed. Not only did this substantially increase the size of herds, but thanks to the tireless experiments of the Leicestershire breeder Robert Bakewell, they became larger and heavier as well. By the mid-eighteenth century a veritable craze for agricultural improvement had swept the country. Even King George III contributed to Young's journal under the pen name "Farmer George."

Spurred by personal competition and the quest for profits, improving landlords hastened to acquire and enclose more and more land. The unquestioned control of Parliament by the gentry facilitated a policy of legalized confiscations. Between 1760 and 1815 some 3,600 acts of Parliament enclosed 6 million acres of land, or roughly a quarter of the arable land in England. By 1840 the communally farmed open field had ceased to exist.

What emerged in its place was a system of great estates worked by tenant farmers and hired laborers—no longer a peasantry but an agricultural workforce. This system, with its vastly greater productivity and efficiency, enabled Britain to feed a population that had begun to grow at an unprecedented rate. In 1700 the population of England was about 5.5 million; by 1801 it had increased to 9 million; and by 1851, to 18 million. This growing population provided both the workforce and the primary market for the products of the Industrial Revolution.

Despite the growth in national wealth, many English men and women, reduced from a real if precarious independence as propertied cultivators to the status of mere laborers, felt dispossessed in their own country. The poet Oliver Goldsmith caught the popular sense of alienation and bitterness in "The Deserted Village," a poem that went through five editions in the year of its publication, 1770:

> *Ill fares the land, to hastening ills a prey*
> *Where wealth accumulates and men decay.*
> *Princes and lords may flourish, or may fade*
> *A breath can make them, as a breath has made*
> *But a bold peasantry, their country's pride*
> *When once destroyed, can never be supplied.[2]*

Even Arthur Young, the foremost propagandist of the new agriculture, came at last to deplore its human cost. "I had rather," he wrote at the end of the eighteenth century, "that all the commons were sunk in the sea than that the poor should in future be treated as they have generally been hitherto."

Apart from Britain, the Low Countries, and Denmark (where Dutch methods were also introduced), the agricultural revolution was slow to spread. Enthusiasm for agricultural improvement ran high in France, particularly among the group of reformers called the Physiocrats, led by François Quesnay (1694–1774); Louis XV wore a potato flower in his lapel in an attempt to popularize the plant. But the French aristocracy was not eager to disturb the system of seigneurial dues that constituted its chief profit from the peasantry, and the revolution of 1789, in abolishing the manorial regime, left France a nation of small proprietors and delayed the introduction of large-scale capitalist agriculture for a century.

The agricultural revolution was a revolution in soil management and animal husbandry rather than mechanization. The scythe gradually replaced the sickle in the eighteenth century, but it was not until the nineteenth that threshers and reapers were introduced, and their use spread slowly. The abundance of cheap labor—and the necessity to absorb a rapidly growing population—made the introduction of laborsaving machinery in agriculture not only less necessary but also politically dangerous. No

similar inhibitions were at work in industry, where machines created more work than they destroyed. But if the agricultural revolution was not in this sense a part of the Industrial Revolution, at least until the introduction of combine harvesters in the 1880s, it was an indispensable precondition of it.

Science, Technology, and the State

The last major element in the Industrial Revolution was the development of machine technology itself. As will now be clear, the new technology was not a cause but rather an effect of conditions that favored and to some degree compelled an attempt to expand productive capacity—the extension of a market economy and the pressure of a growing population.

Bodies such as the Royal Society and the Society of Arts in England as well as informal working groups of scientists and manufacturers coordinated efforts to find solutions for specific industrial problems and sponsored prize competitions. These efforts were addressed particularly to the textile industry, which, accounting for three-fourths of all English exports, was the country's largest. England had traditionally specialized in woolens, but the leading edge of the industry was in cotton, stimulated by the popularity of fine calicoes from India and by the supply of cotton provided by slave labor in the colonial plantations. Raw materials were thus available, and a market was waiting, but productive capacity lagged. The first breakthrough occurred in 1733, when a Lancashire clockmaker, John Kay, invented the flying shuttle. This device enabled weavers to drive the shuttle across their looms by pulling strings attached to hammers. At one stroke it doubled the capacity of the loom. Yet the weavers could produce their cloth no faster than spinners could provide them with thread. The Royal Society offered a prize for a spinning machine, but not until James Hargreaves devised a set of spindles driven by a single wheel, the "spinning jenny," could the supply of thread keep up with the capacity of Kay's loom. A former barber, Richard Arkwright, attached the jenny to the water frame, a system of rollers that drew the thread taut before it was spun. The supply of thread now exceeded loom capacity until the clergyman Edmund Cartwright invented a power loom that could be operated by water or steam. Arkwright made a fortune and was rewarded with a knighthood in 1786, the first ever given to an industrialist, and Cartwright was voted £10,000 by a grateful House of Commons.

The official recognition given these men of humble status indicated the importance the state attached to commercially viable inventions. Yet the British government was far less directly involved in promoting industrial development than mercantilist France, with its state-sponsored factories, or the Prussia of Frederick the Great. The British concentrated instead on seeking raw materials, opening markets, and securing naval supremacy. From the age of the Navigation Acts (1651–1660), designed to ensure control of the colonial trade, the government pursued a consistent policy of commercial advantage. Britain fought not for *gloire* but for trading posts and privileges; what it sought above all from the wars against Louis XIV was penetration of the rich market of Spanish America, and when, 70 years later, it obtained logging rights along 300 leagues of wooded Mexican coastline, a British diplomat noted sagely, "If we manage this area wisely, there ought to be enough wood for eternity." If free enterprise and laissez-faire, the gospel so compellingly preached by Adam Smith in *The Wealth of Nations,* were to prove the formula for industrial expansion at home, it was within the framework of unfettered access to world markets and vital resources opened up by a century and a quarter of deliberate imperial policy.

The Transformation of Britain

Between about 1780 and 1830 Great Britain was transformed more profoundly than any nation in recorded history. This transformation affected the size and distribution of the population and the living conditions of the vast majority. It altered the nature and in some respects the very notion of family life, work, and leisure. It profoundly affected the bonds of social organization and the physical face of the land itself. From Britain the effects of this transformation rippled outward, first to the rest of Europe and then, through the mechanism of imperialism, to the furthest corners of the globe.

During this same period, the eyes of all Europe were fixed not on Britain but on the revolutionary upheavals in France. Yet economically and even socially, France in 1830 was still in many respects the France of 1780, a nation of peasant proprietors tilling the soil much as their ancestors had done for hundreds of years. The events in France were significant certainly, and indeed they were broadly related to the great transformation in Britain. But if we can in the last analysis see the same fundamental change at work in both countries—the triumph of the

Coal-mining operations such as the one depicted here in the county of Northumberland, belching their black smoke for miles around, transformed much of the British landscape in the early nineteenth century.

capitalist mode of production and its integration with the powers of the state—the method of this change was very different in each. In France the drama was played out as a contest for control of the state, while in Britain, where the interests of the commercial classes and the state had been completely harmonized, a social transformation of unprecedented magnitude was achieved with relatively little political disturbance.

The magnitude of economic change in Britain can best be suggested by statistics. In 1700 Britain produced 2.5 million tons of coal; in 1815, 16 million. Pig iron production rose from 17,000 tons in 1740 to 125,000 in 1796 and then doubled again to 256,000 tons in 1806. Much of this production went to service the booming cotton industry, whose output rose from 21 million yards of cloth in 1796 to 347 million by 1830. During this period cotton cloth rose from ninth to first place in the value of British manufactures, accounting for almost half of all exports. Even after 1830 textiles in general and cotton in particular constituted the essential product of the Industrial Revolution.

The Organization of Labor

The enormous increase in production attested by these figures entailed not only new energy sources and new machines but also new methods of commercial and industrial organization. Thus arose the two distinctive institutions of the Industrial Revolution: the bank and the factory. The function of banks was to concentrate capital; that of factories, to concentrate labor. There were still only 12 banks in Great Britain outside London in 1750; by 1793 there were nearly 400, and by 1815 about 900. The intimate connection between banking and industrialization was demonstrated by the fact that some of the leading inventor-industrialists of the period—Richard Arkwright and James Watt among them—formed banks of their own as their business expanded.

The modern factory was the result of the machine. Previously, production had been carried on by four more or less distinct means of organization: the small workshop; the "cottage" or "domestic" system of home labor; the urban "manufactory" (to use Marx's term), which concentrated large numbers of workers under the same roof; and the preindustrial factory, or "arsenal," which assembled workers on an open-air site such as a mine, dockyard, or foundry.

Of these four, the first two were by far the most important. The small workshop, consisting typically of a master craftsman, two or three journeymen, and a like number of apprentices, had been characteristic of the medieval city. The workshops were organized on the basis of craft or trade into guild associations, which set general conditions of work and wages and standards of production. The guild system was in decay in the eighteenth century and in Britain had been legally abolished, although the workshop itself, with its distinction among master, journeyman, and apprentice, still remained. The result was that journeymen increasingly tended to organize in defense of their working conditions and wages, a phenomenon noted with deep disapproval by the German Imperial Diet in 1731.

The cottage or domestic system was particularly widespread in the clothing trade, although it was common as well in metalworking and other pursuits. Under this arrangement the clothier provided the yarn and the looms to spinners and weavers who worked at home and whose product the clothier then collected and marketed, thus combining the function of capitalist and merchant in one. On his travels in the English countryside in the 1720s Daniel Defoe noted that the population of whole villages was engaged in cloth production, "so that no hands being unemployed, all can gain their bread." Cloth-producing centers on the Continent were similarly organized. At its most developed, the domestic system converted rural hamlets into integrated productive units in which the workers were separated only by walls.

The urban manufactory was typical of more specialized textile production, such as hat, lace, and tapestry making. The Gobelins tapestry works established by Colbert was perhaps the most famous example. The manufactory concentrated as many as 500 workers under a single roof, thus making possible a greater division of labor and a closer supervision of the productive process—both typical of the nineteenth-century factory. The manufactory differed from a factory in the modern sense chiefly in that machinery was directly hand-operated and hand-powered; human muscle still supplied the energy.

The eighteenth century reserved the term *factory* itself for industrial or mining operations in which human energy was supplemented by wind, running water, or fire. Iron foundries, arsenals, and shipyards were typical examples. Large-scale water-powered mining was well established in central Europe by the sixteenth century. Yet even though the concentration of labor and the increasing sophistication with which it was organized laid the basis for an industrial breakthrough, it could not of itself bring it about. Far greater concentrations could be found in early Ch'ing China. What made the difference was the development of iron machinery powered by coal and steam and the expanding market economy prepared by commercial capitalism. China had neither. Its immense productive base was devoted primarily to domestic consumption, and its unexcelled craftsmanship had been developed at the expense of its technology.

The factory system of the Industrial Revolution was essentially an adaptation of the urban manufactory to the new machines. These machines doomed the domestic system. The engines that powered them required buildings of unprecedented size and complexity of design. Andrew Ure described one such factory at Stockport:

> **The building consists of a main body, and two lateral wings, the former being three hundred feet long, and fifty feet wide, the latter projecting fifty-eight feet in front of the body. There are seven stories, including the attics. The moving power consists of two eighty-horse steam-engines, working rectangularly together, which are mounted with their great gearing-wheels on the ground floor . . . and are separated by a strong wall from the rest of the building. This wall is perforated for the passage of the main horizontal shaft, which, by means of great bevel wheels, turns the main upright shaft, supported at its lower end in an immense pier of masonry, of which the largest stone weighs nearly five tons.[3]**

Ure described the steam engines as the "two-fold heart" of the factory, whose alternating pulsations caused "an uniformity of impulsive power to pervade every arm of the factory." As this language suggests, the factory was conceived of as a giant organism whose life-blood was the surging force of its engines and whose vital activity—production—depended on the coordination of all its parts. This was why the factory was, much more than a gigantic enclosure for heavy machinery, an integrated system of production. Ure himself defined the na-

WOMAN   DRAGING   COAL   OLD   WOMEN   AT WORK   CHILDREN   PICKING   UP

These horrific images of work in a British coal mine of the 1840s were recorded by a French visitor. Women and children were preferred for work in the coal galleries because they were smaller and more docile than men. Notice that the woman in the left frame is chained to her cart so that she can drag it forward on all fours. The height of the galleries was approximately that of the hold on a slaving vessel.

ture of this system: "The term *Factory System* . . . designates the combined operation of many work-people, adult and young, in tending with assiduous skill a series of productive machines continuously impelled by a central power."[4]

Industrial Discipline

Ure's words reflected a profound transformation in attitudes toward work itself. The work patterns of an agrarian society had been dictated by the rhythms of nature. People satisfied with subsistence quit when they had achieved it. But production for the market was open-ended, and long before the advent of the modern factory, entrepreneurs such as the Scotsman John Law had deplored the fact that many agricultural laborers were "idle one half their time." From this equation of leisure time with idleness it was only a short step to regarding typical workers as lazy and unwilling to work—especially for their employer's profit—except when goaded by necessity. Daniel Defoe was irked when "strolling fellows" refused his offer of day labor, replying that they could earn more money by begging. This did not suggest to prospective employers the desirability of offering better wages; rather, most agreed with Samuel Johnson that "raising the wages of day laborers is wrong for it does not make them live better, but only makes them idler."

In fact, few workers could afford "idleness" in the market-oriented British economy of the eighteenth century, where most of the rural population could make ends meet only by entering the cottage system. But the productivity of workers in their own homes was imperfectly supervised at best; only in factories could a genuine work discipline be enforced. Long before such discipline came to Britain, Colbert had applied it to his state factories in France. No swearing or idleness was permitted; only hymns might be sung; and workers whose output was chronically defective were put in irons.

The mechanized factory carried this process to its logical conclusion. Instead of assigning one class of worker, the overseer, the task of imposing discipline on the rest of the workforce, such discipline was now imposed by the rhythm of the machine itself. No longer did the laborer work a machine; rather, the machine worked the laborer. The penalties for slackness were savage. "Idlers"—often women and children, who comprised the majority of the workforce in the textile mills—were flogged, tortured, and hung with weights; had vises screwed to their ears; or were tied three or four at a time "on a crossbeam above the machinery, hanging by our hands," as a witness told an investigating commission in 1835. Sixteen-hour workdays were not uncommon, and many workers toppled from weariness into their machinery: the grisly image of a worker falling into a vat of lard and becoming a part of the product in Upton Sinclair's novel *The Jungle* (1906) had its counterpart in fact. Some commentators compared the treatment of factory workers unfavorably to that of West Indian slaves, and conditions were even worse in the mines.

Family Life: A Tale of Two Cultures

The early Industrial Revolution had a devastating effect on traditional patterns of child rearing and family life among the rural poor. Child labor among the poor had been common in preindustrial Europe, but parents maintained direct supervision of their children in the field or, in the cottage system, at the wheel or loom. Once families were brought under the discipline of the factory, however, it was no longer the parent who determined the nature, duration, and rhythm of work. Adult males were indeed a minority in the typical textile mill. Employers preferred women and children, the younger the better. Andrew Ure confessed that it was "near impossible to convert persons past the age of puberty . . . into useful factory hands." At the factory of Samuel Greg, seven workers in ten were under the age of 18, one in six under the age of 10. Children entered the factory at the age of 5 or 6 as they enter school today; in some mills children as young as 3 were employed, and in one recorded case a child of 2. Ure depicted these children as "lively elves" whose work "seemed to resemble a sport." Unfortunately, the elves tended not to live very long: the child mortality rate among Britain's working poor in the mid-nineteenth century was two to three times that of the middle class. Children who emerged from what the poet William Blake (1757–1827) called the "dark Satanic mills" of early industrialism were so puny and stunted that they seemed to many observers to belong to another race.

The relative underemployment of adult males in the factories left many fathers to serve as "house-husbands" while their wives and children worked. Many young women went into domestic service in middle- and upper-class households; by the middle of the nineteenth century, female servants made up the second largest occupational category in Britain, after farmworkers. Such women were often sexually exploited by their employers; others went into prostitution in the new factory towns. Under these circumstances the male-dominated family unit that had been characteristic of early modern Europe at all social levels was gravely undermined among the new working class. Many of what we regard as typical family problems of the modern poor—single-parent, female-headed households; high rates of illegitimacy and child delinquency; participation in the underground economies of prostitution and theft—were already in evidence in early industrial Britain. The Poor Law of 1834 dealt savagely with the destitute. The assumption behind it was that unemployment and destitution were the result not of low wage rates and violent fluctuations in the industrial economy but of personal idleness and unwillingness to work. Paupers were herded into workhouses where husbands were separated from wives, as if in jail, and parents from children. Those who died there were denied church burial. Poverty itself was thus made a crime in both this world and the next.

In contrast to the working-class family, the bourgeois household was becoming more closely knit. It was also

Child Labor

This testimony was given by Joseph Hebergam, age 17, before a select committee of Parliament in 1832.

Q.: You had fourteen and a half hours of actual labor at 7 years of age?

A.: Yes.

Q.: What means were taken to keep you at your work so long?

A.: There were three overlookers; there was a head overlooker, and then there was one man kept to grease the machines, and then there was one kept on purpose to strap.

Q.: Was the main business of one of the overlookers that of strapping the children up to this excessive labor?

A.: Yes, the same as strapping an old restive horse that has fallen down and will not get up.

Q.: How far did you live from the mill?

A.: A good mile.

Q.: Was it very painful for you to move?

A.: Yes, in the morning I could scarcely walk, and my brother and sister used out of kindness to take me under each arm, and run with me to the mill, and my legs dragged on the ground. . . .

Q.: Were you sometimes too late?

A.: Yes; and if we were five minutes too late, the overlooker would take a strap, and beat us till we were black and blue.

Source: "Report of the Select Committee on the Factories Bill," in *Industrial Revolution: Children's Employment*, vol. 2 (Shannon: Irish University Press, *British Parliamentary Papers*, 1968–1972), pp. 157–159.

more child-centered than ever before. Children had been viewed traditionally as miniature adults. They were neither the object of family life nor the prime focus of its concern. In peasant families children were put to work as soon as they were able; in aristocratic ones they were boarded out at the age of 7 or 8. But in the wake of such reformers as Rousseau and Pestalozzi childhood was not only defined negatively as the absence of such adult traits as size, strength, and rationality but also seen as a distinct phase of life with its own experiential value. Rousseau and Pestalozzi were succeeded by a torrent of popular manuals on child rearing with titles such as *The Parents' Handbook.* "The child," declared the poet Wordsworth, "is father to the man," and the bourgeois household was gradually reconceived as a kind of factory whose product was the child, an attitude still reflected in our language today when we speak of children as "products" of either good or broken homes.

While thus internalizing the values of industry within the home itself, the bourgeois household was also viewed as a refuge from the competitive pressures of society, "a tent pitch'd in a world not right," in the phrase of the poet Coventry Patmore. The influential Victorian critic John Ruskin called it "the place of peace; the shelter, not only from all injury, but from all terror, doubt, and division." This idealized vision of "home, sweet home" implied a domestic division of labor between a male breadwinner and a woman whose function as wife and mother was to maintain a secure and idyllic refuge. This reinforced the patriarchal dominance of the bourgeois household just when it was being shattered in that of the working class.

The bourgeois wife and mother was expected to subordinate herself totally to her husband and to have no thought or interest beyond his welfare and comfort. Such subordination began in the bedroom. The Victorian woman was taught not merely to put her husband's pleasure before her own but to experience no pleasure at all. As one physician wrote, "A modest woman seldom desires any sexual gratification for herself. She submits to her husband, but only to please him; and, but for the desire of maternity, would far rather be relieved of his attentions."

In every respect, then, the working-class and bourgeois family experience was sharply contrasted. In the bourgeois home the husband was the master and sole provider; in the working-class one it was often the wife who found employment while the husband maintained whatever home life was possible. The bourgeois family exalted the child as the "product" for which it existed, while the children of the working class were expendable units in the dredging of coal or the making of textiles. The result, wrote the novelist and later statesman Benjamin Disraeli, was that Britain had become

two nations between whom there is no intercourse and no sympathy; who are ignorant of each other's habits, thoughts and feelings, as if they were dwellers in different zones, or inhabitants of different planets, who are formed by a different breeding, are fed by a different food, are ordered by different manners, and are not governed by the same laws.[5]

Capital, Labor, and the Rights of Man

Disraeli's two nations might also be given another name: capital and labor. Writing in the 1830s, the French novelist Honoré de Balzac (1799–1850) remarked that the three orders of Old Regime society "have been replaced by what we nowadays call classes. We have lettered [professional] classes, industrial classes, upper classes, middle classes, etc." Balzac's "etc." would include the growing army of industrial laborers, which Marx would call the proletariat and others, more simply, the working class.

The novelty in a social division between classes instead of orders was that it no longer assumed a harmony but rather a conflict of interests between the various groupings, particularly between the two broad categories known as capital and labor. The traditional medieval distinction among those who worked, those who fought, and those who prayed—the peasantry, the aristocracy, and the clergy—was based on the idea that each order had a distinctive function that was essential to the good of the whole and the glory of God: If the role of the fighters and prayers included command over the bodies and souls of the workers, it was on behalf of a common welfare that embraced all. Martin Luther, whose revolution shattered the unity of the priesthood, reinforced the idea of subordination when he preached that each man had a vocation prescribed by God in which it was his duty to labor and to remain content.

The Enlightenment brought with it a fundamental change of attitude. Its prime political documents, the Declaration of Independence and the Declaration of the Rights of Man, asserted the legal equality of all men but said nothing about their economic rights. They thus divorced the political realm, in which citizens might call on the state to enforce their legal rights, from the economic one, in which the state was, optimally, a neutral arbiter of the private contracts that individuals had entered into of their own free will. Implicit in this view was John Locke's distinction between society as a voluntary association of equals and the state as the agency designed to provide a secure arena for the interplay of private interests.

This point of view received its most persuasive expression in the Scotsman Adam Smith's (1723–1790) *Inquiry into the Nature and Causes of the Wealth of Nations* (1776). Smith believed that the generation of wealth was the result of each individual pursuing his or her own private interest in an arena of competitive equality. The public interest was the sum of competitive interactions, since the only generalized interest all actors shared in an economic system was to maximize its total wealth, a goal best achieved by ensuring them the liberty to pursue their interests, whether as producers or as consumers, as they saw fit.

From this premise it followed that the obtrusive government regulation characteristic of mercantilism could only dampen initiative and retard the creation of wealth. Such a viewpoint was welcomed not only by late-eighteenth-century entrepreneurs but, at least in Britain and America, by the government as well; as William Pitt the Younger exclaimed to Smith, "We are all your pupils." To those who predicted that chaos would result from an unregulated market, Smith responded by invoking the idea of an "invisible hand" that guided selfish individual interests toward collective profit and efficiency through the laws of supply and demand. Taking this notion a step further, his successors, notably David Ricardo (1772–1823), argued that the relations between capital and labor were governed by natural laws as fixed and immutable as the laws of physics. Those laws enshrined the clash of interests at the heart of society. Competition, not cooperation, was the law of social life.

For anyone unable to compete, there could be only a struggle to survive. Long before the proletarians began to perceive their employers as class antagonists, however, the spokesmen of the new industrial order had portrayed them as enemies of progress. In effect, the working class was defined negatively as having no interests and hence no social existence. Its only desire, according to writers such as William Temple, was to be as idle as possible. "Great wages and certainty of employment render the inhabitants of cities insolent and debauched," Temple declared. He concluded that "the only way to make [the poor] temperate and industrious is to lay them under a necessity of laboring all the time they can spare from meals and sleep, in order to procure the common necessities of life." Ironically, both Adam Smith and David Ricardo regarded labor as the source of all economic value, an idea that was to be crucial to the thought of Karl Marx. But Smith and Ricardo failed to relate the abstract value of labor to the actual toil of the laborer. In effect, labor was seen as something to be extracted from the recalcitrant body of the worker as coal was hacked out of the side of a hill.

At first, workers' resistance to the new industrial order was directed chiefly at the introduction of new machinery or the importation of foreign labor or products. As early as 1675 the silk weavers of East London smashed 35 mechanical looms imported from Holland. In 1719 the weavers rose again to protest the importation of cheap calico fabrics from India and secured an act of Parliament against them. The use of Irish immigrant labor occasioned the riots of 1736, which included a bomb blast in the houses of Parliament. Anti-Irish feeling also sparked the great Gordon riots of 1780, when London burned for six days.

The most sustained violence occurred between 1811 and 1817, a period marked not only by an intensive mechanization of textile production but by the general depression that set in with the end of the Napoleonic wars. A destitute rioter in East Anglia summed up the plight of many in 1816: "Here I am between Earth and Sky, so help me God. I would rather lose my life than go home as I am." The rioters were called Luddites after a legendary figure, Ned Ludd, who may have destroyed stocking frames in Yorkshire in the 1780s. *Luddism* has gone into the dictionary as a synonym for mindless opposition to change. In fact, the Luddites were chiefly artisans and skilled workers who put forward a platform of political grievances and demands, including the right to organize. Industrialists opposed worker organization for obvious reasons of self-interest but also on the grounds that it interfered with the working of the "objective" laws of economics to the detriment of productive efficiency and hence general prosperity. The doctrine that the free interplay of private market interests produced maximum public benefit in the form of wealth and happiness was known as economic liberalism or, in a phrase borrowed from the French, *laissez-faire* (roughly, "leave it alone").

The philosopher Jeremy Bentham (1748–1832) argued that it was actually possible to calculate social benefits on an arithmetic scale and thereby determine the public good, which Bentham defined as "the greatest happiness of the greatest number." Bentham agreed with Smith and Ricardo that this happiness could be achieved only by noninterference in economic activity, especially by the state. "Every law is an evil because every law is a violation of liberty," he wrote, "so that the government can only choose between evils."

But if nonintervention was enjoined on the state, it applied equally to organizations, such as guilds or unions, that attempted to raise wages artificially or to reduce working hours. The chief economic role allotted the state in the laissez-faire dispensation was to prevent such organizations from arising to do mischief, and the only good laws the state could enact in the economic sphere were those suppressing them. The government did indeed act, spurred in the 1790s by fear of political clubs on the Jacobin model organized by the London shoemaker Thomas Hardy and by tracts such as Tom Paine's *The Rights of Man,* which demanded the establishment of a republic. In 1799 and 1800

Luddism

This declaration by framework knitters, a formerly prosperous class of artisan workers who possessed a royal charter regulating their production of hosiery, illustrates the grievances of skilled craftsmen, which included complaints about the inferior quality of machine-made goods as well as fears of depressed wages and unemployment. "Ned Ludd" was a symbolic signature, referring to an already mythic figure, and "Sherwood Forest" was meant to evoke not only the legend of Robin Hood but also the freedom and independence traditionally associated with England's woodsmen.

Whereas by the charter granted by our late sovereign Lord Charles II, by the Grace of God King of Great Britain, France, and Ireland, the framework knitters are empowered to break and destroy all frames and engines that fabricate articles in a fraudulent and deceitful manner and to destroy all framework knitters' goods whatsoever that are so made. . . . And we do hereby declare that we will break and destroy all manner of frames whatsoever that make the following spurious articles and all frames whatsoever that do not pay the regular prices heretofore agreed to by the masters and workmen—All print net frames making single press and frames not working by the rack and rent and not paying the price regulated in 1810: warp frames working single yarn or too coarse hole—not working by the rack, not paying the rent and prices regulated in 1809. . . . All frames of whatsoever description the workmen of whom are not paid in the current coin of the realm will invariably be destroyed. . . . Given under my hand the first day of January 1812. God protect the Trade.

Ned Ludd's Office
Sherwood Forest

Source: A. Aspinall and E. A. Smith, eds., *English Historical Documents*, vol. 11: *1783–1832* (Oxford: Oxford University Press, 1959), p. 531.

it passed the Combination Acts, which forbade workers to organize for any purpose whatever. However, it did nothing about industrial lobbies such as the General Chamber of Manufacturers, organized by Matthew Boulton and Josiah Wedgwood to promote the interests of capital. Nor did most advocates of laissez-faire seem to regard the thousands of enclosure acts passed by Parliament on behalf of private interests as state intervention.

As the catastrophic effects of industrialization on the working class became apparent, however, widespread demand arose for government regulation of at least the conditions of child and female labor. "A feeling very generally exists," the conservative Thomas Carlyle remarked, "that the condition and disposition of the Working Classes is a rather ominous matter at present; that something ought to be said, something ought to be done, in regard to it." That "something," largely the work of reformers such as Francis Place (1771–1854) and the earl of Shaftesbury (1801–1885), was a series of Factory Acts,

notably the Factory Act of 1833 and the Mines and Collieries Act of 1842, which prohibited the employment of children under the age of 9 in textile mills and children under 10 and women underground in mines, and the Factory Act of 1847, which established a ten-hour day for women and children. Slowly, the pulverizing conditions of industrial labor were relaxed, and its devastating impact on the working-class family was mitigated.

Robert Owen, Industrial Reformer

The most sustained opposition to laissez-faire economics came from Robert Owen (1771–1858), industrialist, philanthropist, and founder of British socialism. Owen

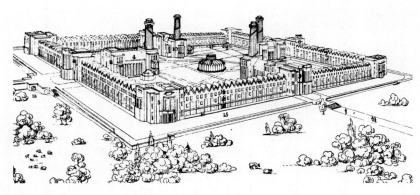

Stedman Whitwell's conception of one of Robert Owen's utopian communities is a cross between a medieval fortress and a planned city, with its fanciful architecture and rigid thoroughfares. The pastoral scene in which it is so incongruously set emphasizes its rejection of commerce. Such communities were designed as self-sufficient living systems for 500 to 2,000 people.

rejected the claim of laissez-faire economics to scientific status. Far from objectively conforming to the immutable laws of economics, he contended, it was only one means among many for ordering society, and a "low" and "inferior" one at that which created not wealth and harmony but misery and conflict.[6]

Owen was born in a small Welsh town, the son of a saddler and ironmonger and a local farmer's daughter. At the age of 15 he migrated to Manchester. Here he shared rooms at one point with Robert Fulton, the inventor of the steamboat, whom he lent £100 out of his first savings. Shy and diffident, Owen was nonetheless manager of a cotton mill employing 500 people by the age of 19. In 1794 he became a partner in the Chorlton Twist Company, one of Manchester's principal textile firms, and five years later he persuaded his fellow partners to purchase the New Lanark spinning mills near Glasgow from the industrialist David Dale, whose daughter Caroline he married.

Thus far Owen's career resembled that of many of the other self-made industrialists of the era. But he was already a member of the Manchester Board of Health and keenly interested in reform. Determined to make New Lanark a model for industrial development, he rebuilt the workers' houses, cleaned and paved their streets, provided cheap coal for heating, and opened a company store that sold goods at cost.

As Owen's views grew more radical (and his profit margins lower), his business partners became restive. In 1813 he bought them out and formed a new company whose partners, including Jeremy Bentham, agreed to limit themselves to a 5 percent return. This enabled Owen to carry out the educational theories that he had gradually developed, which he first spelled out in *A New View of Society* (1813). Owen argued that people were wholly the products of their environment and education. He built a large educational complex at New Lanark, the

heart of which was the first nursery school in Great Britain. His school, which anticipated much of modern progressive education, was run on the principle of play; no child was forced to do anything against his or her wishes, and no punishment was ever imposed. New Lanark became a mecca for reformers of every stripe and a major tourist attraction as well: between 1816 and 1826 nearly 20,000 visitors streamed through its gates.

Owen himself had meanwhile turned his interests to reform on a national level. His agitation was largely responsible for the passage of the early (though ineffective) Factory Act of 1819. By this time he had become convinced of the radical injustice of contemporary society. Always a religious skeptic, he now openly denounced the clergy, thus parting company with mainstream reformers who sought to mitigate the evils of the Industrial Revolution by an appeal to Christian ethics. Owen shocked a meeting of his fellow magnates by declaring that it would be better for the cotton industry to perish altogether than to be carried on under conditions that destroyed the health of its workers.

Between 1817 and 1820 Owen put forward a sweeping plan to reorganize society on the basis of small, cooperative communities. Each community would contain 500 to 2,000 members and would be both agriculturally and industrially self-sufficient. The major buildings, suitably spaced and landscaped, would be contained in a large rectangle, giving everyone access to light and air. Production for profit was prohibited; goods were to be distributed on the basis of labor performed. Each community was to be completely self-governing. Owen envisioned such communities as establishing regional and national federations and, ultimately, a worldwide one. It was, he fervently believed, the social, economic, and political form of the future.

Owen traveled widely over the next several years in Ireland and on the Continent to promote his plan, and in 1825 he set up the model community of New Harmony on a 20,000-acre site in Indiana. Despite initial enthusiasm, it collapsed after three years, having cost Owen the bulk of his fortune. He returned to England in 1829 to find that in his absence he had become a hero to the nascent British labor movement, which, coming into the open after the repeal of the Combination Acts in 1824, had adopted his call for worker self-governance. In October 1833 he launched what was to become the Grand National Consolidated Trades Union, the first nationwide confederation of labor in history. Local unions and associations rushed to join, and the Grand Union claimed no fewer than 500,000 members by the spring of 1834.

Thoroughly alarmed, employers initiated lockouts of workers who joined the Union, and the government cracked down as well, deporting seven Dorset workers who went down in labor history as the Tolpuddle martyrs. What doomed the Grand Union, however, was the very speed at which it had grown, outstripping both its organizational resources and its agreed-on goals. Owen himself was disillusioned, as the union, far from evolving peacefully toward communal living, appeared bent on a bloody confrontation with capital. By late 1834 it had ceased to exist in all but name, and embittered labor militants turned their backs on socialism in Britain for the next 50 years.

Owen continued to promote his ideal communities, seven more of which were founded in Britain between 1825 and 1847. An exchange founded by the flannel weavers of Rochdale in 1844 became the basis of the modern cooperative movement, which still flourishes in the midwestern United States. Owen himself continued to see America as the best hope for the realization of his principles. All four of his sons became U.S. citizens; the eldest, Robert Dale Owen, served in Congress and had a distinguished career as an advocate of educational reform and women's rights. Active to the end, Owen addressed public meetings into his eighty-eighth year. Carried home to die in his native town, he spent the last day of his life planning the reform of education in the parish.

The Population Explosion

An observer visiting our planet about 250 years ago and returning today would probably be struck by two things: first, by how many more human beings are inhabiting it, and second, by how densely concentrated they are in specific areas. The first of these phenomena goes popularly by the name of the population explosion; the second is called urbanization. Both of them are related to the Industrial Revolution, though they are by no means simply its result.

The human population of the earth was probably well under 10 million at the time of the neolithic revolution 10,000 years ago. Agriculture made historical civilization possible, and civilization, from a very early point, was marked everywhere it developed by city-dwelling. Thus a continuous rise in population and a propensity to urbanization have been characteristic of civilization from the beginning. What has been unprecedented is the steady surge of population since about the mid-eighteenth century. In 1750 the world population was under 800 million. It reached 1 billion by about 1830, 2 billion in 1930, 3 billion in 1960, 4 billion in 1975, and 5 billion in 1986. At the same time, the number of people engaged in agriculture has been steadily diminishing. In most places, at least 80 percent of the population was engaged in agriculture in 1750; in most industrialized nations today, the figure is less than 5 percent.

POPULATION GROWTH, 1750–2000 (in millions)

	1750	1800	1850	1900	1950	2000 (projected)
Asia (including territories east of the Urals)	498	630	801	925	1,381	3,458
China	200	323	430	436	560	1,200
India and Pakistan	190	195	233	285	434	1,269
Africa	106	107	111	133	222	768
Europe (including territories west of the Urals)	167	208	284	430	572	880
North America	6	7	26	82	166	354
South and Central America	16	24	38	74	162	638
Australasia and Pacific Islands	2	2	2	6	13	32
World	**791**	**978**	**1,262**	**1,650**	**2,515**	**6,296**

These numbers suggest some obvious conclusions. The population explosion began before the advent of the Industrial Revolution, and it was well under way as a worldwide phenomenon long before the effects of industrialization reached beyond Europe. However, it has unquestionably been sustained by the Industrial Revolution, including the continuous increase in agricultural capacity known today as the "green revolution." Despite the fears of Malthus and others, the food supply has kept pace with population growth; indeed, most of the industrially developed nations suffer at present from excess productive capacity, which has led them to warehouse enormous quantities of food and to subsidize farmers to keep large portions of their acreage fallow. It remains true that world nutritional levels are declining as a whole and that famines have broken out in places like the Sahel region of Africa, but these conditions are the result of unequal economic development and wealth, often compounded by political breakdown rather than by inadequate world capacity as a whole.

Although there is much debate about the causes of the population explosion, it has been associated everywhere not with an increase in fertility but with a decrease in mortality. The difference may be summarized by a single statistical comparison. In 1700 only 475 of every 1,000 people born live would reach the age of 20; by the mid-twentieth century, 960 would do so. The sharp decline in the death rate was essentially the result of a reduction in mortality from infectious diseases and (after the introduction of modern contraceptive devices) infanticide. Emigration and the settling of new lands relieved some of the consequent population pressure. Some 60 million Europeans left the Continent between 1846 and 1924, mostly for the Western Hemisphere, the Siberian hinterland of Russia, and Australasia. Not all of this resulted in net population gain. White settlers in Australia completely exterminated the native population of the large island of Tasmania, and four-fifths of the Maori population of New Zealand and three-fourths of the Indian population of the United States had been destroyed by the 1870s.

The first great surge in population was to a large extent a European phenomenon. In the absence of reliable data (only Sweden kept mortality statistics before 1800), we can only speculate that a cyclic remission in the incidence of microbial diseases and the increase in agricultural productivity in northern Europe combined to trigger growth. Given the enormously high level of mortality, even a marginal increase in the survival rate could have had a significant impact on population.

Not until after 1850 was control of infectious diseases made possible by the introduction of hygiene and sanitation, particularly in the purification of water supplies and the disposal of waste. These two measures did more to reduce mortality rates than any others, including the development of vaccines and so-called wonder drugs (the sulfa family in 1935 and antibiotics, most notably penicillin, in the 1940s). The concern for sanitation was at first provoked by the appallingly high mortality rates among workers in early industrial towns, but it was extended systematically only after the scientific connection between dirt and disease had been established by the research of Pasteur in France, Lister in Scotland, and Koch in Germany in the 1860s and 1870s. The results were dramatic. Deaths from typhoid fell by more than 85 percent in England over a 35-year period, and those from malaria declined by nearly as much in Italy over 20 years. It was not the ability to cure infectious disease but the simple reduction of exposure to it that accounted for this progress.

The population of Europe (including Russia) roughly quadrupled between 1650 and 1900, from about 100 to some 430 million, exclusive of emigration. From less than a fifth of the world's population in the mid-seventeenth century, Caucasians had become a third of it by the dawn of the twentieth. This was the high-water mark of European demographic advance. The introduction of Western standards of sanitation to other areas of the globe—essential to preserve the health of European colonizers in the heyday of imperialism—ignited a similar population explosion in Asia and Africa. By the 1980s non-Western peoples again accounted for approximately four-fifths of the world's population.

Perhaps the most significant and far-reaching effect of the Industrial Revolution was the urbanization of Western society. The city had occupied a distinctive place in the West since the Middle Ages. With its walls and towers, it stood off boldly from the surrounding countryside. No less important were the charters and privileges, often won by long struggle, that gave it a unique degree of self-government and political importance. The late medieval city-states of Italy and the free imperial cities of Germany were the finest flowering of this proudly independent civic culture, and neither the Renaissance nor the Reformation would have been conceivable without them.

The great eighteenth-century cities of London, Paris, and Amsterdam, with their worldwide commercial and financial connections, were prototypes of a new kind of city, the global metropolis. But such cities were still exceptional. With nearly a million inhabitants by 1800, London was ten times larger than the next British city and 100 times or more the size of the majority of Britain's towns, which still served, as they had for hundreds of years, primarily as markets for the local country-

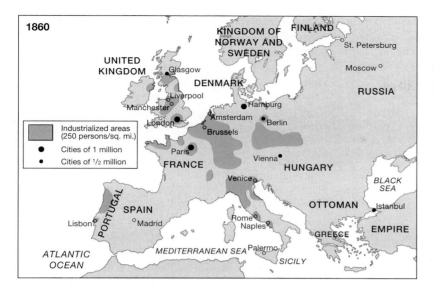

MAP 31.2 URBANIZATION IN EUROPE

side. Although urbanization had reached 50 percent or more in some highly commercialized regions of the Low Countries, in Britain less than a third and in France less than a quarter of the population lived in towns.

The Industrial Revolution changed all that. Factory towns sprang up overnight near the coalfields and iron mines of Britain's industrial heartland. The pulse of manufacturing turned regional marketing centers into points on a nationwide distribution grid and old coastal towns into international seaports. These in turn were now linked by a new mode of transportation ideally designed for hauling large quantities of goods, the steam locomotive. The British census of 1851 distinguished between manufacturing, mining, and hardware towns; re-

gional centers and seaports; and spas and coastal resorts. Like everything else, the city was now a specialized category, a part of the universal division of labor.

And it was to the city that the rapidly growing British population now came—to London above all. From under a million inhabitants in 1800, London swelled to 2.5 million by midcentury and 4.5 million by the early 1900s. Half again as many people lived in its suburbs. No city of its size had ever been seen before in the world. No other British city approached it, but many others achieved rates of growth that were proportionally no less impressive. By 1851 half the population lived in urban areas, and that number would grow to three-quarters by 1900. The percentage of farm laborers declined correspondingly. As the

MAP 31.3   RAILWAYS IN GREAT BRITAIN,
1825–1914

Glasgow
Edinburgh
Ayr
Newcastle
Sunderland
Carlisle
Stockton and
Darlington
Railway (1830)
Lancaster
York
Liverpool and
Manchester
Railway (1830)
Hull
Holyhead
Crewe
Lincoln
Ruabon
Norwich
Birmingham
Rugby
Cambridge
Merthyr
Gloucester
Colchester
Cardiff
Oxford
Bristol
London
Salisbury
Brighton
Dover
Exeter

0   50   100 Miles

Railways by 1836:
1,000 miles built
Railways by 1852:
7,000 miles built
Railways by 1914:
23,000 miles built

olution was about 17,000. The cotton industry transformed it in the 1770s and 1780s, and the grime-blackened factories with their surrounding slums that seemed to mushroom overnight made it the prototype of the new industrial city. By the 1780s its population had grown to 40,000, by 1801 to 70,000, and by 1831 to 142,000: an eightfold increase in 80 years. Visitors commented on the new appearance of what had once been described as the "fairest" town in the region. A Prussian visitor noted in 1814 the pall that hung over it. "The cloud of coal vapor may be observed from afar. The houses are blackened by it. The river . . . is so filled with waste dye-stuffs that it resembles a dyer's vat." Another visitor proclaimed it "abominably filthy" and obnoxious to the senses: "the Steam Engine is pestiferous, the Dyehouses noisesome and offensive, and the water of the river as black as ink." The Frenchman Alexis de Tocqueville summed up contemporary opinion in 1835, when he wrote of Manchester, "Civilization works its miracles, and civilized man is turned back almost into a savage."

A river of humanity streams up this impossibly congested street in Gustave Doré's depiction of nineteenth-century London. The vividly gesturing porters and drivers suggest the vigor and tumult of a great commercial metropolis, and the Dickensian fat boy asleep on the pile of cargo in the center adds a touch of humor, but the picture recedes darkly into a sea of anonymous human faces and forms, an ominous comment on the mass society Doré saw taking shape.

British commentator Robert Vaughan wrote as early as 1843, "If any nation is to be lost or saved by the character of its great cities, our own is that nation."[7]

Manchester: Factory Town

If any city might have served as a test case for Vaughan's assertion, it was industrial Manchester. Situated in Lancashire west of the Pennine mountains and connected to the port of Liverpool by the river Mersey, Manchester had long been a modestly prosperous regional marketing center whose population on the eve of the Industrial Rev-

Nowhere else was the confrontation between the classes more starkly posed. A local clergyman noted:

There is no town in the world where the distance between the rich and the poor is so great. . . . There is far less *personal* communication between the master cotton spinner

and his workmen . . . than there is between the Duke of Wellington and the humblest laborer on his estate.

When Friedrich Engels, the colleague of Karl Marx and himself a Manchester industrialist, tried to engage a "middle class gentleman" in conversation about the

Two Views of Manchester

Two highly contrasting views of Manchester were provided by John Aikin and, some 40 years later, James Kay.

The prodigious extension of the several branches of the Manchester manufactures has likewise greatly increased the business of several trades and manufactures connected with or dependent upon them. The making of paper at mills in the vicinity has been brought to great perfection, and now includes all kinds, from the strongest parcelling paper to the finest writing sorts, and that on which banker's bills are printed. To the ironmongers' shops, which are greatly increased of late, are generally annexed smithies, where many articles are made, even to nails. A considerable iron foundry is established in Salford, in which are cast most of the articles wanted in Manchester and its neighborhood. . . . The tin-plate workers have found additional employment in furnishing many articles for spinning machines; as have also the braziers in casting wheels for the motion-work of the rollers used in them; and the clockmakers in cutting them. . . . To this sketch of the progress of the trade of Manchester, it will be proper to subjoin some information respecting the condition and manners of its tradesmen, the gradual advances to opulence and luxury. . . . Within the last twenty or thirty years the vast increase of foreign trade has caused many of the Manchester manufactures to travel abroad. . . . And the town has now in every respect assumed the style and manners of one of the commercial capitals of Europe.

———

Manchester, properly so called, is chiefly inhabited by shopkeepers and the laboring classes. . . . The rapid growth of the cotton manufacture has attracted hither operatives from every part of the kingdom, and Ireland has poured forth the most destitute of her hordes to supply the constantly increasing demand for labor. . . . The population . . . is crowded into one dense mass, in cottages separated by narrow, unpaved, and almost pestilential streets, in an atmosphere loaded with the smoke and exhalations of a large manufacturing city. . . . The houses . . . are too generally built back to back, having therefore only one outlet, no yard, no privy, and no receptacle for refuse. Consequently the narrow streets, in which mud and water stagnate, become the common receptacle of offal and ordure. . . .

[These districts] . . . are inhabited by a turbulent population, which, rendered reckless by dissipation and want, . . . has frequently committed daring assaults on the liberty of the more peaceful portions of the working classes, and the most frightful devastations on the property of their masters. Machines have been broken, and factories gutted and burned at mid-day. . . . The police form . . . so weak a screen against the power of the mob, that popular violence is now, in almost every instance, controlled by the presence of a military force.

Sources: J. Aikin, *A Description of Manchester* (London: John Stockdale, 1795), pp. 176–184 passim; J. Kay, *The Moral and Physical Condition of the Working Classes Employed in the Cotton Manufacture in Manchester,* 2nd ed. (London: Cass, 1970), pp. 20–43 passim.

condition of the city's slums, he received the brusque reply, "And yet there is a great deal of money made here.
Good morning, sir."[8] It was no doubt the existence of such
attitudes that made an American visitor "thank Heaven
that I am not a poor man with a family in England."

Such despair, as the reformer Francis Place noted,
had turned large sections of the Manchester working class
into potential revolutionaries. In 1817 a band of destitute
weavers set out for London to protest their wages, only to
be turned back by force. Two years later, in August 1819,
troops fired point-blank into a mass rally at St. Peter's
Field in the city, killing 11 people and wounding some
400, including 113 women and children. It was the first
battle of modern labor history, and the "Peterloo Massacre," as it was called in mocking comparison to the Battle of Waterloo, symbolized the threat of class war.

In the 1830s and 1840s Manchester often seemed on
the verge of anarchy. Popular unrest exploded again with
the economic slumps in 1829 and 1836. These were compounded by devastating outbreaks of typhoid and cholera,
which were added to the normal toll of respiratory and in-
testinal diseases taken by air and water pollution and by
the lack of sanitation: it was estimated that there was one
indoor toilet for every 212 inhabitants of the city. Moreover, despite its phenomenal growth, Manchester was still
being governed as if it were a village. There was no regular police force, no provision for social services, and no attempt to regulate growth. Not until 1853, when the population, now in excess of 300,000, had begun to sprawl
over into suburbs as chaotic as the center itself, was Manchester formally incorporated as a city.

*Raw industrial waste was dumped directly into
Manchester's river, the Irwell, whose still and blackened
water were captured in James Mudd's 1854 photograph.*

As the historian Asa Briggs explained:

**All roads led to Manchester in the 1840s. It was the
shock city of the age, and it was just as difficult to be
neutral about it as it was to be neutral about Chicago in
the 1890s or Los Angeles in the 1930s.[9]**

Reformers focused on the city, and novelists such as
Elizabeth Gaskell in *Mary Barton* and Charles Dickens
in *Hard Times* depicted it, as Gaskell said, to "give utter-
ance to the agony" of the poor. Manchester's mill owners, protesting the unflattering portraits of themselves in
such social novels, complained that their services to the
nation in creating new wealth and opportunity were un-
fairly disparaged. But whichever side one took in the
great class debate, all agreed that Manchester was the
crucible of an unprecedented phenomenon, as prodigal
of energy and power as it was of misery and despair: the
industrial city.

Ironically, Manchester itself had already passed the
peak of its industrial importance. Its factories were ob-
solescent in comparison to newer models elsewhere,
and its prosperity rested increasingly on its importance
as a trading center. The Manchester Exchange, first
opened to the public in 1809 and greatly expanded in
1838, was the largest brokerage facility in Europe.
With economic maturity came at least the beginnings
of civic responsibility. A local sanitary code, one of the
first in the country, was drafted in 1845. The next year
Manchester got its first public parks and a bequest to
found what became the greatest of the early civic universities. In 1857 it held an exposition that drew more
than 1.3 million visitors and led to the founding of an
orchestra. By late Victorian times the city that had been
described as "the entrance to hell" by the commander
sent to quell disturbances there in 1839 had become respectable and almost staid.

The Spread of
the Industrial Revolution

The rest of Europe was hardly stagnant while Britain was
undergoing its great revolution. Population and production, both agricultural and industrial, were rising on the
Continent between 1780 and 1830, and cities were growing. Arthur Young was impressed with the progressive

nature of farming in parts of France on his travels in the 1780s, while German farmers introduced a variety of new crops into their country, including potatoes, beets, hops, and tobacco. Nor were industrial improvements confined to Britain. In France new methods of iron and steel production were developed, and Joseph-Marie Jacquard invented a silk loom. In Germany the world's first sugar-beet refinery began operation. Swiss and Dutch banking were highly developed, and the eighteenth century saw major improvements in roads, bridges, and harbors and extensive canal-building projects in northern France and Prussia. An observer looking for the likeliest place for the Industrial Revolution to begin would probably have suggested the Netherlands in 1700 or France in 1750.

Exploitation and Resistance

It was in Britain nonetheless that the spark of the Industrial Revolution caught fire. In France a largely parasitic aristocracy drained off capital investment, a top-heavy governmental bureaucracy often crushed the initiative it was trying to promote, and the absence of a central banking system hampered the flow of credit. Germany suffered from its division into hundreds of tiny principalities and the chaos of internal customs barriers and road and river tolls that this engendered. The Dutch republic, the great commercial success of the seventeenth century, had exhausted itself in struggles with Louis XIV. In eastern Europe, including Prussia, Austria, and Russia, the persistence of serfdom hamstrung the movement of labor so critical to industrial development.

Thus it was not until about 1830 that industrialization per se—the use of power-driven machinery and the organization of labor and production in factories—came to the Continent. It appeared first along a belt that included the Low Countries, northeastern France and western Germany, and northern Italy, where the concentration of a skilled and urbanized workforce, plentiful deposits of coal and iron, good road and river communications, and access to seaports were most favorable. Its spread, however, was notably uneven. It advanced most rapidly in Belgium, which profited not only from its commercial connections with the Netherlands, from which it had just achieved independence, but also from its rich deposits of coal.

France, despite its economic potential, remained primarily a nation of small farmers throughout the nineteenth century; in 1881 its population was still two-thirds rural. A key variable was social attitude. French capital, long sheltered behind government subsidies and high tariffs, was far less entrepreneurial than its British counterpart; the Parisian banker Seillière was all too typical

when, returning from a visit to an ironworks in 1836, he was reported "scared out of his wits by the investment going on." Large-scale financing was still a novelty in France, and much of it was introduced by foreign firms, such as the great international banking house of Rothschild. French industry, which specialized in luxury items—silks, carpets, tapestries, porcelain, fashion clothing, vintage wines, and brandies—was craft-oriented and not easily adaptable to mass production. A British visitor at a French industrial exhibit in 1802 remarked that there was not a single item of ordinary consumption on display.

In fact, it was the British who introduced the first power machines into France. William Wilkinson set up the first coke furnace in the country at Le Creusot in 1785; not until 1819 was another built. John Holker, who settled in France in the mid-eighteenth century, was almost single-handedly responsible for setting up a modernized textile industry in Rouen, and as late as 1840 it was observed that the majority of foremen in its plants were from Lancashire. The pace of British investment stepped up considerably in the 1820s. Aaron Manby and Daniel Manton set up a large ironworks plant at Charenton in 1827 that became an industrywide model, and the same partners introduced the first gas lighting in Paris two years later.

As in Britain, industrial expansion in France was at first largely confined to textile manufacturing; cotton production doubled between 1830 and 1846. A railway-building boom in the 1840s brought increased demand for iron and steel as well. In the two decades after 1848 the French economy entered the industrial era, although many small-scale enterprises continued to flourish. The value of industrial production doubled, foreign trade trebled, internal commerce quadrupled, and railway mileage and total industrial horsepower quintupled.

As in Britain, industrialization was accompanied by ruthless exploitation of the workforce, including women and children. Conditions in France had never been idyllic; in 1776 the bookbinders of Paris had struck to win a 14-hour day. But the regime of the factory intensified the worst abuses of the preindustrial workshop. An observer in the department of Nord described working conditions in 1826:

> **The greed of the manufacturers knows no limits; they sacrifice their workers to enrich themselves. They are not content with reducing these poor creatures to slavery by making them work in unhealthy workshops from which fresh air is excluded, from 5 A.M. to 8 P.M. (and sometimes 10 P.M.) in the summer, and from 6 A.M. to 9 P.M. in the winter; they force them to work a part of Sunday as well. From bed to work and from work to bed—that sums up the life of their victims. . . . They**

never have a moment for their private affairs; they always breathe a polluted atmosphere; for them the sun never shines.[10]

France too had its outbreaks of machine breaking, and the industrial riots in Lyons in 1831 and 1834 paralleled those in Manchester. In Charles Fourier (1772–1837) it had its own utopian reformer as well. Fourier proposed a network of small, self-contained communities called phalansteries similar to Owen's experiments at New Lanark and New Harmony; like Owen's, attempts to found such communities were short-lived. More modest goals of reform lagged behind the British example. Despite official concern about the high rate of physical rejection among French army conscripts, the only industrial legislation passed in the first half of the nineteenth century was the Factory Law of 1841, which prohibited the employment of children under the age of 8 in factories.

The German Giant

The Napoleonic wars were a watershed in German economic development. They caused serious dislocation, but German industry, sheltering behind the Continental System, benefited by a respite from competition with British products. They also simplified Germany's political geography, reducing its hundreds of principalities to 39 states, of which an enlarged Prussia, now in control of the coalfields of the Ruhr and the Saar, the main river systems of the north, and the prosperous cities of the Rhineland and Westphalia, was the most important. Under Prussian leadership, a free trade zone, the Zollverein ("customs union"), had been established by 1834, embracing some 34 million people. This formed the basis for a sustained industrial expansion whose rate of growth was unsurpassed on the Continent.

Textiles and metallurgy flourished, and new mining techniques opened up the great coal deposits of the Ruhr. Railways were introduced in 1835, eight years after the French had built their first line; by 1850 there were twice as many miles of track in Germany as in France. Private and public capital were symbiotic in Germany to an extent unparalleled except in tiny Belgium, which was for all practical purposes an extension of Germany's western frontier. Major capital construction, such as railways, was financed by joint-stock ventures underwritten in part by government funds, and by the late 1840s the first state railways were built. By virtually every measure—population, production, urbanization—Germany was the most economically powerful region on the Continent by 1850, and within a generation it would be challenging the lead of Britain itself.

Industrial Development After 1850

The wealth and productivity of the West increased exponentially after 1850. In part this increase was stimulated by the same factor that had fueled the economic boom of the sixteenth century: the discovery of gold in the New World. The California gold strike of 1848 (and the sizable deposits found later in Australia) added as much gold to the world's stocks in the next 20 years as in the preceding 350. As the new supply leveled off, the European economy contracted in the 1870s and 1880s, only to surge forward again with fresh supplies from South Africa and the Klondike. A second source of cap-

THE INDUSTRIAL REVOLUTION

Economic developments	Political events
Agricultural revolution (c. 1700–1800)	Enclosure Acts (1760–1840)
Spinning jenny, steam engine (1760s)	Population expansion begins (c. 1750)
First industrial factories (1760–1780)	Adam Smith, *The Wealth of Nations* (1776)
First iron bridge (1779); first wrought iron produced (1784)	Thomas Malthus, *An Essay on Population* (1798); Anticombination Acts (1799–1800)
Canal and turnpike system built (1760–1820)	Luddite revolts (1811–1817)
First locomotive (1825)	Great Reform Bill (1832); Factory Act (1833); Poor Law (1834)
Industrialization spreads to the Continent (c. 1830)	Industrial riots in Lyons (1831)
First telegraph line (1844)	Karl Marx and Friedrich Engels, *The Communist Manifesto* (1847); Revolutions of 1848
Bessemer steel furnace (1856)	First public corporations (1859)
Telephone (1876); light bulb (1880); transformer (1881); automobile (1885)	Standard Oil trust (1882)
Wright brothers' airplane (1903)	Sherman Antitrust Act (1890); U.S. Steel (1901)

ital, particularly for Britain and, to a lesser extent, France, was the profits of trade and empire. The traffic of European commerce had constituted 75 percent of the world's trade by 1800. The volume of that trade now skyrocketed, increasing at least 1,200 percent between the 1840s and 1914.

Much of this trade was with the United States, which, already a major economic force by 1860, had become the world's leading industrial power by 1900. The industrialization of the United States marked the triumph of Alexander Hamilton's vision of an America founded on commercial and industrial prosperity over Thomas Jefferson's dream of a pastoral democracy based on independent farmers. Numerous factors created an ideal climate for expansion: vast deposits of iron, coal, and petroleum, which, with a plenitude of gold and silver, provided an unsurpassed source of both raw materials and specie; a domestic labor and consumer market continually fed by immigration; and a political system firmly controlled by northern banking and industrial interests after the Civil War. By 1890 U.S. iron and steel production had surpassed that of Britain; by 1900 the United States was making more steel than Britain and Germany combined; by 1910 its rail network was carrying a billion tons of freight per year. Huge trusts and monopolies dominated the economy, exploiting the cheap labor drawn primarily from southern and eastern Europe. When the United States Steel Corporation was organized in 1901, it was capitalized at $1.4 billion—a sum greater than the total wealth of the country a century before.

The Harnessing of Science

At the same time, new technological developments greatly extended the scope of the Industrial Revolution. A new age of steel resulted from refining processes that permitted both much higher temperatures in blast furnaces and the use of lower grades of ore. In the last three decades of the nineteenth century world steel production increased 50-fold as steel, lighter and more tensile than iron, began to replace it everywhere in rail, ship, and building construction.

For the first time as well, applied science and engineering began to feed directly and systematically into technological development, creating new products, processes, and sources of energy. The age of the amateur inventor, the inspired tinkerer working alone, was rapidly drawing to a close; the American Thomas Alva Edison (1847–1931), the last of the type, ultimately developed his own research team. Large firms began to employ their own scientists and engineers, working directly on product

development and production improvement. At the same time, the lag time between basic scientific discovery and its technological application was sharply diminished.

Electricity was as crucial to the nineteenth century as steam had been to the eighteenth. Following the conversion of mechanical motion into electric current by Michael Faraday in 1831, the American Samuel F. B. Morse produced the first practical telegraph in the 1840s. The telegraph was the beginning of a communications revolution that paralleled that of the steam locomotive in transportation. The telephone followed in 1879, and in 1896 the Italian Guglielmo Marconi adapted radio waves, discovered by Heinrich Hertz a decade before, to a new mass communications device.

The development of electromagnets, the electrolytic process, and the modern dynamo paved the way for the use of electricity in public places such as railways, docks, theaters, and markets, as well as in some factories. The incandescent light bulb, invented independently by Edison in America and Sir Joseph Swan in Britain, brought electrical illumination into the home and the office in the 1880s. In the same decade the steam turbine began to replace the old reciprocal-action engine. It was soon adapted to coal and then to petroleum, the fuel source that would power the twentieth century. The combustion engine followed in 1886, the airplane in 1903. By the early 1900s, European and American cities were lit electrically by huge generating systems, and their streets were crowded with trams and, increasingly, automobiles. At the same time, organic chemistry (the chemistry of carbon compounds), developed especially in Germany, produced a whole range of synthetic dyes, textiles, paints, and other products. No longer were humans confined to working, blending, crushing, and refining the given raw materials of nature; by manipulating the basic organic components of these materials, new, artificial products could be created.

By every measure—energy produced, goods and services provided, miles of railway track and telegraph, telephone, and cable line laid—industrialization and the new, unprecedented standards of living it made possible increased by quantum leaps in Europe and the United States during the nineteenth century. But industrial development remained unevenly distributed geographically, and industrial wealth was even more unequally shared socially. Moreover, the disparity between worker and owner in Europe and the United States was greater still between colonizer and colonized as capital penetration and imperial expansion brought the mines, factories, technical processes, and industrial discipline of the West to the far corners of the globe. As this process intensified

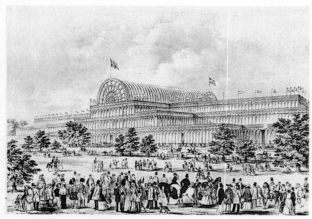

Flags fly proudly over the Crystal Palace, built to house the world's first international industrial exhibition in London in 1851, while a festive bourgeois crowd takes its ease outside the monument. The palace, constructed of cast iron and glass, was itself a triumph of the new technology.

during the last decades of the century, social and political dislocation, and in some cases devastation occurred on a scale that dwarfed the changes that had taken place in Britain and on the Continent. Only a few places outside Europe achieved industrialization on their own before 1900, most notably the United States and Japan. As the twentieth century dawned, European economic and political hegemony in the world was at its zenith.

SUMMARY

The Industrial Revolution and the population explosion that accompanied it began in the middle of the eighteenth century, and both have continued unabated the processes of change and upheaval that have transformed the globe. Population pressure spurred agricultural and industrial development, at first in Britain and then elsewhere, and success in sustaining an ever-expanding population generated the market and product demand that fed technological growth. When in 1851 Britain celebrated its role as the "workshop of the world" with a great international industrial exhibition at the Crystal Palace in London, the most important technological advance in humanity's recorded history was already an accomplished fact. The windmill and the waterwheel had given way to the steam engine, the domestic workshop to the factory, the horse and cart to the locomotive and the telegraph. Metals had replaced wood in the construction of harbors, bridges, buildings, and machinery, as coal had replaced it as the source of power. At the same time, the nature of work and

of the social organization that revolved around it was no less radically transformed. The artisan who saw a job through from start to finish was replaced by the skilled factory worker who was confined to a single part of a process and integrated into a complex market structure that dictated the wages, conditions, and availability of employment. The family circle, the primary preindustrial work unit the world over, began to give way to an impersonal industrial discipline that reshaped and often shattered traditional relationships and modes of living at the most basic level. Inexorably, these changes radiated outward from their European origins to embrace the entire world and to create not merely a new global economy but a new global culture as well.

NOTES

1. K. Marx and F. Engels, *The Communist Manifesto* (New York: New York Labor News Co.), pp. 13–14. First published in 1848.
2. A. M. Lambert, *The Making of the Dutch Landscape* (New York: Seminar Press, 1971), p. 195.
3. A. Ure, *Philosophy of Manufactures* (New York: Kelley, 1967), p. 109. Originally printed in 1861.
4. Ibid., p. 13.
5. B. Disraeli, *Sybil, or the Two Nations.* In *The Works of Benjamin Disraeli* (New York: M. W. Dunne, 1904–1905), bk. 2, chap. 5.
6. M. Cole, *Robert Owen of New Lanark* (New York: Oxford University Press, 1953), p. 152. First published in 1857.
7. A. Briggs, *Victorian Cities* (London: Odhams Books, 1965), p. 55.
8. Ibid., p. 102.
9. Ibid., pp. 92–93.
10. W. O. Henderson, *The Industrial Revolution in Europe, 1815–1914* (Chicago: Quadrangle Books, 1961), p. 107.

SUGGESTIONS FOR FURTHER READING

Ashton, T. S. *The Industrial Revolution, 1760–1830.* London: Oxford University Press, 1961.

Berlanstein, L. R. *The Industrial Revolution and Work in Nineteenth-Century Europe.* New York: Routledge, 1992.

Braudel, F. *Civilization and Capitalism.* 3 vols. London: Collins, 1979–1985.

Briggs, A. *Victorian Cities.* London: Odhams Books, 1965.

Chambers, J. D., and Mingay, G. E. *The Agricultural Revolution, 1750–1850.* New York: Schocken Books, 1966.

Cipolla, C. M., ed. *The Industrial Revolution, 1700–1914.* London: Penguin Books, 1973.

Cole, M. *Robert Owen of New Lanark.* New York: Oxford University Press, 1953.

Crafts, N. F. R. *British Economic Growth During the Industrial Revolution.* New York: Oxford University Press, 1986.

Dennis, R. *English Industrial Cities of the Nineteenth Century.* Cambridge: Cambridge University Press, 1984.

Floud, R., and McCloskey, D., eds. *The Economic History of Britain Since 1700.* 3 vols. Cambridge: Cambridge University Press, 1994.

Heywood, C. *The Development of the French Economy, 1750–1914.* Cambridge: Cambridge University Press, 1995.

Henderson, W. O. *The Industrial Revolution in Europe.* Chicago: Quadrangle Books, 1961.

Hobsbawm, E. J. *Industry and Empire.* Harmondsworth, England: Penguin Books, 1970.

Kidd, A. *Manchester.* Keele, England: Keele University Press, 1993.

Landes, D. *The Unbound Prometheus: Technological Change and Industrial Development in Western Europe from the Seventeenth Century to the Present.* London: Cambridge University Press, 1969.

Mathias, P. *The First Industrial Nation: An Economic History of Britain, 1700–1914.* New York: Scribner, 1969.

McKeown, T. *The Modern Rise of Population.* New York: Academic Press, 1976.

Mokyr, J., ed. *The Economies of the Industrial Revolution.* London: Rowman & Allanheld, 1985.

Perkin, H. *The Origin of Modern English Society, 1780–1860.* London: Routledge & Kegan Paul, 1969.

Stearns, P. N. *The Industrial Revolution in World History.* Boulder, Colo.: Westview Press, 1993.

Thompson, E. P. *The Making of the English Working Class.* Harmondsworth, England: Penguin Books, 1964.

Weber, A. F. *The Growth of Cities in the Nineteenth Century.* Ithaca, N.Y.: Cornell University Press, 1969.

Wilson, C., and Parker, G. *An Introduction to the Sources of European Economic History, 1500–1800.* London: Weidenfeld & Nicolson, 1977.

Zaretsky, E. *Capitalism, the Family, and Personal Life.* London: Pluto Press, 1976.

The Age of Ideology

In the wake of the French Revolution and the Napoleonic conquests, Europe experienced some of its most turbulent and troubled decades. The statesmen of the victorious allies, meeting at Vienna, sought to restore the Old Regime and to find an antidote to revolution. Their attempts foundered on the continuing demands for representative government, free competition, and social justice, often expressed through a fervent desire for national independence or unity. This was in turn linked to the wider cultural movement of Romanticism, which, in its emphasis on the free expressive powers of the individual, questioned traditional values and undermined traditional authority. By 1830 the fragile détente between the old noble elites and the increasingly powerful bourgeoisie had broken down, and a new wave of revolutionary disturbance swept Europe. This was only the precursor of the far more widespread and violent revolutions of 1848, in which the industrial proletariat, fired by the doctrines of socialism, played for the first time a leading role. These revolutions ended largely in apparent failure, but they confirmed the ascendancy of the bourgeoisie as the only barrier to the demand for a new social order.

The Legacy of Revolution

The American Revolution, in declaring all men born "free and equal," and the French Revolution, in asserting liberty, equality, and fraternity to be the goals of a just society, had propounded new political values to the

Detail from Honoré Daumier's painting Les Divorceuses.
At an impassioned meeting of women, one of many held during the Revolution of 1848, a feminist spokeswoman demands reform of the divorce laws. Daumier's portrayal typified the derisive reaction of the press to the new and disturbing phenomenon of feminist activism.

Western world. Freedom or liberty, as the Old Regime understood these terms, meant not general rights applicable to all but privileges enjoyed by particular individuals or corporate groups: the right of a town or locality to charge bridge, river, or road tolls, for example, or the exemption of the clergy from the jurisdiction of secular courts. The foundation of Old Regime society was not equality but hierarchy and subordination; its members were not citizens but subjects.

Even more foreign to the old order was the new revolutionary ideal of fraternity, the solidarity of all citizens with one another, and their patriotic identification with the nation and, beyond borders, with all humanity. In America these principles had inspired the first nation ever created on the basis of citizen equality, though it still excluded women and blacks. The founding of the United States had in turn been a powerful inspiration to the French revolutionaries of 1789. But whereas the United States, an ocean away, had been able to export its revolution only by precept and example, the armies of the French republic, crossing the Alps and the Rhine, had brought theirs by force to much of Europe.

The champions of the old order, led by Britain—whose own revolutions of 1640 and 1688 had been the antecedents of both the French and American ones—had fought and finally defeated the armies of France. Long before Waterloo, however, the ideals of freedom and equality had been tempered in both revolutionary France and democratic America. In the United States the election of senators by state legislatures and of the president and vice-president by an electoral college represented a barrier to direct citizen control of the legislative and executive branches of government. In France a similar retreat was visible as early as 1791 in the distinction between active and passive citizens, and by the time of Napoleon, passive acquiescence in a dictatorial regime was the only function left to citizenship.

Despite this, the ideals of representative government and an egalitarian society remained alive. No longer could the rulers of Europe rely on obedience to authority based on the unquestioned subordination of subject populations to their natural masters, and political agitation everywhere now took the form of demands for basic rights and representation. Of no less importance were the values of freedom and equality in dissolving the traditional barriers to state centralization. The reduction of many particular and individual freedoms was a tedious and sometimes impossible task; the removal of a single set of generalized freedoms required only the suspension of constitutional guarantees by an emergency decree, as the Terror had shown. Liberties extended to all and tyranny exerted over all lay uncomfortably close together in the revolutionary state.

The demand for liberty and equality was often linked to another pervasive political sentiment of the early nineteenth century, nationalism. In its simplest terms, nationalism was a sense of cultural and political identity among a given people. Cultural identity was manifested in shared traditions and the possession of a common language; political identity was expressed in the association with a particular region or territory. The ultimate expression of a people's identity was the possession of a state.

Nationalism was expressed with particular vigor in Germany by the critic Herder, who argued in the 1770s and 1780s that each people had its own organic development and must pursue its own individual destiny. This contention, like many other early manifestations of Romanticism, went counter to the Enlightenment ideal of a universal reason applicable to all. Herder urged his compatriots to look to their own cultural heritage for meaning and direction, rather than to an imported French model that could only be valid for the French, not the Germans.

Herder's work stimulated a cultural nationalism that was displayed in patriotic literature; research into German philology, folklore, and legend; and attempts to define the German "soul." The Napoleonic conquests galvanized political nationalism in Germany as well. Fichte had called on the people of Prussia to regenerate the lost honor of their fatherland, while his fellow Prussian, the philosopher Georg Wilhelm Friedrich Hegel (1770–1831), claimed that the historical dichotomy between the individual and the community was overcome in the unity of the modern nation-state. The highest manifestation of this unity was not, as Fichte expressed it, in the securing of particular benefits such as life, liberty, and personal well-being, but in a noble patriotism and love of country.

This almost mystical sense of the union, or perhaps submersion of the individual in the nation, suggests that nationalism was not an essentially liberal cause, even though liberals often expressed their aspirations through it and used it as a vehicle of rebellion against the established order. In Russia nationalism would be invoked in the 1840s both by liberal westernizers who wished to see Russia become modern and competitive by adopting western European values and institutions and by conservative Slavophiles who believed that Russia could fulfill its messianic destiny in the world only by remaining true to its traditions. In short, nationalism appealed across the spectrum from economic rationalists, who saw the nation-state as an efficient market mechanism, to religious enthusiasts, who saw in it a communal salvation.

The result of these conflicting ideologies was a new and uncertain age in which, for the first time, the very

The Mystique of Nationalism

The nationalist fervor that Napoleon stimulated and that ultimately overthrew him was powerfully fed by the antirationalist elements that also produced the Romantic movement. In this passage, the French philosopher Joseph de Maistre (1753–1821), a conservative opponent of the Enlightenment and of the French Revolution, expresses his sense of the "national soul" inherent in all peoples.

Human reason left to its own resources is completely incapable not only of creating *but also of conserving any religious or political association,* because it can only give rise to disputes and because, to conduct himself well, man needs beliefs, not problems. . . . Religion and political dogmas, mingled and merged together, should together form a *general or national mind* sufficiently strong to repress the aberrations of the individual reason which is, of its nature, the mortal enemy of any association whatever because it gives birth only to divergent opinions. . . .

What is patriotism? It is this national mind of which I am speaking; it is individual *abnegation.* Faith and patriotism are the two great wonder-workers of the world. Both are divine. All their actions are miracles. Do not talk to them of scrutiny, choice, discussion, for they will say that you blaspheme. They know only two words, *submission* and *belief;* with these two levers, they raise the world. Their very errors are sublime. These two infants of heaven prove their origin to all by creating and conserving; and if they unite, join their forces, and together take possession of a nation, they exalt it, make it divine and increase its power a hundred-fold.

Source: J. Lively, ed., *The Works of Joseph de Maistre* (New York: Macmillan, 1965), pp. 108–109 (modified slightly).

---

basis of the social order was in dispute. In the aftermath of Napoleon's defeat, the victorious allied powers set about to restore the world they had known before 1789 as far as they could. Their attempts to do so, against not only the countervailing forces unleashed by the French and American revolutions but also the as yet unreckoned ones of the Industrial Revolution, determined the course of European politics to the middle of the nineteenth century and beyond.

The Congress of Vienna

The major European powers met in Vienna in September 1814 to try to untangle 20 years of war and revolution. It was the first such general congress of the powers since the one that had settled the Thirty Years' War at Westphalia in 1648. Every state on the Continent sent representatives, including defunct members of the old Holy Roman Empire seeking reinstatement. But only five parties really counted—Austria, Britain, Prussia, Russia, and France, represented, respectively, by Prince Metternich, Viscount Castlereagh, Baron Hardenberg,

Tsar Alexander I (the only sovereign taking direct part in the proceedings), and Baron Talleyrand, who after serving Napoleon had brokered the return of the Bourbon dynasty to France.

Collective Security

What the allies wanted at Vienna, broadly speaking, was to restore the old order of kingship and aristocracy, to prevent the domination of Europe by any single state, and to contain the virus of revolution wherever it might spread. To accomplish this, they created a structure of collective security that was essentially a classical balance-of-power system tinctured by the agreement to suppress all forms of radical activity. This meant that collective security would be brought to bear not only against states that threatened the stability of the system by external action but also against those whose internal stability was threatened by domestic discontent.

The framework for this system was already in place in the wartime coalition that had defeated Napoleon. Formalized as the Quadruple Alliance in 1815 and ex-

The Congress of Vienna, which redrew the map of Europe in the wake of the Napoleonic era. Metternich stands in the left foreground, Castlereagh is seated in the center with his legs crossed, and Talleyrand is seated to the right with his right arm on the table.

tended, after a suitable period of probation, to include France in 1818, it formed the basis of the so-called Concert of Europe, which kept the peace of the Continent, or at any rate took the credit for doing so, down to 1914. The novelty of the system was the recognition that war, because it had the potential to unleash revolution, had become too dangerous a luxury for Europe to afford. Alexander I, for whom it represented not merely a political instrument but a spiritual compact, managed to bully his fellow sovereigns (with the exception of the pope, the Turkish sultan, and the regent of Britain) into signing a "holy alliance" against war and for Christian concord. On a more mundane level, Prince Metternich conceived it as a sanction to intervene in the affairs of any state threatened by revolution. The British were suspicious of the uses to which such an unlimited warrant might be put, however. Reverting to a lone hand after years of marshaling coalitions on the Continent, they refused to commit themselves to any joint command. Prussia too was skeptical of any rapprochement between its two powerful eastern neighbors, Austria and Russia.

The Diplomatic Settlement

The strains among the allies at Vienna came into the open over the Polish-Saxon question, which nearly torpedoed the congress. Napoleon had taken away almost all the territory gained by Austria and Prussia in the partitioning of Poland to create a satellite entity, the Grand Duchy of Warsaw. Its collapse with the defeat of his empire again left a power vacuum in eastern Europe.

Alexander I insisted on restoring the original prepartition Poland, with himself as king. To win Prussia's support, he offered to cede it the duchy of Saxony. Metternich, appalled, sought out Castlereagh and Talleyrand, who agreed to resist the Russian plan, by force if necessary.

The Polish-Saxon question was finally settled by compromise. Alexander received a reduced "congress" Poland that was roughly equivalent to Napoleon's Grand Duchy, and Prussia was compensated with two-fifths of Saxony. But the whole episode pointed up the inherent contradiction of the congress system, which presupposed lasting cooperation between historical rivals whose interests were fundamentally opposed.

The Congress of Vienna did, however, decide a wide range of issues, which set the diplomatic framework of the nineteenth century. Uppermost in the minds of the allies was the creation of buffer zones, primarily against France but more subtly against Russia, whose steady westward encroachment had become a major concern over the preceding 100 years. A new Belgo-Dutch kingdom of the Netherlands was erected as a barrier on France's northern frontier, and Prussia was given a solid bloc of territory along the Rhine to perform a similar function. With the acquisition of the Rhineland, Prussia now overarched all of northern Germany, facing France to the west and Russia to the east. Austria was reinstalled in northern Italy and expanded along the Dalmatian coast, where, from a southern vantage, it could serve as a check against Russian designs on Turkey and French ones on Italy. The British, following traditional policy, sought no territory on the Continent but added several key islands and stations in the West Indies and the Far East to their unrivaled sea empire. Bestriding the major ocean arteries of the world, they were uniquely situated to exploit the productive forces of the Industrial Revolution and to enjoy a century of extraordinary world dominion.

The thorniest single issue facing the powers was the settlement of Germany. Beset by the rival demands of nationalists who dreamed of a unified German state and the claimants of liquidated states who wanted a return to the benevolent chaos of the Holy Roman Empire, they chose to preserve the states carved from the empire by Napoleon, loosely linked in a body known as the German Confederation, whose main function was to keep

the smaller states from gravitating toward France. It was a pragmatic solution that left Prussia in a position of greatly augmented influence and postponed for 50 years the final confrontation between Prussia and Austria for control of Germany.

The dramatic return of Napoleon from Elba and the ensuing Hundred Days compelled the allies to impose harsher sanctions on France, which had been treated leniently at first. The congress took away some snippets of French territory, imposed an indemnity of 700 million francs, and posted an army of occupation in France for three years. Nevertheless, France's treatment was still relatively mild. Events bore out the wisdom of the allies'

MAP 32.1   EUROPE AFTER THE CONGRESS OF VIENNA (1815)

moderation; the age of French aggression and French preponderance in Europe was over.

By their lights, the diplomats at Vienna accomplished a good deal. They cleared away the debris of a generation of war and converted a wartime coalition into a permanent instrument for maintaining order. The instrument was flawed, and the values it sought to defend—monarchy, aristocracy, and hereditary privilege—were already in eclipse, but the goal of regulating interstate conflict was a first step toward the containment of war.

What the men at Vienna were unwilling to recognize was the change of their own time. Formed under the Old Regime, their conception of society was still patriarchal; in the words of the Holy Alliance, the sovereigns of Europe were "as fathers of families towards their subjects and armies." In redrawing the map of the Continent, they acted in the high-handed manner of old, parceling out peoples and territories at will. It would never have occurred to them to ask Belgians whether they wanted to be under Dutch rule, Venetians under Austrian, or Poles under Russian. They rightly calculated that nationalism, the new sentiment that a land belonged to its people and not to its ruler, was incompatible with the preservation of the existing order; they wrongly concluded that they could contain it with treaties, armies, and spies.

Reaction and Revolution

The notion of collective security against revolution—what came to be known as the Congress System—was the brainchild of Prince Klemens von Metternich (1773–1859), who as foreign minister of Austria from 1809 to 1848 put his stamp on the diplomacy of the age. Metternich envisioned the system operating through periodic meetings of the great powers that by monitoring developments in each state could scotch any activity that threatened either internal or external stability. As the Troppau Protocol of 1820 put it:

> **States which have undergone a change of government due to revolution, the results of which threaten other states, *ipso facto* cease to be members of the European alliance. . . . If owing to such alterations immediate danger threatens other states, the powers bind themselves, by peaceful means, or if need be by arms to bring back the guilty state into the bosom of the Great Alliance.**

The opportunity soon arose to test the system. The restored regimes in Spain and the Kingdom of the Two Sicilies, both of which had proved reactionary, were violently unpopular. In Spain, Ferdinand VII dismissed an

Metternich's Plea for the Old Order

Prince Klemens von Metternich, the preeminent figure in European politics between 1815 and 1848, here forcefully expresses his conservative credo.

Drag through the mud the name of God and the powers instituted by his divine decrees, and the revolution will be prepared! Speak of a social contract, and the revolution is accomplished! The revolution was already completed in the palace of kings, in the drawing-rooms and boudoirs of certain cities, while among the great mass of the people it was still only in a state of preparation. . . .

The first and greatest concern for the immense majority of every nation is the stability of the laws, and their uninterrupted action—never their change. Therefore let the governments govern, let them maintain the groundwork of their institutions, both ancient and modern; for if it is at all times dangerous to touch them, it certainly would not now, in the general confusion, be wise to do so.

Source: K. von Metternich, *Memoirs*, trans. A. Napier, vol. 3 (London: Richard Bentley & Son, 1881), pp. 461, 474.

elected assembly, the Cortes; restored confiscated clerical and noble estates; and proclaimed a return to divine right absolutism. Rebellion broke out in early 1820, and the king was compelled to restore constitutional rule. In Naples, where King Ferdinand I, like his nephew Ferdinand VII in Spain, had abrogated reforms and alienated both the army and the bourgeoisie, an insurrection broke out at the same time, and revolts and disturbances erupted elsewhere on the Italian peninsula against Spanish, Austrian, and papal rule. In Portugal too the demand for constitutional government led to an uprising, and in 1821 a rebellion broke out in Greece that soon became a revolution against three and a half centuries of Ottoman rule. Within the space of a year, insurrection had sparked across the entire Mediterranean from Cape Finisterre to the eastern Aegean.

Metternich called for action but met a divided response. The British dissented from the Troppau Protocol, and the French, unwilling to serve as the agent of Austrian interests in Italy, sat idle. Metternich was more successful with Prussia and Russia, with whose assent an Austrian army descended on Italy and speedily crushed the rebellions in Naples and Sardinia. France agreed to act in Spain, where it was anxious to restore its influence, and when the revolutionary government in Madrid rejected an ultimatum to modify its reforms in 1823, it sent troops across the Pyrenees to restore Ferdinand VII. Despite promises of clemency, Ferdinand carried out a bloody purge and plunged Spain back into a civil and clerical autocracy that left a bitter legacy.

The case of Greece was more complicated. The Ottoman Empire, battered by the southward expansion of Russia in the eighteenth century, faced revolt among the subject peoples within its own borders. The Serbians had risen in 1804 in the beginnings of a struggle for nationhood that was to have profound consequences for all Europe. Their rebellion aroused little interest, but when the Greeks, whose merchants dominated the trade of the eastern Mediterranean, rebelled with the support of Alexander I (whose horror of revolutions stopped short at those that advanced Russian interests), the Continent took notice.

The powers forced Alexander to back off and waited for the Greek insurrection to burn itself out. But they failed to take into account both the resolve of the Greeks and a new force that the very idea of collective security had helped to create—public opinion. A new classical revival, spurred chiefly by German scholars and archaeologists in the eighteenth century, combined with the nascent Romantic movement to produce a fascination with things Greek. Committees to support the Greek

The poet Byron in Greek dress. Byron died while attempting to raise money and troops for the Greek cause, an act that galvanized European support for Greek independence and symbolized the Romantic quest for freedom and the recovery of the heroic ideal.

cause sprang up spontaneously all over western Europe and the United States. In the face of this, the calculated indifference of the powers could not be kept up. Britain, France, and Russia attempted to impose an armistice on Turkey in 1827 and, failing that, sent out a squadron that first blockaded and then destroyed the Turkish fleet at Navarino in the Peloponnesus. The Turks were compelled to recognize Greek independence by the London Protocol of 1830.

The Troubled 1820s

The revolt of the Greeks was the political cause célèbre of the 1820s. It gave heart to nationalist movements everywhere, although it showed too that such movements could not hope to succeed merely on the basis of elite elements but required mass support. It left the Congress System in ruins as well. The spectacle of an allied fleet playing midwife to a revolutionary state demonstrated that Metternich's dream of a perpetual status quo could not withstand a united demand for change and that in a crisis each power would consult its own interest first and its treaty obligations second. What emerged was a looser, more informal understanding, the Concert of Europe, by which the great powers would attempt to resolve their major differences and avoid general war.

While only Russia among the major powers underwent an actual rebellion within its borders between 1815 and 1830 (the Decembrist revolt of 1825), all experienced significant unrest. We have touched on the Luddite attacks and urban agitation in Britain. In the wake of the Peterloo Massacre, the government passed a series of repressive measures through Parliament, the Six Acts, which suppressed public meetings, curbed the press, and speeded up procedures for prosecuting offenders against the public order. It was not until the late 1820s that a less hysterical atmosphere began to prevail.

In France, Louis XVIII (1814–1824) sought a middle ground between the reactionary Ultraroyalist party, which wanted to turn the clock back to 1789, and the ex-Bonapartists and republicans, whom Louis knew he would have to conciliate to stabilize his regime. He offered a charter that in essence preserved the structure of the Napoleonic Code and set up a bicameral assembly that could veto royal legislation. However, the assassination in 1820 of the duke of Berry, the heir to the throne, set off a new wave of reaction. Under the intransigent Charles X (1824–1830), the political program of the Ultras was enacted. The Law of Indemnity (1825) compensated nobles who had lost their estates during the revolution by devaluing government bonds held by the bourgeoisie, and the Law of Sacrilege, passed in the same year, imposed the death penalty for the theft of sacred objects and other vaguely defined offenses against the church.

Despite its greatly strengthened geopolitical situation, Prussia was content to allow Metternich to play ideological policeman to the rest of Germany, a role he assumed with relish. By the Carlsbad Decrees of 1819, Metternich suppressed the nationalist student societies that had succeeded the quasi-military gymnastic clubs founded during the Napoleonic wars, whose members, wearing gray-shirted uniforms and imbued with a hatred of "foreign" (including Jewish) influence, strikingly foreshadowed elements of Nazi ideology and practice. Student groups that gathered at Wartburg Castle near Eisenach to commemorate the tricentennial of Luther's Ninety-five Theses in 1817 toasted unity and freedom but also burned conservative and antinationalist books after a torchlight procession, a rather dubious way to protest censorship.

In Austria itself Metternich's chief concern was to suppress nationalist stirrings among the many minority groups that comprised the Habsburg empire. The very name Austria had been adopted only in 1804 to describe the patrimonial lands of the emperor, and whereas the yearning for national identity might encourage a sense of unity in such regions as Germany and Italy and strengthen it in states such as Britain, France, or Spain already established on the basis of a common language and heritage, it could only foster division and separatism in the Habsburg realm. By skillfully playing rival minorities off against one another, Metternich delayed his day of reckoning for more than 30 years; by failing to provide a genuine accommodation for nationalist aspirations within the framework of the empire, he ensured that that day would come.

Russia was still by far the most autocratic of all European states. Like Catherine the Great, the eccentric Alexander I (1801–1825) began his reign with a flourish of reform. Men of all classes were legally entitled to hold land for the first time, and masters were encouraged to free their serfs. New schools were founded, and new ideas entered the country, particularly through the medium of the Freemasons and other secret fraternities. The reforming Count Speransky even drafted plans for a system of representative bodies culminating in a national assembly, though without real legislative power. But after the Napoleonic invasions a chastened Alexander, regarding his country's disaster as a divine judgment, lapsed into a reactionary mysticism that made him Metternich's most zealous if not always most reliable ally in the war against reform.

Frustrated liberal aspirations among the officer corps in conjunction with a succession crisis in December 1825 provoked Russia's first attempt at revolution. Alexander's heir, the Grand Duke Constantine, had secretly resigned his claim to the throne in favor of his brother Nicholas, but when the tsar died suddenly, each brother proclaimed the other. In the resulting chaos, disaffected officers raised the standard of "Constantine and constitution," which some of the soldiers apparently thought referred to the tsar and his wife.

Whatever the comic overtones of the Decembrist uprising, it was ruthlessly suppressed. Hundreds were imprisoned or exiled, and five officers were executed; these officers' courageous bearing made them symbols of resistance under the despotic reign of Nicholas I (1825–1855). The latent genius of the Russian people flowered in an extraordinary literary generation that included the poets Alexander Pushkin (1799–1837) and Mikhail Lermontov (1814–1841) and the novelists

Nikolai Gogol (1809–1852) and Ivan Turgenev (1818–1883). Gogol in particular caught the spirit of Nicholas' Russia in his comic novel *Dead Souls* and his play *The Inspector General,* while the young Feodor Dostoevsky (1821–1881), later one of the century's greatest novelists, began his career by facing a mock firing squad in Siberia for allegedly "socialist" activities. Others, like the journalist Alexander Herzen (1812–1870), sought haven abroad, thus initiating the long tradition of the Russian exile.

Liberalism

The term most frequently used to describe the varied forms of opposition to the Restoration regimes was *liberalism,* a word that continues to bear different and sometimes contradictory meanings. The origins of liberalism

go back to the British philosopher and political theorist John Locke (see Chapter 27), who argued for the supremacy of society over the state or, in practical terms, the control of the Stuart monarchy by the propertied classes. Adam Smith drew out the implications of Locke's argument for the freedom of commerce from state interference as well. By the early nineteenth century, liberalism had come to stand broadly for free trade in a laissez-faire marketplace, the limitation of state authority by written constitutions, secular education, and national self-determination. In a general sense, nineteenth-century liberalism may be said to have represented the interests of capitalist enterprise and the aspirations of the commercial bourgeoisie. This was how Karl Marx took it; for him liberalism was simply the ideology of the bourgeoisie. But it was merged as well with a post-Enlightenment skepticism about the role of government

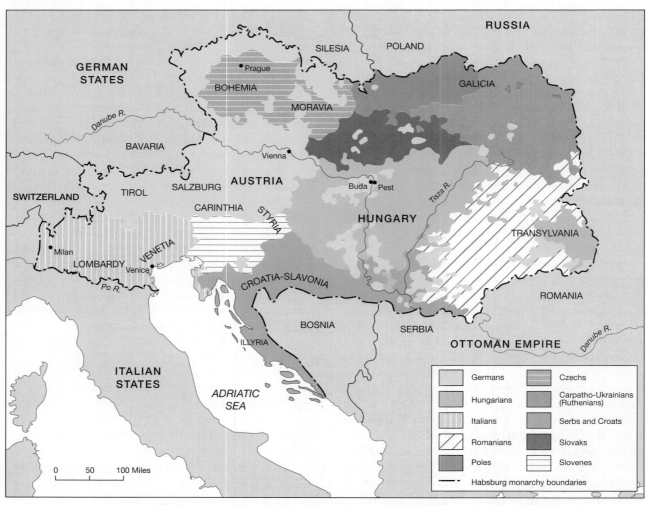

MAP 32.2   ETHNIC COMPOSITION OF THE AUSTRO-HUNGARIAN EMPIRE

and with a profound change in cultural sensibility, Romanticism, to form a complex and potent mixture whose appeal extended far beyond narrow economic interests.

Romanticism and the Quest for Identity

Romanticism may be viewed in many ways. The term *Romantic* is often contrasted with the term *classical* to express a mood or movement of art, thought, and cultural sensibility in which feeling and imagination shape form instead of the other way around and in which the expression of individual personality is valued above conformity to established norms of taste and style. As such, it is a tendency that may be observed in many cultures and periods, particularly in the arts.

The Dethronement of Tradition

Historically, the Romantic movement that began in the West in the mid-eighteenth century represented a final emancipation from the authority of ancient Greece and Rome. That legacy lay heavily over the medieval period in terms of its religion (Christianity, the faith of the late Roman Empire), its law (largely based on the Code of Justinian, itself an adaptation of the Roman civil code), and its thought (influenced first by Aristotle and later by Plato and his followers). So deeply was the culture of the West permeated by the influence of antiquity that even the reaction against scholastic thought and institutions that we call the Renaissance took the form of a renewal of the classical tradition. A similar movement on a smaller scale took place with the classical revival that began in the mid-eighteenth century. This time, however, the reinterpretation of the Greco-Roman tradition took place in the context of a far wider shift in the perspective of Western culture.

Many things contributed to this development. The Renaissance emphasis on the value of the individual and the Reformation idea of personal responsibility for one's own salvation (and one's ethical conduct in the world) laid the first basis for this shift. The scientific revolution, with its repudiation of ancient and medieval cosmogony and its challenge to the traditional Christianity that rested on it, enthroned reason in place of faith and tradition. The Enlightenment doctrine of progress, based on reason, asserted the indefinite improvement if not the perfectability of the species. The French Revolution was the political expression of this hope, and it persisted in the utopian schemes of Owen, Fourier, and others.

The result of all this was a new view of human possibility. At the same time, however, the prospect of an un-

charted future provoked deep anxiety. The past was no longer the model for the present but merely a record of progress to date; culture was not to be inherited but to be created. For the first time the West took on the burden of originality, of the new and avant-garde, that has characterized its culture ever since. Each generation, each decade, was to be reckoned in terms of its difference from its predecessors. The demand for progress and the measure of progress (whether in art, science, politics, or fashion) by originality speeded up the experience of time no less than the factory whistle, the locomotive, or the newspaper.

The Romantic Hero

The dethronement of tradition and the quest for the new put extraordinary emphasis on the role of the individual. A single person, properly placed, could change the destiny of a nation; a single idea could create a new product or industry or a new artistic form. Yet the solitary individual might also suffer defeat. The great political figure, like Napoleon, might endure ignominy and exile; the inventor might fail; the struggling artist might die in obscurity. Emancipated from tradition, society was now dependent on genius; and genius, wayward and unpredictable, was to be found only in the individual.

What emerged was a confidence in the collective destiny of Western culture—whether in the form of nation-building, utopian experiment, missionary zeal, or imperial expansion—that rested paradoxically on the talent and initiative of the isolated individual. The cultural expression of this paradox was Romanticism. The Romantic hero was typically a sensitive, misunderstood young man (much less often a woman) in revolt against his surroundings or a man of destiny boldly seeking knowledge and power. In the former type, Romanticism portrayed the sense of anxiety and vulnerability that beset the individual in a time of change; in the latter, the vaunting self-confidence of a society that had laid claim to the secrets of nature and would soon take the dominion of the earth.

Goethe and the Romantic Spirit

Both kinds of Romantic heroes were represented in the work of the great German poet and dramatist Johann Wolfgang von Goethe (1749–1832), whose career spanned the last decades of the Enlightenment and the first ones of Romanticism. Goethe was the son of a town councillor of Frankfurt. He studied and briefly practiced law before turning to a literary career, which by 1775 was prominent enough to secure him an invitation from the young duke of Weimar, Karl August, who had chosen him to be the star of what he hoped to make the most brilliant court in Europe. Arriving with little thought except to gain a temporary sinecure that would free him for writing, Goethe was to remain at Weimar for the rest of his life.

Goethe was not merely the founding figure of modern German literature but also an artist and natural scientist of distinction. Like Rousseau, he was a keen student of botany, and he put forward an elaborate theory of color in opposition to Newton's. Goethe's scientific pursuits were closely tied to his conception of nature as a unity

This oil painting of the great Goethe with his wife and children, by J. K. Seekatz, is much more than a fancy-dress family portrait. Situated in a pastoral setting typical of eighteenth-century aristocratic portraits, Goethe symbolizes the emergent power of his own bourgeois class and its appropriation of the political and material source of aristocratic power, the land. At the same time, the towering ruin stands for Romantic aspirations and hence Goethe's personal claim to status as an artist.

composed of innumerable individual elements. From this sprang Goethe's profoundly Romantic idea of the cosmos itself as the ultimate living organism, a notion that nationalist thinkers would find easy to apply to the relationship between the individual citizen and the nation.

But it was as an author that Goethe exerted his greatest influence. His early novel, *The Sorrows of Young Werther* (1774), brilliantly captured the mood of the early Romantic movement in Germany and portrayed its quintessential hero in the student Werther, who commits suicide out of frustrated love. *Werther* was a best-seller all over Europe and sparked a rash of real suicides; its fame was so great that the Chinese painted the young hero and his love, Lotte, on porcelain for the export trade. But Werther's sorrows were as much metaphysical as amorous, and he thus embodied the Romantic sense of the individual at odds with the world.

Goethe himself was very much the rebellious young man he wrote about in his early years, tempestuous in his love affairs and radical in his politics. It was only much later, as the venerable Sage of Weimar, that he acquired the image of Olympian wisdom and detachment that has been historically associated with his name. The work that gave continuity to his entire career as well as matchless definition to the Romantic movement itself was his dramatic poem *Faust*. The Faust legend originated in a sixteenth-century German physician, astrologer, and magician who called himself Faustus and was reputed to have made a pact with the Devil, a symbol of the Romantic quest for forbidden knowledge and experience. Equally important, Goethe's literary Devil, Mephistopheles, is not merely an evil tempter but a tormented being who is a larger symbol of Faust himself. Goethe's difficulty in finishing the poem—he worked on it for 60 years—stemmed from his rejection of the legend of Faust's ultimate damnation; like his fellow Romantics, he believed that the quest for knowledge was the essence of man's being and that good and evil could not be disentangled from it. In the end his Faust finds salvation rather than punishment, though not before coming to understand the limitations of all knowledge and the abiding mystery of existence.

In his later years Goethe was the cultural arbiter of Europe, whose favor and blessing was sought by the great and near-great; Napoleon, who met him at Erfurt in 1808, confessed to having read *Werther* seven times. No other poet since Shakespeare had so profound an influence on his fellow artists; the Romantic composers Beethoven, Schubert, Berlioz, Liszt, Mendelssohn, Schumann, and Wagner were only some of the musicians who found inspiration in his work, particularly

Faust. Goethe himself had a wide and sympathetic interest in younger artists, and he was particularly taken by the English poet Lord Byron (1788–1824), whose death he memorialized in the second part of *Faust.* But his most abiding influence was on his fellow German poets and dramatists.

The Spread of Romanticism

The generation that came to maturity with Goethe in the 1770s and 1780s included the playwrights Gotthold Ephraim Lessing (1729–1781) and Friedrich von Schiller (1759–1805), in whom the link between Romantic individualism and Romantic nationalism can be seen clearly. In his *Laocoön,* Lessing called for the creation of a national, heroic literature and the rejection of classical models, which were likened (as in the ancient statue from which he drew his title) to a giant serpent strangling human creativity. Schiller responded to that call in plays such as *William Tell* and *The Maid of Orleans* that described charismatically led movements of national liberation.

Goethe remained the mentor and example for the most important German writers of the next two generations, including the poets Friedrich von Novalis (1772–1801), Friedrich Hölderlin (1770–1843), and Heinrich Heine (1797–1856), and the playwright Heinrich von Kleist (1777–1811). The last decade of the eighteenth century also saw the advent of Romanticism in Britain, with the poetry of William Wordsworth (1770–1850) and Samuel Taylor Coleridge (1772–1834) and the immensely popular novels of Sir Walter Scott (1771–1832). Coleridge's still widely read *Rime of the Ancient Mariner* (1798) combined Christian symbolism with Romantic quest and atonement, while Wordsworth's epic verse autobiography, *The Prelude* (1807), offered the artist himself as hero, a theme that was to preoccupy both the nineteenth and twentieth centuries. Their successors, the tragically short-lived John Keats (1795–1821), Percy Bysshe Shelley (1792–1822), and Byron, brought English Romantic poetry to its finest flowering.

The Romantic Poet

In the preface to his Lyrical Ballads *(1798), William Wordsworth describes the poet as a kind of universal lawgiver, what his younger contemporary Percy Shelley would later call "the unacknowledged legislator of the human race." This proclamation of the sovereign genius of the solitary poet was crucial to the development of Romantic individualism and to the notion of the artist as a uniquely privileged figure in society.*

What is meant by the word Poet? What is a Poet? To whom does he address himself? And what language is to be expected from him? He is a man speaking to men: a man, it is true, with more lively sensibility, more enthusiasm and tenderness, who has a greater knowledge of human nature, and a more comprehensive soul. . . . He is the rock of defense of human nature; an upholder and preserver, carrying everywhere with him relationship and love. In spite of difference of soil and climate, of language and manners, of laws and customs, in spite of things silently gone out of mind and things violently destroyed, the Poet binds together by passion and knowledge the vast empire of human society, as it is spread over the whole earth, and over all time. The objects of the Poet's thoughts are everywhere; though the eyes and senses of men are, it is true, his favorite guides, yet he will follow wheresoever he can find an atmosphere of sensation in which to move his wings. Poetry is first and last of all knowledge—it is as immortal as the heart of man.

Source: The Complete Poetical Works of William Wordsworth (Philadelphia: Porter & Coates, 1851), pp. 664, 666.

It is arguable that France produced the first truly Romantic figure in Jean-Jacques Rousseau, who called for a return to nature as a refuge from the evils of a corrupt civilization and whose candid autobiography, the *Confessions,* was the earliest model of Romantic quest literature. However, the neoclassicism that dominated the arts through most of the eighteenth century retained its hold longer in France than elsewhere. The French Revolution harked back to Rome and Greece for its symbols of republican virtue and patriotism, and Napoleon adapted them for his own purposes. Not until after 1815 did France produce its first Romantic generation. The crucial transitional figures were the novelist Benjamin Constant (1767–1830), the poet and historian François-Auguste-René de Chateaubriand (1768–1848), and Madame de Staël (1766–1817), whose immensely influential book *On Germany* (1813) popularized German Romantic philosophy in France. Chateaubriand was the herald of a Catholic revival in France that rejected the Deism of the Enlightenment and the revolution and signaled a renewal of interest in medieval piety, soon reflected in a neo-Gothic movement in architecture. Madame de Staël caught this new mood as well: "I do not know exactly what we must believe," she declared, "but I believe that we must believe! The eighteenth century did nothing but deny. The human spirit lives by its beliefs." This new, if rather vague, religiosity blended well with Romantic self-absorption, but it clashed with liberalism. The result was that the Romantics tended to sort out either on the extreme right (Chateaubriand in France, Novalis in Germany) or on the extreme left (Shelley in England), with very few in the political middle.

The post-1815 generation in France included the novelist Stendhal (Marie-Henri Beyle, 1783–1842), whose great novel *The Red and the Black* gave the French their own Werther in the character of Julien Sorel; the painter Eugène Delacroix (1798–1863), whose depiction of a Turkish atrocity during the war of Greek independence, *The Massacre at Chios,* profoundly influenced European opinion; and the composer Hector Berlioz (1803–1869), whose *Symphonie fantastique* (1830), with its lavish orchestral coloration and fevered literary program, was the prototypical Romantic symphony.

Romantic music reached its apogee in Germany and Austria, where in the period between 1770 and 1830 four of the greatest geniuses in musical history appeared: Franz Joseph Haydn (1732–1809), Wolfgang Amadeus Mozart (1756–1791), Ludwig van Beethoven (1770–1827), and Franz Schubert (1797–1828). Haydn and Mozart were the supreme masters of the classical style that reigned for most of the latter half of the eighteenth century, with its emphasis on clarity of structure

Ludwig van Beethoven bridged not only the classical and Romantic periods in music but also, as the first musician to support himself primarily from the sale of his own work, the era of aristocratic patronage and of the artist-entrepreneur.

and texture, but their work exhibited elements of the nascent Romantic sensibility as well. Beethoven bridged the classic and Romantic eras, particularly in the nine symphonies that remain to this day the most admired synthesis of personal expression and formal control in music. Beethoven was a critical transitional figure in another respect as well. Whereas Haydn had worn the livery of his aristocratic employers for most of his life and Mozart had been at the mercy of his patrons, Beethoven was the first composer to make an independent living by the sale of his music. The artist too, no longer sheltered (and subordinated) by clerical or noble patrons, had entered the marketplace.

Romanticism Beyond the Arts

Romanticism touched not only the arts but philosophy, history, religious thought, and the natural sciences. Even as the Enlightenment proclaimed the sovereignty of reason, the German philosopher Immanuel Kant undercut its claims by arguing that the human mind was no mere passive receptor of experience, as Locke and other empiricists had believed, but a complex mechanism that gave form and shape to phenomena according to its own internal laws. Accordingly, the world could not be experienced as it was "in itself" but only as filtered through the processes of intellect and emotion and therefore subjectively.

Kant's philosophy was called idealism, after his distinction between the "ideas" we form of reality through the interaction of world and mind and the world as it exists independently of our perception of it. The implications of Kantian idealism were extended by the Prussian philosopher Georg Wilhelm Friedrich Hegel (1770–1831). Hegel argued that all of human history was a great unconscious drama that tended toward the realization of human freedom, which he called the spirit of reason. The agents of this drama were great individuals such as Caesar and Napoleon, through whose personal passions and ambitions this spirit acted; thus Caesar had created the first world empire, and Napoleon had stimulated the sense of national self-identity that Hegel saw as the final phase of the development of freedom.

Hegel's emphasis on the role of great men in history dovetailed neatly with Romantic individualism, while his

Classical philosophy culminated in the work of Georg Wilhelm Friedrich Hegel, whose conception of history as a struggle between dialectically opposed forces embodied Romantic notions of quest and struggle and profoundly influenced Karl Marx.

identification of nationalism with the progress of freedom had immense appeal to liberals in Germany and elsewhere, despite his praise of the conservative Prussian state. He also gave great impetus to the development of nationally oriented histories, such as those written by Jules Michelet in France and Leopold von Ranke (1795–1886) in Germany, as well as such cognate disciplines as ethnology (the study of humankind by racial and cultural divisions) and philology (the study of particular languages). No other thinker of the period made so comprehensive an effort to reconcile the two opposite poles of Romantic thought: the attempt to define oneself in opposition to society, whether as explorer, entrepreneur, or artist, and the desire for patriotic identity within the national group.

Romanticism and the Image of Women

The beginnings of modern feminism coincided with those of Romanticism and may be seen as part of the same process of social transformation. Prior to this time the few women who by sheer force of personality had been able to distinguish themselves were regarded as oddities or freaks. Samuel Johnson's cruel jest that a woman preaching was like a dog walking on its hind legs summarized the dominant male attitude toward female intellectual activity in general, even during the Enlightenment. But with the nineteenth century women began to appear for the first time on a plane of equality with men, particularly as literary artists. If Mary Wollstonecraft still had to struggle for recognition because of her sex in the 1790s, Madame de Staël was much more readily accepted only 20 years later, and in the succeeding decades women came to occupy an increasingly prominent place in the arts, particularly literature. We have noted the immense popularity of the British novelist Elizabeth Gaskell in the 1840s and 1850s (see Chapter 31). An analogous position was occupied by the American author and abolitionist Harriet Beecher Stowe, best known for her novel *Uncle Tom's Cabin* (1852), and the French novelist Aurore Dupin (1804–1876), who, taking the pen name George Sand, became as famous for her daring private life—which included a highly publicized liaison with the great Polish composer-pianist Frédéric Chopin—as for her voluminous literary output. At least four Englishwomen stand in the front rank of nineteenth-century literature: Jane Austen (1775–1817), whose social novels reveal a psychological penetration equaled among her contemporaries only by Goethe; the Brontë sisters, Charlotte and Emily; and Mary Anne Evans (1819–1880), known by the pen name George Eliot, whose novel *Middlemarch* is rivaled only by the major works of Charles Dickens. At the same time the reclusive New Englander Emily Dickinson (1830–1886) was writing some of the finest lyric poetry since Sappho.

Nevertheless, the disabilities faced by women attempting to compete in what was still a man's world were obvious. Elizabeth Gaskell was never known by her own forename but simply as "Mrs. Gaskell"; Dupin and Evans both adopted masculine pen names in an effort to gain more serious attention for their work; and Emily Dickinson's poems were never published in her own lifetime. If, moreover, a place in literature and to a lesser extent in the other arts was reluctantly conceded to women, it served only to confirm age-old prejudices against them in the fields of philosophy, politics, and the professions. Fichte argued that women lacked the "speculative aptitude" for either philosophical inquiry or public office. Hegel made what was to be the fundamental nineteenth-century bourgeois distinction between a public world of work and struggle, in which only men were fit to compete, and the private sphere of "piety and domesticity," for which women were intended by nature. The Frenchman Auguste Comte (1798–1857) doubted that women could be entrusted even with running a household except under male supervision. If women excelled in literature, it only confirmed the stereotype of them as creatures in whom imagination prevailed at the expense of intellect.

The rejection of traditional marriage by women like Mary Wollstonecraft and George Sand and their demand for free sexual companionship reinforced the widespread male belief that women should be confined as tightly within the bounds of "piety and domesticity" as possible. Yet the image of woman had come to stand allegorically for revolution itself. The seal of the French republic depicted a woman armed with a pike, and in Delacroix's famous painting of the revolution of 1830, *Liberty on the Barricades,* a female figure leads a charge over the bodies of fallen sans-culottes, a top-hatted bourgeois at her side. Her bared breast recalls the classical image of the Amazon warrior, but the realistic touches— the stained petticoats, the hair under the arms—proclaim her as well to be a woman of the people. At the same time, her nudity carries an implicit message of sexual aggressiveness that is only partly offset by her averted, impassive gaze. Delacroix's figure conveys the conflicting impulses behind the early Romantic image of woman: the idealized warrior-goddess and the available woman of the street, the symbol of liberation who remains chained in her petticoats, leading a battle that will be fought by the sans-culottes but won by the bourgeoisie.

The Liberal Revival and the Revolutions of 1830

By the late 1820s dissatisfaction with the reactionary Bourbon dynasty in France and the slow pace of reform in Britain had reached the flashpoint of revolution. A neutral observer, asked to predict where it would actually occur, would probably have chosen Britain. The British political system, unreformed since 1689, had refused even a token accommodation to the new social reality created by the Industrial Revolution. Yet Britain alone, of all the major states of Europe, was to avoid revolution in 1830 and the years to come. Not London but Paris was to provide the impetus for the next wave of insurrection.

The July Revolution in France

The new revolutionary crisis began in March 1830, when the French Chamber of Deputies, led by the bankers Jacques Lafitte and Jean-Paul Casimir-Perier, voted no confidence in the government of Charles X and its policies of censorship, suffrage restriction, and clerical control of education. Charles dissolved the assembly, but new elections, even though limited to an electorate of 100,000, produced a decisive opposition majority. The king wavered, but urged on by Metternich among others, he responded on July 26 by dissolving the Chamber before it could meet, imposing new press censorship, reducing the electorate to a hard core of 25,000 aristocrats, and announcing fresh elections on this basis.

The target of these edicts was the regime's bourgeois opposition, but the reaction came from the working-class sections of Paris. The very next day barricades appeared spontaneously in the streets; the army, called out to clear them, refused to do so. Faced with anarchy, Charles abdicated two days later in favor of his grandson and fled into exile. France was left without a government.

The sudden vacuum of power revealed the clear-cut divisions of the French political spectrum. The bourgeois opposition—bankers, industrialists, and merchants— wanted not the overthrow of the Bourbon monarchy but greater favor within it for themselves. The Parisian workers, students, and radical intellectuals who had taken to the barricades and made the revolution wanted a republic, headed by the venerable marquis de Lafayette as president. A compromise was hastily brokered behind the scenes. The duke of Orléans, a collateral relative of the Bourbons but a republican soldier in the army of 1792, was put forward as a constitutional monarch by a coalition consisting of Talleyrand, the liberal journalist Adolphe Thiers, and Lafitte, the duke's personal banker. When Lafayette publicly endorsed him, the republican opposition melted away. Louis-Philippe, as the new king was called, promised to abide by the charter of 1814, flew the tricolor flag of the 1789 revolution rather than the Bourbon lily, and was the first monarch to wear the contemporary equivalent of a business suit in public. With his paunch and his umbrella, he was indistinguishable from the bourgeoisie that had brought him to power and whose interests he faithfully served.

Revolution East and West

The three-day revolution in France was the signal for major uprisings in Belgium and Poland. Catholic Belgium, united with the Netherlands by the Congress of Vienna, chafed under the domination of a Protestant Dutch king, William I. Heartened by the French example, Belgians rose in August 1830 and, after fruitless efforts at conciliation, proclaimed independence under a liberal monarchy of their own. A hastily arranged big power conference in London recognized the new government to forestall French intervention.

The Polish rebellion was triggered by the news that Tsar Nicholas I, who was also king of Poland, was planning to send Russian troops through that country on its way to help suppress the Belgians. Russian rule was desperately unpopular, however, and almost any pretext might have served. The Polish Diet declared Nicholas deposed, but the tsar's army speedily crushed the revolt. Poland was absorbed directly into the Russian empire and ruled under a state of military emergency that lasted technically from 1833 until World War I. Thousands of Poles were executed, imprisoned, or banished to Siberia, and many more fled to the West, among them Chopin.

Lesser disturbances also shook Germany, Italy, Switzerland, Spain, and Portugal, though for the most part without significant result. Yet liberals could, with the tragic exception of Poland, count 1830 as a year of victory. The bourgeoisie had finally cut a king to their own measure. The powers had been forced to acquiesce in an independent Belgium whose constitution acknowledged the sovereignty of the people and provided what was to be for many years the widest electoral franchise in Europe. The autocratic William I was forced to embrace reform in the Netherlands, and liberal gains were made

in Switzerland. Above all, 1830 marked the year when history seemed to move again in Europe. The liberal triumph was far from complete, but its outlines at last seemed visible.

Britain: Revolution Averted

Britain accomplished revolutionary change without revolution. The settlement of 1689 had confirmed the supremacy of Parliament over the king. But neither the size of the electorate—less than 4 percent of the population—nor the distribution of seats had changed in nearly a century and a half, and both were now profoundly unrepresentative of the urban, industrialized society that Britain had become. The long and almost unbroken Conservative domination of British politics from 1760 to 1830 had hardened the nation's rulers in their resistance to change.

Reform, however, was in the air. Tariff duties and colonial trade restrictions, some in effect since the seventeenth century, were relaxed, and the Test Act, which had barred Catholics and Dissenters from public life since 1673, was at last repealed (1829). A gesture was even made toward the lower orders; unions were recognized, and the number of offenses punishable by death was cut by 100. But the one issue that had become symbolic of the liberal cause as a whole—parliamentary reform—remained unaddressed.

The reformers' moment came in 1830, when the duke of Wellington's government fell and a Whig ministry under Lord Grey came to power. Despite bitter Tory opposition, Grey steered a parliamentary reform bill through both houses in 1832, although the Lords acquiesced only when faced with the king's threat to create enough Whig peers to override them. It was just in time; riots had broken out all over the country, a tax strike was being organized, and radicals urged a run on the Bank of England to bring the propertied classes to their knees.

The Reform Act was as important for the revolution it averted as for the rather modest alterations it produced. It changed the image but not the reality of power in Britain. Some 143 seats in the House of Commons, about a quarter of the total, were redistributed. Slightly fewer than half of these went to new industrial towns, such as Manchester, which had previously lacked representation of any kind. Some, but by no means all, of the "rotten boroughs"—decayed constituencies that continued to return members to Parliament with a largely phantom electorate—were eliminated. The franchise was extended from slightly under 500,000 to just over 800,000

Mazzini's Call to Revolution

Despite the failure of the revolutions of 1830, young nationalists took heart at the year that had rocked the kings of Europe on their thrones. Giuseppe Mazzini, the leader of Young Italy, an organization dedicated to the liberation and unification of Italy, here declares both the faith and the method of his revolutionary band. The emphasis on education and guerrilla tactics sounds a particularly modern note.

Young Italy is *Republican*. . . . Republican—because theoretically every nation is destined, by the law of God and humanity, to form a free and equal community of brothers; and the republican is the only form of government that insures this future. . . .

The means by which Young Italy proposes to reach its aims are—education and insurrection, to be adopted simultaneously, and made to harmonize with each other.

Education must ever be directed to teach by example, word, and pen the necessity of insurrection. Insurrection, whenever it can be realized, must be so conducted as to render it a means of national education. . . .

Insurrection—by means of guerrilla bands—is the true method of warfare for all nations desirous of emancipating themselves from a foreign yoke. This method of warfare supplies the want—inevitable at the commencement of the insurrection—of a regular army; it calls the greatest number of elements into the field, and yet may be sustained by the smallest number. It forms the military education of the people, and consecrates every foot of the native soil by the memory of some warlike deed.

Source: N. Gangulee, ed., *Giuseppe Mazzini: Selected Writings* (London: Lindsay Drummond, 1945), pp. 129–134 passim.

---

voters, still little more than 5 percent of the population. The net effect was a token recognition of the industrial bourgeoisie that kept the balance of electoral power safely in the hands of the landed gentry and nobility.

But while on some issues the interests of the two groups were genuinely divided, it would be a mistake to see them as fundamentally opposed. The new magnates of industrial capitalism, like their eighteenth-century predecessors in commerce and finance, had little need of parliamentary representation to make their weight felt. The propertied classes in town and country had adjusted their mutual relations in a manner that more adequately represented the influence of the former. Both agreed that the reins of government would continue to rest with them to the exclusion of the vast majority. The Reform Act of 1832, like the regime of Louis-Philippe in France, reflected that broad consensus. So did the repeal in 1846 of the Corn Laws, which had kept grain prices high by curtailing foreign imports. Industrialists opposed the Corn Laws because high food prices forced them to pay higher wages; the landowners finally endorsed repeal, not least to preserve the ruling consensus.

The Socialist Challenge

It would be accurate to say that the working classes had fought the revolutions of 1830 and the bourgeoisie had won them. The sans-culottes on the barricades in Paris, the workers who defied the Dutch king in Brussels and Antwerp, and the British laborers who seized Bristol and threatened other towns in their demand for parliamentary representation had all taken an initiative that their betters were quick to convert to their own advantage. Nothing could symbolize the irony of mass politics in the early industrial age more than the spectacle of elderly aristocrats like Lafayette and Lord Grey stage-managing the transference or at any rate the sharing of power between the traditional nobility and the industrial bourgeoisie at the behest of the workers.

The Demand for Reform

The experience of the 1830s and 1840s taught at least the more advanced elements of the working class that their interests could not be encompassed by those of the

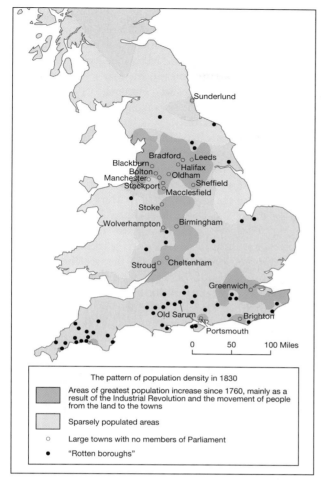

MAP 32.3 PARLIAMENTARY REPRESENTATION IN BRITAIN BEFORE 1832

Map legend:

Sunderlund

Bradford · Leeds
Blackburn · Halifax
Bolton
Manchester · Oldham
Stockport · Sheffield
Macclesfield

Stoke

Wolverhampton · Birmingham

Stroud · Cheltenham

Greenwich

Old Sarum · Brighton
Portsmouth

0   50   100 Miles

The pattern of population density in 1830

Areas of greatest population increase since 1760, mainly as a result of the Industrial Revolution and the movement of people from the land to the towns

Sparsely populated areas

○ Large towns with no members of Parliament

● "Rotten boroughs"

bourgeoisie. The mass movement that Robert Owen led briefly from 1833 to 1834 (see Chapter 31) was prompted in part by disillusion with the Reform Act, and by the end of the 1830s the first sustained workers' movement had emerged in Britain, the Chartists. It began in 1836 when a small shopkeeper, William Lovett, founded the London Workingmen's Association. The association's relatively modest initial demands were presented in the tradition of social deference to one's superiors. Its tone, however, soon grew more radical. In 1838, with the assistance of the veteran reformer Francis Place, it drew up the first People's Charter. This document rejected the piecemeal reform of Parliament, which was all conventional politics could offer. It demanded a secret ballot, equal electoral districts, annually elected Parliaments on the basis of universal manhood suffrage, the removal of property qualifications for office, and payment for all members of Parliament. The effect of this would have been fully to democratize the political system (at least for men) and to enable workers themselves to stand for and occupy seats in Parliament. Here was a genuine break with the politics of deference, with its assumption that the interest of the working class could be represented satisfactorily by its social betters.

In February 1839 a self-styled workers' convention met in London to press for the People's Charter, now attached to a petition bearing a million signatures. When the House of Commons rejected the charter, a general strike was proposed. Lacking organization and experienced leadership, it petered out in sporadic agitation from which many existing unions held aloof. Unlike Owen's Grand Union, however, the Chartist movement did not collapse with its first defeat but remained a powerful force throughout the 1840s.

A similar rethinking of worker interests was going forward in France, where, having consolidated its position, the government of Louis-Philippe set its face against even token reform. In 1839 the journalist Louis Blanc (1811–1882) argued in a widely read book, *The Organization of Labor,* that the state should socialize all major economic services, including banking, transportation, and insurance, and establish "social workshops," or cooperative factories operated by and for workers. Blanc's reformism derived from the Saint-Simonians, followers of the influential Count de Saint-Simon (1760–1825), who had advocated control of public services and enterprises by a technocratic elite of scientists and engineers. What both Saint-Simon and Blanc ignored, however, like more "utopian" socialists such as Owen and Fourier, was the problem of actual political power. The state, whether controlled by aristocrats, by bourgeoisie, or, as in much of western Europe, by an uneasy combination of both, was highly unlikely to cede authority to either workers or engineers.

From Reform to Revolution

Such was the conclusion drawn by revolutionaries such as Louis-Auguste Blanqui (1805–1881) and Pierre Proudhon (1809–1865). Proudhon, unwilling to compromise with any scheme of state ownership, declared roundly that all property was a theft of the value created by labor. He envisioned the abolition of the state in favor of a system of decentralized cooperative enterprises that would produce and exchange goods noncompetitively on the basis of social need. For Blanqui, such an arrangement, however desirable in principle, begged the fundamental question of power: How was such a peaceful system to be established against the resistance of the propertied classes and the state machinery they controlled? Blanqui's answer was armed revolution aimed at establishing a "dictatorship of the proletariat," a phrase he coined. Blanqui spent most of his life in jail or on the run. Tocqueville, observing him in 1848 at a rare moment of liberty, said he had the appearance of a man who had passed his life in the sewers. But with agitators like Blanqui a new kind of figure had appeared on the European scene, convinced of the inevitable struggle between the classes and dedicated to revolution at any cost.

The thinkers and activists we have just considered subscribed to a common critique of the capitalist system. They accepted Adam Smith's definition of labor as the source of all productive value and believed (as Smith did not) that the wealth produced by this labor should be owned socially or collectively; hence the name *socialism* applied to their ideas and demands. The socialists' beliefs were clear-cut: private ownership was the appropriation by force of an excess share of the common social wealth, and unregulated capitalism was the equivalent of unrelieved exploitation. But they disagreed about the remedy. Owen, Fourier, and Proudhon put their faith in small, collectively owned enterprises linked voluntarily into cooperative associations; Saint-Simon and Blanc believed that only state power could break up existing concentrations of private capital and ownership; and Blanqui added that only revolution from below could give the proletariat access to that power. What they all lacked was a theory of social action or, more simply, a credible plan for overthrowing the existing order.

Karl Marx

Karl Marx supplied the theoretical basis for socialism. Marx was the first socialist thinker to challenge the fundamental claims of liberal economists such as Adam Smith and David Ricardo, who argued that private enterprise—economic competition for individual profit—maximized the production of wealth and hence the aggregate social good. Ricardo was sensitive to the high social cost of capitalism: the exploitation of child and female labor, the tendency of worker income to remain at subsistence level, and the "business cycle"—the abrupt spasms of boom and bust to which the industrial system had already shown itself vulnerable. These costs were regrettable but, Ricardo felt, for the most part unavoidable. This was particularly true for income stagnation, which Ricardo formulated as the "iron law of wages." In times of industrial expansion when the demand for labor exceeded the supply, he argued, wages would tend to rise above subsistence level; but the result of relative prosper-

ity was a higher birthrate, which produced excess labor capacity, depressed wages, and caused starvation and misery. For this reason, worker demands for higher wages were self-defeating. Marx challenged this and similar "laws" of economics in his major work, *Capital*, advancing a comprehensive countertheory to demonstrate that capitalism was not merely unstable but also inherently self-destructive.

Marx was born in 1818 in Trier, in the rapidly industrializing Rhineland. He was descended on both sides from a long line of rabbis, but his father, like many other Jews of the time, had submitted to Christian baptism to gain entry into the legal profession. Marx studied philosophy at Bonn and Berlin and joined a circle of young radicals who were attempting to extend Hegelian thought in a leftward direction. As a correspondent for the *Rheinische Zeitung*, he exposed the wretched poverty of the winegrowers of the Trier region in an article that helped lead to the suppression of the newspaper. Quitting Germany in disgust, he settled in Paris, where he produced a series of extraordinary and prophetic essays on worker alienation and shed his last attachments to

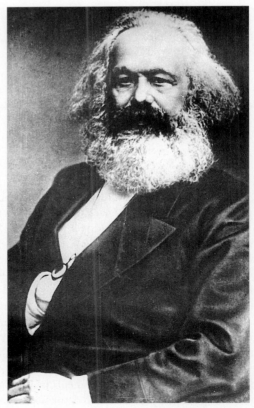

The founder of modern communism, Karl Marx, in a photograph taken in the mid-1870s.

Romantic and Neoclassical Art

Eugène Delacroix, MASSACRE AT CHIOS. This vivid, if stylized, rendering of the massacre of Greek rebels on the island of Chios by the Turks helped mobilize opinion throughout Europe on behalf of the Greek cause. The stereotyped but highly effective images of defenseless womanhood at the mercy of the sword were all calculated to arouse bourgeois outrage.

Eugène Delacroix, THE TWENTY-EIGHTH OF JULY: LIBERTY LEADING THE PEOPLE (also known as LIBERTY ON THE BARRICADES). This famous painting personifies liberty as a female figure leading a charge over the bodies of fallen sans-culottes, a top-hatted bourgeois at her side. Her bared breast recalls the classical image of the Amazon warrior, but her stained petticoats proclaim her to be a woman of the people.

Caspar David Friedrich, TRAVELER LOOKING OVER A SEA OF FOG. Friedrich's striking vision of a solitary climber staring into the abyss evokes the Romantic confrontation with nature. The artist has posed his hero with his back to the viewer, as if turned away from civilization, but his attire and walking stick proclaim him to be essentially urban and bourgeois.

Eugène Delacroix, GEORGE SAND IN MASCULINE COSTUME. To make headway in a man's world, the novelist Aurore Dupin adopted a male pen name, George Sand, and male attire as well. Sand's expression, a mix of sensitivity and severity, conveys the ambiguity of her role and the plight of the woman artist in the nineteenth century.

Gustave Courbet, self-portrait, also called "The Man with the Pipe." Courbet painted many self-portraits in a wide variety of moods. Here his averted gaze and musing expression show him lost in private reverie, as indifferent to the viewer as Friedrich's traveler. At the same time, however, the strong brow and the clenched pipe indicate a man preparing to take determined action in the world.

J. M. W. Turner, Eruption of La Soufrière.
*Turner's image of a volcano suggests the immense force
of natural power but also the ambition of industrial
civilization to channel that power.*

Édouard Manet, Déjeuner sur l'Herbe. Manet's manifesto of sexual and artistic freedom, first exhibited in 1863, caused a scandal. Unlike the nude figures of Delacroix' Massacre at Chios, the nude in Manet's painting is not offered up for pity, protection, or erotic fantasy, nor is she the property of the men whose company she shares. In contrast, the modest, stooping figure in the background represents a submissive femininity (as well as the conventions of academic painting) that the new bohemian freedom rejected.

William Adolphe Bouguereau, Charity. Bouguereau's painting deals with a real contemporary problem, urban poverty and abandonment, but in such a way as to blunt perception. The pleading mother is given the guise of a Renaissance Madonna, an effect emphasized by the neoclassical façade she is crouched against and the Italianate building in the distance. Poverty here is removed from all misery and squalor and is presented as feminine dependence, appealing to chivalry and charity.

Hegelian idealism. On the eve of the revolutions of 1848 he hailed the coming of a new socialist order in *The Communist Manifesto,* written with his lifelong friend and collaborator, Friedrich Engels. After 1848, Marx took refuge in London with his large and needy family. He lived there for the remainder of his life, in part supported by Engels, who owned a factory in Manchester.

Dismissing his predecessors and rivals, Marx declared his work to be the only "scientific" socialism. It was founded on a grand theory that, arguing humanity's intellectual and social development from its material struggle to wrest the necessities of life from nature, proceeded to describe the stages of history in terms of a struggle for control of the technical means of production—land, labor, and machinery. Marx described ancient society as founded on slavery, the medieval West on feudalism, and capitalism on wage labor, which he saw as a modern form of slavery. Since, like other socialists, Marx regarded labor as the only source of productive value (capital itself, he argued, was only the result of previous labor), all profit extracted from labor by means of the wage system was "surplus" or appropriated value.

Marx praised the bourgeoisie for having greatly expanded the material base of civilization by industrialization and urbanization, even as it simultaneously debased its human content by forcing the great mass of the population to live in conditions of unparalleled exploitation and misery. The contradiction between the prosperity of the few and the poverty of the many could not, however, ultimately be ignored. At the same time, the inherent tendency of capitalist competition to contract and profit margins to shrink would lead to ever-severer contractions of the business cycle until the conditions for socialist revolution were ripe.

But revolution could be neither prepared nor accomplished without active class struggle. Marx continually stressed the cooperative nature of that struggle across all borders, rejecting nationalism as a bourgeois phenomenon that reflected the divisive, competitive nature of capitalism itself. In 1864 he was instrumental in founding the International Workingman's Association, later known as the First International, to promote the proletarian cause throughout Europe and America. At his death in 1883, he was clearly the foremost figure of European socialism, as both a thinker and an activist.

Marx never managed to put his mature ideas into finished, comprehensive form. Half his manuscripts lay unpublished at his death, many to remain unknown for decades; even his masterpiece, *Capital,* the first part of which was published in 1867, was only a torso. In part

this reflected his own refusal to settle into any mold, even his own; as he once wittily remarked, "I am not a Marxist." Yet his work helped to shape modern society, and in the universality of his influence he may be regarded as among the few nonreligious thinkers of world significance. Before Marx no theory of societal development had advanced much beyond Plato and Aristotle 2,000 years before. There was no theory of historical change that dealt adequately with the concrete problems of subsistence, organization, or technological innovation. Yet although Marx emphasized material necessity in determining social forms, his ultimate concern was for the creation of a just society in which men and women would be liberated from the iron compulsion of labor and free to realize their human potential.

The Russian émigré Annenkov described Marx as unkempt, domineering, and very nearly offensive in manner; but, he added, "he looked like a man with the right and power to demand respect, no matter how he appeared before you and no matter what he did," a man with "the firm conviction of his mission to dominate men's minds and prescribe them their laws." Much of the twentieth century responded to the force of his vision.

The Revolutions of 1848

When late in the year 1847 Marx and Engels warned of the imminence of revolution in *The Communist Manifesto,* they may have been the only ones in Europe to expect it. Yet within the first four months of 1848 the Continent was rocked by almost 50 separate revolutions in France, Prussia, Austria, and almost all the lesser German and Italian states. Surveying the wreckage of monarchies, Tsar Nicholas I wrote to Queen Victoria that Russia and Britain seemed to be the last two states standing in Europe. His exaggeration was only slight.

The Causes of the Revolutions

Some general causes of the revolutions can be discerned, although they differed with the circumstances of each state or region. The Industrial Revolution, which had begun in earnest on the Continent after 1830, had shaken social and demographic patterns and profoundly altered political ones. Unfulfilled nationalist aspirations were a primary impetus in Germany, Italy, and eastern Europe. These tensions and grievances were also exacerbated, as before 1789 and 1830, by hard times. Harvests were poor in the three years preceding 1848; the Prussian peasantry, lacking bread, survived on potatoes, while in

Ireland famine and emigration reduced the population from 8.5 million to 6.5 million. Urban workers were also squeezed by the rising price of food, and the agricultural crisis soon produced industrial depression as well. The integration of agricultural and industrial markets through capitalist development meant that any disturbance in one sector of the system had immediate repercussions in the rest of it, while the new concentration of population in towns and cities provided natural foci of discontent.

The single most pervasive element in the revolutions of 1848, however, was a general questioning of the existing political order. The monarchs of the Old Regime had based their authority on appeals to divine right and a traditional social order, but the appeal to tradition had little force in a society where the most basic relations of property, production, and authority were being transformed and a new financial, commercial, and industrial elite was busily accumulating power. Still less could rulers legitimate themselves where, as in most of Italy, they served not a native but a foreign interest.

The new bourgeois or quasi-bourgeois regimes established by the events of 1830–1832, though based explicitly or implicitly on popular sovereignty and constitutional guarantees, had proved unwilling to embrace the vast majority of the people in the political process. Except for Belgium, in no European nation did the electorate exceed 5 percent of the population. The Chartists were rebuffed in their demand for universal manhood suffrage in Britain, while in France, with only 300,000 electors in a population of 30 million, the government of François Guizot set itself resolutely against even a token extension of the franchise. After two revolutions and 60 years, the French Assembly was a less representative body than the Estates General of Louis XVI had been.

The Collapse of the Old Order

The revolutions of 1848 began in Italy, where on January 12 the people of Sicily rose against Ferdinand II. By the end of the month Milan and Venice had proclaimed their ancient independence as republics and called on King Charles Albert of Piedmont and Pope Pius IX to help unify the entire peninsula. The French were not far behind. When the authorities abruptly banned a rally in Paris on behalf of the franchise in late February, the events of 1830 swiftly repeated themselves. Riots broke out, barricades went up, and the National Guard, called out to quell the disturbances, joined in instead. Louis-Philippe dismissed the unpopular Guizot in a bid to regain middle-class support. But the Parisian workers were not to be duped a second time. Breaking into the Chamber of Deputies, they forced the proclamation of a republic, and Louis-Philippe fled into exile in London.

The news from Paris galvanized dissidents in Germany and Austria. In Berlin the irresolute Frederick William IV (1840–1861) found himself a virtual prisoner of nationalists who demanded that Prussia take the lead in unifying Germany under a liberal constitution. Student rebels and workers joined in Vienna to extract a promise of reform from the emperor, Ferdinand I, and the aged Metternich fled the city in disguise to join

THE REVOLUTIONS OF 1848 AND 1849

1848

January	Sicilian uprising against the Kingdom of Naples
February	Naples, Tuscany grant constitutions; revolution in Paris, republic proclaimed
March	Uprisings in Vienna, Venice, Milan, Berlin; serfdom abolished in Austria; Venice proclaims a republic; Frederick William IV promises Prussia a constitution
April	Constituent Assembly elected in France
May	Frankfurt Assembly convenes
June	Troops quell popular uprisings in Prague and Paris
October	Austrian army retakes Vienna from radical students and workers
December	Ferdinand I of Austria abdicates in favor of Franz Joseph; Louis Napoleon elected president of the French Republic

1849

February	Rome proclaims a republic
March	Battle of Novara; Charles Albert abdicates
April	Hungary declares independence from Austria; Frederick William IV refuses the crown of Germany from the Frankfurt Assembly
May–August	Frankfurt Assembly dispersed; absolute monarchy restored in Naples; Russia suppresses the Hungarian revolution; Republic of Venice surrenders

MAP 32.4   EURPOE'S REVOLUTIONS OF 1848

Louis-Philippe in exile. In Prague, Bohemian national-ists rose against Habsburg rule, while Hungarians led by Louis Kossuth (1802–1894) demanded virtual indepen-dence from Austria, with a separate army, government, and system of finance. In addition, the Hungarian Diet, composed exclusively of noblemen and long one of the most reactionary assemblies in Europe, voted for consti-tutional government, the abolition of serfdom, and the imposition of taxes on the nobility. By the end of March the Austrian Empire was prostrate, while in Germany a group of liberals, meeting spontaneously in Heidelberg, called for the election of an all-German parliament on the basis of universal manhood suffrage and under the supervision of an electoral body, the *Vorparliament,* sum-moned directly by them. So great was the enthusiasm for unity throughout the country, and so paralyzed were the existing governments, that the election was duly carried out, and on May 18 the 830 delegates of the new parlia-ment convened in Frankfurt to make Germany a nation.

The most striking fact in this whirlwind of revolu-tions was the suddenness and ease with which they were accomplished. Not only had Louis-Philippe, like his pre-decessor Charles X, fallen at what seemed the merest touch, but the most rock-solid thrones in Europe, Prus-sia and Austria, had been shaken by relative handfuls of

protesters who made up their demands as they went along. Nothing could have more vividly demonstrated the ideological bankruptcy of the old order and its help-lessness in the face of even the most disorganized chal-lenge. But the revolutionaries, united for the moment in the flush of success, were soon as divided from one an-other as they had been from the kings who served as the common target of their discontent.

Counterrevolution in Central Europe

Among the first revolutions to unravel were in the Aus-trian Empire. In Italy, Charles Albert had no sooner as-sumed leadership of the anti-Habsburg coalition than it began to collapse; a counterrevolution restored Ferdi-nand II in Sicily, while the Venetians made it clear that they had no intention of abandoning their republic to merge with the House of Savoy. In July, Austria badly defeated Charles Albert's forces at the battle of Cus-tozza, and a last attempt to resuscitate the cause ended in disaster at Novara in March 1849. The Italian conflagra-tion was not quite over; in November 1848, Pius IX fled Rome after the assassination of his chief minister, and a republic was proclaimed in February headed by Giuseppe Mazzini (1805–1872), whose impassioned vision of a united, democratic Italy had made him a hero to a generation of young nationalists. Mazzini's government immediately announced the confiscation of church lands and their redistribution to the peasantry, as well as a program of public housing for the urban poor. Although it controlled only the city of Rome and its immediate environs, the republic declared itself the nucleus of a united Italy. But it fell to a French army in July, and with the surrender of Venice a month later, the collapse of the revolutionary cause in Italy was complete.

In Hungary the Magyar majority under Kossuth alienated the Slavic populations under its control by proclaiming what amounted to racial hegemony: it abolished local assemblies in non-Magyar provinces and prescribed that Hungarian be the exclusive language of all higher education as well as of the Diet. A pan-Slavic congress convened in Prague in June but was suppressed by troops still loyal to the Habsburgs. This victory emboldened the court party to attempt the liberation of Vienna. In October, the Habsburgs reoccupied the city after a bombardment and executed or exiled its radical leaders on the spot. Two months later the feebleminded Ferdinand I was induced to step down in favor of his 18-year-old nephew, Franz Josef I (1848–1916), who completed the process of restoration the following summer by crushing the Hungarian revolt with the aid of 140,000 Russian troops.

In Germany, meanwhile, the Frankfurt Assembly set to its task of providing the country with a national government and a constitution. The fundamental anomaly of its position, however, was soon apparent. Almost all the delegates were members of the upper bourgeoisie whose vision was of free trade, untrammeled growth, an end to the political monopoly of the aristocracy, and a liberal, constitutional regime. But the masses, whose rebellion had cleared the ground for them, wanted none of these things. They were peasants clamoring for land, artisans demanding protection for their trades, and workers who wanted higher wages and industrial regulation. Free enterprise only meant new chains to them, and free speech was less important than bread they could afford to eat.

While the Frankfurt delegates attempted to thrash out their own differences—whether the new Germany should be a federation or a unitary state, a monarchy, an empire, or a republic, and above all whether it should seek to incorporate German-speaking areas of Austria, Denmark, and Poland within its borders—the existing governments of the German Confederation, supposedly awaiting final extinction but still in control of their armies, recovered their authority. By the time the Assembly had drafted its constitution—which included provisions for freedom of speech, assembly, and the press; religious toleration; and

public education—both Prussia and Austria had become strong enough to reject it out of hand. When Frederick William IV was approached in April 1849 to become "emperor of the Germans," he replied that he would not pick up a crown from the gutter. At that the Frankfurt Assembly began to collapse. The more moderate delegations, unwilling to contemplate a republic, went home, and the radical remnant was dispersed by force in June. The revolution in Germany was over.

France: From Revolution to Empire

In France the course of events was quite different. Here alone (apart from Mazzini's short-lived Roman republic), the monarch of an independent state had actually been deposed and a new provisional government established. A hasty compromise among revolutionary factions, it consisted of seven moderate and three radical (socialist) republicans. Among the latter was Louis Blanc, who urged immediate relief for the unemployed through a Ministry of Progress that would establish his workshop system. Behind Blanc was the specter of Blanqui, who showed his power by mounting a demonstration of 100,000 workers in Paris in March 1848. When Blanc failed to win them the concessions they demanded, one of the marchers denounced him as a traitor. The revolution had already been split.

Most of the wealthier bourgeoisie and nobility had already fled Paris, and the United States was the only foreign power to recognize the French republic. The moderates in the government placed their hopes in speedy elections, which they expected to produce a conservative majority that would isolate the radicals. A Constituent Assembly, elected by universal manhood suffrage in April, convened on May 4 and immediately replaced the provisional government with a five-man executive of its own that contained no socialists. On June 22, following an abortive coup led by Blanqui, the government announced the dissolution of the workshop program, which had been set up as a sop to Blanc but had provided only ill-paid road work. The reaction was immediate. The workers took up arms, the government proclaimed martial law, and the class war heralded only six months before by Marx and Engels in *The Communist Manifesto* became a reality in the streets of Paris. Ten thousand people were killed or wounded in a three-day struggle without quarter (June 24–26) until troops under General Louis Cavaignac regained control of the city. An occupation army of 50,000 remained until October.

The so-called June Days sent a shudder of terror throughout bourgeois Europe; one woman likened the

The June Days

The French liberal Alexis de Tocqueville describes the June Days of 1848.

I come at last to the insurrection of June, the most extensive and the most singular that has occurred in our history, and perhaps in any other: the most extensive, because, during four days, more than a hundred thousand men were engaged in it; the most singular, because the insurgents fought without a war-cry, without leaders, without flags, and yet with a marvellous harmony and an amount of military experience that astonished the oldest officers.

What distinguished it also, among all the events of this kind which have succeeded one another in France for sixty years, is that it did not aim at changing the form of government, but at altering the order of society. It was not, strictly speaking, a political struggle, in the sense which until then we had given to the word, but a combat of class against class. . . .

It must also be observed that this formidable insurrection was not the enterprise of a certain number of conspirators, but the revolt of one whole section of the population against another. Women took part in it as well as men. While the latter fought, the former prepared and carried ammunition; and when at last the time had come to surrender, the women were the last to yield.

Source: A. T. De Mattos, trans., *The Recollections of Alexis de Tocqueville* (New York: Columbia University Press, 1949), pp. 150–151.

strife in Paris to the siege of Rome by the barbarians. The feeling was reciprocated, and not by French workers alone. "Every proletarian," wrote the editor of *Red Revolution* in London, "who does not see and feel that he belongs to an enslaved and degraded class is a *fool*." The ideological breach between the classes was complete, and that division remained the formal posture of western European politics for well over a century.

SUMMARY

Looking back on the revolutions of 1848, Karl Marx observed wryly that history repeats itself: the first time as tragedy, the second as farce. There was more than a touch of farce about many of them, but there was much tragedy too, and in the June Days of Paris, an ominous portent of the future. But perhaps the dominant emotion was frustration. For a moment, liberals had dreamed of constitutions, nationalists of unification, and radicals of a classless society in which the workers of every land could embrace as comrades. These dreams were not yet to be.

The European elite of the mid-nineteenth century—an amalgam of the upper bourgeoisie and the traditional landed aristocracy—was still powerful enough to maintain itself, while its opponents were too diffuse in their aims, too divided among themselves, and too little rooted in the political and social realities of the mass of the population they claimed to represent. Yet the demands they made—political equality, national consolidation, and social justice—reflected deeply felt ideological contradictions within European society. Inherited privilege, the basis of political dominance in Europe for centuries, was no longer self-justifying, while acquired privilege—the accumulation of wealth and capital by the bourgeoisie—was equally suspect as a mandate to rule. If the revolutionaries of 1848 had failed to topple the existing order, they had exposed the essential hollowness and vulnerability of any authority not based on popular consent.

SUGGESTIONS FOR FURTHER READING

Abrams, M. H. *The Mirror and the Lamp: Romantic Theory and the Critical Tradition.* New York: Oxford University Press, 1953.

Artz, F. B. *Reaction and Revolution, 1814–1832.* New York: Harper & Row, 1963.

Cranston, M. *The Romantic Movement.* Oxford: Basil Blackwell, 1994.

Chevalier, L. *Laboring Classes and Dangerous Classes in Paris During the First Half of the Nineteenth Century.* New York: Fertig, 1973.

Clark, K. *The Romantic Rebellion.* New York: Harper & Row, 1973.

Dakin, D. *The Greek Struggle for Independence.* Berkeley: University of California Press, 1973.

De Ruggiero, G. *The History of European Liberalism,* trans. R. G. Collingswood. Boston: Beacon Press, 1959.

Droz, J. *Europe Between Revolutions,* 1815–1848. New York: Harper & Row, 1967.

Friedenthal, R. *Goethe: His Life and Times.* Cleveland: World, 1965.

Hammond, J. L., and Hammond, B. *The Age of Chartism.* Hamden, Conn.: Archon Books, 1962.

Hobsbawm, E. J. *The Age of Revolution: Europe, 1789 to 1848.* New York: New American Library, 1962.

Kohn, H. *The Idea of Nationalism.* New York: Collier Books, 1967.

Krieger, L. *The German Idea of Freedom.* Boston: Beacon Press, 1957.

Lichtheim, G. *A Short History of Socialism.* New York: Praeger, 1970.

Lynch, K. A. *Family, Class, and Ideology in Early Industrial France: Social Policy and the Working-Class Family,* 1825–1848. Madison: University of Wisconsin Press, 1988.

Manuel, F. E. *The Prophets of Paris.* Cambridge, Mass.: Harvard University Press, 1962.

McLellan, D. *Karl Marx: His Life and Thought.* New York: Harper & Row, 1973.

Nicolson, H. *The Congress of Vienna.* London: Constable, 1946.

Pinkney, D. H. *The French Revolution of 1830.* Princeton, N.J.: Princeton University Press, 1972.

Pointon, M. "Liberty on the Barricades: Women, Politics and Sexuality in Delacroix," in S. Reynolds, ed., *Women, State and Revolution.* Brighton: Wheatsheaf, 1986.

Sheehan, J. J. *Germany,* 1770–1866. New York: Oxford University Press, 1990.

Sperber, J. *The European Revolutions, 1848–1851.* Cambridge: Cambridge University Press, 1994.

Stearns, P. N. *1848: The Revolutionary Tide in Europe.* New York: Norton, 1974.

Taylor, A. J. P. *The Habsburg Monarchy, 1809–1918.* New York: Harper & Row, 1965.

CHAPTER
33

The Triumph
of Nationalism

The failure of the 1848 upheavals represented at once a crushing blow to the ideals of Romantic revolution and the last desperate stand of the conservative order established by the Congress of Vienna. In the decades that followed, the forces of order gave way to those of change as a powerful, rapidly spreading nationalism triumphed in Europe.

As the dominant theme of European history over the next half century, nationalism had a powerful appeal to a broad cross section of society, from workers to industrialists and from merchants to aristocrats. Many factors explain the success of nationalism in the post-1848 period. Unlike the abortive nationalist movements of the 1820s and 1830s, it now combined the Romantic celebration of the past and its tortured search for self-identity with a new realism based on the understanding and use of power. Moreover, artists, writers, and musicians explored nationalistic themes in their work, while both higher literacy rates and more skillful propaganda made more and more members of the middle and lower classes sensitive to nationalist symbolism. Most important, in regions where nationalistic aspirations were frustrated by foreign domination, a new generation of practical, tough-minded leaders came into power. Raised during the turbulent days of the Napoleonic empire, these men admired the methods of modern warfare and diplomacy, appreciated the benefits of efficient government, and understood the principles of liberal economics and industrial development. Cavour in Italy and Bismarck in Germany were the two most outstanding examples of this marriage between nationalism and power politics. In an age increasingly under the influence of science and technology, Bismarck and Cavour successfully translated the ideals of an earlier generation into the concrete action of the new.

Otto von Bismarck as the victorious leader of Prussian forces outside Paris, 1871.

In Italy and Germany, nationalism assumed the form of nation-building. Where centralized states already existed, as in Britain, nationalism merged with liberalism to forge a new ruling elite dedicated to industrial and commercial expansion through overseas conquest or, as in the case of France, to economic development under a restored empire. In the Austrian, Russian, and Ottoman empires, despotic monarchies struggled to control ethnically diverse populations clamoring for independence or self-determination. While the young republic of the United States struggled to restore unity after a destructive civil war, nationalism promoted independence movements and nation-building in Latin America. Finally, the international Zionist movement added a new element to nationalism as it sought to give expression to the centuries-old quest for a Jewish homeland.

The emergence of nationalism in the second half of the nineteenth century is a development of immense importance. As a worldwide phenomenon, its long-range repercussions would be felt in the national antagonisms that twice in the twentieth century erupted into global war, in the twisted ideas that fed the ideologies of fascism between the wars, and in the national rivalries over which the United States and the Soviet Union fought a dangerous ideological war. Ironically, nationalism also inspired the revolt of former colonies against Western rule, which was itself partly a consequence of nationalism.

The Politics of National Grandeur: Napoleon III in France

Nowhere after 1848 was the beguiling appeal of nationalism stronger than in France. In December 1848, partly as a result of the gruesome violence of the June insurrection, French males overwhelmingly chose as the president of their new Second Republic Louis-Napoleon Bonaparte, the enigmatic nephew of Napoleon I. Much to everyone's amazement, General Louis-Eugène Cavaignac, the conservative republican hero who had crushed the June riots, received only 1.5 million votes, the socialist Alexandre Ledru-Rollin and the poet Alphonse de Lamartine even less, whereas the virtually unknown Louis-Napoleon won the trust of more than 5.5 million Frenchmen.

Louis-Napoleon (1808–1873) had almost no political experience, but the magic of his name was irresistible. For years he had lived abroad, a dreamy youth caught up in the euphoria of revolutionary Romanticism. Implicated in the 1831 revolt in the Papal States and in two ludicrous plots to overthrow Louis-Philippe, he spent time in exile

and then in prison until his escape to England in 1846. French and English reactionaries funded his return to Paris in 1848, whereupon he campaigned for the presidency by invoking the theme of national unity.

Louis-Napoleon's platform, designed to appeal to a strife-torn society, argued that the country needed an authoritarian leader. But Louis-Napoleon was duplicitous. While appealing to Catholics and other proponents of authority, he also cultivated the support of the working classes.

He proposed to eliminate a corrupt Parliament and political parties to establish a direct relationship between the citizens and himself through plebiscites based on universal male suffrage. Unlike the role of the aristocratic Old Regime or the upper-middle-class government of Louis-Philippe, the proper function—indeed, the duty—of government was, in Louis-Napoleon's mind, to wipe out poverty and provide prosperity for all citizens.

These views, expressed in two pamphlets he wrote while in prison, *On Napoleonic Ideas* and *The Extinction of Poverty,* formed the core of Louis-Napoleon's political thought. But his popularity was derived largely from the memory of national greatness attached to Napoleon I. Despite a stocky build and an exaggerated mustache and goatee, Louis-Napoleon had a charismatic appeal that transcended class and social status. He realized that public opinion could be a powerful instrument of authority. He knew almost by instinct what later, twentieth-century dictators would discover, that an authoritarian state based on nationalist pride and popular consensus and promising both social tranquillity and economic prosperity had a strong appeal in times of stress.

The Second Republic lasted three years. Although its constitution provided for a strong president, the chief executive could serve for only one term. Louis-Napoleon therefore played to the conservatives who dominated the National Assembly by enacting measures in favor of the Catholic church, reducing the suffrage, and restricting freedom of education and the press. When the legislature refused to amend the constitution to permit him a second term, Louis-Napoleon seized power. On December 2, 1851, he illegally dissolved the Assembly and proclaimed a temporary dictatorship in the name of the people. With the support of the army, he arrested his opponents and crushed an uprising of the workers. In a plebiscite held that same month, 92 percent of the voters gave him the power to draft a new constitution that made him president for ten years. A second plebiscite a year later confirmed by an even greater margin the hold of the Napoleonic legend

The Napoleonic Myth

In 1839 Louis-Napoleon wrote a pamphlet titled On Napoleonic Ideas. *Praising the reign of his uncle as having been founded on the will of the people, Louis-Napoleon contributed to the popularization of the Napoleonic myth on which he was to base his own rise to power.*

The Emperor Napoleon has contributed more than any other person to hasten the reign of liberty, by preserving the moral influence of the revolution, and diminishing the fears which it inspired. . . .

The government of Napoleon, better than any other, could have sustained liberty, for the simple reason that liberty would have strengthened his throne, though it overthrows such thrones as have not a solid foundation.

Liberty would have fortified his power, because Napoleon had established in France all that ought to precede liberty; because his power reposed upon the whole mass of the nation; because his interests were the same as those of the people; because, finally, the most perfect confidence reigned between the ruler and the governed. . . .

There is no longer any necessity to reconstruct the system of the emperor; it will reconstruct itself. Sovereigns and nations will concur in re-establishing it; because each one will see in it a guaranty of order, of peace, and of prosperity. . . .

In conclusion, let us repeat it, the Napoleonic idea is not one of war, but a social, industrial, commercial idea, and one which concerns all mankind. If to some it appears always surrounded by the thunder of combats, that is because it was in fact for too long a time veiled by the smoke of cannon and the dust of battles. But now the clouds are dispersed, and we can see, beyond the glory of arms, a civil glory greater and more enduring.

Source: Louis-Napoleon Bonaparte, *Napoleonic Ideas,* trans. J. Dorr (New York: Appleton, 1859).

on the national psyche: Louis-Napoleon was proclaimed Napoleon III, emperor of the French.[*]

The Second Empire

The structure of imperial government, inspired by the constitution of Napoleon I, was designed to give the impression of a regime responsive to the popular will. An appointed senate was balanced by an assembly chosen every six years by carefully manipulated elections based on universal male suffrage. Parliament could, however, only discuss items submitted by the emperor and had to debate behind closed doors. Napoleon personally controlled the army and the budget and conducted foreign affairs, advised by a handpicked Council of State.

Napoleon's domestic policies, resting on vigorous government intervention in the economy, produced unparalleled prosperity. The emperor deliberately strengthened the middle class by encouraging investment and the modernization of industry. The state-owned railroad increased its mileage fivefold during the first decade of imperial rule, thus stimulating industrial development and commerce. A law passed in 1865 introduced the concept of limited liability to protect corporate stockholders from excessive risk. Investment capital was raised through the *Crédit Mobilier,* a banking institution that sold shares to the public. A free trade agreement with Britain in 1860 resulted in an increase in French exports and eventually a favorable balance of trade. Between 1859 and 1869, to advance commerce with the East, French capital financed—and a French engineer, Ferdinand de Lesseps, constructed—the Suez Canal. These measures bound the middle class to the government, for industrial production

[*]Napoleon II, son of Napoleon I, died in 1832 without having served as emperor.

Renovation of a Paris neighborhood, showing workmen and supplies in foreground.

had doubled and the vitality of the economy seemed to confirm the wisdom of the French people in putting another Bonaparte on the throne.

Working-class support for Napoleon III was almost as strong as middle-class enthusiasm, for wages kept pace with inflation and the emperor sponsored government health programs, low-cost housing, and numerous public works projects. Despite the fears of many businessmen, in the 1860s he even permitted the formation of trade unions and legalized the right to strike.

The vigorous economic life of the Second Empire was accompanied by a deliberate effort to drape the public image of France in a grand, if at times gaudy, style. The results were most stunning in the imperial capital, where Napoleon appointed Baron Georges Haussmann to direct a massive rebuilding program. Narrow but picturesque medieval streets and unattractive neighborhoods were demolished to make way for 85 miles of broad boulevards and tree-shaded pavements. Along with large squares and stately new buildings, Haussmann also built sewers to provide drainage. Although costly and controversial, these projects not only created jobs but also gave the emperor better security because the wider avenues made it difficult to erect barricades against government troops, as the Parisians had done so often in the past. This experiment in urban renewal transformed Paris into a well-ordered and elegant city. It also created a vast stage on which Napoleon and his consort, Empress Eugénie, performed lavish public ceremonies befitting the renewed splendor of France.

Born Eugénia de Montijo (1826–1920), Eugénie was the beautiful, ambitious daughter of a Spanish father and a Franco-American mother. When she met the French president in 1850, she judged him a man of

greatness and offered to finance his coup d'état the next year. They were married in January 1853, after Napoleon became emperor, in a sumptuous ceremony in Notre Dame Cathedral. Together they presided with great elegance over the Second Empire. Just as Napoleon dreamed of the reemergence of his nation as a great power, so Paris was to become once again the arbiter of Europe in matters of taste and culture. After the drab years of Louis-Philippe's bourgeois monarchy, the new imperial court gave at least the appearance of grandeur.

Despite the considerable domestic achievements of the Second Empire, the economic conditions of the working class were depressed, and Napoleon III did nothing to improve the status of French women. Although his uncle's civil code had declared the equality of all French citizens, women were not included in the definition of citizenship; consequently, the power of men over them was actually strengthened. For example, after marriage, women could not control their own property, engage in a business or profession, or administer children's financial affairs without the consent of their husbands. Divorce laws favored men, and adultery had significantly more serious consequences for wives than for husbands. The law codes thus reinforced women's legal inequality and subordination.

Uniting with the utopian socialists in the 1830s and with the republican socialists in 1848 and 1849, the French feminist movement had been one of the most vigorous and advanced in Europe, pushing hard for women's rights and social reform. But the censorship and restrictive domestic policies of the Second Empire repressed the feminists along with other opponents of Napoleon III's rule. Feminist views were therefore restricted largely to the liberal salons of Paris and the underground press, where women writers—notably Juliette Lamber and Jenny Héricourt—fought against conservative patriarchy and the equally antifeminist views of former socialist and republican allies such as Pierre-Joseph Proudhon and the historian Jules Michelet. Lamber and Héricourt argued for women's rights in education, the professions, and government and exposed the contradictions implicit in the prevalent attitudes toward marriage, divorce, and the double sexual standard. They and women like them kept social debate alive until the repressive phase of the empire came to an end in the 1860s.

The Liberalization of the Empire

Napoleon III protested that he was a man of peace, but foreign entanglements often threatened to disrupt the stability of the Second Empire. Almost unavoidably, the Napoleonic name raised the specter of war, although

Napoleon III had neither the military genius nor the diplomatic astuteness of his uncle. French participation in the Crimean War had been popular, and colonial forays in Africa and Indochina had limited success. But his intervention in Italian affairs backfired when it resulted in the loss of papal territory. More damaging was the disastrous attempt in the 1860s to impose French control over Mexico; even worse was Napoleon's failure to obtain territorial gains from the unification of Germany. The cumulative effect of these mistakes gave rise to domestic criticism, and Napoleon's sensitivity to public opinion led him to make reforms intended to soothe the discontent.

This process of liberalizing the empire, against which Eugénie counseled her husband, began by granting the Assembly increased powers and permitting his political enemies—especially liberals, republicans, and legitimist monarchists—to criticize the government openly. He next lifted the restrictions on parliamentary debate and freedom of the press, a move that encouraged the opposition. The lifting of censorship also led to the emergence of a reinvigorated feminist movement. Women such as Maria Deraismes debated the issue of inequality before

Napoleon III and Empress Eugénie with their son. Napoleon III dreamed of imperial grandeur, but this photograph shows the Bonapartes as a proper bourgeois family.

large audiences, published feminist newspapers, and established the Association for the Rights of Women. Although Deraismes and her friends were few in number and it would be many decades before their movement scored significant victories, they contributed much to the quality of French political life in the last years of the Second Empire. By 1869, when national elections were held, it became clear that the emperor had lost control of the political situation—almost half of the voters supported opposition candidates and elected 30 republicans to the assembly. Early in 1870 Napoleon institutionalized these changes in a new constitution that for all practical purposes created a parliamentary government with the emperor serving as head of state. In May the last of Napoleon's plebiscites showed 7.5 million citizens in favor of the new regime and only 1.5 million against.

Whether these sweeping changes reflected Napoleon III's desire to bring France closer to democracy is uncertain, but his days as emperor were numbered. In the summer, drained and in ill health, he went to war against Prussia, and before it was over the Second Empire had collapsed in defeat and the French people had once again turned to a republic.

Material progress made the first decade of Louis-Napoleon's reign some of the best years economically in the history of modern France, at least for the bourgeoisie, yet the price of prosperity was the suppression of political freedom. The second half of his rule saw the gradual restoration of liberty accompanied by imperialism and war. Once admired as one of the great rulers of the mid-nineteenth century, he died a broken man, scorned by European opinion and repudiated by the French people, a victim of the very Napoleonic legend he represented.

Power Politics and the Unification of Italy

The impact of nationalism was even more dramatic in central and southern Europe. There, by 1871, two new nation-states, Italy and Germany, appeared. Italy, in Metternich's famous phrase, had been merely a "geographical expression." The Italian peninsula comprised less than a dozen independent states; Germany was little more than a name used to describe the region between France and Austria that consisted of some 38 separate kingdoms, principalities, and duchies. Both had had glorious pasts, Italy as the center of the ancient Roman empire and the land of the Renaissance humanists, Germany as the core of the medieval Holy Roman Empire

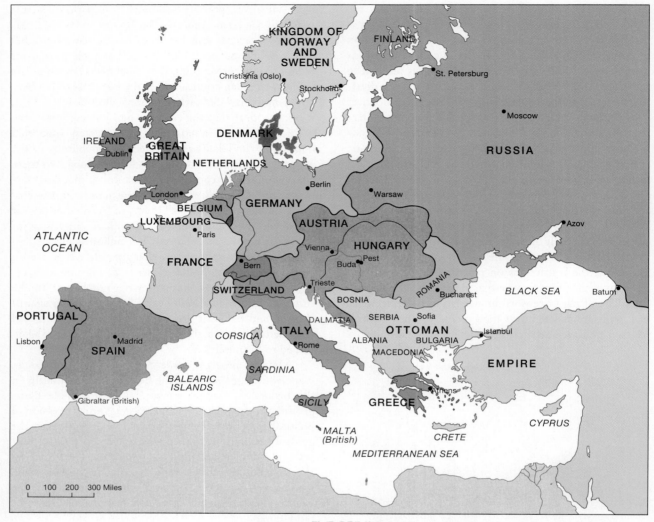

MAP 33.1   EUROPE IN 1871

and the site of Luther's Protestant Reformation. But circumstances and history combined to keep each divided and subject to foreign intervention and manipulation.

Nationalism in Italy and Germany was aroused by the French invasions and the wars of Napoleon I. Bonaparte had reduced and rearranged the states in each region and thereby suggested the possibilities of national unification to Italians and Germans, but their nationalism was in part a reaction against foreign occupation. After Waterloo, the Congress of Vienna restored almost all the original rulers of these states to their thrones and replaced French occupation with Austrian influence. In the 1820s and 1830s revolutionary Romanticism failed to bring down the status quo so anxiously guarded by Metternich, although national feeling continued to mature

during the next decade. As we have seen, the 1848 revolutions gave rise to the first serious attempts to achieve unification in Italy and Germany, but again Austria crushed nationalist hopes.

Out of the defeats of 1849 came one positive result: Piedmont-Sardinia emerged as the only viable Italian state to champion national independence, while Prussian leadership became the focus of the unification effort in Germany. In the 1850s Cavour as prime minister of Piedmont and in the 1860s Bismarck as minister-president of Prussia gave their national movements strong leadership that easily matched Napoleon III in cunning and ambition and, by substituting the principles of power politics for Romantic idealism, achieved unification at last.

Nation-building in Italy and Germany demonstrated that midcentury nationalism had secured the consensus of large portions of the middle classes and eventually the nobility. By 1871, when the process was complete, the entrance of Italy and Germany into the European state system profoundly altered the balance of power on the Continent.

The Italian Risorgimento

Strong local traditions and competition characterized the politics of the Italian peninsula since the appearance of city-states in the Middle Ages. Despite some changes wrought at Vienna in 1815, the congress restored the overall structure of the Italian state system. In the south the Kingdom of the Two Sicilies (combining Naples and Sicily) was ruled by a branch of the Bourbon dynasty related through marriage to the Austrian Habsburgs. In central Italy the Papal States remained the temporal possession of the Catholic church and were ruled from Rome by the popes. The north-central region consisted of a patchwork of small states dominated from Florence by the Grand Duchy of Tuscany, where dynastic and political arrangements also gave the Habsburgs considerable influence. In northeastern Italy the Vienna settlement gave the Habsburgs direct control over the provinces of Lombardy and Venetia, which were ruled from Milan by an Austrian viceroy. Finally, in the strategically important northwest corner lay the Kingdom of Sardinia, consisting of the Piedmont and Savoy regions and the island of Sardinia, ruled by the House of Savoy. This ambitious dynasty had pursued a long-standing policy of expansion in Italy, and in the first half of the century Charles Albert had made two dramatic but unsuccessful bids to oust Austria from the peninsula.

Italian nationalists debated a variety of programs that shared the common goal of an Italian "resurgence," or *Risorgimento,* as the movement for independence and unity was known. Giuseppe Mazzini (1805–1872), one of the great European theorists of nationalism, preached a revolution aimed at creating a united Italian republic based on popular sovereignty and universal suffrage. Mazzini's idealistic propaganda, which educated a generation of Italians to the cause of freedom, posed a radical democratic alternative to the more conservative programs of his contemporaries. The Neo-Guelph* movement, founded by the Piedmontese priest Vincenzo Gioberti, advocated a federation of Italian states led by the papacy

---

*In the Middle Ages the Guelphs were supporters of the papacy against the ambitions of the Holy Roman emperor.

and protected by the king of Sardinia. The election of Pope Pius IX in 1846 gave brief impetus to Gioberti's plan, but ultimately his effort to reconcile Italian unification with the temporal interests of the church proved unrealistic. The third alternative, known as the moderate program, was the work of a group of liberal Piedmontese noblemen. Opposed to the revolutionary tactics and democratic principles of Mazzini, the moderates championed a unification imposed from above by Piedmontese armies and a constitutional monarchy under the House of Savoy. The Risorgimento was the climax of Italian nationalism, but from another perspective it was also an ideological civil war fought between radicals and moderates deeply divided over the form and purposes of the unified state that all desired.

Cavour the Realist

Charles Albert's valiant war against Austria in 1848 and 1849 had given credibility to the moderate program. Despite his abdication in 1849, the hapless monarch had left his kingdom a constitution that became the symbol of Italian liberal hopes, one that his son, Victor Emmanuel II (1849–1878), refused to rescind despite Austrian pressure. In 1850 the young king appointed to the cabinet Count Camillo Benso di Cavour (1810–1861), a brilliant statesman into whose hands the leadership of the Risorgimento passed.

Although born into the nobility, Cavour was also the epitome of the nineteenth-century businessman. Portly, nearsighted, and a dull orator who spoke French better than Italian, Cavour was nonetheless crafty and steel-willed. Above all, he was a master of power politics, unwilling to allow principle to interfere with objectives and capable of outwitting Europe's shrewdest diplomats. With a successful background in agriculture, industry, and banking, he developed an abiding belief in economic liberalism. First as minister of agriculture and commerce in 1850 and then as prime minister from 1852, he modernized Piedmont's economy and forged an alliance of moderate forces within parliament that was responsible for progressive legislation. He understood fully that Piedmont lacked the strength to rid Italy of the Austrians alone, and his policy hinged on securing the support of powerful foreign allies. Nevertheless, Cavour's view of unification was more limited than Mazzini's, for his goal was originally the creation of a large Piedmontese kingdom covering northern Italy but excluding the Papal States and the Bourbon south.

Cavour's first step in the realization of his plan was a masterstroke of political cynicism. Although Piedmont

Count Cavour, whose shrewd policies ultimately unified Italy, is depicted here in a photograph taken at the Congress of Paris in 1856.

had no apparent interest in the Near East, in 1854 he intervened in the Crimean War on the side of Britain and France, thus securing a place for himself at the Paris peace talks that followed. Cavour not only succeeded in raising the "Italian question" at the conference but also won the admiration of Napoleon III. The French emperor, who in his youth had developed a strong affection for Italy, believed that his sponsorship of the Italian cause would further his own prestige. In July 1858 he and Cavour negotiated the secret Treaty of Plombières. The agreement pledged French military support for a war against Austria, the goal of which would be Piedmont's annexation of Lombardy and Venetia. Victory was to result in the creation of a kingdom of upper Italy and an Italian federation under the presidency of the pope. For its help, France would receive from Piedmont the provinces of Savoy and Nice. Cavour and Napoleon further agreed to manufacture a suitable pretext for war with Austria, and they promised not to make a separate peace until their goals had been reached.

In the tension-filled months that followed, efforts to settle the Italian problem peacefully threatened to wreck Cavour's plans. In April 1859, however, the Austrians played into his hands by issuing an ultimatum demanding that Piedmont demobilize its armies. The French declared war and, taking advantage of Austrian delays, quickly moved into Italy to join their Piedmontese allies. Lombardy was liberated, but as the allies prepared to press into Venetia the unpredictable Napoleon III suddenly announced the conclusion of an armistice at Villafranca with the Austrian emperor, Franz Josef. It clearly violated Napoleon's agreement with Cavour, for the Austrians were forced only to surrender Lombardy. Nevertheless, Victor Emmanuel accepted the terms, and the outraged Cavour resigned in protest.

Yet all was not lost. During the fighting in Lombardy, moderate nationalists and liberal businessmen secretly worked in cooperation with Cavour to stage a series of revolts that unseated the rulers of the central Italian duchies. Then, in the wake of the armistice of Villafranca, they engineered popular demonstrations in favor of union with Piedmont. Returning to office in January, Cavour suppressed his anger and struck a bargain with Napoleon that permitted the Piedmontese annexation of these territories. Borrowing one of Napoleon's favorite political tactics, Cavour engineered plebiscites to confirm popular enthusiasm for his territorial aggrandisement. Thus by 1860 Piedmont had been considerably enlarged by the addition of Lombardy and the duchies of central Italy. The first step in the unification of Italy had been taken.

The Crisis of Italian Unification

Until the plebiscites in central Italy, the astute Cavour had managed to shape the course of events, but now the initiative was seized by Giuseppe Garibaldi (1807–1882). A hero in the age of power politics, a determined Romantic in the face of Cavour's cynicism, Garibaldi was nevertheless the greatest guerrilla fighter of the century. Although he believed in Mazzini's republican doctrines, he was above all a patriot determined to see Italy free and united. With a death sentence on his head for having taken part in a Mazzinian plot, Garibaldi fled to South America in 1834 and fought against authoritarian government in the jungles of Uruguay. He returned to Italy in 1848 to fight along with Charles Albert and then went to Rome to lead the dramatic defense of Mazzini's republic against the French troops sent there by Napoleon III to restore the pope. By 1859, when Garibaldi again commanded a volunteer army against Austria, he was a popular figure with a rapidly growing following.

Garibaldi's vision of unification encompassed the entire Italian peninsula. In 1860 he decided to complete

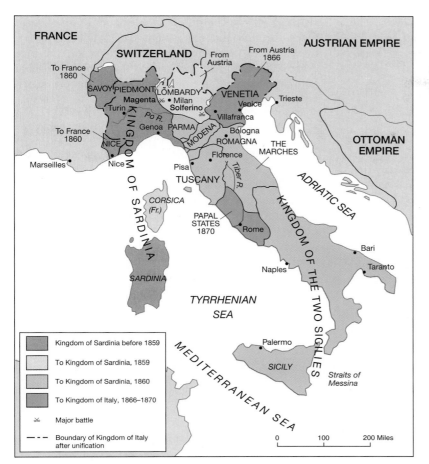

MAP 33.2   THE UNIFICATION OF ITALY, 1859–1870

the process begun by Cavour with a daring military expedition against the Kingdom of the Two Sicilies. Cavour not only mistrusted Garibaldi's republican sentiments but also feared that Napoleon III would intervene if Garibaldi attempted to seize Rome. He therefore played a double game, secretly encouraging Garibaldi's 1,000-man army of "Red Shirts" while simultaneously preparing to stop the guerrilla leader with force should he threaten Rome. Landing in Sicily in May, Garibaldi outmaneuvered the Bourbon armies, recruited additional volunteers among the disaffected peasants, and captured the island. By September he had crossed to the mainland and taken the Neapolitan capital, declaring a provisional dictatorship over the entire Italian south. In the meantime, a worried Cavour had persuaded Napoleon III to agree to the passage of Piedmontese troops through the Papal States in order to protect the pope. Instead, Victor Emmanuel seized all the papal lands except for the area around Rome. In October, as the Risorgimento reached its climax, Victor Emmanuel and Garibaldi met just north of Naples, thus bringing the moderate and the radical forces face to face. Determined to make Italy a nation rather than plunge it into civil war, Garibaldi relinquished his conquests to the king. In March 1861 the Piedmontese sovereign was proclaimed Victor Emmanuel II, king of Italy. Two months later Cavour died.

The euphoria of the Risorgimento quickly faded as the Italians encountered the problems of nationhood. Indeed, the kingdom was still incomplete. Venetia was not incorporated until the Austro-Prussian War of 1866, and Rome itself was not seized until the Franco-Prussian War in 1870. When this did occur, the annexation of Rome produced deep hostility between the Catholic church and the new state that plagued Italian affairs for the next half century. Regional differences and local loyalties remained strong, and the gap between the developing industrial interests of the north and the depressed agricultural economy of the south widened. A host of vital public policy issues, including illiteracy, disease, and extreme poverty, placed enormous pressure on a national debt already burdened by the costs of the wars of unification. Added to these difficulties was an often corrupt parliamentary regime that remained unresponsive to the needs of the largely unenfranchised poorer classes and a ruling elite bent on making Italy a great power. The challenge for Cavour's successors, then, would be to resolve these problems of national development and move Italy toward political democracy.

Iron and Blood: The Making of the German Empire

In Germany, as in Italy, the Congress of Vienna mandated a restoration designed to prevent national unification as well as to guarantee Austrian preponderance in German affairs. The creation of the German Confederation, with a diet, or parliament, at Frankfurt representing 38 sovereign states, recognized the irreversibility of Bonaparte's destruction of the Holy Roman Empire and his simplification of the German state system. The confederation included small states with only a few hundred square miles of territory, such as the Thuringian principalities, and much larger units such as the kingdom of

Bavaria, which comprised more than 10,000 square miles. Religious differences reinforced political divisions, for while northern Germany was Protestant, the predominantly Catholic south tended to regard Austria as a bulwark against Protestant Prussia. In these circumstances, Austria dominated the divided German states.

Nationalism and the German State System

The kingdom of Prussia, with considerably enlarged territories and a formidable army, was the second most powerful state in the German Confederation. Its autocratic and unstable monarch, Frederick William IV (1840–1861), aspired to expand the Hohenzollern position in Germany. Just as Piedmont vied with Austria for mastery in Italy, so Prussian-Austrian rivalry was the heart of the German power struggle after 1815. The stronghold of German nationalism, however, was not the Prussian monarchy, whose motivation was largely one of dynastic power, but the rapidly growing liberal middle class. The Prussian-sponsored *Zollverein* (customs

Cavour Versus Garibaldi

Throughout 1860, while Garibaldi's volunteer army seized the island of Sicily and then the mainland portion of the kingdom of Naples, Count Cavour, the Piedmontese premier, tried to prevent Garibaldi from seizing control of the Italian unification movement. In this letter Cavour describes his political calculations and his efforts to stop Garibaldi.

If Garibaldi proceeds to the mainland of southern Italy and captures Naples just as he has already taken Sicily and Palermo, he will become absolute master of the situation. King Victor Emmanuel would lose almost all his prestige in the eyes of Italians. . . .

We would be forced to go along with his plans and help him fight Austria. I am therefore convinced that the king must not receive the crown of Italy from Garibaldi's hands. . . .

I have no illusions about the grave and dangerous decision I am advocating, but I believe it is essential if we are to save the monarchic principle. Better a king of Piedmont should perish in war against Austria than be swamped by the revolution. The dynasty might recover from a defeat in battle, but if dragged through the revolutionary gutter its fate would be . . . sealed.

Although I have made up my mind how to act if Garibaldi reaches Naples, it is nevertheless my first duty to the king and Italy to do everything possible to prevent his success there. My only hope of foiling him is if I can overthrow the Bourbon regime before Garibaldi crosses to the mainland—or at least before he has had time to reach Naples. If the regime falls, I would then take over the government of Naples in the name of order and humanity, and so snatch out of Garibaldi's hands the supreme direction of the Italian movement.

Source: C. B. di Cavour, letter to Costantino Nigra, August 1, 1860, in D. Mack Smith, ed., *Garibaldi* (Englewood Cliffs, N.J.: Prentice Hall, 1969), pp. 44–45.

union) that developed after 1818 not only stimulated trade throughout Germany and underscored the economic advantages of unification but also anticipated the so-called *kleindeutsch* ("small German") solution that sought to exclude Austria from German affairs.

By 1848 these middle-class elements hoped that Prussia would provide the leadership to unify Germany and give it a constitutional monarchy. Twice during the revolutions of 1848, however, these expectations were dashed by the military-aristocratic forces that ruled Prussia. In the fall Frederick William, encouraged by the army and reactionary elements in his court, withdrew his promise to allow an elected constituent assembly to draft a liberal constitution. In March 1849, when the Frankfurt assembly elected him emperor of Germany, he rejected the "crown from the gutter," later issuing a more conservative constitution of his own. This royal document provided for a two-chamber parliament, an appointed upper house and a lower house elected by an unequal and indirect system of universal male suffrage. Although the constitution was ambiguous about the role of the lower house (Landtag) in formulating budget laws,

it was clear that the king retained extensive authority. Yet Frederick William's efforts to unify Germany failed. In 1850, when he attempted to solicit an imperial crown from his fellow German monarchs, Austria and Russia coerced him to abandon the plan in a humiliating capitulation at Olmütz.

Bismarck and the Liberals

Despite its commercial and industrial primacy, Prussia's repressive domestic policies, together with Frederick William's timidity in foreign affairs, cast doubt on its ability to bring about German unification. These tendencies were reinforced when William, the monarch's brother, became regent in 1858 and then king in 1861. William I (1861–1888) precipitated a constitutional crisis in Prussia that changed the course of German history.

In February 1860, William presented a bill to the Prussian Landtag that proposed to double the size of the regular army and increase compulsory military service from two to three years. Most controversial perhaps was the fact that the king, himself a professional soldier, wished to reduce the role and independence of the civilian militia, whose lack of discipline he regarded with contempt. The liberal middle classes—who, because of the elitist nature of the suffrage law, dominated the Landtag—saw these measures as a constitutional challenge, for they wished both to assert the power of parliament over the king and to reduce the influence of the military in Prussian society. As a result, the military bill was eventually withdrawn. When a later version of the same bill was voted down in 1862, William dissolved the Landtag, but the new elections only increased the liberal majority. Torn between abdicating and forcing a showdown with the liberals, the king appointed Count Otto von Bismarck (1815–1898) as his new minister-president.

Bismarck ranks as one of the dominant figures in modern German history. Although a member of the conservative *Junker* class of aristocratic landowners, he was neither provincial in his outlook nor ideologically wedded to the past. He cut an imposing figure, stubborn, fiercely combative, and oblivious to the constraints of tradition and constitutional theory. Bismarck was also a master political strategist. His early career had given him wide experience in diplomacy, first as a Prussian delegate to the Frankfurt Diet and then as ambassador in St. Petersburg and in Paris. Though he disdained the parliamentary demands of the liberals, he recognized that they had embraced nationalism and that Prussia needed their industrial skills and wealth. Bismarck's view of unification was at first limited—the imposition of Prussian

Princess Victoria of Hohenzollern, the wife of Emperor Frederick William IV of Germany, was at the center of liberal opposition to Bismarck's domestic policies.

mastery over largely Protestant northern Germany, a goal he eventually came to believe would require the expulsion of Austria from the German state system.

For Bismarck, the German question and the conflict with the Landtag were linked, for a strong army was needed to deal with Austria. When he found that compromise with the liberals over military reform was impossible, he reorganized the army with funds earmarked for other purposes. The liberals denounced Bismarck's high-handed tactics, and the issue was further complicated by public criticism from Frederick, the heir to the throne, who had been influenced by his liberal-thinking wife, Victoria (1840–1901), the oldest daughter of Britain's Queen Victoria and Prince Albert. Victoria envisioned a unified Germany ruled not by the military but by the best traditions of German culture. Her role in the constitutional crisis resulted in her exclusion from public life for many years.

Not only was Bismarck oblivious to the protests of the liberal opposition, but he lectured them on *Realpolitik*. In blunt speeches before the Landtag, he declared that only a policy of "iron and blood" would yield results, that power rather than principle determined the outcome of conflict and that results justified means. A vigorous program in foreign affairs, he believed, would win over many liberals and critics of his violation of constitutional procedure. Moreover, since the defeats of 1848, the German intellectuals had either emigrated or abandoned

politics. Bismarck thus set the terms on which German unification would be achieved, for just as Cavour's actions intensified the ideological struggle between Italian moderates and radicals, so Bismarck polarized the German unification movement between liberals and the advocates of power politics.

The Showdown with Austria

Bismarck's determination to extend Prussian authority over northern Germany made a military confrontation with Austria all but inevitable. The showdown evolved between 1863 and 1866 and resulted from a situation involving Schleswig and Holstein, two northern duchies controlled by the king of Denmark, although not an actual part of his kingdom. Holstein, inhabited almost entirely by Germans, was part of the confederation, whereas Schleswig's mixed population of Danes and Germans fought bitterly over the issue of membership. When Denmark moved to annex Schleswig in 1863, Bismarck persuaded the Austrians to join Prussia in what proved to be a short and successful war to reclaim the two provinces. The Peace of Vienna that ended the war against Denmark provided that Austria and Prussia would administer the provinces jointly. Discussion as to their future resulted in a deadlock when the Austrians insisted that the provinces become a single state ruled by a German prince, while Bismarck demanded extensive

Bismarck on Power Politics

On September 30, 1862, Bismarck made the following remarks before the Prussian Landtag in order to secure approval of the military reorganization bill proposed by King William I. His words were the quintessential statement on the nature of power politics.

While it is clear that we cannot avoid complications in Germany, we do not seek them. Germany does not look to Prussia's liberalism but to her power. Because the southern states of Germany—Bavaria, Württemberg, and Baden—would like to indulge in liberalism, Prussia's role will not be assigned to them! Prussia must gather her forces and hold them in reserve for the right moment, which we have already missed several times. Since the Treaty of Vienna, our borders have not been designed to ensure a healthy body politic. Not by speeches and majorities will the great questions of the day be decided—that was the mistake of 1848 and 1849—but by iron and blood.

Source: H. Kohl, ed., *Die politischen Reden des Fürsten Bismarck* (Stuttgart: Cotta, 1892–1905). Translated by P. Cannistraro.

commercial rights that would have made them virtual Prussian provinces. A temporary agreement was established in 1865 according to which Holstein would be run by Austria and Schleswig by Prussia. This awkward arrangement led to continued quarrels between the two allies and eventually gave Bismarck the excuse to provoke a war with Austria.

Like Cavour, Bismarck understood that *Realpolitik* required careful diplomatic preparation among the other European powers. Prussia needed assurance that other nations would not come to Austria's assistance. Because he had offered to help Russia put down a Polish uprising in 1863, Bismarck was fairly certain that Tsar Alexander II would not interfere, but Napoleon III was the unknown element. In the fall of 1865 Bismarck and Napoleon held a secret meeting reminiscent of the Plombières encounter between Napoleon and Cavour. Bismarck secured Napoleon's promise of neutrality in the event of an Austro-Prussian war with vague promises of territorial compensation for France along the Rhine. The following year he negotiated an alliance with Italy that promised Italian military assistance in return for the Austrian-held province of Venetia. After years of preparation, the war came suddenly. On June 1, 1866, the Prussians sent troops into Holstein in protest over what Bismarck claimed was an Austrian violation of their agreement. In response, the Austrians persuaded the German Confederation to vote military action against Prussia. Bismarck's answer was to declare the confederation dissolved and order Prussia's armies into action.

The Austro-Prussian War was important for several reasons. Bismarck tried to make the point that the "national development of Germany" was at stake, although in truth Prussian aggression was the real issue. After seven weeks of fighting, Austria was defeated at Königgrätz in Bohemia. The Prussian victory was due to the ability to deploy troops rapidly by railroad, the use of a new breech-loading gun, and the brilliant strategist Count Helmuth von Moltke. The king's controversial military reorganization bill had proved itself. Although the war was fought against the other states of the German Confederation as well as Austria, the latter had been poorly prepared and had to fight on both the German and the Italian fronts. By imposing deliberately moderate peace terms on Austria in the Treaty of Prague (August 1866), Bismarck demonstrated once again his mastery of *Realpolitik*. No reparations were extracted from Austria, and a separate agreement forced it only to cede Venetia to the Italians. Bismarck's real goal was achieved by the dissolution of the confederation and Austria's withdrawal from German affairs. The Austrians also had to recognize Prussia's annexation of Schleswig-Holstein and a number of German states in the north. While the southern Catholic states remained independent, they had to pay indemnities and sign military alliances forcing them to fight on Prussia's side in any future war.

After the war, Bismarck presided over the creation of the North German Confederation. Dominated by Prussia, it included all German states north of the river Main. A constitution made the king of Prussia its president and Bismarck its chancellor. Local affairs remained in the hands of each state, but the central government controlled foreign policy and military authority. The parliament of the North German Confederation consisted of the *Bundesrat*, or upper house, representing each of the states, and a *Reichstag*, or lower house, elected by universal male suffrage. This system, which later provided the model for the constitution of united Germany, reflected the wide powers of the Prussian king and limited such parliamentary principles as ministerial responsibility. But the liberalized franchise created the sense that wide strata of the people, not just the middle class, now had a stake in Germany's future.

The Franco-Prussian War and the Forging of German Unification

It is difficult to say just how long Bismarck intended the North German Confederation to remain in place. As a Prussian rather than a German nationalist, his vision of unification may well have remained limited despite the events of 1866. But just as Garibaldi had forced Cavour to broaden his view of Italian unification in 1860, so now the diplomatic blunders of Napoleon III pushed Bismarck to complete the process he had begun.

Austria's defeat at the hands of Prussia shocked Napoleon, who had underestimated Prussian power. The suddenness of the Austrian collapse prevented him from intervening, and Prussia's victory had been so complete that Bismarck did not grant the territorial rewards that he had vaguely promised Napoleon. Napoleon's failure to extract concessions from Bismarck, compounded by the fiasco in Mexico, stimulated the emperor's opponents at home, who argued that the war represented a severe blow to French prestige. Napoleon became convinced that the consolidation of German strength on France's borders had to be stopped. For his part, Bismarck came to realize that a war with France would inflame German nationalism and push the southern states, where business circles already favored unification, into a united Germany.

Friction between the two countries mounted steadily, with both Napoleon and Bismarck contributing

MAP 33.3   THE UNIFICATION
OF GERMANY, 1866–1871

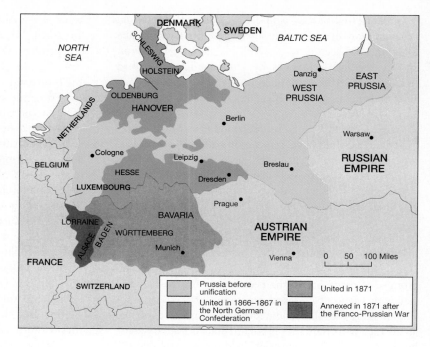

to the tension. The pretext for war arose from a dispute over whether a German prince related to William I would become king of Spain. The immediate cause for the outbreak of the Franco-Prussian War was the so-called Ems dispatch. When William I agreed to withdraw his support of the Hohenzollern candidate, Napoleon demanded that the Prussian king apologize and promise not to raise the Hohenzollern candidacy again. Meeting with the French ambassador at Ems in July 1870, the Prussian ruler refused to give such a promise and telegraphed the details of the talk to Berlin. Bismarck had the dispatch published in the press after changing the wording to create the impression that William had insulted the French. Newspapers in Paris and Berlin sensationalized the telegram and enraged public opinion. On July 19 the French declared war.

As in the case of the struggle with Austria four years earlier, the swiftness of the Franco-Prussian War and the superiority of Prussia's military forces stunned Europe. Thanks to Bismarck's lenient treatment of Austria in 1866, it remained neutral, as did the other great powers; moreover, the military treaties he had forced on the southern German states brought them into the war on the side of Prussia, so that the war became, at least in name, a "national" one. On September 1 the Prussian armies captured Napoleon III along with more than 100,000 French soldiers at Sedan. The news of Napoleon's surrender was followed a few days later in Paris by the proclamation of a republic. The republican

forces continued to fight for five additional months despite the siege of the capital and the outbreak of an uprising in March known as the Paris Commune. While Paris held out against starvation and the violence sparked by the Commune, Bismarck consolidated Germany. On January 18, 1871, in the Hall of Mirrors in the palace of Versailles, William I was proclaimed German emperor, and all of Germany was at last unified under a political system virtually identical to the one that had governed the North German Confederation.

At the end of the month the French republic capitulated, and in February a National Assembly was elected and the liberal monarchist Adolphe Thiers chosen as chief executive. Thiers, who made peace with the Germans, had little room to negotiate, for Bismarck was in no mood to be generous. The peace of Frankfurt, signed on May 10, was harsh. France had to pay an indemnity of 5 billion francs and accept German occupation until it was paid. Most distressing to the French, however, was the loss of Alsace and most of Lorraine to Germany. These provinces, which contained iron deposits and a prosperous textile industry, were inhabited by German-speaking people who preferred the French to the Prussians, and their annexation remained for the next half century a source of bitterness between Germany and France.

The Franco-Prussian War had profound repercussions. Along with the unification of Germany came the victory of Bismarck's political strategy, which had wedded German nationalism to the conservative-aristocratic forces that ruled Prussia and cowed the liberals into abandoning their opposition in the face of unification. The completion of Italian territorial unity was an unexpected by-product of the Franco-Prussian War, for when Napoleon III brought home the troops stationed in Rome to protect the pope, King Victor Emmanuel III seized the city and made it the capital of Italy. Most immediately the war led to the collapse of Napoleon's Second Empire. Perhaps its most far-reaching result was the shift in the balance of power. By 1871 Italy was demanding recognition as a great power, and the collapse of Austria and France demonstrated that Germany had emerged as the most powerful European state. The Treaty of Frankfurt confirmed the end of the Concert of Europe created by the Vienna peace settlement in 1815, for not only had Austria and France been defeated by the new German colossus, but Britain and Russia had remained aloof from the wars. Napoleon III, Cavour, and Bismarck, each in his own way an embodiment of the nationalist doctrines that dominated the age, had wrought profound changes in the structure of the European state system.

Eastern Europe and the Ottomans

Austria's role in Italian and German affairs after 1815 was symptomatic of its status as a multiethnic empire in an age of rising nationalism. This last dynastic state, ruled by the Habsburgs since the Middle Ages, survived the waves of Romantic nationalism of the 1820s and 1830s, as well as the upheavals of 1848, but its existence was seriously challenged in midcentury as its many nationalities clamored for independence. Twelve million Germans controlled political power and enjoyed special status in a state that reached 50 million by 1914 and included 24 million Slavs to the south, 10 million Magyars and 4 million Romanians to the east, as well as Czechs, Slovaks, Poles, Croats, Serbs, Italians, and a variety of other ethnic groups. The Habsburgs made a number of attempts to bring the forces of nationalism under control, but neither reforms, the granting of limited provincial autonomy in 1859, nor the new constitution of 1861 was effective.

The Austro-Prussian War of 1866 demonstrated just how divided and weak the Austrian Empire was, and defeat provoked still one more effort at reform. After difficult negotiations, Emperor Franz Josef reached a compromise (*Ausgleich*) with Hungarian leaders. The new constitution created the Dual Monarchy, in which Franz Josef was both king of Hungary and emperor of Austria. Foreign affairs, finance, and military matters were conducted by common ministers, but otherwise the two parts of the monarchy were autonomous, each with its own constitution, official language, and parliament.

The *Ausgleich* did not, of course, eliminate the serious problems facing the empire but merely enabled the Hungarians to share with the Germans in its rule. The other nationality groups continued to demand their freedom. Some industry and a middle class thrived in Bohemia and the area surrounding Vienna, and serfdom had been abolished in 1848. However, in both halves of the Dual Monarchy most inhabitants were landless, backward peasants burdened by conservative landowners and heavy taxes. Despite the ancient lineage of the Habsburgs and the importance of its strategic position in Europe, the Dual Monarchy remained an anachronism in a Europe rapidly dividing along national lines.

Vienna in the Age of Franz Josef

As the capital of Austria, Vienna was a microcosm of the empire, reflecting its strengths and weaknesses, its brilliance and its contradictions. Since 1278, when the Habsburgs selected the town on the banks of the Danube for their capital, the city had been a center of bureaucracy and aristocratic splendor. Vienna grew rapidly in the modern period, and by the opening of the nineteenth century it contained more than a quarter of a million people. Yet although the Habsburg capital was the government center for a vast multiethnic empire, it remained an essentially German city in language and culture.

Because its economy was built around the court and the government, Vienna had little industry or industrial proletariat until the mid-nineteenth century. It collected and spent tax revenues, and its economic life centered on banking, crafts, and the production of luxury goods, including silk and porcelain. Similarly, the social structure of the city included a wealthy aristocracy, a variety of civil servants, artisans and shopkeepers, a small but prosperous business class, and workers. With the coming of the Industrial Revolution to Vienna in the 1830s and 1840s, tens of thousands of peasants streamed into the city, and by the eve of the revolutions of 1848 its population had increased to 400,000.

As long as Austria remained a great European power, Vienna was a center of European diplomacy, a role it played never more splendidly than as host of the great peace settlement following the Napoleonic wars. In the generation before the revolutions of 1848, the city of Metternich became the capital of the European conservative order, crowded with diplomats, reactionary politicians, and police agents bent on uncovering revolutionaries. Metternich's office, and therefore the nerve center of the bureaucracy, was housed in the Ballhaus chancery, built in the early eighteenth century, but the true grandeur of the Habsburg empire was displayed in the rich array of luxurious royal palaces. Emperor Franz Josef, who died in 1916 after 68 years on the throne, was installed in the vast Hofburg Palace and moved in the summer months to the ornate Schönbrunn Palace. The important aristocratic families of the realm built lavish residences, of which the most remarkable was the Belvedere, the summer palace of Prince Eugène of Savoy. While the bulk of the population lived in middle-class housing and ugly tenements, much of the European nobility that visited Vienna saw only the splendors of the ruling class. In the 1860s Vienna's beauty was enhanced still further by the demolition of the city's medieval wall and the building of the Ringstrasse, a majestic tree-lined boulevard encircling the city that rivaled Haussmann's work in Paris.

Vienna's importance to Western culture was unequaled in the sphere of music. The city nurtured the greatest concentration of musical brilliance in modern times, for the patronage of the Habsburgs and the nobility attracted the musical giants of Europe—Mozart and Haydn, Beethoven, Schubert and Schumann, Johann and Richard Strauss, Brahms and Mahler. Although the second half of the nineteenth century was a period of crisis and decline for the Habsburg empire, its capital thrived as a refined city basking in sentimentality. The light operatic themes of Franz Lehar's *Merry Widow* (1905), together with the late Romantic lushness of the music of Anton Bruckner and Gustav Mahler, had wide popular appeal. The aging Emperor Franz Joseph, who stood stiffly in uniform braced by his sword while the imperial court danced to the waltzes of Johann Strauss, was the symbol of a fragile and once great empire.

In this time of unabashed nostalgia, Vienna also gave birth to avant-garde movements that challenged the values of the past. Richard Strauss' *Der Rosenkavalier* (1911) represented the swan song of Romantic opera in the classical style—a young composer, Arnold Schönberg, had already broken from the Western tradition of tonality, and two young followers, Alban Berg and Anton Webern, were pushing the revolution in music even further by abandoning the standard Western conception of key. Painters and writers were experimenting with new forms of expression that would later lead to the

movement in the arts known as the Vienna Secession. But it was perhaps in the study of a Viennese physician named Sigmund Freud that the most profound transformation was taking place. Freud's investigations suggested that deep-rooted instincts struggled for release and dominance within the human psyche, and the popularization of his work shattered nineteenth-century rationalism.

Vienna also saw the emergence of political movements that challenged the roots of European liberalism, among them the Christian Socialist party of Karl Lüger and the Social Democratic party led by Victor Adler. But whereas the Social Democrats appealed to the city's growing industrial working class, Christian Socialist membership came largely from the petite bourgeoisie. Lüger and his followers identified closely with a growing anti-Semitic sentiment in the city. Lüger was mayor of the city when, in 1907, a teenage German first came to Vienna to study painting. In Vienna the young man discovered anti-Semitism and came to loathe the mixing of nationalities that he saw in the capital. His name was Adolf Hitler.

Russia Between Reaction and Reform

The dilemmas facing a multiethnic empire such as Austria were perhaps more serious still in Russia, where the problems of national minorities were compounded by the vast size of its territory and the complexity of its population. Stretching thousands of miles across two continents, the peoples of the Russian empire included a wide diversity of Europeans and Asians, and for centuries Russia struggled unsuccessfully to define its national identity between the pulls of two civilizations.

Despite its complexity, the social structure of Russia's population was rigidly divided between a small and highly privileged nobility and a huge, impoverished peasant population. Perhaps 95 percent of Russian subjects fell into the peasant category, the great majority of them serfs with no civil rights or property who owed heavy dues and services to the landowning masters. The wealthy nobility owned almost all the land and were exempt from taxes and military service. Because Russia's economy was predominantly agricultural throughout most of the nineteenth century, a small middle class existed only in the larger cities.

In an age when autocracy was disappearing in Europe, the Russian tsar remained an absolute monarch. His will was law, and only the poverty, backwardness, and ineffective bureaucracy of imperial Russia limited his authority. Because no legitimate forms of protest existed, conspiracy and local insurrection were frequent. When faced with such threats, the Romanov dynasty swung between extremes of enlightened reform and brutal repression.

Tsar Alexander I (1801–1825), who recognized that the political and social structure of the empire needed to be modernized, had experimented with constitutionalism and federalism before reverting to autocracy. His brother, Nicholas I (1825–1855), was so obsessed by the fear of revolution that he appointed secret police to hunt down subversives. Nicholas proclaimed the principles of "autocracy, Orthodoxy, and nationalism," by which he meant obedience to the Romanov dynasty, adherence to the Russian Orthodox church, and the advancement of Russian national interests. Censorship and restrictions on intellectual life were combined with the exile of political prisoners to Siberia.

The tsar also ordered a program of Russification of ethnic minorities and supported the Slavophiles, who believed that Russia should live according to its traditional Slavic values in an agrarian society based on Orthodoxy, mysticism, and despotism. Opposed to this position were the Westerners, who argued that Russia should modernize by adopting the European model of industrial society built on rationalism. This debate split the intelligentsia, Russian intellectuals who wanted to achieve political goals.

Alexander II and the Dilemma of Russian Reform

The great issues confronting Russian society in the mid-nineteenth century came to a head after Russia's defeat in the Crimean War. The crisis began when Russia and Turkey went to war in 1853 over the Balkan territories of Moldavia and Wallachia. The next year Britain and France, concerned over Russian attempts to control the Christian holy places in Jerusalem and Palestine and to expand into the eastern Mediterranean, came to the aid of the Turks by invading Russia's Crimean peninsula in the Black Sea. Eventually Piedmont and Austria also sided against Russia, thus involving most of the European powers in a military conflict for the first time since the Congress of Vienna. The Crimean War ended in 1856 with Russia's defeat on the battlefield and diplomatic losses at the Paris peace conference.

Nicholas I died during the war. Like many other Russians, his more liberal son, Alexander II (1855–1881), realized that the Crimean disaster was due in part to the country's military and industrial backwardness,

and he at last gave in to demands for reform. In 1861 he issued an imperial edict that emancipated more than 22 million serfs and gave them communal title to a portion of the land on which they worked. A system of local government was begun at the level of the village commune (*mir*), which held the land in common. District councils administered the courts and collected taxes, while indirectly elected provincial councils (*zemstvos*) acted as forums for open discussion of political and social issues and provided elementary education. But the emancipated serfs were forced to compensate their former lords, and their land parcels were generally too small for profitable cultivation. The emancipation edict was thus a step forward in relative terms only, for most of the former serfs quickly fell into debt and wound up as agricultural laborers on the estates of their former masters. Moreover, Alexander began to doubt the wisdom of some of his measures after an assassination attempt in 1866, and in the mid-1870s he reimposed censorship on the press and the universities and curtailed freedom of debate in the *zemstvos*.

The new wave of repression sparked widespread discontent. Socialists such as Alexander Herzen (1812–1870) inspired many of the radical intelligentsia to live in the small villages in an attempt to raise peasant political consciousness. But as these so-called *Narodniki* (from the Russian word *narod*, "people") became disillusioned by the obstacles they faced, many began to proclaim themselves "nihilists," who believed in nothing. In the face of Alexander's return to repression, some of the nihilists came under the influence of the anarchist Mikhail Bakunin (1814–1876), who preached the destruction of the government through "propaganda of the deed," by which he meant individual acts of violence. In 1881 Alexander II was assassinated by such a terrorist act.

Russia descended into deep reaction during the reigns of Alexander III (1881–1894) and his son, Nicholas II (1894–1917). The only positive developments were the economic reforms carried out in the 1890s by Count Sergei Witte (1849–1915), a tough finance minister bent on modernizing the Russian economy along Western lines. Under Witte's leadership, government initiative rather than private capital stimulated industrialization. Until reactionary agrarian interests forced his dismissal in 1903, Witte succeeded in attracting Western investments by putting Russia on the gold standard, launching the trans-Siberian railroad, and stimulating industry. The French, eager for an alliance with Russia, poured capital into the empire. According to one estimate, industrial production doubled in a decade. Yet Witte's programs did not begin to come to

Tsarist Russia on the Edge of Revolution

In 1881 Tsar Alexander II was assassinated by an anarchist group known as the "Will of the People." In March that same year the terrorist organization addressed an open letter to the new tsar, Alexander III, of which the following is an excerpt.

A dispassionate glance at the grievous decade through which we have just passed will enable us to forecast accurately the future progress of the revolutionary movement, provided the policy of the government does not change. The movement will continue to grow and extend; deeds of a terroristic nature will increase in frequency and intensity. Meanwhile the number of the discontented in the country will grow larger and larger; confidence in the government, on the part of the people, will decline; and the idea of revolution—of its possibility and inevitability—will establish itself in Russia more and more firmly. A terrible explosion, a bloody chaos, a revolutionary earthquake throughout Russia, will complete the destruction of the order of things. Do not mistake this for a mere phrase. We understand better than anyone else can how lamentable is the waste of so much talent and energy—the loss, in bloody skirmishes and in the work of destruction, of so much strength which, under other conditions, might have been expended in creative labor and in the development of the intelligence, the welfare, and the civil life of the Russian people. . . .

These are the reasons why the Russian government exerts no moral influence and has no support among the people. These are the reasons why Russia brings forth so many revolutionists. These are the reasons why even such a deed as killing a Tsar excites in the minds of a majority of the people only gladness and sympathy. Yes your Majesty! Do not be deceived by the reports of flatterers and sycophants; Tsaricide is popular in Russia.

Source: J. H. Robinson and C. Beard, eds., *Readings in Modern European History*, vol. 2 (Boston: Ginn, 1909), pp. 364–366.

grips with the monumental social and political problems the country faced.

The Dissolution of the Ottoman Empire

By the start of the nineteenth century, the Ottoman Empire still ruled an estimated 40 million people, but corruption and administrative chaos were rife and, as in the Austrian Empire it bordered, the nationalist aspirations of its subject populations were already threatening to tear it apart. Revolts by Serbs and Greeks were followed later in the century by Bulgarian and Romanian uprisings, while some of the sultan's ambitious regional commanders, such as Muhammad Ali, governor of Egypt, pursued independent policies. The Western view of the Ottoman Empire was summed up by Tsar Nicholas I, who during a state visit to England in 1844 referred to it as a "dying man."

While nationalist movements challenged the unity of the Ottoman Empire, the great powers posed a more serious threat to its existence. By 1830 the Russians had occupied the Danubian principalities of Moldavia and Wallachia, the French had seized Algiers, and with the help of foreign intervention the Greeks had won their independence. As the internal decay of the Turkish system accelerated and the territorial ambitions of the European states grew, the so-called eastern question emerged. Although on one level it involved the interaction between the Ottoman Empire and the great powers, the eastern question may more clearly be understood as the conflict among the great powers over the future of the sultan's domains. One major complication arose from the growing competition between Austria and Russia for predominance in the Balkans; another was due to the centuries-old Russian ambition to gain control over the Turkish Straits in order to have free access from the Black Sea into the Mediterranean. The fate of the Ottoman possessions in the Middle East interested both Britain and France, for the British regarded the area as the gateway to India and the French were concerned over the protection of Christian holy places. Similarly, in North Africa the French were intent on expanding their foothold in Algiers into Morocco and Tunisia at the same time that the British consolidated their interest in Egypt following the completion of the Suez Canal.

The web of competing interests that comprised the eastern question made the Ottoman Empire a sensitive issue in European diplomacy. The Crimean War and the Paris peace conference of 1856 confirmed the neutrality of the Black Sea, ended the Russian occupation of Moldavia and Wallachia (the provinces were merged into the kingdom of Romania a few years later), and left the protection of the Christian populations of the Middle East to the sultan. But if the peace conference basically preserved the Ottoman Empire, succeeding events speeded its disintegration. In 1875 revolts against Turkish rule in Bosnia led to a declaration of war against Istanbul by the semiautonomous states of Serbia and Montenegro, which were eventually assisted by Russia. When the resulting Treaty of San Stefano (1878) threatened to shift the balance of power in the Balkans in favor of Russia, Austria and Britain became alarmed. That summer, therefore, the Russians were forced to the conference table at the Congress of Berlin. Despite Bismarck's claim that he would act as an "honest broker" at the confer-ence, Russian gains from the Treaty of San Stefano were severely reduced. Serbia, Montenegro, and a new state, Bulgaria, were recognized as fully independent from Turkish rule, while the provinces of Bosnia and Herzegovina were placed under Austrian administration. The Ottoman Empire lost half of its European territory. During the next 30 years European powers would strip Turkey of its remaining possessions in North Africa.

The dismemberment of the Ottoman Empire aroused discontent among the sultan's younger, Western-educated subjects and in the army, where opposition to the inefficient rule of the sultans was growing. In 1856 a far-reaching reform edict, the *Hatt-i Humayun*, established a progressive political structure for the empire, but a new sultan, Abdul Hamid II (1876–1909)—known for his brutal tyranny as "Abdul the Damned"—crushed the hopes of the reformers. After issuing a new constitution, Abdul Hamid reimposed tyranny. In the Ottoman Empire, as in Russia, the weight of centuries of repression seemed to move toward revolution.

The Jewish Question and the Birth of Zionism

The Enlightenment had significantly advanced the theoretical equality and the actual emancipation of the Jews, and during the nineteenth century the remaining legal restrictions on them were eliminated in virtually every major country of Europe, although quasi-official sanctions such as educational and professional quotas remained. Despite the fact that religious and social prejudices against them were still deeply rooted in Europe, most Jewish populations were being assimilated into Europe's social, economic, and cultural life.

In an age of self-conscious nationalism, however, the Jewish question grew increasingly complicated. The development of "scientific" theories of race in the late nineteenth century and the resulting merger of nationalism and racism stimulated anti-Semitic discussion. In countries where Catholic and Christian influence blended with political conservatism, anti-Semitism emerged as a political movement with widespread appeal. In Germany, Adolf Stöcker's Christian Socialist Workingman's Union, the Conservative party, and even an Anti-Semitic League advocated an end to Jewish influence in national life, and in 1882 an international anti-Semitic congress was held in Dresden. In France, Edouard Drumont's book *La France juive* (1886) inflamed popular attitudes, and the shocking Dreyfus affair revealed the depth of anti-Semitic sentiment. In the Dual Monarchy, the Christian

Abdul Hamid II, a cruel despot, ruled the Ottoman Empire until the Young Turks deposed him in 1909.

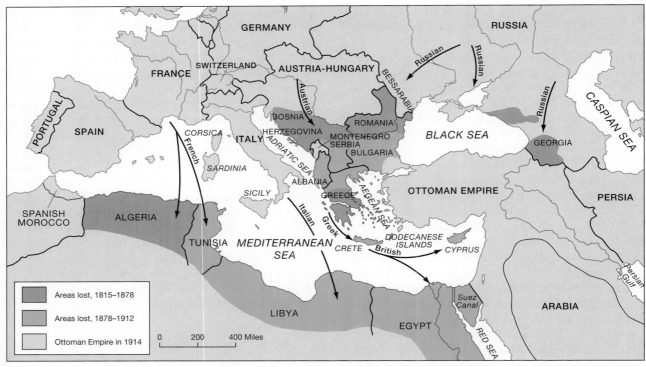

MAP 33.4   THE DECLINE OF THE OTTOMAN EMPIRE TO 1914

Socialist party elected Karl Lüger mayor of Vienna on a distinctly anti-Semitic platform.

It was in Russia, where the partitions of Poland in the late eighteenth century had made millions of Jews subjects of the tsar, that systematic repression became state policy. Anti-Semitic measures coincided with the reactionary policies of Alexander I and Nicholas I, and in the wake of the assassination of Alexander II in 1881, violent anti-Semitic campaigns, or pogroms (*pogrom* is Russian for "devastation"), were unleashed, often with official connivance, as Jews were killed and beaten and their homes and shops burned and looted. The infamous May Laws of 1882 provided the basis for the expulsion of Jews from villages and rural centers outside Poland, and even fiercer pogroms broke out in 1902 and 1903. In the period from 1881 to 1910, millions of Russian Jews fled, most of them to the United States.

As a reaction to these persecutions and a defense against the assimilation and secularization of Jewish life, the end of the century saw the development of an organized movement of Jewish nationalism called Zionism. Advocates of Zionism argued that Jews would never find justice and equality until they returned to their biblical homeland and formed their own national state. Rabbi Zevi-Hirsch Kalischer and a number of other Jewish

thinkers had already proposed the establishment of a homeland in Palestine, and in 1869 an agricultural colony named Mikveh Yisrael ("Hope of Israel") was founded there. In 1882 Leo Pinsker, a Russian Jewish physician, published an influential pamphlet, *Autoemancipation*, advocating a similar program.

Theodor Herzl and the Quest for a Jewish Homeland

The founder of modern political Zionism was Theodor Herzl (1860–1904). Against overwhelming odds, and at times almost single-handedly, Herzl set in motion the movement that years after his death resulted in the establishment of the state of Israel.

Herzl was born in Budapest to a merchant family of assimilated Jews. After taking a law degree from the University of Vienna, he turned to writing, immersing himself in the world of sentimental bourgeois culture that characterized the Austrian capital in the 1880s. Although he wrote successful plays, journalism was Herzl's real talent, and he made an international reputation as foreign correspondent for the prestigious *Neue Freie Presse.* A handsome man with a Romantic, narcissistic personality, he moved in literary and aristocratic circles. But in 1891 his Viennese paper sent Herzl to Paris, where his life took a sudden and dramatic turn. In Paris, Herzl discovered his identity as a Jew. France was then in the throes of the Dreyfus scandal, and Herzl witnessed the anti-Semitic frenzy firsthand. Thereafter, Jewish issues began to preoccupy him. The result was his famous pamphlet, drafted in a few intense months in late 1895 and published the following year as *Der Judenstaat (The Jewish State).*

Written in a powerful, crisp style, *The Jewish State* was a radical analysis of the Jewish question. Herzl argued that although many Jews had attempted to assimilate into European society, anti-Semitism had made this impossible. "I consider the Jewish question," he wrote, "neither a social nor a religious one, even though it sometimes takes these and other forms. It is a national question." His solution, therefore, was that Jews all over the world should organize to obtain a land of their own. In his mind, Palestine was the natural site for a Jewish state. But unlike earlier leaders, he insisted that Palestine should be secured not through unofficial immigration and infiltration but through an international charter.

Herzl threw himself into the task. Sacrificing his marriage, his wealth, and eventually his health, he spent the rest of his life in a tireless campaign to convince his fellow Jews and to secure the support of world opinion. His efforts resulted in the establishment of the World Zionist Organization. In 1897 he presided over the First Zionist Congress, in Basel, Switzerland, which proclaimed that "Zionism seeks to establish for the Jewish people a publicly recognized, legally secured home in Palestine" and to strengthen "Jewish self-awareness and

On Anti-Semitism

The reemergence of anti-Semitism assumed new and more virulent forms in the late nineteenth century and led Jewish leaders such as Theodor Herzl and his friend Max Nordau to found the Zionist movement. Here are two moving statements by them on the nature of anti-Semitism.

Stunned by the hailstorm of anti-Semitic accusations, the Jews forget who they are and often imagine that they are the physical and spiritual horrors which their deadly enemies represent them to be. The Jew is often heard to murmur that he must learn from the enemy and try to remedy the faults ascribed to him. He forgets, however, that the anti-Semitic accusations are meaningless, because they are not a criticism of facts which exist, but are the effects of a psychological law according to which children, wild men, and malevolent fools make the persons and things they hate responsible for their sufferings.

I believe that I understand anti-Semitism, which is really a highly complex movement. I consider it from a Jewish standpoint, yet without fear or hatred. I believe that I can see what elements there are in it of vulgar sport, of common trade jealousy, of inherited prejudice, of religious intolerance, and also of pretended self-defense. I think the Jewish question is no more a social than a religious one, notwithstanding that it sometimes takes these and other forms. It is a national question which can only be solved by making it a political world-question to be discussed and controlled by the civilized nations of the world in council.

We are a people—One people.

Sources: M. Nordau, speech to the First Zionist Congress, 1897, in A. Hertzberg, ed., *The Zionist Idea* (Garden City, N.Y.: Doubleday, 1959), p. 241; T. Herzl, *The Jewish State: An Attempt at a Modern Solution of the Jewish Question* (New York: Maccabaean Publishing Co., 1904), pp. 4–5.

national consciousness." By 1901 there were local Zionist organizations throughout the world, including 1,034 in Russia and 135 in the United States, and branches as far afield as New Zealand, Chile, and India. Herzl gained the help of influential Jewish leaders and met with heads of state, including Kaiser William II and the Turkish sultan, in efforts to realize the Basel program. In 1903 the British government offered part of its East African possessions as the basis for a Jewish state. Through the work of Herzl's successor, Chaim Weizmann (1874–1952), and the support of the British statesman Arthur Balfour, the British government became increasingly sympathetic to the Zionist cause, but not until World War I did it support a Jewish homeland in Palestine.

Herzl's program provoked great controversy, even within the ranks of the Zionist movement. Some biographers have portrayed him as a man with a messianic complex—he demanded blind obedience from his followers, and everywhere he traveled, especially in eastern Europe and Russia, throngs of poor Jews greeted him with adulation. His argument that assimilation had failed suggested to many that he despaired of liberalism, yet his vision of the new Jewish state was so grounded in tolerance and progressive ideals that it often provoked resentment from cultural Zionists who saw nothing specifically Jewish about it. Similarly, he failed both to understand the importance of socialism within the Zionist ranks and to anticipate the clash between Jews and Arabs that would result from the occupation of Palestine. Yet his methods yielded results, and he galvanized millions of Jews the world over. His despondency over the failure of assimilation, together with his warnings about the dangers of anti-Semitism, gave an urgency to his search for a solution to the Jewish question. Some of his critics charged that he was obsessed by the Zionist program, but his forebodings about the fate of Europe's Jews would prove tragically prophetic.

The Struggle for National Unity: The United States and Latin America

The struggle for national identity in the nineteenth century was by no means limited to Europe. Similar developments were occurring as far away as China and Japan. Perhaps the closest parallels were to be found in newly independent Latin America and the United States, for the governments there had been set up by people who considered themselves European in culture and values and who were inspired by the same Enlightenment principles that nourished the French Revolution.

Even after the American union had adopted its constitution in 1787, the United States continued to wrestle with ideological issues concerning the nature of its democracy. Indeed, the struggle between the Federalists, who represented the conservative northern landowners and the commercial classes, and the southern landowner Democratic-Republicans, who championed the small yeoman farmers of the young republic, was not unlike the European conflict between conservatism and liberalism. The passage of the Bill of Rights in 1791 and the subsequent election of Thomas Jefferson (1801–1809) as president signaled the rejection of a powerful central government dominated by privilege and wealth, a tendency later confirmed in the democratic principles of Andrew Jackson (1829–1837).

The advance of democratic attitudes in the United States went hand in hand with its territorial expansion.

The founder of the modern Zionist movement, Theodor Herzl, was driven by the revival of anti-Semitism in the late nineteenth century as well as by the centuries-old aspirations of Jews for a homeland in Palestine.

In less than half a century huge tracts of land, each larger than most European countries, were added to the United States. The Louisiana Purchase in 1803, the settlement of the old northwestern territories, and the conquest of Texas and California in the Mexican-American War all fulfilled what Americans came to call their "manifest destiny," an attitude first expressed by the Russians in their expansion across Siberia. As more settlers pushed westward into the frontier territories, the pioneer values of hard work, individual worth, and self-reliance were deemed more valuable than birth and status. The seemingly unlimited American continent, with its fertile farmland and natural resources, gave Americans self-assurance and unbridled optimism.

The American Civil War

Yet the American experience was not without serious problems. Sectional disputes, particularly between the agricultural south and the industrializing north, threatened to disrupt the republic. By the 1850s the institution of slavery, on which the southern economy depended, had become a deeply divisive issue. The test of nationhood came in the bitter civil war between 1861 and 1865, in which Abraham Lincoln (1861–1865) sought to preserve national unity just when Cavour had forged an Italian state and Bismarck was striving to create a united Germany. As war leader, Lincoln put the preservation of the nation before the question of abolition. But in response to growing demands, he issued the Emancipation Proclamation on January 1, 1863, abolishing slavery in the secessionist Confederate states. The defeat of the Confederacy achieved both goals of ending slavery in the United States (long after it had been abolished in most other places in the Western world) and preserving the American union.

Following the civil war, the United States entered a period of unrestrained economic development and industrialization. By the end of the century almost 200,000 miles of railroads crisscrossed the continent, and American mills produced a third of the world's steel. The population of the nation, swelled by almost 30 million immigrants from Europe and Asia between 1860 and 1914, settled hundreds of millions of acres of land in the west and swarmed into the burgeoning cities. On the eve of World War I almost half of the nation's 100 million people lived in urban centers. The rapid transformation of the American continent from a frontier society to an industrial giant and the resulting leap in America's status to global power were to have profound consequences for the world.

National Development in Latin America

In Latin America the struggle for national liberation began in 1808, when Napoleon's armies drove the rulers of Spain and Portugal into exile, thereby providing an opportunity for republican nationalists in the colonies to seek self-government. Yet political consolidation did not go as far as in North America, where, apart from Mexico, the entire continent eventually came under the jurisdiction of either Canada or the United States. For one thing, the population of Latin America was more ethnically complex: that of the Spanish colonies was about 45 percent Indian, 30 percent mixed Indian and European (mestizo), 20 percent white, and 5 percent black. In Brazil, where slavery was common, some 50 percent of the population was black, 30 percent mixed (*mamelucos*), and 20 percent white.

By 1821 Mexico and the Central American states— Costa Rica, Salvador, Nicaragua, Guatemala, and Honduras—had secured their independence. Despite an experiment between 1823 and 1839 to unite the five smaller states in a federal republic known as the United Provinces of Central America, regional unity was not permanent. In South America a similar attempt in the 1820s to join Venezuela, Colombia, and Ecuador into Gran Colombia failed, and by 1830 the present grouping of nations—Argentina, Chile, Bolivia, Peru, Ecuador, Colombia, Venezuela, Uruguay, and Paraguay—had been established in what had been Spanish regions of South America.

Brazil: From Empire to Republic

Brazil, the largest nation in Latin America, became independent in 1822, when the Portuguese ruler's son, Dom Pedro (1798–1834), declared its separation from the mother country. As emperor (1822–1831) Pedro proclaimed a constitution that gave him great power and established a parliamentary regime. The emperor's autocratic behavior culminated in an opposition movement that forced him to abdicate in 1831 in favor of his infant son. A regency ruled Brazil until 1841 and enacted a series of constitutional amendments that gave considerable authority to provincial assemblies. Local revolts were widespread in the northern regions, where the sugar and cotton economy experienced difficult times; the coffee-growing areas proved more stable. After the 15-year-old Dom Pedro was proclaimed emperor as Pedro II (1841–1889), order was restored to the country during most of his long reign.

The major issue facing Pedro II was slavery, on which Brazil's social and economic order rested. The agricultural system of large landed estates had been built on slave labor, and when the slave trade ended after 1850, a serious labor shortage resulted. Nevertheless, the abolitionist movement gained in strength, and in 1888 Brazil at last ended slavery. By then the demand for labor was beginning to be met by European immigrants.

The abolition of slavery brought an end to the only remaining monarchy in Latin America, for the wealthy planters resented the emperor's support for abolition and his failure to indemnify them for the loss of their slaves. In November 1889 a military revolt replaced the imperial government with a republic. Political reforms were followed in 1891 by a new constitution that established a federal system of government that still left numerous powers to provincial assemblies.

While the vast interior remained an agricultural region, Rio de Janeiro, the capital, and other cities became centers of modern economic life. Demands for government subsidies, credits, tariffs, and infrastructures led to the printing of paper currency and inflation, which in turn hurt coffee prices. Domestic manufacturing and the middle classes expanded under the presidency of Marshal Floriano Peixoto (1842–1895), known as the "consolidator of the republic," but the coffee planters combined to drive him out of office in 1894. Over the following decades, overproduction of coffee became a persistent problem, which the government attempted to solve through support programs.

Dictatorship and War

Economic and political development was often hampered in Latin America by two factors: most governments fell at one time or another to dictators, known as *caudillos,* who subverted the constitutional systems, and the region also experienced violent and costly wars as competing states clashed over territory and position. Among the most important of these struggles was the Paraguayan War (1865–1870). When Paraguay declared independence in 1813, it was the only landlocked state in South America. Despite economic dependence on Argentina, Paraguayan leaders created a prosperous and progressive country. Nevertheless, border disputes, especially over the area known as the Banda Oriental, poisoned relations between Paraguay and Brazil. In 1828 that region secured its independence as the state of Uruguay, but Brazil continued to intervene in its affairs. In May 1865, Brazil, Argentina, and the Brazilian-backed government of Uruguay formed the Triple Alliance against Paraguay. The war ended five years later with the disastrous defeat of Paraguay, whose population of 500,000 was reduced by as much as three-fourths as a

result of both the fighting and starvation, disease, and occupation. Paraguay lost large portions of its territory. In the War of the Pacific (1879–1883), Chile defeated Bolivia and Peru, seized the valuable nitrate-rich area of southeastern Peru, and cut Bolivia off from the sea.

Argentina and Mexico

In Argentina, attempts by the wealthy port city of Buenos Aires, the federal capital, to impose its control over the rest of the country created political tensions. In 1829 Juan Manuel Rosas (1793–1877) became governor of Buenos Aires and arranged a federal pact that allowed the provinces to run their own internal affairs while leaving foreign policy to him. Nevertheless, the vast plains provinces of the pampas, ruled by tough and independent-minded cattlemen known as *gauchos,* offered continual resistance to centralized government. Rosas, who ruled Argentina as a tyrant and suppressed civil liberties, was overthrown in 1852. The resulting constitution of 1853 resembled that of the United States, creating a federal republic run by an elected president and a two-chamber national legislature. The provinces elected governors and their own legislatures. Over the next 50 years economic development and the creation of an infrastructure—especially the railroad and telegraph networks and

Benito Juárez, the son of Indian parents, served as president of Mexico during a difficult period in his country's history.

a public school system—slowly brought genuine unity to the country. Argentina's population doubled to 4 million between 1870 and 1900, much of the increase owing to migration from Europe.

Unlike most countries in Latin America, Mexico in the nineteenth century had a number of important leaders of mestizo and Indian origin. The Mexican constitution of 1824 was a compromise between middle-class liberals and conservative landowners and military officers. Nineteen states, each with its own legislature, chose the president of the republic. In 1833 Antonio López de Santa Anna (1794–1876), a general of Creole descent, was elected president. Although this period is sometimes called "the age of Santa Anna," he only served intermittently as president for six years. The United States annexed Texas in 1845 and acquired California and New Mexico in the Mexican War of 1846–1848.

Benito Juárez (1806–1872), a Zapotec Indian who had been elected governor of Oaxaca, replaced the ousted Santa Anna. Juárez led a coalition government that reduced the influence of the military and the church. A new constitution enacted in 1857 sparked a violent civil war—the War of Reform—that ended in victory for Juárez and the liberals.

The war so disrupted economic conditions that the government had to suspend payment on foreign loans. This prompted Napoleon III to send a French army to Mexico in 1862 that toppled the government. Napoleon selected the Austrian Archduke Maximilian (1832–1867) to rule as emperor of Mexico. Maximilian's downfall resulted from a combination of Mexican resistance, his alienation of his conservative allies, and Napoleon's decision to recall French troops to Europe after Prussia's victory in the 1866 war with Austria. Juárez captured the hapless Maximilian, who was tried and executed in 1867. Juárez then served as president of Mexico until his death.

In 1876 the Mexican government was again overthrown, this time by Porfirio Díaz (1830–1915), a former follower of Juárez of mixed Creole and Indian descent. Díaz ruled Mexico for more than 30 years. He encouraged the investment of foreign capital and sold off the country's natural resources while the condition of the workers and peasants deteriorated. When he was finally forced to resign in 1911, the Mexican revolution had already begun.

SUMMARY

In the second half of the nineteenth century, European history was shaped largely by triumphant nationalism, which underwent a profound transformation. In midcentury a pro-

ponent of nationalism such as Giuseppe Mazzini saw no contradictions between his demands for Italian national liberation and the aspirations of other nationalities. Indeed, Mazzini had cast his nationalist ideas in broad international terms, envisioning an interdependent Europe in which free, equal, self-governing peoples cooperated in a spirit of harmony. Mazzini, who died in 1872, lived to see nationalism triumph in Italy and Germany, yet by the end of the century he would hardly have recognized the concept as the same idealistic doctrine he had once preached. Nationalism also encouraged state-building and overcame sectionalism in the United States and Latin America.

Nation-building had been a complex interaction in which patriotism and middle-class liberalism had first joined forces against conservatism. Ironically, however, success subverted nationalist movements, for as military, industrial, and conservative aristocratic elites embraced nationalism, many liberals subsumed or abandoned their political values to the more immediate goal of unification. Once national unity was achieved under the leadership of men such as Bismarck and Cavour, the Mazzinian vision of a new civilization nurtured by a spirit of freedom and equality gave way to an aggressive chauvinism that perceived history as the struggle between nations for power and dominance. Bitter national rivalries resulting from the wars of unification in Europe and Latin America gave concrete form to the larger political and intellectual changes taking place. The nationalists of the post-unification period absorbed and twisted the theories spawned by the Darwinian revolution in science, substituting the doctrine of supremacy for belief in equality, rejecting cooperation in favor of competition, and preaching imperialist expansion instead of self-determination. By the end of the century nationalism, which once had promised a new age of peace and security, pointed to an unstable and dangerous future.

SUGGESTIONS FOR FURTHER READING

Binkley, R. C. *Realism and Nationalism, 1852–1871.* New York: Harper, 1935.

Crankshaw, E. *Bismarck.* New York: Macmillan, 1981.

Emmons, T. *The Russian Landed Gentry and the Peasant Emancipation of 1861.* Cambridge: Cambridge University Press, 1968.

Florinsky, M. T. *Russia: A History and an Interpretation.* New York: Macmillan, 1953.

Griffith, G. O. *Mazzini: Prophet of Modern Europe.* London: Hodder & Stoughton, 1932.

Hamerow, T. S. *The Social Foundation of German Unification, 1858–1871.* 2 vols. Princeton, N.J.: Princeton University Press, 1969.

Hertzberg, A., ed. *The Zionist Idea.* Garden City, N.Y.: Doubleday, 1956.

Keen, B., and Wasserman, M. *A History of Latin America,* 3rd ed. Boston: Houghton Mifflin, 1988.

Kohn, H. *The Idea of Nationalism.* New York: Macmillan, 1944.

Mack Smith, D. *Cavour*. London: Weidenfeld & Nicolson, 1985.

———. *Garibaldi*. London: Hutchinson, 1957.

———. *Mazzini*. New York: Knopf, 1995.

McPherson, J. M. *Battle Cry of Freedom: The Civil War Era*. New York: Oxford University Press, 1988.

Mosse, W. E. *Alexander II and the Modernization of Russia*. London: English Universities Press, 1958.

Pflanze, O. *Bismarck and the Development of Germany,* vol. 1, rev. ed. Princeton, N.J.: Princeton University Press, 1990.

Schorske, C. E. *Fin-de-Siècle Vienna*. New York: Knopf, 1979.

Seton-Watson, H. *The Decline of Imperial Russia, 1855–1914*. New York: Praeger, 1952.

Shaw, S. J., and Shaw, E. K. *History of the Ottoman Empire and Modern Turkey*. 2 vols. Cambridge: Cambridge University Press, 1977.

Stavrianos, L. S. *The Balkans, 1815–1914*. New York: Holt, Rinehart and Winston, 1963.

Taylor, A. J. P. *Bismarck: The Man and the Statesman*. New York: Knopf, 1955.

———. *The Habsburg Monarchy, 1809–1918*. New York: Harper & Row, 1965.

———. *The Struggle for Mastery in Europe, 1848–1918*. Oxford: Clarendon Press, 1960.

Thompson, J. M. *Louis Napoleon and the Second Empire*. New York: Norton, 1967.

Williams, R. L. *Gaslight and Shadow: The World of Napoleon III*. New York: Macmillan, 1957.

Woolf, S. *A History of Italy, 1700–1860*. London: Methuen, 1979.

Wright, G. *France in Modern Times*. Chicago: Rand McNally, 1960.

CHAPTER
34

Industrial Society
and the Liberal Order

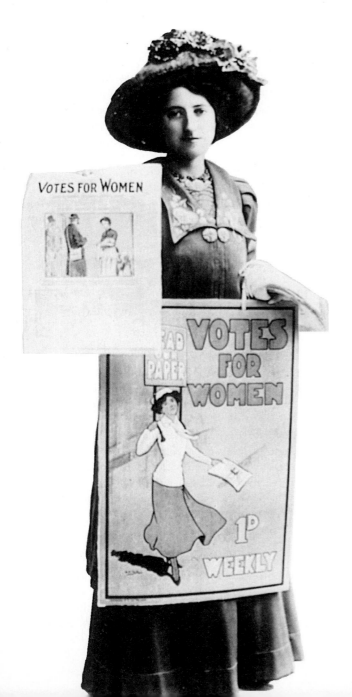

During the last third of the nineteenth century Europe achieved a higher level of material well-being than any previous civilization. Its population was healthier, more nutritiously fed, better educated, and longer-lived, and it enjoyed more physical comforts than any other people in history. Europeans of this generation made remarkable progress in understanding and controlling the physical world. By the end of the century they moved themselves and the products of their industrial culture efficiently not only by steam but also by the internal combustion engine; they turned machines with steam turbines and electrical energy, communicated rapidly around the globe with the telegraph, underwater cable, and telephone; and illuminated the darkness with the light bulb.

These advancements in science and technology, together with unprecedented prosperity, determined how the post-1871 generation thought itself. Most Europeans looked at the world with faith in the limitless capacity of reason to solve problems. "Progress," inexorable and continuous, was their religion. Believing that they were moving steadily toward an ideal future, Europeans were self-assured about the achievements and superiority of their civilization.

The materialist culture of the era reflected the fact that the middle class had become an influential elite in European life. Liberal doctrines shaped the governments of most Western nations, while entrepreneurs and industrialists extolled unregulated, growth-driven capitalism. As the middle class achieved status and political power, bourgeois notions of order and respectability defined public attitudes toward family, sexuality, the roles of men and women, and social behavior. Middle-class values also set standards of style and comfort as well as artistic taste.

A worker for the national Women's Social and Political Union selling Votes for Women, *a suffragette paper.*

865

Still, the age was by no means as well ordered as many contemporaries believed. Industrial capitalism spawned unanticipated problems. Beneath the surface of middle-class prosperity lay widespread poverty and dehumanizing drudgery in the workplace, loudly denounced by social critics. Some demanded social and political reforms and a wider suffrage. As the right to vote spread, radical opponents of liberalism, inspired by the Marxist critique of capitalism, joined industrial workers in forming labor unions and socialist parties in an effort to wrench power from the bourgeoisie.

The social implications of the industrial system were enormous. By the end of the century factories had drawn millions of farmers from the countryside and had transformed a once rural and agricultural Europe into a predominantly urban civilization with pressing problems of public welfare. Higher factory wages had also attracted women to the workplace in large numbers, altering the pattern of family life, modifying sexual behavior, and challenging traditional models of male–female relationships.

Industrial Development and Monopoly Capitalism

In the last third of the nineteenth century, Europe's economy was transformed in three important ways: the Industrial Revolution spread more widely to other European nations, new sources of energy and products were developed, and business elites evolved new forms of control over industry and capital. These trends brought the earlier industrialization process to a climax and shaped Western economic life for generations.

The Second Phase of the Industrial Revolution

The first phase of industrialization had been marked by the application of steam power in the manufacturing of two important commodities, iron and textiles. Subsequent changes in science and technology led to a second and equally important phase. Although steam remained the major source of industrial energy until 1914, electric power and internal combustion engines fueled by petroleum products increasingly replaced steam-driven machinery. The new energy sources led to the development of more sophisticated machines that greatly expanded efficiency and output and lowered production costs.

During the second phase of the Industrial Revolution, steel replaced iron as the basic metal, and the chemical industry grew rapidly. Both developments resulted from the application of scientific discoveries to industry.

Through the process developed by Henry Bessemer (1830–1898) at midcentury, steel could now be manufactured in large quantities. The strength and flexibility of steel had a profound impact on construction, manufacturing, and transportation. As railroad networks spread across Europe and America, the production of locomotive engines, cars, and tracks stimulated industry and capital investment and opened significant new markets. Methods for the mass production of chemical substances revolutionized industry by allowing for the creation of such new products as fertilizers, dyes, explosives, plastics, synthetic fabrics, and medicines such as aspirin.

Germany, France, Italy, Russia, the United States, and Japan became industrial nations. Coal and steel provided useful indices of the growth of production during the second phase of the Industrial Revolution. Between 1870 and 1913 world output of coal had risen from 230 million to more than 1.5 billion metric tons, while steel production rose from 550,000 to more than 80 million tons. By 1914 the "inner zone" of Britain, Germany, and France produced 80 percent of Europe's coal, steel, and machinery and 70 percent of its manufactured products. Germany emerged as Europe's industrial giant and outdistanced Britain. By 1900 German steel production had outpaced Britain's, and on the eve of World War I it was more than double that of Britain and second only to that of the United States, which manufactured almost twice as much as Germany. Germany also led the field in the cast-iron and chemical industries. In the four decades after 1870 Britain's annual growth rate was 2.2 percent, compared to 2.9 percent for Germany and 4.3 percent for the United States.

The sharp increase in productivity after 1870 resulted not only from new energy sources and the spread of industrialism but also from more efficient machines that reoriented production techniques toward standardized parts and specialized tasks. Pioneered by the American automobile manufacturer Henry Ford (1863–1947), the division of labor on assembly lines made cheaper, mass-produced consumer goods widely available. Although these trends contributed to the material improvement of daily life, they also resulted in overproduction, the further dehumanization of the work process, and a decline in the quality of many products.

The Rise of Big Business

The second phase of the Industrial Revolution bore out Karl Marx's prediction of a trend toward the concentration of wealth in fewer hands. The large numbers of small factories and businesses characteristic of early in-

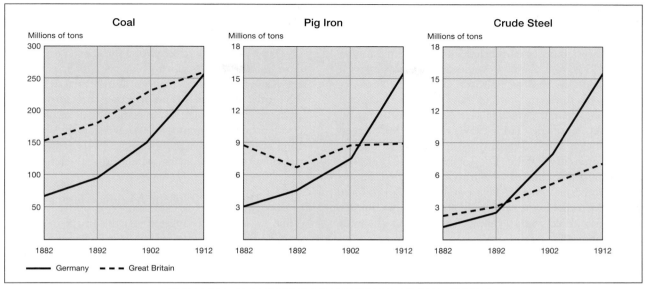

FIGURE 34.1   GERMAN AND BRITISH INDUSTRIAL PRODUCTION, 1882–1912

dustrialization gave way to fewer, larger concerns. Business legislation encouraged the trend by extending the concept of "limited liability," which insured the personal assets of investors against business losses. In retail sales, department stores forced many independent shopkeepers out of business by buying in large quantities and selling at lower prices. Moreover, as the cost of such large-scale operations as steel foundries and chemical refineries increased, entrepreneurs required enormous capital, which was unavailable to smaller producers. Partly for this reason, but largely because competition drove down the margin of profit, investors created monopolies.

Entrepreneurs often operated through "horizontal integration," whereby they controlled a sector of industry or business such as steel, coal, or oil. Such huge combinations—called amalgamations in Britain, cartels in Germany, and trusts in the United States—dominated industry by the end of the century by absorbing or driving out competitors and limiting production, fixing prices, dividing markets, and controlling labor. Through "vertical integration" steel manufacturers could buy up coal and iron mines, chemical plants, blast furnaces, and rail companies to control the entire industrial process.

The giant Krupp manufacturing complex at Essen, Germany (1912), reflected both the new era of early-twentieth-century industrialization and the industrial power of Germany.

Unregulated, monopoly capitalism had long-range implications. Investment banking grew in importance, especially with the adoption of the international gold standard for all major currencies. John Pierpont Morgan (1837–1913), the famous American banker, financed governments as well as railroads and steel companies through his firms in New York and London. Industrial monopolies were the work of such "captains of industry" as Andrew Carnegie (1835–1919), who in 1901 merged his Carnegie Steel Company with the United States Steel Corporation; John D. Rockefeller (1839–1937), owner of the Standard Oil trust; and Alfred Krupp (1812–1887) and August Thyssen (1842–1926) in Germany. Such men were ruthless in their pursuit of profit and accumulated vast fortunes that enabled them to wield unprecedented economic and political power. The social ramifications of the second phase of the Industrial Revolution were far-reaching, especially as the emergence of the private-sector bureaucracy enlarged the white-collar class.

The Social Hierarchy

The political and economic changes that transformed Europe in the nineteenth century profoundly affected society. Despite unprecedented material progress, social and economic differences remained sharp, and the quality of life varied greatly between classes.

The Aristocracy: Adjustment and Change

The aristocracy had been the dominant elite before 1789. Most nobles, whose wealth and status had been determined by land ownership, failed to make the transition to modern capitalist agriculture or industrialization. Although land continued to be important, the real wealth of the aristocracy declined along with their income and access to liquid capital. In countries that remained predominantly agricultural, competition from cheaper overseas grain further reduced farm income. Yet in Britain the aristocracy remained stable well into the nineteenth century. The declining influence of the aristocracy appeared sharper than it actually was because of the rapid rise of the middle class. Liberal constitutions gave the bourgeoisie political power, but aristocrats dominated the upper chambers in parliaments. While the spread of civil service examinations and higher education opened administrative positions to the middle classes, the aristocracy remained largely closed. Ancient lineage and ac-

cess to royal courts sustained the status of nobles, who continued to be the point of reference in matters of social prestige and style.

After 1870 the line separating the aristocracy and the upper middle class began to blur, as it had in the sixteenth and seventeenth centuries, as industrial wealth and noble titles sometimes came together through mutually advantageous marriages. Businessmen with surplus capital often bought sumptuous estates as symbols of their rising status. Increasingly, the upper levels of the industrial class copied the living standards of the aristocracy.

The Growth of the Middle Classes

While the aristocracy underwent adjustment in the late nineteenth century, the middle classes enjoyed expansion, though not uniformly. Grouping economic interests and social strata so diverse that they were often mutually antagonistic, the middle classes included wealthy industrialists and bankers as well as shopowners and white-collar workers. In industrialized countries the middle classes constituted perhaps one-fifth of the inhabitants, and the powerful industrial and banking families formed a very small percentage of the general population. This elite reaped great benefits from expanded industrial production, earning a third of all national income. Consisting of no more than several hundred families in any given country, this group tended to merge with the old aristocracy, aping their manners and elitist attitudes.

Most middle-class Europeans were members of less wealthy and powerful subgroups: the middle bourgeois class of small entrepreneurs, professional experts, and managers or the lower middle class of shopkeepers and white-collar workers. The ranks of the middle range swelled after 1870 with scientists, engineers, lawyers, and accountants—whose occupations grew more professional—as well as with corporate managers and bureaucrats.

The number of shopkeepers and small business owners grew along with teachers, nurses, and other salaried, nonpropertied members of the lower middle class. The most dramatic increase, however, was among the white-collar employees—clerks, salespeople, secretaries, and low-ranking bureaucrats, most of whom came from the working class. White-collar wages were sometimes less than those of skilled workers, but the status conferred by carrying a briefcase, wearing a tie, or having uncallused hands was often seen as compensation for low salaries. The lower middle class expanded rapidly between 1870 and 1900, doubling in Britain to 20 percent of the population.

This photograph of an upper-middle-class English family at tea reveals the Victorian ideal of social and domestic property.

Although middle- and lower-middle-class groups did not control great wealth, they tended to lead comfortable lives that reflected the values and aspirations of the upper-class bourgeoisie. Yet the status of most of the middle class was precarious in comparison to other groups. Easy social mobility encouraged the lower ranks to strive for greater status and income, but tensions were equally strong. Economic pressure from large industries and corporations threatened small businessmen and shopkeepers, while people living on fixed incomes from savings and pensions feared that business cycles and recessions could suddenly wipe them out. For white-collar employees, who made every effort to distance themselves from the workers, the greatest fear was that economic adversity would force them back to their working-class origins.

The Decline of the Working Class

Four-fifths of all people lived by physical labor. Industrialization made Europe a predominantly urban civilization, so by the end of the nineteenth century agricultural workers were a distinct minority in most western and central European countries. The agricultural crisis that began in 1873 as a result of huge imports of wheat from the United States reduced the price of European grains. Landowners cut wages and pushed peasants, many of whom already lived close to subsistence, into more extreme poverty. The decline in agricultural earnings, compounded by natural disasters in the 1870s and 1880s, also struck peasant owners, whose land decreased in value. The rural standard of living improved after 1890 with changes in crops and cultivation methods, as well as the introduction of protective tariffs, but agricultural wages remained less than half the average of factory rates.

Behind the exuberant prosperity of Victorian London lay the poverty of much of Britain's working class. This photograph shows an alley in a working-class section of the city.

In industrialized countries the urban working class represented the largest social stratum and was even more diverse than the middle classes. Among skilled workers, industrialization brought stressful changes as artisans gave way to factory workers who required less skill. Yet there was also a growing need for new kinds of skilled jobs, including metalworkers, machine tool makers, and locomotive engineers. Skilled workers, whose wages were at least twice as high as those of unskilled laborers, saw themselves as an elite with middle-class pretensions. Semiskilled and unskilled workers vastly outnumbered the artisans and the skilled elite. The semiskilled, such as masons, carpenters, plumbers, and some factory workers, earned less money, while the unskilled workers, among whom the largest number were domestic servants, were the lowest paid.

Between the years 1873 and 1896 the West experienced a series of economic crises known collectively as the Long Depression. Primarily an agricultural phenomenon sparked by competition from North American farms, the Long Depression nevertheless affected industry and trade. Rising costs, increased competition, and shrinking markets reduced profits and triggered financial panics. Periods of high unemployment resulted. In Britain, for example, unemployment among unionized workers rose from 1 percent in 1872 to 11 percent in 1879, from 2 percent in 1882 to 10 percent in 1886, and from 2 percent in 1890 to 7.5 percent in 1893. Such sharp cycles of unemployment not only caused severe hardships among working-class families but also fanned enthusiasm for militant labor unions. Yet even though fluctuations in wages accompanied the crises, during the three decades after 1870 real wages rose by about 37 percent, increasing by a third in France and Germany and by more than half in Britain.

Urban working-class diets improved and became more varied as food prices declined and purchasing power increased, and health conditions in the cities improved with the development of sewage systems, clean water supplies, and the scientific control of disease. Industrial productivity reduced the cost of clothing, so workers were better dressed. The expansion of urban construction made less cramped housing available, and the development of inexpensive railway, subway, and tram services gave workers access to better housing in the suburbs, although they still had to devote large portions of their budgets to rent.

Despite advances in the standard of life for urban workers, production outpaced wages. Although working-class purchasing power expanded and living standards improved for all social groups, the gap between workers and the middle classes widened.

POPULATION OF THE MAJOR CITIES OF CONTINENTAL EUROPE AROUND 1910

City	Population	City	Population
Paris	2,888,000	Kiev	469,000
Berlin	2,071,000	Turin	428,000
Vienna	2,031,000	Rotterdam	418,000
St. Petersburg	1,908,000	Frankfurt	415,000
Moscow	1,481,000	Lodz	394,000
Hamburg	931,000	Düsseldorf	359,000
Budapest	880,000	Lisbon	356,000
Warsaw	781,000	Stockholm	347,000
Naples	723,000	Palermo	342,000
Brussels	720,000	Nuremberg	333,000
Milan	599,000	Riga	318,000
Madrid	598,000	Charlottenberg	306,000
Munich	596,000	Antwerp	302,000
Leipzig	590,000	Hanover	302,000
Barcelona	587,000	Bucharest	295,000
Amsterdam	568,000	Essen	295,000
Copenhagen	559,000	Chemnitz	288,000
Marseilles	551,000	Stuttgart	286,000
Dresden	548,000	Magdeburg	280,000
Rome	539,000	Genoa	272,000
Lyons	524,000	The Hague	270,000
Cologne	517,000	Bordeaux	262,000
Breslau (Wroclaw)	512,000	Oslo	247,000
Odessa	479,000	Bremen	247,000

The Urban Landscape

The urbanization of European society—the movement of people from country to city, the growth in the number of urban centers, and the dense concentration of huge populations in them—continued well beyond 1900. Between 1871 and 1911 England's urban population rose from 62 to 78 percent of the whole and France's from 33 to 44 percent. In Germany, which was industrializing rapidly, the increase was spectacular—from 36 to 60 percent. Moreover, 90 percent of Germany's population growth in the same period was in cities. The culture of western Europe had become predominantly urban.

Improved transportation, particularly that provided by the railroad, spurred urban growth, and most important cities became hubs of rail lines or port facilities, and frequently both. In large cities the basic infrastructure—drainage systems, water supply, police and fire protection—had already been established by midcentury, and these services were expanded.

Baron Haussmann's redevelopment of Paris during the Second Empire provided the model for a similar project in Vienna, whose Ringstrasse was inspired by Haussmann's grand boulevards. London and Berlin permitted the reconstruction of inner-city zones in the 1870s, when town planning revived. By the end of the nineteenth century, advances in engineering, building materials, and construction techniques began to change the face of cities. Reinforced concrete and steel permitted multistory office and apartment buildings, and both the American skyscraper and the metal tower designed by French engineer Gustav Eiffel in the 1890s became symbols of the new, aggressive city. Sewers, sidewalks, and electric lights made urban centers more pleasant places in which to live and work.

France led the way with other distinctive features of the modern city. Using wrought iron and steel, Parisian developers built large, glass-covered galleries in which independent shops and cafés were situated, and by the 1880s Moscow had followed the example. The first major department store was the Bon Marché in Paris. By buying in quantity, department stores could sell a wide range of mass-made goods inexpensively, thus making the products of industrial civilization available to workers and the lower middle class.

Working-class housing, which in the early industrial revolution had consisted of squalid, crammed tenements, improved considerably in this period as a result of health and welfare legislation. The French pioneered middle-class apartment complexes, New York exploited that concept, and British cities added the notion of garden apartments. As urban transportation systems grew, more people escaped urban living for tranquil suburbs, and the city became the metropolis.

Everywhere cities adopted from each other, equipping themselves with London-style parks and suburbs, Paris-style boulevards and cafés, and New York-style office blocks and gridded street plans. They all acquired grand public buildings and cultural centers such as opera houses, concert halls, museums, and public libraries, and all were afflicted with pollution, noise, and overcrowding. By the end of the century the urban landscape had assumed its modern appearance.

Sexuality, Women, and the Family

The Industrial Revolution and the consequent movement of populations from the country to the cities had significant repercussions on relationships between men and women, as well as in the family. Urban life tended to erode moral codes and traditional forms of courtship and marriage that were more easily enforced in small villages. At the same time, the employment opportunities and higher wage scales that drew workers to the factories often enabled young men and women to escape family supervision. In the period before 1850 the result had been a dramatic increase in premarital sex (among partners who intended to marry), illegitimate births, and common-law marriages, but this pattern diminished by the last third of the century.

The spread of birth control information contributed to a decline in the birthrate. The French took the lead in contraception, and such traditional methods as the sponge, sheepskin condoms, and the vinegar douche were widely used among the upper classes. In Britain laws prohibited the publication or distribution of contraceptive information until Annie Besant, a socialist, and Charles Bradlaugh, a radical, won a celebrated court case in 1878. Between 1880 and 1900 they distributed more than a million copies of birth control pamphlets that advocated the use of the sponge, syringing with zinc or alum solutions, cervical caps, and rubber condoms. Although Besant aimed her information at the poor, it was the middle class that first made widespread use of these methods. Only by the end of the century did urban workers use them widely. Moreover, middle-class men could more easily afford recourse to brothels, where they found women who were often driven to prostitution by unemployment and poverty.

Industrialization brought mixed results. During the nineteenth century roughly two-thirds of all single women and more than a quarter of married women worked. Life was especially difficult for working women, for most had to function as mothers and wives as well. Married generally in their early and mid-twenties after experiencing the relative independence derived from their jobs, working women subordinated themselves to their husbands. The men ate better food, dressed better, went out without their families in the evenings, and often abused their children and wives. Yet despite the grueling physical and psychological pressures, working mothers managed to keep the basic family structure intact.

The principal female employment categories—domestic service, textile work, and garment making—remained fairly constant into the early twentieth century, but the female workforce consisted increasingly of single women; by 1911 only 9.6 percent of married women were employed. The notion that women should "retire" when they married was a product of urban industrial culture. In the cities domestic service employed more women than any other activity in the nineteenth century.

The Cult of Domesticity

The development of the cult of domesticity, which limited women largely to home maintenance and child rearing, contributed greatly to the social construction of gender roles. In this nineteenth-century handbook for housewives, Mrs. Isabella Beeton explains the principles of household management.

Of all those acquirements, which more particularly belong to the feminine character, there are none which take a higher rank, in our estimation, than such as enter into a knowledge of household duties. . . .

Early rising is one of the most essential qualities which enter into good household management, as it is not only the parent of health, but of innumerable other advantages. Indeed, when a mistress is an early riser, it is almost certain that her house will be orderly and well-managed. . . .

Cleanliness is indispensable to health, and must be studied both in regard to the person and the house, and all that it contains. Cold or tepid baths should be employed every morning, unless, on account of illness or other circumstances, they should be deemed objectionable. . . .

Frugality and economy are home virtues, without which no household can prosper. . . . The necessity of practising economy should be evident to every one. . . .

The treatment of servants is of the highest possible moment, as well to the mistress as to the domestics themselves. On the head of the house the latter will naturally fix their attention; and if they perceive that the mistress' conduct is regulated by high and correct principles, they will not fail to respect her.

After this general superintendence of her servants, the mistress, if the mother of a young family, may devote herself to the instruction of some of its younger members, or to the examination of the state of their wardrobe, leaving the latter portion of the morning for reading, or for some amusing recreation.

Source: I. Beeton, *Book of Household Management* (London: Beeton, 1861), pp. 2–9 passim.

Because it promoted such virtues as hard work, cleanliness, and obedience, domestic service was regarded as ideal training for future wives of the working class.

Bourgeois Respectability

The expanding demand for domestic servants reflected both the growing prosperity of the middle class and the new ideal of womanhood that it cultivated. The separation between the male sphere of work and business and the female sphere of home and family reached its most fully developed form among the middle class. Bourgeois respectability required that the home be comfortable, well furnished, and characterized by an atmosphere of warmth and safety from the outside world. Middle-class sensibilities idealized women as gentle and virtuous creatures devoted to bearing and raising children and looking after their husbands. The Victorians evolved a "cult of

domesticity" for women that stressed duty, submissiveness, and devotion. A close and emotionally intimate family life was extolled as the social bedrock of the age.

The middle-class family concentrated legal power in the hands of the husband and father. Until midcentury contracts were often used in upper-class families to safeguard the property rights of daughters about to be married, for a husband ordinarily gained control of a wife's property. Most states in America passed married women's property acts, as did Britain in 1882, but these were designed largely to enable fathers who had no sons to pass inheritances to their daughters. Widows almost always had to defer to the relatives of their deceased husbands regarding such matters as their children's education and upbringing. Similarly, divorce was still generally obtainable only by women who could prove that their husbands were impotent or unfit fathers; in most countries husbands could gain a divorce on the grounds of adultery but women could not. Educational patterns perpetuated the inferior status of women. While middle-class boys usually went to school to receive classical education or professional training in law, medicine, or accounting, girls stayed home to learn painting, needlework, and religion.

Sexual Attitudes

The ideology of bourgeois respectability had a powerful impact on attitudes toward sexuality, though not on its practice. Sexual pleasure was regarded as a male preserve. The assumption that women were not supposed to enjoy sex was a powerful form of male dominance. Public attitudes toward sexuality encouraged a double standard according to which men might, with proper discretion, visit brothels and maintain mistresses to fulfill their "natural" needs. Victorian moral strictures were also imposed on children, whose clothing and physical activities were regulated to repress masturbation and sensations that might lead to sexual arousal. Menstruation—known as "the curse"—was little discussed, and pubescence was regarded as a profoundly disturbing and disagreeable experience.

Diaries and letters, the proliferation of sex manuals and pornography, and the literature of the period demonstrate that despite the strictures fostered by middle-class sexual codes, men and women continued to enjoy sex. The sensational trial and imprisonment in 1895 of the writer Oscar Wilde (1854–1900) because of his love affair with Lord Alfred Douglas made Victorians uncomfortably aware of other sexual orientations. Wilde's account of this experience, *The Ballad of Reading Gaol* (1898), had to be published anonymously, and his "open letter" to Douglas, *De Profundis* (1905), did not appear until after his death. The tension created by the dissonance between moral theory and behavior produced a psychological anxiety that pervaded the late Victorian age.

Liberalism and the Political Order

The middle class had been a driving force behind the political upheavals that stretched from the American Revolution in 1776 to the revolutions of 1848. They had reacted strongly against the excesses of the French Revolution, but their demands for a share in political power, expressed through the doctrine of liberalism, had made them the foe of absolutism and aristocracy. After 1815 the bourgeoisie stood in sharp opposition to the conservative political principles of the Restoration. In France they brought the "bourgeois king," Louis-Philippe, to

power in 1830, while in England, where the 1832 Reform Act had enfranchised the industrialists, the propertied classes enjoyed significant political influence. In 1848 and 1849 they came close to establishing constitutional regimes in central and eastern Europe.

The political triumph of the middle classes came after 1850, when they joined forces with elements of the aristocracy in supporting unification movements in Germany and Italy and Napoleon III in France. Thereafter, as the middle classes gained power, they reversed their historical role; whereas once they had acted as a powerful force for change, now they emerged as the champions of order. Liberalism, the doctrine that expressed middle-class aspirations, changed as well.

Over the course of the nineteenth century, liberalism had proved to be a flexible doctrine capable of encompassing a wide range of objectives, from the Enlightenment belief in individual rights to Romanticism and from nationalism to Bismarck's *Realpolitik*. After 1870 the industrial and financial bourgeoisie began to appropriate political liberalism as their special preserve, making it the philosophy of the capitalist establishment.

Though liberalism underwent a transformation after 1870, it continued to stand for the basic premise that government should be based on a written constitution (except in Britain, where an unwritten agreement prevailed), with the middle classes and aristocracy represented in parliamentary institutions elected by limited male suffrage. Liberal parliamentary systems reflected a number of trends: a widening suffrage that eventually encompassed most of the working classes, the appearance of modern political parties representing a range of class and special interests, free elementary education, compulsory military service, the secularization of national culture, and the growing role of the state in social legislation and public policy. Individual countries produced variations in this pattern, but as the century drew to a close, liberalism had permeated the political culture of western Europe almost everywhere. By 1900 all but one of the great European states were part of the "liberal" order; only Russia stood outside the system.

Britain in the Victorian Age

No nation more completely represented the liberal order than Britain, and no European monarch symbolized that ideal more completely than Queen Victoria (1837–1901). She inherited the throne from her uncle, William IV, at the age of 18. In 1840 she married a German cousin, Prince Albert of Saxe-Coburg-Gotha, who had a formative influence on her character. She learned to express her wishes and opinions forcibly to her ministers and had a strong though discreet influence on politics. After Albert's death in 1861, Victoria lapsed into seclusion as the "widow of Windsor." Her 64-year reign as queen (she was also crowned empress of India in 1876), together with the fact that she was the grandmother of both Kaiser William II of Germany and Tsar Nicholas II of Russia, made Victoria the venerable matriarch of Europe's royalty. But as the symbol of Britain's political stability and industrial power, she was no glittering incarnation of imperial splendor. When she reappeared in public in the 1880s, it was as a matronly icon of bourgeois virtue, dressed in black and wide in girth.

Midway through Victoria's reign, British politics underwent a crucial transformation that resulted in the emergence of new leaders at the head of modernized political parties. Under William Gladstone (1809–1898), the old Whig-radical coalition evolved into the Liberal party. An eloquent orator, Gladstone, the pious son of a merchant, was trained as a classical scholar before entering politics. As chancellor of the Exchequer, he had pushed for a policy of free trade as well as reforms that included a postal savings and insurance system widely used by workers and a reduction in taxes. In 1864, when only one adult male out of six had the right to vote, Gladstone pressed for an extension of the franchise, which had not changed since 1832.

Queen Victoria and her husband, Prince Albert, were the ideal royal couple, devoted to each other and serious about their duties.

At this time Benjamin Disraeli (1804–1881) was molding the aristocratic, agrarian-based Tories into the new Conservative party. More flamboyant than Gladstone, the brilliant Disraeli was the descendant of Spanish Jews and the author of political novels. He was convinced that the Conservatives needed to broaden their support by appealing to the middle classes. After a successful record of leadership in the House of Commons, he overcame the suspicion of his colleagues, who regarded him as opportunistic, and eventually won the support of Queen Victoria, who preferred the Conservatives to the Liberals.

Gladstone and Disraeli made possible the passage of the Reform Act of 1867. After Gladstone had tried without success to secure passage of a similar bill in 1866, Disraeli—who saw an opportunity for the Conservatives to reap the political credit—maneuvered the measure through the House of Commons. By giving the vote to all middle-class males and the highest-paid urban workers, the second Reform Act doubled the size of the electorate by adding almost a million voters to the rolls.

From 1868 to 1914 the Liberal and Conservative parties alternated in power. First Gladstone and Disraeli, and then their successors, outdid each other in sponsoring political and social legislation. Competitive civil service examinations were introduced in 1870, the secret ballot a year later. After 1884, when Gladstone passed another reform bill that increased the electorate by the addition of 2 million agricultural laborers, Britain continued to evolve toward parliamentary democracy, at least for men.

Before the end of the century the great mass of British workers and farm laborers benefited from a range of reforms—largely modeled on similar legislation introduced in Germany by Bismarck—that included free elementary education; minimum-wage laws; accident, health, and unemployment insurance programs; old-age pensions; and a graduated income tax. Marxist socialism, which was gaining a foothold in less democratic Continental states, had little appeal in Britain. By the eve of World War I, England's upper bourgeoisie believed that their country offered compelling testimony to the wisdom of the alliance between political liberalism and industrial capitalism. Still, as late as 1892 a report found that almost a third of the inhabitants of London—Britain's largest city and the hub of the British Empire—lived in poverty.

The Third Republic in France

For 70 years after 1870 France was governed by a republic born out of military defeat and civil war. The French surrender following the Battle of Sedan had resulted in the overthrow of Napoleon III and the proclamation of a republic (see Chapter 33). The National Assembly chose the liberal royalist Adolphe Thiers (1797–1877) as president. Thiers negotiated the humiliating peace terms with Bismarck that ended the Franco-Prussian War.

In March 1871 the National Assembly moved the government to Versailles, the traditional seat of the French monarchy. There the liberal-monarchist majority further aroused the fury of the Parisians by canceling the debt moratorium and the pay of the civilian National Guard, measures that had kept tens of thousands from starvation during the Prussian siege of the capital. Thiers then tried to confiscate the 200 cannon that had been cast by public subscription during the siege. Angry mobs dragged the cannon to safety and drove off government troops.

Civil war erupted. Extremists in Paris took control of the rebellion and established the Commune, modeled on the revolutionary government of 1792. When the regular army broke through the city's defenses in May, the Communards executed hostages, including the archbishop of Paris, while the Assembly's soldiers summarily shot everyone found with weapons. By the time government troops had secured the city, as many as 20,000 Communards had been executed, and twice that number were deported to penal islands. The repression of the Commune had been bloodier than any civil clash in modern French history. It left a permanent legacy of class bitterness that polarized French politics and intensified social division.

The Third Republic proved both politically unstable and unpopular. Although the monarchists had a majority in the National Assembly, they could not agree on a suitable candidate for king and in effect continued the republic by default. The constitution of 1875 created a democratic government in which the prime minister and his cabinet were fully responsible to Parliament, whose lower house, the Chamber of Deputies, was elected by universal male suffrage.

Unlike the British, the French failed to develop modern political parties until the end of the century. Poorly organized political groups were held together only by immediate concerns. Royalist sentiment, which remained strong, was the focus of opposition to the Third Republic, but the monarchists remained divided on whether to support the Bourbon, Orléanist, or Bonapartist claimant to the throne. Republican supporters were equally divided. Radical republicans, led by Georges Clemenceau (1841–1929), were anticlerical and anti-German. Moderate republicans were more willing to compromise on major issues. Together, the moderate royalists and the republicans represented the liberal tradition in French politics. The left, which took more than a decade to recover from the disaster of the Commune, was also split into factions. In Parliament, majorities were difficult to form and still more difficult to maintain. More than 50 coalition cabinets governed France during the first 40 years of the republic.

The republic was no friend of social revolution. Reform legislation was slow in coming, and it was 1910 before earlier work and health laws were complemented by accident and social insurance programs. Still, moderates established the supremacy of Parliament and a system of secular state education that slowly engendered republican values in the post-1870 generation.

The strange career of General Georges Boulanger (1837–1891) mirrored the discontent that beset the Third Republic. Originally a radical republican and protégé of Clemenceau, Boulanger became war minister in 1886. He was a popular figure who made a habit of riding a magnificent black horse through the streets of Paris. Chafing under the humiliation of defeat in the Franco-Prussian War, royalists and patriotic admirers saw him as a symbol of French glory. Boulanger lost his cabinet position in 1887 and was sent to the provinces, where he drummed up support for a new constitution and a more authoritarian regime. With the help of right-wing politicians, he planned a coup d'état in 1889 but lost his nerve at the last minute and fled to Brussels.

More serious in its repercussions was the dramatic Dreyfus affair. In 1894 Captain Alfred Dreyfus (1859–1935), a Jewish officer attached to the French General Staff, was court-martialed for treason on charges that he had supplied military secrets to the Germans. A military court ignored evidence that another officer had been guilty. This aroused the radical republicans, who believed that the military had falsely condemned Dreyfus while protecting the real traitor. While Dreyfus languished in prison on Devil's Island, the notorious penal colony, Clemenceau and the novelist Émile Zola (1840–1902) took up his cause and accused the General Staff of harboring clerical, royalist, and anti-Semitic prejudices. In 1899 the army found Dreyfus guilty "with extenuating circumstances" and pardoned him, but his supporters continued to demand a full acquittal, which came only in 1906.

The episode widened the wedge that already separated radicals, socialists, and intellectuals from army leaders, monarchists, and the Catholic church. The crisis unleashed a wave of anti-Semitism that fueled right-wing forces. The Dreyfus case, like the Boulanger affair, revealed that the enemies of the government were strong. Yet the legacy of the French Revolution was equally

After toppling this column bearing a statue of Napoleon I in Paris, the Communard rebels erected the red flag of revolution in its place.

powerful, and the Third Republic survived for another half century.

Germany Under the Reich

Liberalism in Germany was weaker than in Britain or France because it had been tied so closely to the triumph of Bismarck's unification program. Bismarck had been appointed minister of Prussia to overcome a deadlock between the king and the liberals in the Landtag, which he did by circumventing its control of the budget. In September 1866, however, after his stunning victory over the Austrians, the liberals and others sanctioned his violation of the Prussian constitution.

While Bismarck cowed the liberals, he also forged a powerful alliance between bourgeois industrialists and aristocratic landowners that enabled him to impose political unity on the German states. Prussia ran the federal structure of the German empire through its monarchy, bureaucracy, and army, and, with 236 of 397 seats in the lower house of parliament, the Reichstag, dominated the national assembly. Outwardly, the German parliament conformed to the liberal formula: the Reichstag, which approved laws and budgets but had no real authority over foreign affairs or the imperial ministers, was elected by universal male suffrage. The upper house, the Bundesrat, represented the 26 federated units of the empire and could initiate laws and block measures proposed by the Reichstag. The powers of the emperor were extensive, for he was commander in chief of the army and, in his role as king of Prussia, remained almost an absolute monarch. Moreover, the kaiser appointed the imperial chancellor, who was responsible to him alone.

Bismarck presided over the empire as chancellor for 19 years. Disdainful of his critics, the "Iron Chancellor" rammed his programs through parliament with the support of the conservative landowners and the upper middle class. The interests of the industrialists and bankers were represented by the National Liberals, while the great landowners backed the Conservatives. The Progressives, who spoke for the more radical liberals who had initially opposed Bismarck; the Center party, which

The headstrong Kaiser William II dismissed Bismarck in 1890 and assumed personal direction of German affairs.

spoke for the Catholics; and the Social Democrats, representing the socialist party, were Bismarck's chief sources of opposition.

Bismarck's ruthless methods and high-handed policies were designed to forge a single nation out of the patchwork of states that made up the new empire. He tried to extinguish local loyalties and crush opposition to the central state.

The first target of this policy was the Catholic church, against which he unleashed the so-called *Kulturkampf,* or "battle for civilization"—a campaign to make loyalty to Germany supreme over devotion to the Catholic church. Although the *Kulturkampf* was an extreme example of a growing trend toward secularization all over Europe, Bismarck saw it essentially as a political issue. Germany was predominantly Protestant, but Catholics comprised a third of the population and were strong in Alsace-Lorraine. Bismarck clashed with the church when he sponsored laws that abolished religious orders, imposed state supervision over Catholic education, made civil marriage compulsory, and required government approval of ecclesiastical appointments. When he removed bishops and hundreds of priests, Bismarck succeeded only in making political martyrs of them and found that German Catholics rallied to their church. In the next elections, the Catholic-oriented Center party nearly doubled its representation in the Reichstag. Always the realist, Bismarck eventually reached an accommodation with Pope Leo XIII (1878–1903).

Bismarck also dealt with what he considered the other major national problem, the threat of socialism. The formation of the Social Democratic party in 1875 led him to fear that the socialists would capture the loyalties of workers for the cause of revolution and internationalism. He persuaded the Reichstag to pass legislation restricting socialist activities. Denied an open forum, the socialists organized support underground and elected their candidates to the Reichstag in ever larger numbers. Faced with another political disaster, Bismarck switched his tactics in the 1880s by sponsoring social welfare programs designed to wean the workers away from the socialists while keeping the antisocialist laws intact. Bismarck's social security laws, the most advanced in Europe, provided workers with accident and health insurance and retirement benefits. After 1890 workers were given additional rights, including labor arbitration and better working conditions. These measures failed to reduce working-class support for the socialists, but they did demonstrate that organized political pressure could win substantial material benefits for workers without revolution. As a result, the Social Democratic party grew enormously in electoral strength and by 1912 was the largest party in the Reichstag. At the same time, however, it lost much of its revolutionary impetus.

Bismarck virtually ruled the German empire until 1890, when Kaiser William II (1888–1918) forced him to retire. As erratic as Bismarck was strong-willed, William had come to the throne when he was 29. Strict training had made him deeply attached to military discipline and the spirit of manly virtue that infused the aristocratic Prussian officer corps. Determined to rule Germany himself and unwilling to be dominated by Bismarck as his predecessors had been, William proclaimed, "There is only one master in the Reich [empire], and that is I." Heaping honors on Bismarck, the kaiser retired the man who had created the German empire.

In assuming command of the Second Reich (German nationalists considered the medieval Holy Roman Empire to have been the First) William II ruled the most powerful state in Europe. Its population was large and growing rapidly, and its modern industrial plant was outpacing those of other nations in producing coal, steel, chemicals, and electrical energy. Spectacular economic growth and a system of higher education that stressed technical training produced the most literate and scientifically advanced population in Europe. The German army was the most efficient military force in the world. Stridently nationalistic, the kaiser launched Germany on a new and dangerous course in world affairs.

The Liberal State in Italy

Britain and Germany offered examples of the liberal order at its extremes, one strong and stable, the other weak and shallowly rooted. Italian liberalism evolved between the two extremes. As in the case of Germany, Italian unification owed a great deal to the efforts of one man, Count Cavour. Unlike Bismarck, however, Cavour had been an admirer of British political traditions and was a moderate liberal by conviction.

Much as Prussia had done in Germany, Piedmont had imposed its traditions and institutions on the Italian states along with unification. The king was commander in chief of the armed forces and had the authority to declare war and make treaties. He also appointed the prime minister, who was declared to be "responsible," although whether to the king or to parliament remained unstated. The Chamber of Deputies, or lower house of the Italian parliament, was elected on the basis of limited male suffrage, with only 2 percent of the population able to vote. The Chamber controlled budget appropriations and could initiate legislation. The Senate, or upper house, could veto measures passed in the Chamber, and its members, appointed by the king for life, tended to be conservatives, nobles, and public officials.

As in France, organized political parties did not emerge in Italy until after the turn of the century.* Instead, parliamentary deputies considered themselves members of either the right or the left. These were largely meaningless labels that had been used during the unification struggle to describe, respectively, the supporters of Cavour's program of constitutional monarchy and Mazzini's republican followers. After 1870 the terms denoted degrees of liberalism, although the differences in outlook were often more a matter of emphasis than substance. In the first years of the kingdom, when the right was in power, the government pursued a fiscally conservative program of high taxation and low expenditure for social reform. When the left came into power in 1876, it repealed some of the more onerous taxes, widened the suffrage, and instituted compulsory elementary education. Significant social and economic progress came slowly. The lack of clearly defined political parties and programs contributed to the practice of *trasformismo*, whereby prime ministers formed coalitions that changed constantly, depending on the specific issue and the patronage to be distributed.

The pride that had accompanied unification quickly faded as Italians faced the problems of nationhood. The annexation of Rome in 1870 produced deep hostility between the Catholic church and the new state that was to plague Italian politics for the next half century. Through the Law of Guarantees, parliament recognized papal sovereignty over Vatican City and offered financial compensation to the church. But Pius IX, who declared himself a "prisoner of the Vatican," would not compromise. He refused to recognize the kingdom and prohibited Italian Catholics from taking part in political life. The stalemate, known as the "Roman question," weakened the legitimacy of the new state in the eyes of Italy's overwhelmingly Catholic population.

Regional differences and local loyalties remained strong in Italy after unification. The gap between the industrial interests of the north and the depressed agricultural economy of the south widened after 1870, and illiteracy, disease, and poverty put pressure on a national debt already burdened by the costs of the wars of unification. Despite the reforms of the left after 1876, the ruling liberal elite remained unresponsive to the needs of the unenfranchised poor for many years. Unemployed migrant workers turned increasingly to brigandage in the south, while peasant anarchism was widespread in Sicily and central Italy. In the industrial centers of Milan and Turin, workers turned to socialism.

The last two decades of the century were a period of crisis that tested liberalism. From 1887 to 1891 and again from 1893 to 1896 leadership was in the hands of Francesco Crispi (1819–1901). Like Bismarck, Crispi was determined to stem the rise of socialism by suspending constitutional rights and smashing the Socialist party with massive arrests and police harassment. He was also anxious to make Italy a great power through military alliances and colonial conquest, but scandals and military defeat in Africa brought him down. Vigorous action against socialists and anarchists by Crispi's successors climaxed in the bloody suppression of labor demonstrations in 1898. The liberal state in Italy demonstrated its deep hostility to working-class movements.

The accession of Victor Emmanuel III (1900–1946) to the throne in 1900 brought Giovanni Giolitti (1842–1928) to the forefront of national politics. Giolitti served off and on as prime minister for most of the years before World War I. A shrewd politician, he toned down the level of confrontation with labor, coopted moderate socialists into the parliamentary system, and ended strikes through negotiation. Giolitti sought a reconciliation with the church, presided over the development of industry, and sponsored significant factory and social legislation. Finally, in 1911 Giolitti introduced near-universal male suffrage. The liberal state had begun its first tentative steps toward democratic reform when World War I intervened.

Spain and the Smaller Powers

Instability and unrest, due largely to intrigues surrounding the succession to the throne, marked Spanish political life in the mid-nineteenth century. After a revolution unseated Queen Isabella II (1833–1868), a number of governments—first under the Cortes, then under a king imported from Italy, and finally as a republic—failed to find support and encouraged the church and the army to interfere in politics. Only when Alfonso XII (1874–1885) became king under a liberal constitution did a measure of stability return.

Thereafter, Spain struggled with the problems of social and economic modernization. Small areas of industry existed within an agrarian nation dominated by conservative landed interests. Anarchist and regionalist movements were strong, especially in the Basque region and Catalonia, while industrial growth in Barcelona prompted the rise of socialism. In 1890 universal male suffrage was instituted, but the constant struggle be-

---

*The Italian Socialist party, founded in 1892, was the exception.

tween the Liberal and Conservative parties made social reform difficult.

Events in Spain's colonies added to the nation's problems. When a combination of repressive policies and ineffective administration led to the outbreak of guerrilla resistance in Cuba in 1898, the United States seized the opportunity to wage war with Spain over its possessions. The Spanish-American War resulted in the loss of Cuba and the cession of the Philippines, Puerto Rico, and Guam to the United States. By the end of the century intellectuals known as the Generation of 1898 were engaged in reassessing Spain's culture and turned increasingly to mystical nationalism in their search for national purpose.

Belgium, the Netherlands, Denmark, Sweden, and Norway followed a more stable pattern. All were constitutional monarchies that by 1914 had introduced universal male suffrage. Belgium was the most industrialized nation on the Continent, but the other states underwent rapid economic development that enlarged the middle class.

By 1900 Britain, France, Italy, and Germany represented the range of liberal experience in the European political order. Almost without exception, other nations were variants on the liberal theme. The pace of social and political change differed, depending on the strength of liberalism and the ability of elites to maintain their authority against the emerging political challenge of the working class. As widening suffrage laws involved larger numbers in political life and as governments assumed a greater responsibility for social welfare, the state also claimed more loyalty from its citizens.

The Rise of Feminism

In 1879 the Norwegian dramatist Henrik Ibsen (1828–1906) published a play, titled *A Doll's House,* that exposed the frustration of a wife who felt trapped in what appeared to be a "perfect" marriage. The play ends with Nora, the wife, walking out of her husband's house and slamming the door. Nora became a symbol of female independence for women who sought to escape patriarchy and the middle-class family.

Modern feminism has its roots in the social transformations caused by industrialization as well as in the rebellion against the constraints imposed on women by the ideology of bourgeois respectability. The gulf separating lower-class from middle-class women widened, and not simply because of differences in income and status. Prosperity increased the leisure of middle-class females, who were relieved of household tasks by servants and labor-saving devices. Yet many bourgeois women resented their removal from the workplace, their inferior education, and their confinement in the home.

Social Activism and Women's Rights

To escape their constricted lives, bourgeois women sought outlets in such activities as philanthropy, church work, and temperance drives. British and American women were zealous proponents of abolitionism, although they were forced to take second place to males in abolitionist groups. In the second half of the nineteenth century they did volunteer duty in workhouses, hospitals, and urban tenements, thereby opening up new professions for women in nursing and teaching. After Jane Addams (1860–1935) had established Hull House, Chicago's famous social welfare center, and Beatrice Potter Webb (1858–1943) had disguised herself as an unemployed worker in order to investigate poverty in London's slums, social work also gave women employment opportunities.

Women could not help but be struck by the bitter irony of their efforts to combat racial and industrial slavery while they themselves remained oppressed, and many turned from social activism to feminist militancy in an effort to secure political equality. The beginnings of the modern women's liberation movement can be traced to the world antislavery convention that met in London in 1840, where Elizabeth Cady Stanton (1815–1902) and other women delegates were forced to sit in a curtained galley, separate from the men. In July 1848, Stanton organized a women's rights convention in Seneca Falls, New York, which issued an 18-point "declaration of sentiments" demanding the vote, property and divorce rights, and equal employment opportunities.

In Europe feminists found support in the British reformer John Stuart Mill (1806–1873). Mill was a disciple of the philosopher Jeremy Bentham, who had argued that the best government was one that gave its citizens access to the greatest pleasure and the least pain. In 1859 Mill published *On Liberty,* which posited that society should permit every individual the fullest degree of liberty consistent with the freedom of others. Government, argued Mill, may restrict freedom only to protect society. Conversely, Mill's democratic sentiments led him to urge government action to eliminate poverty, the exploitation of child labor and economic injustice, and the repression of women.

During the debate over the Reform Act of 1867, Mill, a member of the House of Commons, introduced an amendment to give women the vote. Though defeated 194 to 73, the minority vote was surprisingly large. With contributions from his wife, Harriet Taylor (1807–1859), Mill incorporated the women's rights issue into his theory of liberty in a ground-breaking essay, *The Subjection of Women* (1869). The principle of utility, said Mill, demanded that society eliminate inequality and prejudice, which had prevented women from bringing their talents to bear on public issues. Mill had been arrested in his youth for advocating birth control methods and was convinced that women were the victims of sexual domination. His essay pointed out that men had convinced women of their own inferiority. Later the social scientist Lester Ward (1841–1913) extended Mill's arguments by asserting in *Dynamic Sociology* (1883) a theory of the natural superiority of women.

The Suffrage Struggle

The women's movement spread throughout Europe in the nineteenth century. Often divided over tactics and goals, feminist leaders nevertheless constituted a kind of women's international as they fought against male privilege, government and church policy, and tradition. In 1868 British women founded the National Society for Women's Suffrage. The following year Susan B. Anthony (1820–1906) and Elizabeth Stanton established the National Woman Suffrage Association, which merged with other groups in 1890 to form the National American Woman Suffrage Association. By the 1870s unmarried propertied women had received the municipal franchise in Britain, Sweden, and Finland, and American women had gained the suffrage in a few states.

On the European continent, especially where the Catholic church was strong, the women's movement generally incorporated the suffrage into broader campaigns. In France two generations of feminist activism had been repressed after the 1848 revolutions, but the women's rights struggle revived during the Third Republic under the leadership of Hubertine Auclert, who demanded the vote on the principle of "perfect equality of the sexes before the law and before customs and morality."[1] Anna Maria Mozzoni translated Mill's essay on women into Italian and published a women's journal, while Luise Otto-Peters, who had fought for women's rights during the 1848 revolutions, cofounded the General Association of German Women in 1865. Efforts to forge unity among suffrage forces climaxed in 1902 in the International Alliance of Women, which held congresses in Berlin, Copenhagen, Amsterdam, London, Stockholm, and Budapest.

Emmeline Pankhurst and the Politics of Confrontation

The suffrage movement captured public attention in Britain after the turn of the century under the fiery leadership of Emmeline Pankhurst (1858–1928), a woman of immense determination and eloquence. The daughter of a Manchester textile printer, Pankhurst was educated in Paris and was influenced by French feminists. In 1879 she married Richard Pankhurst, an advocate of women's suffrage with whom she promoted the Women's Property Act.

After working with suffrage groups in Manchester, Pankhurst became convinced that women had to use confrontational, and at times violent, tactics to publicize their cause and win the right to vote. In 1886 she participated in a strike of female workers in a London match factory, an experience that taught her the advantages of direct action. Three years later she helped establish, in affiliation with the Liberal party, the Women's Franchise League. Because it met with resistance from the Liberals, she subsequently switched her political allegiance to the Independent Labour party. When the death of her husband in 1898 left her alone to raise a son and three daughters, she took a civil service job but was fired because of her suffrage work.

Inspired by her daughter Christabel, also an ardent feminist, in 1903 Pankhurst created the Women's Social and Political Union (WSPU), a London-based suffrage organization without party affiliation. The WSPU opposed candidates for elected office who did not support the women's vote. Together with her daughters Sylvia and Christabel, Pankhurst led an army of women—called "suffragettes" to distinguish them from the "suffragists" of the moderate National Union of Women's Suffrage Societies—in public meetings, marches to Buckingham Palace, and demonstrations before Parliament.

In 1911, after the government's continued refusal to adopt a prosuffrage platform, Pankhurst took control of the WSPU and, with Christabel, directed a window-smashing campaign along fashionable shopping streets, for which Emmeline received a nine-month prison term. Nevertheless, the WSPU's tactics grew more violent. One woman chained herself to the railings at 10 Downing Street, the residence of the prime minister, while shouting "Votes for women!" Some resorted to bombings and arson; one woman smashed the Rokeby Venus, a painting in the National Museum, and another tried to

Emmeline Pankhurst, whose radical strategies emboldened British suffragettes, was repeatedly arrested.

strike the Tory Winston Churchill with a horse whip. Following an attempt to bomb the house of Lloyd George, Pankhurst was sentenced to three years' penal servitude. During repeated jail terms, she and her daughters went on hunger strikes to dramatize their cause and had to be force-fed. In 1913 Emily Davison was killed after flinging herself in front of King George V's horse at the Epsom Derby. As the American suffrage leader Carrie Chapman Catt observed, the Pankhursts were "in a state of insurrection" against the British government.[2]

The efforts of Emmeline Pankhurst and other courageous women contributed to the development of feminist consciousness as well as to the vote issue, but the women's movement achieved only limited success before World War I. Pankhurst threw herself into war work after 1914 despite fading health. Her lifelong struggle for women's suffrage bore fruit in 1918 with the passage of the Representation of the People Act.

Science and the Doctrine of Progress

The worship of science and the belief in progress that marked European attitudes in this period weakened the eighteenth-century emphasis on the efficacy of human will. In broad terms, the Enlightenment had taught that people could shape their own destinies and mold society to their needs. Nineteenth-century developments, by contrast, reinforced the view that the scientific method could merely reveal the laws governing the physical and social environment. The process of discovery offered the promise of unending material improvement, but the laws of science could not be changed or suspended. Hence the optimism of the eighteenth century was replaced by a vision of perfectability that portrayed humans as part of a larger process of change.

The Darwinian Revolution

Scientific discoveries and technological advances had made possible Europe's Industrial Revolution and the improvement in its standard of living. The growth of literacy encouraged the popularity of science and the spread of its methods to other disciplines. The French philosopher Auguste Comte (1798–1857) was the first major figure to apply scientific principles to the study of society. In his *System of Positive Philosophy,* worked out in the 1830s, Comte argued that laws of social behavior paralleled the physical laws governing the universe and that both were discoverable through the study of specific data. Observation of individual phenomena, he believed, would demonstrate the similarities between them, which would in turn reveal natural laws. Comte described human thought as having moved from an early "theological" stage in which it was believed that the world operated by divine action to a "metaphysical" phase that sought to understand nature through abstract principles. Comte saw the thought of his own day as the final, "positive"

The Suffragette Revolt

The radical suffragettes of the pre–World War I period declared a feminist war against middle-class society in their efforts to win the vote for women. In this speech, made in London in 1912 after having been released from prison, the British suffragette Emmeline Pankhurst delivered her challenge in no uncertain terms.

Ladies and gentlemen, the only recklessness the militant suffragists have shown about human life has been about their own lives and not about the lives of others, and I say here and now that it never has been and never will be the policy of the Women's Social and Political Union recklessly to endanger human life. We leave that to the enemy. We leave that to the men in their warfare. It is not the method of women. . . . There is something that governments care far more for than human life, and that is the security of property, and so it is through property that we shall strike the enemy. From henceforward the women who agree with me will say, "We disregard your laws, gentlemen, we set the liberty and the dignity and the welfare of women above all such considerations, and we shall continue this war as we have done in the past; and what sacrifice of property, or what injury to property accrues will not be our fault. It will be the fault of that government who admits the justice of our demands, but refuses to concede them. . . ."

Be militant each in your own way. Those of you who can express your militancy by going to the House of Commons and refusing to leave without satisfaction, as we did in the early days— do so. . . . Those of you who can express your militancy by joining us in our anti-government by-election policy—do so. Those of you who can break windows—break them. Those of you who can still further attack the secret idol of property, so as to make the government realize that property is as greatly endangered by women's suffrage as it was by the Chartists of old—do so.

And my last word is to the government: I incite this meeting to rebellion! . . . Take me, if you dare, but if you dare I tell you this, . . . you will not keep me in prison.

Source: E. Pankhurst, *My Own Story* (New York: Hearst's International Library, 1914), pp. 264–266.

stage, when observable data rather than metaphysical forces explained human behavior and the physical world.

Although Comte rejected theories of evolution, his work dovetailed with that of a number of natural scientists. Jean-Baptiste Lamarck (1744–1829) had tried to show that plants and animals, including humans, had evolved by adjusting to the environment. Sir Charles Lyell (1797–1875), in his *Principles of Geology* (1830–1833), explained the formation of the earth as the result of a slow process of geologic evolution rather than a sudden cataclysm or act of creation. Lamarck and Lyell relied on the painstaking accumulation of evidence in the development of their theories.

These theories formed the intellectual climate in which the British naturalist Charles Darwin (1809–1882) formulated his theses about evolution. His famous book

On the Origin of Species by Means of Natural Selection (1859) was not the first work to posit a theory of evolution, but it explained in unprecedented detail how the evolutionary process worked. Darwin's principle of natural selection involved a number of points. Because every species produced more individual life forms than could survive, a struggle for existence took place within and between species. Variations, he asserted, gave some organisms advantages in the competition, so that only the fittest survived. But changing environmental conditions demanded alterations in the definition of fitness. In *The Descent of Man* (1871), Darwin argued that, like other forms of life, humans also evolved—from an ancestral type common to anthropoid apes—by the same principle of natural selection.

Darwin's theory was startling because it challenged both the deistic notion that the universe had been designed by God and the biblical account of creation. By claiming that the survival and development of organisms was a mechanistic process, Darwin rejected the notion of divine purpose in nature. His vision of a constantly changing world in which humans were simply another form of animal life seemed to support the spirit of materialism.

Science and Society

Darwin had been influenced by social theorists, including Thomas Malthus, whose *Essay on the Principle of Population* (1798) had predicted that population growth would outstrip food supplies. Social scientists, in turn, used Darwin to support their arguments, but in doing so they took evolution far beyond Darwin's intent. The British political philosopher Walter Bagehot (1826–1877) applied natural selection to politics, asserting the superiority of nations that conquered others. His fellow countryman Herbert Spencer (1820–1903) made the classic case for what, ironically, came to be called Social Darwinism—Darwin himself never endorsed this doctrine. In his *Synthetic Philosophy,* Spencer contended that the economic competition of individuals advanced social progress by eliminating the weak. His arguments reflected an extreme form of laissez-faire liberalism that opposed state assistance to the poor and similar social legislation. By the end of the nineteenth century the Darwinian concept of the survival of the fittest had even been used to justify imperial conquest and racism.

Culture and Industrial Society

European artists and writers were profoundly affected by the new culture of science and industry. The contradictions of industrial civilization gave rise to two opposing trends in the arts during the second half of the nineteenth century. The idealistic fervor of Romantic painting was replaced by an "academic" style descended from the official canons of seventeenth- and eighteenth-century painting that deemphasized the individual's quest for meaning through an encounter with nature. Academic portraits conveyed the values of the middle class, while bucolic landscapes presented orderly treatments of nature.

Other artists responded to industrial society with a powerful "realism" that rejected an idealized version of industrial civilization. The call for a new artistic conscience was sounded by critics such as John Ruskin (1819–1900), who, like many of the realists, was influenced by socialist critiques of industrial capitalism and sought to make painting and literature responsive to the problems of the age.

Painting: New Visions of Reality

Scientific developments affected culture profoundly. Some artists saw the development of the camera in the early decades of the century (the first photograph dates from around 1826) as a threat to painting, especially if they defined art as the reproduction of observable experience. But artists such as the Frenchmen Édouard Manet (1832–1883) and Edgar Degas (1834–1917) and the American Thomas Eakins (1844–1916) used photography to study form and motion. Moreover, the realist painters found inspiration in daily life and approached their subject matter with sensitivity.

The British artist J. M. W. Turner (1775–1851) had taken an important step in this direction with his controversial *Rail, Steam and Speed: The Great Western Railway* (1845). Although Turner claimed that the scene represented a literal depiction of a train in a snowstorm, the public rejected his energy-charged treatment of a locomotive as subject matter unsuited to true art. The French painters Gustave Courbet (1819–1877) and Honoré Daumier (1808–1879) were the major proponents of realism. Courbet believed that the search for truth required the artist to reveal the ugly as well as the beautiful. Influenced by socialism, Courbet made the working class the focus of his work because modern life relied on its labor. He was a realist not in the sense that he rendered the details of every object but in his portrayal of the harsh reality of workers and peasants without idealizing his subjects. *The Stonebreakers* (1849) depicts two workers whose hidden faces betray the anonymity of grueling labor. Daumier, who had been a cartoonist for a radical newspaper, executed watercolors and drawings of common people that deliberately avoided a romanticized vision of poverty.

In the last third of the nineteenth century some artists moved beyond realism under the impact of scientific theories. From recent discoveries in optics, artists learned that air and light are waves of color joined by the human eye into patterns. Their use of short, broken brushstrokes and specific hues captured the way in which changing sunlight affected objects. In doing so, these artists rejected a frozen rendering of reality in favor of a view that was at once scientific and subjective.

The painting by the Frenchman Claude Monet (1840–1926) titled *Impression: Sunrise* (1873) inspired a hostile critic to dub the new style "Impressionism."

Monet's fellow Impressionists, including Camille Pissarro (1830–1903), Auguste Renoir (1841–1919), Henri de Toulouse-Lautrec (1864–1901), and Edgar Degas, were similarly committed to these concerns. The Impressionists depicted subject matter that varied from Monet's early railroad station, *Gare Saint-Lazare, Paris,* to the chorus girls of Toulouse-Lautrec's posters and Manet's *Bar at the Folies-Bergères.* While their vision still concerned how the world appeared to the human eye, it was sharply different from that of realists such as Courbet and Daumier.

The Literary Response

If poetry was the major literary mode of the Romantic era, the novel best suited the industrial age. By midcentury an older generation of writers such as Honoré de Balzac (1799–1850) and Victor Hugo (1802–1885) was already making a transition from Romanticism to realism to express injustice. Whereas Hugo's *Les Misérables* (1862) combined political radicalism with emotionally evocative social criticism, Balzac and Gustave Flaubert (1821–1880) shaped a consciously un-Romantic form. Balzac launched the realist movement with a series of novels collectively titled *The Human Comedy,* and Flaubert's *Madame Bovary* (1857), which was prosecuted for its candid treatment of adultery, revealed the sordid underside of bourgeois life. One of the most powerful works in this genre was Émile Zola's *Germinal* (1885), a portrayal of socialist hopes among French miners. Flaubert and Zola led the way from realism to naturalism by applying the principles of scientific observation to the human condition. Influenced by Darwin, the naturalists demonstrated the effect of social environment on personality.

The works of two Russian writers, Ivan Turgenev (1818–1883) and Leo Tolstoy (1828–1910), and of the Norwegian dramatist Henrik Ibsen revealed the universal character of realism. Flaubert had a pronounced influence on Turgenev. Turgenev's first important work, *A Sportsman's Sketches* (1852), was a strenuous protest against serfdom. His novel *Fathers and Sons* (1862) introduced the term *nihilism* to express his protagonist's rejection of all forms of authority. In the tragic story of *Anna Karenina* (1877), Tolstoy depicted a character similar to Flaubert's Madame Bovary. His masterpiece, the monumental novel *War and Peace* (1869), set against the background of the Napoleonic wars, reflected his sense of Russian nationalism as well as the detailed analysis of characters and events many realists employed.

Ibsen's plays explored the conflict between individual freedom and the bourgeois, materialist culture of the late nineteenth century. Whereas Flaubert and Tolstoy examined the theme of adultery, *A Doll's House* (1879) portrayed a wife who suddenly realizes that she has been living for years with a distant husband who considers her simply a precious possession. Like Mill, Ibsen believed in the obligation of society to further individual freedom, but he was disillusioned by political theories. In *An Enemy of the People* (1882), Ibsen lashed out at the cupidity of the majority who, because their income is endangered, refuse to accept a physician's discovery that the mineral waters of their town are polluted.

The greatest popular success of the realist genre was achieved by the British writer Charles Dickens (1812–1870). His novels were widely read through serialization in newspapers and magazines. His grotesque characters and often improbable plots took Dickens beyond the realm of conventional realism. Yet his novels vividly portrayed the social problems of his times, and his most compelling plots were set in the cities, where social classes played out the contradictions of industrialism. The protagonist of *Oliver Twist* (1838) is an orphan brought up in a workhouse for pauper children, where he is mistreated by a cruel master. Dickens reveals how poverty leads to injustice, crime, and tragedy. In *Hard Times* (1854), Dickens deals with the human consequences of aggressive economic individualism in an industrial city called Coketown, where a selfish businessman obsessed with sales and money destroys the lives of his children.

From industrial Britain to agrarian Russia, nineteenth-century novels and plays came to grips with the harsh realities of industrial capitalism and bourgeois society, adding a powerful voice to the protests of the working class.

Socialism and the Labor Movement

Working-class militancy in Europe struggled against the misery and alienation of industrial capitalism. The sansculottes of the French Revolution and the Luddites of eighteenth-century Britain, like the utopian idealists Robert Owen and Saint-Simon and the British Chartists and the revolutionaries of 1848, had vented worker rebellion against exploitation. As liberalism triumphed after 1850, some of the harsher aspects of industrialism were blunted by reforms. Nevertheless, laborers devised strategies aimed at improving working conditions, and some advocated the elimination of capitalism itself.

In the second half of the nineteenth century the working-class movement focused around three traditions: trade unionism, anarchism, and the scientific socialism derived from the principles of Karl Marx and Friedrich Engels. Unionism accepted industrial capitalism as a permanent feature of modern life but sought to mitigate its impact by improving wages, benefits, and working conditions. Unionists gradually won a legal basis for organizing and the right to strike. Anarchism and Marxist socialism, by contrast, rejected the permanence of capitalism and saw private property as a source of repression and inequality that could not be reformed. Although Marx himself in later life advocated a political path to socialism, many of his followers continued to believe in violent revolution. Anarchists and Marxists were divided in their attitudes toward the state. Anarchists, rejecting all forms of authority, sought to destroy government, while Marxists wanted to seize control of the state and install the proletariat in power, leaving the destruction of the state for a later stage. These divisions weakened the working-class movement.

Socialism, Anarchism, and the Paris Commune

Initially, socialists, anarchists, and other radicals collaborated in the creation of the International Workingmen's Association, founded in London in 1864. The First International, as it was generally known, tried to coordinate labor activities throughout Europe and provide a vehicle for socialist debate. Marx, who was its dominant figure, clashed with Mikhail Bakunin (1814–1876), the exiled Russian anarchist, and eventually drove nonsocialists from the International.

Marx's triumph came a year after the Paris Commune, a pivotal event in international socialism. Marx contributed to the legend surrounding the Commune with a pamphlet titled *The Civil War in France,* in which he argued that it represented the first clear-cut case of proletarian violence. A few international socialists and anarchists had been involved in the Commune uprising, along with large numbers of radicals and ordinary citizens who had no clear program, but the Commune was by no means a Marxist revolution. Yet socialists everywhere came to regard it as a symbol both of the class struggle and of the bourgeois determination to crush worker agitation. Throughout Europe liberal governments reacted to the Commune by imposing restrictions on the working-class movement.

The First International dissolved in 1872 in the wake of the Commune and the socialist-anarchist split. For two decades thereafter, militant action remained largely in the hands of the anarchists, who increasingly adopted terrorist tactics, which they termed "propaganda of the deed." Anarchists tried twice in the 1870s to assassinate Kaiser William I and succeeded in killing a number of statesmen and heads of state, including Tsar Alexander II of Russia (1881), the French president François Sadi-Carnot (1894), the Spanish prime minister Antonio Cánovas del Castillo (1897), Empress Elizabeth of Austria-Hungary (1898), King Umberto I of Italy (1900), and the American president William McKinley (1901). Despite these acts of terrorism, many anarchist leaders repudiated violence. Prince Peter Kropotkin (1842–1921), a Russian noble exiled in London, argued for peaceful cooperation among workers, and the Italian anarchist Errico Malatesta (1853–1932) stressed the humanitarian nature of anarchism and saw himself as an antiauthoritarian socialist.

Trade Unions and the Labor Movement

Although Marx had predicted the growth and concentration of capitalist wealth, the condition of the working class itself did not worsen. Indeed, the general prosperity that began in the 1850s improved the standard of living of most workers, moderating the attitudes of labor and slowing the growth of unions. By the latter part of the century, however, craft unions, representing skilled trades, were again organizing. In the 1870s the Liberal ministry of Gladstone recognized such unions and legalized the strike. The London dockworkers' strike of 1889 provided the impetus for the organization of unskilled laborers and gave rise to industrial unions representing both skilled and unskilled workers throughout an entire industry. By the end of the century Britain's 2 million union members represented the largest and most successful union experience in Europe.

Beyond Britain, modern unions developed largely during the two decades of economic depression that stretched into the 1890s, largely under the banner of socialism. Napoleon III had permitted unions in 1864 in France, but they were suppressed after the Commune, and only in 1884 did the Third Republic grant them legal status. In Germany, Bismarck's antisocialist campaign retarded their formation until the Imperial Industrial Code of 1891 permitted the right to strike. By 1900 organized labor counted some 850,000 members in Germany and 250,000 in France; in Italy and Austria-Hungary unions were slower to develop.

In the 1890s unionism on the Continent took a more radical turn under the influence of syndicalist leaders. The Frenchman Georges Sorel (1847–1922) was the major proponent of syndicalism (from the French word *syndicat,* "trade union"). He argued that

The Spirit of Revolution

Peter Kropotkin (1842–1921), a Russian noble by birth, was one of Europe's leading anarchists. A follower of Bakunin, Kropotkin had been arrested in Russia and France before settling in London, where he lived in exile for thirty years. In "The Spirit of Revolt" (1880), he explained how in times of social crisis revolutionary ideas can be translated into action through individual acts of courage.

There are periods in the life of human society when revolution becomes an imperative necessity, when it proclaims itself as inevitable. New ideas germinate everywhere, seeking to force their way into the light, to find application in life. . . . One arrives at the conviction that the revolution was indeed inevitable, and that there was no other way out than by the road of insurrection. . . .

But between this pacific arguing and insurrection or revolt, there is a wide abyss—that abyss which, for the greatest part of humanity, lies between reasoning and action, thought and will—the urge to act. How has this abyss been bridged? How is it that men who only yesterday were complaining quietly of their lot . . . a few days later were capable of seizing their scythes and their iron-shod pikes and attacking in his castle the lord who only yesterday was so formidable? . . . How was it that *words*, so often spoken and lost in the air like the empty chiming of bells, were changed into *actions?*

The answer is easy.

Action, the continuous action, ceaselessly renewed, of minorities brings about this transformation. Courage, devotion, the spirit of sacrifice, are as contagious as cowardice, submission, and panic. . . .

When a revolutionary situation arises in a country, before the spirit of revolt is sufficiently awakened in the masses to express itself in violent demonstrations in the streets or by rebellions and uprisings, it is through *action* that minorities succeed in awakening that feeling of independence and that spirit of audacity without which no revolution can come to a head. . . .

By actions which compel general attention, the new idea seeps into people's minds and wins converts. One such act may, in a few days, make more propaganda than thousands of pamphlets.

Source: Walter Laqueur and Yonah Alexander, eds., *The Terrorism Reader: A Historical Anthology,* rev. ed. (New York: Meridian, 1987), pp. 90–95.

unions rather than political parties were the logical institutions through which working-class leaders could take power from the middle class and reorganize society. In 1895 syndicalists formed the General Confederation of Labor, a union umbrella organization that undertook strike action and rivaled the socialists for leadership of the labor movement. Syndicalism spread to Italy, where leaders attempted an unsuccessful general strike in 1904. After the 1905 Russian revolution, Rosa Luxemburg (1870–1919), a Polish Jew active in politics, published a pamphlet titled *The Mass Strike, the Party, and the Trade Unions* (1906) in which she defined the strike as a political weapon. In *Reflections on Violence* (1908), Sorel proclaimed the general strike as the only means of achieving socialism. The general strike, he argued, would provoke violent state repression, which would incite the workers to revolt.

Socialist Parties: Between Reform and Revolution

Socialist parties grew rapidly in the years after the Paris Commune. Despite Bismarck's efforts to crush it, German socialism flowered. In 1869 two Marxists, August Bebel (1840–1913) and Wilhelm Liebknecht (1826–

Women were active in organizing labor unions and in strike activity. Here is a women's labor parade held in New York City in 1913.

1900), founded the Social Democratic Labor party, which elected several deputies to parliament. In 1875 the Social Democrats joined forces with the more moderate followers of Ferdinand Lassalle (1825–1864) to issue the so-called Gotha program, combining Marxist theory with pragmatic Lassallian reforms. Although Marx denounced the mixture of revolutionary doctrine and reformist objectives, the resulting German Social Democratic party (SPD) became the strongest socialist party in Europe.

The German example inspired socialists elsewhere. In Belgium socialists founded a party in 1879. A non-Marxist Italian Worker party developed in 1882, although the socialists did not develop an organization of their own until ten years later. Meanwhile, Russian exiles in Switzerland formed the Russian Social Democrats in 1883. In both Italy and Russia police repression against socialists and anarchists was particularly severe and forced many radicals to spend years in exile. In France doctrinal disputes led to the creation of separate parties that did not unite until 1905.

British socialism followed the same moderate path as its unions. In 1884 a group of middle-class intellectuals founded the Fabian Society.* Led by the Irish play-wright George Bernard Shaw (1856–1950), Sydney Webb (1859–1947), Beatrice Webb, and the novelist H. G. Wells (1866–1946), the Fabians rejected violent revolution. In 1900 socialists formed the Labour party.

As socialist parties gathered strength throughout Europe, their leaders attempted to reawaken international solidarity with the creation in 1889 of the Second International. It served largely to organize congresses, coordinate May Day celebrations in honor of the working class, and provide a forum for consultation. National parties continued to provide the impetus for the socialist movement.

In the two decades before World War I the international working-class movement was dominated by the opposing models offered by German and French socialists. In 1899 Éduard Bernstein (1850–1932) published a theoretical work titled *Evolutionary Socialism*. Bernstein, who had been influenced by the British Fabians, was both a revisionist and a reformist. His revisionism derived from his conviction that Marxist doctrine had to evolve as social, political, and economic conditions changed. In the context of a parliamentary system and an expanding industrial economy such as that in Germany, Bernstein challenged Marx's beliefs in the coming crisis of capitalism, the increasing polarization of classes, and the certainty of working-class revolution. This position led him to abandon revolutionary tactics in favor of achieving concrete gains for workers through parliamentary

---

*Named after the ancient Roman general Quintus Fabius Maximus, who avoided pitched battles with the Carthaginians in favor of harassing operations.

reform and collaboration with non-Marxist parties. In effect, Bernstein's arguments reflected German socialist policy since the 1870s, although his reformism was bitterly denounced by orthodox Marxists. Indeed, the reformist-revolutionary controversy split socialist parties everywhere.

Bernstein's counterpart in France was Jean Jaurès (1859–1914), a fiery speaker and humanist scholar who urged socialist collaboration with middle-class governments to secure reforms. Under pressure from the International, which condemned revisionist "opportunism" and urged French socialists to unite into one party, Jaurès reverted to orthodoxy.

The development of socialist parties gave added impetus to the women's movement. Although women did not often rise to top positions in labor organizations, they found more acceptance from male comrades than in other parties. Socialists eschewed civil marriage as a bourgeois institution and practiced free love in radical circles. Most socialist parties eventually advocated universal suffrage, divorce laws, and birth control.

The SPD took the lead in organizing women. After the party accepted their right to work, a law forced the creation of separate groups for women. In 1878 Bebel issued his *Women in the Past, Present, and Future*, the first sustained study of the women's question from a socialist perspective. Six years later Engels published *The Origins of the Family, Private Property, and the State*. The core of their arguments remained the idea that the sup-

Socialist Women

The Russian-born Angelica Balabanoff (1869–1965) was one of the most important figures in the pre-war socialist movement. After leaving her wealthy family, she studied and worked in the movement throughout Europe, serving on the executive committee of the Second International for many years. Here she describes her early collaboration with Maria Giudice, an Italian socialist, while both were in St. Gall, Switzerland, in 1904.

One day . . . I received word that a young Italian teacher, an ardent propagandist for Socialism, was coming to St. Gall. She had only recently fled from Italy to escape imprisonment for an article she had written. I wrote the comrades at St. Gall that Maria was to have the use of my room. When I returned I found . . . Maria was experiencing her first pregnancy. She eventually became the mother of seven children and the object of considerable gossip. . . . Several years later, in Italy, the editor of a clerical journal made slurring remarks about Maria's morals. Meeting him in the marketplace one day, Maria, in a loud voice that all round her could hear, inquired of a vegetable woman if this was the man who had gossiped about her. The startled woman . . . nodded her head affirmatively. Maria then stepped in the path of the astonished editor and, before the crowd which had already assembled, gave him a resounding slap in the face. There was little more talk of Maria and her children after that. . . .

At the time Maria lived with me in St. Gall, the Italian Socialists had no special propaganda paper for women. We conceived the notion that one should be started. . . . Both Maria and I were hostile to any form of "feminism." To us the fight for the emancipation of women was only a single aspect of the struggle for the emancipation of humanity. It was because we wanted women, particularly workingwomen, to understand this, to learn that they had to fight not *against men* but *with* them against the common enemy, capitalist society, that we felt the need of this paper. Moving to Lugano, Maria and I founded *Su, Compagne! (Arise, Comrades!)*. It was an almost instant success. . . .

Source: A. Balabanoff, *My Life as a Rebel* (New York: Harper, 1938), pp. 34–35.

pression of women evolved as the concept of private property developed.

The party's major theoretician of Marxist feminism was Clara Zetkin (1857–1933), who pioneered female militancy within the SPD as well as in the Second International and edited the magazine *Equality*. Zetkin's theories started out from Marx and Engels' position concerning the nature of the middle-class family. She argued that housework and child rearing represented exploitation in the form of unpaid labor. Bourgeois morality had made women little more than property controlled by men. Hence women's liberation was impossible in isolation but had to take place as part of the broader socialist struggle against capitalism. Because Zetkin believed that female labor was a precondition for the liberation of women from sexual slavery, she urged them to participate in the workforce as well as in socialist politics. The Gotha program of 1875 had advocated universal suffrage but refused to support more radical feminist views. Zetkin and other women eventually forced the SPD to adopt a broader feminist position.

Together with Rosa Luxemburg, Zetkin opposed revisionism, a position that separated them from other women in the SPD as well as from nonsocialists because they argued the incompatibility of the socialist women's movement and bourgeois feminism. Nonsocialist feminists, they asserted, sanctioned capitalism, a system of exploitation that repressed men and women alike. The hostility of the revisionist leadership drove Zetkin and Luxemburg further to the left, and on the eve of World War I they were among the extremists who formed the German Communist party.

SUMMARY

*T*he rise of feminism and socialism after 1870, like the work of realist painters and novelists, revealed the deep contradictions that beset the liberal order in Europe. The political order moved toward democracy, while advances in education, health, and communications contributed to the modernization of a society in which workers and peasants were more fully integrated into national life. Yet industrial capitalism, which had produced remarkable prosperity, also engendered economic and cultural oppression in the organization of work, gender and family relations, and the accumulation of unprecedented wealth by a new business-financial elite. Nor was the prosperity of the period evenly distributed. Workers' wages rose except during the Long Depression, but poverty was still widespread. Illiteracy, infant mortality, and illness remained higher among the workers than in the middle classes.

Constitutional monarchies and parliamentary regimes based on universal male suffrage had replaced absolute monarchy almost everywhere in Europe by the opening of the twentieth century. Nevertheless, in some Western states liberal governments proved no less vigorous than the old autocrats in preserving a stable social order and protecting the interests of industrial capitalism and patriarchy. While Europe remained generally at peace for almost half a century, the international order spawned by liberalism also produced militarism and new forms of nationalism, racism, and imperialism.

NOTES

1. C. G. Moses, *French Feminism in the Nineteenth Century* (Albany: State University of New York Press, 1984), p. 213.
2. E. F. Hurwitz, "The International Sisterhood," in *Becoming Visible: Women in European History,* ed. R. Bridenthal and C. Koonz (Boston: Houghton Mifflin, 1977), p. 337.

SUGGESTIONS FOR FURTHER READING

Anderson, B. and Zinsser, J.P. *A History of Their Own: Women in Europe from Prehistory to the Present.* vol. 2. New York: Harper & Row, 1989.

Bridenthal, R., and Koonz, C., eds. *Becoming Visible: Women in European History.* Boston: Houghton Mifflin, 1977.

Burrow, J. W. *Evolution and Society: A Study in Victorian Social Theory.* Cambridge: Cambridge University Press, 1966.

Cahm, C. *Peter Kropotkin and the Rise of Revolutionary Anarchism.* New York: Cambridge University Press, 1989.

Clark, M. *Modern Italy, 1871–1982.* London: Longman, 1984.

Friedberg, A. L. *The Weary Titan: Britain and the Experience of Relative Decline, 1895–1905.* Princeton, N.J.: Princeton University Press, 1989.

Girouard, M. *Cities and People: A Social and Architectural History.* New Haven, Conn.: Yale University Press, 1985.

Harrison, F. *The Dark Angel: Aspects of Victorian Sexuality.* New York: Sheldon Press, 1977.

Hayes, C. J. H. *The Generation of Materialism, 1871–1900.* New York: Harper, 1941.

Joll, J. *The Second International, 1889–1914.* New York: Harper & Row, 1966.

Joyce, P. *Visions of the People: Industrial England and the Question of Class, c. 1848–1914.* New York: Cambridge University Press, 1991.

Landes, D. *The Unbound Prometheus: Technological Change and Industrial Development in Western Europe from 1750 to the Present.* Cambridge: Cambridge University Press, 1969.

Linder, M. *European Labor Aristocracies: Trade Unionism, the Hierarchy of Skill, and the Stratification of the Manual Working Class.* Frankfurt: Campus, 1985.

Marsden, G., ed. *Victorian Values: Personalities and Perspectives in 19th-Century Society.* New York: Longman, 1990.

Milward, A. S., and Saul, S. B. *The Development of the Economies of Continental Europe, 1850–1914.* Cambridge, Mass.: Harvard University Press, 1977.

Mosse, G. L. *The Culture of Western Europe.* Chicago: Rand McNally, 1961.

Nettl, J. *Rosa Luxemburg*. New York: Schocken Books, 1989.

Pflanze, O. *Bismarck and the Development of Germany*, vols. 2–3. Princeton, N.J.: Princeton University Press, 1990.

Pugh, M. *The Making of British Politics, 1867–1939*. Oxford: Blackwell, 1982.

Rewald, J. *The History of Impressionism*. New York: Museum of Modern Art, 1961.

———. *Post-Impressionism*. New York: Museum of Modern Art, 1978.

Sheehan, J. J. *German Liberalism in the Nineteenth Century*. Chicago: University of Chicago Press, 1978.

Stearns, P. N. *European Society in Upheaval: Social History Since 1800*. New York: Macmillan, 1967.

Thoennessen, W. *The Emancipation of Women: The Rise and Decline of the Women's Movement in German Social Democracy, 1863–1933*. London: Pluto Press, 1973.

Thompson, D. *Democracy in France Since 1870*. New York: Oxford University Press, 1969.

Vicinus, M., ed. *Suffer and Be Still: Women in the Victorian Age*. Bloomington: Indiana University Press, 1972.

Vincent, J. *Disraeli*. New York: Oxford University Press, 1990.

GLOBAL ESSAY

Writing and Communication (II)

Throughout the ancient and medieval world, literacy was relatively uncommon, but in time improved printing techniques encouraged its spread. In the Arab world and in Europe the production of books was limited by two factors: each copy of a text had to be written by hand, and the material used for manuscripts was generally either parchment, made from split sheepskins, or vellum (calfskin), both of which were expensive. These limitations were first overcome in China, where paper had been manufactured since the first century A.D. Around the eighth century the Chinese invented a system of printing using blocks of wood. The idea of binding several sheets of paper together followed shortly; the first printed book, consisting of six pages, was published in 868.

The notion of movable type originally had little appeal to the Chinese, whose script is made up of thousands of different characters. But in the eleventh century the Chinese developed movable type in wood, a technique later adopted by the Koreans, who were the first to use it on a large scale. Both the Chinese and the Koreans soon made metal type, which obviously lasted longer and made mass printing possible.

By the eighth century the Arabs had borrowed the Chinese method of manufacturing paper, but they had little interest in block printing, perhaps because the art of writing had become an important skill in itself. Toward the end of the twelfth century the Arabs introduced papermaking into Spain, from where the technique spread slowly into northern Europe; by the beginning of the fifteenth century it had reached Germany and Switzerland.

The introduction in Europe of movable type occurred much later than in China and Korea, in the mid-fifteenth century. The material used for the type was metal, since medieval craftsmen were skilled at engraving medals and coins. The first printed book, the so-called Gutenberg Bible, was published in 1455 at Mainz.

In China the production of books had generally been limited to works for the educated classes. The first major printing project was an edition of the Confucian classics in the tenth century, followed by the Buddhist scriptures, and during the Sung period books on art, literature, science, and philosophy appeared in large numbers. Literacy remained primarily an elite preserve, given the difficulty of the written language, but popular fiction began to grow, and literacy rose among the urban merchants, themselves an expanding group.

The effects of printing in Europe may have been more widespread or more immediate than in Asia, especially as

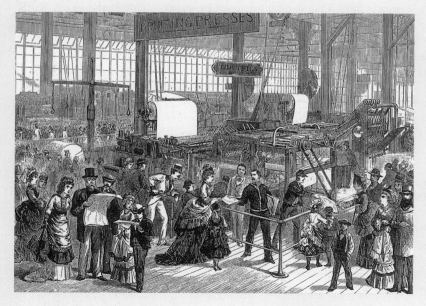

This web press, which was capable of printing on both sides of the paper, was featured at a Philadelphia exhibition in the 1870s.

universities and other schools enlarged their enrollments to educate the children of merchants and craftsmen. The demand for texts could now be met. Furthermore, the process was self-reinforcing: the more books there were, the more people learned to read. Thus the impact of printing was not merely to facilitate the circulation of ideas among educated people but also to make available on a popular level a vast range of material to which access had formerly been difficult, such as almanacs, herbals, and prophecies.

It soon became apparent that the new technology could be employed in conducting political, religious, and scholarly debate, and controversial positions were circulated quickly. Among the first masters of the medium was the Protestant Martin Luther, who published a series of printed tracts on church reform in 1520 and a German translation of the Bible (New Testament in 1522, Old Testament in 1534) that became a cornerstone of the Reformation. The Reformation introduced printed pamphlets, hymns, religious texts, and sacred pictures to much of northern Europe, calling for not only religious changes but social ones as well. Subsequently, debate in the Western world has been conducted in large measure in print, now supplemented by radio and television. Print has not been replaced for scholarly, scientific, or religious debate, and access to the media on social issues (except for talk shows) is generally limited to people who have established their positions in print. Only political debate has partly replaced print as the medium of prime communication, but even here print remains indispensable.

Between the Reformation and the French Revolution mass literacy began to develop in Europe and to spread among European colonizers elsewhere in the world. The first battleground for printed texts had been a sacred one, but pamphlets could now be distributed and books published to advocate or even galvanize social and political change, and the spread of popular literature had an enormous impact on the English, American, and French revolutions. Not only did pamphleteers advance specific causes or claim individual wrongs, they also served to make accessible at a popular level ideas that had hitherto been limited to intellectuals.

The pamphleteers of the French wars of religion at the end of the sixteenth century and the English Revolution in the mid-seventeenth argued fundamental religious and political ideas, and their works, often cheaply printed, attracted wide circulation. The London bookseller George Thomason collected nearly 30,000 books, pamphlets, broadsides, and news sheets published in England between 1640 and 1661, an astonishing output in a country of only 5 million people. The appetite for news persisted, and the seventeenth century saw the first newspapers established in Augsburg, Strasbourg, London, and Paris. The role of print expanded in the eighteenth century, making it possible for growing numbers of westerners in particular to keep abreast of public events and political issues. "Every Englishman, nowadays," said Samuel Johnson, "expects to be promptly and accurately informed upon the condition of public affairs." But not until the advent of the "penny press" in the next century were newspapers fully accessible to the masses. Such exposure required not only literacy and the availability of an extra penny to spend for a paper but also a desire to use the money to acquire the news rather than other goods.

The Enlightenment would have been unthinkable without the printing press, which enabled the philosophes to appeal over the heads of established authority for fundamental reform. Often, however, the most radical thought became available on a popular level only in times of crisis. Tom Paine crystallized revolutionary attitudes in America with a pamphlet appropriately titled *Common Sense*, and the ideas of Jean-Jacques Rousseau became crucial to the thinking of French revolutionaries when they were expressed in popular form by Sieyès in his pamphlet *What Is the Third Estate?*, published in January 1789. In China, with its far greater population, there was from the eleventh century a major increase both in popular fiction and in printed manuals and pamphlets, although, unlike their European counterparts, the latter were rarely critical of the established order.

At the same time, the growth of knowledge and its relatively easy transmission were fundamental to the sudden surge of scientific development in the West. In the eyes of thinkers such as Francis Bacon and René Descartes, it was pointless to continue to depend on ancient writers and their books: new research was needed, and fresh ideas had to be circulated. In medicine and astronomy, chemistry and physics, the basis of modern scientific practice was laid in books published as early as the sixteenth and seventeenth centuries.

Books were also vehicles of popular instruction and entertainment. From the beginning, many of the most popular books were horoscopes and prophecies, cookbooks, collections of tales, and reports of extraordinary events. New literary forms such as the novel, the short story, and science fiction were created to meet popular demand for fiction and to express new social values and aspirations. All these forms, including manuals, novels, and even detective stories, appeared in print in China several centuries earlier than in the West, although overall literacy in China probably lagged behind after 1600. In the nineteenth century, the great age of the novel in the West, New York's dockside was often crowded with readers eagerly awaiting the arrival of the latest installment of a Charles Dickens book from England.

If the inventions of writing and printing represent two giant steps in the development of world civilization, the mass communication systems of the twentieth century represent a third. Today's virtually instantaneous global communication was foreshadowed in a series of nineteenth-century inventions that did much to change the role of the written word. A government postal system was introduced in Britain in 1840, much facilitated by the rapid growth of the railway system. Four years earlier, in 1836, the stamp tax on newspapers had been reduced, and by the middle of the century press circulation was three times its former level. The American Samuel Morse invented the telegraph, first used in 1844, and it soon became a valuable means of communication for Julius Reuter's news agency, the first international news service. The Prussian chancellor Otto von Bismarck effectively combined the telegraph and the press in 1870 when he edited a captured French telegram, the Ems dispatch, for publication, knowing that it would probably provoke the French to declare the war he sought; he was right, and the way was prepared for the completion of German unification.

The laying of the first permanent transatlantic cable in 1866 and Alexander Graham Bell's invention of the telephone a decade later made direct, instantaneous communication between Europe and North America possible. During World War II British prime minister Win-

Roving photographers such as this one provided valuable documentation for social historians. This photograph shows a couple in an early Duryea automobile. The Duryea was built between 1893 and 1917.

ston Churchill and American president Franklin Roosevelt conferred frequently by telephone, using the undersea cable. In the aftermath of the 1961 Cuban missile crisis, Soviet and American leaders approved the creation of a direct communications link, or "hot line," between the Kremlin and the White House to facilitate rapid discussion in the event of future crises.

Another revolutionary development in communications involved the technology of the camera and film. Graphic materials, of course, had been reproduced on printing presses for centuries, but beginning in the 1830s it was possible to transmit, through the new process of photography, the immediate pictorial image of an event. Photographs were vehicles of emotion as well as information, reaching both the illiterate and the educated. The photographs of Mathew Brady (c. 1823–1896) enabled Americans to grasp the horrors that were occurring on the civil war battlefields; his work laid the foundation for modern newsphoto services. Cameras could do more than record battles; they could shape them, particularly after aerial photography became practicable. Although the first aerial shots (from balloons) dated from 1858, the development of the airplane half a century later permitted extensive use of aerial photographs for military purposes, a vital advantage in World War I. Aerial photography has also played an important role in mapping and surveying natural resources, thus facilitating communication about our physical environment.

The initial impact of these changes was limited to Europe and North America, but they were spread

Alexander Graham Bell demonstrated the telephone he invented by calling Boston from Salem, Massachusetts, on March 15, 1877.

elsewhere in part by the Western colonial powers. In India the British founded universities in Calcutta, Bombay, and Madras, and public opinion expressed itself through newspapers. In China the foreign-run Maritime Customs Service began an efficient Western-style postal and telegraph system after 1860, and missionaries published huge numbers of tracts and founded Western-style schools, colleges, and universities. The Dutch colonial administration of Indonesia, the British in Burma and Malaya, and the Americans in the Philippines did much the same. Japan was first widely exposed to Western influence in 1853 and soon began to employ Western technology.

In Africa the principal beneficiaries of technological progress were the colonial powers themselves. Many parts of Africa had a rich tradition of song and story that went back centuries, but little of it became known beyond the immediate oral range until the twentieth century. In general, the African communicative tradition was a spoken one; some of the works of Somali and Swahili poets of the eighteenth and nineteenth centuries were written down, but virtually everything else that is known of earlier times was collected by modern anthropologists. With the arrival of European colonizers and missionaries, a limited number of Africans learned the languages and writing systems of their conquerors, but only the liberation struggles of the twentieth century produced any level of general literacy. Many African writers thus faced the dilemma of having to decide whether to produce works in an alien language for the outside world or use their own tribal language. The same problem still confronts writers in other areas whose native languages and cultures—Basque, Gaelic, and Welsh, for example—struggle to survive in the face of more widely spoken rivals.

The appearance of new inventions—radio, movies, the phonograph—combined with earlier changes to enhance the ability to communicate. In the case of sound transmission, war was again crucial in accelerating the technological development that had begun in the mid-nineteenth century. The transmission of sound using electromagnetic waves rather than wires was discovered by the Italian Guglielmo Marconi in 1895, and within 20 years transmission was possible across both the Atlantic and the Pacific. After World War I, the radio came into common use, bringing with it revolutionary possibilities for political leaders to communicate directly with the masses of their people. Among the early masters of this medium were Franklin Roosevelt, who used the radio for his "fireside chats," and Josef Goebbels, Hitler's propa-

In the early 1920s the radio became very popular. Early sets required the use of headphones.

ganda minister. The integration of sight and sound in the cinema was achieved in 1927, when Al Jolson spoke and sang in the first "talkie," *The Jazz Singer;* by 1930 silent pictures were antiquated. The stage was set for the filming of not only movies for entertainment but also the massive spectacles staged by Hitler at Nuremberg and the patriotic newsreels shown in movie theaters that bolstered morale during World War II.

The phonograph also had roots in the mid-nineteenth century, though only in the 1890s did serious manufacturing commence. Improved electrical reproduction came in the 1920s and fine-grooved records arrived in the following decade. It was now possible for people in one part of the world to hear and appreciate music from other continents. Perhaps there is no better example of this than the present Japanese fondness for Beethoven's Ninth (Choral) Symphony, performed widely in Japan each year. Moreover, Chinese, Japanese, and Korean conductors and soloists are now some of the best performers of Western music.

Perhaps the most revolutionary development in communications has been television. Although development of electronically transmitted images was under way as early as 1924, only after World War II was intercity network television launched, using coaxial cables. Microwave radio transmission began the same year, 1946, and in 1951 microwave relay made possible the first coast-to-coast television broadcast. The historical ramifications were enormous. In addition to the educational and cultural possibilities television afforded, the medium's ability to provide viewers with virtually immediate coverage of major events created new pressures as well as opportunities for political leaders. Mounting American anger over military involvement in Vietnam in the 1960s resulted at least in part from what people saw on their television screens. The widespread outpouring of sympathy and aid for famine-stricken areas in North Africa in the 1970s and early 1980s was triggered by television pictures of the victims, and television brought home unprecedentedly graphic images of violence and carnage in the Los Angeles riots and the civil war in Bosnia in 1992.

Improved communications are changing modern society. Radio and especially television have substantially altered industrial societies by creating mass markets, which have in turn altered labor-management relations and created a greater homogeneity of manufactured goods. Mass communications also facilitate the creation of a consensus for action, while simultaneously providing minorities—in the absence of censorship—with the means to alter majority thinking and behavioral patterns, as Martin Luther King, Jr., demonstrated in the U.S. civil rights movement of the 1960s. Through modern technology, ideas and tastes can be increasingly homogenized, yet it is also possible to use the same means to facilitate the rapid acceptance of new styles and ideas. Television and the movies have even intensified urbanization by popularizing the lure of the cities, which are increasingly attractive both because of their employment possibilities and for their culture and lifestyle.

The pace of the communications revolution still varies considerably from region to region. For every 1,000 people in the United States, for example, there were 408 television sets and 1,417 radios in 1968, compared to 208 and 255, respectively, in Japan and 3 and 74 in South Korea. Indonesia and India lagged even further behind, with only 14 television sets and 13 radios per 1,000 people, respectively; Nigeria had only one television set for every 1,000 persons in 1968. Such countries are only now experiencing the full brunt of the print revolution. Between 1948 and 1968 the number of daily newspapers declined slightly in the Western industrial countries of the United States, Great Britain, France, Italy, and the Netherlands; doubled in India; nearly tripled in Pakistan; and jumped nearly sevenfold in Turkey. There are, of course, exceptions to these patterns, often because of political factors such as the rise or fall of authoritarian regimes. The main problem facing developing countries seeking to implement new communications technology is the extraordinary capital outlay required, a problem that will perpetuate the communications gap in the foreseeable future.[1]

Nevertheless, the introduction of communication satellites in the 1970s made possible a global communications network. Even in areas without electricity, a transistor radio can enable people to hear the news, political messages, and cultural events. But instantaneous communications can complicate international relations. In the nineteenth century, reports of hostile action on another continent could take a week or more to reach a concerned government, but at least that provided time for a considered response. With the advent of the telegraph, and later communication satellites, the pressure for rapid decisions at the expense of deliberative analysis increased, thereby intensifying the risks of war.

The ability of computers to store and retrieve information is a recent technological advance with major implications for communications. Computers can be programmed with artificial languages to facilitate high-speed transmission of information. Used responsibly,

Sophisticated programming has given the virtually omnipresent computer seemingly human qualities with respect to its ability to perform rational calculations and tasks. This drawing for a computer advertisement in 1968–1969 clearly shows the computer as a living thing.

computers are valuable for uses ranging from complex mathematical calculations to scientific experiments. But they can also be programmed to act in the absence of human reflection, as in the case of the massive computer-generated trading that triggered enormous losses on the New York Stock Exchange in 1987. Ironically, revolutionary advances in communications technology, often generated by wartime research, have simultaneously presented the world with possibilities both deadly and visionary.

NOTES

1. Statistics in this paragraph from W. P. Davison, "The Media Kaleidoscope: General Trends in the Channels," in *Propaganda and Communication in World History*, ed. H. D. Lasswell, D. Lerner, and H. Speier, vol. 3 (Honolulu: University Press of Hawaii, 1980), pp. 191–248.

SUGGESTIONS FOR FURTHER READING

Abel, E., et al. *Many Voices, One World: Communications and Society.* Paris: UNESCO, 1984.

Birkerts, Sven. *The Gutenberg Elegies: The Fate of Reading in an Electronic Age.* Boston: Faber and Faber, 1994.

Craig, J. *Thirty Centuries of Graphic Design: An Illustrated History.* New York: Watson-Guptill, 1987.

Frawley, W. *Text and Epistemology.* Norwood, N.J.: Ablex, 1987.

Lasswell, H. D., Lerner, D., and Speier, H., eds. *Propaganda and Communication in World History,* vols. 2 and 3. Honolulu: University Press of Hawaii, 1980.

Logan, R. K. *The Alphabet Effect: The Impact of the Phonetic Alphabet on the Development of Western Civilization.* New York: Morrow, 1986.

Lowenthal, L. *Literature and Mass Culture: Communication in Society,* vol. 1. New Brunswick, N.J.: Transaction Books, 1984.

Schiller, H. I. *Information and the Crisis Economy.* Norwood, N.J.: Ablex, 1984.

Siegel, L., and Markoff, J. *The High Cost of High Tech: The Dark Side of the Chip.* New York: Harper & Row, 1985.

Whalley, J. I. *Writing Implements and Accessories: From the Roman Stylus to the Typewriter.* Detroit: Gale Research, 1975.

Art of Modern Asia and Africa

This Congolese carving of a Belgian official and his native driver comments wittily yet perceptively on imperial relationships.

The "iron horse" in Japan: early Meiji woodblock artists were fascinated by the new railways, as most Japanese were intrigued with the artifacts of the modern West that flooded into their country.

Portuguese merchants, greeted by Jesuits, unload goods from India and East Asia at Nagasaki, Japan, in the sixteenth century. Painted by a Japanese artist on gold-leafed paper.

Western painters, especially the Impressionists, were profoundly influenced by
Chinese and especially Japanese styles. Here are two Hiroshige originals from
the mid–nineteenth century (top) and two paintings by his Dutch contemporary
Vincent van Gogh (bottom), obvious copies but with some idiosyncratic touches.

Japanese ladies follow the Meiji trend of westernization by learning to play the piano. But they keep their traditional Japanese hairstyles and the cherry tree screen, despite their Western dresses.

The Japanese were quick to portray the westerners who had forced their way into the country. Here are two representations from 1854, showing Commodore Perry (right) and his second in command, Adams (left). Like the Chinese, the Japanese clearly saw westerners as savages.

IA ORANA MARIA

Paul Gauguin, *La Orana Maria* ["We Greet Thee, Mary"]. Gauguin's images of a placid yet sensually inviting South Seas world far removed from the scramble of nineteenth-century Western materialism had great appeal. Gauguin himself had at one time been a stockbroker.

CHAPTER
35

The Age of
Western Domination

Contemporary world history began during the last three decades of the nineteenth century, when a handful of European countries imposed their domination over major portions of the globe. Britain, France, Germany, and to a lesser extent Italy and Belgium exercised control over a large portion of the earth's land surface and population. Russia continued to push its borders eastward into Asia, while the United States and Japan extended their presence into the Pacific region. One result of this grab for colonial possessions was the establishment of complex forms of interdependency among world civilizations that still shape our lives. This first major phase in the creation of a "global village" as a product of imperialism is the background of the contemporary age.

The New Imperialism

The process by which this transformation took place is known as the new imperialism, to distinguish it from the earlier phase of European expansion that took place between the sixteenth and eighteenth centuries. This newer form of imperialism was characterized by a number of unique features.

The earlier overseas empires lay chiefly in the Americas and included extensive European-run areas in India and Southeast Asia as well as footholds on the East Asian and African coasts. After 1870 the Western powers moved into the interiors of Asia and Africa. Although the older empires traded with local populations, they were generally regarded as sources of direct revenue for the home country—tribute from local rulers, taxation from the indigenous populations, and the expropriation of gold and silver.

Battle scene between African Zulu warriors and British garrison in 1879. Warriors carrying spears and shields against British on horseback. Slain warrior in the foreground.

Because the new imperialism was the work of advanced industrial-capitalist nations rather than of mercantile economies, it involved the commitment of significant financial investment as well as the deliberate exploitation of the material and human resources of the colonial areas. The economic function of the new imperialism, whether real or perceived, led in turn to the establishment of direct political control over the colonies. By the opening of the twentieth century, therefore, a new and direct relationship of unequal exchange had been established among the civilizations of the world, marked by a vast difference between the industrial and technological power of the West and the relative weakness of less technologically developed cultures.

Conflicting Interpretations

Scholars debate the causes and consequences of the new imperialism. One basic fact appears to be generally accepted: by 1870 conditions in Europe were ripe for overseas expansion. The breakdown of the Concert of Europe and the creation of nation-states in Germany and Italy heightened aggressive national rivalry. Moreover, power status was increasingly equated with overseas colonies, so empire became a matter of national honor. The Long Depression of 1873–1896 convinced some business and government leaders that overseas colonies would solve the problems caused by shrinking European markets and increasingly higher wages. Though policymakers often used economic arguments to explain the necessity for expansion, imperialism had support among all classes, including workers. Even trade union leaders and some socialists were enthusiastic about colonial expansion.

Economics and Empire

Economic rivalry between older industrial states such as Britain and France and newly industrializing states such as Germany and the United States added to the competition for colonies, especially as tariff barriers restricted European markets after 1880. Unprecedented prosperity and military-industrial power produced by the second phase of the Industrial Revolution and advances in science, technology, and industrial organization gave Europeans confidence in the superiority of their civilization. The climax of European development in the last decades of the century thus brought together a thirst for national pride and security, the desire for continued economic expansion, and an appetite for cultural dominance.

The connection between economics and imperialism is hardly in doubt, although its exact nature is debated.

The economic slump that began in the 1870s had increased unemployment, reduced prices for manufactured goods, and diminished exports, which forced industrial nations to compete fiercely for markets for their manufactured goods at a time when the abandonment of free trade limited the European market. This competition prompted some observers to argue for sheltered colonial markets limited to trade with the home country. An additional stimulus to imperialism arose from the demand for raw materials unavailable in Europe, especially copper, rubber, tin, cotton, jute, and petroleum, as well as foodstuffs such as coconut, coffee, and tea, on which Europeans had come to rely. Not only were raw materials necessary to the new industrial products, but their value was enhanced because cheap colonial labor made mining, extraction, and agriculture especially profitable.

The debate over economic factors centers on accumulated surplus capital. This argument, which later became the major interpretation of Marxist writers, was first proposed in 1902 by the British economic liberal John A. Hobson (1858–1940) in *Imperialism: A Study*. Hobson believed that capitalism suffered from underconsumption—that is, wealth in capitalist societies was poorly distributed as a result of overaccumulation by the rich. The business and financial interests that controlled such surplus capital soon discovered that it could be more profitably invested overseas, where cheap labor and raw materials made a greater return possible. Hobson saw imperialism as the effort of capitalists to find investment outlets for their surplus wealth. He argued that surplus capital could be eliminated if workers were paid higher wages and the rich were taxed more heavily; because these measures would result in greater purchasing power for the working class, the need for new markets—and hence imperialism—would disappear.

In 1916 V. I. Lenin (1870–1924), the future Communist leader of the Russian Revolution, wrote the classic Marxist analysis of the subject, *Imperialism: The Highest Stage of Capitalism*. The scramble for colonies, Lenin noted, coincided with the change in Europe's economy from a phase of free competition to one of intense monopoly through combines, trusts, and the control of finance capital. Imperialism emerges from this "highest" stage of capitalism when business and financial interests in each country seek to extend their monopolies overseas in the search for greater profits. Imperialism was therefore an inevitable response to the "internal contradictions" of monopolistic capitalism. For Lenin, imperialism would result in the breakdown of capitalism.

Hobson and Lenin were partly correct. Between 1860 and 1900 the value of British capital invested abroad grew from $7 billion to $20 billion. By the eve of

World War I, one-fifth of the foreign investments of France and Germany was in colonial regions, and about half of Britain's overseas investment was in the colonial world. In many instances, however, foreign rulers needed and requested Western capital, and financial investment hardly explained the imperialist expansion of less developed nations such as Italy and Russia, which had little surplus capital. Nor does colonialism explain the equally large British investments in noncolonial areas, such as Latin America and the United States. Finally, although some colonial possessions were profitable, the military and bureaucratic costs of occupation usually exceeded the financial return.

Imperialism caught the imagination of the European mind and responded to a popular interest in the exotic. Scientists, missionaries, hunters, and adventurers poured into Africa and Asia in the late nineteenth century. Yet even the humanitarian instincts of the mission-

aries, intent on bringing Christianity and modern medicine to "heathens," involved a conviction about the superiority of their own civilization. When the British writer Rudyard Kipling spoke of the "white man's burden," he reflected the view of many Europeans that the civilizing mission was a sacred duty of "more advanced" races—a view supported in more ruthless fashion by believers in Social Darwinism.

Africa and the Colonial Powers

The most intense phase of the new imperialism unfolded in Africa, a continent four times the size of Europe. For centuries westerners had viewed sub-Saharan Africa as the "Dark Continent," a vast, unexplored expanse where inhospitable climate, diseases, and geography conspired to keep them out. Muslim traders crisscrossed much

Imperialism and Economics: The Debate

Among analysts of the economic causes of the new imperialism, two major authors stand out: Hobson and Lenin.

By far the most important economic factor in imperialism is the influence relating to investments. The growing cosmopolitanization of capital is the greatest economic change of this generation. Every advanced industrial nation is tending to place a larger share of its capital outside the limits of its own political area, in foreign countries, or in colonies, and to draw a growing income from this source.

Imperialism is capitalism in that stage of development in which the dominance of monopolies and finance capital has established itself; in which the export of capital has acquired pronounced importance; in which the division of the world among the international trusts has begun; in which division of all territories of the globe among the great capitalist powers has been completed.

More recent students of imperialism, however, have questioned these earlier views.

In the second half of the twentieth century, it can be seen that imperialism owed its popular appeal not to the sinister influence of the capitalists, but to its inherent attractions for the masses . . . and the adoption of a creed based on such irrational concepts as racial superiority and the prestige of the nation. . . . Imperialism cannot be explained in simple terms of economic theory and the nature of financial capital.

Sources: J. A. Hobson, *Imperialism: A Study* (New York: Pott, 1902), p. 30; V. I. Lenin, *Imperialism: The Highest Stage of Capitalism* (New York: International Publishers, 1939), p. 89; D. K. Fieldhouse, "Imperialism: A Historiographical Revision," *Economic History Review*, 2nd ser., 14 (1961): 209.

of West Africa and the Sahara, but as late as the mid-nineteenth century only the coastal settlements and a few interior regions were represented on European maps.

Africa on the Eve of Imperialism

Despite Western ignorance, however, Africa had undergone a major transformation in the centuries before the new imperialism. Iron metallurgy, agricultural techniques, and the introduction of new crops had spread across the continent, and a large increase in population had caused migrations into central and southern Africa. Diversity of geography and ethnocultural patterns determined development. Sophisticated cultures and effective states marked some regions, especially in the savanna zone of West Africa, where the kingdoms of Ghana, Mali, and Songhay had once flourished, and in Zimbabwe and the Swahili city-states of southeastern Africa. In the rain forests and the southern regions, inhabited

German bacteriologists, including the famous Robert Koch (third from left), scrutinize blood samples in East Africa in a search to isolate the microbe that causes sleeping sickness, a major tropical disease. The attitudes of weakness and dependence of the African subjects contrast vividly with the brisk assurance and soldierly dress of the Europeans.

mainly by San and Khoikhoi, political organization revolved around village communities that relied on traditional food-gathering techniques and pastoralism.

Although the British navy tried to suppress the slave trade along the African coast after 1805, slavery continued to flourish inside Africa. Indeed, the decline of the transatlantic slave trade actually drove the price of slaves up, and in many African societies, especially on the west and east coasts and in Ethiopia, slavery became a cornerstone of social and economic life. The Swahili city-states and Dahomey, for example, developed huge plantation systems of slave-based agriculture, similar to those that developed in the United States. In Dahomey and Ashante slaves were also used to mine gold. In the port cities of West Africa slavery contributed to the rise of a new class of African merchants.

Along with the persistence of slavery, many regions of Africa witnessed an increase in legitimate trade, especially in ivory, palm oil, cloves, and other agricultural products. In the Niger delta the commercial revival encouraged a unique governing-trading arrangement that extended organized trade into the interior. As a result the inland forest empires of Oyo and Benin, which could not adjust to the new commercial economy, began to decline and were eventually overrun by the Muslim Fulani, who expanded their control as far west as Senegal.

In East Africa the early and mid-nineteenth century saw the development of long-distance caravan routes, first by the Nyamwezi and other African merchants and then by Arab traders. The region experienced serious social upheaval, especially in Malawi, Tanganyika, and northern Mozambique, into which tens of thousands of warriors from southern Africa moved, displacing the local populations. Arab slavers and merchants also pushed their way into the interior regions west of lakes Victoria and Tanganyika, where political and social conditions approached chaos. An important exception, however, was the kingdom of Buganda, a powerful centralized state that was in the process of territorial expansion. In southern Africa the numerous culturally related Bantu societies had been settled for centuries in the fertile coastal plains. Lacking political cohesion or modern military defenses, they now found themselves overrun by encroaching white settlers from the Cape Colony and Portuguese slavers from Mozambique. One Bantu group, the Zulu, were a highly disciplined society of warriors with large, well-organized cities that had steadily expanded into the surrounding countryside, absorbing neighboring populations and chiefdoms. Under their ambitious leader, Shaka (1818–1828), the Zulu steadily conquered new territory. The subsequent introduction of firearms by the British and the Muslims had even more serious consequences. The breech-loading rifle and the Gatling gun enabled the British to subdue the Zulu in a series of bloody wars in the 1870s. These and other struggles resulted in a massive scattering of populations out of the region, which in turn displaced other societies and caused considerable social dislocation.

Only two states in Africa were able to maintain their independence in the face of mounting European aggression—Ethiopia and Liberia. After centuries of isolation, the feudal kingdoms of Ethiopia were reunited by a Shoa warrior who dubbed himself Emperor Theodore. He created a modern army and a state administration, although the most fertile lands of the realm continued to be held by nobles and the Coptic Christian church.

Liberia, founded in 1821 by Americans as a home for freed blacks returning to Africa from the United States, was politically sovereign but remained dependent on American economic interests.

Explorers and Missionaries

Western interest in Africa intensified in the early nineteenth century as a result of the debate over the abolition of the slave trade. Curiosity about the interior of the continent combined with humanitarian concerns to bring a host of explorers and missionaries to Africa. Exploration focused on two unsolved geographic mysteries: the source of the Niger River in West Africa and the source of the Nile in East Africa. As early as 1795 Mungo Park,

The Inhumanity of Imperialism

In the tropical rain forests of the Zaire basin, company agents used private armies of former slaves to control the local labor supply and extract the valuable rubber from the region. In this report for the Times of London, *an American missionary, the Rev. J. B. Murphy, described the inhumanity of imperialism.*

It has reduced the people to a state of utter despair. Each town in the district is forced to bring a certain quantity [of rubber] to the headquarters of the commissaire every Sunday. It is collected by force. The soldiers drive the people into the bush. If they will not go they are shot down, and their left hands cut off and taken as trophies to the commissaire. The soldiers do not care who they shoot down, and they more often shoot poor helpless women and harmless children. These hands, the hands of men, women and children, are placed in rows before the commissaire, who counts them to see that the soldiers have not wasted the cartridges. The commissaire is paid a commission of about 1d. a pound upon all the rubber he gets. It is therefore to his interest to get as much as he can. . . .

Let me give an incident to show how this unrighteous trade affects the people. One day a State corporal, who was in charge of the post of Lolifa, was going round the town collecting rubber. Meeting a poor woman whose husband was away fishing, he said, "Where is your husband?" She answered by pointing to the river. He then said, "Where is his rubber?" She answered, "It is ready for you," whereupon he said, "You lie," and, lifting his gun, shot her dead. Shortly afterwards the husband returned, and was told of the murder of his wife. He went straight to the corporal, taking with him his rubber, and asked why he had shot his wife. The wretched man then raised his gun and killed the corporal. . . . The commissaire sent a large force to support the authority of the soldiers; the town was looted, burned, and many people killed and wounded. In November last [1894] there was heavy fighting upon the Bosira, because the people refused to give rubber, and I was told upon the authority of a State officer that no fewer than 1,890 people were killed.

Source: Quoted from Kevin Shillington, *History of Africa* (New York: St. Martin's Press, 1989), p. 336.

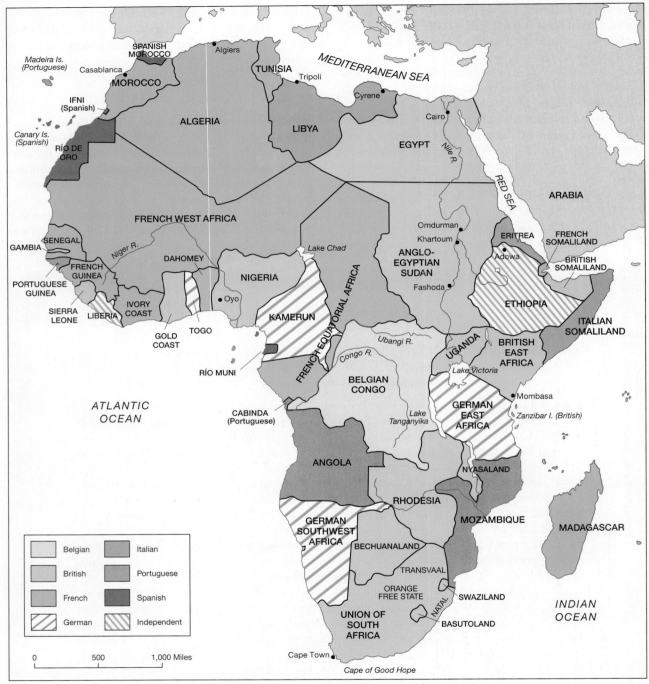

MAP 35.1   AFRICA ON THE EVE OF WORLD WAR I

a Scottish doctor, led an expedition up the Niger, but not until 1830 was the river fully traced. Successive British adventurers—including Sir Samuel White Baker and his wife, Lady Florence Baker—made their way from the coast of East Africa in search of the sources of the Nile.

In 1864 the Bakers were the first Europeans to see a huge lake, which they called Lake Albert in honor of Queen Victoria's husband.

The most famous African explorer of the period was David Livingstone, whose humanitarianism and courage caught the imagination of Europe. His expeditions in the 1850s sparked public interest. From 1857 to 1863 Livingstone explored the Zambesi River region and in 1866 set out on his last journey, intending to settle the question of the source of the Nile. When no word reached the outside world for five years, an American newspaper sent Henry M. Stanley, a well-known correspondent, to find the lost missionary. The two men met in 1871, but Livingstone, sick and exhausted, refused to return to Britain. When Stanley returned to the Congo in 1878 on behalf of King Leopold of Belgium, he paved the way for a new phase in the history of Western imperialism.

The Scramble for Africa

Portugal had held Angola and Mozambique since the age of exploration, but before 1870, European powers had seized only a few footholds along the coast. France had occupied Algeria and portions of Senegal, and Britain already controlled the Cape of Good Hope, Gambia, and Sierra Leone and had imposed its commercial influence on the Niger River region and Zanzibar. Following the midcentury explorations, the pace of expansion became intense as Western powers scrambled for territory.

King Leopold, who planned to exploit the Congo through the privately financed International Congo Association, sparked the race for colonies. Establishing a pattern that would be used by other entrepreneurs, hundreds of tribal chieftains were tricked into signing treaties granting the association some 900,000 square miles of land. Karl Peters, founder of the German Colonization Society, followed suit in East Africa, and the Germans seized Southwest Africa. The French army officer Pierre de Brazza secured control over vast tracts north of the Congo River.

In 1885 Bismarck called a conference in Berlin to establish international guidelines for the acquisition of African territory. The conference recognized the Congo Free State as a neutral region. Although the Congo was to be governed by the Belgian king, all nations were to have free access to trade and navigation, and the slave trade was to be suppressed. The diplomats agreed that henceforth a power with coastal possessions had a right to the adjacent hinterland only if it effectively occupied the territory. Future disputes were to be settled by arbitration.

The Congo under Leopold's rule suffered unimaginable exploitation. Private firms used forced labor to squeeze maximum profit out of the rich rubber and ivory resources. Atrocities committed by the labor

overseers, together with the toll of disease and climate, claimed more than 10 million lives during the next 20 years. Conditions did not improve until Leopold turned his private ownership of the Free State over to the Belgian government in 1908, when it was renamed the Belgian Congo.

Following the Berlin conference, nine-tenths of the African continent was rapidly divided among the European powers. Italy and Germany joined the scramble. When France blocked Italy's ambitions in Tunisia, Italy instead occupied Eritrea and Somaliland, desolate areas along the Red Sea. In 1896 the Italians attempted to conquer the Christian state of Ethiopia, but the forces of its emperor, Menelik, four times the size of the Italian army, defeated the invaders at Adowa. Although Bismarck was personally opposed to African colonization, he yielded to domestic pressure. Germany proclaimed a protectorate over Southwest Africa and German East Africa (Tanganyika) and eventually added Togo and Cameroon to its empire. When Kaiser William II dismissed Bismarck in 1890, German colonial activities intensified.

Britain, France, and the Perils of Empire

The largest empires in Africa were acquired by France and Britain, whose conflicting ambitions at times brought the two powers to the brink of war. The de Brazza expedition had enabled France to claim a huge portion of equatorial Africa, and by 1896 France had occupied Madagascar as well. The focus of French efforts, however, was in the Sahara. From Algeria, Senegal, and the Ivory Coast the French pushed south, east, and north across the great desert, establishing military outposts while fighting nomads. In 1881 they occupied Tunisia, and by the end of that decade they had gone beyond Lake Chad to the borders of the Sudan. Eventually the French hoped to reach the Nile and perhaps the Red Sea, a plan that brought them into conflict with British aspirations.

By the time the Berlin conference convened, Britain held the Cape Colony in southern Africa and had imposed its control over Egypt. In 1875 Ismail, Egypt's ruler, was unable to repay huge loans from French and British bankers. When, as a result, he was forced to sell his stock in the Suez Canal Company, representing 44 percent of all shares, the British prime minister, Benjamin Disraeli, bought them, giving Britain a vital stake in the strategic waterway. The next year Ismail suspended interest payments on Egypt's foreign debts, and France and Britain assumed joint control of its finances. Foreign intervention sparked nationalist reaction among

Women and African Society

Travelers in precolonial Africa encountered long-established social customs that appeared alien to them and that their own cultural arrogance or ethnocentrism made them perceive as primitive. Even David Livingstone, who had a deeper respect for African traditions than most westerners of his day, sometimes misunderstood the import of what he found. This anecdote, which Livingstone's Victorian mind found humorous, revealed the strength of women's roles in one African community.

The person whom Nyakoba appointed to be our guide, having informed us of the decision, came and bargained that his services should be rewarded with a hoe. I showed him the article; he was delighted with it, and went off to show it to his wife. He soon afterward returned, and said that, though he was perfectly willing to go, his wife would not let him. I said, "Then bring back the hoe"; but he replied, "I want it." "Well, go with us, and you shall have it." "But my wife won't let me." I remarked to my men, "Did you ever hear such a fool?" They answered, "Oh, that is the custom of these parts; the wives are the masters.". . . When a young man takes a liking for a girl of another village, and the parents have no objection to the match, he is obliged to come and live at their village. He has to perform certain services for the mother-in-law, such as keeping her well supplied with firewood; and when he comes into her presence he is obliged to sit with his knees in a bent position, as putting out his feet toward the old lady would give her great offense. If he becomes tired of living in this state of vassalage, and wishes to return to his own family, he is obliged to leave all his children behind—they belong to the wife. This is only a more stringent enforcement of the law from which emanates the practice which prevails so very extensively in Africa, known to Europeans as "buying wives." Such virtually it is, but it does not appear quite in that light to the actors. So many head of cattle or goats are given to the parents of the girl "to give her up," as it is termed, i.e., to forego all claim on her offspring, and allow an entire transference of her and her seed into another family. If nothing is given, the family from which she has come can claim the children as part of itself: the payment is made to sever this bond.

Source: D. Livingstone, *Missionary Travels and Researches in South Africa* (New York: Harper, 1858), pp. 667–668.

Egyptian intellectuals and army officers, and in 1882 riots in Alexandria led to a British bombardment of the city and the establishment of a protectorate over the country. For the next 25 years Egypt was ruled by a British governor.

The British next moved to secure the Sudan, an Egyptian dependency to the south. In 1885 a British garrison at Khartoum under General Charles ("Chinese") Gordon was massacred by the armies of the Mahdi, the leader of fierce Muslim tribesmen. Not until 1898 did the British send an expeditionary force, commanded by General Horatio Kitchener, to retake the Sudan. This time the nationalist fervor of the Muslims was no match for the new British machine guns. More than 10,000 tribesmen were wiped out at Omdurman. A few months earlier a French expedition under Captain Jean-Baptiste Marchand had arrived at Fashoda, where it planted the French flag. On September 18, only a few weeks after Omdurman, Kitchener, with a superior force, met Marchand there. An open clash was avoided only when the French government backed down.

British and French imperial plans ran directly counter to each other, for while France sought to create an east-west empire that stretched from the Atlantic to the Red Sea, Britain dreamed of a north-south domain that reached from Egypt to Cape Town. Along with Egypt and the Sudan, Britain already controlled Uganda and British East Africa (Kenya), and a determined British push north from the Cape might connect the parts.

South Africa and the Boer War

The British Cape-to-Cairo scheme was the brainchild of Cecil Rhodes (1853–1902), who had become fabulously wealthy in diamond and gold mining. A fierce nationalist and Social Darwinist, Rhodes became prime minister of the Cape Colony in 1890 and began to formulate a scheme to bring more of Africa under British rule.

The other European powers represented a lesser obstacle to Rhodes than internal conditions in South Africa. The Cape had been settled in the seventeenth century by Dutch immigrants, staunchly independent Calvinist farmers and cattlemen. When Britain annexed the colony after the Napoleonic Wars, these Afrikaners (the British called them Boers, from the Dutch word for farmer) migrated north in the Great Trek, eventually establishing the Orange Free State and the Transvaal Republic. As they carved out new settlements, the Boers encountered opposition from the Bantu and Zulu populations as well as from the British, and more than 30 years of continuous fighting ensued. Just when a compromise appeared possible, the discovery of gold and diamonds intensified the conflict between the British and the Boers. In the 1880s and 1890s hundreds of thousands of Englishmen poured into the mining towns of the Transvaal, Bechuanaland, and the area later known as Rhodesia, overwhelming the Boers and making open conflict all but inevitable.

The principal Boer spokesman was Paul Kruger (1825–1904). As president of the Transvaal, Kruger pressured the *uitlanders* ("foreigners") by levying dis-

criminatory taxes on them, curbing the use of English, and curtailing the exercise of political rights. In 1895 Rhodes and his agents attempted to overthrow Kruger when a small British force invaded the Transvaal under the command of Dr. Leander Jameson. The Jameson raid failed, but public opinion in Europe condemned the British, and Kaiser William II telegraphed Kruger that the Germans had been ready to help the Boers. In 1899 Britain and the Boer republics went to war; the Boers were defeated and surrendered in 1902. The British eventually granted self-government to the region, and in 1910 the Cape Colony, Natal, the Orange Free State, and the Transvaal were joined as the Union of South Africa.

Imperialism and Its Consequences

Imperialism affected both the European conquerors and their colonial subjects. Economic and industrial development in the West responded to the influx of raw materials and the opportunities for overseas investment, and it is probable that the resulting lower prices had a positive effect on the real wages of some European workers. On the diplomatic level, however, competition for colonies increased tensions among the great powers. The impact on Africa was incalculable as the full weight of Western technology descended on the continent, which for centuries had been relatively undisturbed by outside influences. In less than a generation Africans found their social and political structures shattered, their agrarian economy transformed, and their values undermined. Europeans exploited the natural and mineral resources of Africa, extracting huge quantities of gold, diamonds, ivory, rubber, and copper. White settlers seized fertile agricultural land formerly occupied by tribal communities, especially in southern and eastern Africa. The construction of roads, railroads, and telegraph lines stimulated internal trade across long distances and, together with the introduction of a wage-earning structure, transformed the barter economy into a monetary system. Yet enormous manpower was needed to reshape the African economy and build an infrastructure, and the labor supply, poorly paid, was often conscripted by force and treated brutally.

The "modernization" of the continent took a terrible toll on the cultural and political pattern of African life. Broken family and kinship patterns often resulted as workers were required to move over wide distances and tribal communities were stripped of their land. Moreover, imperialism resulted in artificially drawn political boundaries that divided many tribes and merged hostile

The Boer farmers of southern Africa took up arms against the British and fought a guerrilla war in the bush. Here several generations join in the fight.

groups. Even Western humanitarian programs had a mixed impact on local populations. The missionary efforts improved sanitation and agricultural methods and provided Africans with Western education. But these benefits also subverted African identity and undermined traditional values and social mores, for young Africans who were exposed to Western education or converted to Christianity often rejected family and tribal authority.

The speed and relative ease of European conquest obscure the fact that Africans resisted imperialism. The nomads of the Sahara, the Muslims of the Sudan, and the Zulu of southern Africa fought vigorously against Europeans. After the conquest, resistance took more subtle forms. A new class of westernized Africans, many trained at European universities and then appointed to posts in the colonial administrations, eventually emerged. Ironically, these Africans, having absorbed Western political attitudes and values, returned home to provide leadership for their people and sometimes spearheaded the drive for independence.

The West in Asia

Many of the same trends were set in motion by the pressures for westernization in Asia. This was most true in the countries incorporated in Western colonial systems—India, Ceylon, Burma, Malaya, Indochina, Indonesia, and the Philippines—but similar trends were evident in China and even in Japan. Traditional Asian cultures and states were, however, more highly developed than in Africa and could more readily resist or choose from among Western ideas and institutions. For example, a major Christian missionary effort was made, but it produced few converts, although as in Africa it was an important means of introducing Western medicine and education. Much of traditional Asian culture remained vigorous, especially the family system. At the same time, many Asian institutions were remade under Western influence or were augmented by new ones introduced by westerners.

The arrogance as well as the success of Western imperialism was galling to most Asians, especially given their own pride in their ancient traditions of greatness. Western colonialism and the unequal treaties forced on Siam (Thailand), China, and Japan, stimulated a renewal of the national Asian traditions and an effort to make them relevant to a world dominated by the West and its standards. Thus India witnessed the Hindu Renaissance and related movements (often under British pressure) to eliminate or restrict such institutions as *sati* and child marriage. In China similar movements arose against foot-binding, chaste widowhood, and concubinage; in Japan, against premarital promiscuity, class-based restrictions on clothing, and more or less open pornography (known as "spring pictures").

Asians found this forced reexamination of much of their cultural heritage under the eyes of an alien conqueror deeply disturbing. Now more than ever they needed to hold their heads up and to believe that to be Indian, Chinese, Japanese, or Southeast Asian was something to be proud of. Many convinced themselves that although the West might have a temporary material advantage, the East was still superior spiritually and in the arts of civilization.

Industrialization was in time pursued vigorously, first in India, then in Japan, and finally in China, although it lagged in Southeast Asia. At least as important as technological change were such institutions as banking and joint-stock companies and the particularly Western idea of nationalism. The great Asian empires and states of the past had been cultural and bureaucratic structures different from the nation-states of modern Europe, whose national coherence and drive Asians rightly saw as a source of strength that they lacked but that they must have if they were again to be masters in their own house.

British Imperial India

A divided and weakened India had progressively fallen under the domination of the English East India Company (as described in Chapter 29), and by 1857 most of it was being administered, directly or indirectly, as a single unit. Most Indians exposed to the new British model of Western-style progress admired it, but in the long run being united for the first time yet treated as second-class citizens in their own country led to Indian nationalism. The insurrection of 1857 (discussed in Chapter 29) was not yet a war of independence, but it marked the beginning of Indian response to a foreign control increasingly tinged with arrogance. In the wake of the insurrection, the English East Company was dissolved and the so-called Dual System abolished.

The mutiny marked a watershed between the earlier stages of company rule, which saw considerable racial and cultural mixing, and the rise of full-blown imperialism. The British crown assumed direct imperial authority under the Government of India Act (1858), although the façade of Indian principalities was maintained until independence. To complete the transfor-

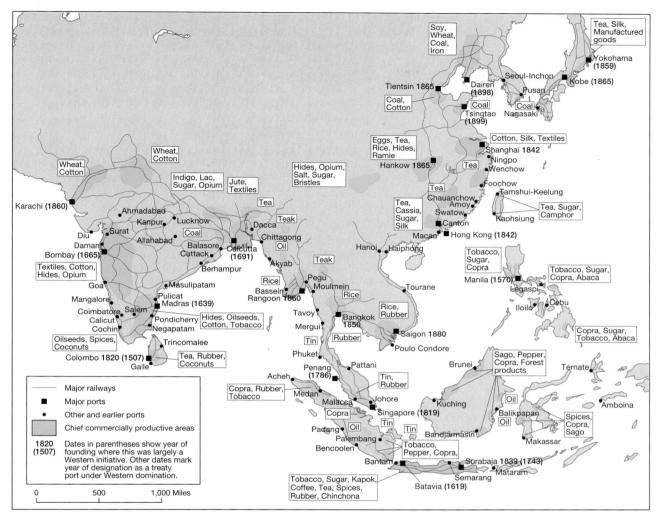

MAP 35.2   MAJOR PORTS AND COMMERCIALLY PRODUCTIVE AREAS
N EAST ASIA, 1600–1940

mation, Queen Victoria adopted the title Empress of India in 1877. She took a special interest in her new dominions, which her prime minister, Benjamin Disraeli, called "the brightest jewel in the crown," and is said to have prayed nightly for her Indian subjects. Although she never went there, many Indians revered her as their own empress, part of the long Indian imperial tradition even under alien rulers, and her picture was widely displayed in people's homes.

The British were careful not to displace any more of the native rulers or to take over more territory, a policy kept until Indian independence in 1947. British residents were placed in each of the hundreds of small and a few large Indian-ruled states, but intervention or threats were rarely needed to keep the roughly half of India still for-

mally in native hands in line with British policy. The army remained largely Indian, but the proportion of British officers and troops was increased, and elite regiments of Sikhs, Rajputs, and Gurkhas (from Nepal) were formed. Indians joined the colonial civil service as well and held responsible positions in all fields under overall British supervision.

Modern Growth

The opening of the Suez Canal in 1869, the shift to steam navigation, and the rapid spread of railways brought India much closer to Europe, greatly accelerating the commercialization of the economy. By the end of the century India had by far the largest rail network

(25,000 miles) in all Asia, on a par with many European countries but on a far bigger scale. This too had obvious commercial consequences, but there were social ones as well. British women could now join their husbands more easily in India and raise their families there, thus creating another wedge of separation between the races and cultures. Colonial social life centered in the buildings and grounds of the British Club in each city or town, from which Indians were excluded. This social barrier not only delimited the Indians' inferior status but also kept many of the British in a kind of prison of their own making, cut off both from the subjects they ruled and from fresh ideas and attitudes from home. Thus developed what came to be called the colonial mentality, which preserved a mid-Victorian code of conduct and mores well into the twentieth century.

Indians were the first Asians to experience the impact of Western capitalism and industrialization in their country on a large scale. Many were quick to respond as entrepreneurs to the new economic opportunities in commerce and machine manufacturing. As in Britain, industrialization began first with machine-made textiles in Bombay and Calcutta, then in a widening range of other manufacturing. Railways stimulated the growing commercialization of agriculture, especially in industrial crops such as jute (fibers), cotton, indigo, and new plantation production of tea, grown mainly in the hills of Assam, which captured most of the world market. New irrigation projects, especially in the semi-arid Punjab and the Indus valley, opened productive farming areas to feed India's booming cities and increased output elsewhere. By 1900 India had the world's largest irrigation system.

Calcutta remained the country's largest city, closely followed by Bombay and then by Madras. Bombay, with its magnificent harbor and its closeness to cotton-growing areas in Gujarat and Maharashtra, became the premier port and the chief center of Indian-owned textile manufacturing. Large new industrial cities also grew inland as the railway linked most of the country in a single market: Ahmedabad in Gujarat; Lucknow, Kanpur, and Allahabad in the central Ganges; Salem and Coimbatore in the south; and many more. Karachi became the port for cotton and wheat from the Indus valley. British industrial and commercial investors, managers, and traders made money and sold goods in this vast new market, but Indians were increasingly prominent as well in the growing modern sector. Indians also entered and in time dominated the new Western-style professions such as law, medicine, engineering, and education. By 1900 India had the world's fourth largest textile industry and by 1920 the biggest steel plant in the British Empire, both, like many other industries, owned and managed largely by Indians.

Colonial Government

The British saw themselves as the bringers of order and civilization to their empire, a role that many of them likened to that of the Romans 2,000 years earlier in Europe. Britain was the greatest power in the world from the mid-eighteenth century to the early twentieth. It was also the nursery of industrialization and modern representative government. These things bred a sense of pride and greatness. Britons were fond of describing theirs as an empire on which the sun never set, since it stretched almost around the globe. Indians, they felt, should be grateful to be included, and indeed many were.

British-style education, conducted in English, continued to shape most Indian intellectuals and literate people to a large degree in the British image. The law of British India, based on English common law, was practiced and administered overwhelmingly by Indians themselves. Nonetheless, the British retained firm control of all senior positions. The prestigious Indian Civil Service (ICS), staffed until the twentieth century almost entirely by Britons trained in Indian affairs, long remained an exclusive supervisory group under the viceroy, the effective head of state in India appointed by London. The ICS was referred to proudly as the "steel framework" whose roughly 900 members ensured the smooth operation of the colonial government.

Despite colonial achievements in agriculture, public health, education, and transportation, however, most Indians remained poor, illiterate, and powerless. Occasional regional famines continued, as in China. Tenancy and landlessness grew with the increasing commercialization of agriculture, and industrial growth was far too slow to absorb or produce adequately for the rising population.

Between 1800 and 1947 the total population of India probably at least doubled, in itself a sign of order and greater economic opportunity, as in eighteenth-century China. The official census begun in 1871 showed a more or less continuous growth of population together with a falling death rate. But this surge in population was barely matched by overall economic growth, which was in any case unbalanced. There was thus little new margin for improved living standards, and while some commercial, professional, and landed groups prospered, much of the peasantry sank deeper into poverty. India remained poor

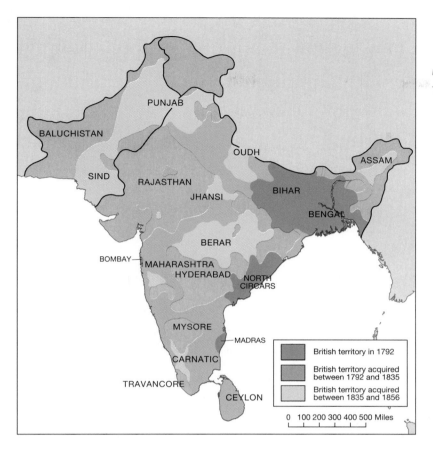

MAP 35.3 GROWTH OF THE BRITISH EMPIRE IN INDIA

PUNJAB
BALUCHISTAN
OUDH
ASSAM
SIND
RAJASTHAN
JHANSI
BIHAR
BENGAL
BERAR
BOMBAY
MAHARASHTRA
HYDERABAD
NORTH CIRCARS
MYSORE
MADRAS
CARNATIC
TRAVANCORE
CEYLON

British territory in 1792

British territory acquired between 1792 and 1835

British territory acquired between 1835 and 1856

0 100 200 300 400 500 Miles

in part because it was poor to begin with after the extravagances, exploitation, and collapse of the Mughals. Industrialization and commercialization directly impoverished some groups and benefited others, as also happened in the West. The hand spinners of cotton, India's single largest manufacturing workforce, were devastated by factory production and British imports, although hand weavers benefited from the cheaper machine-spun yarn. The widening market also gave new employment to many farmers, craftsmen, factory or railway workers, and laborers. The pattern in textiles was repeated in other industries and markets and occurred in China as well.

The colonial government was chronically pinched for funds; London insisted that all expenses had to be covered from Indian revenues. The army took much of these, in part for the conquest of Burma, and there was little to spare. Planning was thus difficult, and problems were addressed piecemeal or not at all. Reformers accused the government of playing the role of night watchman while most Indians remained in poverty. Even so, the colonial administration required indirect support, costs that were necessarily borne by ordinary British tax-

payers. Thus the imperial system was supported by the middle and lower classes of both countries for the benefit of British and Indian elites.

It would have been impossible for the relative handful of British in India to control the subcontinent and its 350 million people by the 1930s without the support or the active help of most Indians. The British officer contingent in the Indian army reached 40,000 only in the special circumstances of the two world wars. The total number of Britons of all levels and in all branches of the civil service, including district officers, judges, and police, was never more than 12,000. In short, colonial India was run mainly by Indians, who until relatively late supported the British raj, or government, willingly. By 1910, for example, the police force comprised about 5,000 Britons and more than 600,000 Indians. The rest of the civil service employed about 600,000 Indians with only some 5,000 Britons, and the army consisted of about 150,000 native troops and approximately 25,000 British officers.

In contrast, the higher echelons of government remained a British preserve. As if to show their aloofness

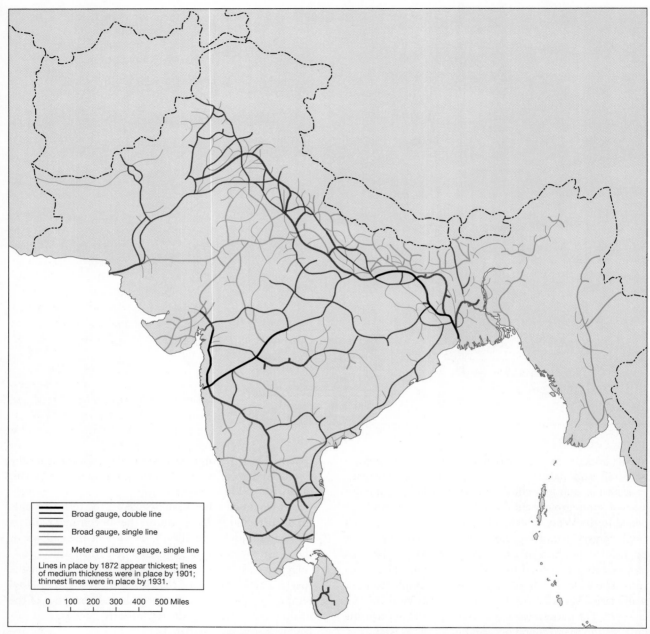

Broad gauge, double line

Broad gauge, single line

Meter and narrow gauge, single line

Lines in place by 1872 appear thickest; lines of medium thickness were in place by 1901; thinnest lines were in place by 1931.

0   100   200   300   400   500 Miles

MAP 35.4   GROWTH OF INDIA'S RAILWAY NETWORK

from the country, they governed in the blazing hot months of summer from stations in the Himalayan foothills, first at Darjeeling in northernmost Bengal and later from Simla, north of Delhi. From both they enjoyed spectacular views of the snow-covered mountains; cool, bracing air; Western-style lodges and cottages that reminded them of home; and a round of parties, picnics, and receptions.

As more colonial officers served longer, young British women came or were sent out to India to find a husband, an annual migration at the beginning of the cool weather in autumn irreverently referred to as the "arrival of the fishing fleet." Those who remained unspoken for by the time the hot weather resumed in mid-March often went back to England as "returned empties." As the British community grew, many families by the twentieth century had lived in India for several generations and thought of it as home. They called themselves Anglo-Indians and lived in separate residential areas built for them some distance from the Indian towns where they worked. These were known as "civil lines" or "cantonments," since many of them had begun as quarters for troops or garrisons. Their households were staffed by large numbers of Indian servants, whose labor was cheap.

Another group was also known as Anglo-Indians. These were the products of intermarriage, which had been common in the eighteenth and early nineteenth centuries and occasionally took place in later years. These Anglo-Indians were rejected by both the Indian and British communities, but they usually tried to pass as English and spoke wistfully of "home," meaning an England that most of them had never seen. Many of them became Christians in an effort to raise their status, as did many Untouchables. Missionary efforts made few converts otherwise, although mission schools remained an important means to Western education for many non-Christians as well as for the few Christians.

New Delhi: Indian Summer of the Raj

Calcutta had long seemed inappropriate as the capital of a British India that had expanded to cover the subcontinent, thousands of miles from Bengal. Although now a thoroughly Indian city, it had been founded by the British themselves and had no indigenous roots or history. Its marginal coastal site further emphasized the foreignness of British rule. For several years after 1900 alternative capital sites were considered, and Delhi, the former Mughal capital, was chosen. At the head of the Ganges valley, Delhi controlled routes both east and south to the heart of India. Successive invaders had to capture Delhi first, mounting their campaigns and ruling their empires from there. The British raj moved too in 1911 to rule from where so many others had before.

It was decided to build a new planned city as an imperial statement, adjacent to the old city and with open space around it but still well within sight of Shah Jahan's Red Fort (see Chapter 20). The remains of other imperial Delhis of the past also showed on the skyline. An artificial hill was built as the setting for the monumental residence and gardens of the viceroy, flanked on each side by two large and stately government buildings known as the Secretariat. From this low rise, broad boulevards and wide vistas led to other buildings and monuments to empire, including the parliament house, by the 1920s filled with mainly Indian members.

Like Paris and Washington, New Delhi was planned before the age of mass transit and the automobile. It was built in a star-shaped pattern with broad tree-lined streets intersecting at angles and punctuated by circles of green area around which traffic had to move. The plan included a large separate commercial and shopping district, with buildings in neoclassical and Anglo-Indian styles, grouped around an immense circle, still called Connaught Circus. Related enterprises lined the streets

Social life in the hill stations: a fete at Simla, in a glade nostalgically named Annandale, painted by A. E. Scott around 1845.

leading into it at various angles. Pleasant shaded avenues with British names occupied most of the rest of the new planned city, most of them filled with gracious residences and beautiful gardens for civil servants, Indian princes (most of whom maintained extensive establishments in New Delhi), and other members of the upper classes. Lesser officials, workers, and servants commuted the mile or so from Old Delhi, mainly by bicycle, or were housed in the unplanned developments that soon grew around the edges of New Delhi.

The ambitious building plans of 1911 and 1912 were delayed by World War I, but by 1930 the new imperial capital was complete. The architects of New Delhi were of course British, but they made a generally successful effort to combine Western and Indian monumental and imperial traditions, consciously using the same red sandstone of which the Red Fort had been built and creating buildings that fit their Indian setting far better than the earlier Victorian extravagances in Calcutta and Bombay. Old Delhi remains a traditional Indian city, centered around the Red Fort. A confusing maze of tiny streets and alleys surrounds the bazaar near Shah Jahan's great mosque, the Jama Masjid. The large unbuilt area in front of the Red Fort remains a vast open-air market and a frequent scene of political

rallies. New Delhi became almost automatically the capital of independent India, with no sense of inappropriateness for the world's largest parliamentary democracy, still based on British colonial foundations. Since 1947 Delhi has boomed and become a major industrial center. But Old and New Delhi represent different strands in India's varied past and now also show the two faces of contemporary India, traditional and modern.

The Rise of Indian Nationalism

British-educated Indians, despite their prosperity, were increasingly resentful of the racial discrimination to which they were subject. Many began to demand a larger role in their country's government. Gradually, a movement for independence developed. Liberal Englishmen agreed, contending that alien rule was contrary to the British tradition of representative government and political freedom. Gestures toward increasing the participation of Indians in the administration and civil service and elections for some officials and advisers came too slowly to satisfy either Indian or British critics.

The Indian National Congress, which was to become the core of the independence movement, was actually founded by an Englishman in 1885. Indian political leaders made nationalist appeals, among them highly effective and articulate figures such as M. G. Ranade (1842–1901), B. G. Tilak (1856–1920), G. K. Gokhale (1866–1915), and Motilal Nehru (1861–1931), the father of Jawaharlal Nehru (1889–1964), independent India's first prime minister. Their language, culture, and education were as much English as Indian, and they could speak eloquently in terms of British tradition itself against the colonial rule of their country by foreigners.

Meanwhile, fear of the still expanding Russian empire in central Asia prompted yet another disastrous invasion of Afghanistan in 1878 to install a British puppet on the throne of Kabul. The Afghans murdered the British resident and his entire staff and military escort within a year, and guerrilla fighters stalemated a second invasion until it was withdrawn in 1880 and the Afghans were again "permitted" to choose their own ruler. Opinion in Britain was outraged by both the brutality and the cost of this futile military adventure, and the Disraeli government fell as a result.

The colonial government in India spearheaded other costly ventures as well. In addition to the conquest of Burma, it launched an armed reconnaissance against Ti-

An example of colonial architecture: Victoria Station, Bombay, with a statue of Queen Victoria atop its dome.

bet in 1903 and 1904 to forestall illusory Russian influence there. The mission showed the flag and obtained an agreement about the frontier. While imperial posturing preoccupied the colonial government and drained the country's resources, poverty in India remained largely unaddressed. Indian nationalists blamed the severe economic distress in many areas on colonial rule. Boycotts of British imports were begun, cutting their value by 25 percent between 1904 and 1908. The government's response was often repressive, and many political leaders were jailed. There were still many British in government with more liberal ideas, and many more outside government, who strove to reduce racial discrimination and urged Indian self-government as Britain's ultimate goal. In 1883, for example, it was agreed that Indian judges could preside over cases involving Europeans. But imperialist attitudes and bureaucratic inertia retarded giving Indians a larger and more appropriate role in their own government.

More than a million Indian troops and noncombatants served the British effort in World War I in Europe and the Middle East. Many hoped that this would speed progress toward self-government. When change lagged after the war, civil disobedience movements spread, led by Mohandas "Mahatma" Gandhi (1869–1948), among others; this was met by more government repression. In 1919 Indian troops under British command, called in to put down rioting in Amritsar near Lahore, fired on a peaceful and unarmed crowd celebrating a festival, leaving 400 dead. The massacre was a watershed in Anglo-Indian relations. It turned most Indians away from the idea of reform and toward the goal of full independence, creating almost overnight a greatly expanded nationalist movement.

In 1907 the British Parliament had declared that independence was Britain's objective in India, a point the British government reaffirmed in 1917 and 1921, but the colonial administration remained slow to move. Although the electoral system was greatly broadened in the 1920s and 1930s and Indian legislatures and officials were given far more power and responsibility, it was too little, too late. Time had run out for British rule in India.

The Amritsar Massacre of April 1919 was followed by further repression in the wake of renewed protests and demonstrations. Here British police officers in Amritsar watch while their Indian assistants search a demonstrator.

Colonial Regimes in Southeast Asia

The Dutch came to control the largest amount of territory and population in Southeast Asia, incorporating the whole of what is now Indonesia in their colonial empire, from which they largely excluded other Western trade or investment competition. Many Chinese were already there, however, and their numbers increased to some 3 million as they expanded their control of smaller-scale domestic trade and retailing. The British, along with other westerners, had been trading in Burma since the seventeenth century, but as their Indian empire and imperial ambition grew, they progressively annexed Burma. Malaya was thinly settled and unimportant in trade until the tin and rubber boom of the late nineteenth century, but the British hoped to use bases there in an effort to tap the trade with Southeast Asia and with China, a role ultimately performed by Singapore. By the end of the nineteenth century all Malaya was under British colonial administration, but primarily on an indirect basis through local Malay sultans. French and American colonialists arrived late on the scene. France acquired the Indochinese states of Vietnam, Cambodia, and Laos through conquest by 1885, and the Americans inherited control of the Philippines as a consequence of their defeat of Spain, the former colonial master of the area, in 1898. Each of these Western colonial regimes followed policies with many similarities and some differences. Siam (now Thailand) remained independent as a buffer between rival

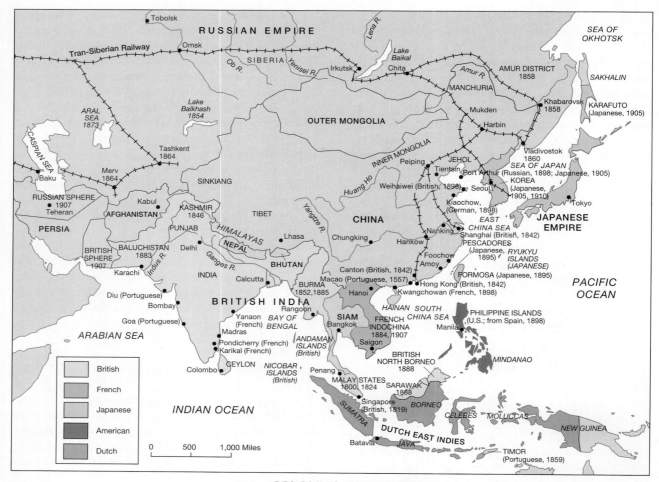

MAP 35.5   COLONIAL EMPIRES IN ASIA

colonial empires but had to accept the same set of "unequal treaties" as was imposed on China and Japan.

The British in Burma and Malaya

Britain's activity in Southeast Asia had been incidental to its concerns in India and its efforts to break into the China market. It was at first confined to founding bases on the fringes of Dutch power in Malaya. In 1786 a settlement was made at Penang on the northwestern Malay coast, where the British hoped to attract Chinese traders. This was only moderately successful, and they established what soon became their major Southeast Asian trade base at Singapore in 1819.

From the start, Singapore, with its large and excellent harbor commanding the southern entrance to the Molucca Strait, was a commercial center for all Southeast Asia. Malaya itself remained thinly populated and largely undeveloped until the end of the nineteenth century. Burma was India's immediate geographic neighbor to the east. Its antiquated monarchy periodically made difficulties for British merchants and ignored or insulted British representatives. A brief war from 1824 to 1826 gave the British special rights in the important coastal provinces of Burma. Two more minor wars in 1852 and 1885–1886, for the most part provoked by the British, annexed lower Burma and the rest of the country. Burma was then administered as a province of British India until it was granted separate colonial status in 1937.

Burma and Malaya were rapidly commercialized after 1880 under British rule. Railways were built, and steam navigation was developed. The Irrawaddy delta in lower Burma, including much newly cultivated land, became a major exporter of rice. Upper Burma produced timber, especially teak, for export, and the central valley yielded oil from wells drilled by the British. All this moved out for export through the port of Rangoon, which served as the colonial capital. In Malaya were found rich deposits of tin, a metal in great demand in the industrializing West, and toward the end of the century Malaya also became the world's major producer of plantation rubber. Labor for tin mining and rubber tapping had to be imported, since the local Malays, subsistence farmers, were not interested in such work. The gap was filled mainly from overcrowded South China, and Chinese settlers soon comprised nearly half the population of Malaya. In time many of these Chinese immigrants, who also entered the booming commercial economy of Singapore, became wealthy. The Malays increasingly resented Chinese domination of the commercial economy. Indians also entered, as both laborers and merchants, and with the Chinese and the British controlled the commercial production and foreign trade of both Burma and Malaya. The colonial government of Malaya ruled as much as possible through local sultans and tried to preserve traditional Malay culture, but both countries were economically transformed.

French, Dutch, and American Colonialism

Largely eliminated from India by the end of the eighteenth century, the French sought their own colonial sphere in Asia. They used the persecution of French Catholic missionaries in Vietnam as a pretext for conquering the southern provinces in 1862, including the port of Saigon. Later they annexed Cambodia and Laos and in 1885 took over northern Vietnam after defeating Chinese forces sent to protect their tributary state. Under French control, southern Vietnam became a major exporter of rice and rubber grown in the delta of the Mekong River and exported through the chief port of Saigon, which became the colonial capital. Cambodia and Laos remained little developed commercially. Northern Vietnam was already too densely populated to produce surpluses for export, but there was some small industrial growth around the city of Hanoi and in the northern port of Haiphong. The colonial administration tried to impose French culture on these territories, collectively called Indochina.

French rule was oppressive and often ruthless in suppressing all gestures toward political expression. The army was augmented by special security forces and had much of the apparatus of a police state, which executed, jailed, or drove into exile most Vietnamese leaders. These included the young Ho Chi Minh (1890–1969), later the head of the Vietnamese Communist party, who went to Europe in 1911 and later left Paris for Moscow and Canton.

The Dutch left most of Indonesia to native rulers until late in the nineteenth century, content with controlling trade from Batavia (now Djakarta), their colonial capital. Batavia was situated on the tropical island of Java, which produced a variety of plantation crops the Dutch promoted after 1830, including sugar, coffee, tea, and tobacco. By the early 1900s rubber was an important commodity, and Indonesia was second only to Malaya in its production. Oil was also found and exploited. The discovery of more oil and tin and the cultivation of prime land for rubber and tobacco prompted the Dutch to conquer first the neighboring island of Sumatra and then Borneo, Celebes, the Moluccas, Bali, and the hundreds of smaller islands in the archipelago south of the Philippines. New railways and ports were built to expedite trade.

Dutch rule was fiercely contested on some of the islands, especially Sumatra, and it never penetrated effectively into the mountain and jungle interior of Borneo. (The British controlled the northern coast of Borneo.) Dutch rule became increasingly oppressive. Indonesians were excluded from government, prevented from exercising political rights, and denied access to more than elementary education. Java was systematically exploited by forcing its peasants to grow export crops for Dutch profit. Production and population grew very rapidly, but living standards and quality of life declined.

In 1898 the United States went to war with Spain over Cuba and acquired the Philippines as its first overseas colony. The 43 years of American control had a greater effect on the culture and economy of the islands than 400 years of Spanish rule. The Americans built roads and hospitals and established an education system up to the university level. In Asia only Japan had higher literacy and public health. But America's economic impact was exploitive. In partnership with rich Filipinos, it concentrated on growing commercial crops for export, especially sugar, and often neglected the basic needs of the people as a whole. Manila, the colonial capital, became a rapidly growing commercial center and the chief base of the Filipino middle class and educated elite. The Americans declared as their goal the creation of a democratic society in their own image. To a degree this was achieved, but Philippine politics remained under the control of a landed elite supported by others who profited from the American connection and paid little attention to the dominantly peasant population, which remained exploited. The country had been subjugated only by a brutal war against Filipino nationalist resistance from 1899 to 1902 in which the Americans pursued policies that foreshadowed their later misadventures in Vietnam. Most peasants, still largely illiterate, could not take advantage of free public education or free expression. The United States granted independence to the Philippines in 1946 on terms that ensured its continuing influence and left huge American military bases there.

Independent Siam

While the rest of Southeast Asia was being taken over by imperialist powers, the Thais kept their independence. This was in part the result of geography. Siam lay between the British in Burma and Malaya and the French in Indochina. Neither was willing to let the other dominate the country. British preponderance in Thai foreign trade and investment was balanced by French annexation of territory claimed or occupied by Siam in western Cambodia and Laos. British Malaya detached Siam's southern provinces. Nonetheless, the Thais benefited from a series of able kings who adroitly played the French off against the British and urged the advantages to both of leaving at least part of their country as a buffer state. They had to grant special trade, residence, and legal privileges to the colonial powers, a system like that imposed on China, but there was no foreign effort to take over the government. Nevertheless the Thai economy developed along the same lines as those of colonial Southeast Asia, with a big new export trade in rice from the delta area, followed later by rubber and tropical hardwoods. Bangkok, the capital, grew rapidly as the chief port for foreign trade and spreading commercialization.

Overseas Chinese

Western development had important demographic consequences for Southeast Asia. Immigrant Chinese began to flood into all the commercially developed parts of the region in growing numbers after 1870, as plantation and mining workers and as traders. They soon largely monopolized the retail trade in all the cities of Southeast Asia, although they shared it with immigrant Indians in Burma and Malaya. In Bangkok they constituted more than half the population and, as in Burma and Vietnam, controlled most of the large export trade in rice. Southeast Asians resented them, especially since they also served as moneylenders and owned most of the shops, but they were often welcomed by the colonialists as useful labor and commercial agents. In Siam, unlike the rest of Southeast Asia, most Chinese were quickly assimilated into society through intermarriage and acculturation. Elsewhere they tended to remain confined to their own quarters and suffered discrimination from the local people. Altogether, Chinese settlers in Southeast Asia totaled about 15 million by the outbreak of World War II.

China Besieged

The Opium War of 1839–1842, in which the British demolished the Chinese forces, was ended by the Treaty of Nanking, which granted Britain most of its demands

WESTERN COLONIZATION, 1800–1900

The Americas	Africa	Asia
Dissolution of the Spanish and Portuguese empires (c. 1810–1825)	Britain occupies the Cape Colony (1806)	Britain completes conquest of India (1818), acquires Singapore (1819)
U.S. proclaims Monroe Doctrine (1823)	French occupy Algeria (1830)	Opium War against China (1839–1842); Hong Kong ceded to Britain
French empire in Mexico (1864–1867)	Boers begin Great Trek (1833)	United States forces Japan to end policy of isolation (1853–1854)
Canada gains Dominion status (1867)	Britain begins systematic exploration of central Africa (1849)	Sepoy Rebellion in India (1857–1858); Second Anglo-Chinese War (1858–1860)
Spanish-American War; United States acquires Puerto Rico, the Philippines; Cuba becomes U.S. protectorate (1898)	Gold discovered in the Transvaal (1868); scramble for Africa begins (1870)	France colonizes Indochina (1858–1885); Russia annexes Transcaucasus and central Asian steppe (1859–1879), founds port of Vladivostok (1860)
U.S. detaches Panama from Colombia, begins Panama Canal (1903)	Berlin Conference (1884–1885); German empire; Congo Free State recognized Anglo-Boer War (1899–1902)	Britain annexes Burma to India (1886); U.S. naval base at Pearl Harbor (1887) Boxer Rebellion (1899–1900)

Opium

The imperial commissioner sent to Canton in 1839 to stop the opium trade wrote a letter in the same year to the young Queen Victoria that read in part as follows:

Magnificently our great emperor soothes and pacifies China and the foreign countries. . . . But there appear among the crowd of barbarians both good and bad persons, unevenly. . . . There are barbarian ships that come here for trade to make a great profit. But by what right do they in return use the poisonous drug [opium] to injure the Chinese people? . . . Of all that China exports to foreign countries, there is not a single thing which is not beneficial. . . . On the other hand, articles coming from outside China can only be used as toys; they are not needed by China. Nevertheless, our Celestial Court lets tea, silk, and other goods be shipped without limit. This is for no other reason than to share the benefit with the people of the whole world.

Source: S. Y. Teng and J. K. Fairbank, *China's Response to the West* (Cambridge, Mass.: Harvard University Press, 1954), pp. 24–26.

for trading rights and concessions. The war was provoked by Chinese efforts to end British and American imports of opium, but the larger issues were China's refusal to deal with foreigners as equals or to permit them to trade where they liked. The port of Hong Kong was ceded outright, and five mainland ports, including Shanghai and Canton, were opened to British trade and residence. Other Western powers, including the United States, negotiated similar treaties the following year. These included the right of extraterritoriality, whereby foreign nationals in China were made immune from Chinese jurisdiction and were dealt with according to their own laws. The war had finally cracked China's proud isolation.

Foreign trade immediately began a rapid increase that continued until the world depression of the 1930s. Tea and silk remained the dominant exports and opium the main import, although it was overtaken after 1870 by cotton yarn, textiles, kerosene, and a variety of other foreign manufactured goods. The treaties further impinged on China's sovereignty by limiting the import tariffs it might impose to 5 percent. This had the effect of giving Western goods virtually unrestricted access to the vast Chinese market. Although China continued to provide most of its own needs, the treaties reduced the country to semicolonial status.

Peking's reluctance to abide by the terms of the treaties led to a second war from 1858 to 1860. British and French troops captured Tientsin (Tianjin) and Peking and burned the imperial summer palace. They

saw this as retaliation for Chinese "treachery"—the breaking of successive agreements to observe earlier treaties and to receive the British ambassador in Peking, as well as firing on British forces and imprisoning their representatives.

Traders and Missionaries

The Treaty of Tientsin, which ended this second war, opened still more ports to residence and trade and allowed foreigners, including missionaries, free movement and enterprise anywhere in the country. Missionaries, the largest number of them American, often served as a forward wave for imperialism, building churches and preaching the Gospel in the interior and then demanding protection from their home governments against Chinese protests or riots. The trouble that missionaries or foreign traders encountered might be answered by sending a warship to the nearest coastal or river port to threaten or shell inhabitants, a practice known as "gunboat diplomacy." When antiforeign mobs assaulted missionaries or their converts, Western governments often used this as a pretext for extracting still more concessions.

Most Chinese were not receptive to the Christian message, especially in the evangelical form of most missionary preaching, and they resented foreigners with special privileges and protection encroaching on their country. Nor did they understand the missionary practice of

Through Each Other's Eyes

After the Opium War, foreign arrogance increased. Here is a sample from 1858.

It is impossible that our merchants and missionaries can course up and down the inland waters of this great region and traffic in their cities and preach in their villages without wearing away at the crust of the Chinaman's stoical and skeptical conceit. The whole present system in China is a hollow thing, with a hard brittle surface. . . . Some day a happy blow will shiver it [and] it will all go together.

But the Chinese returned the compliment.

It is monstrous in barbarians to attempt to improve the inhabitants of the Celestial Empire when they are so miserably deficient themselves. Thus, introducing a poisonous drug for their own benefit and to the injury of others, they are deficient in benevolence. Sending their fleets and armies to rob other nations, they can make no pretense to rectitude. . . . How can they expect to renovate others? They allow the rich and noble to enter office without passing through any literary examinations, and do not open the road to advancement to the poorest and meanest in the land. From this it appears that foreigners are inferior to the Chinese and therefore must be unfit to instruct them.

Sources: G. W. Cooke, *China: Being the Times Special Correspondence from China in the Years 1857–58* (London: Routledge, 1858), p. v; "A Chinese Tract of the Mid-Nineteenth Century," in E. P. Boardman, *Christian Influence on the Ideology of the Taiping Rebellion* (Madison: University of Wisconsin Press, 1952), p. 129.

buying or adopting orphans for charitable and religious purposes and so assumed the worst motives for these practices. Stories circulated that they ate babies or gouged out their eyes for medicine. In 1870 a mob destroyed a French Catholic mission in Tientsin and killed 10 nuns and 11 other foreigners; gunboats and heavy reparations followed.

Unlike the British, the French had no important trade with China and often used protection of their missionaries as a means of increasing their influence. In 1883 they went to war with China over Vietnam when Chinese troops crossed the border to eject them. The French destroyed part of the new Western-style Chinese navy and the dockyards at Foochow on the South China coast, which they had earlier helped to build. China was humbled again.

The Taiping Rebellion

Meanwhile, the greatest of all uprisings against the Ch'ing government erupted in 1850, the Taiping Rebellion. Westerners tend to overemphasize their own role in China as the major influence on events after 1840. China

was huge, westerners were few, and their activities were limited to the treaty ports and outlying mission stations. China continued to respond primarily to its own long-standing internal problems, chief among which was a burgeoning population. Having outstripped production, it was falling into poverty and distress in many areas. The Taiping leader, Hung Hsiu-Ch'uan (Hong Xiuquan), was a frustrated scholar who had failed the rigid imperial examinations several times and then espoused an idiosyncratic version of Christianity adapted from missionary teaching. Hung became the leader of a largely peasant group from the impoverished mountain region of southern China, which resented its exclusion from the treaty ports and sought the overthrow of the Manchus. The rebels picked up massive support as they moved north and captured Nanking (Nanjing) in 1853. A northward thrust from there was turned back later that year near Tientsin, but rebel forces won at least a foothold in 16 of China's 18 provinces and dominated the rich Yangtze valley.

The efforts of the Taiping rebels to govern were relatively feeble. Large-scale fighting against the imperial forces continued without significant breaks until its final suppression in 1864. The cost in destruction and loss of life was horrendous. As many as 50 million people died, and much of the productive lower Yangtze region was laid waste. During the same period the Ch'ing also faced three other mass uprisings, in the north, the southwest, and the northwest. The latter two were primarily Muslim rebellions against Ch'ing rule, which lingered until 1873. As one Ch'ing official said, these revolts were like a disease of China's vital organs. In contrast, the activities of the Western powers were a marginal affliction only of the extremities.

Attempts at Reform

One foreign power, however, was still advancing by land: the Russians. Sensing China's weakness, they penetrated the Amur valley in northern Manchuria, from which they had been excluded in 1689. In the treaties following the war of 1858–1860 they detached the maritime provinces of eastern Manchuria and added them to their empire; among their acquisitions was the port of Vladivostok. Muslim rebellion in the northwest after 1862 served as a pretext for Russian intervention in northern Sinkiang (Xinjiang). The Ch'ing government decided that this threat must be met head on, marched an army 2,500 miles from its base in eastern China, and to general surprise defeated both the rebels and the Russians by 1878.

Survival of the Ch'ing regime against the appalling challenges it faced showed that it was still capable of successful action. After 1860 it undertook a policy of "self-strengthening," which included the establishment of new Western-style arsenals, gun foundries, and shipyards. These and other efforts to modernize were handicapped by government red tape, but they achieved some progress. Several outstanding senior officials who realized the need for change rose to power. For a decade or two the Ch'ing seemed to have a new lease on life and to show surprising vigor.

It was not to last. The reformers never won full support from the still archconservative throne or from most of the people. Both remained essentially antiforeign and opposed to adopting Western tactics even to fight westerners. In 1862 a weak boy-emperor came to the throne, dominated by his scheming mother, Tz'u Hsi (Cixi, 1835–1908), a former imperial concubine who had plotted her way to the top. When the emperor died in 1875 at the age of 19, she put her 4-year-old nephew in his place, retaining all real power for herself as the empress dowager until her death in 1908. Tz'u Hsi was clever and politically masterful but narrow-minded and deeply conservative. She had no understanding of what was required to cope with the foreign threat to Chinese sovereignty.

Tz'u Hsi, the empress dowager, was a powerful and unscrupulous ruler. In keeping with the degeneracy of the late Ch'ing period, she favored the overly ornate style in which she decorated many rooms in the Imperial Palace in Peking.

China's first tentative efforts at change were thus for the most part aborted. The Confucian reactionaries, who with few exceptions again dominated the government, grudgingly acknowledged the potency of Western arms but insisted that there could be no abandoning or even altering the traditional Chinese view of the world to deal with them.

Treaty Ports and Mission Schools

Meanwhile the treaty ports, which numbered more than 100 by 1910, grew rapidly, attracting Chinese as merchants, partners, and laborers. Manufacturing also began to grow in the treaty ports, especially after 1895, when the Japanese imposed a new treaty that permitted foreign-owned factories to operate in the ports; these produced mainly textiles and other consumer goods. This was the real beginning of modern industrialization in China.

Chinese entrepreneurs and industrialists, many of whom had been blocked or discouraged by the conservative government, welcomed the more enterprising world of the treaty ports. As elsewhere in Asia, imperialist arrogance was growing, and the Chinese found themselves excluded from foreign clubs and parks and treated as second-class citizens in their own cities. Many were torn between their ancient cultural pride and their sense of humiliation by westerners on the one hand and their reluctant admiration for the West's power and success on the other. As with their Indian counterparts in colonial Calcutta and Bombay, these conflicts produced the first stirrings of modern nationalism.

The most widespread Western influence on Chinese society came through the efforts of missionaries. The total number of Chinese Christians remained discouragingly small, and many, perhaps most, of them were so-called rice Christians, who attended church for handouts. Most Chinese looked down on Christian converts as traitors or simply as the dregs of society. Many of the missions came to realize that education and medical help were more attractive than Christian doctrine and might pave a smoother path toward the goal of conversion. Mission-run schools spread rapidly, as did their hospitals. The schools drew many students, in time most of the young Chinese who wanted to study English and Western learning or science. Although most graduates did not become converts, they adopted Western ways of thinking in many respects. Most twentieth-century Chinese nationalists were influenced by mission schools, and most of China's universities were founded by missionaries.

Government schools that included Western curricula were also established, and in 1905 the traditional examination system was abolished. Missionaries and others translated a wide range of Western works, which were read avidly by the new generation of Chinese intellectuals, many of whom began to call for the overthrow of the Ch'ing regime. Ironically, they used the treaty ports, notably Shanghai, as their base, where they were protected from Ch'ing repression by living under foreign law.

The Boxer Rebellion

Missionaries in rural areas continued to provoke antiforeign riots as their activities spread. In the late 1890s the empress dowager adroitly turned a group of impoverished bandits and rebels in the eastern part of northern China against the missionaries instead of against the dynasty and by extension against all foreigners. By early 1900 this group, which called itself the "Fists of Righteous Harmony" but was known more simply to westerners as the Boxers, went on a rampage, burning mission establishments and killing missionaries and Chinese converts. Converts were resented for their use of foreign intervention in their disputes with other Chinese. By June 1900, with covert imperial support, the Boxers besieged the foreign legations in Peking, which barely held out until relieved by a multinational expedition in mid-August. Having earlier declared war officially against all the foreign powers, the court fled to Sian (Xian). After brutal reprisals, the Western powers (now including a large Japanese contingent) withdrew, and a peace was patched up a year later. A staggering indemnity was forced on China, on top of one already extracted by Japan in 1895. The empress dowager and her reactionary councillors, who had seen the Boxers as the final solution to the "barbarian problem," were left nominally in power.

The Ch'ing dynasty was moribund, but no workable alternative was yet at hand. China had still to learn the lessons of national unity and shared political purpose, which had been unnecessary in the past, when the empire controlled "all under heaven" and China had no rivals. The government finally fell in 1911, more of its own weight and incompetence than from the small, disorganized group of revolutionaries whose uprising joined the defection of disgruntled troops. The fall of the Ch'ing dynasty was hardly a revolution, but it ended the imperial rule by which China had been governed for more than 2,000 years and opened the way for fundamental change.

Japan Among the Powers

As indicated in Chapter 30, the antiquated Tokugawa shogunate was toppled in 1868 and 1869 by a new group of reformers. Their goal was the rapid modernization and westernization of Japan in order to save their country from colonialism and to remove the unequal treaties that had been forced on it. That effort was spectacularly successful. By 1895 new Western-style technology and industry had progressed far and had given Japan new power. With power came new ambition. In a conflict over dominance in Korea, Japan's new navy and army easily defeated China's poorly coordinated forces in 1894–1895 and detached both Korea and Taiwan from Chinese control, adding them to what was now the Japanese colonial empire. In 1904–1905 Japan's new strength enabled it to win early victories against a more formidable opponent, Russia, and then to conclude a treaty that replaced Russian dominance in Manchuria with Japanese. Confidence was high, as Japan was clearly established as a major power in East Asia, and by the early years of the twentieth century Japan was able to get rid of the unequal treaties and to deal with Western powers as an equal. But imperial ambition and military adventuring led the nation into what the Japanese call the "dark valley," beginning with their efforts to take control of much of eastern China in 1915, their formal takeover of Manchuria as part of their empire in 1931, and the morass of their full-scale invasion of China from 1937, a road that led to Pearl Harbor and Hiroshima. Nevertheless, the Meiji period, from 1868 to 1912 (the death of the Meiji emperor), was one of great and constructive progress that laid the foundation of modern Japanese society and economy.

The Meiji Restoration: Response to the West

In contrast to China, the Meiji Restoration in Japan ushered in a period of rapid change and wholesale westernization. Meiji was the reign title of the young emperor, who moved to Tokyo ("eastern capital") in 1869 as the restored head of state, although his role remained symbolic. He and his successors served as a rallying point for new nationalist sentiment, and most Japanese took inspiration from the fact that their country was once again under imperial rule.

The goal of the new government was to strengthen and modernize Japan and thereby to free it from the unequal treaties (see Chapter 30). Like China, Japan had suffered loss of control over its tariffs and had been forced to concede extraterritoriality and other special privileges to the Western powers. In contrast to the Chinese, however, Japan's leaders realized that regaining their independence depended on mastering Western technology. They also saw that military technology could not be separated from overall industrialization or from the institutional structures that had produced and accompanied it in the West.

Whereas pride rendered these truths unacceptable to the Chinese, Japan showed little hesitation after 1869 in transforming or abolishing traditional institutions. Many Japanese urged wholesale westernization, arguing, "If we use it, that will make it Japanese." Some radical enthusiasts in the early years of Meiji actually tried to destroy traditional temples in their zeal to sweep away the old and make way for the new Japan. Japanese national pride did not rest so much in the culture as in the people's sense of themselves. Although change proved largely bloodless and was accompanied by relatively minor political reorganization, Meiji Japan produced in many ways a real revolution.

Economy and Government

The first priority was rapid industrialization, especially in heavy industries and armaments. Foreign advisers were hired to expedite this growth—from Britain for a modern navy, from Germany for a modern army and armaments

industry, and so on. Railways were quickly built to link the major cities, and new ports and facilities were created. The machinery of government and law was wholly remade, modeled on a judicious combination of Western systems. What emerged was a modified constitutional monarchy with a parliament and a largely Western-derived legal system. Such change was important also to demonstrate that Japan was a "civilized" country where foreigners did not need extraterritoriality to protect them.

All Western institutions, and even such details of Western culture as dress and diet, were seen as sources of strength. Samurai discarded their swords and traditional garb, put on Western business suits, learned to waltz, and dominated the new bureaucracy. Some samurai found careers as officers in the new army, and others went into business, government, or manufacturing. The ranks of the army were filled with peasant conscripts; war was no longer a gentlemen's preserve.

The Japanese were rapidly mobilized toward the new goals. They were accustomed to direction, from daimyo, samurai, or other hierarchical superiors, and most came to share the national objectives with genuine enthusiasm. Japan's almost ready-made nationalism, the fruit of an island country with a long history of separateness, was a strong asset. Its people were also linguistically, racially, and culturally homogeneous (as the Chinese and Indians were not), and the country was small and more easily integrated as a unit. In landmass and population, approximately 50 million by 1910, Japan was about the size of one of China's larger provinces, and some 90 percent of its people were concentrated in the corridor between Tokyo and Osaka. What was decided in Tokyo was quickly carried out everywhere as national policy. Farm output tripled between 1870 and 1940 as a result of both new Western technology and hard work. In many ways it was the latter that accounted for Meiji Japan's astounding success.

Japanese Imperialism

By the 1890s Japan had a modern navy and army and a fast-growing industrial base. Japanese steamships had won a major place in East Asian trade, and Japanese merchants had acquired a rising share of the China market. In 1894 Britain agreed to relinquish the unequal clauses of the old treaty with Japan by 1899, and other nations soon followed suit.

Having followed the Western lead in modern development, Japan now joined the other imperialist powers in colonial conquests. Korea was the handiest target, and in brief campaigns in 1894 and 1895 the new Japanese fleet and army demolished Chinese forces sent to protect China's tributary dependency. The peace treaty made

Japan dominant in a still nominally independent Korea; the Chinese also ceded to them the island of Taiwan (Formosa), a huge indemnity, and the right to operate factories in the China treaty ports.

At the same time, the Russians were extending their influence, railways, and concession areas in Manchuria, whose southern tip they leased from China. The Japanese saw this as a threat to their position in Korea, but in any case they had their own plans for Manchuria. They struck there in 1904 without declaring war, winning a rapid series of land and naval battles against Russia by a combination of dash and willingness to take heavy casualties. The Russians were far from their home base and inadequately prepared; in time their much greater resources would have prevailed, but the Japanese persuaded the American president, Theodore Roosevelt, to arrange a peace at Portsmouth, New Hampshire, in 1905. The Russians were concerned by then with the first stirrings of revolution at home, and the war was expensive and unpopular in Russia. Japan inherited Russia's position in Manchuria and tightened its grip on Korea, which in 1910 became an outright colony in a growing Japanese empire.

Japan's first steps toward empire profited from the tacit support of the Western powers, who saw it as a counterweight against Russia's geographic advantage in the Far East. Japan had been encouraged to attack Russia by the Anglo-Japanese treaty of alliance and friendship signed in 1902, which was welcomed in Japan as a mark of international equality. Theodore Roosevelt saw the Japanese as promising allies, "bully fighters," as he called them. The Russo-Japanese War of 1904–1905 inaugurated a period of new pride, confidence, and continued economic progress.

Japan joined the Allies in World War I, ostensibly as an equal partner, although it took no part in the fighting in Europe apart from sending a few destroyers to join the British Mediterranean fleet. The opportunity was used instead to take over the German concession areas in China, centered in the province of Shantung (Shandong) in the eastern part of northern China. In 1915 Japan presented China with a list of 21 demands that would have made it in effect a Japanese colony. By such bullying tactics, Japan quickly lost the admiration and goodwill built up by its progress since 1869. The Twenty-one Demands also infuriated Chinese patriots and more than any other event spurred the rise of broad-based Chinese nationalism. The demands were rejected, although Japan hung on to the German concessions in Shantung. Meanwhile, the Japanese continued to develop Taiwan, Korea, and Manchuria.

Taiwan offered rice, sugar, and tropical crops to feed Japan's booming population. Korea had rich resources of coal, iron ore, and timber, which Japan appropriated. The Japanese drained the country of every useful commodity, including food crops, to support their growth, leaving the Koreans as an impoverished and exploited labor force. Koreans were forced to adopt Japanese names, and most were denied even elementary education; the public use of their own language was forbidden. Manchuria, still formally part of China but in effect a Japanese sphere, was a storehouse of coal, ores, timber, productive agricultural land, and potential hydroelectric power. Japan exploited all these resources while building an infrastructure of railways, mines, irrigation systems, dams, port facilities, and a colonial administration. In Korea too, railways, mines, factories, and roads were built and basic economic growth was begun, although for Japanese benefit. In Taiwan the infrastructure for economic redevelopment was also laid, primarily in agriculture, leading to new prosperity.

In Manchuria the Japanese built the largest single industrial complex in Asia, including closely integrated mines and factories in the Mukden (Shenyang) area, a dense rail network, and a highly productive commercialized agriculture that generated large surpluses of wheat and soybeans for export to Japan and to world markets through the port of Dairen. Large power dams were built on Manchuria's rivers. The population increased by nearly a million a year from 1900 to the outbreak of the Pacific war in 1941, consisting almost entirely of Chinese who migrated from a disordered and impoverished North China in search of new economic opportunity. Japan's huge investment in Manchuria laid the basis for China's industrialization after Japan's defeat in 1945. But Japan's record as a colonial power, despite the constructive achievements, was marred, as in Korea, by an exploitive approach as well as a disregard for local interests or aspirations.

Ito Hirobumi: Meiji Statesman

The leading statesman of Meiji Japan, Ito Hirobumi, was born in one of the outer daimyo domains of southwestern Japan in 1841. As a youth, he wanted passionately to save his country from the foreign threat, and at the age of 21 he tried to burn the newly established British embassy in Tokyo. But when he visited Britain the next year, he realized that it was impossible to drive the westerners out by such tactics, and he returned to work for Japan's modernization. After the Meiji Restoration he went with government missions to Europe and America to learn how to make his country strong and in 1881 became Japan's first prime minister under the new Western-style government. A later visit to Prussia convinced him that a constitutional monarchy was best suited to Japan. Ito was the chief architect of the new constitution proclaimed by the emperor in 1889, which contained many elements of the German imperial constitution. He understood, however, that constitutional government, and the cooperation of the new parliament, could not be made to work without political organization and popular support. In 1898 he left office to form a political party for that purpose, which was dominant in Japan until 1941.

After the Russo-Japanese War in 1905, Ito became the first Japanese resident-general in Korea. The Koreans deeply resented Japanese control, but Ito saw a civilian-based policy as preferable to the complete military occupation urged by powerful voices at home and hoped, against the odds, that he could win the Koreans' goodwill and cooperation in developing their country. In 1909 he was assassinated by a Korean patriot while on a visit to northern Manchuria—an abrupt end to the career of a man who might have played a vital moderating role in subsequent

Japanese policies. Ito was an enthusiastic modernizer, especially after his visits to the West, but he also understood the need for compromise in politics and for adapting Western ways to Japanese traditions, circumstances, and values. In some ways he remained at least as traditional as he was modern. His objective was the preservation and development of his country, and westernization was only a means to that end. He believed deeply in the restoration of the emperor's personal rule and aimed to accomplish his goals by working through the throne. But he also understood the rising yearning for a less authoritarian form of government and the need for political parties, a constitution, and a parliament. These aspirations he served well, never letting personal ambition or power cloud his judgment or his dedication to the public welfare.

Australia and the Pacific Islands

Western expansion came late to the Australian continent and most of the Pacific islands. Australia, however, had been inhabited by aborigines for some 50,000 years, and

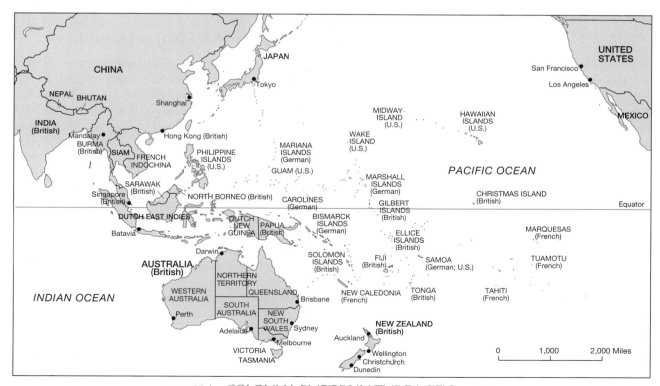

MAP 35.6   COLONIAL EMPIRES IN THE PACIFIC, c. 1900

more recently peoples from Southeast Asia had migrated to Australia and the myriad islands of the Pacific. The culture of these peoples varied from that of the aborigines, who lived until Western colonization very much as their Paleolithic ancestors had, to the Maori of New Zealand, skilled seamen whose delicate, filigreed woodcarving had no equal in the world. Western explorers called this region Oceania. In addition to Australia and New Zealand, Oceania included Melanesia, extending from New Guinea to Fiji; Micronesia, to the north, embracing the islands from the Marianas to the Gilberts; and Polynesia, the easternmost islands, encompassing Samoa and Hawaii.

Australia: Convicts, Wool, and Gold

Although Spanish explorers and traders had plied the Pacific throughout much of the sixteenth century, the Dutch were the first westerners to reach Australia, which they called New Holland, in the early 1600s. The English displayed some interest late in the same century, but not until 1770 did a British expedition under James Cook discover land suitable for settlement and claim Australia for Britain. Because the great island continent was not astride the trade routes, it had hitherto been ignored, but the British soon found a use for the latest acquisition to their empire. Having lost the war with the American colonists and having failed to establish penal settlements in West Africa, they could dump unwanted convicts in Australia.

The first British colony was founded at Sydney on the southeast coast in 1788 by Captain Arthur Phillip, who became the first governor. Because the colony was so distant from Britain and so difficult to supply, it was slow to attract free settlers. Many of the earliest free colonists were soldiers who decided to stay in Australia after serving in the British garrison, notwithstanding the fact that the land was described by one officer as "very barren and forbidding." By the mid-nineteenth century it had become the home of some 160,000 transplanted convicts, many of whom were assigned to work a specified number of years for the free colonizers. New South Wales, as the region around Sydney was called, was difficult to farm, especially because of insufficient water, but in the early 1800s the woolen industry developed rapidly, aided by the British government's termination of import duties on colonial wool. Between 1821, when wool was first shipped to Britain, and 1845, wool export increased from 175,000 pounds to 24 million pounds.

By that point exploration was moving rapidly forward, and there were key settlements at Melbourne in the south, Perth in the southwest, and Brisbane to the north. Interest in Australia increased substantially when gold was discovered in New South Wales and its southern neighbor, Victoria, in 1851, two years after the great rush had begun in California. In the ensuing decade the population of New South Wales jumped from 200,000 to 350,000, and Victoria's rose from 77,000 to 540,000. As the population of the continent as a whole passed 1 million, more attention had to be given to food production, especially when the supply of gold dwindled. As in the American west, bitter conflicts arose between ranchers and farmers, with the latter additionally plagued by water shortages and inadequate transportation facilities. The crisis was gradually resolved only as roads, railways, and irrigation systems were built and as farmers learned to dry-farm and to apply chemical fertilizers.

During the late nineteenth century interest grew in uniting the six Australian colonies, each of which had been given its own legislature by an 1850 British statute. Federation would not only eliminate internal economic barriers but also enhance Australia's ability to withstand potential aggression from one or more of the imperial powers. The resulting commonwealth of Australia, founded in 1901, was a constitutional federation, with the central government, as in the United States, possessing only limited authority.

New Zealand: Maori and Missionaries

The Australian aborigines had been spread too thinly and were too pacific to have posed a serious threat to colonizers. In New Zealand, however, the native Maori were not only relatively more populous, considering New Zealand's smaller size (one-thirtieth the size of Australia), but much better organized and temperamentally more militant. Although Captain Cook had claimed New Zealand for Britain in 1769, interest in settling the islands was slow in developing. Missionary efforts to the Maori, begun in 1814, made striking progress by midcentury. Simultaneously, however, some of the Maori began acquiring European guns, which they turned against rival tribes in an orgy of violence. The island also became a battleground in a different kind of war—one fought ideologically and politically between missionaries, who wanted the land preserved for Christianized Maori, and imperial colonizers, who envisaged a country dominated by white settlers.

Matters came to a head in 1840, thanks largely to the colonizing schemes of Edward Gibbon Wakefield and his New Zealand Land Company. The island, he truthfully told a parliamentary committee, was "the most beautiful country" with a fine climate and productive soil.

The British decision to annex New Zealand may have been stimulated as well by a French show of interest in the island nation. The British government formally annexed New Zealand in 1840; the newly appointed governor negotiated a treaty with the Maori, obtaining their recognition of British sovereignty and promising them secure land tenure. But many of the Maori were soon disillusioned as whites from Australia and Britain poured into the islands, and fighting was frequent until 1872, when the Maori finally accepted defeat. By that point the population of the islands was approximately 250,000, of whom less than 40,000 by one estimate were Maori. They were victims not only of the fighting but, like the Australian aborigines and the Amerindians, of the new diseases transmitted by Europeans. Peace provided fresh opportunities for growth, and in the next 30 years the population more than tripled, modern transportation and communications systems were developed, and a democratic political constitution evolved that in 1893 extended suffrage to women.

Islands of the Pacific

Although Spanish and Dutch explorers had discovered some of the islands of Melanesia, Micronesia, and Polynesia, it was not until the late eighteenth century that Europeans began to show serious interest in them. At first their motives were largely economic: whalers and sealers from America, Britain, and France used some of the islands as bases, and merchants traded tools, cloth, and guns for sandalwood, which found a ready market in China. As in New Zealand, much of the early interest in the islands was also religious. Spanish missionaries sought converts in the Marianas, British Protestants in 1797 launched their campaign in Tahiti, and American Protestants began working in Hawaii in 1820. Where the missionaries went, the political interests of their home governments were usually quick to follow. In Tahiti, however, the English Protestants who virtually ran the island were ousted by the French navy in 1843, after which Catholic missionaries taught the natives their version of Christianity.

As imperial rivalry intensified among the great powers in the late nineteenth century, the Pacific islands were increasingly coveted. The interest in converting the native populations continued but was clearly subordinate to economic considerations and imperial advantage. Britain, France, the United States, and Germany competed for the spoils, toppling native states, such as the kingdom of Fiji, in the process. The most notorious example of this occurred in 1893, when American planters, aided by a contingent of 150 marines, overthrew Hawaii's Queen

Samoan chieftains and their king listen to the reading of a Western peace treaty in 1881. Note the guard of soldiers in the rear.

Liliuokalani (1891–1893). Despite the fact that the United States had recognized Hawaii's independence in 1842, the American government waited only until 1900 to annex it, as it had annexed the Philippines and Guam two years earlier. "We need Hawaii just as much and a good deal more than we did California," insisted President William McKinley; "it is manifest destiny."

Thus in 1900 every island in Polynesia, Micronesia, and Melanesia was a colonial possession of Britain, France, Germany, or the United States. Once mighty Spain, after losing the Philippines and Guam, had sold its remaining Pacific islands—the Carolines, Marianas, and Marshalls—to Germany the previous year. The Germans, however, would lose those islands to Japan in 1914, the same year they lost northeastern New Guinea to Australia and their part of Samoa to New Zealand. Less than three decades later, conflicting Japanese and American ambitions in the Pacific resulted in the attack on Pearl Harbor that propelled the United States into World War II.

SUMMARY

The age of domination saw European powers take control of most of Africa, India, Ceylon, Burma, Malaya, Indochina, Indonesia, and the Philippines, while they and the Americans exercised a strong influence and enjoyed special concessions in Thailand, China, and Japan. The Japanese, taking a lesson from their Western teachers, created their own colonial empire in Korea, Taiwan, and Manchuria.

Imperialism radically challenged the traditional values and structures of the societies it conquered or dominated. The result was dislocation, suffering, and cultural trauma. Much of value was weakened or destroyed. But the West also brought advances in technology, productivity, and medicine that raised the standard of living and increased life expectancy. For better or worse, the colonial impulse united most of the globe in a broad, overarching web of economic and political interdependence for the first time in history. Some of the West's values would be adopted, some contested, some rejected. Many of them would be accepted only after being assimilated to the older cultural patterns that reasserted themselves as the yoke of Western dominance was shaken off. The four great civilizations of Asia each responded differently to the Western challenge. British dominion in India stimulated the development of a nationalist movement that created a modern state on the subcontinent. Similar developments came later in Southeast Asia and were retarded by repressive French and Dutch colonial policies. China, too large to be conquered, would find its own path to modernity after a century of confusion and anarchy. Japan made the most rapid and apparently the easiest transition from a traditional society to a modern, industrial one and in mere decades achieved the status of a world power.

SUGGESTIONS FOR FURTHER READING

Imperialism and Africa

Barone, C. A. *Marxist Thought on Imperialism.* Armonk, N.Y.: Sharpe, 1985.

Baumgart, W. *Imperialism: The Idea of British and French Colonial Expansion, 1880–1914.* New York: Oxford University Press, 1982.

Curtin, P. D. *Africa and the West: Intellectual Responses to European Culture.* Madison: University of Wisconsin Press, 1972.

Denoon, D., and Nyeko, B. *Southern Africa Since 1800,* rev. ed. New York: Longman, 1984.

Fieldhouse, D. K. *Economics and Empire, 1830–1914.* Ithaca, N.Y.: Cornell University Press, 1973.

Freund, B. *The Making of Africa.* Bloomington: Indiana University Press, 1984.

Gifford, P., and Louis, W. R. *France and Britain in Africa: Imperial Rivalry and Colonial Rule.* New Haven, Conn.: Yale University Press, 1971.

Hallett, R. *Africa Since 1875.* Ann Arbor: University of Michigan Press, 1974.

Langer, W. L. *The Diplomacy of Imperialism, 1890–1902,* 2nd ed. New York: Knopf, 1965.

Lewis, D. L. *The Race to Fashoda: European Colonialism and African Resistance in the Scramble for Africa.* London: Weidenfeld & Nicolson, 1988.

Oliver, R., and Atmore, A. *Africa Since 1800,* 3rd ed. Cambridge: Cambridge University Press, 1981.

Perham, M., and Simmons, J., eds. *African Discovery: An Anthology of Exploration.* London: Faber & Faber, 1961.

Robertson, C., and Berger, I., eds. *Women and Class in Africa.* New York: Africana, 1986.

India

Davis, L. E., and Huttenback, R. A. *Mammon and the Pursuit of Empire.* Cambridge: Cambridge University Press, 1988.

Forster, E. M. *A Passage to India.* New York: Harcourt, Brace, 1924. (Fiction)

Mason, P. *The Men Who Ruled India,* rev. ed. New York: Norton, 1985.

Seal, A. *The Emergence of Indian Nationalism.* Cambridge: Cambridge University Press, 1968.

Southeast Asia

Bastin, J., and Benda, H. J. *A History of Modern Southeast Asia.* Englewood Cliffs, N.J.: Prentice Hall, 1968.

Hall, D. G. E. *A History of Southeast Asia,* 4th ed. New York: St. Martin's, 1984.

Harrison, B. *Southeast Asia: A Short History.* London: Macmillan, 1975.

Orwell, G. *Burmese Days.* New York: Harcourt, Brace, 1934.

Osborne, M. E. *Southeast Asia: An Illustrated Introductory History.* New York: HarperCollins, 1981.

Stanley, P. W. *Reappraising an Empire: The American Impact on the Philippines.* Cambridge, Mass.: Harvard University Press, 1984.

Steinberg, D. J., ed. *In Search of Southeast Asia.* Honolulu: University Press of Hawaii, 1987.

China

Fairbank, J. K. *The Missionary Enterprise in China and America.* Cambridge, Mass.: Harvard University Press, 1974.

Gasster, M. *China's Struggle to Modernize.* New York: Knopf, 1972.

Hsu, I. *The Rise of Modern China.* New York: Oxford University Press, 1975.

Murphey, R. *Shanghai: Key to Modern China.* Cambridge, Mass.: Harvard University Press, 1953.

Pruitt, I. *Daughter of Han.* New Haven, Conn.: Yale University Press, 1945.

Schrecker, J. *Imperialism and Chinese Nationalism.* Cambridge, Mass.: Harvard University Press, 1971.

Japan

Beasley, W. G. *The Meiji Restoration.* Stanford, Calif.: Stanford University Press, 1972.

——. *The Rise of Modern Japan.* New York: St. Martin's, 1990.

Borton, H. *Japan's Modern Century.* New York: Ronald Press, 1955.

Myers, R. *The Japanese Colonial Empire.* Stanford, Calif.: Stanford University Press, 1984.

PART FIVE

The Twentieth Century

Culture, Society, and the Great War

The German philosopher Friedrich Nietzsche challenged Christian morality and conventional values. His ideas were later distorted and used by the Nazis for their racist propaganda.

Until a second global conflict erupted in the 1930s, modern memory recalled only the "Great War" of 1914–1918. World War I was called "great" because its toll on human life, its monetary cost and physical destruction, and the human trauma it caused made all others pale in comparison. It started because rulers and government officials blundered in the summer of 1914, but a half century of diplomatic, social, and cultural history lay behind the immediate events. Many artists and writers had rejected traditional moral and social values, and some glorified violence as a catharsis that would strengthen what they believed was a civilization in decay. Such views anticipated the political breakdown of Europe by creating a climate in which war seemed acceptable, even desirable.

Although the fighting stopped in November 1918, its impact was felt for decades. Four empires disappeared as a result of the conflict—Hohenzollern Germany, Habsburg Austria-Hungary, Ottoman Turkey, and Romanov Russia. This last was replaced by the world's first state to describe itself as socialist with the goal of transforming itself into a communist society. The shock of the war experience, no less than the conditions of peace imposed on the vanquished, helped shape the twentieth century.

The Great War was not the first worldwide war, for earlier struggles had also been waged on several continents and oceans. In this war military engagements took place in Africa, Asia, and the Middle East, but the fighting was concentrated in Europe. Although imperialism formed part of the background to the war, its causes were almost entirely in the West. Nevertheless, the Great War had worldwide repercussions. In its

929

aftermath, Europe's overseas empires disintegrated as its global supremacy collapsed.

The Crisis of European Culture

In the three decades preceding World War I, European culture underwent a revolution that transformed thought: antirationalists challenged the optimism inherited from the Enlightenment and the materialism of the nineteenth century, while the literary and artistic avant-garde experimented with new ways of experiencing time and space. Philosophers increasingly favored instinct over reason to explain human behavior, while students of the mind proclaimed that beneath the fragile veneer of civilization lurked dark forces. Scientists, who had previously explained the physical world through the observation of recordable data, confronted a universe in which measurement itself was relative to the observer. Literary narrative, which once expressed motives and character, spoke increasingly in the language of ambiguity. The crisis also overturned aesthetic values as artists questioned conventional expressions of reality. Most disturbing, new strains of antidemocratic and racist thought were introduced into politics.

The Revolt Against Positivism

As we have seen (Chapter 34), in the early nineteenth century Auguste Comte had argued that human behavior can be explained by "positive" observable data rather than by metaphysical forces. By the end of the century many intellectuals had turned against materialism and reason in what came to be known as the antipositivist revolt. Its most outspoken proponent was the German Friedrich Nietzsche (1844–1900). A philosopher repelled by the hypocrisy and pettiness of his time, Nietzsche assaulted traditional morality. His scathing criticism of bourgeois values extended to the roots of Western culture, from Greco-Roman rationalism to the Judeo-Christian belief in compassion, sin, and humility—concepts he said were more suitable to slaves and weaklings than to the free and the strong.

To realize freedom and human potential, Nietzsche urged the abandonment of these traditions in favor of instincts and emotions. He called on heroic leaders to guide the masses: "All gods are dead," he proclaimed, "so we now want the superman to live." While he condemned democratic liberalism and equality, he also repudiated militarism and anti-Semitism, although apologists for Nazism later seized on his writings as justification for their doctrines of national and racial superiority. These justifications were part of the philosophical underpinning for European anti-Semitism. Misunderstood during his lifetime, Nietzsche's ideas had a profound influence on European culture. Literary and artistic rebels drew inspiration from his attack on the establishment, and in the 1920s political demagogues were influenced by his concept of the superman.

Nietzsche's stress on the irrational was echoed by the French philosopher Henri Bergson (1859–1941). Distinguishing between the rational intellect and intuitive understanding, Bergson believed the former a useful tool for analyzing knowledge but not for understanding reality. Only intuition could grasp the "life force," which informed all experience and expressed itself in a continuum, or "duration," that instinct alone could describe. Bergson's chief influence lay in underscoring nonrational experience. Although he did not reject science, he undermined the scientists' claim to a monopoly on knowledge.

Sigmund Freud (1856–1939), a Viennese physician, confirmed Bergson's arguments about the limits of reason. Freud's treatment of psychiatric disorders, based on clinical data, convinced him that behavior is the result of powerful and primitive desires such as aggression and sex. These drives usually remain in an irrational uncon-

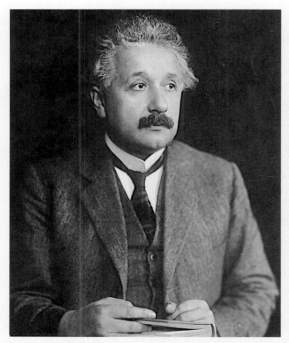

Albert Einstein, whose theories of relativity revolutionized our concepts of the universe, is shown here in his middle years. He received the Nobel Prize for physics in 1921.

scious, which he called the id. Freud believed that the id struggles constantly against the ego, which rationalizes and channels these desires according to the constraints of reality and the socially implanted values of the superego.

The superego functions as a kind of conscience, but instead of reflecting absolute moral values or rational truths, it is the product of social conditioning. Because the mind tends to repress the id, the conflict generally remains unconscious. Nevertheless, the resulting tensions can cause crippling experiences of guilt and fear or even mental breakdown. Freud's theories, particularly those concerning infantile and childhood sexuality, shocked bourgeois notions of human nature. Moreover, by positing that some people live emotionally in a frozen past, Freud and other psychoanalysts altered human perception of time as a forward-moving concept.

Like Nietzsche, Freud emphasized the irrational basis of human behavior and social values. For Freud, civilization is built on the repression of powerful individual urges, particularly sexual ones. Socialization, and hence "progress," rests not on reason but on the frustration of instincts that, held continuously in check, threaten to overwhelm it. Nietzsche had questioned whether civilization was worth its cost in terms of human fulfillment. Freud assumed that repression and self-denial are the necessary price of society. World War I seemed to bear out his pessimism about human nature and the stability of civilization, and his influence on postwar thought was enormous.

Freud's leadership within the movement he founded for the study and treatment of the human psyche—psychoanalysis—was challenged by his former disciple, Carl Jung (1875–1961), who elaborated his own theory of a collective unconscious. In recent decades Freud's theories have been sharply challenged. Nonetheless, he has remained one of the most influential thinkers of the century, and his indirect impact on sexual attitudes, artistic expression, and the concept of mental illness has been incalculable. Perhaps no one has done more to change the modern conception of human nature.

The Dilemmas of Science

Ironically, advances in the realm of physical science seemed to reinforce antirationalist arguments. Since the days of Newton, science had sustained the idea that the physical world operated according to immutable laws and predictable mechanical processes. The modern scientific age, which began with investigations into the nature of matter following the discovery of X-rays in 1895 by Wilhelm Röntgen (1845–1923), shattered these illu-

sions. Experiments by Marie Curie (1867–1934) and her husband, Pierre Curie (1859–1906), showed that the atomic weight of elements such as radium changed as they emitted energy in the form of "subatomic" particles. These findings suggested a relationship between matter and energy. By the end of the 1920s a radical revision of the basic assumptions of classical physics had totally recast scientific understanding of the universe.

Early in the twentieth century the German physicist Max Planck (1858–1947) conducted studies of radiation that revealed that contrary to earlier theories, light energy moves not in steady waves but in discontinuous yet calculable spurts, which he called quanta. Working independently, Albert Einstein (1879–1955) also began to revolutionize physics. His "Special Theory of Relativity" (1905) rejected the notion that space and time were absolutes, suggesting instead that both were relative to the position of the observer. Einstein showed that light moves through space in particles known as photons and calculated that the energy contained in a photon was equal to its mass multiplied by the square of the speed of light—a concept expressed in his famous formula, $E = mc^2$. Hence not only do mass and time vary with velocity, but energy and mass are interchangeable. Einstein's "General Theory of Relativity" (1915), which explained gravitation, further shook standard views of the physical world: it described the universe as curved, so that when light waves are deflected as they pass through a gravitational field, they eventually return to their point of origin. Einstein's universe was a four-dimensional one in which length, breadth, and height also had to be conceived in terms of time.

In the years between the evolution of Einstein's theories of relativity, Ernest Rutherford (1871–1937) forced contemporaries to abandon still another basic assumption about matter. Rutherford theorized that the atom, which since ancient times had been regarded as a solid, indivisible mass, was actually an arrangement much like a solar system, consisting of a central particle (the nucleus) with a positive electrical charge, surrounded by orbits of negatively charged electrons. He demonstrated that by bombarding substances with subatomic particles, the structure of atoms could be changed.

In the popular mind these theories and findings led to a doubly disturbing conclusion about the physical universe: that it was shifting and uncertain and that knowledge of it might lie beyond human comprehension. While almost all countries, in an effort to coordinate wireless communications and transportation schedules, were adopting World Standard Time at the beginning of the twentieth century, scientists such as

Einstein were shattering the concept of a uniform public time into the infinite variations of private times relative to each individual.

Realism Abandoned: Literature and Art

The revolt against positivism was reflected in literature and painting. Writers and artists not only expressed the social criticism that rejected the values of materialist culture but also probed beyond the conscious mind. Alienation impelled literary figures to take refuge in obscure symbolism, decadence, or aestheticism, while artists provided visual evidence of the breakdown of traditional forms.

The rebellion in literature had begun at midcentury with the publication of *Flowers of Evil* (1857) by the French poet Charles Baudelaire (1821–1867). Like the British poet Algernon Swinburne (1837–1909) and others, Baudelaire was hostile to bourgeois values and deliberately shocked conventional morality. The 1880s saw the birth of the Decadents and Symbolism, two literary movements derived in part from these earlier sources. The Decadents were sophisticated aesthetes such as Oscar Wilde (1854–1900), J. K. Huysmans (1848–1907), and Gabriele D'Annunzio (1863–1938), who extolled the idea of art for art's sake and cultivated exoticism and artificiality.

The Symbolists, represented by Stéphane Mallarmé (1842–1898) and Paul Verlaine (1844–1896), sought to express the inexpressible in experimental verse that relied on symbols to convey images that logic alone could not fathom. They rejected conventional perception in favor of a subjective, inner world. Often proclaiming the values of aestheticism and decadence, the Symbolists portrayed emotions derived from immediate experience, much as Bergson had urged.

In the 1870s Impressionism assaulted both realism and academic art by depicting the disintegrative effects of light. By the 1880s Impressionism was under attack by Postimpressionists, who, like the Symbolists, were moving away from the outer world of visible reality to an inner realm of the individual artist. In his later years, Claude Monet (1840–1926), the leading Impressionist, painted huge canvases depicting waterlilies. These shimmering pools of color, almost devoid of form, represented a transition between the perceived reality of Impressionism and the emotion of Postimpressionism.

One of the most powerful Postimpressionists was Vincent van Gogh (1853–1890), whose works conveyed an imaginative vision of the world. Like Paul Gauguin (1848–1903), who left the materialistic society of France to settle in Tahiti, van Gogh was interested in using the formal, abstract elements of art—line, color, and form—to express an intensely personal view of truth. Paul Cézanne (1839–1906), however, wanted to free art of subjectivity and emotionalism. Following classical principles, he used color to stress the underlying weight and volume of objects. His landscapes define objects only in the most general sense by using contour, color, and mass to convey abstract equivalents for conventional objects.

Barcelona and the Modern Temper

No city better reflected the cultural ferment of turn-of-the-century Europe than Barcelona. Located on Spain's northeastern plain at the edge of the Mediterranean Sea, Barcelona was the center of Catalan regionalism. In many ways the capital of Catalonia province represented the outstanding example of a modern European city, an innovative, rapidly modernizing enclave in a traditional, agrarian nation. By the late nineteenth century Barcelona had become a city marked by bold cultural experimentation.

Founded at the end of the first century B.C. as a Roman administrative center, the town had grown up in the Middle Ages around a military fortress. Its location on the sea made it a natural focus of trade and shipbuilding. The Industrial Revolution reached Spain through Barcelona, where an enterprising middle class emerged in the late eighteenth century. By the 1850s chemical and machinery manufacturers had joined bankers, shipping magnates, and textile producers in forming a powerful liberal oligarchy. Although its members pressed for urban development and economic modernization, they also fought the labor and socialist movements with support from the government.

At midcentury greater Barcelona had a population of several hundred thousand that exhibited the class characteristics of an advanced capitalist society. Demographic growth forced the adoption in 1859 of a new town plan, similar to the plans followed in Paris and elsewhere, that consisted of a square grid pattern of streets and parks cut across by broad diagonal avenues. Less than a generation later, when more than 500,000 people lived there, Barcelona hosted the Universal Exhibition of 1888. The project, which incorporated a huge complex of exhibition halls, hotels, apartment buildings, factories, and urban services into the city plan, gave a strong thrust to construction and the arts.

Despite their reactionary politics, the economic elites that sponsored the Universal Exhibition encouraged an atmosphere of cultural innovation that made Barcelona synonymous with the most avant-garde trends in Europe. Brilliant local architects, working in the so-called *modernista* style, designed new buildings in a wide range of exciting idioms. This eclectic movement found inspiration in Moorish, Romanesque, and Gothic patterns, in the strong craft tradition of Catalonia, and in the international Art Nouveau style of the period.

The most creative architect of the period, Antonio Gaudí (1852–1926), developed a unique style that reconciled form with function and expressed his militant Catholic beliefs. Gaudí's creations, such as the Guell Palace, incorporated organic forms that resembled sculptural modeling. While his designs were derived from both Gothic and Art Nouveau styles, they represented an original architectural vocabulary that was a reaction against what he saw as the falsity of fin-de-siècle design. Many of his ambitious creations remained unrealized or incomplete; a society exists even to this day that seeks to finish his most famous project, the Church of the Holy Family.

While Gaudí and other architects gave the city a bold new face, Barcelona also became a haven for the avant-garde, which included some of Europe's major artists and writers. Four important Spanish-born artists lived and exhibited in Barcelona in the early years of the twentieth century: Pablo Picasso (1881–1973), usually associated with Paris, executed his first mature works in Barcelona, along with Joan Miró (1893–1983), pioneer abstract painter and a native of the city; Julio Gonzalez (1876–1942), a craftsman turned sculptor; and Salvador Dalí (1904–1989), the famed Surrealist painter. The economic boom that Barcelona experienced during World War I drew many foreign artists from war-torn countries to neutral Spain. The French Dadaist and Surrealist painter Francis Picabia (1879–1953) came into contact with Dalí, worked in Barcelona, and was later joined by the Belgian Surrealist René Magritte (1898–1967). In the 1930s the American photographer and painter Man Ray (1890–1976), the Italian sculptor Alberto Giacometti (1901–1966), and the German painter Max Ernst (1891–1976) all exhibited there.

While these and other creative talents pushed art and design toward modernism, the Spanish writer Eugenio d'Ors (1882–1954) founded a more conservative cultural movement known as *Noucentisme* ("Twentieth Century"), which stressed a revival of Mediterranean classicism in the arts. Nevertheless, as Spain headed toward dictatorship and conflict in the 1920s, Barcelona remained a bastion of cultural discourse. The International Exhibition of 1929 was the last symbol of

The highly original talent of the Barcelona architect Antonio Gaudí is seen here in a photograph of the Casa Mila, an apartment house completed in 1910.

Barcelona's cultural primacy. The brilliant architect Ludwig Mies van der Rohe designed the exhibit's German pavilion in the Bauhaus style, which had come to stand for internationalism and modernity. Ironically, his "Barcelona chair," a pivotal example of modern furniture design, was intended as the official seat for Spain's King Alfonso XIII.

Postimpressionists, Cubists, and Futurists

Postimpressionists such as Cézanne brought painting to the edge of modernism. At the Paris Salon of 1905, the works of a number of Postimpressionist artists—Matisse, Rouault, and others—were hung together because of certain common characteristics. Their distortions, flat patterns, and preoccupation with line and form rather than with objective reality, combined with violent, bold colors and stark contrasts, earned these men the title of *fauves* ("wild beasts"). Closely related to Fauvism were two German Expressionist groups, the Bridge and the Blue Rider, formed between 1905 and 1911, whose proponents emphasized bold colors and psychological portraiture.

The most significant step away from the traditional portrayal of reality came with Cubism, launched in Paris by the Spaniard Pablo Picasso and the Frenchman Georges Braque (1882–1963) in 1907. Influenced by Cézanne, Picasso and Braque developed a concept of form and context that enabled them to render the whole structure of an object as well as its position in space. Abandoning the bright colors and striking contrasts of the *fauves,* they focused on the subtleties of intersecting lines and angles and the reduction of objects to abstract forms. The Cubists not only set in motion the revolution in abstract painting, but, by fracturing objects into separate elements and fixing them in time-space relationships, transformed traditional views of reality.

The only major prewar art movement to develop independently of Paris was Futurism, founded by Filippo T. Marinetti (1876–1944) and a group of young Italian writers and artists in 1909. In contrast to most of the avant-garde of the period, the Futurists rejected humanist culture in the name of the machine and industrial civilization. Exalting the speed and energy of modern life, painters such as Umberto Boccioni (1882–1916) and Carlo Carrà (1881–1966) moved toward the elimination of traditional forms. Futurists advocated the destruction of libraries and museums and, influenced by the ideas of Nietzsche, Sorel, and Bergson, preached violence as an act of liberation. Futurism found other disciples in art and literature, notably in the English painter Wyndham Lewis (1882–1957) and the Russian poet Vladimir Mayakovsky (1893–1930).

Nationalism and Racism

The Futurists may have been the most extreme example of the crisis of European culture, but such disturbing concepts also affected public affairs. Some political theorists and social critics rejected the positivist doctrines on which both liberalism and socialism were based. Georges Sorel founded his syndicalist theories on the belief that the working masses could be stimulated to violent action through the general strike. Sorel's ideas were reinforced by the psychologist Gustav Le Bon (1841–1931), whose book *The Crowd* (1895) argued that mobs responded to pathological suggestion, and by others who maintained that instinct determined social conduct.

The characterization of mass behavior as essentially irrational led the Italian sociologist Vilfredo Pareto (1848–1923) to assert the need for government by an elite rather than by the people. The French monarchist Charles Maurras (1868–1952) founded a reactionary political organization known as *Action Française* on the the-

ory that "the mob always follows determined minorities." Such thinking would influence important political leaders of both the right and the left, from Benito Mussolini to V. I. Lenin.

A further manifestation of these trends was the rise of racism and a new form of nationalism. Whereas nationalists of the 1830s and 1840s fought oppression on behalf of subjected peoples, a chauvinistic nationalism now pitted races and nation-states against one another. Influenced by Social Darwinism, the virulent nationalism of the late nineteenth century preached aggression and dominance. In the 1870s the pan-Slavic movement proclaimed Russia's historic mission to unite all Slavic peoples into a great federation for an inevitable struggle against the West, while the Pan-German League, founded in 1893, demanded territorial expansion and a German-dominated central Europe.

The exaggerated nationalism of the period was linked to racist doctrines, which owed much to the Frenchman Arthur de Gobineau (1816–1882), author of "An Essay on the Inequality of the Races." Gobineau argued that the white races—especially the "Aryans" descended from Germanic tribes—had created civilization but had degenerated as a result of intermingling with "inferior" races. His theories impressed the German musical genius Richard Wagner (1813–1883), who condemned "Jewish" influence in music and whose cycle of four powerful operas in *The Ring of the Nibelungen* (1848–1876) glorified Germanic mythology. Wagner's son-in-law, the British expatriate Houston Stewart Chamberlain (1855–1927), espoused the creation of a superior race through genetic breeding. Chamberlain's *Foundations of the Nineteenth Century* (1899) blamed Europe's racial "degeneration" on the Jews.

Although anti-Semitism had existed for centuries, it reappeared in the vicious Russian pogroms of the late nineteenth century and as the basis for political movements spawned by racial doctrines. In Germany political parties inspired by Adolf Stöcker (1835–1909) elected deputies to the Reichstag on anti-Semitic platforms, while the mayor of Vienna, Karl Lüger (1844–1910), used anti-Semitism to generate popular support for his Christian Socialist party. In France, Charles Maurras led a campaign against the Jews during the Dreyfus affair. Nazi anti-Semitism was rooted in the racist atmosphere of the 1890s.

The Breakdown of the European Order

Few topics in modern history are more controversial than the causes of World War I. During and after the conflict, governments on both sides issued volumes of

The Futurist Manifesto

The Futurists were symptomatic of the crisis of prewar European culture. Not only did they rebel against reason, tradition, and conventional standards of beauty, but they also demanded a new civilization based on the aesthetic of the machine. Here is the first Futurist manifesto, drafted by Filippo T. Marinetti and originally published in Paris on February 20, 1909.

We want to praise the love of danger, the attitude of energy and fearlessness.

Courage, audacity, and revolt will be essential elements of our poetry.

Until now literature has exalted pensive immobility, ecstasy, and sleep. We want to exalt aggressive action, a feverish insomnia, the racer's stride, the mortal leap, the punch, and the slap.

We assert that the beauty of the world has been enriched by a new beauty: the beauty of speed. A racing car . . . is more beautiful than the *Victory of Samothrace.*

We want to praise the man at the wheel, who hurls his spiritual lance across the earth, along the circle of its orbit. The poet must give himself with ardor, splendor, and generosity, to swell the enthusiastic fervor of the primordial elements.

There is no beauty except in struggle. No work without an aggressive character can be a masterpiece. Poetry must be conceived as a violent attack on unknown forces, to reduce and prostrate them before man.

We stand on the last promontory of the centuries! . . . Why must we look back, when what we want is to break down the mysterious doors of the impossible? Time and space died yesterday. We already live in the absolute, because we have already created eternal, omnipresent speed.

We want to glorify war—the world's only hygiene—militarism, patriotism, the destructive gesture of liberators, beautiful ideas worth dying for, and scorn for woman.

We want to destroy museums, libraries, academies of every kind, and want to fight moralism, feminism, every opportunistic or utilitarian cowardice.

We will sing of great crowds excited by work, by pleasure, and by riot; we will sing of the multicolored, polyphonic tides of revolution in modern capitals; we will sing of the vibrant nocturnal fervor of arsenals and shipyards blazing with violent electric moons; of hungry railway stations that devour fire-breathing serpents; factories hung on clouds by the twisted lines of their smoke; bridges that stride the rivers like giant gymnasts, gleaming in the sun with a glitter of knives; adventurous steamers that cut the horizon; deep-chested locomotives whose wheels gallop along the tracks like the hooves of huge steel horses bridled by tubing; and the sleek flight of planes whose propellers flutter in the wind like banners and seem to cheer like an enthusiastic crowd.

Source: L. De Maria, ed., *Per conoscere Marinetti e il futurismo,* trans. P. Cannistraro (Milan: Mondadori, 1973), pp. 5–7.

documents to justify their positions. In the wake of the Allied victory, a defeated Germany was forced to accept the blame. Since then, historians have taken a more balanced view of the war's origins, separating the long-range developments in which all European nations had participated from the immediate circumstances that led to its outbreak. The controversy erupted again in the 1960s when a German scholar, Fritz Fischer, maintained that his country had deliberately planned a far-reaching program of conquest before 1914. The response to Fischer's thesis has been heated, and today most historians would argue that his explanation focused too narrowly on Germany and underemphasized the broader European causes of the war.

For decades historical antagonisms, colonial rivalries, economic competition, and expansionist aspirations, all fueled by chauvinistic nationalism, had propelled Europe into an arms race and hostile alliances.

Diplomatic confrontations increased tensions among the powers, so that most nations came to believe that only military alliances provided safety. When the final crisis came in the summer of 1914, the diplomatic order collapsed through a combination of fear and miscalculation. Science and technology, the twin sources of power and pride that had enabled the West to dominate the globe, made what most statesmen hoped would be an easy war a long and agonizing ordeal from which Europe never fully recovered.

Bismarck and the Concert of Europe

For more than half a century after the defeat of Napoleon in 1815 Europe's international system had been based on the notion that the great powers would act "in concert" to keep the peace established by the Congress of Vienna. The system worked remarkably well until the creation of the German empire in 1871 drastically altered international politics. Bismarck's triumph, won on the ruins of the second French empire, gave birth to a powerful state whose unsurpassed military strength was quickly equaled by its industrial and economic power.

The rapid emergence of Germany upset the European balance of power. Upon achieving unification, Bismarck denied having any further territorial ambitions. For the next 20 years his foreign policy goals remained the preservation of the Concert of Europe and the protection of Germany. Bismarck saw two potentially troublesome situations. On the western frontier the French were obsessed with achieving revenge against Germany after their humiliating defeat in the Franco-Prussian War. For the Iron Chancellor the worst scenario was a military pact between France and Russia that would sandwich Germany between them in a two-front war. To avoid such a "nightmare," as he described it, Bismarck sought to keep France isolated from diplomatic alliances with other powers.

The east presented a more complicated security problem. The rise of nationalism threatened to destabilize east-central Europe and the Balkans by pulling apart both Austria-Hungary, which had been severely weakened by Prussia's lightning victory in 1866, and the deteriorating Ottoman Empire. The Balkans became the focus of this regional instability, for there Austria-Hungary and Russia competed for territory and influence at the expense of the Turks. Conflict between Vienna and St. Petersburg over the Balkans could drag Germany into a major war in the east and allow France to invade from the west. Bismarck responded by creating secret and often mutually contradictory diplomatic and military pacts.

His strategy placed Berlin at the center of a complicated web of alliances that exploited competing national interests and fears.

Bismarck took his first step in 1873, when he concluded a mutual consultation treaty, the League of the Three Emperors, with Russia and Austria-Hungary. The league faced a serious crisis in 1877 and 1878. Russia, motivated by a desire for expansion, joined Serbia, Montenegro, and Bulgaria in a war against Turkey. The Treaty of San Stefano freed the Balkan states from Turkish control and gave the tsar a foothold in the region. Assuming the self-professed role of an "honest broker," Bismarck tried to engineer peace at the Congress of Berlin and redress the balance of power. Austria secured the right to administer the provinces of Bosnia and Herzegovina, which technically remained Ottoman possessions, and the size of Bulgaria was reduced. Nevertheless, the Berlin congress aroused Slavic hostility against Germany and Austria-Hungary, for the Russians were angered by what they considered Bismarck's perfidy, while Serbia and Montenegro were bitter over Austria's occupation of Bosnia and Herzegovina. Romania and Greece were disappointed at not having gotten territories from the Turks. The Balkans had become a powder keg.

Bismarck moved immediately to protect Germany from reprisal. In 1879 he concluded the Dual Alliance with Austria-Hungary, a defensive military pact. The Russians, sensing their isolation, responded in 1881 by agreeing to a mutual-security pact with Germany. Not only did this ease Russia's fears of encirclement, but it also gave Germany a measure of security by reducing the possibility of a joint attack by France and Russia. Bismarck had successfully played off Austria and Russia.

Two additional treaties closed the circle of Bismarck's diplomatic policy. In 1882 the Triple Alliance drew Italy into a defensive agreement with Germany and Austria. Finally, in 1887 Bismarck secretly negotiated the Reinsurance Treaty with Russia, guaranteeing neutrality by one power if the other was attacked. Thus Russia did not have to worry about Germany in the event of a war with Austria, while Germany no longer feared what Russia would do in case of a war with France. Bismarck could now be confident that German interests were protected—at least as long as he managed German affairs.

The Triple Entente

When Kaiser William II forced Bismarck into retirement in 1890, German foreign policy changed drastically. The new emperor rejected the necessity of an alliance with Russia and friendship with Britain, two vital premises of Bismarck's diplomacy. Convinced that Austria was Germany's natural ally, William refused Russian requests to renew the Reinsurance Treaty. The inevitable happened: in 1894 France and Russia signed a defensive military agreement that created the "nightmare alliance" Bismarck had dreaded.

Britain had remained aloof from Continental alliances, adhering instead to its traditional "balance of power" policy. But the kaiser, who resented Britain's preeminent world position, was determined to raise German prestige by winning colonial territories and brandishing German power. Britain, whose industrial growth had fallen behind Germany's, grew alarmed at the kaiser's hostility. Abandoning Bismarck's opposition to imperial conquest, William attempted to block the consolidation of British interests in Africa and in 1896 enraged London by expressing pro-Boer sentiments. Between 1898 and 1900 British security interests were again put at risk when Germany began constructing a powerful fleet that challenged Britain's goal of maintaining a two-to-one margin over Germany's naval forces.

German aggressiveness forced Britain to end its diplomatic isolation. An Anglo-Japanese agreement in 1902 was followed two years later by the Entente Cordiale ("friendly understanding") with France, which settled colonial disputes between the two nations. France agreed to a British sphere of influence in Egypt in return for French predominance in Morocco. Outraged by this, Kaiser William visited Tangier to support Moroccan independence. The Algeciras conference of 1906 affirmed the Entente agreements, rebuffing Germany.

In 1906, in the wake of the Moroccan crisis, the British launched the first of a series of battleships known as dreadnaughts, with greater range, speed, and firepower than any previous type of military vessel. The next year the Germans followed suit, unleashing a costly naval race between the two powers. Tensions increased as German plans to construct a Berlin-to-Baghdad railroad made Britain, France, and Russia uneasy over their interests in the Middle East. Encouraged by the French, Russia and Britain negotiated a treaty in 1907 that settled colonial rivalries in Tibet, Afghanistan, and Iran and, like the Entente Cordiale, made possible closer cooperation in Europe.

In the 20 years after Bismarck's retirement, Europe's great powers had aligned themselves into two blocs. Germany, Austria, and Italy were bound by the terms of the Triple Alliance, while Britain, France, and Russia were tied less formally by treaties that together formed a Triple Entente. Separating these military and diplomatic blocs was a pattern of growing hostility. Disputes between members of the rival blocs heightened tensions and made the alliance systems more rigid, for the fear of being left without the protection of friends led nations to support their partners, regardless of the merits of the issue. The most dangerous consequence of this development was that in times of crisis the alliances limited the options available to each power.

The Arms Race

Even before the division of Europe into opposing blocs, firms such as Krupp in Germany, Schneider in France, and Armstrong-Whitworth in Britain reaped enormous profits from the sale of weapons and exercised great influence on the defense policies of their governments. International rivalries over colonies and markets stimulated armaments industries and were used to justify huge military expenditures. French per capita arms spending more than doubled between 1870 and 1914; Germany's increased more than sixfold. By the eve of World War I both countries were spending almost 5 percent of their national income on weapons.

Improvements in weapons advanced rapidly, yet the nature of technological development made permanent advantage impossible. Reinforced concrete and steel alloys improved defensive systems. Nevertheless, the enormous firepower of heavy artillery—especially long-range howitzers—and more powerful explosives made impregnable fortresses a thing of the past. The British dreadnaughts, designed to revolutionize sea warfare, were mounted with ten 12-inch guns, each capable of hurling an 850-pound shell 10 miles. But the thick armor plating and turbine engines of the dreadnaughts were vulnerable to enemy guns as well as to torpedoes from newly developed submarines and destroyers. Military planners were convinced that the outcome of warfare on land and sea would be determined by artillery.

Despite the technology, infantry soldiers were the basis of war strategy. By 1874 all the great powers except Britain had introduced compulsory military service. France and Germany doubled their standing armies between 1870 and 1914, each keeping almost half a million men under arms in peacetime. The function of the infantry was modified in the 1880s with the introduction of the magazine rifle and the machine gun, which gave great advantage to defensive positions and guaranteed huge casualties to attacking armies. Despite these changes, European tactics were still based on the Prussian campaigns of 1866 and 1870, with their emphasis on speed, mobility, and surprise. Military plans, based on elaborate transportation networks and exact timetables, contributed to the possibility of war, for generals insisted on rapid mobilization during international crises.

Such was the case with the Schlieffen Plan, worked out in 1905 by the German general staff. Based on the likelihood of a two-front war against France and Russia, the strategy assumed that the Russians would take longer to mobilize than the French. Hence Schlieffen proposed that while Germany remained on the defensive against Russia, two armies—a powerful one sweeping through Luxembourg and Belgium and a weaker force moving from the south to lure the French away from the real attack—would swing rapidly around a central "hinge" and crush the French in a giant pincer. Having defeated France, the Germans could then concentrate their military strength against Russia.

With mass conscription came the introduction of the general staff, also based on the German model, and the growing prestige of a professional officer caste. Although strongest in Germany, the link between the landed nobility and the military command was present in every country. Their aristocratic lineage gave high-ranking officers special access to and influence over their sovereigns, even in representative governments, while their conservative outlook in domestic politics weakened the position of liberal civilians in government circles.

Government propaganda, the sensationalism of the press, and the nationalism imbued in citizens by universal elementary education conditioned the public to conscription and the high cost of armaments. Compulsory military training in turn convinced the public to accept the possibility of war.

Europe on the Brink

Relations between the Triple Alliance and the Entente deteriorated as one international crisis succeeded another. The Austro-Russian struggle for hegemony stirred nationalist fervor in the Balkans, where Serbian nationalists sought to create a united Slavic state and looked to Russia—the Slavic "big brother"—for support. Austria-Hungary, which regarded Slavic nationalism as a threat to its multinational empire, opposed Serbia. These forces came to a head in 1908 when Austria attempted to prevent Serbian expansion to the Adriatic Sea by annexing Bosnia and Herzegovina. The angry Serbs, who had hoped to incorporate Bosnia into their greater Slavic state, could do little without Russia, which felt too weak to respond in the face of British and Austrian pressure.

European aggression speeded the disintegration of the Ottoman Empire. In 1911 the kaiser dispatched the

MAP 36.1   THE BALKANS IN 1914

gunboat *Panther* to the Moroccan port of Agadir under the guise of protecting German nationals, but his real purpose was to challenge French and British domination in Africa. The crisis dissipated when the French agreed to cede part of Equatorial Africa to Germany, but it had the effect of alarming British opinion and solidifying the Anglo-French Entente. Later that year Italy went to war against the Ottoman Empire and wrested Libya from the Turks.

Encouraged by these events, the Balkan states attacked Turkey in 1912. The Balkan League, consisting of Serbia, Bulgaria, Greece, and Montenegro, easily defeated the Turks. Bulgaria emerged with the lion's share of the spoils. Austria intervened again to prevent the Serbs from gaining access to the Adriatic Sea, and when Russia protested, an international conference resolved the dispute by creating the state of Albania and compensating Serbia with inland territory. No one was satisfied. A month later, in June 1913, a second Balkan war erupted in which Serbia, Romania, Greece, and Turkey stripped Bulgaria of many of its territorial gains.

The Serbs, who had now doubled the size of their country, reoccupied parts of Albania, but their Russian protectors again failed to back them when an Austrian ultimatum forced their withdrawal. In fact, both Vienna and St. Petersburg remained deeply anxious. Throughout 1912 and 1913, the Austrians were bitterly critical of Germany, to whose lack of support they attributed Serbia's expansion. The Russians simultaneously blamed Britain for having prevented Serbia from gaining access to the sea. On both sides an uneasy feeling prevailed that neither the Triple Alliance nor the Entente could survive further internal tensions.

Sarajevo: The Failure of Diplomacy

On June 28, 1914, three students assassinated Archduke Franz Ferdinand (1863–1914), nephew of the emperor of Austria-Hungary and heir to the throne, while he attended military maneuvers in Bosnia. The three terrorists—members of Young Bosnia, a Slavic nationalist group—had been trained by Serbian army officers in a secret organization called Unity or Death (also known as the Black Hand). The Austrians did not know that Serbian cabinet members had been aware of the plot for some weeks, although they had not approved of it. Nevertheless, the Austrians expressed outrage and accused Serbian officials of complicity in the assassination. Some officials pushed for quick military action, hoping to crush Serbia permanently. The danger lay in the probability that conflict with Serbia would spark Russian intervention. Austria thus sought the support of Germany before acting.

In response, Kaiser William gave Austria-Hungary a "blank check" on July 5—that is, clear assurance of military support, along with advice to strike while world opinion was still hostile to Serbia. His chancellor, Theobald von Bethmann-Hollweg, acknowledged the risk of a general European war but believed that decisive Austrian action supported by Germany would deter Russia. Britain, he assumed, would not intervene. On July 23, Austria presented Serbia with a stiff ultimatum, in-

cluding a demand that Austria be permitted to hunt for Franz Ferdinand's assassins on Serbian territory. Although Belgrade's reply was conciliatory, the Serbians refused to accept this provision, which would have undermined their independence. On July 28, Austria declared war on Serbia.

When a reluctant Tsar Nicholas II ordered partial Russian mobilization on July 30, General Helmuth von Moltke, the kaiser's chief of staff, appealed for an immediate German mobilization in order to put the Schlieffen Plan into operation. Bethmann-Hollweg belatedly tried to persuade the Austrians to negotiate, to no avail. The Austrians announced mobilization against Russia on July 31, and Nicholas responded in kind. The Germans immediately demanded that the tsar pull back, but before he could reply, Germany declared war on Russia on August 1.

The elaborate diplomatic calculations continued to go awry. On August 2 the German ambassador in Brussels delivered an ultimatum demanding free passage through Belgian territory, presaging a preemptive strike against France. The British foreign secretary, Sir Edward Grey (1862–1933), intimated to Berlin that a violation of the international treaty guaranteeing Belgian neutrality would be regarded as a serious matter, but Bethmann-Hollweg ridiculed the idea that Britain would fight over "a scrap of paper." Two days later Germany declared war on Belgium and France and set the Schlieffen Plan in motion. On August 4, Britain declared war on Germany. "The lamps are going out all over Europe," Grey is supposed to have said; "we shall not see them lit again in our life-time."[1]

The Ordeal of the West

Most countries greeted the coming of war with relief and even enthusiasm; almost no one thought it would last very long. Within a few weeks, however, these expectations proved illusory. Europe found itself locked in a prolonged ordeal that brought unprecedented death and destruction.

War of Attrition

The rapid war of movement and assault anticipated by military planners turned into a bloody stalemate almost at once. The German armies crossed into Belgium on August 4, but unexpected resistance and last-minute changes in strategy threw off their timetable. By September they

Archduke Franz Ferdinand and his wife Sofie on June 28, 1914, the day they were assassinated.

THE ROAD TO WORLD WAR I

1870	Franco-Prussian War; second French empire collapses
1871	German empire created; France cedes Alsace and Lorraine
1878	Congress of Berlin; partition of Ottoman Empire begins
1879	Dual Alliance between Germany and Austria-Hungary
1882	Italy joins Germany and Austria-Hungry in the Triple Alliance
1890	Bismarck dismissed as chancellor of Germany
1894	Franco-Russian Alliance
1898	Fashoda crisis; Britain and France on the brink of war in the Sudan
1902	Anglo-Japanese alliance
1904	Anglo-French Entente
1905	First Moroccan crisis; Germany challenges French hegemony in North Africa
1908–1909	Bosnian crisis; Austro-Russian tension in the Balkans mounts
1911	Second Moroccan crisis
1911–1913	First and second Balkan wars
1914	Sarajevo crisis; outbreak of war (June 28–August 4)

had advanced to within 25 miles of Paris, but the French halted them at the Marne River and forced retreat. With the Schlieffen Plan in shambles, the Anglo-French allies and Germany tried to outflank each other; the line of battle soon reached from the Swiss border to the sea.

Once the Germans failed to strike a death blow against France, their dream of a rapid victory vanished. Instead, the equally matched combatants now faced each other in a war in which defense proved stronger than attack. On either side of the front, the combatants dug

The Trauma of Trench Warfare

As millions of young men poured into the trenches during World War I, the unimagined horrors of modern warfare crushed both the values and the optimism of a generation of Europeans. Here two British soldiers describe their experiences during the Battle of the Somme in the summer of 1916.

There was a terrific smell. It was so awful it nearly poisoned you. A smell of rotten flesh. The old German front line was covered with bodies—they were seven and eight deep and they had all gone black. The smell! These people had been laying since the first of July. Wicked it was! Colonel Pinney got hold of some stretchers and our job was to put the bodies on them and, with a man at each end, we *threw* them into that crater. There must have been over a thousand bodies there. I don't know how many we buried. I'll never forget that sight. Bodies all over the place. I'll never forget it. I was only eighteen, but I thought, "There's something wrong here!"

As far as you could see there were all these bodies lying there—literally thousands of them. . . . Some without legs, some were legs without bodies, arms without bodies. A terrible sight. . . . It didn't seem possible. It didn't get inside me or scare me, but it just made me wonder that these could have been men. It made me wonder what it was all about. And far away in the distance we could see nothing but a line of bursting shells. It was continuous. You wouldn't have thought that anybody could have existed in it, it was so terrific. And yet we knew we were going up into it, with not an earthly chance.

Source: L. Macdonald, *Somme* (London: Michael Joseph, 1983), pp. 113–114.

hundreds of miles of trenches, protected by barbed wire, land mines, and machine guns, in which millions of infantry soldiers lived and died. After preparatory artillery barrages, soldiers were ordered to charge the enemy trenches and cross the "no man's land" that separated them, only to be cut down by deadly machine gun fire and artillery. The first four months of fighting alone resulted in 1.64 million casualties, yet after the first battle of the Marne the front line hardly moved. Generals clung stubbornly to the same tactics for three and one-half years, squandering the lives of their men. The conflict had become a war of attrition in which the infliction

of casualties rather than the capture of terrain became the measure of success.

The Eastern Front and Italian Intervention

Conditions were far different on the eastern front, where men and supplies had to move over vast distances. In August the Russians won unexpected victories by moving two separate armies deep into East Prussia. The Germans panicked and withdrew four divisions from Belgium, while the kaiser put the retired general Paul von

MAP 36.2   WORLD WAR I, 1914–1918

Hindenburg (1847–1934) in charge of operations and made the major general Erich Ludendorff (1865–1937) his chief of staff. By dealing separately with each of the Russian armies Hindenburg and Ludendorff won major victories at Tannenberg and the Masurian Lakes, and by mid-September the Russians had lost 250,000 men.

Russia fared better against the Austrians, overrunning Galicia and driving into Hungary. The Austrians suffered further setbacks in the Balkans, where the Serbs twice repelled their armies. But Russian fortunes declined with the entrance of Turkey into the war on the side of the Central Powers, for the closing of the Dardanelles straits cut Russia off from critical supplies. Winston Churchill (1874–1965), Britain's First Lord of the Admiralty, conceived a daring plan to force the straits open, but a joint Anglo-French fleet failed to break through in March 1915. This effort was followed by landings on the Gallipoli peninsula, which were commanded by Mustapha Kemal (1881–1938), the future dictator of Turkey. By January the British had withdrawn.

The war widened further in 1915. The Germans struck, advancing some 200 miles against Russia, inflicting more than 2 million casualties and capturing or destroying almost a third of its industries. Allied reverses on the eastern front were mitigated in part by Italy's entrance into the war in May in return for promises of territory on the Italo-Austrian border and on the Dalmatian coast. In September, Bulgaria joined Germany and Austria.

The War Beyond Europe

Although the most crucial military operations took place in Europe, the Great War was a truly global conflict. Some 640,000 Canadians, 329,000 Australians, and 117,000 New Zealanders fought in the Allied forces, as did more than 1 million Indian troops and hundreds of thousands of African soldiers from the French colonies.

Military activity beyond Europe was of little importance to the outcome of the war, but in the Middle East the fighting was to have a direct bearing on postwar events. Arab nationalists meeting in Paris in 1913 had insisted on autonomy within the Ottoman Empire, but during World War I the British deliberately encouraged the Arabs to revolt, thus foiling Turkish efforts to mobilize them against the Allies. When the Ottoman Empire joined the Central Powers in November 1914, the British Indian army sent an expeditionary force to the Persian Gulf and Iraq, nearly reaching Baghdad before being driven back by Turkish forces. Another Indian force guarded the Suez Canal. During the Gallipoli and Dardanelles campaigns, British diplomats pledged to support an Arab revolt and gained the cooperation of Abdul-Aziz ibn-Saud (1880–1953), the sultan who ruled the Nejd region of south-central Arabia.

British promises to the Arabs were designed to help the war effort, not to bring independence to the region. In 1916 Hussein ibn-Ali (1856–1931), a proclaimed descendant of the prophet Muhammad and protector of the holy city of Mecca, instigated a revolt against the Turks, frustrating efforts to launch a holy war against the Allies. With British approval he declared himself king of the Arabs, claiming control over a vast area stretching from the Hejaz along the Red Sea to the Persian Gulf. That same year the British and French concluded the Sykes-Picot Agreement, which divided much of the region into spheres of influence: France would get Syria and Lebanon; Britain, Iraq and Palestine. Throughout 1917 and 1918, T. E. Lawrence (1888–1935), a British archaeologist and soldier—later known as Lawrence of Arabia—assisted Prince Faisal (1885–1933), Hussein's son, who commanded the Arab forces that seized Damascus and Jerusalem.

The dual nature of British policy in the Middle East became clear in November 1917, when Foreign Secretary Arthur James Balfour formally supported Zionist aspirations for a Jewish homeland in Palestine. The Balfour Declaration did not specifically promise Jewish control over all Palestine, but it contradicted other statements on behalf of Arab nationalist interests.

Elsewhere in the world the war posed a long-range threat rather than an immediate military danger for the West, for Britain and the Dominions feared Japanese expansionism. Allied with Britain since 1902, Japan declared war against the Central Powers in 1914 and swept over the German Pacific islands north of the equator. Australia occupied New Guinea and New Zealand took German Samoa to forestall Japanese expansion in the South Pacific. China declared war against Germany and Austria-Hungary only in 1917, but a 200,000-man Chinese labor battalion served with the Allies in Europe. Yet the Japanese seized the German holdings in China's Shantung province and presented China with the infamous Twenty-one Demands (see Chapters 35 and 37). Unlike China or India, Japan took no part in the war in the West beyond sending several destroyers.

In Africa, British colonial armies, made up of Indian, African, and Afrikaner troops, had little difficulty in taking Togo and Southwest Africa from Germany. But the German commander in East Africa, Paul von Lettow-Vorbeck, matched the daring exploits of T. E. Lawrence in organizing native resistance and conducting guerrilla warfare. He stopped an assault led by the South African general Jan Smuts and invaded Kenya, successfully defending German East Africa until the end of the war.

The British feared German attempts to foment rebellion in Afghanistan and Japanese propaganda in India, but with minor exceptions, the Indian army remained loyal. India was notified that it was automatically at war as part of the empire. Most Indian nationalists, including Gandhi, supported the war, hoping that a British victory would hasten India's freedom. Yet the contributions made by the colonies, together with Allied promises of "liberation" both in the Middle East and in the German possessions, raised questions about the future.

Agony on the Western Front

In 1916 and 1917 the killing on the western front intensified. In February 1916 the Germans massed their forces for an assault against Verdun, hoping that the French would make a costly defense. They were not disappointed. On the first day of the battle the Germans fired about 1 million artillery shells, and when the siege was over months later, 700,000 French and German soldiers were dead. Verdun held, but the bloodletting left deep scars on France. Oblivious to the lessons of Verdun, the British embarked on an offensive at the Somme River in June. Despite a massive preliminary bombardment, 60,000 British soldiers were cut down the first day. The British introduced primitive tanks into the battle with minimal effect, and by November this offensive too was over with little result but slaughter—600,000

British and French and 500,000 German soldiers had been killed or wounded.

In the spring of 1917 the Allies suffered a major blow in the east. On March 12, St. Petersburg erupted in revolution, and three days later Tsar Nicholas abdicated. While awaiting what they now regarded as an inevitable Russian defeat, the Germans retired behind the Hindenburg Line, a fortified defensive position in the west. The French vainly attacked it in April, suffering 250,000 casualties. From July to November the British fought the Germans at Ypres in the fields of Flanders, despite the new horrors of poison gas. The British suffered another 300,000 casualties.

Europeans could hardly grasp the fearful toll that the fighting had taken—more than 2.5 million dead and wounded alone in the four major western engagements of 1916 and 1917. The enthusiasm of 1914 turned to shock and a sense that civilization had reached the point of collapse. "The higher civilization rises," observed a German general, "the viler man becomes."[2] Churchill, writing about the war a few years later, was equally bleak: "When all was over, Torture and Cannibalism were the only two expedients that the civilized, scientific, Christian States had been able to deny themselves: and these were of doubtful utility."[3]

The Social Consequences of Total War

The futility of the war brought opposition and sometimes revolt. During the spring 1917 offensive in Champagne, some French units had refused to leave the

German dead at the Battle of Verdun.

trenches, and the Russian army was rife with mutiny long before the revolution. The shock of the war also spread defeatism among civilians. In Turin, Italian socialists staged an abortive uprising, and in July the German Reichstag passed a peace resolution.

The collapse of morale on both sides raised serious concerns about the home front, for in a war of such gigantic proportions, industrial production was as important as front-line fighting. Attrition created huge shortages not only of manpower but also of food, clothing, and munitions. To cope with the economic and political strains, leaders formed cabinets of national unity, representing in some cases even socialist parties. Governments instituted rationing, placed controls on prices and wages, restricted union activity, and set up planning boards to coordinate production of war matériel.

The trend toward the greater militarization of society that had begun in the late nineteenth century accelerated sharply. The military assumed more authority in civilian affairs, and governments imposed censorship on the press and suspended constitutional procedures. Official propaganda called for a "total" war effort that demanded the regimentation of civilian life. Soldiers and civilians were regarded as one in the struggle. To dehumanize the enemy, Allied propaganda spread stories of "Huns" committing barbaric atrocities in Belgium and northeastern France. As civilian morale fell in the face of mounting casualties at the front, propaganda increased the stakes in victory so as to justify the enormous sacrifices. Both sides claimed to be fighting not just for national defense but in the name of civilization and democracy.

The ceaseless demands of war resulted in full employment, an unprecedented situation that provided wages for women and the poor. Hundreds of thousands of women left the home for the factories, and by the end of the war they comprised more than a third of all industrial workers in most countries. Women also filled white-collar jobs ordinarily occupied by men. Their independence grew with their importance to the war effort, and they broke social customs that had previously restrained them in behavior and dress. Women contributed to the war effort by serving as nurses, orderlies, and ambulance drivers. The huge number of casualties created a serious shortage of medical facilities and overwhelmed trained personnel, so that thousands of volunteers staffed field hospitals along with professional nurses. The primitive conditions under which they worked exposed these women not only to infection and disease but also to the dangers of artillery bombardment and the threat of capture, for nursing and Red Cross units were often immediately behind the front.

Women served at or near the front lines in a number of capacities during World War I. Here a British ambulance driver is shown in France.

The most famous nurse of the war was Edith Cavell (1865–1915), a Briton in charge of a Red Cross station in Belgium. She remained at her post to care for the wounded while Germans overran the area. When they learned that she was also helping captured British and French soldiers escape, they shot her for espionage. Although her nonnursing activities had removed her from the protection of international law, Allied propaganda made her death a symbol of enemy "barbarism."

Class distinctions tended to break down under the impact of the common struggle for survival. Aristocratic ladies volunteered for nursing duties along with working women, and union leaders worked side by side with industrialists on government boards. Moreover, although the enlisted ranks of the armies were filled overwhelmingly with workers and peasants, young aristocrats and educated middle-class men made up the lower officer corps. The dynamics of trench warfare, in which the junior officers led the charges over the top, meant that the upper classes actually spilled a larger proportion of their blood on the battlefields.

Total war targeted civilians as part of an overall military strategy that sought to break morale. German zeppelins dropped bombs over British cities, and Austrian artillery shelled Venice. More effective, however, were efforts to starve entire populations into submission through naval blockades. Britain and France continued to receive food and supplies from the United States and the British Empire, while Russia and the Central Powers, virtually cut off from overseas trade, felt the shortages acutely. Germany instituted rationing as early as 1915. During the bitter winter of 1916–1917, the German people suffered from hunger and cold, subsisting on turnips and substituting synthetic products for natural goods.

The British violated international agreements by interfering with neutral shipping to Germany. The Germans responded with a major innovation in naval warfare, the U-boat, or submarine. To be effective, submarines had to fire on ships by surprise from below the surface, without being able to ascertain whether they were enemy or neutral vessels or whether they were carrying war contraband. Submarine warfare antagonized American opinion, especially after the sinking of a commercial liner, the *Lusitania,* in May 1915 with the loss of more than 1,000 lives, 128 of them American. That summer U-boat commanders were given restricted orders.

American Intervention and the German Collapse

The submarine was a devastating weapon, sinking 750,000 tons of shipping in 1915 alone. After the stalemate of Verdun and the Somme, the Germans believed it might be decisive as well, despite the risk of bringing the United States into the war. Unrestricted submarine warfare was unleashed on February 1, 1917, and President Woodrow Wilson broke diplomatic relations with Germany two days later. Allied and neutral shipping losses more than doubled in 1917. The U-boats, together with German diplomatic intrigue, Allied propaganda, and the influence of American munitions manufacturers and other trading and banking interests, influenced Congress to declare war against Germany on April 6, 1917. By September 1918 more than 1 million American men had reached Europe; they included 200,000 African-American soldiers who served in labor units, in four infantry regiments attached to the French army, and the entire U.S. 92nd Division.

American supplies began to tip the balance in favor of the Allies, but before the end of 1917 they suffered two serious setbacks. In October the Battle of Caporetto nearly knocked Italy out of the war. In March 1918 the new Bolshevik government in Russia signed the Treaty of Brest-Litovsk with Germany, taking Russia out of the war. The events of 1917 were partly offset when Wilson seized the political initiative by announcing American commitment to war aims that he hoped would bring "peace without victory." His Fourteen Points, issued in January 1918, proposed an end to secret diplomacy, freedom of the seas, unimpeded international trade, disarmament, self-determination for the peoples of eastern Europe, the adjustment of imperial claims based on the interests of colonial peoples as well as those of the pow-

ers, and the creation of an international peacekeeping organization, the League of Nations, among other things.

The last year of the war saw a desperate effort by the Germans to win a military victory. In March, Ludendorff regrouped German troops from the former Russian front and made a massive assault against France, driving once again to the Marne River but failing to break through the Allied lines. On July 18 the Allies, reinforced by some 300,000 American soldiers, began their counteroffensive. By the end of September the German armies, having lost another million men, were in retreat, and civilian morale was on the point of collapse. Convinced that victory was impossible, Ludendorff advised the kaiser to sue for peace.

Germany's request for an armistice on the basis of the Fourteen Points met with a stiff response from Wilson, who demanded that the Germans first implement political reforms. In the meantime, Bulgaria, Turkey, and Austria-Hungary collapsed. On November 3 the German fleet at the port of Kiel mutinied, setting off revolutions in Munich and Berlin. Six days later socialists proclaimed a republic in the capital, and the kaiser abdicated. The armistice, signed on November 11, officially ended the fighting.

The Reordering of Europe

At the close of the Great War, people knew that Europe would never be the same. Thirty-four nations had been engaged in the struggle. Vast tracts of once productive land lay in ruins, and the populations of cities such as Berlin and Vienna were at the edge of starvation. More than 10 million fighting men and at least 1 million civilians had been killed and 20 million wounded. The war had also bled Europe's financial resources of $3.3 billion, turning a continent that had once exported huge amounts of capital into a debtor to the United States. Disillusioned by the experience of total war, Europeans were hopeful that the peace would bring a better world.

The Paris Peace Conference

In January 1919 representatives from 27 victorious nations assembled in Paris to draw up peace treaties with five vanquished states—Germany, Austria, Hungary, Bulgaria, and Turkey. Two reasons accounted for the air of expectancy that surrounded the conference. First, Wilson's presence suggested that the treaties would be equitable, since both sides had accepted his Fourteen Points as the basis for peace. Second, each nation brought a delegation of technical experts who promised to arrange the settlements according to objective, "scientific" principles instead of old-fashioned power politics.

Like the Congress of Vienna 100 years earlier, the Paris peace conference was an impressive gathering of national leaders. Britain was represented by its prime minister, the Welsh Liberal David Lloyd George (1863–1945); France, by the Republican premier, Georges Clemenceau (1841–1929); and Italy, by its prime minister, Vittorio E. Orlando (1860–1952). Most of the major decisions were the result of negotiations among the "Big Three," Wilson, Lloyd George, and Clemenceau.

Operating in the shadow of the Bolshevik revolution in Russia and the fear that its example would spread, the Big Three excluded Lenin's government from the deliberations. Moreover, public opinion among the victors demanded harsh peace terms for the defeated enemy. Unlike the Congress of Vienna, where France was accorded full diplomatic representation, Germany was permitted to have only observers at the conference and to await terms dictated by the Allied Powers.

The Treaty of Versailles

The most pressing problem was what to do with Germany. Three issues were paramount: French insistence on future security against Germany, the disposition of

The leaders of the principal Allied Powers gather at the Paris peace conference (1919): (from left) David Lloyd George, Vittorio E. Orlando, Georges Clemenceau, and Woodrow Wilson.

German colonies, and the reparations the Germans would pay. Because France had twice been invaded within 50 years, Clemenceau demanded the creation of a separate buffer state in the Rhineland between his country and Germany. Wilson objected that such a plan would violate the principle of self-determination, and his debate with Clemenceau became so acrimonious that the American president threatened to leave the conference. In the end, Clemenceau compromised: the Rhineland would be demilitarized and occupied by Allied troops for 15 years, during which time the coal-rich Saar region was to be administered by the League of Nations for the economic benefit of France and Britain, and the United States promised to conclude a defensive military alliance with France.

France, Britain, and Japan all coveted German colonies. The "mandate principle" offered a solution under which these powers were each given control over some of the territories under League supervision, with the object of preparing them for independence. The principle did not apply, however, to China's Shantung peninsula, which came under full Japanese authority. Reparations were another contentious issue. Britain and France insisted that Germany be responsible for all damage done to civilians, including pensions and family support. As a result, the Allies drafted Article 231, which held German aggression responsible for the war. The exact amount was fixed two years later at the staggering sum of $33 billion.

Some economists, including John Maynard Keynes (1883–1946), who was attached to the British delegation, believed the peace treaty put Germany in an untenable position that spelled future disaster. He argued that the enormous reparations anticipated were impossible in view of the other economic provisions of the treaty. Large amounts of German coal were allocated to France, many of Germany's ships were given to Britain, and billions of dollars of its foreign assets were confiscated. Territorial losses stripped Germany of half its iron mines and a fifth of its iron and steel industries. The treaty forced Germany to return Alsace and Lorraine to France; on its eastern borders, Germany ceded parts of East Prussia and Upper Silesia to a revived state of Poland, lost the city of Danzig to League control, and gave up territory to newly independent Czechoslovakia. *Anschluss*, or union, was forbidden between Germany and Austria.

Determined that Germany would be in no position to wage another aggressive war, the Allies reduced its army to a 100,000-man volunteer force and limited its navy to a handful of small ships. They also prohibited all offensive weapons, including submarines, airplanes and

Nightmare at Versailles

When the Allies assembled at Paris in 1919 to work out the terms of the peace treaties with Germany and the Central Powers, a range of motivations guided their decisions, from a spirit of revenge to the pressures of domestic politics, which demanded a harsh treaty against the Germans. John Maynard Keynes, a British economist at the peace conference, wrote a devastating critique of the harsh economic terms imposed on the German people and warned of dire consequences for the peace of Europe. Here he describes the atmosphere he witnessed at Paris.

Paris was a nightmare, and everyone there was morbid. A sense of impending catastrophe overhung the frivolous scene; the futility and smallness of man before the great events confronting him; the mingled significance and unreality of the decisions; levity, blindness, insolence, confused cries from without—all the elements of ancient tragedy were there. Seated indeed amid the theatrical trappings of the French Saloons of State, one could wonder if the extraordinary visages of Wilson and of Clemenceau, with their fixed hue and unchanging characterization, were really faces at all and not the tragi-comic masks of some strange drama or puppet-show.

The proceedings of Paris all had this air of extraordinary importance and unimportance at the same time. The decisions seemed charged with consequences to the future of human society; yet the air whispered that the word was not flesh, that it was futile, insignificant, of no effect, dissociated from events; and one felt most strongly the impression . . . of events marching on to their fated conclusion uninfluenced and unaffected by the cerebrations of Statesmen in Council. . . .

In Paris, where those connected with the Supreme Economic Council received almost hourly the reports of the misery, disorder, and decaying organization of all Central and Eastern Europe, allied and enemy alike, and learnt . . . unanswerable evidence of the terrible exhaustion of their countries, an occasional visit to the hot, dry room in the President's house, where the Four fulfilled their destinies in empty and arid intrigue, only added to the sense of nightmare.

Source: John Maynard Keynes, *The Economic Consequences of the Peace* (New York: Harcourt, Brace and Howe, 1920), pp. 5–7.

---

zeppelins, heavy artillery, tanks, and poison gas. Finally, the treaty provided for the trial of the former kaiser as a war criminal, but the Netherlands, to which he had fled, refused to extradite him. The threat of renewed war forced representatives of the new German government to sign the treaty on June 28, 1919.

The peace terms with Germany's allies were hardly less severe. Austria was reduced to a third of its former size, while Hungary was left with a fourth of its former territory. Bulgaria also lost land, and all three states had to reduce their armies. Turkey remained only with Asia Minor and a small strip of territory around Istanbul, and

the Turkish straits were demilitarized and opened to international shipping.

The Search for Security

Wilson had insisted that permanent peace rested on the creation of an international body known as the League of Nations. The Covenant, or constitution, of the League was incorporated into each of the peace treaties. It provided for a system of "collective security" by which the League would encourage disarmament and prevent war by arbitrating disputes and applying economic sanctions.

The Covenant also established a system of mandates by which the European powers assumed the right to rule a number of non-Western areas that they argued were incapable of self-government. Granting self-determination to some European states, such as Poland and Yugoslavia, while denying the same right to the colonized peoples of Asia, Africa, and the Pacific reflected racist assumptions. Because it had no armed force to coerce violators, the League lacked the power to enforce its principles. Moreover, when Congress refused to ratify the Treaty of Versailles, the United States itself failed to join the organization; neither Germany nor the Soviet Union was to become a member for years.

France and Germany sought alternatives to the League of Nations to ensure their security. American withdrawal from European diplomatic affairs denied France the defensive treaty that Britain and the United States had promised. Consequently, France created a "little entente" by aligning itself with Czechoslovakia, Romania, and Yugoslavia, hoping thereby to encircle Germany on its eastern borders. Isolated from the community of nations, Germany made common cause with Soviet Russia, another outcast nation. In 1922 they signed the Treaty of Rapallo, opening diplomatic relations and pledging economic cooperation as well as secret military contacts.

France remained uneasy over German intentions, and when the Germans failed to meet their reparations quota in 1923, French and Belgian troops occupied the Ruhr Basin on the eastern bank of the Rhine. Passive resistance among Ruhr factory workers and miners and British and American protests eventually forced a withdrawal, but the fear and hatred between the nations remained deeply rooted.

In 1925 German Foreign Minister Gustav Stresemann (1878–1929) proposed that Germany, France, Britain, Italy, and Belgium guarantee the western European status quo. The result was the Locarno Pact, which relieved some of the international political tension. In 1926 Germany finally joined the League of Nations. In 1927 the French foreign minister, Aristide Briand (1862–1932), and the American secretary of state, Frank Kellogg (1856–1937), sponsored a treaty renouncing war as an instrument of national policy. The Kellogg-Briand Pact of 1928, eventually signed by 65 states, "outlawed" war.

Society and Culture: The Impact of War

The postwar generation was deeply disturbed by the war. As Europeans rebuilt their cities and mourned their dead, they were haunted by the memory of their former confidence in the superiority of their civilization. This explains why the West experienced a profound crisis of belief after 1919 despite the victory of the democracies and the return of peace.

Although European intellectual and cultural life in the postwar period was creative and varied, it was marked by a mood of anxiety. The sense of futility was particularly acute among the veterans who returned to a civilian society beset with political and economic problems and intent on getting back to "normalcy." To these dashed hopes was added the horror of modern warfare. The German author Erich Maria Remarque (1898–1970) captured the shock experienced by soldiers in two bestselling novels, *All Quiet on the Western Front* (1929) and *The Road Back* (1931). The mood of despair seemed to confirm the prewar intuitions of Nietzsche and Freud that civilized society was irrational and that humans were unable to control their "primitive" instincts. This atmosphere of skepticism stimulated a transformation of Western culture. A decade after the war's end, the "modern" temper of twentieth-century life had been established.

Distrust of established beliefs, uncertainty about the meaning of life, and anxiety about the future produced what the author Gertrude Stein (1874–1946) termed a "lost generation." The triumph of communism in Russia and the rise of fascism in the 1920s suggested a willingness to abandon democracy. Frustrated material expectations added to the disorientation, for the economic boom after 1919 proved to be only a prelude to the Great Depression.

Social Change and Economic Crisis

The impact of the war was felt differently in each country and class. Everywhere the status and power of the old nobility were seriously weakened, especially in the new states of eastern Europe. The aristocracy had been systematically eliminated in Russia after the Bolshevik revolution, and a large number of young British nobles had been killed in the war. Peasants had been conscripted into military service more heavily than any other class, so the toll in death and disablement among them was also high. After the war many peasants refused to go back to their villages and often formed the rank and file of militant veterans' groups in the cities. When they did go back to the countryside, they frequently led protest movements.

Postwar society in western Europe was predominantly urban. In France, the most agrarian of the industrialized nations, the percentage of the working population engaged in agriculture fell from one-half before 1914

MAP 36.3   TERRITORIAL SETTLEMENTS IN EUROPE, 1919–1926

to one-third by 1931. Nevertheless, the number of industrial workers remained fairly stable over the following decades as advances in technology and assembly-line processes made labor more productive. During the first years of the war severe labor shortages had produced higher wages and a modicum of prosperity for the working classes, but government controls and inflation eventually forced wages to lag behind prices, resulting in significant discontent. The support and cooperation that socialist parties and unions gave to the war effort had conditioned many labor leaders to moderate policies. Some working-class leaders, however, reverted to more radical doctrines after the war, and many looked to the Russian Revolution for inspiration. As real wages rose between 1924 and 1929, particularly for the unskilled, worker discontent was once again mitigated, a trend reinforced by new social welfare measures in many countries.

The war affected the middle classes most severely. Greater educational opportunities and the growth of the service sector increased the number of white-collar workers, many of whom came from working-class families. The economic slump of the 1920s, however, slowed middle-class mobility. The pressure was particularly acute on the lower middle class, whose opportunities for advancement into managerial positions in the private sector shrank as the economy slowed. Inflation also limited the earning power of this group and threatened its status. The most extreme distress occurred in Germany, where by 1925 inflation had eaten up more than 50 percent of the capital held by the lower middle class. Retirees, widows, and others living on fixed incomes were hit especially hard, as were property owners whose incomes were frozen by rent regulations. Lower-middle-class earnings fell markedly in the 1920s, and millions of

The Mood of Postwar Pessimism

In the decade after World War I, many aspects of nineteenth-century civilization were abandoned in the West as religious belief, political principles, defined gender roles, and public morality were consciously rejected by the "lost generation." Here the Spanish philosopher José Ortega y Gasset (1883–1955) reveals this sense of postwar pessimism and lack of intellectual leadership behind it.

To the XIXth Century many things seemed no longer possible, firm-fixed as was its faith in progress. Today, by the very fact that everything seems possible to us, we have a feeling that the worst of all is possible: retrogression, barbarism, decadence. This of itself would not be a bad symptom; it would mean that we are once again forming contact with that insecurity which is essential to all forms of life, that anxiety both dolorous and delicious contained in every moment. . . . Generally we refuse to feel that fearsome pulsation which makes of a moment of sincerity a tiny fleeting heart; we strain in the attempt to find security and to render ourselves insensible to the fundamental drama of our destiny, by steeping it in habits, usages, topics—in every kind of chloroform. It is an excellent thing, then, that for the first time for nearly three centuries we are surprised to find ourselves with the feeling that we do not know what is going to happen to-morrow. . . .

Can we be surprised that the world today seems empty of purposes, anticipations, ideals? Nobody has concerned himself with supplying them. Such has been the desertion of the directing minorities, which is always found on the reverse side of the rebellion of the masses.

Source: José Ortega y Gasset, *The Revolt of the Masses* (New York: W.W. Norton, 1957), pp. 44–46.

---

workers were forced back into the factories, where salaries equaled or exceeded those of white-collar employees. Hence the lower middle class felt squeezed between two groups: the wealthy capitalists, whose income was still increasing, and the workers, from whose ranks many of them had risen. Lower-middle-class resentment of big business and labor often found political expression in radical right-wing groups.

The New Morality: Women, Work, and Sex

The middle class, which had experienced prewar optimism most fully, now found its values under assault. Wartime conditions disrupted social arrangements and family structures: husbands at the front, women in the factories, strangers crowding into the cities, and the uncertainty of survival had loosened the restrictions of bourgeois society and contributed to the breakdown of traditional morality. Psychological and social stress encouraged a new style of life that celebrated "liberation" from conventional behavior. In the 1920s Europeans were caught up in the spirit of the "jazz age," a name re-

flecting the popular perception that American life was more modern and less tradition-bound.

Public manifestations of the new morality appeared everywhere. Women's skirts were shorter and dresses more revealing, slinky adaptations of the "flapper" style made famous in Prohibition America. Young people drank and smoked in public, bars and nightclubs proliferated, and dancing took on more expressive—and suggestive—forms. Motion pictures, perhaps the most popular mass entertainment of the period, created the cult of the "vamp," and the private lives of film stars were spread across the front pages of the popular press. The use of chaperons and arranged marriages declined sharply, while illegitimacy and divorce rates rose. Such changes produced a more open attitude toward sexual matters.

Social developments reflected the new morality. Greater tolerance toward sexual minorities evolved. Events once thought sensational, such as Oscar Wilde's trial in the 1890s, seemed quaint to Europeans of the 1920s who openly professed their differing sexual orientation. Paris and Berlin, the two centers of postwar avant-garde culture, were havens for artists, writers, and musicians that included homosexuals as well as American blacks. Gertrude Stein and Alice B. Toklas, the most famous lesbian couple of the period, presided over a brilliant artistic and literary scene in Paris. Sexual minorities still faced formidable obstacles to equality and acceptance, but the more tolerant attitudes of the 1920s brought the issue into the open.

The emancipation of women was another result of the social transformation. An earlier generation of feminist agitation had made important advances in raising the consciousness of women and calling public attention to their demands for equality. Yet despite the work of the middle-class suffragists and the socialist women's movement, Finland and Norway were the only Western nations in which women had won the right to vote before 1914.

Wartime labor shortages created a situation in which women made significant progress toward representation in the workplace. As women crowded into the munitions industries and the service sector, governments made propaganda appeals to them, thus raising expectations for change. Some nations granted women the right to vote: in 1918 the British Parliament extended suffrage to women over 30, and shortly thereafter both the United States and the new German republic gave the vote equally to men and women. Austria, Poland, and Czechoslovakia joined Belgium, the Netherlands, Sweden, and Denmark in following suit.

While these were crucial gains, the suffrage was not made universal in Spain, France, Switzerland, and Italy until after World War II. Moreover, in many countries marriage and property laws favoring husbands also remained largely intact. After 1919 more women gained access to educational opportunities and a wider range of jobs, although many were forced out of their wartime work by returning soldiers, and in practice some professions remained closed to women. Nor was progress in regard to the status of women and sexual minorities permanent, for serious setbacks occurred in the interwar years, when right-wing regimes repressed both with renewed vigor.

The American jazz singer and dancer Josephine Baker was a great celebrity in Paris during the years between the wars.

Josephine Baker: An American in Paris

One of the most celebrated figures in Europe between the wars was the African-American entertainer Josephine Baker. Born in St. Louis in 1906 to a black mother and a father reputedly of Spanish descent, Baker left school at the age of 8 to help support her family. While living in East St. Louis, she witnessed the race riots that broke out there in 1917, and the sight of white bands burning and killing with impunity left an indelible mark on her.

Baker's talent soon surfaced. She starred in basement musicals as a child and ran away with a vaudeville troupe at the age of 13. Four years later she appeared at Radio City Music Hall in New York in a musical featuring African-American performers titled, stereotypically, *Shuffle Along.* In 1925 she went to Paris with a show called *La Revue Nègre,* which sought to capitalize on the topical vogue for jazz and for "exotic" black entertainers. The show failed and the company was stranded, but Baker caught on with the Folies Bergère, a club famous for its lavish sets and its scantily dressed performers. She created a sensation in her debut, in which she appeared clad only in a tutu made of rhinestone-studded bananas and three bracelets.

Baker's multiple talents as a singer and dancer, wed to a style of inimitable comic abandon, soon made her an international celebrity. Billed only as Josephine, the former slum child earned and spent enormous sums of money; mimicking her own exotic image, she strolled down the streets of Paris with a pet leopard. After a hugely successful world tour, she appeared in films opposite such French stars as Jean Gabin and ventured into light opera as well.

In 1937 Baker married a wealthy industrialist, Jean Lion, converted to Judaism, and became a French citizen. At the outbreak of World War II she joined the Red Cross and was later recruited into the French Resistance, gathering intelligence and also entertaining Free French forces. At the end of the war she was awarded France's highest decorations, the Croix de Guerre and the Légion d'Honneur, as well as the rosette of the Resistance. Baker's wide travel and her experience of poverty and discrimination led her in 1947 to found what she called a World Village at Les Milandes, her estate in southwestern France. Here she and her second husband, Jo Bouillon, adopted a "rainbow family" of 12 children of all races and religions. She became a center of controversy in 1951 after she protested the refusal to serve her at the Stork Club in New York, but the National Association for the Advancement of Colored People (NAACP) named her its Woman of the Year. Baker began a crusade against segregation in her native country and succeeded in integrating theaters and nightclubs from Las Vegas to Miami. In 1963 she stood with Dr. Martin Luther King, Jr., at the climax of his march on Washington, D.C., and delivered an impassioned speech in front of the Lincoln Memorial.

Bankrupted finally by her debts at Les Milandes, Baker was provided a villa for herself and her children by Princess Grace of Monaco. In 1973 she triumphed at Carnegie Hall in another comeback tour, and despite failing health she repeated her success in Paris in a performance commemorating her fiftieth anniversary in France on April 10, 1975. Two days later, she died of a stroke.

On or off the stage, in or out of controversy, Josephine Baker was for half a century a uniquely vivid symbol of glamour, vitality, compassion, and commitment to the struggle for human equality. At the end of her life a film biography (since released) was planned, but she was skeptical: "I would like to meet the woman who has the courage even to play my life story in a film. . . . I do not believe the woman exists who could have had the courage to have *lived* it as I have done." Certainly, few

women of the twentieth century have combined careers and interests so daringly, served the human cause so passionately, and triumphed so indomitably.

Science, Literature, and Art

The postwar crisis of belief was especially acute among artists and writers, whose search for meaning led to creative ferment and experimentation. Proclaiming a "crisis of the mind," the French poet and critic Paul Valéry (1871–1945) articulated the state of anxiety and pessimism. His gloomy prognosis of the future was echoed by the German scholar Oswald Spengler (1880–1936). Spengler's immensely popular book *The Decline of the West* (1918) compared the development of Europe with the historical pattern of other civilizations. He argued that the West had entered a period of decay that could be reversed only by an authoritarian "Caesar" capable of imposing peace and order on a chaotic world. In a similar vein, Ortega y Gasset's *Revolt of the Masses* (1930) warned that democratic society would result in the decline of education and culture.

Science offered no antidote to these laments. Building on the advances in physics at the turn of the century, the Danish physicist Niels Bohr (1885–1962) had formulated a theory of the atom in 1913 that attempted to reconcile Max Planck's quantum theory with Ernest Rutherford's view of atomic structure. By the mid–1920s, however, more complex ideas challenged Bohr's conclusions. The abstract language of differential equations took the place of concepts such as orbits, while Bohr and others revised their earlier hypotheses. In 1927 the German physicist Werner Heisenberg (1901–1976) announced his "uncertainty principle": the behavior of atomic particles did not conform to the laws of cause and effect. The futility of attempting to find a comprehensive explanation of physical phenomena to replace the old Newtonian model became increasingly apparent.

Postwar developments in philosophy both reflected and reinforced the findings of science. Ludwig Wittgenstein (1889–1951), the most forceful advocate of the movement called logical empiricism, maintained that traditional ethical and metaphysical systems were meaningless because philosophy was nothing more than statements of fact clarified by logic. Logical positivists asserted that unless such concepts as "freedom" and "God" could be reduced to the precise language of mathematics and symbolic logic, they were meaningless. Similarly, existentialism, derived from the Danish philosopher Søren Kierkegaard (1813–1855) and later associated with the French philosophers Jean-Paul Sartre (1905–1980) and Albert Camus (1913–1960), presented an image of human helplessness and despair in the face of an existence devoid of meaning and a supreme being. Although the existentialists argued that humans exist without a predetermined purpose, they still asserted the necessity of responsible moral action.

In the world of literature, a no less startling revolution took place. Language and structure gave way to experiments that reflected new theories of the human personality as well as a conscious desire to break away from traditional forms. Authors extended the path opened by Marcel Proust (1871–1922), the French author of *Remembrance of Things Past,* with a new "stream of consciousness" of subjective experience. The year 1922 saw the publication of two influential works in this genre, *Ulysses* by the Irishman James Joyce (1882–1941) and *Jacob's Room* by the Englishwoman Virginia Woolf (1882–1941), followed in 1929 by *The Sound and the Fury* by the American William Faulkner (1897–1962). Each of these works probed the random thoughts and emotions of everyday consciousness and the obscure sources of human motivation that Freud had suggested.

D. H. Lawrence (1885–1930), whose controversial novel *Lady Chatterley's Lover* (1928) was censored for its explicit description of sexual desire, exemplified the postwar liberation from bourgeois mores. The German Thomas Mann (1875–1955), in *The Magic Mountain* (1924), evoked the collapse of meaning. Franz Kafka

(1883–1924), a German Jew who lived in Prague, wrote frightening tales of nightmares that haunt the imagination, most notably *The Trial* (1925) and *The Castle* (1929).

While much of the literature of the period between the world wars was so innovative as to confuse and repel readers, the poetry of the Irishman William Butler Yeats (1865–1939) had a more direct appeal, for he combined traditional lyricism with a stoic view of the world. In a similar manner, the German Rainer Maria Rilke (1875–1926) attempted to evoke harmony with nature.

The Italian dramatist Luigi Pirandello (1867–1936) and the poet T. S. Eliot gave the most representative expression to the concerns of the period. In Pirandello's *Six Characters in Search of an Author* (1918), two sets of players, a family and a group of actors, appear on stage at the same time, with the family members asking actors to portray their roles. Both family and actors present versions of the truth peculiar to their own viewpoints. Much as in Einstein's theories, Pirandello's play offered relative truths from which the observer—or the audience—could choose. The absurdity of a world without fixed guideposts was a pervasive theme of interwar European culture. Eliot, in *The Waste Land* (1922), captured most poignantly the sense of desolation that so many creative thinkers of the postwar world felt. Eliot portrayed the spiritual emptiness of modern London and brought the mood of Symbolism into English poetry. He eventually resolved his personal crisis by joining the Anglican church.

The plastic arts, like literature, caught the spirit of the period. As early as 1915 the horrors of the war had begun to produce the deliberately nonsensical antiart

Walter Gropius founded the Bauhaus, the most important school of modern architectural design, to reconcile art with technology. His functionalist style is apparent in the workshop building, completed in 1926.

movement known as Dada (from the French meaning "hobbyhorse"). Other artists embraced a "return to order" that restored representational forms to painting so as to express human alienation and isolation. Surrealism drew from a variety of sources, including the new realism, prewar Cubism, Dadaism, and Freudian psychology. Surrealists such as Salvador Dalí and Giorgio de Chirico (1888–1978) created visions of a dream world and hallucinatory landscapes according to the irrational dictates of the subconscious. Other artists, such as Wassily Kandinsky (1866–1944) and Paul Klee (1879–1940), moved from their earlier Expressionist concerns toward greater abstraction, a trend that Piet Mondrian (1872–1944) brought to its extreme in rigidly nonobjective paintings.

Klee and Kandinsky taught at the Bauhaus, the most famous school of architecture and design in modern times. Founded in Weimar by the architect Walter Gropius (1883–1969), the Bauhaus sought to reconcile art with science and technology. It advanced an architectural style emphasizing functionalism, the use of glass and prefabricated concrete, and a rejection of ornamentation. The Bauhaus "international style," also championed by the French architect Le Corbusier (1887–1965) and the American Frank Lloyd Wright (1869–1959), testified to the triumph of the modern temper.

SUMMARY

The generation that grew to maturity between 1890 and 1919 experienced the stress and excitement of living through the end of one historical era and the birth of another. The second half of the nineteenth century had been generally a period of material growth, optimism, and self-confidence. Science and technology had made life in the West more comfortable and had enabled the Western powers to impose their rule over much of the globe.

Many of the same factors that caused European expansion contributed, however, to a mounting crisis among the Western states. To a litany of old grievances were added new rivalries and competition for increasingly limited resources. While political leaders and capitalist entrepreneurs in one nation worked to outmaneuver their counterparts elsewhere, military officers and ideologues planned strategies of defense and domination. Once the crisis erupted, the West discovered that it had become much better at waging war than it had imagined. But unlike the wars of imperial conquest, the great European powers were more or less evenly matched, and the war consequently became an exercise in self-destruction.

The strain of total war had produced major change. Socialists shared power in wartime governments, and monarchies were overthrown in three major states. In some countries the bloodletting decimated the ruling classes, while in others revolution eradicated or severely wounded traditional elites. Prewar social arrangements were further altered as a result of the massive conscription of peasants, the mobilization of women into the workforce, and the disruption of family life.

The postwar age was a new world. Not only had the European map changed with the shifting of frontiers, but new states also appeared on the ruins of old empires. Positive thinkers saw liberal democracy installed in central and eastern Europe for the first time; the more pessimistic questioned the chances for its survival. New forms of political extremism arose everywhere; in Russia and Italy, they soon came to power and threatened to spread. Nor did Europe's world supremacy survive much beyond the war. As the forces of nationalism took hold in the colonies, Western control of the subject peoples of Asia, Africa, and the Middle East weakened.

Science, literature, and art undermined the optimism of an earlier age, expressed the despair of a generation that had experienced shattering trauma, and forged new directions. Some intellectuals turned back to religion as a source of hope and comfort. Even Carl Jung rejected the teachings of Freud, his intellectual mentor, by advocating the therapeutic value of religious faith. In 1934, with the world in the throes of the Great Depression, the British historian Arnold Toynbee published the first of a series of volumes, titled A Study of History, *that likened the development of civilizations to the biological process of life, with cycles of birth, growth, and decline. Unlike Oswald Spengler, however, Toynbee entertained the prospect that Western civilization might revive itself. In the search for meaning, others turned instead to political movements of protest and violence.*

NOTES

1. Viscount Grey of Fallodon, *Twenty-five Years, 1892–1916*, vol. 2 (New York: Stokes, 1925), p. 20.
2. K. Robbins, *The First World War* (New York: Oxford University Press, 1984), p. 88.
3. W. S. Churchill, *The World Crisis* (New York: Scribner, 1923), p. 3.

SUGGESTIONS FOR FURTHER READING

Calder, N. *Einstein's Universe.* New York: Penguin Books, 1980.
Cantor, N. F., and Wertman, M. S., eds. *The History of Popular Culture Since 1815.* New York: Macmillan, 1968.

Cecil, L. *Wilhelm II.* Chapel Hill: University of North Carolina Press, 1989.

Ellenberger, H. F. *The Discovery of the Unconscious.* New York: Basic Books, 1970.

Evans, R. J. W., and Strandmann, H. P. von, eds., *The Coming of the First World War.* New York: Oxford University Press, 1989.

Fussell, P. *The Great War and Modern Memory.* New York: Oxford University Press, 1975.

Hughes, H. S. *Consciousness and Society: The Reorientation of European Social Thought, 1890–1930.* New York: Knopf, 1958.

Hughes, R. *The Shock of the New: Art and the Century of Change.* New York: Knopf, 1981.

Joll, J. *The Origins of the First World War.* London: Longman, 1984.

Kern, S. *The Culture of Time and Space, 1880–1918.* Cambridge, Mass.: Harvard University Press, 1983.

Lee, D. E. *The Outbreak of the War, Causes and Responsibilities,* 4th ed. Lexington, Mass.: D.C. Heath, 1975.

Martin, M. W. *Futurist Art and Theory, 1909–1915.* Oxford: Clarendon Press, 1978.

Masur, G. *Prophets of Yesterday: Studies in European Culture, 1890–1914.* New York: Macmillan, 1961.

Mayer, A. J. *The Politics and Diplomacy of Peacemaking.* New York: Knopf, 1968.

Mosse, G. *The Culture of Western Europe.* Chicago: Rand McNally, 1969.

Offer, A. *The First World War: An Agrarian Interpretation.* New York: Oxford University Press, 1990.

Pulzer, P. G. *The Rise of Political Anti-Semitism in Germany and Austria.* New York: Wiley, 1964.

Remak, J. *The Origins of World War I, 1871–1914,* 2nd ed. Fort Worth: Harcourt Brace, 1995.

Rewald, J. *The History of Impressionism.* New York: New York Graphic Society, 1980.

Robbins, K. *The First World War.* New York: Oxford University Press, 1984.

Sontag, R. V. *A Broken World.* New York: Harper & Row, 1971.

Stearns, P. N. *European Society in Upheaval: Social History Since 1800.* New York: Macmillan, 1967.

Williams, J. *The Other Battleground: The Home Fronts, Britain, France, and Germany, 1914–1918.* Chicago: Regnery, 1972.

Wohl, R. *The Generation of 1914.* Cambridge, Mass.: Harvard University Press, 1979.

GLOBAL ESSAY

The Human Image (II)

Since the primitive carvers of the Old Stone Age some 25,000 years ago, the human figure has been a central theme of artistic representation. Each civilization has accorded it a different emphasis, and artists of every culture have interpreted it from the aesthetic and religious points of view of their times and societies. Throughout much of the ancient period and during the first millennium A.D., the human figure served a number of important purposes, principally as the embodiment of religious themes, as a means of representing notions of beauty, or as a general commentary on the human condition.

While these functions continued to be served by the human image, important changes began to occur in the modern age. The sixteenth century saw a more secularized portrayal of the human figure in cultures as diverse as Europe and India, together with greater stylistic naturalism. At the same time, an exceptionally active artistic patronage began to emerge throughout much of the world. From the court of Ming China to the Mughal Empire in India and the Medici of Florence, rulers turned to painters and sculptors to produce memorials to the greatness of their regimes. Artists had, of course, always served political purposes, but in some cases rulers now developed a new respect for their creative powers. Figures such as Michelangelo achieved the stature of a culture hero in the late European Renaissance, a phenomenon enshrined in Giorgio Vasari's *Lives of the Painters*. Moreover, while patronage elsewhere in the world remained largely in the hands of rulers, in the West private parties began to commission artists to paint their portraits, so that the human figure increasingly represented the wider elite.

Mughal culture in India revealed the diversity of Muslim artistic response to figurative art. The court of Akbar and his successors was the center for the production of portrait miniatures, exquisitely delicate works that meticulously recorded their subjects in a narrative style. Unlike Persian miniatures of earlier times, with their fairy-tale decorations, these paintings display an almost unnerving detachment, as in the portrait of a courtier dying of opium addiction. They testify as much to the virtuosity of the artist as to the representation of an individual.

The emperors of Ming China treated artists with less respect than the court of Akbar: Chinese artists

Dying Courtier, *c.1618. Portrait of a man dying of opium addiction.*

worked in palace workshops under tight supervision, a custom that drove many of the more progressive among them to flee the capital for the cities of the south. Free from the demands of the emperors, many painters of the period seem to have deliberately avoided the depiction of human beings, thus reinforcing the Chinese preference for landscapes.

During the Ch'ing dynasty (1644–1912) sculptors reverted to smaller-scale works in porcelain, exceeding the technical skill of earlier Chinese ceramists. A small white porcelain statue of Kuan-yin (the Chinese goddess of compassion) from the seventeenth century reveals the softness of form and the deeply humanized rendering of a goddess achieved in this medium. Large quantities of such ceramics were exported to Europe in the eighteenth century, and to this day the term *china* is used to describe fine ceramic wares, especially porcelain.

In contrast to the detached aestheticism of the Mughal image and the refined delicacy of later Chinese porcelains, artists of the early Edo period in Japan depicted the human figure as a means of memorializing historic events. Chinese travelers observed that like their own painters, their Japanese neighbors tended to use scroll paintings to narrate events, often without philosophical meaning. A pair of painted Japanese screens from 1610 depicts westerners playing music. These are among the interesting works that show Portuguese and Dutch influences on Japanese painting as well as Japanese curiosity at the appearance of the "southern barbarians," as the Jesuit missionaries were known. The figures show little interest in the individuals represented but depict their customs, together with their costumes, so drab to Japanese eyes.

Toward the end of the seventeenth century the principal artistic medium in Japan shifted from scroll painting to the woodblock print, which increasingly reflected the lives and tastes of an emerging commercial society. The woodblock allowed for the inexpensive reproduction and wide distribution of popular images and themes, such as the Kabuki actors so admired by the middle class.

When the Portuguese arrived at Benin, West Africa, in the fifteenth century, they found a rich and sophisticated kingdom, whose sculptural tradition may well have been related to that of the earlier civilization of the neighboring city of Ife. Climatic conditions in sub-Saharan Africa have not favored the survival of early wooden carvings, but sculptures made of ivory and metal reveal skillful renderings of the human form both realistically and in more abstract styles. A fifteenth-century zinc brass head is a delicate and idealized portrait of a king. Like the Japanese, Benin artists recorded the appearance of the newcomers, though in a much more symbolic and stylized form. An ivory portrait mask made

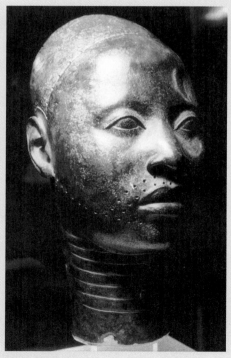

Zinc brass head from Benin, twelfth to fifteenth century.

for a ruler is topped by a crown composed of a band of long-haired, bearded Portuguese. The carver of this piece is more interested in hairstyles than in dress but shows the same curiosity at strange customs and appearance. The ruler's portrait expresses elegance and power out of all proportion to its size.

No such record survives of the arrival of westerners in the Americas. The art of the last Aztecs retains a strong element of decoration, as in the statues of deities carved to embellish temples. Yet the last period of Aztec art provides at least one outstanding example of an artist's use of the human figure to depict a primal event: the carving of a woman (perhaps a goddess) giving birth. The realism of the straining and the cold, damp look of the skin, produced by a careful working of the stone, are powerfully contrasted with the stylized miniature adult emerging from the womb.

From the sixteenth to the late nineteenth centuries, European art was molded by the principles of the Italian Renaissance style, which flourished in the fifteenth and early sixteenth centuries. In their efforts to combine the splendors of classical antiquity with Christian values, Renaissance artists turned to the human figure as an image of the highest form of beauty. The face and body reemerged in a way that has been as important for the subsequent development of Western art as its appearance in ancient Greek art in the fifth century B.C. The Renaissance stress on mental and physical prowess and on the ability to control and change environment resulted in the triumph of the human figure as the chief focus of artistic representation in the Western world. Its treatment of the body may best be understood by examining two categories of painting and sculpture: the nude and portraiture.

After centuries of neglect, the female nude was reemphasized in European art in the late fifteenth century. Several of Sandro Botticelli's paintings, including his *Primavera,* were inspired by Hellenistic statuary, especially depictions of Venus, yet they also reflect the early Renaissance philosophical interest in ideal beauty. The classical Venus figure offered the artist an opportunity to depict the female nude, something that could not be done with the Virgin Mary, hitherto the most popular female subject in European art. Titian, the brilliant Venetian painter, displayed the female nude in a reclining form that would remain popular for centuries. His *Venus of Urbino,* vividly and sensuously colored, reflects the Renaissance artist's interest in rendering the human figure in a wholly natural condition, in contrast to the late medieval renditions of naked bodies, often shown at the Last Judgment or in hell. Donatello's famous statue of a virtually nude David is a particularly fine example of

Aztec woman, perhaps a goddess, in childbirth.

the combination of Christian and pagan elements in the Renaissance. The subject is a figure from the Old Testament, but the classical stance and the provocative nudity are Greek.

In portraiture Renaissance painters combined an interest in personality and the external world. Leonardo da Vinci's *Last Supper* is both the re-creation of a famous biblical episode and a masterpiece of psychological study in which the viewer is implicitly invited to interpret the emotional responses of Christ's disciples through expressions and physical gestures when they learn one of them is a traitor. No less psychological were the late works of Donatello and Michelangelo, both of whom rejected external beauty in their quest to understand the depths of the penitent soul. A half century later, when the art of the late Renaissance had begun to give way to the sophisticated Mannerist style, the Florentine artist Bronzino brilliantly depicted the individualized Renaissance man in his *Portrait of a Young Man.* Here is an elegant, affected youth whose aloof demeanor, handsome face, and elegant hands reveal the haughty arrogance of an educated gentleman of high social position. While Mannerists such as Bronzino emphasized the neck and hands to convey a sense of grace, others, such as El Greco, distorted their figures to highlight the spiritual values of the Counter-Reformation.

The baroque art of the seventeenth century in Europe was characterized by the expression of strong emotions, often religious, and a virtuoso technique. These characteristics can be seen in the works of the Italian sculptor Bernini. In his *St. Theresa in Ecstasy,* the body of the enraptured saint, her robes, and the cloud on which she rests combine to create the illusion of mystical drama. Unlike Michelangelo, Bernini uses the facial expression of his subject, suffused with a passion at once mystical and sensual, to enhance the dramatic effect. Rubens, the Flemish baroque master, concentrated on the human figure as the epitome of the animal body straining against the physical forces around it, whether in the form of soft, luminous female flesh or muscular, tanned male bodies. Unlike the bodies of El Greco or the late works of Donatello and Michelangelo, those of Rubens vividly represent the zest for physical life that was a dominant element of the baroque spirit.

A more traditional use of the human figure as political icon appears in Hyacinthe Rigaud's portrait of Louis XIV (see page 616), painted at a time when the grandeur of the baroque style was beginning to yield to the more graceful, intimate rococo. Much rococo art was more concerned with shallow aristocratic pastimes than with the use of the human form to explore deeper values. However, a strong interest in portraiture, firmly rooted

Bronzino's Portrait of a Young Man.

Scene from a Japanese bathhouse, c. 1800.

in the Renaissance, continued throughout the period, especially in Britain.

By the late eighteenth century a similar kind of style had developed in Japan, which depicted day-to-day human activities with a directness that marks a distinctly independent school. Much of earlier Japanese art was strongly influenced by Chinese traditions, but no Chinese artist would have produced prints of the kind known as *ukiyo-e* ("pictures of the floating world") or even recognized them as works of art. One print depicts the scene in a bathhouse, with both naked and dressed figures casually going about their business. In strong contrast to the imposing image of Louis XIV, these figures are given an intentional anonymity, expressing as they do the universality of human experience. This and other prints of the kind made a great impression in Europe when they were first seen there in the nineteenth century. Their influence was strongly felt by the Impressionists.

The later years of the Mughal court saw an increasing informality in the treatment of the human figure, although eighteenth-century Indian art never approached the candor of the *ukiyo-e* prints. The paintings often deal with romantic themes, as in the depiction of a prince embracing his favorite mistress. Lacking the precision of earlier Mughal art, the work remains within the same framework of stylistic refinement, and a common human experience becomes transformed into an episode of elegance and grace: it hardly seems to matter that the faces of the women in the scene are virtually indistinguishable.

Love scene by Muhammad Yusuf al-Husaini, c. 1630.

Most of the works discussed so far either commemorated an individual or used the human figure to symbolize universal human experience or values. These traditions continued during most of the nineteenth century. The austere Neoclassicism of Jacques-Louis David glorified the French Revolution and the Napoleonic period. But by the end of the century European artists had begun to employ human images to express anxiety about the state of their world. There are few more disturbing images of tension and neurosis than *The Scream*, by the Norwegian Edvard Munch, in which the distortions of the human body in the painting are reflected in the cosmic upheaval of land and sky.

The years preceding World War I produced traumatic changes throughout the world, in politics and society as well as in cultural life. Munch's attempt to unify figure and landscape to express a transcendent emotion characterized much of the art of the late nineteenth and early twentieth centuries in Europe. In many respects Munch's projection of human emotion onto landscape recalls fourteenth-century Christian art in Italy, but now devoid of religious context.

Years before Munch, the Frenchman Paul Cézanne had begun the effort among modern Western artists to reduce visual experience to simple, abstract forms. This movement was in turn influenced by European contact with the art of Asia, Africa, and Oceania. Western artists found universal messages in the highly stylized art forms of these regions, an impact that may be clearly seen in the paintings of Picasso and Gauguin and the sculptures of Constantin Brancusi. The brutally stylized representations of prostitutes in Picasso's *Demoiselles d'Avignon* (see "The Visual Experience: Art of the Modern Western World") caused a great scandal and presaged his even more radical experiments in abstraction a few years later, in which recognizable images disappeared altogether.

The so-called Expressionist style of Munch, which was taken up by German and Austrian artists shortly before World War I; the flat, abstracted style perfected by Picasso and his colleague Georges Braque, known as Cubism; and the wholly abstract canvases and watercolors of the Russian Wassily Kandinsky all foreshadowed a crisis in the representation of the human image in Western art. The cultural shock of World War I and the impact of Freudian psychology brought further distortions of the image in the form of Surrealism, a movement that dominated European art between the world wars. Seeking to penetrate psychological states, Surrealist art was, like Expressionism, an attempt to probe beyond the image into inner realms of feeling, and much of it was overtly erotic.

But, although it was often accused of being obscure, Surrealism was also capable of powerful political statement, as in Salvador Dalí's *Soft Construction with Boiled Beans—Premonition of Civil War*.

At the same time, Soviet Russia and Nazi Germany were demanding a new official art that would represent their propaganda objectives—the depiction of happy and contented workers in the first case, racially pure Aryans in the second. Hitler banned all abstract or Expressionist art in the Third Reich, and in 1937 he organized a notorious exhibit of "degenerate" art, which showed the work that had been purged from German museums. The exhibition backfired, as audiences streamed in not to mock but to admire some of the finest German painting of the century.

Some artists of the period, such as the British sculptor Henry Moore (1898–1986), continued to represent the human figure in simplified, monumental forms of great power, and Picasso, the most protean and prolific painter of the human image in history, returned to it after World War I. The image was banished again when Abstract Expressionism became the dominant international style after World War II, only to return with the Pop Art of the 1960s. Pop Art, whose images were derived largely from advertising and comic strips, sought to satirize consumerism and both cinematic and political cults of personality, as in the portraits of Marilyn Monroe and Mao Tse-tung by the American Andy Warhol

Salvador Dalí, Soft Construction with Boiled Beans—Premonition of Civil War, *1936.*

Philip Guston, Untitled, *1980.*

(1928–1987). Pop Art was soon assimilated into a new style of "magic realism," which aimed for photographic illusion, while the former Abstract Expressionist Philip Guston (1913–1980) returned to the image with an effect at once comic and chilling, as in the disembodied head that rolls up an inclined plane in *Untitled*. More recently, the German Anselm Kiefer (born 1945) has turned to the long-disfavored genre of historical portraiture in his remarkable representations of German cultural history.

It is hardly surprising that the history of art has been marked by a continual recourse to the human figure as a source of expression and communication. The range of treatment reflects the diversity of human experience. Works have served religious, political, and aesthetic purposes, have documented events, and sometimes have tried to control them, as in fascist and Soviet art. Differences between cultures seem stylistic rather than reflective of profound divergences: the statue of an Egyptian pharaoh and the portraits of a European, Indian, Chinese, or African sovereign reflect a similar political aim, the exaltation and commemoration of the ruler. If anything seems unexpected, it is that at the end of the twentieth century, a period of unprecedented upheaval both in life and in the arts, naturalistic depictions of human beings continue to fascinate us. Such works suggest that the need to "see ourselves as others see us" remains constant.

SUGGESTIONS FOR FURTHER READING

Clark, K. *The Nude: A Study in Ideal Form.* Princeton, N.J.: Princeton University Press, 1956.

De Dilva, A., and Von Simson, O. *Man Through His Art,* vol. 6: *The Human Face.* New York: Graphic Society, 1968.

Garland, M. *The Changing Face of Beauty.* New York: Barrows, 1957.

Lee, S. *A History of Far Eastern Art.* New York: Abrams, 1974.

Man: Glory, Jest, and Riddle: A Survey of the Human Form Through the Ages. San Francisco: M. H. de Young Memorial Museum, California Palace of the Legion of Honor, and San Francisco Museum of Art, 1965.

Mayor, A. H. *Artists and Anatomy.* New York: Artist's Limited Edition, 1984.

Mode, H. *The Woman in Indian Art.* New York: McGraw-Hill, 1970.

Neumeyer, A. *The Search for Meaning in Modern Art,* trans. R. Angress. Englewood Cliffs, N.J.: Prentice Hall, 1964.

Relouge, I. E., ed. *Masterpieces of Figure Painting.* New York: Viking, 1959.

Rowland, B. *The Art and Architecture of India.* Baltimore: Penguin Books, 1967.

Segal, M. *Painted Ladies: Models of the Great Artists.* New York: Stein & Day, 1972.

Selz, P. *New Images of Man.* New York: Museum of Modern Art, 1959.

Smart, A. *The Renaissance and Mannerism in Italy.* New York: Harcourt Brace Jovanovich, 1971.

Walker, J. *Portraits: 5,000 Years.* New York: Abrams, 1983.

Wentinck, C. *The Human Figure in Art from Prehistoric Times to the Present Day,* trans. E. Cooper. Wynnewood, Pa.: Livingston Publishing, 1970.

Willett, F. *African Art: An Introduction.* New York: Praeger, 1971.

CHAPTER
37

Upheaval in Eurasia and the Middle East

Leon Trotsky arriving in Paris in 1929, an exile from the Bolshevick USSR he helped found a decade earlier.

The twentieth century has been characterized by rapid change, particularly in the transformation of the world's biggest countries, China, Russia, and India, and the similar transformation of the Middle East. Together the four regions hold half the world's population. In China and Russia this change has appropriately been called revolutionary, entailing not only the overthrow of old governments by violence and civil war but also a radical restructuring of social, economic, and political systems in a short period of concentrated effort. The upheavals in each country were engineered and directed by native Communist parties, which made use of mass support by workers and peasants, groups that had previously been excluded from power. Each revolution also created a new set of ideological values.

Like the French and American revolutions, those in Russia and China inspired others and served as models for change elsewhere in the world. The Chinese Revolution did not prevail until 1949, but its early stages from 1919 to 1934 were strongly influenced and for a time directly guided by Russian communists. When these early revolutionary efforts failed, China left the Soviet path. The ultimate success of the Chinese Revolution in 1949, and its later development, was far more an indigenous phenomenon than a response to the Russian experience.

Although strong differences marked the struggles for independence in India and the Middle East, neither can properly be viewed as a revolution. The Arabs fought Ottoman control with arms during World War I but then came under British and French authority. Indian protests against the British emphasized a nonviolent strategy. In both regions political power was eventually handed over peacefully to nationalist leaders. In the Middle East the League of Nations mandate system and the influx of Jewish settlers into Palestine, negligible until the rise of Nazism but significant thereafter, stimulated resistance from the native Arab population. Yet in the interwar years Arab nationalism failed to become a genuine mass movement as it did in India. There the independence effort, as in China and Russia, involved peasants and workers under the direction of political organizers. While the nationalist regimes in Turkey and Iran attempted to modernize their countries after World War I, little effort went into radical restructuring of Indian society or its values.

Nevertheless, the changes that took place in India and the Middle East were in some ways revolutionary, for the awakening of nationalism and the end of the colonial system were to have long-range repercussions. India is the outstanding case of a drive for change that used traditional vehicles and symbols to attract support and to accelerate transformation, a pattern that repeated itself in the form of Muslim fundamentalism among Arab states after World War II.

In all these regions powerful leaders played a key role in planning and directing change, among them Lenin and his successor, Stalin, in the USSR; Mao Tsetung in China; Gandhi and his successor, Nehru, in India; and Faisal, ibn-Saud, Mustapha Kemal, Chaim Weizmann, and Reza Shah Pahlavi in the Middle East. Each of these leaders could claim to have made an enormous impact on his own country and on states far beyond its borders. The twentieth century has been called the century of revolution primarily because of the massive upheavals in Russia, China, India, and the Middle East. The ripples that each of these revolutions sent around the world helped to spawn fundamental changes in Asia, Africa, and Latin America. The century of revolution began with dramatic events in Russia in 1917.

The Russian Revolution

In March 1917* the first of two revolutions erupted in war-weary Russia, shattering 300 years of history in the space of a few days: the Romanov dynasty, the last absolute monarchy in Europe, was toppled from the throne it had occupied since 1613. Though laden with drama, the events of March were only a prelude to an even farther-reaching transformation. As if one revolution was insufficient to shift the weight of Russian history, with

---

*Russia still used the ancient Julian calendar, which had been abandoned in the West centuries earlier. By this time it was 13 days behind the modern Gregorian calendar. Throughout this chapter Gregorian dates will be used.

its virtually unbroken pattern of political and social repression and economic hardship, a second revolution erupted in November. The communist state that arose out of the November revolution became a major force in shaping the twentieth century.

The Twilight of the Romanovs

The 1905 uprising had been a clear symptom of crisis. Provoked by Russia's defeat in the war with Japan, the "revolution" had climaxed on "Bloody Sunday" (January 22, 1905), when troops fired on protesting workers in St. Petersburg. In October the growing unrest and strikes finally persuaded Tsar Nicholas II (1894–1917) to create an imperial Duma, or assembly, to be elected by broad male suffrage. Within two years, imperial decrees undid most of these reforms. Nicholas was determined to restore his absolute authority. After 1911, following the assassination of Peter Stolypin, a reformist minister who had tried to repress terrorists and reactionaries, he further alienated the educated and professional classes by surrounding himself with conservative advisers. By 1914 some ministers even saw a European war as a positive catalyst for national unity.

After the outbreak of war, Nicholas took direct command of the Russian armies—the only European head of state to do so—despite his lack of military training. At first his gesture had a positive symbolic value for the millions of peasants who rallied to the call for arms, but as the imperial armies suffered defeat after defeat, even the least sophisticated Russians began to hold the tsar personally responsible. However, most military officers had been poorly trained in modern strategy. Soldiers sent to the German front were among the worst-fed and worst-equipped in Europe. Tens of thousands lacked even a rifle and were told to take one from a fallen comrade or a dead enemy; thus their greatly superior numbers failed to compensate for the country's lack of preparedness. In addition to the incompetence of the generals and the enormous logistical problems stemming from Russia's vastness, Russian society was not sufficiently modernized to organize effectively for or sustain a major war effort. The Romanov dynasty collapsed in part because of the retarded development of the country's industries and infrastructure.

While Russia's war effort deteriorated, Nicholas left the government in the hands of his wife, Tsarina Alexandra (1872–1918), a religious zealot and absolutist. Her uncompromising attitude was in part shaped by Grigori Rasputin, an eccentric Russian Orthodox monk whose great influence derived from his ability to convince

Tsar Nicholas II and his five children a few years before the revolution that overthrew the Romanov dynasty.

Alexandra he could relieve her son's hemophilia. Rasputin's power over the tsarina and his manipulation of official policy outraged officials and members of the imperial court who hoped that political reforms would defuse popular discontent. Between September 1915 and November 1916 the Duma was suspended, while severe shortages of food and fuel provoked massive resentment in the cities. In December, hoping to free the royal family from his influence, conservative aristocrats murdered Rasputin. By then, however, the domestic situation had deteriorated so severely that revolution was imminent. Within the reconvened Duma even conservatives and constitutional monarchists opposed the royal family.

The March 1917 Revolution

On March 8, 1917, disorder erupted in Petrograd.* Food riots led by women spread to the workers, and both a factory lockout and a socialist-inspired Woman's Day celebration filled the streets with protesters. The crisis came

---

*The tsar had changed the name of the city from St. Petersburg to the Russian form, Petrograd, to emphasize the patriotic nature of the war. Under the Soviets the city was renamed Leningrad, only to revert to the name St. Petersburg in 1991.

when the tsar, still at the front, ordered the revolt suppressed. On March 11 troops fired into a crowd, but the government's inexperienced reinforcements then mingled with the demonstrators. As cries of "Down with the tsar!" rang out, officials found their orders unenforceable. The next day the Duma proclaimed a provisional government under Prince Georgi Lvov and called on Nicholas to step down. With the generals unable to assure him of the army's loyalty—indeed, military leaders supported his stepping down—the last of the Romanov tsars abdicated. He and the imperial family were held under house arrest and were later captured by the Bolsheviks.

After centuries of absolutism and repression, Russia experienced a sudden liberalization. The provisional government planned the election of a constituent assembly on the basis of universal male suffrage and introduced civil liberties. It also implemented the eight-hour workday, ended the persecution of the Jews, and released thousands of political prisoners, although it maintained that only a legally constituted government could resolve the land problem. The new regime enjoyed the support of Western-educated Russians and of the business and professional classes, while the Duma was dominated by liberals who favored a constitutional monarchy. Even the Entente Powers generally preferred the provisional government to the rule of the tsar, hoping that it would reinvigorate the Russian war effort.

From its inception, however, the provisional government was challenged by the more radical Soviet (council) of Workers' and Soldiers' Deputies, formed in March. Modeled after the organization that had led the 1905 general strike, the Petrograd soviet was in the hands of workers' representatives who had served on the tsar's War Industries Committee. While hundreds of similar groups soon sprang up in army units, industrial centers, and the countryside, the Petrograd soviet maintained its preeminence because of its location in the capital.

In contrast to the Duma, led by liberal elements, the membership of the soviets consisted largely of socialists of various types. The Social Revolutionaries looked to the peasants and their village councils for instituting change and favored the use of violence. The Mensheviks and the Bolsheviks, factions within the Social Democratic party, were both Marxist in ideology, though sharp differences divided them. The reform-minded Menshevik ("minority") faction sought to build a large party organization along the lines of the Western social democratic movements. They hoped to achieve their goals through peaceful evolution but did not expect to establish socialism in Russia until industrial development was more advanced.

The Bolshevik ("majority") group accepted Marxist goals but followed the teachings of Vladimir Ilyich Lenin (1870–1924), their exiled leader. Lenin rejected Marx's idea that socialist revolution was premature in an under-developed country like Russia, where the industrial proletariat was small. He also opposed the evolutionary strategy of the Mensheviks, arguing that only violent revolution would achieve socialism. Lenin argued for a "vanguard" of professional revolutionaries that would control a disciplined party, educate the workers and peasants, and prepare to seize the initiative.

The soviets, composed of these competing factions and without a clearly articulated ideology, supported the spontaneous actions of the urban crowds and landless peasants. They thereby competed with the provisional government for the people's loyalty. As this struggle progressed, the provisional government found itself at a growing disadvantage. The Bolsheviks, the only major group of the left not represented in the government, remained free of responsibility for unpopular policies.

The weaknesses of the provisional government proved to be fatal. The new leaders made no attempt to address the demands of the urban proletariat or to satisfy the land hunger of the peasants. Of more immediate significance, however, was its war policy. Despite the desperate unpopularity of the conflict, the Duma felt duty-bound to honor the alliance with the Entente against Germany. When the government renewed its pledge to support the war effort in May, popular opposition forced many members to resign.

Lenin and the Bolshevik Coup

The Bolsheviks exploited the shortsightedness of the provisional government as Lenin began to dominate events. A short, stocky man, mostly bald, with a moustache and a goatee, he did not look charismatic. But John Reed, a young left-wing American writer, understood that although Lenin was a "colorless" man, he had a gift for "explaining profound ideas in simple terms" that any unschooled Russian peasant could understand. He led, said Reed, "purely by virtue of his intellect."[1] Born Vladimir Ilyich Ulyanov, Lenin had been a radical since age 17, when the government had executed his older brother for plotting to assassinate Alexander III. During his twenties he became a Marxist, and his revolutionary activities brought him nearly five years of imprisonment and exile in Siberia. In 1900 he found refuge in western Europe, where he led the Bolshevik break from the Mensheviks.

When the March revolution erupted, Lenin, still in exile in Switzerland, persuaded the German government to grant him passage to Russia. The Germans, hoping that the Bolsheviks would disrupt the Russian war effort, transported him in a sealed train across their lines to the border, and Lenin arrived in Petrograd on April 16. His famous April Theses declared total opposition to the provisional government and instructed his followers to work for a second revolution in Russia. A communist victory, he said, would contribute to Russia's industrial base and help sustain Marxist socialism permanently.

Early in July soldiers and sailors led an uprising in Petrograd. The provisional government put down the revolt and blamed the Bolsheviks. Lenin, disguised as a locomotive fireman, fled to Finland, while a number of his followers—among them Lev Kamenev and Leon Trotsky—were arrested. When the provisional government launched a final military offensive against the Germans in July, soldiers deserted en masse, while in the countryside millions of peasants seized large estates. In an effort to broaden its support, the provisional government replaced Prince Lvov with Alexander Kerensky (1881–1970), a moderate Social Revolutionary. Kerensky's refusal to negotiate a withdrawal from the war served only to discredit him and his Menshevik allies. The final blunder came in September, when Lavr Kornilov, a reactionary military officer, attempted to crush the soviets. Kerensky appeared to welcome the general's action, but he came to believe that Kornilov intended to turn against him as well; he therefore armed the Red Guards, volunteer units from the Petrograd soviet. Pro-soviet railway workers refused to transport Kornilov's equipment, and many of his troops fraternized with the Red Guards.

While Kerensky had prevented a military coup, his power now depended to a great extent on the soviets, who bitterly opposed his determination to continue the war. In the meantime, Bolshevik strength grew rapidly. Lenin's program of "peace, land, and bread" presented a compelling alternative to the provisional government's promises, and his slogan of "all power to the soviets" was a shrewd appeal for popular support. In late October, as the Bolsheviks gained a majority in the Petrograd soviet as well as in Moscow, Lenin secretly returned to Russia.

With Trotsky, now freed from prison, Lenin planned the seizure of power. Trotsky (1879–1940), born Lev Bronstein, was a brilliant intellectual and strategist who had spent some of his own political exile in the United States. He was the real architect of the Bolshevik coup. He secured control of military power by persuading the Petrograd soviet, which he headed, to appoint him commander of a military revolutionary committee to protect the city. After winning over the soldiers

Lenin's April Theses

Lenin arrived in Petrograd from Switzerland on April 16. The next day he issued his famous April Theses before a conference of Mensheviks and Bolsheviks called to discuss the possibility of uniting the Social Democrats. He declared his opposition both to Lvov's provisional government and to party unification, and demanded a second revolution in Russia.

1. . . . under the new government of Lvov and Co., owing to the capitalist nature of this government, the war on Russia's part remains a predatory imperialist war.

    The class-conscious proletariat may give its consent to a revolutionary war actually justifying revolutionary defencism, only on condition (a) that all power be transferred to the proletariat and its ally, the poorest section of the peasantry; (b) that all annexations be renounced in deeds, not merely in words; (c) that there be a complete break, in practice, with all interests of capital. . . .

2. The peculiarity of the present situation in Russia is that it represents a *transition* from the first state of revolution, which . . . led to the assumption of power by the bourgeoisie—to its second stage which is to place power in the hands of the proletariat and the poorest strata of the peasantry. . . .

3. No support to the Provisional Government. . . .

4. It must be explained to the masses that the Soviet of Workers' Deputies is the only possible form of revolutionary government and that, therefore, our task is, while this government is submitting to the influence of the bourgeoisie, to present a patient, systematic, and persistent analysis of its errors and tactics, an analysis especially adapted to the practical needs of the masses. . . .

5. Not a parliamentary republic—a return to it from the Soviet of Workers' Deputies would be a step backward—but a republic of Soviets of Workers', Agricultural Labourers' and Peasants' Deputies throughout the land, from top to bottom.

    Abolition of the police, the army, the bureaucracy.

    All officers to be elected and to be subject to recall at any time. . . .

6. In the agrarian programme, the emphasis must be shifted to the Soviets of Agricultural Labourers' Deputies.

    Confiscation of all private lands. . . .

7. Immediate merger of all the banks in the country into one general national bank, over which the Soviet of Workers' Deputies should have control.

8. Not the "introduction" of Socialism as an immediate task, but the immediate placing of the Soviet of Workers' Deputies in control of social production and distribution of goods.

9. Party tasks:

    a. Immediate calling of a party convention.

    b. Changing the party programme, mainly (1) concerning imperialism and the imperialist war, (2) concerning our attitude toward the state, and our demand for a "commune state" [named after the Paris Commune], (3) amending our antiquated minimum programme.

    c. Changing the name of our party [from Social Democracy to the Communist Party]

10. Rebuilding the international. . . .

Source: Robert P. Browder and Alexander F. Kerensky, eds., *The Russian Provisional Government, 1917: Documents,* vols. II and III (Stanford: Stanford University Press, 1961).

Lenin and Trotsky planned the Bolshevik revolution and won the Russian civil war. They are shown here in a doctored photo, with Stalin added at the left.

in the Petrograd garrison, his forces captured the telephone exchange, railroad and electric stations, bridges, and government buildings on the night of November 6. Sailors from the Kronstadt naval base brought the cruiser *Aurora* up the Neva River to within firing range of the Winter Palace, seat of the provisional government. The Bolshevik majority in the Congress of Soviets, meeting the next morning in Petrograd, proclaimed that power was now in the hands of the soviets and announced that Lenin was the head of the new government. On November 8, Kerensky fled. With almost no bloodshed, the Bolsheviks had won control of Russia.

Building the Communist State

The seizure of Petrograd and the overthrow of the Kerensky government by no means guaranteed the Bolsheviks a lasting victory. Lenin still had to extend his control to the rest of the country. Setting up an enduring Bolshevik regime would require three more years of bitter struggle amid civil war, political opposition from anti-Bolshevik groups, and invasion by the troops of 14 foreign countries.

Lenin's immediate strategy was to achieve popular support and a measure of stability by ending war, hunger, and peasant unrest. The Social Revolutionaries had the largest following among Russia's landless peasants, but Lenin stole their thunder by declaring the nationalization and distribution of all land. Although in theory the soviets were to keep the large estates intact as collective farms, in practice the peasants, who were already seizing land on their own, were permitted to keep what they had taken. As revolutionary as these actions were, they failed to solve the hunger crisis. Small property holders withheld their crops from urban consumers. Hoarding increased as a result of the civil war and poor harvests; for years starvation plagued millions.

The promise of peace proved costly to keep. The Germans now sensed victory in the east, but their peace terms were so harsh that some Bolshevik leaders, including Trotsky and Nicolai Bukharin, wanted to continue the war as a revolutionary struggle. Lenin's insistence on ending the hostilities prevailed, and on March 15, 1918, his representatives signed the Treaty of Brest-Litovsk. It ceded to Germany all its wartime conquests as well as eastern Poland, the Ukraine, and the formerly Russian areas of Finland, Estonia, Latvia, and Lithuania. Not until the Nazi-Soviet Pact of 1939 would Russia recover its 1914 frontiers, but the treaty provided Lenin with the much needed opportunity to solidify his authority. Lenin quieted opposition to it within the Communist party—the new official name the Bolsheviks adopted in March 1918—by arguing that the spread of "world revolution" into western Europe would eventually render Russia's losses meaningless.

Despite the euphoria that had greeted the provisional government following the March revolution, political liberalism grew in shallow soil. Initially, the revolutionaries took democracy far beyond conventional practice, with popular choice entering virtually every area of life. In the soviets a kind of direct democracy prevailed, while in army units soldiers elected officers and in the factories workers organized management councils. Yet there was no tradition of self-government above the village level in Russia. The revolution left a vacuum that inexperienced local councils of semiliterate peasants could hardly fill. Into this void Lenin moved his disciplined organization after the November revolution. Yet his own forces were small and lacked experience.

The Bolsheviks had never pretended to value democracy, and Lenin's program demanded peace and economic well-being, not freedom in the traditional Western sense. He knew too that after the distribution of land, universal suffrage would produce a majority representing small landowners. In fact, when the elections for a constituent assembly previously scheduled by the provisional government were held in late November, the Social Revolutionaries won nearly twice as many delegates as the Bolsheviks. When the assembly met in January 1918, Lenin demonstrated his intention to create a Marxist-style "dictatorship of the proletariat," disbanding the assembly after only one day of deliberation. For several months Lenin governed in a coalition with left-wing Social Revolutionaries, but when the latter withdrew their support in June, Russia came under one-party rule that retained power until 1991.

During 1918 and 1919 the Bolsheviks began to implement their political and economic policies. Grassroots government yielded to centralized state administration by the Communist party, soldiers' councils were replaced by appointed officers, and factory committees gave way to trade unions controlled by party officials. In the countryside independent peasants now had to deliver their "surplus" produce to hungry urban populations. Advances toward self-determination for ethnic minorities and border peoples were eventually replaced by Russian-dominated centralization thinly disguised as a federal state. Lenin believed this system of "war communism" to be necessary under the dual pressure of civil war and foreign invasion. The pressing need for industrial production was not being met by the factory committees, which often lacked technical skills and sometimes resisted state efforts to coordinate labor. Moreover, Lenin saw industrial cartelization as the basis of a socialist economy. Each branch of industry was therefore nationalized and centralized into state trusts. By 1920 about 90 of these trusts existed, all subordinated to the Supreme Council of National Economy, which attempted to direct industrial production throughout the country.

Revolution Under Siege

Early Bolshevik policies and Leninist authoritarianism were shaped in large part by the return of war and strife to Russian soil. The infant Communist regime had to fight for its survival against an array of domestic and foreign enemies: counterrevolutionary legions made up of conservatives, moderates, and even some Social Revolutionaries, known collectively as the White Army; border nationalities seeking independence from Russia; more than 100,000 troops from 14 foreign nations, including the United States, Britain, France, and Japan; and peasants waging a so-called green revolution against the Reds who requisitioned their crops. Between 1918 and November 1920 the Red Army defended Russia's borders in a desperate effort to save the Communist regime.

A combination of military and ideological motives led to the Allied invasion of Russia. The Entente Powers had supported Kerensky's government in order to bolster the war on the eastern front. Lenin's demands for a separate peace aroused Allied suspicion that he was a German agent, but they failed to convince the Bolsheviks to reject the German peace terms. With their troops no longer tied down on the Russian front, the Germans broke through Allied lines in the west and marched to a position less than 40 miles from Paris. The German advance was repulsed, but the Allies, fearful that the Bolshevik revolution might spread to their own war-weary population, determined on a preemptive strike.

In June 1918 the Allies decided on military intervention. The French and British sent nearly 24,000 soldiers to Murmansk and Archangel. On July 16 the Bolsheviks, worried that the Allies might try to liberate the tsar, executed the entire royal family. In Siberia, 40,000 Czech prisoners of war, formerly Austro-Hungarian conscripts, revolted against their Russian guards and commandeered the trans-Siberian railroad in an attempt to reach their homeland, where they hoped to fight for Czech independence. To assist the Czech legion, President Wilson approved a landing at Vladivostok, where 72,000 Japanese and 8,000 American troops eventually arrived. During the winter of 1918–1919 two British divisions seized the rail lines that connected the Black and Caspian seas along the oil-rich Russo-Turkish border. French units, joined by Greek forces, also landed at Odessa on the Ukraine's Black Sea coast.

Allied soldiers remained in Russia after the armistice was signed in November, giving support to the White Army. Against difficult odds, the Bolsheviks possessed a number of advantages. Party discipline and Lenin's leadership kept their forces together while the White Army factions, united only in their opposition to the Communists, were rent with political division. The Bolsheviks also controlled the Russian heartland and could wage war along interior lines, whereas their enemies were scattered along the periphery. Moreover, the Red Army generally had the support of the peasants, who knew the Bolsheviks would never restore the power of the large landowners. Finally, in ethnically Russian areas Bolshevik propagandists shrewdly combined revolutionary rhetoric with a patriotic appeal in the face of foreign invasion.

Bolshevik military operations were commanded by Trotsky, whose abilities as a speaker and Marxist theoretician were matched by brilliant organizational talent. Trotsky raised, equipped, trained, and directed the Red

MAP 37.1 RUSSIA IN WAR AND REVOLUTION, 1917–1921

Army, rushing from one front to another in a special train outfitted as a mobile headquarters. He kept troop morale high by means of political propagandists, called commissars, who were attached to Red Army units. His forces repulsed assaults from Siberia, the Ukraine, and the newly independent state of Poland. Late in 1920, Allied ships evacuated more than 100,000 soldiers from Odessa. By the end of the struggle the Bolsheviks had recovered much of the old imperial lands on the western

front, except for the Baltic states and the territory lost to Romania and the new states of Czechoslovakia and Poland. With the civil war won, they also regained control over Azerbaijan, Russian Armenia, and Georgia, which separatist forces had threatened to make independent. These and other nominally autonomous states were eventually incorporated into the Union of Soviet Socialist Republics (USSR), established in December 1922. After two years of desperate fighting against invasion,

What Price Revolution?

The great loss of human life during the Russian Revolution and the civil war, criticized by the enemies of bolshevism, was defended by Leon Trotsky as a necessary price for great historical change.

But the misfortunes which have overwhelmed living people? The fire and bloodshed of civil war? Do the consequences of a revolution justify the sacrifices it involves? The question is teleological and therefore fruitless. It would be as well to ask in the face of the difficulties and griefs of personal existence: Is it worth while to be born? Melancholy reflections have not so far, however, prevented people from bearing or being born. Even in the present epoch of intolerable misfortune only a small percentage of the population of our planet resorts to suicide. But the people are seeking the way out of their unbearable difficulties in revolution.

Is it not remarkable that those who talk most indignantly about the victims of social revolutions are usually the very ones who, if not directly responsible for the victims of the world war, prepared and glorified them, or at least accepted them? It is our turn to ask: did the war justify itself? What has it given us? What has it taught?

Source: L. Trotsky, *The Russian Revolution* (Garden City, N.Y.: Anchor/Doubleday, 1959), p. 483. (Originally published in 1930.)

---

civil war, and famine, the Communist regime was secure but exhausted.

Alexandra Kollontai and the Women's Question

On important role in radical movements. Daring women such as Vera Zasulich, who assassinated a cruel provincial governor in 1878, and Olga Liubatovich, who was exiled in Siberia and conspired in St. Petersburg, were but two of the many Russian revolutionary women. Others, such as Angelica Balabanoff and Anna Kulischiov, achieved prominence as exiled socialists, Balabanoff as secretary to the Second International and Kulischiov as a leader of the Italian socialist women's movement. The career of Alexandra Kollontai (1872–1952) illustrates both the role of women in the anti-tsarist movement and the tense relationship between women's liberation and the Bolshevik revolution.

Born into a wealthy family as Alexandra Domontovich, she married a young engineer but after three years left her husband, who viewed her sympathies for the working class as willful defiance of his authority. After studying in Zurich, she returned to St. Petersburg and joined the Menshevik wing of the Social Democratic party. At the time of the 1905 revolution Kollontai recognized "how little our Party concerned itself with the fate of women of the working class and how meager was its interest in women's liberation." She also came to believe that liberation for women "could take place only as the result of the victory of a new social order and a different economic system."[2] Forced into exile, she lived in western Europe and the United States from 1908 to 1917. In 1915 she broke with the Mensheviks over the war and began to correspond with Lenin, returning to Russia in March 1917.

As a member of the Bolshevik Central Committee, Kollontai supported Lenin's call for an armed uprising. After the November coup she was appointed commissar for social welfare in Lenin's cabinet. Within the party and the government she argued that the revolution

An early Bolshevik and an ardent feminist, Alexandra Kollontai took part in the first stages of Lenin's government.

others—especially young urban middle-class Russians and intellectuals—agreed.

When Stalin became general secretary of the Communist party in 1922, the Workers' Opposition movement was purged and Kollontai's lover, Alexander Shylapnikov, was killed. Kollontai herself was virtually banished for the next two decades: from 1924 until her retirement in 1945 she served as Russian ambassador to Norway, Mexico, and Sweden and as a representative to the League of Nations. In her last lonely years Kollontai suffered from the knowledge that the revolution she had helped make had fallen short of her hopes.

would be betrayed unless it destroyed bourgeois moral standards and the authoritarian family. These ideas and her efforts to establish a state-supported system of maternity and infant care drew sharp criticism from her male comrades, who accused her of wanting to "nationalize" Russian women. Her position was undermined when she joined the anti-Leninist faction and pushed to democratize the Communist party through direct worker participation in policymaking. In March 1918 she resigned from the government and later joined the Workers' Opposition movement. Following the civil war, during which she worked as a propagandist with the Red Army, Kollontai criticized the new marriage laws established by the Bolshevik regime, which she felt maintained inequality, and demanded full rights for women. Her controversial ideas on women's liberation and sexual freedom were explained in *The New Morality and the Working Class* (1920), the publication of which alienated her still further from the Communist leadership. Although Kollontai's advocacy of sexual relationships based on affection and equality rather than on socially imposed codes offended her more conservative comrades, many

Stalin Versus Trotsky: The Struggle for Power

Even without the military struggles of the 1918–1920 period, chaotic economic and social conditions would have threatened the Bolshevik regime. Millions of Russians had died as a result of war, epidemics, and famine. Cities and villages lay in ruin, and the transportation system barely functioned. A lack of managers, technicians, and raw materials had brought factories to a virtual standstill, and industrial production had fallen to about 20 percent of its prewar level. Hoarding and drought continued to cause severe food shortages. Popular support for the Bolsheviks eroded. A wave of peasant uprisings and factory strikes preceded a military revolt, in March 1921, when sailors at the Kronstadt naval base, once a pro-Bolshevik bastion, seized the Winter Palace and proclaimed a "third revolution" against Lenin's regime. The Red Army crushed the movement with much bloodshed, and Lenin knew he had to act swiftly.

In March 1921, Lenin announced the New Economic Plan (NEP), a retreat from Marxist orthodoxy. The NEP permitted a degree of private enterprise in small industries and the retail trade, ended food requisitioning, and allowed peasants to sell their produce on the open market after paying a small tax. The state, however, continued to own and operate major industries, banking, and transportation and to control wholesale and foreign trade. The NEP slowly achieved success, and by 1928 agricultural and industrial production had returned to prewar levels. The controversial plan resulted in the revival of the rural middle class of kulaks ("large peasants") that ran counter to the Marxist goal of a classless society. The kulaks leased or owned large parcels of land, which they farmed with hired laborers, and raised crops for the market.

As long as Lenin lived, he and the Old Bolsheviks—the group that had made the revolution in 1917—retained control of the Communist party, but he was concerned over the increasing number of bureaucratic careerists entering its ranks. The Soviet constitution of 1923 created the All-Union Congress of Soviets, a representative body in which the highest power theoretically resided. The Congress—its name was changed to the Supreme Soviet in 1936—elected the Council of People's Commissars (changed to the Council of Ministers in 1946), the Executive Committee, and the small Presidium, which acted for the Congress between sessions. In reality, however, the Communist party ran the country through its Central Committee, composed of just under 50 members, which met several times each year. The Central Committee in turn elected the ten-member Politburo, which convened weekly and chose a secretariat of from one to three members to perform executive duties.

In 1922 Lenin suffered two strokes, which removed him from day-to-day leadership. Trotsky appeared to be the logical choice to succeed Lenin, but party members began to unite against him. A temporary troika, or three-member leadership, emerged late in 1922 to carry on Lenin's work, consisting of Grigori Zinoviev, party leader in Petrograd (later named Leningrad); Lev Kamenev, the Communist boss of Moscow; and Joseph Stalin, general secretary of the party and the least known of the three.

Tough, clever, and power-hungry, Stalin (1879–1953) was the only Old Bolshevik of lower-class origin. Born Joseph Djugashvili in the province of Georgia, he was the son of a shoemaker and the grandson of serfs. After being expelled from a theological seminary, he joined the Bolshevik movement at the turn of the century and took the underground name of Stalin, meaning "man of steel." He performed some of the party's most reprehensible tasks, including the robbing of treasury transports to acquire operating funds. Hardened in the tsar's prisons and Siberian exile, Stalin possessed none of the broader culture of his colleagues, most of whom had lived in western Europe. As general secretary he dispensed patronage to build a personal following and came to that office at a time when a new generation of bureaucrats was developing within the party.

Lenin recognized Stalin's power at the very time that the other Old Bolsheviks were growing suspicious of

Trotsky. After his second stroke in December 1922, Lenin began to consider the problem of succession. With the help of his wife and closest political assistant, Nadhezhda Krupskaya (1869–1939), he dictated a "testament" in which he reviewed possible successors, chiefly Trotsky and Stalin. Although he seemed to favor Stalin, he expressed doubts as to whether Stalin knew how to use his power wisely. Less than two weeks later Lenin added a "codicil," or supplement, to these notes denouncing Stalin as "too rude" and advising the party to appoint someone "more tolerant, more loyal, more polite and more considerate to comrades, less capricious, etc."[3]

Though Lenin had always held reservations about Stalin, his opinion hardened when he learned that Stalin had tried to intimidate Krupskaya. Following Lenin's death early in 1924, the testament and the codicil were read before the party's Central Committee. That summer Krupskaya attempted to have the documents presented before the entire party congress, but Stalin managed to have only minor commissions hear them. Krupskaya survived Stalin's brutal purges and remained on the Central Committee, but her husband's denunciations of the man who became the dictator of Soviet Russia went unpublished until after Stalin's death.

In 1924 Stalin, who was never known for his mastery of Marxist theory, put forward the novel concept of "socialism in one country." He argued that the Soviet Union could create the industrial economy necessary to sustain socialism without exporting revolution. Against this position Trotsky offered the doctrine of "permanent revolution," an unceasing struggle aimed at the elimination of capitalism everywhere. Stalin believed that the extension of communist revolution to all capitalist societies required resources that Russia did not have and meant continual armed strife with the West. Stalin eventually won the struggle with Trotsky because he secured control over the party apparatus and won the support of other party leaders. Even leftists such as Zinoviev and Kamenev, whose views corresponded more closely to the permanent revolution theory, feared Trotsky's ambitions, and in 1925 they helped the supposedly safer Stalin strip Trotsky of his position as war commissar. In 1929 Trotsky fled into exile, where, after years of opposition to Stalin's regime, he was murdered in Mexico by a Soviet agent in 1940.

Stalin's skill at maneuvering was consummate. Having used the support of the party's left to weaken Trotsky, he joined forces with Nicolai Bukharin, leader of the right. Together they removed Stalin's opponents from the Central Committee while Stalin increasingly controlled the smaller Politburo. He then turned against his former allies. After the failure of a communist uprising in Bulgaria in 1925, he secured the dismissal of Zinoviev as head of the Communist International and then destroyed Kamenev's authority by having the Moscow party apparatus placed in the hands of the Politburo. In 1928, having crushed the party's left wing, Stalin broke with the right. He did this by favoring the collectivization of agriculture and forced industrialization, positions long associated with the left. When Bukharin opposed these policies, Stalin drove him from office. With Trotsky in exile and the old-guard Bolsheviks outmaneuvered, Stalin emerged as the unchallenged master of the Soviet state.

The Comintern: Russia Between East and West

Stalin's formula for one-country socialism rejected not only Trotsky's insistence on the need for continuing revolution but Lenin's legacy as well. In March 1919, Lenin had invited the world's socialist leaders to Moscow to create a new global organization known as the Communist International, or Comintern. The purpose of this so-called Third International was to convert the Russian Revolution into a world struggle. The instability of the immediate postwar period—marked by the fall of the monarchies in Austria-Hungary and Germany; riots in China, India, and Japan; the seizure of factories by Italian workers; and the establishment of a communist

regime in Hungary—gave Comintern leaders hope. However, their optimism was premature, for except in the Soviet puppet state of Mongolia, communism failed to seize permanent power beyond Russia. The Comintern sent agents to every corner of the world to organize and strengthen indigenous communist movements, but Stalin's policies and the organization's internal limitations hampered its effectiveness.

The Comintern had a divisive impact on the European left. Demanding disciplined followers among the socialists in other countries, Lenin established 21 conditions for foreign parties seeking membership in the Comintern. These included purging themselves of reformists, restructuring their organizations along Bolshevik lines, supporting all communist governments, preparing for the seizure of power in their own countries, and fighting social democrats as well as capitalists. Lenin believed that the moment for world revolution had arrived, but many Western socialist leaders were reluctant to gamble their previous gains on the chance of revolution. Social democrats preferred to achieve socialism without resorting to dictatorship. The result was that socialist parties outside the USSR split into two camps between 1920 and 1921, with most rejecting Lenin's demands in favor of achieving socialism through parliamentary reform. Lenin accused them of wasting a historic opportunity.

THE RUSSIAN REVOLUTION AND THE WORLD

Events in Russia	Events abroad
Alexander II emancipates Russia's serfs (1861)	Lincoln's Emancipation Proclamation in the United States (1863)
	Scramble for Africa (1870–1914)
Alexander II assassinated (1881)	Congress of Berlin; Russian gains against Turkey partly annulled (1878)
Accession of Nicholas II (1894)	Franco-Russian Alliance (1894)
Revolution of 1905: tsar promises civil liberties and constitutional government	Russo-Japanese War (1904–1905)
First Duma convenes (1906)	
Reforms of Stolypin (1906–1911)	Instability in the Balkans (1908–1914)
	Revolution in China (1911)
Influence of Rasputin; massive strikes and shortages (1914–1917)	World War I; Russia incurs devastating casualties (1914–1917)
February 1917 revolution; tsar abdicates; Kerensky heads provisional government	United States enters war (April 1917)
October 1917 revolution; Lenin leads Bolshevik coup, leaves war (March 1918)	Allied armies invade Russia (March 1918); war ends in Allied victory (November 1918)
War communism (1918–1920); civil war and famine ravage Russia	Paris Peace Conference (1919)
	Chinese May 4 movement (1919); Gandhi begins nonviolent movement in India (1919)
Kronstadt mutiny; leftist opposition crushed (1921)	Jewish immigrants settle in Palestine (1920–1929)
New Economic Plan (1921–1927)	Fascist seizure of power in Italy (1922)
Lenin dies (1924); Stalin replaces him (1924–1929)	Mustapha Kemal takes power in Turkey (1923)
	Great Depression begins (1929)

The Comintern: East Versus West

At the Congress of the Peoples of the East, called by the Communist International in 1920, the representatives of non-Western countries complained bitterly that their concerns were being ignored by Russian leaders. One of the most vocal critics was M. N. Roy, an Indian Communist, who argued that the official report on colonial questions maintained that the fate of the revolutionary movement in Europe depended entirely on the course of the revolution in the East.

Without the victory of the revolution in the Eastern countries, the Communist movement in the West would come to nothing. . . . This being so, it is essential that we divert our energies into developing and elevating the revolutionary movement in the East and accept as our fundamental thesis that the fate of world Communism depends on the victory of Communism in the East.

Here is Lenin's response to Roy's arguments.

Comrade Roy goes too far when he asserts that the fate of the West depends exclusively on the degree of development and the strength of the revolutionary movement in the Eastern countries. In spite of the fact that the proletariat in India numbers five million and there are 37 million landless peasants, the Indian Communists have not yet succeeded in creating a Communist Party in their country. This fact alone shows that Comrade Roy's views are to a large extent unfounded.

Source: F. Claudin, *The Communist Movement: From Comintern to Cominform*, vol. 1, trans. B. Pearce (New York: Monthly Review Press, 1975), pp. 247–248.

Despite these divisions, the Comintern caused panic in Western countries. In the United States a "Red scare" in 1919 led to a government witch-hunt for radicals of every kind. In Europe many frightened members of the middle class abandoned liberalism in favor of fascism and other anti-Communist movements.

The hysteria the Comintern aroused in the West was ironic in view of the fact that revolutionary communism was so unsuccessful elsewhere in the world. The early socialists were essentially Eurocentric in outlook, a characteristic derived in part from Marx's belief that revolution was likely only in advanced capitalist societies. "The founders of Marxism," noted one scholar, "judged non-European civilizations through the prism of European civilization. The road to progress for the backward peoples they saw as the road of Europeanization, not only from the socio-economic standpoint but also culturally."[4]

Comintern leaders gave little attention to the needs and aspirations of non-Western communists. At the third congress of the Comintern in 1921, the Indian Marxist M. N. Roy attacked the meeting for allowing him only five minutes to report on revolutionary activities in the subcontinent. The next year the Indonesian communist Tan Malaka condemned the Comintern for opposing the pan-Islamic movement, which he said had isolated his party from the Muslim peasants of his country. At the 1924 congress Mexican representatives warned Soviet leaders that they were ignoring potential allies in Latin America, while Sen Katayama of the Japanese Communist party assailed Zinoviev for hardly mentioning the Eastern question. Ho Chi Minh (1890–1969), the Vietnamese activist, complained bitterly that westerners were ignoring revolutionaries in colonial areas and misunderstood the liberation movements.

When the Comintern did support revolutionary activities in the Third World, its approach reflected Soviet concerns. In 1924 the Comintern sent the able but inexperienced Michael Borodin to China to establish a Communist military college at Whampoa, near Canton. The principal of the college was young Chiang Kai-shek (1887–1975), recently returned from a visit to Russia. Despite Chiang's involvement in the Chinese Nationalist party (Kuomintang) and his close ties to bankers, the Comintern ordered the Chinese Communists to integrate themselves into the Kuomintang. On April 12, 1927, Chiang's troops, aided by gangs hired by Shanghai businessmen, launched a surprise attack against Borodin, the Communists, and the trade unions, murdering thousands and imprisoning many more. Nevertheless, for a time the Comintern attempted to mend the ill-fated alliance with the Kuomintang.

Of all the factors that undermined the Comintern, none was more important than Stalin's rise to power. His one-country socialism was essentially a defensive strategy designed to protect the Soviet state. His concern that revolutionary activities elsewhere could endanger the USSR resulted in his using the Comintern only to keep foreign Communist leaders in line. Under Stalin the Communist International became an anachronism, and in a gesture to antifascist unity during World War II, he disbanded it in 1943.

The inability of the Comintern to establish Communist regimes beyond the Soviet Union should not obscure the profound impact of the Russian Revolution. The Bolshevik seizure of power shook the West to its foundations and altered international relations. Stalin was shortsighted only in failing to recognize the Russian Revolution as the first of a series of momentous upheavals that would transform the world.

China: Rebels, Warlords, and Patriots

In contrast to the Russian Revolution, the upheaval in China began almost tentatively, then sputtered and apparently died, and finally broke out in full force only after nearly 40 years of false starts and setbacks. In China too there were perhaps revolutionary implications in the Taiping Rebellion of 1850–1864. All revolutions have their antecedents, but China's was particularly slow in the making. China had first to develop a national political consciousness and a political organization that could pursue revolutionary change, both of which were lacking in its historical experience. The Chinese were accustomed to the overthrow of dynasties grown old and ineffective and their replacement by a new group, which would then administer the traditional system more successfully. The system itself, however, enshrined by the Mandate of Heaven, appeared to be beyond challenge.

But by the twentieth century the traditional model had lost its ability to deal with the now overwhelming problems of mass poverty, technological backwardness, and political weakness. These problems were vividly symbolized by China's helplessness in the face of the imperial powers of the West. It was to take another century to create a new set of solutions and a political structure to pursue them. Meanwhile, China's material welfare and ancient pride continued to suffer.

The Ch'ing dynasty collapsed in 1911, with the gentlest of shoves from a small and poorly organized group of revolutionaries (see Chapter 35). The Ch'ing was widely seen as a failure and was equally resented as an alien dynasty of conquest. Most of the revolutionary support rested on one or both of these grounds rather than on the still only half-formed plans for change. The end of Manchu rule is considered a revolution because the government was overthrown in an armed uprising by people who called themselves revolutionaries and had some new and radical ideas. But they were too few and too politically inexperienced to establish an effective government of their own, and to make matters worse, they were split into factions. The most important revolutionary organization was the Kuomintang, founded around the turn of the century and led by Sun Yat-sen (1866–1925), an idealist with great personal charisma but little sense of practical politics.

Sun Yat-sen and the 1911 Revolution

Sun was born to a peasant family near Canton (Gwangzhou), traditionally a hotbed of separatism and political ferment. At the age of 13, like many Cantonese, he emigrated, joining his older brother in Honolulu, where he went to a church boarding school and became a Christian. At 16 he returned to study in Hong Kong and finished a medical degree there in 1892 at a British mission hospital. After practicing only briefly in Macao, he founded a secret society to overthrow the Manchus, drawing support from overseas Chinese. In 1895 he was forced to flee to Japan, from where he made repeated trips to build Chinese contacts in the United States, Britain, and Hawaii. Other radical leaders and groups in China were also active, and several abortive attempts were made to seize power until an uprising at Wuhan in 1911 was joined by some troops among its garrison. Its successful defiance brought the fall of the imperial government. Sun returned from abroad and became the first president of the newly proclaimed republic. The last Ch'ing emperor, a 6-year-old boy named Pu Yi, abdicated early in 1912, marking the end of an imperial tradition more than 2,000 years old.

China was still hopelessly divided, and even Sun saw that he could not provide unity and strong central government. He agreed to step down in 1912 as president in favor of Yuan Shih-kai (Yuan Shikai, 1859–1916), a leading Ch'ing military man who had thrown his lot in with the republicans. Sun had earlier put together a set of guidelines for a new government called the Three Principles of the People. These were nationalism, democracy, and the people's livelihood, none of which was clearly defined. Nationalism in the modern sense was still a new idea to most Chinese, but they could at least make common cause against the foreign Manchu dynasty in the name of Chinese self-determination. Sun's notion of democracy was heavily indebted to Western models. It implied but did not spell out social and political equality, a notable departure in itself from the hierarchical forms of Confucianism. Democracy was to be assured by a constitution largely on an American pattern, while "livelihood"—a partial redistribution of wealth on behalf of the poorer peasantry—was to be achieved through tax reforms.

China was far from having the requisite basis for democracy, however. There were no true political parties as yet, only a variety of elite or intellectual groups, divided among themselves. When the new Kuomintang won national elections in 1913, Yuan, who had busily concentrated real power in his own hands, arranged the assassination of its leading organizer, Sung Chiao-jen (Song Jiaoren), who had pressed for constitutional government. Sun again fled to Japan, while Yuan tightened his grip as military dictator by force, bribery, and intimidation. In 1915 he had himself declared president for life and took to riding around in an armored car for fear of attack by frustrated revolutionaries. Meanwhile, he dared not confront Western and Japanese imperialism in China because he was dependent on foreigners who looked to him as a strongman who could ensure order. The revolution had been betrayed.

Several southern and western provinces, where disgruntled military men and revolutionaries were active, broke away from Yuan's control. In 1916 he died suddenly after failing to have himself declared emperor. Political and ideological change had gone much too far to permit any return to such traditional forms, although there was still neither a consensus on what should succeed them nor a semblance of national unity. During the next 12 years China dissolved into virtual anarchy, divided among a number of regionally based warlords and other local military leaders. The Kuomintang and the early revolutionaries had a political ideology of sorts but no army; the warlords had armies but little or no program or party organization. Their troops marched around the countryside like a scourge on the peasants, while a bewildering variety of short-lived regimes or po-

litical cliques succeeded each other in Peking as the nominal government of China.

In 1917 Sun returned to Canton, formed a rival government, and began building a more effective political organization. He complained that trying to get the Chinese people to work together was like trying to make a rope out of sand. But although he tried to arouse mass support, he appealed mainly to intellectuals and the few Chinese who were as yet politically conscious. What began to spark Chinese nationalism more effectively were new Japanese encroachments on the nation's sovereignty and spontaneous popular protests against them.

The May Fourth Movement

Japan's Twenty-one Demands on China, issued in 1915, provoked immediate protests from patriotic Chinese, especially after Yuan accepted most of them. China joined the Allied side in World War I in 1917, sent labor battalions to the Western front, and hoped thus to get a hearing at the Paris peace conference. But Japan had secretly obtained Allied agreement to keep what it had taken in China's Shantung province, and it soon appeared that the lofty Western talk about self-determination did not apply to Asia.

When news broke that the warlord government in Peking had also signed secret agreements with Japan, mass demonstrations erupted on May 4, 1919. Chinese nationalism boiled over in what came to be called the May Fourth movement. A new and increasingly radical generation of students in government and mission schools and universities emerged, imbued with Western ideas and dedicated to building a new China. Student protesters beat up a pro-Japanese official and burned a cabinet minister's house. They went on to organize a union and to seek support among the large group of westernized businessmen, industrialists, and shopkeepers in the treaty ports. Strikes and boycotts of Japanese goods attracted widespread support. The cabinet resigned, and China refused to sign the Versailles Treaty.

The May Fourth movement stimulated renewed intellectual ferment as well, especially in Peking and Shanghai, where hundreds of new political and literary periodicals attacked traditional culture, deplored China's weakness, and advocated a variety of more or less radical solutions. The model of the Confucian scholar steeped in the classics gave way to that of "progressive" thinkers who wrote in the vernacular and tried to appeal not only to fellow scholars or intellectuals but to the people as a whole. Parental and family controls, arranged marriages, and the subjugation of women and the young became targets of attack. Women, especially students, played a prominent part in the May Fourth movement; they and their male colleagues urged full-scale female emancipation and an end to the rigidity of the traditional system as a whole. Lu Hsun (Lu Xun, 1881–1936), the greatest modern Chinese writer, voiced bitter indictments of the old society, whose supposed ideals of "benevolence" and "virtue," he alleged, were hypocritical masks for oppression and exploitation. Foreign imperialism was deeply resented, but such critics as Lu Hsun saw it as the result of China's weakness rather than as the cause. The May Fourth movement sought to build a new China in which modern Western ideas of democracy, equality, science, and nationalism would have a prominent place. The example of Meiji Japan was much admired, despite Japanese aggression against China. Like the Meiji leaders, China's new voices called for a clean slate and a national renewal that would incorporate Western ideas.

China and the Marxist Model

Among the Western concepts with particular appeal was Marxism, especially after the success of the Russian Revolution in 1917. Russia too had been a relatively undeveloped country that had embraced the Marxist-Leninist doctrine of centralized organization and collective effort. The Soviet formula seemed to fit China's circumstances, and Marx himself had suggested the relevance of his ideas to China many years earlier. In 1921 a small group of intellectuals, including Mao Tse-tung (Mao Zedong, 1893–1976), then a young student, founded the Chinese Communist party. Representatives from the Comintern helped the new party set up its organization. Soviet experience in political mobilization was also attractive to the Kuomintang, which, like the Communist party, remained largely without any mass base. Sun Yat-sen, still head of the Kuomintang, agreed to an alliance with the Communist party under Comintern direction. Sun's military assistant, Chiang Kai-shek, was sent to Moscow to study Soviet methods. Party dictatorship was seen as necessary in the early stages of national unification, but Sun's Three Principles of the People and some form of representative government were reasserted as the ultimate goal. Sun may have been moving in the direction of socialism during his last years, but he died suddenly in 1925, and party control passed to Chiang Kai-shek. Chiang, despite his Soviet experience, was a far more conservative figure. With his military background, Chiang saw China's first priority as the achievement of national

unity, through force if necessary. He began promisingly by mounting a military and political campaign with Communist help. Moving north from the Kuomintang base in Canton with his Communist allies to defeat the warlords, he established a new national capital at Nanking (Nanjing) in 1927.

The Nanking Decade

Chiang never completely eliminated warlord power in several of the outlying provinces, and although he dominated the Kuomintang, he led it far from its radical origins and progressively lost support. He tried to wipe out his Communist allies in a military coup in Shanghai in 1927 and then in a series of campaigns from 1930 to 1934. Some of the Communists, including Mao, were not in Shanghai in 1927 but in rural areas trying, without success, to organize peasant rebellion. Their small remaining forces retreated to a mountain stronghold in the southeast. Chiang's forces finally drove them out in 1934, forcing them into a retreat known as the Long March. An increasingly ragged column of Communists dodged ahead of Chiang's troops in a zigzag route across western China. The precariously few survivors finally reached a new base area in the remote and mountainous northwest in 1935, centered on Yenan (Yanan). Relatively safe from Chiang's army, they pursued land reform policies and slowly extended their support base in this border area, from which they were to emerge after World War II in 1945 to lead a victorious revolution.

The decade of the Nanking government between 1927 and 1937 was, despite its repressive aspects, a period of at least modest recovery and growth. Chiang permitted no genuine democracy, with the excuse that order and unity must come first. But at least the forms of constitutional government existed, and the economy underwent considerable modernization. Western-trained Chinese developed a central banking system, and a national rail network began to take shape. Industrial growth was still confined almost entirely to the treaty ports but increasingly under Chinese management.

These developments, however, were on a small scale compared to the needs of the country and had little or no impact on most of its predominantly peasant population. Poverty grew in the countryside. The Kuomintang's political base had become largely a coalition of businessmen from the treaty ports and rural landlords, which sought to suppress agrarian reform and prevent the rise of a politicized peasantry. The Communists, meanwhile, clung to their small base in the northwest, biding their time.

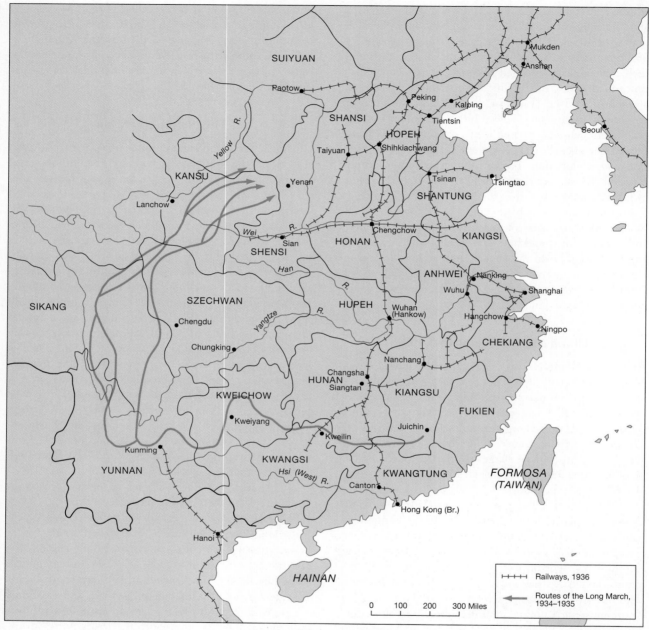

MAP 37.2   CHINA IN THE 1930s

Japan's invasion of China transformed the situation. The Japanese, having reduced Manchuria to an economic colony, invaded in 1931 and annexed it outright. They watched with concern as Chiang made progress toward national unification and began to build China's military strength. When the militarists who controlled Japan after 1930 saw their hopes for dominance in China and East Asia threatened, they launched a general assault on China in 1937, attacking first at Peking and then at Shanghai; later in the year they moved on to sack Nanking. With its capital in flames, the Kuomintang retreated up the Yangtze, largely to sit out the rest of the war, while the Communists in the north perfected a guerrilla strategy against the invaders and captured the leadership of Chinese nationalism.

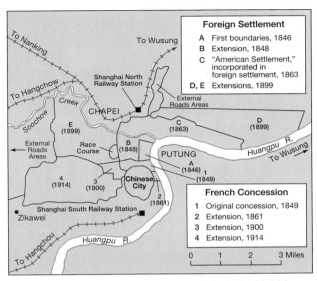

Foreign Settlement
A First boundaries, 1846
B Extension, 1848
C "American Settlement," incorporated in foreign settlement, 1863
D, E Extensions, 1899

French Concession
1 Original concession, 1849
2 Extension, 1861
3 Extension, 1900
4 Extension, 1914

MAP 37.3 THE GROWTH OF SHANGHAI

Shanghai: The Model Treaty Port

While the Communists retreated to remote Yenan behind its mountain barriers and began to work out their program for a new China under the leadership of Mao, Shanghai remained a bastion of foreign privilege and Chinese collaborators. But it also harbored the growing group of Chinese dissidents, radicals, and revolutionaries who lived there under the protection of foreign law. Chinese police could not pursue suspects in the foreign settlements, which were ruled by a foreign-dominated municipal council with its own police. The Chinese Communist party had been founded there in 1921 for that reason, by a small group of revolutionaries and writers, part of the much larger number of political refugees living in the city, many of whom were periodically hounded or captured and executed by the Kuomintang secret police. Chiang Kai-shek's military coup in 1927 killed many of them and drove some of the survivors out, but many remained underground and continued to produce literary and political magazines with titles like *New China, New Youth,* and *New Dawn,* which were avidly read by intellectuals in the rest of China.

After Shanghai passed Peking as China's biggest city about 1910, it became the country's chief center of literature, publishing, and cultural and political ferment. The May Fourth movement spread immediately from Peking to Shanghai; student organizers persuaded many Shanghai merchants to boycott Japanese, and later British, goods. Shanghai joined Peking as a major base for the New Culture movement, sometimes called the Chinese Renaissance, and its efforts to remake Chinese society. Lu Hsun and many other New Culture writers lived in Shanghai.

At the same time, Shanghai remained by far the largest port and commercial center in China, through which more than half its foreign trade passed. It also

Cosmopolitanism in Shanghai, 1933: (from left) the American journalist Agnes Smedley, the playwright George Bernard Shaw, Madame Sun Yat-sen, Ts'ai Yuan-p'ei (a leading intellectual), and Lu Hsun. Shaw was on a visit to China and is here being welcomed by the founders of the China League for Civil Rights.

housed more than half the country's modern industry. Chinese entrepreneurs, both traditional and westernized, competed and collaborated with foreigners in trade, banking, and manufacturing, and many adopted a Western style of living. The foreign settlements at Shanghai were replicas of the modern Western city and looked much like Manchester or Chicago. The muddy foreshores of the Huangpu River, a Yangtze tributary that ran along one edge of the city and constituted the harbor, were covered in the nineteenth century by an embankment known as the Bund. It became Shanghai's main thoroughfare, lined with imposing Western banks and hotels. Nanking Road, the main shopping street, ran at right angles to it, away from the river, and extensive residential areas featured houses in the Western style. The foreign population peaked at about 60,000 in the 1930s, in a city that by then totaled about 4 million, many of whom lived outside the foreign concession areas in sprawling slums or in the walled Chinese city next to the concessions. But the commercial and industrial heart of Shanghai was largely run by foreigners (the Japanese had edged out the British as the majority interest by the 1930s), and they built it in the Western image. They spoke of it as a beacon of "progress" in a vast Chinese sea of "backwardness."

Shanghai was described as "in China but not of it." The city brought silk, tea, and other agricultural goods from the Chinese hinterland for export in return for metals, machinery, and manufactured goods. Overall, however, Shanghai's economic example made relatively little impact, except in the other treaty ports. Elsewhere, it was largely rejected as alien and unsuited to China. The Communists labeled Chinese collaborators in Shanghai and the other treaty ports "running dogs" of the imperialists and were contemptuous of their departure from Chinese ways in favor of westernization.

Shanghai and the other treaty ports cut a deep wound of humiliation in the Chinese psyche, but they also offered an example of the kind of industrial and organizational strength without which China could not hope to chart its own destiny. Shanghai played a major role in stimulating the rise of modern Chinese nationalism and with it a determination to rid the country of its foreign oppressors. The foreign way was rejected, but its technological and industrial achievements were to be adapted to serve Chinese needs. The residents of Shanghai were, of course, the most affected by its example, and it was primarily there that China's modern revolution began. In the end, all foreign privileges were swept away by the revolution, but Shanghai remains

The Bund, Shanghai, 1986. Except for the vehicles, little has changed since Shanghai's heyday as a treaty port. Most of the buildings shown here date from the 1920s and 1930s. The Huangpu River and floating docks are on the right.

China's biggest city and its most advanced industrial and technological center. Shanghai's modernity thus survived the expulsion of the foreigners and shaped basic aspects of the new China.

India: Toward Freedom

In India the pressures for change were narrowly concentrated on winning freedom from colonial rule. Like China, India suffered from mass poverty, technological backwardness, and foreign domination. Indian nationalists tended to blame colonial oppression for their problems and to see the solution as getting rid of their British overlords. But as in China, a new national consciousness had first to be developed and a national political organization built. India had functioned throughout most of its past not as a national political unit but, like China, as a cultural tradition. It took time to get Indians or Chinese to work together for a common political goal. The Indian independence movement did respond to the need for attacking poverty and injustice and for pursuing modern development, but the immediate objective was political freedom. While its final achievement was in some ways a revolutionary change, most Indians saw no need to reject either their own tradition or aspects of the British colonial experience that could help the new nation adapt to the modern world.

India's progress toward freedom is in large part the story of the careers of two men, Mohandas K. Gandhi (1869–1948), often called the Mahatma, or "Great Soul," and Jawaharlal Nehru (1889–1964). Gandhi gave the independence movement what it had not yet had, mass appeal and a mass following. Nehru, in close cooperation with Gandhi, gave practical leadership but acknowledged the charismatic power of Gandhi's example. In the years after World War I the Congress party was transformed under Gandhi's direction from a small group of intellectuals into a truly national party representing a wide range of regional interest groups and mobilizing millions of Indians. Gandhi proved adept at using aspects of the Indian tradition as vehicles of protest against British im-

perialism and as rallying points for nationalist sentiment and organization.

Gandhi and Mass Action

The son of a minor official in commercial Gujarat, Gandhi followed the path of many upwardly mobile Indians in a rapidly changing society. At 19 he went to London to study law and there became thoroughly westernized. Soon after his return to India, he took a job with an Indian law firm in South Africa, where he spent the next 20 years defending Indian merchants and other immigrants against racist oppression and developing tactics of nonviolent protest and noncooperation.

Back home in 1914, he supported Indian participation in World War I on the Allied side, hoping, as many Indians did, that loyalty to Britain in its hour of need would be rewarded by self-government. The British secretary of state for India announced in 1917 that the government's policy was "the gradual development of self-governing institutions" and an increase of Indians in responsible positions, but with the end of the war it became clear that such change would be painfully slow. Meanwhile, peasant economic suffering and distress among exploited industrial workers were growing. Gandhi traveled through India dressed as a poor peasant, reaching out to the masses and gaining a reputation for personal sanctity. But he also organized and led successful strikes and protest movements, using nonviolent

Gandhi the ascetic, spinning cotton yarn. He made it a point to spin 200 yards of yarn every day as a symbolic act, no matter how busy he was.

Gandhi's Message to the British

Gandhi knew England and British culture well, in part from his time there as a student, and he had many British friends. In his Hind Swaraj (Independent India), *he addressed them.*

I admit you are my rulers. . . . I have no objection to your remaining in my country, but . . . you will have to remain as servants of the people. . . . We do not need any European cloth. We shall manage with articles produced and manufactured at home. . . . This is not said to you in arrogance. You have great military resources. . . . If we wanted to fight with you on your own ground, we should be unable to do so but [we must] cease to play the part of the ruled. . . . If you act contrary to our will, we will not help you; and without our help, we know that you cannot move one step forward. . . . You English who have come to India are not good specimens of the English nation, nor can we, almost half-anglicized Indians, be considered good specimens of the real Indian nation. If the English nation were to know all you have done, it would oppose many of your actions. . . . If you will search into your own scriptures, you will find that our demands are just. Only on condition of our demands being fully satisfied may you remain in India; and if you remain under those conditions, we shall learn several things from you and you will learn many from us. So doing we shall benefit each other and the world. But that will happen only when the root of our relationship is sunk in a religious soil.

Gandhi's ideas and personal qualities are well brought out in that passage. Nehru said the following of him in 1935.

I have never met any man more utterly honest, more transparently sincere, less given to egotism, self-conscious pride, opportunism, and ambition. . . . It has been the greatest privilege of our lives to work with him and under him for a great cause. To us he has represented the spirit and honor of India.

Sources: W. T. de Bary, ed., *Sources of Indian Tradition,* vol. 2 (New York: Columbia University Press, 1964), pp. 265–266; J. Nehru, "Mahatma Gandhi," *L'Europe* (February 1936), p. 21.

methods with great effect. These and other signs of ferment appeared to members of the government as "seditious conspiracy." Repression followed, culminating in the Amritsar Massacre of 1919, when Indian troops under British command fired on an unarmed and peaceful crowd, leaving 400 dead.

From then on, more and more Indians came to see colonialism as unacceptable. The Congress party began to press for independence, and Gandhi's weapon of nonviolent protest and noncooperation attracted more and more followers. Gandhi based his tactics on the ancient Hindu idea of *ahimsa,* or reverence for life, and drew on the redemptive power of love to convert even brutal opponents by its "soul force," or *satyagraha.* Traditional Indian values stressed the avoidance of conflict and the importance of self-control, seeking resolution through compromise and consensus. Nonviolent action was also a practical means for unarmed and powerless people to confront an oppressive state. As the American civil rights leader Martin Luther King, Jr., was later to demonstrate, it worked, both to build a dedicated following and to make its protest against injustice effective.

Gandhi organized boycotts of British imports, an action that caught the popular imagination, as it had in China, and helped build a larger following. He urged Indians to wear only their own cottons and wherever possible to spin and weave for themselves. The spinning wheel became a powerful nationalist symbol, linked also to 5,000 years of the country's history. Some of the Congress party's intellectual elite were scornful of Gandhi's methods, the style of a traditional sadhu (holy man) he adopted, his embrace of the poor, and his personal asceticism. But as both an astute politician and a saintly figure he attracted more support and got more results than the party's politicians had ever done. Gandhi gave the Indian people a sense of their own national identity and inspired them to action through traditional methods and symbols. He succeeded where others had failed in attracting Muslims, Sikhs, Christians, and agnostics to his cause, thus creating India's first truly national movement. He urged his fellow Indians to "get rid of our helplessness" and stand together. As Nehru said of him, "He has given us back our courage, and our pride."

Strikes, boycotts, and demonstrations spread in the early 1920s, but with millions of people now involved, Gandhi could not always guarantee nonviolence. Thousands were jailed, violence occurred on both sides, and in 1922 Gandhi was sentenced to prison for six years. He was released for medical reasons after two but did not resume political agitation until 1930, distressed that his nonviolent campaign had gone astray.

Hindus and Muslims

Meanwhile, the government, affected by Gandhi's popular movement, began to implement many of the reforms previously demanded by the Congress party. It greatly increased the number of Indian officers in the civil service and the army and moved toward the abolition of the tax on cotton. By 1937 all the British Indian provinces had become self-governing, with legislatures elected by Indian voters. Nehru became mayor of his home city of Allahabad. During this time, rioting between Muslims and Hindus broke out in many areas, a symptom of the general atmosphere of turmoil but also of the efforts of special groups to ensure a better place for themselves in the independent India that was clearly coming. Hindus and Muslims had worked together for many years in the Congress party. Now Muslims were warned that they had to safeguard their interests against the Hindu majority and that their own party, the Muslim League, led by Mohammed Ali Jinnah (1876–1948), was their only sure protector.

Jinnah pressed for a separate Muslim electorate to vote for candidates for the new posts being opened to Indian officeholders and Indian voters. Meanwhile, Nehru increased his organizational control of the Congress party, although he maintained his loyalty to Gandhi as India's spiritual and symbolic leader. Nehru insisted that the Congress party was the party of all Indians, including Muslims, and that the independence movement would be weakened by factionalism. He was proved tragically right.

The worldwide depression that began in 1929 bore heavily on India and greatly increased its economic distress. When Gandhi resumed political action in 1930, he chose as his targets the tax the government imposed on salt and the official ban on private saltmaking from the sea, arguing that the tax and the monopoly especially

The Declaration of Indian Freedom

Nehru, as president of the Congress party, declared January 26, 1930, a special day for the assertion of India's right to independence and issued this pledge, which was recited throughout India by millions of nationalists. Note the close similarity, quite conscious on Nehru's part, to the American Declaration of Independence.

We believe that it is the inalienable right of the Indian people, as of any other people, to have freedom and to enjoy the fruits of their toil and have the necessities of life, so that they may have full opportunities of growth. We believe also that if any government deprives a people of these rights and oppresses them, the people have a further right to alter it or abolish it. The British government in India has not only deprived the Indian people of their freedom, but has based itself on the exploitation of the masses, and has ruined India economically, politically, culturally, and spiritually.

Source: S. Wolpert, *A New History of India* (New York: Oxford University Press, 1982), pp. 314–315.

hurt the poor. He led a protest march on foot across India to the coast, where he purposely courted arrest by picking up a lump of natural salt and urging Indians to do likewise, as many thousands did. Gandhi, Nehru, and many others were jailed, and there was a wave of strikes. Gandhi had again stirred the conscience of the nation. After eight months in prison, he was released to meet with the viceroy in New Delhi. Gandhi agreed to discontinue civil disobedience; in return, the government sanctioned a movement to promote the use of Indian-made goods and invited Gandhi to a London conference on India later in 1931, together with Jinnah as a representative of the Muslims.

The conference ended in stalemate, and Gandhi was taken back to jail a week after his return. Boycotts, strikes, and violent demonstrations erupted again without Gandhi to restrain them. Meanwhile, economic distress deepened as world markets for India's exports shrank, and a new, more conservative viceroy was appointed. In England, however, popular and parliamentary opinion was turning more and more toward self-government for India. In 1935 a new constitution for India was announced, followed by nationwide elections in 1937 in which nearly 40 million Indians voted. Congress candidates swept the election, and the Muslim League did not even win most of the seats reserved for Muslims. The new constitution granted "safeguard" powers to the colonial government, but Congress ministries took over the provinces. Jinnah was outraged, and until his death he devoted his energies to building first an effective party for Muslims and finally a separate state. Nehru pointed out in reply that the Congress party was a national, not a special-interest party and that more than 100,000 Muslims belonged to it.

By the outbreak of war in 1939, India was well along the road to self-government, but the war brought the proimperial Winston Churchill to power in Britain and postponed all talk of independence until fascism could be defeated in Europe and Asia. Indians were informed that they were automatically at war with Germany, and later with Italy and Japan. Neither the Congress party's representatives nor other Indian leaders were consulted. Nationalists once again felt betrayed. The Congress party's provincial ministries resigned in protest, leaving the political field to Jinnah and his Muslim League. A belated British offer, reduced at Churchill's insistence from independence to dominion status once the war was over, was rejected. Gandhi called it "a postdated check on a failing bank." He began a series of nonviolent campaigns, culminating in the "Quit India" movement of 1942, a slogan that was scrawled on walls all over the country and

shouted at Britons. Nehru spent most of the war in jail, and Gandhi was confined periodically. Jinnah exploited their absence to press for a separate state for Muslims, to be called Pakistan. Independence would come too late to avoid the bloody tragedy of partition.

The British had begun in India as a small group of merchants competing with Arabs, Portuguese, Dutch, French, and Indians for a share of the trade and a few ports. Trading and maintaining the security of routes and warehouses led imperceptibly to more and more political influence and control in an India that lapsed into chaos after 1707. In time the lure of imperial glory captured the British imagination, but there was a kernel of truth in the observation some made that the Indian empire was acquired in "a fit of absence of mind." After 1774 Parliament began to supervise the governance of India, and by 1858 virtually the whole of the subcontinent had been brought under direct or indirect British control.

As early as the 1830s, most Britons agreed that India would one day be independent and that long-term British policy should prepare for this. Indians were quick to learn Western ideas and techniques wherever they saw them as useful, including business and industrial methods and British-style education, law, and parliamentary government. India is still governed today by institutions derived from Britain. The assimilation of British ways also greatly enhanced and accelerated the growth of the independence movement, which Indians saw as itself within the British tradition of political freedom.

If independence had come in 1907, when Parliament first declared it to be Britain's objective, or in the 1920s, when the policy was reaffirmed, it would have been possible to look back on the British era in India in relatively positive terms, though marred in the late eighteenth century by plunder and by the arrogance that led to the 1857 mutiny and its bitter aftermath. But however one assesses the balance or weighs it with other aspects of British rule, especially the failure to combat the fundamental modern Indian problem of poverty, Britain's clearest political error was its delay in giving India independence. Nevertheless, there is little bitterness over the colonial legacy in India, in contrast to much of the rest of Asia, which underwent a harsher rule under the Japanese, French, or Dutch. Many originally British institutions are now firmly a part of South Asian civilization. India has much in common today with other former British colonies, including the United States and Canada, as joint inheritors of many aspects of a common culture.

The Nationalist Awakening in the Middle East

The same nationalist forces that challenged European imperialism in India and China had an equally pronounced impact on the Middle East. Despite ethnic disunity and traditional theological differences within Islam, Arab consciousness had been stimulated by the common experience of Turkish and European exploitation. By the eve of World War I, independence movements, often used as an entering wedge for Western interests, had already dismembered large portions of the weakened Ottoman Empire. The Greeks and most of the Slavic peoples of the Balkans either had freed themselves from Turkish rule or had fallen under Austro-Hungarian control. In North Africa, France had taken Algeria and established protectorates in Morocco and Tunisia, Britain had imposed a sphere of influence over Egypt and the Sudan, and Italy had occupied Libya and Somalia. Besides Turkey proper, only Iraq, Syria, Palestine, and Arabia still remained within the Ottoman sphere.

The Mandate System and the Palestine Question

British success in arousing Arab hostility against the Turks during the war, together with the success of the British adventurer T. E. Lawrence in coordinating Arab resistance, had helped free most of the Middle East from Ottoman control by 1918. When the war was over, Faisal of Iraq and Lawrence lobbied the Paris peace conference for Arab rights, while Chaim Weizmann, who had succeeded Theodor Herzl as the leader of the Zionist movement, continued to push for the creation of a Jewish state. Neither party succeeded. After Faisal's appeals were rejected, an Arab congress declared him ruler of Syria, Palestine, and Lebanon.

While Faisal and Lawrence were in Paris, Abdul-Aziz ibn-Saud took to the deserts with his troops, extending his control over central Arabia. In 1925 he finally forced Hussein to abdicate as ruler of the Hejaz, which he united with his own Nejd sultanate. The British quickly recognized these conquests, and in 1932 ibn-Saud formally changed the name of his realm to the kingdom of Saudi Arabia. Vast oil deposits were soon discovered, and ibn-Saud's hereditary absolute monarchy eventually grew wealthy through the concessions granted to Western oil companies.

Although the Saudi dynasty was successful in Arabia, Arab nationalism continued to be frustrated elsewhere. Faisal's rule over Syria was short-lived, for in 1920 the Allies tacitly recognized the terms of the Sykes-Picot Agreement by approving the League of Nations mandate system, and Turkish control formally gave way to Western domination. The French ejected Faisal from Syria, engendering bitter resistance from the Arab population, and created Lebanon as a separate mandate. In 1926 Lebanon was made a republic, with borders similar to those of the now independent state. The roads, buildings, and irrigation systems constructed under French occupation did not make up for the suppression of civil liberties and the divisive efforts to gain the allegiance of the Christian Arabs of Lebanon. The Lebanon mandate had a rich religious diversity, for in ancient times it had been a place of refuge for religious sects of all kinds. The Maronite Christians, a Roman Catholic group that followed Eastern Orthodox rites, with roots that went back to the seventh century, comprised about 40 percent of the population; Muslims of various sects made up the bulk of the remaining inhabitants. When the French eventually evacuated the area after World War II, they left behind a legacy of deep hostility.

The British were more successful in their mandate areas. Following an Iraqi rebellion in 1920, which they put down with much bloodshed, they made the popular Faisal king of Iraq, although they continued to run his financial and military affairs for another decade and supervised the creation of a constitutional monarchy. In 1922 Britain granted nominal independence to Egypt but refused to withdraw its troops from the country, and it followed a similar path in Iraq, where independence was recognized in 1930 in exchange for a military alliance that maintained British influence there. Nor did the discovery of rich oil fields in Iraq benefit the population of the region, for foreign companies secured lucrative concessions, further inflaming Arab resentment against the West.

The Palestine problem remained another source of anti-Western hostility as well as a cause of regional unrest. Britain's contradictory policies in the Middle East satisfied neither Arab nor Jewish demands, and throughout the interwar period British governments continued to shift between the two. Arab riots erupted in Palestine immediately after the creation of the British mandate over the area, prompting London to issue assurances that the Balfour Declaration would not be implemented in a way that would damage Arab interests. Yet British statesmen agreed with the Zionist position that the anguished history of the Jews made the creation of an independent Jewish homeland in Palestine a moral necessity. The Jewish community there—the Yishuv—had had a nearly uninterrupted residence since biblical times. It increased as a result of Zionist efforts in the late nineteenth century. By 1919 Jews in the mandate numbered around 60,000, or less than 10 percent of the population. In the early 1920s Britain permitted many Jews to join the Yishuv; by 1939 it had grown to 450,000, almost a third of the total.

Serious violence against Jews, provoked in part by aggressive settlement and the exclusion of Palestinians from newly established factories, broke out in 1929. When Nazi racial policies in Germany and anti-Semitism elsewhere caused another large wave of illegal Jewish immigration in the 1930s, the violence escalated to a virtual state of civil war. The British responded with proposals to create two separate states in the area, but both sides rejected the plan. The bitter struggle between Arab and Jew would reemerge after World War II with far-reaching results.

Despite overwhelming obstacles, Jewish immigrants achieved remarkable success. Although most came from European cities, they adjusted quickly to the rural conditions in Palestine, buying up Arab farmland as well as turning formerly arid terrain into fertile farms and citrus orchards through irrigation, much as the Arabs themselves were doing. The socialist beliefs of many of the early settlers encouraged collective agricultural labor through a farm unit known as the *kibbutz*, where men and women worked on an equal basis and shared nurseries, dining facilities, and schools as well as the defense of the community. Another form of enterprise was the *moshav*, a mixture of capitalist and socialist economic features. By 1939 the Jews had created, on socialist principles, an economic infrastructure that encompassed transportation networks, irrigation schemes, and other forms of industrial and agricultural productivity unique in the Middle East at that time. They also built new and prosperous cities, such as Tel Aviv, where a rich intellec-

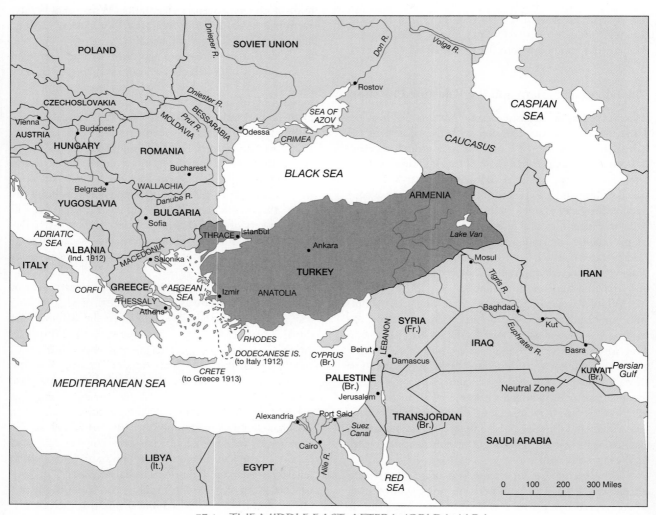

MAP 37.4 THE MIDDLE EAST AFTER WORLD WAR I

tual life thrived, based on the Hebrew language. This intellectual revival was facilitated by a Hebrew-language publishing industry and theater. Other institutions that elaborated biblical and medieval Jewish cultural themes in a twentieth-century context included art and music academies, a philharmonic orchestra, and the Hebrew University of Jerusalem and its Jewish National Library. By the late 1930s Jewish claims to Palestine, both biblical and historical, were reinforced by their achievements in constructing the foundations of a modern society.

The Modernization of Turkey and Iran

In the second half of the nineteenth century internal problems had made it difficult for the Ottoman Empire to deal effectively with external challenges. The reactionary excesses of the Sultan Abdul Hamid (1876–1909) stimulated opposition among Western-educated reformers and army officers (see Chapter 33). These groups formed the Young Turk movement, which in 1908 forced Abdul Hamid to restore the constitution and the parliament. When the sultan attempted a counter revolution, the Young Turks unseated him. They soon imposed rigid centralization based on Turkish supremacy on a state that included substantial Arab, Armenian, and Slavic minorities. Wooed by German agents, who trained their army, the Young Turks brought Turkey into World War I on Germany's side.

Military defeat precipitated the final demise of the Ottoman Empire. While the subject Arabs were breaking away from Istanbul, the Allies imposed a harsh peace treaty on Turkey that provided for the partition of its empire. In these circumstances, patriotic Turks turned to Mustapha Kemal (1881–1938), who had defended Gallipoli against the British in 1915. The Western-educated Kemal, charismatic and strong-willed, became the focus of a nationalist movement that revolutionized Turkish life. Setting up a new capital at Ankara, in central Anatolia—a site chosen as deliberately remote from European influence—he won popular acclaim by defying the Allies, abolishing the privileges that foreigners once had in Turkey, and repelling the Greek armies that attempted to wrest further territory from the Turks. While recognizing the inevitability of Arab independence, he was unwilling to surrender Asia Minor, eastern Thrace, or the Dardanelles. In 1923, after creating a republic and defeating a Greek thrust against Asia Minor, he forced a revised peace treaty on the Allies that permitted Turkey to keep Asia Minor and a small strip of territory around Istanbul on the European side of the Turkish Straits.

Kemal—who was given the name Atatürk, or "Father of the Turks"—embarked on a program of massive change designed to bring Turkey into the modern era. Although technically president of the republic, he governed as a dictator under a one-party system with a national assembly elected by indirect vote of a limited electorate, made universal only in 1934. His ability to introduce far-reaching change stemmed in part from an appeal to Turkish nationalism. As the Japanese had done so successfully in their own drive for westernization, Kemal now played on the fear and resentment that Western imperialism had provoked while simultaneously stressing Turkey's historic role as the dominant force in a region of lesser states. With ruthless determination, he abolished ancient customs and swept away cultural patterns that he felt impeded Turkish modernization. Outwardly, the most visible signs of Kemal's revolution were the changes in dress that he decreed. Government officials were required to substitute Western business suits and hats for robes and fezzes. Western-style family names were introduced, and place names were altered to symbolize the break from an archaic past. But other changes had a more profound impact. Kemal, who professed no religious beliefs, struck deeply at Islamic tradition by separating church from state and secularizing the nation's educational and legal systems. A simpler, more phonetic alphabet replaced the intricate Arabic script as the written language, and the government launched a far-reaching educational campaign among millions of previously illiterate Turkish citizens.

Mustapha Kemal Atatürk, the architect of modern Turkey and its first president.

Kemal's vigorous social reforms inspired a similar modernization experiment in Iran. In a move much like the revolt of the Young Turks, nationalistic Iranian reformers forced the despotic and backward shah to grant a constitution in 1906. The reform momentum was shattered the next year when the British and the Russians divided Iran into spheres of influence and assumed substantive control of the country. When the British tried to impose their authority over the entire country after the war, Reza Khan Pahlavi (1877–1944), a colonel in the Persian Cossack Brigade, took power and assumed the title of shah in 1925.

Reza Shah Pahlavi greatly admired Kemal Atatürk and imitated his modernization program, though with less success. The shah's secularization efforts met with fierce opposition from the powerful Islamic religious leaders, who resented all Western influence and were as strong as the small group of European-trained reformers. Like Kemal, Reza Shah Pahlavi changed place names and westernized dress. He built an efficient army and encouraged trade and industry, but he was personally corrupt, and his government proved tyrannical.

In Turkey, Kemal's reforms radically altered the status of women. Polygamy, still practiced by a minority, was abolished in 1926, and marriage laws were modeled after Western examples. Wealthy women began to attend universities and abandoned their veiled costumes in favor of modern European dress. In 1934 women were enfranchised and made eligible for election to the National Assembly. Reza Shah Pahlavi introduced similar policies in Iran, although there Islamic influence kept a stronger hold on women. These and other changes marked a sharp departure from tradition, whose tribal and Islamic practices had kept women in bondage to men, secluded from public life, and confined by strict codes of behavior. The older customs continued to prevail in Saudi Arabia and elsewhere. Nevertheless, the new social norms fostered by Kemal Atatürk and Reza Shah Pahlavi, together with the emergence of a cohesive Jewish community in Palestine where women labored on an equal basis with men, broke the centuries-old pattern of female subservience in the Middle East.

SUMMARY

Early in the twentieth century the largest and oldest societies in the world broke sharply with the patterns of the past. In Russia, China, India, and the Middle East, half the world's people rejected the political systems that had governed them and strove to remake their societies.

In Russia a corrupt, ineffective, and repressive regime was toppled by an alliance of workers and intellectuals under the charismatic leadership of Lenin. In November 1917 his Bolsheviks swept away the provisional government that had replaced the Romanov dynasty and began a radical experiment in economic and social mobilization. They instituted a program of forced modernization that would enable the Soviet Union, as Russia was now called, to catch up with western Europe and improve the economic condition of its people. On Lenin's death in 1924, leadership passed to the more ruthless, power-conscious Stalin. Lenin's dream of a workers' democracy quickly faded, but Russia's industrial and military power grew rapidly, and the Soviet example of successful revolution and modernization exerted worldwide influence.

In China the revolutionary Kuomintang party succeeded the antiquated Ch'ing dynasty, which collapsed in 1911, but the revolutionaries were too few and too divided to form an effective government. The revolution was betrayed by a military strongman, Yuan Shih-kai, and upon his death in 1916 China disintegrated into a civil war among rival warlords. Under the leadership of Chiang Kai-shek, the Kuomintang managed to form a national government in 1927 but failed to unite the country or to eliminate the rival Chinese Communist party. The Japanese invasion of 1937 mortally weakened the Kuomintang, and civil war after 1945 soon brought the Communists to power with their radical solutions to China's urgent problems of poverty and weakness.

In India the long struggle for independence from British rule made real progress only after 1919, when Mahatma Gandhi greatly widened the movement's support by appealing to mass sentiment. Gandhi restored Indians' pride in their own tradition and identity. With the help of Jawaharlal Nehru, he forged a political instrument, the Congress party, into a successful vehicle for freeing India from colonialism and addressing its inherited problems of economic backwardness and inequality.

In the Middle East both Turkish and European colonial domination was also rejected, and new regimes were created in each country. In 1919 the League of Nations replaced the centuries-long rule of the Ottoman Empire in the Middle East with British and French mandates, designed to provide a transition to independence. The seeds of Arab nationalism grew slowly in the interwar period, for rulers such as Faisal in Iraq and ibn-Saud in Saudi Arabia remained heavily dependent on the European powers, while leaders such as Kemal Atatürk in Turkey and Reza Shah Pahlavi in Iran attempted to modernize their countries according to Western models. The colonization of Palestine by Jewish settlers under British patronage further exacerbated Arab nationalism. Only in the post–World War II era did true independence develop, when several factors combined to bring the new Arab *states together against the lingering dominance of the West: the enormous financial strength achieved through the regional coordination of oil resources, a newfound cultural identity inspired by a return to Islamic fundamentalism, and common opposition to the Jewish state of Israel.*

Each of these regions linked approaches based on its individual historical experience to the goal of creating new national strength and development. Each swept away unacceptable political systems and built in their place new governments designed to be more effective in responding to urgent national needs. Taken together, the revolutionary changes in these four major regions did indeed shake the world, by fundamentally transforming the half of it that they governed and by inspiring millions in the other half to do the same.

NOTES

1. J. Reed, *Ten Days That Shook the World* (New York: Random House, 1960), pp. 170–171.

2. A. Kollontai, *The Autobiography of a Sexually Emancipated Communist Woman,* trans. S. Attanasio (New York: Herder & Herder, 1971), p. 13.

3. D. N. Jacobs, ed., *From Marx to Mao and Marchais: Documents on the Development of Communist Variations* (New York: Longman, 1979), pp. 104–105.

4. F. Claudin, *The Communist Movement: From Comintern to Cominform,* vol. 1, trans. B. Pearce (New York: Monthly Review Press, 1975), pp. 72–73.

SUGGESTIONS FOR FURTHER READING

Balfour, Baron J. P. *Atatürk: The Rebirth of a Nation.* London: Weidenfeld & Nicolson, 1964.

Bondurant, J. *The Conquest of Violence: The Gandhian Philosophy of Conflict.* Berkeley: University of California Press, 1969.

Brown, J. *Gandhi and Civil Disobedience.* Cambridge: Cambridge University Press, 1977.

Carr, E. H. *The Russian Revolution: From Lenin to Stalin.* New York: Free Press, 1979.

Chen, J. T. *The May Fourth Movement in Shanghai.* Leiden, Netherlands: Brill, 1971.

Clark, R. W. *Lenin.* New York: Harper & Row, 1988.

Daniels, R. V. *Red October: The Bolshevik Revolution of 1917.* New York: Scribner, 1967.

Deutscher, I. *The Prophet Armed: Trotsky, 1879–1921.* New York: Viking, 1965.

Dirlik, A. *The Origins of Chinese Communism.* New York: Oxford University Press, 1989.

Eastman, L. E. *The Nationalist Era in China, 1927–1949.* Cambridge: Cambridge University Press, 1990.

Edwardes, M. *The Last Years of British India.* London: Cassell, 1963.

Gasster, M. *Chinese Intellectuals and the Revolution of 1911.* Seattle: University of Washington Press, 1969.

Irving, R. G. *Indian Summer: Luytens, Baker, and Imperial New Delhi.* New Haven, Conn.: Yale University Press, 1982.

Iyer, R. *The Moral and Political Thought of Mahatma Gandhi.* New York: Oxford University Press, 1986.

Lincoln, W. B. *Red Victory: A History of the Russian Civil War.* New York: Simon & Schuster, 1989.

Low, D. A., ed. *Congress and the Raj: Facets of the Indian Struggle, 1917–47.* Columbia: University of Missouri Press, 1977.

Majumdar, R. C. *History of the Freedom Movement in India.* Calcutta: K. L. Mukhopadhyay, 1962.

Pandey, B. N. *Nehru.* London: Macmillan, 1976.

Reed, J. *Ten Days That Shook the World.* New York: Random House, 1960.

Sachar, H. M. *The Emergence of the Middle East, 1914–1924.* New York: Knopf, 1969.

Sheridan, J. E. *China in Disintegration: The Republican Era.* Glencoe, Ill.: Free Press, 1975.

Ulam, A. B. *The Bolsheviks.* New York: Macmillan, 1965.

———. *Lenin and the Bolsheviks.* London: Collins, 1969.

Upton, J. M. *The History of Modern Iran.* Cambridge, Mass.: Harvard University Press, 1960.

Visram, R. *Women in India and Pakistan: The Struggle for Independence.* Cambridge: Cambridge University Press, 1992.

Von Laue, T. H. *Why Lenin? Why Stalin?* London: Weidenfeld & Nicolson, 1966.

Wilbur, C. M. *Sun Yat-sen: Frustrated Patriot.* New York: Columbia University Press, 1976.

Wolfe, B. D. *Three Who Made a Revolution,* rev. ed. New York: Dial Press, 1964.

Wright, M. C. *China in Revolution: The First Phase, 1900–1903.* New Haven, Conn.: Yale University Press, 1968.

Young, E. P. *The Presidency of Yuan Shih-kai.* Ann Arbor: University of Michigan Press, 1977.

CHAPTER

38

Totalitarianism and the Crisis of Democracy

As 1919 opened, Europeans were optimistic about the prospects for democracy. Widespread confidence prevailed that the leaders of the victorious Allied Powers who assembled at Paris in January would arrange a lasting peace and fulfill President Wilson's dream of making the world "safe for democracy." The collapse of the autocracies in Russia, Germany, and Austria-Hungary was followed by the creation of parliamentary governments throughout central and eastern Europe. Within two decades, however, liberal ideals and democratic governments were in crisis as fascist movements or authoritarian regimes developed in almost every country. By 1933 fascists had seized power only in Italy and Germany, but their appeal was so pervasive that one historian has characterized the entire interwar period as the "epoch of fascism."* Equally pervasive was the allure of totalitarianism, a political system favored by both fascist and Soviet dictators.

Fascism, in contrast to communism, proclaimed itself a spiritual rather than a materialist philosophy, but its appeal increased dramatically during periods of economic hardship. The financial crisis that began in 1929 plunged the world into an economic collapse of unprecedented dimensions, causing extreme social distress and challenging capitalism itself. The political consequences of the Great Depression were equally disastrous. The political systems of Britain, France, and the United States, where democracy was deeply rooted, were threatened, though without succumbing to fascism. In central and eastern Europe, however, where democracy had been the product of the 1919 settlements, liberal governments often fell victim to dictatorship and spawned fascist movements. Together, fascism and the Great Depression posed a deadly challenge to democracy.

---

*In this chapter *Fascism* refers to Italian Fascism, *fascism* to the generic variety.

Hitler in the summer of 1934 in Venice.

Totalitarianism as a form of government imposes complete control over its citizens in order to implement an ideology that seeks to transform society according to supposedly immutable historical laws. Both fascism and communism are totalitarian.

Totalitarian governments are single-party dictatorships in which constitutional rights are severely restricted or eliminated. All political organizations but the official party are outlawed, and in totalitarian states the bureaucracy and the party are closely intertwined. Such regimes are characterized by state terrorism, coercion, police surveillance, government monopoly of the communications media, and strong state economic control. Educational systems indoctrinate citizens from an early age, and social and leisure organizations are designed to mobilize the masses.

Totalitarian rulers are ideological dictators. Men such as Lenin and Mussolini, Stalin and Hitler were driven to put their doctrines into practice. Though they often compromised for expediency, ideological goals took precedence over traditional values. These dictators relied on modern technology—loudspeakers, radio, motion pictures—to achieve social control as well as to reinforce their leadership. In the hands of Mussolini and Hitler the totalitarian state became the instrument for the mobilization of huge industrial, economic, and military resources to unleash wars intended to reshape human life.

The Nature of Fascism

Many Europeans, dissatisfied with liberal governments but unwilling to adopt communism, regarded fascism as an alternative, a "third way" capable of solving the problems of industrial society. Fascists claimed that their system would supersede class struggle and transform society.

Scholars still debate the nature of fascism. Some regard it as a universal phenomenon that possessed a core of similar characteristics in all countries. Despite these similarities, however, Italian Fascism and German Nazism had deep ideological differences, and each in turn differed from fascist movements elsewhere. Although the term *fascist* continues to be applied to noncommunist authoritarian regimes, some observers doubt that we can speak of fascism outside the European setting and beyond the chronological period 1919–1945.

Was fascism a movement of the right or of the left? Was it a revolutionary, a conservative, or a reactionary force? These questions may be resolved in part by recognizing the distinction between fascism as a movement before it came to power and fascism as a regime after it seized control of a government. Once in office, fascist leaders often compromised with traditional power elites to consolidate their authority, and these compromises changed the original aims of their movements.

General Characteristics

Certain characteristics are found in virtually all such movements. The fascists rejected the concept of liberty inherited from the French Revolution and nineteenth-century liberalism. They argued that democracy corrupts the human spirit with greed, sacrifices national interests

Mussolini (left) leading the Fascist march on Rome in the fall of 1922.

for the sake of party and class concerns, and fosters alienation and a loss of community. Fascists claimed that they would eliminate the class conflict implicit in Marxism, which divided the national community. In the place of Enlightenment rationalism, fascism proclaimed the superiority of instinct, feeling, and blood, and it glorified violence and action. The fascists promised to restore idealism and youthful activism and to integrate every class and citizen into the all-embracing totalitarian state.

Fascist regimes were sustained by the cult of the charismatic leader, whose authority was unquestioned and to whom all loyalty and obedience were directed. Dictators such as Benito Mussolini (1883–1945) and Adolf Hitler (1889–1945) played crucial roles in the success of fascism. Propaganda and public rituals instilled in the population a fanatical faith in the leader, who, with an elite party, ruled in the name of a single national will. Future leaders would be trained through the party, which acted as a link between the people and the state.

The mass base of fascism came chiefly from the lower middle class. White-collar workers, civil servants, artisans, and shopkeepers resented wealthy capitalists just as they feared the working classes. This lower-middle-class group, from which the early movements filled their ranks, hoped that fascism would solve the postwar economic crisis and restore traditional values—respect for authority, family, and nation. It shared the fascists' alienation from the existing social and political order, whose elites monopolized power and restricted advancement. Fascist programs were, however, tailored to attract diverse interests so that segments of the aristocracy, big business, urban labor, and the peasantry found them appealing.

Fascism's major appeal was to nationalism or racism. Such appeals cut across class lines and economic interests, and fascist propaganda played successfully on the popular desire for national greatness and ethnic dominance. Mussolini's dream of re-creating a Roman empire and Hitler's prophecy of a "thousand-year Reich" reflected the fascist thirst for expansion, and the foreign policies of both dictators were aggressive. For some fascist movements—particularly the German National Socialists—racism was the core of their ideologies, but for others—such as the Italian Fascists—racism represented a later addition. Nevertheless, many fascists emphasized the biological or spiritual distinctiveness of their national "races" and exalted the unity of "blood and soil" in their national histories. Fascism systematically eliminated entire populations as the extreme logic of its racism unfolded: hundreds of thousands of North Africans were slaughtered by Italian Fascist armies, and millions of Jews were murdered by the Nazis in central Europe.

The Origins of Fascism

Some historians regard fascism as a reaction against ruling elites, while others consider it a strategy adopted by those elites to forestall revolution from below. Many scholars agree that we must look for the sources of fascism in the nineteenth century. In Italy and Germany the circumstances in which national unification was

University Professors and Fascism

In November 1931, Mussolini approved a decree requiring all professors in Italian universities to pledge their faith to Fascism and to indoctrinate their students to Fascism. Of the approximately 1,200 professors, only 12—all of whom were eventually dismissed—refused to swear allegiance to the regime. Here is the oath:

I swear to be loyal to the King, to his royal successors and the Fascist regime, to observe loyally the *Statuto* [Constitution] and the other laws of the State, to exercize the office of teacher and fulfil all the academic duties with the purpose of forming citizens, industrious, honest and devoted to the Fatherland and the Fascist regime. I swear that I do not belong and will not belong to associations or parties whose activity is not conciliable with the duties of my office.

Source: Herman Finer, *Mussolini's Italy* (New York: Henry Holt and Company, 1935), p. 482.

achieved may have had an important bearing on the origins of fascism. Unification was the work of political and economic elites who excluded the masses from nation building and used the instruments of power politics—war and diplomacy—to achieve their purposes. These elites shaped the new national states according to their own interests. Large segments of the populations were therefore not integrated into national life and looked to fascism to give them a share in the benefits of nationhood.

The Marxist interpretation asserts that fascism is the product of class struggle common to all capitalist societies. It argues that as the counterrevolutionary form adopted by capitalists to suppress the workers, fascism is an attempt by the industrial and financial interests to save dying capitalism. Most Marxists now consider fascism an independent force distinct from capitalism itself. In this view, capitalists supported and used fascism as a weapon in their struggle against the working classes. The "Red scare" that spread throughout Europe following the Russian Revolution provided the atmosphere in which fascism rose to power.

Other scholars argue that the origins of fascism are to be found in the moral and cultural crisis that Europe experienced at the turn of the century. The late-nineteenth-century revolt against positivism undermined many of the ideals inherited from the Enlightenment and the French Revolution and challenged the underlying Judeo-Christian ethical principles on which Western civilization was based. The decline of these values affected political behavior and produced social disintegration, and World War I was seen as an irrational triumph over reason. Accordingly, fascism emerged out of the dislocation of the postwar period as an extreme revolt against positivist values.

Marxist and non-Marxist scholars agree that fascism was an immediate result of World War I. In the postwar crisis, a number of elements—the presence of unemployed and alienated veterans, thwarted lower-middle-class aspirations, capitalist fears of revolution, the outrage of nations humiliated in the war or in the peace settlements—were skillfully manipulated by fascist leaders.

Italy: The Fascist Triumph

The life of Benito Mussolini and the history of Italian Fascism were inextricably linked. Italian Fascism and its regime bore the indelible stamp of his personality and ideas, but he never dominated his movement as Hitler did Nazism.

Benito Mussolini

The founder of Fascism was born in 1883 in a small village in northeastern Italy. Mussolini's father, a blacksmith, was a socialist from whom he inherited a radical, anticlerical bias. He displayed a violent personality but a keen intelligence. His mother, a devout schoolteacher, sent him to a Catholic seminary, from which he was expelled for stabbing another pupil. By 1901 Mussolini was teaching elementary school and active in local socialist politics. The next year he fled to Switzerland to avoid the draft, remaining there until 1904. As a center for revolutionary exiles from many countries, Switzerland afforded Mussolini the opportunity to develop his socialist ideas. He read widely and worked as a propagandist for the Italian Socialist party (PSI). After his return to Italy, he distinguished himself as a revolutionary socialist, a public speaker, and a journalist. During the Italo-Turkish War (1911–1912) he was a staunch pacifist and anti-imperialist, earning a prison term for antiwar agitation. In 1912 he helped the revolutionary socialist faction seize control of the PSI and was made editor of its official daily, *Avanti!*

By the outbreak of World War I, Mussolini had become a prominent socialist leader. During the "interventionist crisis" (1914–1915), in which Italy remained neutral while arranging to enter the war on the Allied side, he rejected some of his socialist principles, particularly his antiwar stance. Concluding that the war could act as a catalyst for revolution, he advocated Italian intervention and as a result was expelled from the PSI in 1915. That year, with money from industrialists and foreign sources, he founded his own newspaper, *Il Popolo d'Italia,* which became the official Fascist organ.

Following a brief stint as a soldier, during which he was wounded and made a sergeant, Mussolini returned to political agitation. He had meanwhile absorbed nationalist ideas and abandoned his belief in the class struggle. By the end of the war Mussolini was a revolutionary without an ideology, a leader in search of a movement.

Postwar Crisis in Italy

Peace was accompanied by a crisis in Italy. To bolster wartime morale the government had promised land for peasants, jobs for workers, and political and social equality. These promises created expectations among Italians of all classes, but postwar realities brought swift disillusionment. Italy's national debt had risen dramatically, the value of its currency had fallen sharply, and foreign trade had been seriously curtailed. The spiraling cost of living hit the working and middle classes hard. Demobilized soldiers demanded jobs, many of which had been filled by women during the war, and the difficulties of converting the economy to peacetime production resulted in more than 2 million unemployed by the end of 1919.

Economic hardships were compounded by a crisis of national prestige. The Treaty of London (1915) that brought Italy into the war had committed the Allies to extensive territorial concessions for Italy, including the Trentino and southern Tirol, the port of Trieste, the Istrian peninsula, the Dalmatian coast, and the Dodecanese islands, which the Italians had occupied since 1912. But at the Paris peace conference Wilson and Lloyd George not only gave Dalmatia to the new Yugoslav state but also refused to compensate Italy with the port city of Fiume, which Prime Minister Orlando demanded. The Italians felt betrayed, and a patriotic frenzy swept the country. Nationalists blamed Orlando's liberal government for what they termed the "mutilated victory," and Fiume became the symbol of Italy's frustrated hopes.

In September 1919 the nationalist writer and adventurer Gabriele D'Annunzio (1863–1938) invaded Fiume with a group of veterans and set up an independent state. Although the Italian government drove him out after a year, the Fiume adventure set a dangerous precedent for military coups and demonstrated the extent of nationalist sentiment. While he ruled Fiume, D'Annunzio adopted symbols and techniques that Mussolini later copied, including the Roman salute, fiery rhetoric, mass torch-lit rallies, and the title of *Duce* ("leader").

Italian frustrations were directed against the liberal regime. In the postwar elections of November 1919, the liberals, who had enjoyed a large majority in the Chamber of Deputies since unification, suddenly found themselves reduced to the third-ranking party, behind the Socialists and the Italian Popular party, which combined progressive Catholic principles with demands for social and economic reform. The Socialists and Catholics together held enough seats to control the Chamber of Deputies but failed to form a coalition, and King Victor Emmanuel III (1900–1946) continued to select his prime ministers from among the discredited liberals.

Against this background, industrial and agrarian unrest intensified, with more than 1,600 strikes in 1919 alone. In the impoverished south, landless peasants led by veterans and socialists seized uncultivated land, and in September 1920 a major factory sit-in in the northern industrial centers threatened to develop into a revolution. This "occupation of the factories" helped push the industrialists into the arms of the Fascists.

The Fascist Movement

In this context Mussolini founded the Fascist movement. At a meeting of about 100 followers in Milan in March 1919, he established the first *fascio di combattimento* ("combat group"), a mixture of nationalist intellectuals, former socialists and syndicalists, and war veterans. The name of the movement was derived from the Latin word *fasces,* a bundle of rods tied around the shaft of an ax, which had been used by the ancient Romans to symbolize unity and authority. Fascist groups spread throughout northern and central Italy, and membership grew from less than 1,000 in the summer of 1919 to 20,000 by late 1920 and to more than 250,000 by 1922. Most were veterans who sought a sense of community based on the "spirit of the trenches"—comradeship, loyalty, bravery, and action. These alienated young men formed Mussolini's paramilitary squads, whose members came to be known as Squadristi. Their parades and rallies, black-shirted uniforms, and nihilistic slogans vividly symbolized Italy's postwar crisis.

The Squadristi unleashed a reign of terror across the nation under the command of local Fascist chieftains. They launched "punitive expeditions" against socialist and trade union offices, urban strikers, and peasant protesters. By 1921 the antisocialist campaign was bringing Fascism financial backing from industrialists and landowners, and the liberal government took no steps to halt Fascist violence. Fascist assaults against city halls and provincial officials were followed by open threats to take over the state.

The March on Rome

While the Blackshirts' violent tactics weakened the Socialists and created the impression that Fascism possessed a strength beyond its numbers, Mussolini maintained the profile of a respectable politician. In 1921 he signed and then violated a peace pact with the PSI and converted the Fascist movement into the National Fascist party (PNF), which won 35 seats in Parliament. Mussolini now had the prestige of being a deputy. The Liberal premier, Giovanni Giolitti, hoped to co-opt the Fascists into the established order by luring Mussolini into a coalition of moderate and conservative parties. Like other liberals, Giolitti failed to understand that Fascism was not a conventional political force.

In 1922 Mussolini marched on Rome to frighten the government into conceding power to Fascism. Between

October 26 and 28, tens of thousands of Blackshirts moved toward the capital while Mussolini waited in Milan. The king, uncertain of the army's loyalty and fearful of civil war, refused to impose martial law. On October 29 he asked Mussolini to become prime minister. Mussolini arrived in Rome the following day, dressed in top hat and tails. Only then did the Blackshirts enter Rome, but now to cheer Mussolini before the royal palace. The liberal state had collapsed in the face of a bluff.

Mussolini took office by legal means, but with only 35 Fascist deputies in a chamber of more than 500, he moved cautiously. Over the next year and a half he assumed extensive authority, muzzled the press, and passed a new election law designed to ensure a Fascist majority in Parliament. According to this measure, the party that received the largest popular vote, with a minimum of 25 percent, would have two-thirds of the seats in the Chamber of Deputies. In 1924 the Fascists swept the elections by rigging the polls and intimidating opponents with violence, thus securing control of Parliament. Mussolini grew more confident when the army agreed to support the regime in return for the creation of a Fascist militia that would absorb the Blackshirts.

That summer the courageous Socialist leader Giacomo Matteotti (1885–1924), who had exposed the illegality of the Fascist electoral victory, was murdered by Fascist thugs. Popular reaction against Mussolini was so strong that he feared dismissal by the king. Opposition deputies withdrew in protest from the Chamber, and Blackshirt leaders pressured Mussolini to complete the seizure of power. In January 1925, in a forceful speech to Parliament, he assumed total responsibility and proclaimed the Fascist dictatorship. This speech was followed by a "second wave" of violence against the opposition. Over the next four years Mussolini created the first fascist regime in history.

Mussolini's Italy

In the aftermath of the Matteotti crisis, Mussolini laid the foundations of his totalitarian state. He abolished all political organizations except the Fascist party, censored the press, set up a political police force, instituted loyalty oaths for civil servants, created a military court to prosecute anti-Fascists, and secured power to rule by decree. Once Fascists were installed in key government posts, he sought a broad popular consensus.

On the surface Italy was still a parliamentary state with a monarch. The 1861 constitution remained in force, and Mussolini supposedly held office as prime minister at the pleasure of the king. Imposed above this system was the Fascist Grand Council, which in theory combined party and state functions. The council, appointed by Mussolini, selected candidates for election to the Chamber of Deputies and approved policy decisions. In 1939 this body was replaced by the Chamber of Fasci and Corporations, which represented trades and professions rather than parties. Traditional institutions therefore coexisted with new Fascist bodies, and the totalitarian state never fully superseded them.

Economic Policy

The Fascists established strong state control over the economy while preserving capitalism. Mussolini abolished the non-Fascist unions, prohibited strikes, and recognized the rights of industrial associations. In return, the industrialists supported his regime and dealt only with Fascist unions. Having abolished the economic rights of workers, Mussolini established the "corporate state" in the late 1920s by combining unions and employer associations into "corporations" for each major economic sector and industry. The corporate system was touted as an original form of economic organization in which state-supervised cooperation between capital and labor would replace class conflict. In reality, private business continued largely unhindered, and the corporate structure had little impact on economic life, except to control workers.

Mussolini failed to solve Italy's economic problems or temper the long-range effects of the Great Depression. Efforts to impose autarchy, or economic self-sufficiency, made matters worse. Marshlands were drained and cultivated, and farmers were coerced into growing more wheat and less of other crops. Nevertheless, overall agricultural production declined. Higher tariffs to stimulate industry increased consumer prices and shortages. Despite welfare programs and subsidies to large families, the standard of living of industrial and farm workers declined throughout the 1930s.

The Church and Fascism

Mussolini was more successful in relations with the Catholic church. Though an atheist, he understood the importance of Catholicism in Italian life and saw the church as a bulwark against communism. He thus ended the hostility that had existed between church and state since 1870, when the kingdom of Italy seized Rome from

Mussolini's Seizure of Power

In late 1924 Mussolini was accused by the opposition of having ordered a secret Fascist police force to assassinate socialist deputy Giacomo Matteotti. After weeks of hesitation, during which pressure from both his enemies and radical Fascist leaders mounted, he assumed full authority and declared a dictatorship in a speech on January 3, 1925.

It is I who in this chamber make accusations against myself. . . . If I had founded a secret police, I would have done so through the kind of violence that is an integral part of history. I have always said . . . that violence, to be effective, must be surgical, intelligent, and high-minded. . . .

I declare here, before the entire Chamber and before the Italian people, that I and I alone assume political, moral, and historical responsibility for everything that has happened.

If this surprising statement is sufficient to indict me, then bring forth the scaffolds! If Fascism has been only castor oil and clubs instead of the superb passion of Italy's best youth, the fault is mine. If Fascism has been a gang of criminals, then I am their leader.

If all the violence in this country has been the result of a special historical, moral, and political climate, I am responsible for that climate because I created it. . . .

When two elements are in inevitable conflict, the solution is force. History has never known another solution.

I tell you now that the problem will be solved. Fascism, the government, the party are all in working order.

You are all under an illusion. You believed that Fascism was finished because I compromised it, but this is not at all the case. Italy wants peace, tranquility, and calm labor. We will give it these things, with love if possible, but with force if necessary.

Rest assured that within the next twenty-four hours the situation will be clarified in every way.

Source: E. Susmel and D. Susmel, eds., *Opera omnia di Benito Mussolini,* vol. 21, trans. P. V. Cannistraro (Florence: La Fenice, 1953), pp. 235–241 passim.

the papacy. The Lateran Pacts of 1929 recognized the independence of Vatican City, which became a separate state within the city of Rome; anticlerical laws were repealed; Catholic youth groups were to be free from interference; the Vatican was to have its own newspaper and radio station; religious instruction in state schools became compulsory; and the government paid the Vatican an indemnity. The Lateran Pacts secured the church's cooperation and gave the regime a respectable image. Most important, Mussolini won the support of many devout Italians. Pope Pius XI (1922–1939) proclaimed him "the man sent to us by Providence."

Regimentation, Propaganda, and Art

The regimentation of life under Fascism affected both thought and behavior. Mussolini created a secret police agency (called OVRA), spied on anti-Fascists, and introduced a new penal code. Nevertheless, a variety of circumstances—Mussolini's penchant for compromise, a long tradition of Italian resistance to bureaucratic authority, and the more limited ideological goals of Fascism—combined to make his system of terror less severe than that in Nazi Germany or the Soviet Union.

Control of the media and cultural life was placed under the Ministry of Popular Culture. Young people were trained in the party's youth organization, which included separate groups for males and females aged 6 through 17. They provided military training, sports, and political indoctrination; by the mid-1930s they had over 3 million members. Leisure activities for workers and peasants were controlled through the party's Dopolavoro ("afterwork") organization. By 1940 the party, once an elite vanguard, had been opened to practically all Italians, many of whom viewed membership as a career necessity.

Although Mussolini's early movement had included several female Blackshirts, Fascism held a rigidly chauvinist attitude toward women, who were viewed exclusively as housewives and "mothers of the race." The Duce's highly publicized mistresses enhanced his reputation as a virile lover, and Fascists in general regarded women as objects to be "conquered" by men. The regime fostered conservative social values that reinforced traditional mores. The party trained young females to be wives and mothers, while state agencies provided maternity assistance, hygiene instruction, and child care information. Mussolini had supported giving the vote to women, but once in power he buried political equality. During the Fascist period the percentage of women making up the working population dropped as the depression affected both agriculture and industry.

The party glorified the leader. Mussolini was virtually deified as the farsighted "man of destiny." His skills as an orator, combined with his studied poses and facial expressions, captivated huge throngs. Slogans glorified the Duce and Fascist achievements: "Mussolini is always right," "A minute on the battlefield is worth a lifetime of peace," "Believe! Obey! Fight!"

In the mid-1930s the party introduced programs designed to alter Italian customs. Males were to be molded into the Fascist "new man"—obedient, virile, ruthless, efficient, and selfless. The military salute supplanted the handshake, black shirts were to be worn instead of business suits, and bourgeois pastimes such as golf and tennis were replaced with team sports. Many Italians privately scoffed at such measures, which were observed only superficially. The Fascists idealized imperial Rome as their inspiration, and Mussolini promised to create a new empire in which his people would recapture the Roman traditions of sacrifice and discipline. Mussolini was to be Italy's new Caesar.

With Mussolini in power, Margherita Sarfatti (1880–1961), his constant companion and adviser, emerged as the most influential woman in Italy. She wrote a regular art column and edited Mussolini's official monthly. An international array of prominent writers paid court at her salon in Rome, and she patronized intellectuals and painters, for whom she secured commissions and arranged exhibits.

Sarfatti advocated the "return to order"—the abandonment of abstractionism that had marked prewar artistic modernism—and supported painters who remained committed to a modern style while appreciating older Italian traditions, especially perspective, portraiture, and classical landscape painting. Sarfatti believed that this artistic transformation suited the Fascist emphasis on nationalist values and social order. In 1922 she

Margherita Sarfatti, Italian art critic and the author of a popular biography of Mussolini, was the Fascist dictator's lover and cultural mentor for 20 years. This photo was taken in 1931.

organized the artists whose work combined modernism and classical ideals into a movement called the Twentieth Century (*Novecento*) and persuaded Mussolini to inaugurate its first group exhibit. Until the early 1930s the movement came close to representing Fascism's official artistic style, and thus Mussolini's regime encouraged the kind of avant-garde culture that Hitler condemned as "decadent." In promoting the Twentieth Century, Sarfatti struggled against anti-intellectual Fascists who viewed modernism as a product of a corrupt civilization and wanted a "social realist" art that was little more than posterlike propaganda.

Rome, the Fascist Capital

With its ancient grandeur and rich archaeological remains, Rome was ideally suited for Mussolini's imperial dreams. Its history spanned 2,000 years. Rome's ancient ruins and monuments stood against medieval buildings, Renaissance palaces, and baroque churches. Fountains and squares provided relief from the winding, dark streets and bustling shopping districts.

Besides its role as a cultural center, Rome was a seat of government. After the collapse of the empire, the city became the site of the papacy and the Catholic church, later dominated by the Vatican and St. Peter's Basilica. When Rome became the capital of Italy in 1870, it began to assume its modern appearance. The influx of white-collar workers to staff the bureaucracy increased the size of the urban community significantly. Rome's population of 200,000 in 1870 doubled by the turn of the century, and by 1936 it had reached almost 1.2 million. During the reign of King Umberto I (1878–1900) the city underwent a construction boom to accommodate its growing population, and elaborately ornate Umbertine architecture took its place alongside older styles.

Like emperors and popes before him, Mussolini determined to redo Rome in order to accent its imperial past, thus making the city the capital of the new Fascist empire. He ordered archaeological excavations and the renovation of ancient sites. He demolished entire residential districts to build a grand concourse, the Via dell'-Impero ("Imperial Way"), running from the Colosseum along the Forum to the Piazza Venezia, where his office was located. On the walls of the Basilica of Maxentius he placed massive marble maps of the ancient Roman conquests, followed by one showing the Fascist domain. The Piazza Venezia, dominated by a huge monument to Victor Emmanuel II, was the core of Fascist Rome. From the balcony of the Palazzo Venezia, Mussolini harangued enormous crowds. He also gave the city a modern appearance by constructing monuments and buildings in a modernized classical style characteristic of the regime's taste in architecture. In the 1930s a new complex for the University of Rome was built, as was the Italic Forum, a stadium surrounded by statues of nude athletes to symbolize Fascism's emphasis on physical strength. After the Lateran Pacts of 1929, Mussolini again destroyed residential districts to build a wide boulevard from the Tiber River to St. Peter's.

By the end of the decade, plans had been laid for a new minicity in the suburbs between Rome and the ancient port of Ostia. Here modern public buildings were designed in the Fascist style for a world's fair in 1942, but the coming of World War II ended the project.

The Anti-Fascist Opposition

In spite of the enthusiasm Mussolini engendered, many Italians opposed Fascism. Mussolini's enemies came from all political parties and all walks of life. By 1926 most of the well-known anti-Fascists who escaped Blackshirt brutality had been forced into exile, where they established groups with such names as Justice and Liberty. In the early 1930s an underground Communist network had been set up in Italy and, together with Justice and Liberty, kept the hope of freedom alive while refuting Fascist propaganda. Mussolini's irresponsible foreign adventures gave anti-Fascism an added impetus, and his anti-Semitic laws alienated many Italians, who regarded the small Jewish population of 50,000 as loyal and productive. The degree to which Italians were repelled by Mussolini's anti-Semitic policies reflected their humanist traditions.

Germany: From Weimar to Hitler

Nazism, the German variety of fascism, developed after Mussolini founded his Fascist group, but it took more than a decade longer to come to power. Outwardly, the two movements appeared to be almost identical—radical parties with ideologies inspired by elements of socialism, syndicalism, and nationalism; the cult of the charismatic leader; a rank-and-file membership consisting largely of the lower middle class and veterans disaffected by the postwar crisis; a paramilitary organization with uniforms, slogans, and a philosophy of violence; resentment toward capitalists and hatred for the communists; and a revolutionary determination to destroy parliamentary government.

Despite these similarities, the Nazi regime was generally acknowledged to have been more totalitarian than Mussolini's system. The racial component in Nazi ideology represented a major difference between the two movements and in part explains the greater brutality of the Third Reich. In its early stages, Mussolini's cabinet included several Jewish ministers, a situation inconceivable in Nazi Germany, and his mistress for almost 20 years, Margherita Sarfatti, was a Jew. During the 1920s Hitler had regarded Mussolini as a mentor, the elder statesman of international fascism; after the Nazi takeover in Germany, however, Hitler emerged as the senior partner in what became known as the Rome-Berlin Axis. This change reflected the disparity between the industrial and military capacities of Italy and Germany.

Revolution and the Weimar Republic

The military collapse of 1918 had a profound impact on Germany. Revolutionary unrest erupted, and worker and soldiers' councils similar to those in Russia were formed. On November 8, communists in Munich set up a separate Republic of Bavaria that was put down only after a civil war between rightists and leftists. When Kaiser William II abdicated on November 9 and his chancellor resigned, the government was placed provisionally in the hands of Friedrich Ebert and Philipp Scheidemann, both moderate Social Democrats. That same afternoon Scheidemann proclaimed a republic with Ebert as its first chancellor. Extremists on both the left and the right, however, attempted to seize power. To maintain order, Ebert offered the German high command guarantees of protection if the army remained loyal. Revolutionary Marxists, known as Spartacists (after the Thracian gladiator Spartacus, who led a slave uprising against Rome in 73 B.C.), revolted in 1919 under the leadership of Rosa Luxemburg and Karl Liebknecht. During "Spartacist Week" (January 6–15) they battled the government in the streets of Berlin. Luxemburg and Liebknecht were killed by soldiers sent to arrest them. The government also turned for support to private military groups known as the Free Corps, headed by embittered former officers and armed veterans. The Free Corps, from which would come many of the early adherents to the Nazi movement, would eventually turn against the government itself.

After the Spartacist revolt, an array of moderate political parties—the largest of which were the Social Democrats, the Catholic Center party, and the Democrats—met in the National Assembly at Weimar to draft a new constitution. This document (adopted in July 1919), which created the German Republic, reflected progressive social ideas and democratic principles. It provided for universal suffrage, a cabinet system of government with an elected president and an appointed chancellor, and a bill of rights that guaranteed civil liberties, education, and employment.

Although the so-called Weimar Republic was one of the most liberal governments in Europe, it was burdened from the start with serious problems. In March 1920, militarists led by Wolfgang Kapp attempted a putsch, or coup, by marching on Berlin. Kapp's putsch was suppressed by a socialist-led general strike. In the first election under the new constitution, held three months later, the three-party centrist coalition that had dominated the National Assembly fell from 76 to 47 percent of the popular vote, while the parties on the extreme right and left almost doubled their support. Moderate forces never again regained a majority, and the 13 years of the Weimar government produced 20 different cabinets. The German people looked on the republic with suspicion, especially since the Allies had forced the kaiser to abdicate. Rightist and leftist extremists regarded the

regime as an enemy and plotted against it. Although the army had agreed to protect the government, its high command was uncomfortable with the democratic system and blamed the republic for the humiliating Treaty of Versailles.

Germans found it difficult to understand how their country, once an industrial giant with the best army in the world, could have lost the war. Moreover, they resented the fact that the Allies had forced them to accept total responsibility for the war. Right-wing extremists, monarchists, and army officers manufactured the legend that Germany had been "stabbed in the back" by traitors, whom they identified as Marxists and Jews. Reactionaries pointed to the helpless new republic, shorn of its army, as a symptom of decadence. Extremists assassinated two progressive ministers—Matthias Erzberger in August 1921 and Walther Rathenau a year later.

The economic problems that beset postwar Germany fueled the feeling that the Weimar Republic was too weak to rule. The government responded to the severe unemployment that struck the country by printing huge quantities of paper currency to finance assistance programs and prevent massive starvation. The resulting inflation devastated much of the middle class, a condition exacerbated by the French occupation of the Ruhr valley in 1923. The German mark, worth about 12 U.S. cents at the end of the war, was now virtually worthless—German shoppers paid for a loaf of bread or a newspaper with sacks of currency. The almost daily rise in the cost of living left salaries far behind, and people on fixed incomes—pensioners, widows, disabled veterans—were virtually wiped out. By 1925 inflation had destroyed 50 percent of the capital of the lower middle class, more than half a million of whom were forced into factory work. The devastating economic collapse caused widespread despair and further undermined public confidence in the republic.

Adolf Hitler and the Rise of Nazism

Adolf Hitler, the founder of the Nazi movement, was born in 1889 in Braunau, Austria, near the Bavarian border. His father, a minor customs official, was unsympathetic to his son's aesthetic leanings, and the young Hitler was always much closer to his mother. Frustrated by his desire to be an artist, he did poorly in his studies and never graduated from high school. In Vienna, where Hitler lived between 1908 and 1913, he evolved his theories of history, politics, and racism. He lived a harsh, bohemian existence, working odd jobs and earning money

Hitler's Architectural Megalomania

Beginning in 1936, Hitler planned to completely redesign Berlin as the capital of the Nazi world empire. At the center of the new city was to be a huge triumphal arch, five hundred and fifty feet wide and three hundred and eighty-six feet high, as well as a gigantic domed hall that would be many times the size of Rome's St. Peter's Basilica. Here, Albert Speer, the official Nazi architect, explains Hitler's obsession with the monumental buildings he craved.

This love for vast proportions was not only tied up with the totalitarian cast of Hitler's regime. Such tendencies, and the urge to demonstrate one's strength on all occasions, are characteristic of quickly acquired wealth. . . .

Hitler's demand for huge dimensions, however, involved more than he was willing to admit to the workers. He wanted the biggest of everything to glorify his works and magnify his pride. These monuments were an assertion of his claim to world domination. . . .

Designs of such scale naturally indicate a kind of chronic megalomania, which is reason enough to dwell on these grandiose plans. . . . Perhaps it was less their size than the way they violated the human scale that made them abnormal. . . .

[The domed hall], the greatest assembly hall in the world ever conceived up to that time, consisted of one vast hall that could hold between one hundred fifty and one hundred eighty thousand persons standing. . . . The hall was essentially a place of worship. The idea was that . . . it would acquire an importance similar to that St. Peter's in Rome has for Catholic Christendom. Without some such essentially pseudoreligious background the expenditure for Hitler's central building would have been pointless and incomprehensible.

Source: Albert Speer, *Inside the Third Reich: Memoirs,* trans. R. Winston and C. Winston (New York: Macmillan, 1970), pp. 81–82, 165–166, 183.

by painting watercolors and postcards. Although he developed some skill as a draftsman, his ambitions were frustrated when he was refused admission to the Vienna School of Architecture.

Hitler absorbed a muddle of ideas and attitudes that ultimately formed the basis of Nazi ideology. Racism, in particular anti-Semitism, had the most powerful impact on him. Vienna's population reflected the mixed ethnic composition of the Austro-Hungarian Empire, and in the late nineteenth century Karl Lüger and Georg von Schönerer channeled Austria's anti-Semitic traditions into political movements. Lüger was the dominant figure in the Christian Socialist party, a Catholic organization supported by reactionary conservatives who elected him mayor of Vienna on an anti-Semitic platform. Schönerer, leader of the lower-middle-class Liberal party and a member of the Austrian parliament, organized student clubs in Vienna on the basis of anti-Semitism and

generated widespread worker support for a campaign against the alleged influence of Jewish bankers in the imperial government. Moreover, he believed that the "superior" German race should rule over the "inferior" Slavs of central and eastern Europe—Czechs, Serbs, Poles, and others.

Under the influence of these sources, Hitler became obsessed with the idea of race. He came to see Judaism and Marxism as twin forms of degeneracy and to identify the Jews as the principal source of moral and cultural decline in Europe. From Schönerer's pan-German ideology he concluded that Germany and Austria must be united into a "greater Germany," while Lüger's political success suggested that the key to a radical movement was the ability to generate and channel the enthusiasm of the masses.

When World War I broke out, Hitler volunteered in the Bavarian infantry, for he considered himself a Ger-

As unemployment and inflation mounted in postwar Berlin, scenes of poverty became painfully familiar. Here Berliners sell tin cans for scrap during the severe inflation of 1923.

man. He fought at the front, was promoted to corporal, and was twice awarded the Iron Cross. The end of the war found him recuperating in a hospital from the effects of poison gas.

At the end of World War I, Hitler worked in Munich as a political informant for the army. In this capacity he joined a small group known as the German Workers' party, one of many such organizations that sought to stimulate German patriotism and infuse the working class with the spirit of nationalism. Hitler spent the next five years developing his political talents and leadership within the party. Like Mussolini, he had a natural oratorical ability and spoke frequently in public, expounding the views he had evolved in Vienna. He was unimpressive in appearance, yet he projected a personal magnetism that gripped a nation. To a far greater degree than Mussolini, Hitler had an uncanny ability to sway the masses and evoke worship. These qualities enabled the Nazi Führer ("leader") to convert his small group into a mass party.

In 1920 the German Workers' party was renamed the National Socialist German Workers' party (NS-DAP), shortened in popular usage to "Nazi." It acquired its own newspaper, and its 25-point program called for a Greater Germany incorporating all German-speaking peoples, annulment of the Treaty of Versailles, denial of citizenship to Jews, and socioeconomic reforms to benefit the workers and the middle class. Although Hitler himself regarded the socialist provisions as propaganda,

some Nazi leaders, such as Gregor and Otto Strasser, took them seriously.

The party also developed a paramilitary wing of storm troopers called the *Sturmabteilung* (SA), with its brown shirts, outstretched-arm salute, "Heil Hitler!" and swastika symbol. Rallies, marches, songs, and banners were incorporated in techniques that Hitler's propaganda machine later developed on a massive scale. The SA membership, like that of Mussolini's Blackshirt squads, consisted of disaffected veterans and Free Corps volunteers, rootless young men, and thugs and criminals. Ernst Röhm, the SA leader, believed that violence and terror would bring about the Nazi revolution.

In 1923 Hitler determined to seize power by force. Inspired by Mussolini's march on Rome, he planned a putsch in Munich with the connivance of local officials and the backing of a popular World War I general, Erich Ludendorff. On the evening of November 8 the Brownshirts surrounded a beer hall in which a political meeting was scheduled. The putsch ended in fiasco the next day as the police scattered the participants and arrested Hitler. The abortive revolt brought Hitler a five-year prison term, of which he served less than nine months. In jail he wrote his famous testament *Mein Kampf* ("My Struggle"), outlining his racial theories, domestic policies, and plans for world conquest. He also concluded that the Nazi conquest of Germany must combine legal electoral methods with violence.

Nazism: The Philosophy of Domination

The Nazis viewed life—and therefore history—as a Darwinian struggle for existence in which the fittest triumphed over the weak. Hitler's call for German rearmament was therefore only the first step in a plan for world domination. Hitler preached his brutal message in a speech in Munich on March 15, 1929.

If men wish to live, then they are forced to kill others. The entire struggle for survival is a conquest of the means of existence which in turn results in the elimination of others from these same sources of subsistence. As long as there are peoples on this earth, there will be nations against nations. . . .

There is in reality no distinction between peace and war. Life, no matter in what form, is a process which always leads to the same result. Self-preservation will always be the goal of every individual. Struggle is ever-present and will remain. This signifies a consistent willingness on the part of man to sacrifice to the utmost. Weapons, methods, instruments, formations, these may change, but in the end the struggle for survival remains. . . .

One is either the hammer or the anvil. We confess that it is our purpose to prepare the German people again for the role of the hammer. For ten years we have preached, and our deepest concern is: How can we again achieve power? We admit freely and openly that, if our Movement is victorious, we will be concerned day and night with the question of how to produce the armed forces which are forbidden us by the peace treaty. We solemnly confess that we consider everyone a scoundrel who does not try day and night to figure out a way to violate this treaty, for we have never recognized this treaty. . . .

We confess further that we will dash anyone to pieces who should dare to hinder us in this undertaking. . . . Our rights will never be represented by others. Our rights will be protected only when the German Reich is again supported by the point of the German dagger.

Source: G. W. Prange, ed., *Hitler's Words* (Washington, D.C.: American Council on Public Affairs, 1944), pp. 10–11.

After the Munich failure, Röhm attempted to wrest control of the Nazi movement from Hitler. Röhm saw the SA as the instrument for the conquest of the state and the party. But in Hitler, who wanted to subordinate the SA to the party, Röhm met his match in duplicity. Using murder, blackmail, and slander to reassert his position, Hitler defeated Röhm, who went into exile in Bolivia in 1925. Hitler had become the undisputed leader of the movement.

The inner core of the Nazi leadership, attached to Hitler by loyalty and fear, began to take shape. The hierarchy included the gluttonous Hermann Göring, future air marshal; the tireless party organizer Rudolf Hess; the brilliant propagandist Josef Goebbels; the rabid ideologue Alfred Rosenberg; and the chilling technocrat of police terror, Heinrich Himmler. The party also developed its organizational apparatus, creating youth groups and the infamous *Schutzstaffel* (SS), an elite defense corps later used in the mass exterminations of World War II. In 1929 Himmler took control of the SS and turned it into one of the principal instruments of Hitler's power. The black uniforms and death's-head insignia of the SS became synonymous with the Nazi terror state.

Weimar Culture

German cultural life between 1919 and 1933 was marked by a feverish brilliance. In theater, cinema, art, architecture, and literature, Germany exploded with a creative energy that was at once modern, experimental, and tormented. Berlin, with a population of more than two million, emerged as the center of Weimar's cultural ferment. War and defeat had combined to transform the grim solemnity that had once marked Germany's capital into an irreverent spirit that made the city a mecca for young, talented Germans in search of a faster-paced, modern life. By the early 1920s restaurants, bathhouses, dance halls, and nightclubs—including the dozens of gay and lesbian bars described by British writer Christopher Isherwood in his *Berlin Stories*—gave the city a rowdy allure that rivaled even the attractions of Paris. American jazz became the rage, and the iconoclastic atmosphere also gave rise to a peculiar Berlin institution, cabarets in which political and social satire took the form of musical comedy. The air of unreality became starker in the aftermath of the terrible inflation that struck in 1923 and put a quarter of a million Berliners out of work.

No artist better symbolized Germany's postwar culture than George Grosz (1893–1959). After being court-martialed from the army for insubordination, Grosz went to Berlin, where he joined in succession the Dada movement, the Expressionists, and the Spartacists. Inspired by the bitter irony he saw in the cabarets, Grosz' political drawings satirized fat industrialists, militarists, and corrupt politicians and assaulted bourgeois morality. Grosz detested the Nazis and in 1923 executed a star-

The brilliant artist George Grosz made a series of drawings depicting the military and bourgeois influences on German society in the 1920s.

tlingly prescient drawing of a monocled officer with a swastika, the first of many anti-Nazi works depicting storm troopers and other symbols of the political reaction stalking Germany.

Grosz' counterpart in theater was Bertolt Brecht (1898–1956), whose plays and poems explored the agony of human isolation and the dilemma of moral and political commitment. A pacifist repelled by the horrors of World War I, Brecht's first critical success came in 1922 with a play titled *Spartacus* (later renamed *Drums in the Night*), about a veteran who chose a comfortable life instead of joining the Spartacist uprising.

In 1924 Brecht moved to Berlin, where the theatrical producer Max Reinhardt and the composer Kurt Weill recognized his genius. In his plays as in his personal life, he struggled to detach himself from the irrationality of violence, sex, and aggression and strove to understand how modern society transformed individuals into groups. In *Man Is Man* (1927) he described how a worker had been changed into a bloodthirsty soldier.

After 1929 Brecht's work revealed a growing commitment to Marxism. *The Three-Penny Opera* (1928) expressed his cynical distaste for bourgeois materialism by taunting his audiences for their gluttonous appetites and lack of ethical values. Under growing Communist influence, Brecht shifted to an austere didactic style. His controlled language and aesthetic precision urged self-discipline and self-denial in the interests of humanity—he was, he said, interested in the ideas his characters represented rather than in the characters themselves. These influences led him to the development of the Epic Theater, in which plays were conceived on a grand scale and the audience kept at a distance through the use of signs, posters, and light.

In 1932 his full-length play *St. Joan of the Stockyards*—based in part on Upton Sinclair's novel *The Jungle*—depicted the Great Depression as the story of greedy speculation in the Chicago stock market. Despite his Marxism, Brecht never made himself a blind servant of party discipline. *The Measures Adopted* (1930) brought criticism from German Communist officials because it depicted the murder of a young comrade by party militants. Brecht refused to dramatize revolutionary events, believing that to use the theater for political purposes was to undermine its revolutionary fervor.

Darker forces began to encircle Brecht in the early 1930s. The creative genius that had given Berlin's cultural life its brilliance seemed unreal in the midst of the Great Depression, which by 1932 had raised unemployment in the city to 636,000. The contrast between Berlin's cabaret culture and Germany's political realities grew sharper as Hitler's storm troopers spread violence and bloodshed. Brecht left Berlin in 1933, eventually emigrating to the United States.

The Nazi Seizure of Power

At first the Nazi party's electoral prospects were not promising. When the economy began to recover in 1924, political instability seemed to abate. The next year the country elected a new president, the revered Field Marshal Paul von Hindenburg (1847–1934), who provided middle-class Germans with a sense of security. Although Nazi membership increased from 27,000 in 1925 to 178,000 in 1929, the number of Nazi deputies in the Reichstag fell from 32 to 12. By the end of the decade the future of National Socialism was by no means clear. The Great Depression created the mass base Hitler needed to seize power.

By 1932, German production had fallen by 39 percent and unemployment hit almost 6 million. The economic collapse encouraged extremist movements. Although other factors enhanced the appeal of Nazism, the hardship and fear generated by the crisis produced the ideal environment for Nazi success. The depression po-

larized German politics. In parliamentary elections held between 1929 and 1932, Nazi representation rose to 230 seats, while the Communist delegation increased from 54 to 89. Moderate elements were pushed aside as these two sworn enemies battled physically and verbally. When the 85-year-old Hindenburg decided to run for a second term as president in 1932, Hitler and Communist leader Ernst Thälmann opposed him. Hindenburg and Hitler faced each other in a runoff, but although the now senile field marshal won, Hitler had received more than 13 million votes. The Nazis slipped to 196 seats in the November 1932 elections as the Communists raised their total to 100, encouraging some people to believe that the radical left would assume control of the government.

Hitler's followers urged him to seize power in a coup d'état, while conservative antidemocratic forces—aristocratic landowners, army officers, industrialists, wealthy merchants, and financiers—were both terrified at the prospect of a Communist victory and attracted to Hitler's nationalist slogans. Hoping to manipulate him to stem mass discontent and advance their own interests, some began supplying funds to the Nazis.

On January 30, 1933, Hindenburg, fearful of civil war and pressured by his advisers, appointed Hitler chancellor of the German Republic. Hitler promptly dissolved the Reichstag and called for new elections. When the parliament building was destroyed in a fire of unknown origin, the Nazis blamed the Communists and conducted the balloting in an atmosphere of anti-Communist hysteria and intimidation. Although the Nazis won only 44 percent of the vote, support from extreme nationalists added another 8 percent to give the coalition a legislative majority. Declaring a national emergency, Hitler expelled the Communist deputies from the Reichstag, which then voted him dictatorial powers for four years. After using this authority to outlaw all other political parties, he completed the transition to dictatorship when he combined the office of president with that of chancellor following the death of Hindenburg in August 1934. Hitler destroyed the shortlived Weimar Republic and became the unchallenged ruler of a Germany that was anxious to restore its economy and regain its place in international affairs.

Nazi Germany

With great self-assurance and clear policies already formulated, Hitler embarked on a total reshaping of German life, thereby establishing the second—and even more brutal—fascist totalitarian state in Europe.

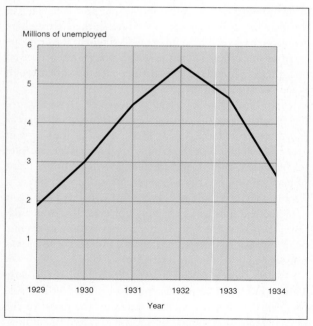

FIGURE 38.1 UNEMPLOYMENT IN GERMANY, 1929–1934

The Nazi State

Hitler created new political and administrative systems. The former states of the German Republic, such as Prussia and Bavaria, were abolished, and a highly centralized government replaced the federal structure established in 1871. Hitler christened his new regime the Third Reich and proclaimed that it would last 1,000 years. He was the Führer, the supreme commander who embodied the sovereignty of his nation. Nazi party members replaced high-ranking officials in the central and local bureaucracies. The party itself was reorganized so that local leaders occupied positions equivalent to their bureaucratic counterparts in government. Although the Reichstag remained intact, it served only to provide Hitler with a forum for public declarations and the legitimation of Nazi programs.

The new German legal system also conformed to Nazi philosophy. Law was defined as the will of the German people acting in the interests of the state and its Führer. "People's courts" replaced the regular judicial system to dispense Nazi justice arbitrarily. To enforce compliance, Hitler established a secret political police—the dreaded Gestapo—and, six months after the Nazi seizure of power, concentration camps—the first one was at Dachau, outside Munich—to hold political prisoners. Under the command of SS leader Heinrich Himmler (1900–1945), ten or more such centers were built in Germany. Prisoners were used as slave labor, while others were beaten, tortured, or starved to death. Medical personnel performed fiendish experiments on living inmates. The Nazi state deliberately abandoned all traditional moral values.

Hitler was cautious in dealing with the armed forces. The officer corps, drawn largely from the elite of Prussian society, had been a powerful and independent force in German life. The generals regarded Hitler and his followers as rabble-rousers who could be cast aside once they had generated a renewed sense of patriotism and crushed the Communist threat. Hitler brought the generals under his control by compromising his own movement and agreeing to preserve the army's independence.

In 1930 Hitler had persuaded Ernst Röhm, the exiled leader of the SA, to return to Germany and resume command of the Brownshirts. After Hitler became chancellor, Röhm pressed him to eliminate the regular army and turn the SA into a revolutionary people's force. But Hitler needed the army both to consolidate his power and to realize his larger plans for world power. In April 1934 he cut a deal with the officer corps: it would support his policies in exchange for the elimination of the SA. The result was a dramatic demonstration of Hitler's ruthlessness. On June 30—the "Night of the Long Knives"—Hitler unleashed a bloody purge of the SA in which Röhm, scores of his associates, and most of Hitler's political enemies were murdered.

Economic Policy

To pull Germany out of the depression and make it economically self-sufficient, Hitler launched extensive public works programs that changed the appearance of Germany through reforestation, swamp drainage, and the construction of superhighways and housing. Farmers received subsidies and protection against debt foreclosure.

Seamstresses sew Nazi flags in 1933.

To avoid dependence on imported raw materials, German scientists developed artificial rubber, plastics, synthetic textiles, and other substitute products.

While unemployment virtually disappeared and living standards began to rise, both employers and workers lost much of their economic freedom. Strength Through Joy, an organization similar to Mussolini's Dopolavoro, offered low-income citizens entertainment, vacations, and travel. Industry and commerce remained privately owned but were placed under strict government control. In 1936 Hitler proclaimed the first of two 4-year plans that regimented economic life, including wages, profits, and production decisions. Business and professional associations became arms of the Nazi economic system, and independent labor unions were replaced with the National Labor Front, in which membership was compulsory. Strikes were prohibited, and all labor relations were regulated by the state. Hitler's economic policies and rearmament program did pull Germany out of the worst aspects of the depression, restoring relatively full employment. Yet workers paid a heavy price—the loss of their liberty and a devastating war.

Society and Culture

State coordination also affected social and cultural affairs. Conscious of the need for future soldiers and workers, Hitler promoted the enlargement of German families through a rising birthrate and improved health care. Some 20 percent of Nazi party members were women in the early 1920s, but once in power, Nazi ideologists, like the Fascists in Italy, limited the role of women in national life. In *Mein Kampf,* Hitler had written that for women "the chief emphasis must be on physical training, and only subsequently on the promotion of spiritual and intellectual values. The goal of female education must invariably be the future mother." Official propaganda projected women as symbols of Germanic female virtue in contrast to the warrior image of men.

Nazi women were generally enthusiastic about restoring traditional social values, and Hitler established a large corps of female officials to organize women in local communities. After 1937, when he began to prepare for war, women were encouraged to work in industry, agriculture, and the service sector.

For males Hitler removed many of the social barriers that had previously limited economic or political opportunities. Most middle-class citizens perceived the Nazi regime as a promoter and guardian of this social transformation.

Organized religion posed a challenge to the new order and hence came under growing pressure to accept government control. Catholic and Protestant clergy were prohibited from criticizing official policies and found it difficult to maintain ties with churches outside Germany. The state discouraged children from attending religious schools while supporting the revival of anti-Christian movements that worshiped ancient Teutonic gods.

The cultural sphere drew special attention as a means both to promote the cult of the Führer and to construct the Nazi world view. Under the vigilance of the minister of propaganda, Josef Goebbels (1897–1945), every facet of intellectual and artistic life was harnessed to generate enthusiasm for Nazi doctrine and its leader.

A group of young Nazis confiscating books to be taken to the Operplatz in Berlin for burning in May 1933.

Publishing houses came under the control of the government, which eliminated all literature not conforming to officially endorsed ideas; "offensive" books were publicly burned. The government assigned themes to writers, artists, architects, and musicians. As in Fascist Italy, sports were seen as a physical demonstration of Nazi virtues. Radio and film, whose potential for shaping mass opinion was immense, were perhaps Goebbels' most powerful propaganda weapons. Leni Riefenstahl, a talented film director, won international acclaim for the seductive power of her visual imagery in such documentary films as *Triumph of the Will* (1935).

Hitler took a keen interest in art and architecture. Viewing modern styles as alien to the "Germanic spirit," he dismissed modern-minded artists and museum curators and in 1935 regimented artists under Nazi party orders. In his inaugural address at the opening of the House of German Art in Munich in 1937, Hitler denounced Impressionism, Futurism, and Cubism as Jewish-inspired "cultural bolshevism." He demanded an art that reflected German values. To illustrate the "depravity" of modernism, the government set up a permanent Exhibition of Degenerate Art. Nazi painting and sculpture reflected a Romantic hero worship inspired by the themes of Nordic mythology made famous by Wagner's operas. This official art lacked originality or creative expression, let alone aesthetic value. Instead, it glorified the Führer as a Germanic warrior, extolled the concept of "blood and soil," idealized the image of mothers and children, and depicted muscle-bound nudes as the embodiment of German strength. The Nazis also attacked modern architecture, closing down the Bauhaus and driving its architects out of Germany. Hitler and his architectural consultant Albert Speer planned to erect in Berlin monumental buildings designed in a pseudo-Greek classicism that would make the city the world capital of the Third Reich.

Underpinning all these efforts was the educational system. Schools and universities underwent a thorough reconstruction of their curricula and faculties to ensure that all students received indoctrination and only carefully screened information. The Nazi party formed a comprehensive youth movement—the Hitlerjugend, or Hitler Youth—that reinforced intellectual, psychological, and political conformity.

Hitler and the Jews

The ultimate horror of the Nazi regime began to reveal itself soon after Hitler came to power. More than any other authoritarian or totalitarian movement, National Socialism was based on racial and ethnic hatred. Nazi ideologues considered the Germans a superior race who deserved to be masters over such "undesirables" as Slavs, gypsies, and Latins. But Hitler, whose anti-Semitism had been formed during his Vienna days, reserved his special animosity for the Jews, whose persecution and ultimate annihilation became his obsession.

Hitler swiftly launched a campaign of official persecution against the Jews. In April 1933 the government barred Jews from the civil service, while racial laws forbade them to study or teach in the universities or to practice medicine, law, and other professions. In 1935 the notorious Nuremberg Laws deprived Jews of all civil rights, including the freedom to marry non-Jews. A campaign of terror against German Jewry followed. "Jewish" became the characteristic term of official disapproval for everything considered negative in Nazi eyes—democracy, communism, liberalism, or individual rights.

As the anti-Semitic drive intensified, thousands of Jews fled Germany. The assassination of a German diplomat in Paris by a young Polish Jew in 1938 was the pretext for the infamous *Kristallnacht* ("Night of Broken

A stylized realism characterized much official art in the Third Reich, as in this depiction of an example of the brave, dedicated young people of Germany by Anton Hackenbroich titled New Youth.

Glass"), a coordinated wave of violence that destroyed Jewish homes, businesses, and synagogues and took many lives; later the Jews were heavily assessed to pay for the damage. The Western democracies, unwilling to assume the burden of caring for millions of refugees, refused to accept mass Jewish immigration. Although some international protests were lodged against these outrages, most Germans accepted them.

The Jews still in Germany now found it virtually impossible to leave, having become hostages for whom the worst horrors still lay ahead. Nazi anti-Semitism drew on a long tradition of persecution, prejudice, and superstition, but the Nazis went far beyond that tradition in imposing the domination of the German "master race" on the "inferior" peoples of Europe. During World War II the fate of Germany's Jews would be tied to that of Jews throughout the Continent as Hitler drove anti-Semitism to its ultimate conclusion: the methodical extermination of European Jewry.

Fascism as a World Phenomenon

To many Europeans the postwar world seemed to be rapidly dividing into two antagonistic systems, communism and fascism. In Europe a struggle unfolded between left and right, between "revolution" and "reaction," that polarized around these extreme ideologies. No European nation escaped the trauma of ideological divisiveness or the specter of fascist radicalism. Societies as advanced as Britain's and as underdeveloped as Romania's experienced their own peculiar brands of fascism: in each state, segments of the population looked to extreme solutions for seemingly unmanageable problems.

Varieties of European Fascism

In France and Britain fascism was not a genuine threat to the established order, for right-wing movements failed to establish a mass base. But France produced fascistlike political groups, some of which modeled themselves after Mussolini's or Hitler's example, that challenged the country's democratic traditions. During the depression the Parti Populaire Français (French People's party) had perhaps as many as a half million members, but it was unable to unify the right. France also produced more traditional conservative movements that capitalized on nationalism and adopted antidemocratic, anti-Semitic principles.

In Britain, where Mussolini was a popular figure in the 1920s, fascist organizations were also established. In the early 1930s the wealthy aristocrat Sir Oswald Mosley founded the British Union of Fascists. An admirer of

Mussolini, Mosley modeled his union on the Blackshirts. Like Hitler, to whom he gravitated after 1933, Mosley dreamed of a Greater Britain in which all citizens were integrated into a regimented society to revive national glory. Mosley's advocacy of political violence resulted in the outlawing of the movement, and during World War II he was imprisoned.

In Spain, where the struggle between right and left was largely the result of a government unable to solve national problems, a military dictatorship under Miguel Primo de Rivera (1870–1930) emerged after 1923. His son, José António Primo de Rivera, founded a fascist movement called the Falange. In the mid–1930s Spain became the bloody battleground in the conflict between communism and fascism. The Spanish civil war was marked by the military intervention of Hitler and Mussolini on the fascist side as well as that of the Soviet Union on the side of the republican government and ended with the installation of the dictatorship of General Francisco Franco.

In Belgium, a nation bitterly divided between Dutch- and French-speaking ethnic groups, the Rexist movement of Léon Degrelle aimed at national unification in a spiritual and racial sense. A different form of fascism developed in Romania, an agrarian society with a strong Orthodox tradition rooted in peasant society. There Corneliu Codreanu's Iron Guard movement appealed to the traditional associations of soil and religion. In Austria two armed organizations, the urban Social Democratic Schutzbund (Alliance for Defense) and the rural Christian Socialist Heimwehr (Home Guard), vied with each other and with the Austrian Nazi party. Led by Prince von Starhemberg, the reactionary Heimwehr opposed democracy as bitterly as it did Hitler's attempts to Nazify the country. Under the Austrian chancellor, Engelbert Dollfuss, the Heimwehr was given representation in the government, which forged the Fatherland Front to block the union (*Anschluss*) of Austria and Germany. These movements, together with the Nazis, gained ground with the assassination of Dollfuss in 1934.

Fascism in Asia

Mussolini had predicted that fascism would be the dominant political philosophy of the twentieth century, and admirers of fascism were to be found the world over. Demagogues who modeled themselves after Mussolini and Hitler were so popular in the United States that Anne Morrow Lindbergh, wife of the famous aviator Charles Lindbergh, spoke of fascism as "the wave of the future." In India and the Arab countries of the Middle East some nationalist leaders gravitated to fascism in the hope that it would lead to independence from colonial rule. Fascist influence may even have inspired a group of radical army officers in China to establish the so-called Blue Shirts (more properly, the "Cotton Cloth People"), although their militaristic, authoritarian program was little more than a variant of the nation-building doctrine of the Kuomintang regime of Chiang Kai-shek.

In Japan, as early as 1934 Marxist writers identified the authoritarian, militaristic, expansionist tendencies of the country as a form of fascism. The code of the samurai and emperor worship suggest that the roots of a native fascism were to be found in Japanese history. Young army officers and small ultranationalist groups pressed for radical changes in politics and the economy, and the leading nationalist ideologue of the period, Kita Ikki (1883–1937), seemed to be a Japanese counterpart of Mussolini. Kita was a former Marxist socialist who called for nationalization of some industries, state regulation of the economy, authoritarian government under the emperor, and the creation of a greater East Asian empire. None of the Japanese groups became a significant movement capable of seizing power, and Japan's constitution and political system remained largely unchanged. After Kita Ikki and some of his followers staged a revolt in Tokyo in 1936, they were executed. The continuity of Japan's political and cultural traditions proved stronger and more entrenched than the new fascistlike ferment. Moreover, the military aggression of the 1930s was not due to an indigenous Japanese fascism but was rather the result of a broad nationalist consensus in favor of expansion among Japan's traditional political and military leaders.

Brazil's Estado Novo

In Latin America fascistlike military dictatorships were widespread in the years between the wars. The rule of Getulio Vargas (1883–1954) in Brazil offers the best example of a regime strongly influenced by European fascism but shaped largely by local conditions.

The Brazilian republic, founded by the military in 1889 after the overthrow of Emperor Dom Pedro II, had proved itself unable to deal with problems of national development. The central government, representing a federation of autonomous states, was undermined by regionalism and the power of local bosses. Because the agrarian economy rested largely on coffee production, the conservative plantation owners dominated Brazil's society and its politics. Poverty and illiteracy afflicted the rural population, and the government repressed the labor movement. Only the small Brazilian middle class, represented chiefly by intellectuals and a group of young military officers known as the *tenentes*, wanted industrialization and agrarian reform.

The Great Depression, which ruined the coffee market and made it impossible for the government to repay its staggering foreign debts, brought down the republic. In October 1930 a military coup put Vargas in power as provisional president. He was to rule Brazil, with one interruption, for almost 20 years. Vargas came from a wealthy ranching family and had run unsuccessfully for president. A shrewd leader, his enemies denounced him as an unprincipled dictator while his followers revered him as the "father of the poor."

Vargas tried to create worker consensus through labor legislation and government-controlled unions while simultaneously encouraging the development of a strong middle class. He diversified agriculture, limited coffee production, and extended tax incentives and government loans to business. Like Mussolini, Vargas expanded his personal power by balancing the conflicting economic and political interests that dominated the country. The left-wing *tenentes* pushed for basic reforms, while the conservatives, resenting his centralization efforts and alarmed by his economic reforms, made an unsuccessful attempt to seize power. On the surface his reforms seemed to support greater democracy and social justice—the electorate was expanded and given the secret ballot, women received the vote, social security laws and educational reforms were enacted, and labor unions were formed. In 1934 Vargas pushed through a new constitution that reduced state autonomy and established government authority over the economy. The new Chamber of Deputies reflected Mussolini's corporatist doctrine by providing for the election of representatives not only by population and area but also by class and profession. The Chamber appointed Vargas president for four years.

Vargas soon shifted to the right. He stripped the *tenentes* of their influence and suppressed the Communists. At the same time, he encouraged the growth of Integralismo, a fascist movement secretly financed by Mussolini. The Integralists, who adopted green-shirted uniforms and a paramilitary organization, railed against democracy, communism, and Jews while preaching rabid nationalism and "Christian virtues."

In 1937 Vargas assumed dictatorial power and ruled Brazil under the Estado Novo (New State), a totalitarian government that strongly resembled European fascist regimes. The Estado Novo abolished political parties, imposed rigid censorship, established a special police force, and filled the prisons with political dissidents. Although Vargas did not attempt the kind of mass mobilization that Mussolini and Hitler had undertaken, he denounced democracy as "decadent" and courted the workers with populist rhetoric. In 1938 he banned all

The Brazilian Experience: The Estado Novo

In June 1940, Getulio Vargas outlined his vision of the authoritative state to a group of his officers.

We and all humanity are passing through a historical moment of great repercussions, resulting from a violent shifting of values. We are marching to a future different from the one we knew in the realm of economic, social, and political organization, and we feel that old systems and anti-quated formulae have entered into decline. It is not, however, as die-hard pessimists and conservatives maintain, the end of civilization, but the tumultuous and fruitful beginning of a new era. Vigorous peoples, fit for life, need to follow the direction of their aspirations, instead of pausing to contemplate what has crumbled and fallen into ruins. . . .

Balanced economy no longer allows privileged classes to enjoy a monopoly of comfort and benefits. . . . The State, therefore, should assume the obligation of organizing the productive forces, to provide the people with all that is necessary for the collective welfare. . . . The era of improvident liberalism, sterile demagoguery, useless individualism, and disorder has passed.

Source: J. W. F. Dulles, *Vargas of Brazil: A Political Biography* (Austin: University of Texas Press, 1967), p. 210.

paramilitary groups, and when the Integralists tried to seize power, he crushed them.

The economic policies of the Estado Novo were similar to Mussolini's Fascist programs. Vargas banned strikes and lockouts and stripped workers of the right to organize independently of the government. The regime set wages and hours, but although industrial workers benefited from some legislation, Vargas appeased the landowners by excluding agricultural workers from the new laws. He industrialized Brazil through a policy of economic planning and government investment in development ventures that combined public and private ownership. State technocrats expanded and rationalized Brazilian business, while Vargas preached an economic nationalism designed to free Brazil from its dependence on foreign capital. In the end he forced Brazil through a period of rapid social change and economic modernization, and his efforts eventually antagonized the traditional elites as well as his supporters.

During World War II, Vargas attempted to liberalize his regime, but in 1945 the army deposed him in a bloodless coup. Vargas, who retained his popularity among Brazilians, was again elected president in 1950. Four years later, when the army tried to force him out of office again, he committed suicide.

Brazil's Estado Novo suggests that fascism can be regarded not only as a political movement in individual countries but also as a model for resolving social and economic problems. Fascism was seen as either a means for speeding up modernization in underdeveloped countries or a method whereby old power elites could retain their authority and status. On still another level, fascism provided an example of how expanded government authority could alter the nature of society. Fascism offered new and brutally direct methods for social organization and control.

Why did fascism succeed in some cases in destroying its liberal enemy? In Italy and Germany the answer seems clear. Liberalism was in crisis at the end of World War I in Italy and poorly rooted in Germany, and traditional leaders were incapable of understanding both the new social forces unleashed by the war and the fascist response. On a more general level, the success of fascism was due to the fear and despair among people whose lives and values were threatened by economic collapse and loss of social status. This sense of desperation that led ordinary people to join fascist movements is aptly expressed in the title of the 1932 novel by German author Hans Fallada, *Little Man, What Now?*

Stalin's Soviet Union

Unlike Hitler or Mussolini, Stalin inherited an established, if not completely shaped, revolutionary system. He had several goals, the first of which was the consolidation of his hold over the country and its Communist

Joseph Stalin, the bloody and paranoid Soviet dictator, portrayed himself to his people as a benevolent father figure.

party. He also wished to make Russia economically independent of the hostile capitalist powers, particularly by modernizing industry. Committed to socialism as they perceived it, Stalin and his supporters were uneasy about the NEP policies introduced by Lenin, which had created a kind of market socialism based on nationalized industry, mixed private retail trade and state distribution, and capitalistic agriculture strongly influenced by state prices and quotas. Eliminating the vestiges of capitalism and introducing a new model of development became a priority, now that the economy had recovered from its wartime prostration and Stalin's political power was secure.

The Five-Year Plans

Stalin adopted a series of five-year plans to replace private property and economic activity with a system of production quotas formulated by a central authority under the party's direction. The plan established production goals for every citizen. Heavy industry and transportation received most of the resources at the expense of consumer-oriented manufacturing and agriculture. The quotas were unrealistic—projected increases of 250 percent for heavy industry, 300 percent for steel production, and 150 percent for agriculture. Workers and managers who met or

exceeded their targets received bonuses; stiff penalties awaited those who fell short. A new government agency, GOSPLAN, translated party directives into performance. In sum, the plans attempted to impose centralized state control on resources and labor that capitalism regulated through such market forces as supply and demand or changes in wages, prices, and interest rates.

The initial plan (1928–1932) had mixed success. Frequent breakdowns in planning and implementation caused waste, surpluses, or shortages, and quotas were rarely met. Moreover, the emphasis on quantity resulted in shoddy products. Nonetheless, owing in part to the substantial importation of machinery, skilled workers, and technicians from industrial countries, production doubled in five years.

Agriculture was another story. Stalin was determined to gain control over the countryside and punish the land-owning peasants who had resisted state authority. Moreover, he wanted to collect grain efficiently and pay for his industrialization programs by controlling grain prices. The method adopted was to consolidate the thousands of small family farms into a few hundred large agricultural enterprises that could use the latest mechanization and management techniques. Each huge farm would focus on a specific crop, which could be grown more efficiently. This would result in agricultural surpluses for sale abroad to finance industrialization.

In 1929 Soviet peasants were ordered to surrender their land and farm animals to the state and to become members of cooperative farms known as collectives. Under state control, each collective would receive quotas. Except for their houses and personal belongings, members were to turn over their property to the collective and to share the work and whatever profit or loss the farm recorded. Much of the peasantry—especially the well-to-do kulaks—rebelled against this system, burning crops and seed reserves or slaughtering livestock rather than surrendering them to the collectives. The police and, occasionally, Red Army troops attacked villages that resisted collectivization. The most capable farmers were either killed or dispatched to labor camps. The scheme was disastrous for Soviet agriculture. Livestock declined by over half, and the output of grain barely increased between 1928 and 1938, when it finally reached the prewar level. A famine swept the country in 1932 and 1933, the direct result of forced collectivization. Together Stalin's agrarian policy and the famine killed between five and eight million people in the Ukraine alone.

Collectivization also had important political implications. The systematic and brutal intrusion into the countryside saw a significant extension of the Communist party's power, for until then its direct control over the vast majority of Soviet citizens had been limited. Stalin's radical measures represented a vital step toward totalitarian control.

Declaring the five-year plan a success, Stalin announced a second in 1932 and a third six years later. In the later versions, steps were taken to improve quality and eliminate shortcomings in production and distribution. The results in industry were impressive. During the first two plans, the output of iron and steel expanded fourfold, that of coal three times; by 1938 the Soviet Union had become the world's largest producer of tractors and locomotives. Many of the new plants featured the latest equipment from America or western Europe. Agriculture, however, continued to present major problems. Grain production crept upward very slowly, and the country faced constant shortages of meat, fruits, vegetables, and dairy products. By the end of 1932 some 60 percent of all surviving peasant families had joined collective farms; by 1938 the proportion reached 93 percent. The government could count on a reasonably steady supply of basic goods for the cities. Collectivization provided Stalin with at least a political triumph.

Industrial expansion coincided with urbanization, as modern cities rose up in previously isolated areas of Siberia and central Asia. To populate them and meet the demand for labor, millions migrated from rural regions to the new manufacturing centers. Workers lost their independence as their unions became instruments of the state and their employment was decided by the central authorities.

Life in Stalin's Russia was harsh. Adequate housing was scarce, and wages failed to keep pace with prices—in 1937 a nonagricultural worker could afford only 60 percent of what he could have purchased in 1928. To material hardships was added the psychological strain of political indoctrination. Everyone was required to attend lectures by party activists, who extolled the virtues of Soviet socialism while warning of capitalist plots. Artists, writers, film producers, playwrights, musicians, and other communicators took seriously Stalin's command that they become "engineers of human minds" and competed as composers of Communist propaganda.

By the mid-1930s another major propaganda theme was added: virtual deification of Stalin. Unlike other dictators, Stalin shunned public appearances at mass rallies and similar functions. Yet his presence, in the form of portraits, statues, and books, was inescapable. Indeed, he became the focal point of a cult of personality comparable to those in Nazi Germany and Fascist Italy.

Social Policy

Stalin's regime offered positive incentives to labor. Unemployment virtually disappeared, and the foundation was laid for free state medical services, pensions for the elderly, subsidized housing, and day-care facilities for children. Perhaps the most meaningful benefit to many was the extension of free education to all. The government declared war on illiteracy, bringing basic schooling to isolated portions of the Soviet Union. Advanced education was provided free to students demonstrating superior aptitude, and a reward system of high salaries, bonuses, and privileges awaited successful graduates. Indeed, a managerial and technocratic class soon emerged that, together with the political and artistic elites, formed a new aristocracy in this supposedly classless society. The welfare system, combined with fear of the consequences of any criticism, muted discontent among the masses.

The status of women underwent significant change. The hopes of early Bolshevik feminists such as Alexandra

In the Soviet Union, women were mobilized into virtually all sectors of the labor force. Here a female tractor driver leads a procession to the fields.

Kollontai that the revolution would achieve equality for women were never fully realized. In 1918 the Zhenotdel, or Party Women's Bureau, was established to educate and recruit women for the Communist party. The Zhenotdel also acted as an advocate for women's interests in the workplace and sponsored women candidates for local elections. Even though it had no powers of enforcement, the Zhenotdel had an uneasy relationship with party officials, and Stalin abolished it in the 1920s.

In that decade, however, Russian women were given legal access to abortion and divorce, and although Stalin minimized the rhetoric of sexual equality, industrial policy and economic necessity resulted in wider opportunities for women. The collectivization of agriculture brought women into the fields in greater numbers, while subsistence salaries for male workers pushed millions of wives and daughters into factory jobs, public works projects, and heavy construction. The most significant change, however, came in educational opportunities, which were now open to women, especially in science, technology, and medicine. Despite the advances in education and employment, the Soviet mobilization of women increased their physical and psychological burdens, for most women were expected to care for children and do housework while working or going to school. Nevertheless, unlike the fascist regimes, which limited women to the roles of wives and mothers, Soviet totalitarianism proclaimed the goal of female equality and made important strides in breaking the pattern of traditional roles for women.

The Great Purges

Stalin's development programs had employed totalitarian mechanisms that used police terror against the peasants. But as uneasiness over his brutal methods mounted, the internal security forces, known as the NKVD, were soon turned against the Communist elite. Between 1936 and 1938 Stalin unleashed a reign of terror that engulfed party members, administrators, and military leaders. Eventually it expanded to include ordinary citizens, many of whom fell victim to sudden arrest and summary execution or exile to a remote labor camp without apparent cause. The reasons behind these "great purges" remain obscure. There is evidence that paranoia may have so consumed Stalin that he struck out blindly against presumed enemies.

The terror began with the assassination in December 1934 of Sergei Kirov, a close associate of Stalin's and, according to some, his chosen successor. Claiming that Kirov's murder was part of a vast conspiracy led by sup-

porters of the exiled Trotsky, Stalin, who had in reality arranged for the murder himself, ordered mass arrests. In 1936 there began a series of public trials that captured world attention. Sixteen "Old Bolsheviks"—activists who had joined the party before 1917—were charged with conspiring to topple Stalin and restore Trotsky to power. All confessed and were executed. Similar trials claimed other Old Bolsheviks, including the theoretician Nikolai Bukharin; all offered identical confessions followed by summary execution. Next the purge reached the army. A secret court-martial in 1937 found Marshal Mikhail Tukhachevsky and other officers guilty of conspiring with the Germans and the Japanese as well as with Trotsky, and all were executed. In addition, thousands of prominent party members, union officials, business executives, and intellectuals lost their liberty or their lives. Stalin culminated the purges by executing the leaders of the very police force that had implemented his program of terror. When the purges were over, millions had fallen victim to his obsession.

The great purges served to remove upper and middle-level officials in the party, state, military, and economic institutions, and Stalin replaced them with younger functionaries who would dutifully obey him. Yet the purges also had the effect of halting the revolutionary changes that had been going on in the Soviet Union since the early 1920s. Thenceforth the regime would follow the path set by Stalin's totalitarian dictatorship.

The Great Depression and the Crisis of Capitalism

By the eve of World War I the capitalist system had grown complex and global in scope. In theory, a free international market set the prices of most basic commodities, although imperialism had long since made the law of supply and demand obsolete in many sectors of the world economy. Moreover, some regions enjoyed special status as the sole producers of specific items sold to the rest of the world. Traditionally, industry and commerce were financed through a system of credit resting on the assumption that lenders or investors could collect the money owed them and that borrowers could earn enough income to repay their loans while continuing to purchase agricultural or industrial products. It was a resilient system, having weathered numerous financial crises—what today might be termed recessions—prior to 1914. But the crisis that erupted in 1929 and lasted in some respects until the outbreak of World War II was more than simply an adjustment in the world economy. Along with major changes in economic theory and practice, it brought untold suffering to millions and raised serious doubts about the viability of capitalism and the liberal political systems on which it rested.

The Economic Collapse

After an initial postwar slump, the 1920s exhibited a surge of economic vitality that brought prosperity to more people than ever before. Much of this growth derived from international trade, construction, and the development of new industries such as the automobile, radio, and motion pictures. The economic expansion had been financed largely by personal, corporate, and international credit—a shaky foundation whose flaws were exposed in the October 1929 stock market crash. Securities purchases relied heavily on margin trading, whereby investors bought stocks and bonds by putting up only a fraction of the purchase price; the remainder was borrowed from brokers, who in turn obtained credit from banks. Such unregulated practices led to widespread speculation in stocks, whose market value was often many times their actual worth. With installment credit readily available, consumers were encouraged to buy houses, automobiles, and other major items without having the cash to pay for them. Here, too, retailers and wholesalers borrowed funds from banks to pay their suppliers. Manufacturers easily obtained credit for plant expansion, and small nations received foreign loans far beyond their ability to repay. If one link in this credit chain suddenly demanded immediate repayment, the others would be forced to come up with large amounts of cash to meet their debt obligations.

The availability of easy credit concealed other serious flaws in the post–World War I economy. The new prosperity was not evenly distributed, for profits far surpassed wages for nearly all working people, and farm prices continued to lag far behind the prices charged for manufactured goods and basic services. Consequently, despite the abundance of credit, mass purchasing power was never based on solid financial ground. Furthermore, the economic optimism of the day resulted in high levels of production and huge inventories, with the possibility that unsold goods could force cutbacks and eventual job layoffs. At the international level the appearance of new states in central and eastern Europe introduced further volatility into the world economy. Since the economies of these states were immature and their finances precarious, their vulnerability to credit difficulties weakened the global economy in time of trouble.

Strictly speaking, the Great Depression began with the financial collapse touched off by the sudden deflation of the New York Stock Exchange in October 1929. In reality the world agrarian sector had already been experiencing severe hardship as the prices of basic agricultural goods followed an unchecked downward spiral. The stock market crash produced a sudden rush by creditors to call in loans at all levels, and the consequent failure of a major European lender (Austria's *Creditanstalt*) in 1931 gave the crisis an international dimension. The panic soon passed to industry, and even large corporations were

Anxious crowds gather outside the New York Stock Exchange in October 1929, following the crash.

forced to halt production as the markets for their goods dried up. By 1933 world production had declined 38 percent and world trade had dropped to one-third its pre-1929 level. When farmers who had escaped previous difficulties were hit by the evaporation of credit and customers, the collapse of the modern capitalist economy appeared complete.

The resulting Great Depression caused mass suffering and fear to an extent hitherto unknown in the modern West. Unemployment reached epidemic proportions—Great Britain reported 3 million unemployed in 1933, Germany 6 million, and the United States 13 million. Worldwide, some 30 million people were without jobs when the depression reached its depth in 1932. People living on fixed incomes or running marginal businesses saw their savings disappear, often literally overnight. Skilled and productive employees were reduced to supporting families on what meager welfare was available. As the depression dragged on, demoralization turned to frustration and resentment. Families disintegrated, suicides rose dramatically, and the very fabric of society seemed torn apart.

Government Response

Nations dealt with the crisis in various ways. The reactions of Britain, France, Germany, Italy, the United States, and the Soviet Union are considered individually in this and later chapters, but some general observations will prove useful here.

At first, governments pursued deflationary policies that made the problem worse but then switched to pump-priming strategies, including deficit spending, to stimulate economic revival. All states, whether democratic or totalitarian, undertook measures to generate work for their citizens and to limit the economic hardship as much as possible: public works programs, spending cuts, currency controls, and tariffs were among the most widespread efforts. Governments assumed a greater degree of control over economic and social life than ever before as they attempted to come to grips with the immediate consequences of the economic collapse and its long-range implications.

The Great Depression affected the future in ways that were not immediately apparent but had a lasting impact. What had once been an integrated world economy disintegrated into highly competitive national economic systems. Economic competition bred distrust between countries and fostered a spirit of nationalism that shattered post–World War I dreams of international cooperation. Extremist political movements that promised

quick solutions to the crisis spread rapidly. While representative government survived in long-established Western democracies, even France, Britain, and the United States experienced profound trauma that altered their political and social traditions.

Britain, France, and the United States: The Trial of Democracy

The Great Depression challenged liberal democratic systems, yet the problems facing each of the three major democracies were unique. Common to Britain, France, and the United States, however, were an extension of state welfare measures, stronger government control over the economy, and the basic survival of democratic institutions.

Politics and Society

After 1919 Britain had to cope with a serious economic slump brought about by the end of the war and the reorientation of the global economy. In the 1920s British governments, led in succession by the Liberals, the Conservatives, and finally the Labour party, grappled with two closely related issues: chronic unemployment—which rose to 18.5 percent in the next decade—and a growing deficit produced in part by social welfare programs. Despite serious labor unrest, most notably a 1926 coal miners' general strike, in periods of severe crisis the Labourites and the Conservatives tended toward ideological convergence. Moreover, the currency policies of successive governments sheltered the British population, particularly its middle class, from the devastating inflationary cycles that ruined other countries.

The postwar period in the United States saw the economic boom of the so-called Roaring Twenties, especially in the construction and automobile industries, and America became obsessed with material wealth. Under Republican presidents Warren G. Harding (1921–1923) and Calvin Coolidge (1923–1929), the country pursued a "return to normalcy" that aimed at a nostalgic re-creation of the atmosphere of the prewar era. Although Americans were suspicious of foreign political entanglements, government policies spread American economic influence into Latin America and the Pacific. The labor movement found organized action increasingly difficult in the face of government hostility, and the rapid economic growth that produced nearly full employment and better wages undercut the appeal of unions. Only farmers seemed excluded from the prosperity. Facing declining prices and rising costs well before the depression, farmers received little support from the government, and hard times had begun to grip rural America in the early 1920s.

The difficulties experienced by the farmer were often obscured by the glare of Jazz Age life in the big cities. Despite the Eighteenth Amendment to the U.S. constitution, which banned the production and sale of alcoholic beverages, popular culture was indulgent and iconoclastic. Flashy automobiles, speakeasies, gangster heroes such as Al Capone, and "flappers"—women considered bold and unconventional in behavior and dress—became symbols of America's frenzied modernism, while the election of Republican president Herbert Hoover (1929–1933) epitomized the belief in uninterrupted prosperity.

Britain and the United States both represented relatively stable political states. In France, by contrast, chronic instability had long appeared to be the rule. This was due in part to the tremendous financial investment needed to rebuild the economy after the wartime destruction the country had suffered. Successive cabinets advanced—and then under fierce opposition retreated from—plans for tax increases and other measures designed to finance reconstruction. The result was a large deficit and a serious inflationary spiral. In addition, the electoral system, based on proportional representation, stimulated political factionalism with a multiparty system that necessitated coalition government.

One of the few islands of stability in the period came with the "government of national union" formed in 1926 by Raymond Poincaré (1860–1934). A careful and temperate man, Poincaré governed France for three years, during which time he restored a measure of equilibrium to the country. He stabilized the franc, halted the deficit-spending programs of previous administrations, and introduced social legislation that rejuvenated the economy and eased social tensions. As living standards improved by the end of the decade, France reestablished its reputation for cultural leadership. Although Paris again became a thriving center of avant-garde artists and writers, its fame in the 1920s rested largely on its colony of brilliant expatriates, which included the writers James Joyce, Ernest Hemingway, and Gertrude Stein.

Toward the Welfare State

The Great Depression shattered the complacency that had permeated life in the three major democracies. Britain, with the apparatus of the modern welfare state well in place by 1930, endured the economic crisis with the least shock to its political system. British Labour prime minister Ramsay MacDonald (1929–1935) converted his cabinet into a national coalition government in 1931 to eliminate partisan policy disputes. He reduced

unemployment compensation in 1931 and sought to stimulate economic recovery by raising taxes, reducing the budget, lowering interest rates, and changing currency and tariff policies. The Conservative governments that followed under Stanley Baldwin (1935–1937) and Neville Chamberlain (1937–1940) continued this approach. Britain weathered the crisis and experienced an economic revival in the late 1930s, based largely on the continued low prices of raw materials from abroad. However, conditions in northern England, Scotland, and Wales remained far more depressed than in the south, encouraging a flight of capital and population from what had once been Britain's industrial heartland that has continued ever since.

Although unemployment in France was not as severe as in other countries, the depression had a critical impact on the country's political system. The government failed to deal effectively with the economic collapse, so as prosperity disappeared after 1932, political tensions resurfaced. The radical right in particular posed such a serious threat that the socialists, Communists, and other leftist elements formed a coalition government under socialist Léon Blum (1936–1937), the so-called Popular Front. Social reforms aimed chiefly at the working and lower classes appeared to reduce social stress, but concerted resistance from the financial and business communities halted the recovery program. By the end of the decade France was economically worse off, more bitterly divided, and more politically unstable than any other leading European power.

The United States underwent the greatest transformation as a result of the depression. Firmly committed to the principles of a free enterprise market economy, the Hoover administration did little to halt the financial collapse of the stock market. By 1932 unemployment had reached 25 percent. Yet the mounting despair of the American people, who increasingly demanded action, did not turn against the fundamental principles of the economic and political system. Hence when Democrat Franklin D. Roosevelt (1933–1945) was elected president by a large majority, he assumed that he had received a mandate for fundamental change that would reform capitalism in order to save it.

Roosevelt represented an alternative to socialism and fascism, favoring forceful intervention by the federal government in economic life. Along with regulating the economy and stimulating business recovery through deficit spending, Roosevelt's New Deal introduced several basic social welfare programs. The result was a resurgence of industrial, commercial, and agricultural activity that, though never attaining predepression levels, stimulated significant recovery and partly cushioned the im-

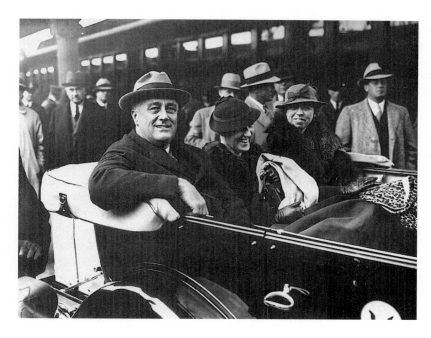

President Franklin D. Roosevelt inaugurated major changes in U.S. economic and social life.

pact of the economic crisis. By 1938, when deficit spending was reduced, a new recession had set in, and it required the massive production needs of World War II to pull the nation completely out of this economic slump. Despite criticism of Roosevelt's programs, the economic turnabout his policies induced was so successful that most Americans were willing to accept them.

The United States, Britain, and France thus retained both the form and the essence of their democratic systems in the face of severe trials. Although fascistlike demagogues developed followings in all three countries, their citizens did not succumb to dictatorship, in part because these governments adopted public works projects, unemployment and health insurance, and old-age pensions to help blunt the impact of economic adversity. The real welfare state was created after World War II, but its origins were found in the social programs of the 1930s.

Central and Eastern Europe

The strength of liberal institutions in the United States and western Europe was not duplicated in most of eastern Europe. New states had arisen after 1919 out of the remnants of the shattered German, Austro-Hungarian, Russian, and Ottoman empires. These "successor states" were Poland, Czechoslovakia, Yugoslavia, Hungary, Austria, Turkey, and the Baltic republics of Estonia, Latvia, and Lithuania. In these nations democracy

proved less resistant to the political and economic stress of the postwar period.

The Successor States

Together with the already independent countries of Bulgaria, Greece, Romania, and Albania, the successor states formed a bastion of small nations in the strategic heartland of Europe. They were governed either by constitutional monarchies with representative institutions or by republican systems modeled after Western democracies. The new democracies were considered important in London and Paris as barriers against the spread of communism and the revival of German power. Most of these states eventually abandoned democracy for authoritarian dictatorship. Although a genuinely fascist regime never ruled in any of these nations before World War II, the reactionary right came to dominate the political and economic systems throughout the region. The special circumstances of the successor states demanded unique approaches to governing and to socioeconomic organization that the liberal system often could not manage.

In retrospect, it is surprising that there was such confidence in eastern Europe as a proving ground for democracy. Without exception, these nations faced problems that would have staggered wealthier, well-established states. A variety of factors retarded economic development. Before 1918 the region had functioned, directly or indirectly, as colonial territory for larger powers, which had supplied it with investments and manufactured goods in return for agricultural products and raw materials. When the war ended, the area faced the sudden loss of secure markets and the inexpensive resources necessary for industrial modernization. To these problems were added a lack of native investment capital, outmoded commercial and agricultural structures, and inadequate communication and transportation systems. Indeed, except for portions of Czechoslovakia, Poland, and Austria, the economies of eastern Europe resembled those of colonial areas in Asia, Africa, or the Middle East.

Social weaknesses contributed to the economic difficulties in eastern Europe. These societies had been dominated by landowning or entrepreneurial nobility and a religious hierarchy that ruled peasants who lived as virtual serfs, despite the formal abolition of serfdom in the nineteenth century. Again with the exception of Austria, Poland, and Czechoslovakia, there was no substantial middle class of merchants, financiers, or managers to provide the expertise and resources needed for modern industrial and commercial development. The small but influential intelligentsia provided the real leadership on a local level. Much of the middle class that did exist was German or Jewish. Finally, these nations were beset with problems common to underdeveloped societies. Illiteracy, high birth and death rates, primitive health conditions, and poor nutrition combined to retard modernization and undermine the democratic systems.

In addition to the clash of interests between landowners and peasants or between the emergent urban dwellers and the much larger rural population, these states were characterized by enormous ethnoreligious diversity. For historical reasons, nearly all of them had a heterogeneous population composed of groups whose ethnic and religious affiliations were different from those of the ruling majority. In some cases, notably Poland, Czechoslovakia, Yugoslavia, Hungary, and Romania, these minorities formed a substantial proportion of the inhabitants. Except for Greece and Turkey, which solved this problem by exchanging minority groups, governments faced ongoing challenges from the minorities. The minorities' reluctance to accept the supremacy of national states, coupled with the failure of most governments to treat their minorities fairly, was a major barrier to the formation of integrated societies.

The Decline of Liberalism

Liberal democracy in eastern Europe also suffered from political liabilities. The lack of experience in representative government meant that the normal give-and-take and compromise of parliamentary systems were absent from local and national politics, with the result that policy making was often paralyzed. Many states had a multiplicity of political parties, which made legislative activity difficult. Perhaps the most serious political liability was the intense nationalism that pervaded the region and colored the perceptions of leaders and common people alike. Some areas, such as Poland, Hungary, and Bohemia, had long-established nationalist traditions, but national animosities were deepened by the wartime experience. Those on the losing side—Austria, Hungary, Turkey, Bulgaria—were determined to regenerate patriotic pride and regain lost territory; the victors who were already independent—Romania, Greece, Albania— viewed nationalism as a device to keep the hard-won spoils of war. In the states formed from territory of the defeated empires—Poland, Czechoslovakia, Estonia, Latvia, and Lithuania—uncompromising nationalism was seen as the basis for protecting their newly won sovereignty. Nationalism in eastern Europe produced aggressive international behavior that impeded cooperation among the countries and rendered impossible the formation of regional organizations that might have resolved economic problems.

It is hardly surprising that parliamentary democracies often failed to cope with these difficulties and gave way to authoritarian dictatorships. The first nation to adopt a dictatorial government was Hungary, which turned to Admiral Miklós Horthy after a short-lived Communist regime under Béla Kun in 1919. Authoritarian leaders soon came to power elsewhere: Marshal Józef Pilsudski in Poland (1926), Antanas Smetona in Lithuania (1926), King Zog in Albania (1928), and King Alexander in Yugoslavia (1929). The Great Depression intensified the problems these nations faced and accelerated the trend toward dictatorship. King Carol began to assume dictatorial power in Romania in 1931, and within three years Engelbert Dollfuss in Austria, Konstantin Päts in Estonia, and Karlis Ulmanis in Latvia had followed suit. In 1935 and 1936 King Boris of Bulgaria and General John Metaxas of Greece completed the transformation to authoritarianism in the region. Only Czechoslovakia, under the leadership of Tomáš Masaryk and Edvard Beneš, managed to retain its democratic government, despite authoritarian tendencies and serious internal problems.

Whether they were royal, civilian, or military dictatorships, these regimes shared certain characteristics. All retained the façade of democratic institutions, but all developed secret police systems, curtailed civil liberties, suppressed political opposition, and relied on centralized bureaucracies to enforce dictatorial decisions. Fascist movements appeared throughout the region, although none came to power before World War II. Instead, the dictators claimed that their regimes represented protection against exploitation, revolutionary unrest, or the persecution of minorities and posed as the embodiment of the national will. The appeals to nationalism and stability in an area beset with competition, mistrust, and insecurity ultimately proved too strong for the democratic experiment in eastern Europe.

SUMMARY

As an ideology, fascism drew on the elitist, antidemocratic radicalism and nationalist-racist doctrines that emerged out of Europe's cultural ferment at the turn of the century. At the same time, modern concepts of political communication and social mobilization provided skillful leaders with the techniques for developing a power base and a new style of authoritarian leadership. The impact of World War I and the subsequent economic crisis helped discredit democratic systems and enabled these leaders to channel popular discontent into mass movements. Once in power, Mussolini and Hitler among the fascist dictators and Stalin in the Soviet Union established totalitarian states that aimed to control all aspects of life and indoctrinate their populations with new ideological values.

For contemporaries in the 1930s the world appeared to be engaged in a series of ideological struggles: a battle between democracy and totalitarianism or between capitalism and communism. Fascist victories in Italy and Germany made the prospects for democracy seem dark, while in the USSR Stalin created an equally brutal police state. The Western democracies came through the economic crisis with their political institutions changed but fundamentally intact. Yet little of the democratic experiment in eastern Europe survived the decade. More dangerous still, in Italy, Germany, and the Soviet Union the totalitarian restructuring of political, social, and economic life offered compelling alternatives to the liberal order.

Finally, the spread of totalitarianism had important international repercussions. Both in Europe and in Asia militarism and the thirst for expansion began to undermine peace. With Mussolini and Hitler in power, one of the compelling forces behind the rise of fascism—nationalist frustration over the 1919 settlements—drove the dictators relentlessly toward the destruction of the postwar international order.

SUGGESTIONS FOR FURTHER READING

Arendt, H. *The Origins of Totalitarianism*, 2nd ed. Cleveland: World Publishing, 1958.

Bracher, K. D. *The German Dictatorship*. New York: Praeger, 1970.

Bullock, A. *Hitler: A Study in Tyranny*. New York: Harper & Row, 1964.

Cassels, A. *Fascism*. New York: Crowell, 1975.

Conquest, R. *The Great Terror: A Reassessment*. New York: Oxford University Press, 1989.

De Felice, R. *Interpretations of Fascism*. Cambridge, Mass.: Harvard University Press, 1977.

Deutscher, I. *Stalin: A Political Biography*, 2nd ed. New York: Oxford University Press, 1967.

Dulles, J. W. F. *Vargas of Brazil: A Political Biography*. Austin: University of Texas Press, 1967.

Gay, P. *Weimar Culture*. New York: Harper & Row, 1968.

Greene, N. *From Versailles to Vichy*. New York: Crowell, 1970.

Hinz, B. *Art in the Third Reich*. New York: Pantheon Books, 1979.

Kershaw, I. *The Hitler Myth: Image and Reality in the Third Reich*. New York: Oxford University Press, 1987.

Kindleberger, C. P. *The World in Depression, 1929–1939*. Berkeley: University of California Press, 1973.

Laqueur, W., ed. *Fascism: A Reader's Guide*. Berkeley: University of California Press, 1976.

Larsen, S. U., et al., eds. *Who Were the Fascists?* Oslo: Universitets-forlaget, 1982.

Lyttelton, A. *The Seizure of Power: Fascism in Italy, 1919–1929*. London: Weidenfeld & Nicolson, 1973.

Mack Smith, D. *Mussolini*. London: Weidenfeld & Nicolson, 1981.

Maruyama, M. *Thought and Behaviour in Modern Japanese Politics*. London: Oxford University Press, 1963.

Morris, I., ed. *Japan, 1931–1945: Militarism, Fascism, Japanism?* Boston: Heath, 1963.

Payne, S. G. *Fascism: Comparison and Definition*. Madison: University of Wisconsin Press, 1980.

Peukert, D. J. K. *Inside Nazi Germany*. New Haven, Conn.: Yale University Press, 1987.

Schoenbaum, D. *Hitler's Social Revolution: Class and Status in Nazi Germany*. New York: Anchor Books, 1967.

Seton-Watson, H. *Eastern Europe Between the Wars, 1918–1941*. Cambridge: Cambridge University Press, 1962.

Shannon, D. A. *Between the Wars: America, 1919–1941*, 2nd ed. Boston: Houghton Mifflin, 1979.

Tannenbaum, E. R. *The Fascist Experience: Italian Society and Culture, 1922–1945*. New York: Basic Books, 1972.

Taylor, A. J. P. *English History, 1914–1945*. New York: Oxford University Press, 1965.

Toland, J. *Adolf Hitler*. Garden City, N.Y.: Doubleday, 1976.

Ulam, A. *Stalin: The Man and His Era*. New York: Viking, 1973.

CHAPTER 39

The Second World War to the Cold War

Mushroom cloud from the atomic bomb.

Some historians see the 20 years separating the two world wars as little more than a pause in an ongoing conflict that began in 1914. Clearly, the origins of World War II are to be found in part in the Great War and in the peace settlements that followed it. Nor is there any doubt that the European war that erupted in 1939 was due chiefly to the aggression of the fascist powers.

World War II was a truly global conflict that unfolded in two distinct theaters, Europe and Asia. The Asian war had actually begun much earlier, as Japan began its own expansionist thrust into China. Japanese ambitions in Asia and the Pacific inevitably drew the United States into the war. The impact of the war on the lives of millions of people was enormous. The waging of "total" war—war in which entire populations were engaged in a life-and-death struggle—proved more devastating than in 1914–1918. When it was over, the world had changed drastically, not least in that the old international system had given way to a new era dominated by the United States and the Soviet Union. Even as Europe and the Soviet Union began the arduous task of reconstructing their societies and economies, a tense and dangerous "Cold War" began to unfold between the two superpowers.

The Rising Sun: Japanese Expansion in East Asia

In the 1920s the Japanese came to view China, with its large territory but internally weak government, as their sphere of interest and had begun to extend their influence on the mainland. In addition to providing an opportunity for territorial expansion, the Great War had also quickened the pace of Japanese industrial growth and enabled Tokyo to capture many regional markets from the Western powers. In the post-World War I period Japan became the main source of textiles and other consumer products for the rest of Asia.

But this thriving economy rested on a precarious base. Lacking essential raw materials, Japan's chief asset was its highly motivated, well-disciplined workforce. Japanese leaders were able to mobilize workers even more effectively than Europe's totalitarian dictators, producing a modern industrial machine and related commercial and financial institutions, largely controlled by a few great family trusts known as the *zaibatsu*. Political and economic leaders realized that their nation would continue to prosper only if it had a guaranteed flow of raw materials, together with secure foreign markets for its products. A disruption of this balance would halt the growth of Japanese power and expose its vulnerability.

The Japanese political system vigorously pursued the interests of the nation's economic elite. On paper Japan possessed a government strikingly similar to that of many European powers—a written constitution adopted in 1889, universal male suffrage since 1925, and modern parliamentary and judicial systems. But this institutional structure was largely misleading. The Diet (parliament) had limited powers, and ministers governed in the name of the supreme and holy emperor, to whom they were completely responsible. A spirit of militarism pervaded Japanese life and gave the professional officer corps a political influence comparable to that enjoyed by the German military caste before World War I. In the 1930s Japan was the only modern nation that required its war and naval ministers to be generals and admirals on active-duty status. Many of its younger officers, influenced by the national revival that had begun in the mid-nineteenth century, were drawn from a segment of the small landowning nobility that followed the warrior code of the old samurai. The powerful combination of nationalism, militarism, and authoritarianism that dominated Japanese politics determined that in time of crisis, ultimate authority passed to the military leaders.

After World War I, Chinese tariff barriers and the Great Depression threatened Japan's access to raw materials and markets. Younger army officers proposed the conquest of nearby territory from which materials could be obtained and to which manufactured goods—as well as surplus population—could be sent. Military spokesmen added a messianic tone to these arguments by insisting that the prosperity and progress of all Asia depended on the Japanese, who would liberate Asia from Western exploitation. Japan's imperial program thus assumed the guise of a broader campaign in defense of Asian interests.

Manchuria was the first target of Japanese expansionism. Russia, whose territory bordered Manchuria on the north and east, had dominated the area until its defeat in the 1905 war. Thereafter, although it remained nominally part of China, Manchuria became a Japanese sphere. In September 1931, Japanese colonels took advantage of a minor incident involving the South Manchuria Railway at Mukden to invade Manchuria. The civilian government reluctantly approved the army's initiative, and by early 1932 the Japanese conquest of Manchuria was complete.

When the Chinese boycotted Japanese goods, Tokyo landed 70,000 troops at Shanghai, then withdrew them under pressure from the Western powers. Japan nonetheless renamed its conquered Manchurian territory Manchukuo ("Country of the Manchus") and proclaimed it an independent state under Henry Pu Yi, the last Manchu emperor, who remained a Japanese puppet. Condemned by the League of Nations, the Japanese withdrew their membership, presenting the League with the first real test of its ability to stop aggression. The League failed to meet the challenge, imposing neither economic nor military sanctions. Japan's ambitions were emboldened by the signing of the Anti-Comintern Pact with Germany in 1936, which bound both partners to withhold aid from the Soviet Union should either party go to war with the Soviets.

Aggression and Appeasement in the West

Japan's success in defying the League of Nations encouraged Hitler's and Mussolini's quest for expansion. Mussolini's emphasis on the virtues of war, combined with his dream of creating a new Roman Empire, impelled him toward conquest. Hitler was even more outspoken about his plans for a Greater German Reich in Europe, the corollary of a racial policy that aimed at bringing the "inferior" peoples of the Continent under the domination of the "master" Germanic race.

Europe and Africa: The Axis Advance

Hitler laid the groundwork for expansion while rebuilding German military strength. In October 1933, Germany withdrew from the League of Nations and the

The Italian campaign against Ethiopia pitted modern weapons and technology against traditional warriors and civilians. Here Ethiopian chieftains display their rifles.

following July instigated a coup in Austria aimed at bringing about the union (*Anschluss*) of Austria and Germany. Nazi conspirators murdered Austrian chancellor Engelbert Dollfuss but were halted by Mussolini, who intervened to protect Austrian independence, which he considered vital to Italy's security.

In January 1935, Hitler won a huge majority in the Versailles-mandated plebiscite that returned the Saar region to Germany. In March he openly defied the postwar settlement, declaring that Germany had formed an air force and had reinstituted the military draft. Despite protests, Britain tacitly endorsed Hitler's actions in June 1935 by signing a naval agreement with Germany.

In the summer of 1934 Mussolini had begun preparations for the conquest of Ethiopia, one of the two remaining independent nations in Africa (the other was Liberia). Arousing enthusiasm with a propaganda campaign at home, the Duce launched his invasion in October 1935. The League of Nations promptly imposed economic sanctions, but it omitted oil from the list of products that member nations could not sell to Italy. This important exception, together with the abstention of the United States, Japan, and Germany from the boycott, virtually assured Italy of victory. In May 1936, when Mussolini proclaimed the incorporation of Ethiopia with Italian Somaliland and Eritrea into a new empire called Italian East Africa, the collective security system created at Versailles crumbled.

Hitler took full advantage of these developments. In March 1936, while the conquest of Ethiopia was under way, he ordered German troops into the Rhineland,

which the Versailles treaty had established as a demilitarized zone. At the same time, he repudiated the 1925 Locarno treaties that guaranteed Germany's frontiers with Belgium and France and recognized the demilitarized status of the Rhineland. Although the French mobilized their troops, Britain refused to act. Hitler and Mussolini had shown that the democracies were unwilling to preserve the postwar settlement. In October 1936 the Führer and the Duce agreed to coordinate an anticommunist campaign in what Mussolini later called the Rome-Berlin Axis.

The Spanish Civil War

The Axis partnership demonstrated its military capacity during the Spanish civil war. When Spain became a democratic republic after the collapse of the Bourbon monarchy in 1931, the new government launched a campaign of social and economic reform. Conservative elements, especially the military, the Catholic church, and the aristocracy, opposed the reforms and gained control of the government in 1933. In response, leftist and democratic groups formed the Popular Front, which regained power in the 1936 elections. Unwilling to accept this, army officers under the leadership of General Francisco Franco (1892–1975) revolted in July. Franco was soon joined by extreme nationalists and Spanish fascists, known as the Falange, and the nation was plunged into civil war.

The Spanish civil war was a major barometer of the willingness of democratic and totalitarian forces to

Hitler and Mussolini review military plans.

act. Hitler and Mussolini poured tanks, planes, and military personnel into Spain on behalf of the Nationalists. Stalin countered by shipping equipment and military advisers to the republican Loyalists. Fearful of escalation, the British and the French adopted a policy of nonintervention. Thousands of liberals, socialists, communists, and anarchists from Europe and America who viewed Spain as an ideological battleground fought as volunteers in international brigades against the Franco forces. The agony of the Spanish people was exemplified by the German bombing of the town of Guernica on April 26, 1937. By the beginning of 1939, the Nationalists had won, and Franco became dictator of Spain.

The Czech Crisis

Emboldened by the timidity of the Western powers, Hitler annexed Austria, occupying it with German troops in March 1938. He then turned to Czechoslovakia. The three million ethnic Germans who lived in the Sudeten border region had never been reconciled to

Franco's victory in the Spanish civil war forced thousands of civilians to seek refuge across the border in France.

Pablo Picasso produced Guernica *to express the agony of the German bombing of the village of Guernica during the Spanish civil war.*

Czech rule. In the aftermath of the Austrian *Anschluss,* the Czech Nazi leader, Konrad Henlein (1898–1945), demanded autonomy for the Sudetenland, a move that Hitler promptly endorsed. The democratic Czech government, headed by President Edvard Beneš (1884–1948), appealed to France and the Soviet Union, with which it had defensive alliances, and mobilized its own forces. Hitler responded by threatening an invasion. War appeared imminent.

The French, unprepared to fight, yielded the diplomatic initiative to Britain's prime minister, Neville Chamberlain (1869–1940). Determined to avoid war, Chamberlain held a series of meetings with Hitler. A final conference, held in Munich with Mussolini and French premier Edouard Daladier (1884–1970) on September 29 and 30, settled the fate of Czechoslovakia. Chamberlain and Daladier accepted the demand for German annexation of the Sudetenland and forced the Czechs to acquiesce. Chamberlain then returned to London to proclaim "peace in our time." Six months later Hitler violated the agreement, moving German troops into Prague and dismembering what was left of Czechoslovakia. It, like Austria, had ceased to exist as a sovereign state.

The Munich settlement represented the culmination of the Western policy of appeasement. The strategy of appeasement had been calculated to eliminate the dangers of war by satisfying the aggressor states through negotiation. At the time the policy did not seem as short-sighted as it does in retrospect. Many agreed with Hitler and Mussolini that some aspects of the postwar peace settlements had been unfair, while others saw the instability of the new states in eastern Europe as proof of the failure of Wilsonian self-determination. Appeasement was the policy of people who had survived the horrors of World War I and were determined to avoid another at almost any cost.

Appeasement was all the more compelling because some European statesmen, still haunted by the specter of the Russian Revolution, believed that the upheavals of war would unleash communism in the West. The Great Depression had seriously weakened the economic and social order of capitalism and had shaken Western faith in democratic political systems. The lack of military preparedness in Britain and France reflected these post-1919 developments, whereas for some Western leaders the armed strength of the aggressors made appeasement seem necessary. The policy, however, only whetted the territorial appetites of Mussolini and Hitler.

World War II

At the end of March 1939—when it was clear that Poland would be Hitler's next victim—Chamberlain publicly assured Warsaw that Britain and France would defend Polish independence. By then the dictators had no reason to believe the Western powers meant what they

MAP 39.1   CENTRAL EUROPE, 1939

said. On April 3, Hitler secretly ordered the invasion of Poland in September, and five days later Mussolini invaded Albania. In May, after Britain and France extended guarantees to Greece and Romania, Hitler and Mussolini signed the Pact of Steel, a formal military alliance.

In preparation for his assault against Poland, Hitler sought to guard against two possible contingencies: the intervention of Russia and, in the event that the Western powers did fight, a two-front war between Russia in the east and an Anglo-French campaign in the west. The Soviet Union had been negotiating with both sides since early spring, but mutual mistrust in Moscow, London, and Paris prevented an agreement. From Stalin's perspective, whereas an alliance with Britain and France might mean a war against Germany with no prospect of gain, Hitler offered him tangible benefits—neutrality in the event of war between Germany and the West and a division of eastern European territory. For Stalin the choice was clear. On August 23, Germany and Russia announced a nonaggression treaty, which contained a secret protocol that divided Poland into German and Russian spheres, gave Lithuania to Germany, and ceded Finland, Latvia, and Estonia to the Soviet Union, thereby almost restoring Russia's 1914 frontiers. The Nazi-Soviet Pact was a consummate act of *Realpolitik*

Hitler's War Plans

On November 5, 1937, Hitler held a secret meeting with his military leaders in which he sketched his plans for aggression and war. Hitler's comments were recorded by his aide, Colonel Hossbach.

The aim of German policy is to make secure and to preserve the racial community and to enlarge it. . . .

Germany's future was therefore wholly conditional upon the solving of the need for space. . . .
Germany's problem could only be solved by means of force. . . .
If the *Führer* was still living, it was his unalterable resolve to solve Germany's problem of space at the latest by 1943–45.
Our first objective, in the event of our being embroiled in war, must be to overthrow Czechoslovakia and Austria simultaneously. . . . Our agreements with Poland only retained their force as long as Germany's strength remained unshaken. . . .
Actually, the *Führer* believed that almost certainly Britain, and probably France as well, had already tacitly written off the Czechs. . . .
Military intervention by Russia must be countered by the swiftness of our operations. . . .

Source: Documents on German Foreign Policy, 1918–1945, Series D, I (Washington, D.C.: U.S. Government Printing Office, 1949), Document No. 19.

concluded by two bitter ideological enemies. It shattered the loyalty of many communists and supporters of the Soviets around the world. On September 1, German planes and armored columns attacked Poland. Two days later Britain and France declared war on Germany. World War II had begun in Europe.

The Nazi Onslaught

Poland fell in less than four weeks, in what the Germans called a *Blitzkrieg* ("lightning war"), which coordinated air and ground forces in a sudden furious attack. Stalin rushed troops into eastern Poland to secure the territory promised him in the Nazi-Soviet Pact. Poland was obliterated.

Unable to launch an offensive before the onset of winter, Hitler held back from an all-out assault to the west. Between late September 1939 and April 1940, this "phony war" was interrupted only by German-British naval engagements. In the meantime, the Soviet Union moved troops into Estonia, Latvia, and (as a result of a new agreement with Germany) Lithuania and on November 30 invaded Finland, conquering it by March 1940 after unexpected resistance. In April, Hitler suddenly struck at Norway and Denmark. The latter fell in less than a day, Norway by the end of the month. Then, on May 10, the German war machine was flung against Belgium and the Netherlands. The same day, Chamber-

lain resigned and was replaced as prime minister by Winston Churchill (1874–1965).

Although the combined British, French, Belgian, and Dutch forces matched Germany's 134 divisions, the Allies were deficient in planes and antiaircraft power and overwhelmed by German *Blitzkrieg* tactics. By the end of May the Germans had pushed the Allied armies to the English Channel, where more than 330,000 French and British troops were evacuated from Dunkirk to England. Bypassing the Maginot Line, a chain of static fortifications that ran north from Switzerland, the Germans pushed rapidly through Belgium into France, outflanking French forces. On June 10, Mussolini, who had kept Italy neutral but now feared that the war might be over before he could act, declared war. French premier Paul Reynaud turned over the government to 84-year-old Marshal Henri Pétain (1856–1951), the hero of Verdun. Determined to salvage what he could, Pétain sued for terms. The armistice, signed on June 22, 1940, granted the Germans occupation of more than three-quarters of France, leaving the southern portion of the country to Pétain, who established a puppet regime in the city of Vichy. A small resistance group led by General Charles de Gaulle (1890–1970) escaped to London and formed the Free French organization. In less than two months, France, the mainstay of democracy in continental Europe, had fallen.

THE ROAD TO WORLD WAR II

1931	Japan invades Manchuria and leaves the League of Nations (September)
1933	Hitler becomes chancellor of Germany (January)
	Reichstag grants Hitler dictatorial powers (March)
	Germany withdraws from League of Nations (October)
1935	Hitler announces German rearmament (March)
	Mussolini invades Ethiopia (October)
1936	Hitler reoccupies the Rhineland (March)
	Outbreak of Spanish civil war (July)
	Rome-Berlin Axis; Anti-Comintern Pact between Germany and Japan (November)
1937	Japan invades China (July)
	Italy withdraws from the League of Nations (December)
1938	Germany annexes Austria (March)
	Munich Pact dismembers Czechoslovakia (September)
1939	German troops occupy Prague (March)
	Italy invades Albania (April)
	Pact of Steel: military alliance between Germany and Italy (May)
	Nazi-Soviet Nonaggression Pact (August)
	Hitler invades Poland (September 1)
	Britain and France declare war on Germany (September 3)

Allied Resistance and Axis Setbacks

With France defeated, Hitler was certain that Britain would make peace. To hasten this, he unleashed his air force against Britain in July to wreck civilian morale by terror bombing. Churchill, Britain's new leader, was a veteran of its imperialist wars and had served as First Lord of the Admiralty during World War I. In the face of adversity, he also proved to be a stirring orator. A convinced anticommunist, he had once expressed admiration for Mussolini but since 1936 had strongly opposed appeasement. Now he personified the British will to resist. Outnumbered by more than 2 to 1, the Royal Air Force (RAF) fought in the skies over London and other cities, inflicting unexpected casualties on the German *Luftwaffe*. In London, St. Paul's Cathedral remained almost alone in the midst of devastated streets as a symbol of survival, while Churchill rallied the nation in eloquent speeches. Unable to launch an amphibious invasion against a superior navy and facing mounting air losses, Hitler broke off what came to be called the Battle of Britain.

MAP 39.2   WORLD WAR II IN EUROPE

Stymied in Britain, the Axis turned to eastern Europe and North Africa. The Italians assaulted the British stronghold in Egypt in September and were repulsed into Libya, but Hitler salvaged the operation and pushed to within 100 miles of the Suez Canal. The pattern was repeated in October, when Mussolini invaded Greece. Valiant Greek resistance, British aid, and poor Italian equipment required Hitler to intervene again. Together with Hungarian and Bulgarian troops, the Germans overran Yugoslavia and defeated Greece.

As early as July 1940, Hitler ordered preparations for an invasion of the USSR. Despite the Nazi-Soviet Pact, Hitler remained obsessed by the desire to destroy Bolshevism and to gain control of the grain-rich fields of the Ukraine. Once Russia was defeated, he believed,

Britain would be forced to capitulate. The Soviet invasion began on July 22, 1941. "Operation Barbarossa" moved the mightiest army in history—some 175 German divisions—against a vast, unfortified front. The Germans took the Soviets by surprise and, shattering their weak defenses, killed or captured two million soldiers in the first months of the campaign. By late October, the USSR appeared about to collapse. But instead of allowing his generals to make a concentrated push against Moscow, Hitler insisted on dispersing his forces along the front. An early winter brought the German offensive to a halt, just as it had Napoleon's Grand Army in 1812. When Stalin's troops counterattacked, first in November and again in December, the Nazi war machine suffered its first setbacks. With Britain holding out in the west and the USSR having survived in the east, Hitler now faced the prospect of a two-front war.

The United States and Japan: The Road to Pearl Harbor

Among the great powers, only the United States remained at peace. Disillusionment over the outcome of World War I had nurtured isolationist sentiment among many Americans, and when President Franklin Roosevelt came into office, he moved cautiously to make the nation aware of the precarious state of world affairs. Roosevelt wanted the United States to exert its influence against fascist and Japanese expansionism. But as the threat of war mounted, isolationists in Congress passed neutrality laws that prohibited the export of arms. Nevertheless, the Japanese drive into northern China in the summer of 1937 moved the American government into an openly anti-Japanese position. That October, Roosevelt, in a public statement known as the Quarantine Speech, declared that war was a contagion that had to be contained.

The outbreak of war in Europe found the American public sympathetic to Britain and France but unwilling to become directly involved. Roosevelt, determined to supply France and Britain with weapons, secured a revision of the neutrality laws that enabled the Allies to buy arms on a cash-and-carry basis. As the Nazis stormed across western Europe, he obtained a $1 billion defense appropriation. Public opinion began to rally behind the president during the Battle of Britain, and in September 1940, Congress implemented the first peacetime draft in American history. Two months later, as British resources neared exhaustion, Roosevelt devised the lend-lease program, which extended unlimited goods, instead of credit, to Britain. In the wake of the Nazi invasion of the USSR, munitions were also sent to the Soviet Union under the same plan. America had become, in Roosevelt's words, "the arsenal of democracy."

In August, Roosevelt and Churchill met on a cruiser off the Newfoundland coast to sign a statement of principles tantamount to war aims. This Atlantic Charter, signed on August 14, not only called for national self-determination, disarmament, and "freedom from fear and want" but also looked forward to "the final destruction of the Nazi tyranny" and unconditional German surrender.

Asian events finally brought America into the war. United States policy toward Japan had already hardened over China. Now, with the Western powers fighting in Europe, Japanese expansionists saw their opportunity. In September 1940, Japan signed a defensive Tripartite Pact with Germany and Italy, extending the Axis alliance to Asia. America responded by banning the sale of essential raw materials, including iron, steel, and aviation fuel, to Japan. Negotiations initiated with the United States in the spring of 1941 by Prince Konoye, the Japanese premier, resulted in deadlock. Hitler's invasion of Russia freed Japan to move without fear of Soviet interference, and in July it occupied Indochina. Roosevelt immediately froze Japanese assets and joined with Britain in imposing economic sanctions. The failure of negotiations, together with the stiff American response to Japan's conquest of Indochina, played into the hands of the extremists in Tokyo. In October, General Tojo Hideki (1885–1948), a militarist, became premier. On the morning of December 7—without a declaration of war and while Japanese envoys were meeting with American officials in Washington—two waves of Japanese planes attacked the United States naval base at Pearl Harbor, Hawaii, striking a devastating blow at American power in the Pacific. The next day the United States declared war on Japan.

The War in China

The Second World War was far more a global conflict than the first, and the major theater outside Europe was Asia. More territory and people in Asia were involved in the fighting than in any other part of the world. Asia experienced the first and so far the only use of nuclear weapons, by the Americans against the Japanese, and China suffered the greatest number of war casualties of any nation.

For China the war had actually begun in 1931 with the Japanese invasion of Manchuria and escalated to an all-out battle for survival when the Japanese attacked Peking and Shanghai in 1937 and fought their way to the Kuomintang capital of Nanking. Japanese troops, with the full knowledge of their commanders, went on an orgy of killing when Nanking fell, vowing to punish the Chinese for holding up the imperial army by their resistance in Shanghai and on the route to Nanking. Chiang Kai-shek had committed most of his best soldiers and modern weapons to slowing the Japanese drive for Nanking, but it was innocent civilians—probably as many as 300,000 dead—who suffered in the so-called Rape of Nanking once the Japanese entered the city. Survivors described horrifying sights of raped women impaled on stakes and children sliced in two.

Aftermath of the Japanese bombing of Shanghai in 1937.

Chiang's government and the remnants of his army retreated westward to Chungking (Chongqing). The Kuomintang war effort was largely spent, its best troops and equipment gone. New conscription drives in the western provinces brought the army to some five million men, but they were poorly clothed and fed, often virtually starved, and tyrannized by their officers; they had few or no weapons and very poor morale. The Japanese invasion was stalled by the mountains of western China, by overextended supply lines, and by the effective guerrilla resistance of the Communists in the north, who pinned down one million enemy troops but were never themselves eliminated. Japanese planes bombed the cities left under Chinese control almost at will after 1937 but had little military effect except to kill many thousands of civilians.

A few small battles took place, largely ineffective retreating actions by demoralized and poorly led Chinese forces easily brushed aside by Japanese columns probing westward. Near the Burma border in the far southwest, periodic artillery duels across the gorge of the Salween River broke out, but no real battles. In the north a different kind of war hurt the Japanese far more. Chinese Communist guerrillas controlled most of the countryside at night, especially west of the coastal plain, bombing bridges, roads, and railways and ambushing Japanese patrols but avoiding pitched battles, given the vast Japanese superiority in equipment. The guerrillas confined the invaders to the cities and towns, and as the war progressed,

they won control of much of the rural north while they too depended on mountains and distance to limit enemy occupation to urban areas in the east. When Japan surrendered in August 1945, its armies still held most of the eastern half of China.

Although there were only skirmishes rather than major battles after 1937, more than 21 million Chinese died at the hands of the Japanese between 1937 and 1945, most of them civilians. The occupying army was at least as ruthless as the Nazis in Europe, exterminating whole villages as part of a policy of terror and slaughtering noncombatants indiscriminately. Their officially sanctioned slogan was "Kill all, burn all, loot all!" In the occupied territories the Japanese forced Chinese to bow or even kneel to their officers and beat or shot them if they were not sufficiently deferential. The record of the Japanese was equally bad elsewhere in Asia, but in China they began much earlier and made no real effort to win local support. Like Nazi terror, Japanese brutality stemmed also from a conviction of their own cultural and even racial superiority and from their contempt for the people they conquered. It was a grim period in the history of East Asia. At the end of the war, the Kuomintang had been fatally weakened, and the Communists had grown from a tiny and hunted band to a major military presence in the north. Their effectiveness against the Japanese had won them a broad base of popular support even among many in the Kuomintang-controlled areas, and by mid-1945 they were the real government of much of the north.

Chungking: Beleaguered Wartime Capital

Just before the fall of Hankow (one of the three cities now part of Wuhan) on the central Yangtze in October 1938, China's capital moved farther upriver to Chungking, where it remained for the rest of the war. Chungking sprawled over steep hills at the junction of the Chialing (Jialing) River and the Yangtze near the center of the generally hilly Red Basin of Szechuan (Sichuan), which was in turn surrounded on all sides by mountains. The steep and narrow gorges of the Yangtze about halfway between Hankow and Chungking along the provincial border were easily blocked by a boom. These natural defenses kept Chungking secure from the Japanese army, but it had few defenses against air attack, and Japanese bombing caused great destruction and loss of life. By 1941, before Pearl Harbor, an unofficial American group, the Flying Tigers, paid by the Chinese but with their own fighter planes, had greatly reduced the bombing raids. Chinese morale was high for the first two or three Chungking years, and the wartime capital was a symbol of patriotic resistance. Whole arsenals and factories had been disassembled and carried on the backs of workers to Chungking and elsewhere in Szechuan to escape the Japanese; university faculties and students made the same journey, carrying what they could of their libraries and laboratories. America's entry into the war against Japan in late 1941 gave morale another boost.

But disillusionment spread as the Kuomintang army largely sat the war out while the increasingly corrupt government of Chiang Kai-shek and his cronies stockpiled arms for use against the Communists. Chungking was also notorious for its gray, cloudy weather; its drizzle; its suffocatingly hot summers and cold, damp winters; and its painful overcrowding. More than a million people from all parts of China, including officials and army personnel, were added to the original small population, with too few additions to housing, water supply, and other basics. Fires set by Japanese bombs often burned out of control, and air raid shelters were grossly inadequate. Chungking's main link with the outside world was the extension of the Burma Road through mountainous

southwest China and, after the Japanese took Burma, the American airlift from India over the "hump" of the Himalayas. The main airport was a sandbank in the Yangtze hemmed in by steep hills on both sides, flooded every spring and summer by rising river levels and obscured most of the time by heavy low clouds. The summer airport was on the edge of a cliff above the river, which was equally dangerous. There were no railways anywhere in Szechuan. People understandably felt isolated. Prices for everything skyrocketed through a combination of wartime shortages, government ineptitude, and a swollen population. The Szechuanese blamed it on "downriver people," who in turn were contemptuous of "ignorant provincials."

Tight "thought control" and the secret police suppressed all free political expression, and people with "dangerous thoughts" or caught with "improper" books in their dwellings were jailed or executed. Those with money and connections lived luxuriously in guarded villas with American-made limousines, but most people in Chungking lived in poverty, mud, and squalor. By 1940 inflation began to rise at about 10 percent per month, accelerating wildly after 1943. Currency might lose half or more of its value between morning and afternoon. The government printed more notes of larger denominations, while its finance minister, H. H. Kung, brother-in-law of Chiang Kai-shek, obtained gold from the United States for his own accounts in overseas banks, as did other Kuomintang officials. Salaries and wages fell hopelessly behind inflation, and malnutrition, tuberculosis, and other diseases of poverty were widespread. Furniture, clothing, books, and heirlooms were sold in a vain attempt to stay afloat. Nearly all officials succumbed to bribery and other forms of corruption, whatever their original principles, if only to save their families. By the end of the war the Chinese were universally demoralized and had lost faith in the Kuomintang. The Chungking years saw the death of Kuomintang hopes to remain the government of a China now sick of its ineffectiveness, corruption, and reaction.

India and Southeast Asia

India was only marginally involved in the war, although two million Indian troops fought under British command in several theaters, and India itself became a major military base and supply center for the Allied war effort in Asia. A few Japanese bombs fell on Calcutta, but the

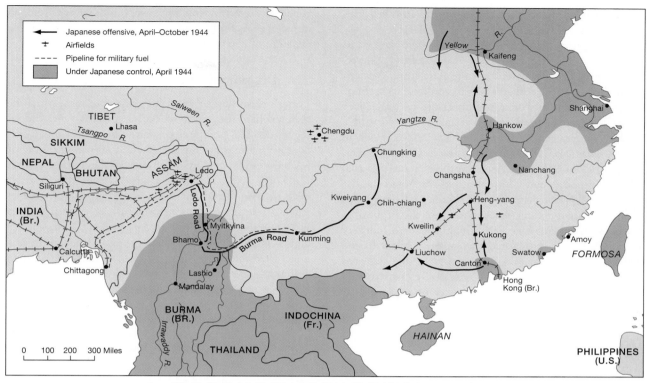

MAP 39.3   THE CHINA-BURMA-INDIA THEATER IN WORLD WAR II

big invasion push through northwestern Burma was stopped by British and Indian troops at Imphal, just inside the Indian border, in the spring of 1944, followed by the accelerating collapse of the Japanese position in Burma as British and Indian forces advanced. Ceylon served as a major Allied base and became the headquarters of the Allied Southeast Asia Command under Lord Louis Mountbatten (1900–1979), who directed the reconquest of Burma and Malaya.

A frustrated Bengali and Indian nationalist, Subhas Chandra Bose (1897–1945), who had been passed over for leadership in the Congress party, saw his chance for power in alliance with the Japanese. Bose had visited Mussolini and Hitler in Europe. He escaped from British arrest in 1941, made his way to Berlin, and in 1943 went by German submarine around Africa to Singapore, where the Japanese gave him command of 60,000 Indian prisoners of war. He called them the Indian National Army for the "liberation" of their homeland, but they were used as cannon fodder in the advance wave for the bloody and fruitless assault on Imphal. Bose escaped and was later killed in an air crash, but he remained a national hero to some Indians.

Japan and the Pacific Theater

The chief military action in Asia took place in the Pacific. Following the attack on Pearl Harbor, the Japanese conquered Malaya, Burma, Indonesia, and the Philippines in rapid succession. This onslaught was aided by Japanese use of French bases in Indochina, granted by the Vichy government in mid-1940 and vital to the assault on Southeast Asia.

The speed of the Japanese advance paralleled that of the Nazis in Europe. Japanese dive bombers destroyed the major ships of the British Asian fleet off Singapore as they had sunk most of the American fleet at Pearl Harbor. The Americans now lacked the naval capacity to defend or supply the Philippines, where much of their air force had been destroyed on the ground a few hours after the Pearl Harbor raid. The Japanese had developed a light, fast, maneuverable fighter plane, the Zero, which gave them air supremacy. The Dutch East Indies (Indonesia) were weakly defended, and no help was available for the greatly outnumbered Dutch. Thailand remained neutral, but at the price of granting Japan use of bases there. By early 1942 Japan had occupied all the smaller islands in the western Pacific and installed garrisons even in the western Aleutians off Alaska.

Japan's thrust southward had long been planned as part of the "Greater East Asia Coprosperity Sphere." Japan claimed that it would liberate Asia from Western colonialism, but the real aim was to combine its technological, industrial, and organizational skills with the labor and resources of the rest of East Asia, thereby creating a single economic entity dominated by Tokyo. Poor in natural resources, Japan sought access to the oil, rubber, tin, and rice of Southeast Asia and the iron ore and coal of the Philippines and China. But Japan ignored the rising force of nationalism, first in China and then in its Southeast Asian conquests. Almost from the beginning, Japanese racist arrogance and brutality made a mockery of "coprosperity" and earned the Japanese bitter hatred everywhere. Western prisoners, including the defeated American forces in the Philippines, were treated with special cruelty. Japan was now master of Asia, and its warrior tradition had only contempt for soldiers who surrendered even when their position was hopeless.

The Price of Victory

The brutality of Japanese rule in Asia was on a massive scale, but it lacked the carefully organized, systematic scope of Nazi atrocities in Europe. As the year 1942 opened, Hitler controlled, directly or indirectly, a huge empire that stretched from the English Channel to the gates of Moscow and from Norway to North Africa. His goal, after victory, was to create out of this area a "New Order" with Germany as its center and around which Europe and the world would revolve. Hitler never developed detailed plans for his empire. Yet the war provided ample evidence of what the New Order would have entailed.

Descent into the Abyss: The Holocaust

Hitler's plans derived from his notions of race, which he believed held the key to world history. Nazi racial ideologues divided Europe's population into three broad categories: the master "Aryan" race of German-speaking or related peoples, below which stood the Latins, and at the bottom the Slavs, Jews, and gypsies. Hitler dealt with the conquered territories according to this scale of values. The inferior populations of the eastern regions would provide Germany with *Lebensraum* ("living space") and a huge supply of cheap or slave labor. Immediately after the conquest of Poland, pockets of German colonists were established there, and more than one million Poles were brought to Germany as forced workers. Later even greater numbers of Russian prisoners suffered the same fate.

Nazi policy in eastern Europe was a vital part of Hitler's geographical scheme, but the Jews were at the core of his obsession about race. He spoke repeatedly of making Germany *Judenrein,* or free of Jews, and in *Mein Kampf* he described how the Nazi state would breed a population of Aryans free of the sick, the weak, and, most important, the Jewish "contagion." As early as 1919, Hitler had written that "the final objective" of anti-Semitism must "unswervingly be the removal of the Jews altogether."[1]

After the seizure of power, Nazi policies had forced the vast majority of German Jews to emigrate, so that by

The inhumanity of war: Polish Jews from the Warsaw ghetto rounded up by German soldiers. From Warsaw they were deported to extermination camps.

1939 few were left in the Reich. Once the war began, large-scale emigration from areas under German control became impossible, and Nazi officials evolved barbaric plans to deal with the millions of Jews in the conquered territories of Poland and eastern Europe. They first schemed to concentrate Europe's Jews in "reservations" in the Lublin district of Poland or on the island of Madagascar. As plans for the invasion of Russia progressed, the removal policy gave way to the Final Solution—the extermination of European Jewry.

Hitler gave SS leader Himmler orders for the Final Solution in the spring or early summer of 1941. As the German army pushed eastward, special SS units—*Einsatzgruppen* ("special-duty groups"), commanded by police chief Reinhard Heydrich—herded Jews into ditches behind the front lines and shot them. Mobile gassing vans were also used. By fall the extermination process had been organized on a massive scale as Jews and other victims were transported by rail from all over the Continent to death camps in Poland.

The SS murdered millions in extermination camps such as Auschwitz, Treblinka, and Bergen-Belsen, where tens of thousands of men, women, and children were gassed to death each day. A precedent for the killing had been set earlier by the gassing of 70,000 mentally ill Germans. The bodies of the victims were stripped of clothing, hair, and gold teeth. Corpses were either processed for soap and fertilizer or burnt. Outside the camps, in Poland and Russia, SS squads continued to slaughter many thousands more, shooting and burying their victims in mass graves.

The Nazis murdered a startling range of victims in their effort to purge Europe of "undesirable" elements, including gypsies, the infirm and mentally ill, Jehovah's Witnesses, and some 60,000 known German homosexuals. But their primary focus remained the Jews. Some estimates suggest that more than six million Jews perished in the Holocaust, more than three-fourths of Europe's Jewish population. Beyond the statistics lies the memory of the planned elimination of entire categories of human beings by a modern, technologically advanced society. Modern history has known no more heinous example of human barbarism.

Isabella Katz and the Holocaust: A Living Testimony

No statistics can adequately render the enormity of the Holocaust, and its human meaning can perhaps only be understood through the experience of a single human being who was cast into the nightmare of the Final Solution. Isabella Katz was the eldest of six children—Isabella, brother Philip, and sisters Rachel, Chicha, Cipi, and baby Potyo—from a family of Hungarian Jews. She lived in the ghetto of Kisvarda, a provincial town of 20,000 people, where hers was a typical Jewish family of the region—middle-class, attached to Orthodox traditions, and imbued with a love of learning.

After the liberation of an extermination camp, German civilians are forced to witness the unspeakable horrors of the Final Solution.

In 1938 and 1939 Hitler pressured Hungary's regent, Miklós Horthy, into adopting anti-Jewish laws. By 1941 Hungary had become a German ally, and deportations and massacres were added to the restrictions. Isabella's father left for the United States, where he hoped to obtain entry papers for his family, but after Pearl Harbor, Hungary was at war with America and the family was trapped. In the spring of 1944, when Hitler occupied Hungary, the horror of the Final Solution struck Isabella. On March 19, Adolf Eichmann, an SS officer in charge of deportation, ordered the roundup of Jews in Hungary, who numbered some 650,000. On May 28, Isabella's nineteenth birthday, the Jews in Kisvarda were told to prepare for transportation to Auschwitz on the following morning. Isabella recalled:

> **And now an SS man is here, spick-and-span, with a dog, a silver pistol, and a whip. And he is all of sixteen years old. On his list appears the name of every Jew in the ghetto.... "Teresa Katz," he calls—my mother. She steps forward.... Now the SS man moves toward my mother. He raises his whip and, for no apparent reason at all, lashes out at her.[2]**

En route to Auschwitz, crammed into hot, airless boxcars, Isabella's mother told her children to "stay alive":

> **Out there, when it's all over, a world's waiting for you to give it all I gave you. Despite what you see here ... believe me, there is humanity out there, there is dignity.... And when this is all over, you must add to it, because sometimes it is a little short, a little skimpy.[3]**

Isabella and her family were among more than 437,000 Jews sent to Auschwitz from Hungary.

When they arrived at Auschwitz, the SS and camp guards divided the prisoners into groups, often separating family members. Amid the screams and confusion, Isabella remembered:

> **We had just spotted the back of my mother's head when Mengele, the notorious Dr. Josef Mengele, points to my sister and me and says, "Die Zwei" [those two]. This trim, very good-looking German, with a flick of his thumb and a whistle, is selecting who is to live and who is to die.[4]**

Isabella's mother and her baby sister perished within a few days.

> **The day we arrived in Auschwitz, there were so many people to be burned that the four crematoriums couldn't handle the task. So the Germans built big open fires to throw the children in. Alive? I do not know. I saw the flames. I heard the shrieks.[5]**

Isabella was to endure the hell of Auschwitz for nine months.

The inmates were stripped, the hair on their heads and bodies was shaved, and they were herded into crude, overcrowded barracks. As if starvation, forced labor, and disease were not enough, they were subjected to unspeakable torture, humiliation, and terror, a mass of living skeletons for whom the difference between life and death could be measured only in an occasional flicker of spirit that determined to resist against impossible odds. Isabella put it this way:

> **Have you ever weighed 120 pounds and gone down to 40? Something like that—not quite alive, yet not quite dead. Can anyone, can even I, picture it? ... Our eyes sank deeper. Our skin rotted. Our bones screamed out of our bodies. Indeed, there was barely a body to house the mind, yet the mind was still working, sending out the messages "Live! Live!"[6]**

In November, just as Isabella and her family were lined up outside a crematorium, they were suddenly moved to Birnbäumel, in eastern Germany—the Russians were getting nearer and the Nazis were closing down their death camps and moving the human evidence of their barbarism out of reach of the enemy. In January, as the Russians and the frigid weather closed in, the prisoners were forced to march through the snows deeper into Germany, heading toward the camp at Bergen-Belsen. Those who could not endure the trial fell by the side, shot or frozen to death. On January 23, while stumbling through a blizzard with the sound of Russian guns in the distance, Isabella, Rachel, and Chicha made a successful dash from the death march and hid in an abandoned house. Two days later Russian soldiers found them. Philip had been sent to a labor camp, and Cipi made it to Bergen-Belsen, where she died.

Isabella later married and had two children of her own, making a new life in America. Yet the images of the Holocaust remain forever in her memory. "Now I am older," she says, "and I don't remember all the pain.... That is not happiness, only relief, and relief is blessed.... And children someday will plant flowers in Auschwitz, where the sun couldn't crack through the smoke of burning flesh."[7]

The Grand Alliance: Victory in Europe

By 1942 the Grand Alliance of the USSR, Britain, and the United States had been formed against Hitler's New Order. From the first the Allies were plagued by mutual distrust: Churchill feared Soviet territorial designs in Europe and what he believed was America's ignorance of European affairs; Roosevelt suspected Churchill's imperialist ambitions in the Mediterranean and Stalin's political motives; and Stalin suspected both Western statesmen, who hated communism, of wanting to deny the Soviet Union the fruits of victory. Nevertheless, they agreed to make military objectives—defeating first Germany and Italy, then Japan—their immediate goal, postponing political issues until the war was won. In January 1942 the three powers joined with 23 other nations in a declaration that reaffirmed these goals as well as the principles of the Atlantic Charter.

The tide of battle began to turn in favor of the Allies in 1942. In May and June, American forces stopped the Japanese advance in the Pacific in crucial battles in the Coral Sea and at Midway Island. In November the United States and Britain launched Operation Torch, the invasion of North Africa.

Under the pressure of the gigantic battles that were consuming Soviet forces on the eastern front, Stalin had repeatedly insisted on the opening of a major second front in the west. No nation sustained a greater burden of physical destruction and death than the Soviet Union, which lost some 20 million men, and no nation contributed more to the defeat of Germany. Since the winter of 1941 the German armies had continued to batter the Soviets along an 1,800-mile front, but in August 1942 the German war machine was flung at the southern zone in a protracted battle for Stalingrad. The situation ap-

peared hopeless when the Germans stormed the city in September. But Stalin's armies, circling around from the south and north, caught Hitler's forces in a gigantic pincer movement. Although winter fast approached, Hitler refused to withdraw his soldiers. On February 2, 1943, the last of the 500,000-man Sixth German Army surrendered. That July, German and Soviet forces fought bitterly along the Kursk salient, southwest of Moscow, in the biggest tank battle of the war. A clear victory for the Soviets, the engagement cost another half million German casualties and spelled ultimate defeat for Hitler.

Churchill and Roosevelt had met in January 1943 in Casablanca, where they made plans for opening the second front. To forestall the Soviets in central Europe, they chose Italy as the target, and in July, Allied troops landed in Sicily from their base in North Africa. The Sicilian invasion precipitated a coup d'état against Mussolini by dissident Fascists and involved King Victor Emmanuel III and Marshall Pietro Badoglio. The king arrested Mussolini and appointed Badoglio prime minister, but Hitler quickly moved German troops into northern Italy and rescued the Duce. By early September, when the Italians signed an armistice and joined the Allies as a cobelligerent against Germany, the Allies had crossed to the mainland. In the north Mussolini established a puppet regime, the Italian Social Republic, under German auspices. Thereafter, for 18 months Italy became the scene of bitter fighting, not only between the Allies and the Axis but also between Fascist loyalists and a massive partisan resistance movement.

British Prime Minister Winston Churchill inspects the damage from a German air raid.

The female labor force in the United States more than doubled during World War II. Here women riveters work on an airplane. "Rosie the Riveter" became a popular icon.

In October 1943, Allied foreign ministers meeting in Moscow reiterated their demand for unconditional surrender. They also agreed to the joint occupation of Germany, the purge of Nazism, and the creation of a United Nations organization to replace the discredited League of Nations. A month later Churchill and Roosevelt met with Stalin in Tehran for their first face-to-face conference. The talks focused on plans for the final attack against Hitler's "Fortress Europe." The three agreed to an invasion of western Europe in the spring of 1944.

Operation Overlord began on June 6, 1944—"D day." Under the supreme command of General Dwight D. Eisenhower (1890–1969), the Allies carried out the greatest amphibious landing in history on the coast of Normandy. More than two million men and millions of tons of equipment poured into northwestern France over the next few months. By the end of August, Allied armies had driven the *Wehrmacht* to the frontiers of Germany, but the drive stalled. In a desperate effort to stave off defeat, Hitler launched a counteroffensive in December, driving deep into the Allied sector in Belgium and Luxembourg, but the bloody Battle of the Bulge proved to be Germany's last major effort. From the east, Soviet armies poured into Germany in January, coming within 100 miles of Berlin, while British and American troops pushed toward Germany from the west, crossing the Rhine in March.

While the Allies were closing the ring around Germany, Churchill, Roosevelt, and Stalin met in February 1945 at Yalta, on the Black Sea. The Yalta conference re-

vealed the growing tensions that would divide the Allies after the war. Roosevelt, eager to secure Soviet entry into the war against Japan, conceded some of Stalin's demands regarding the future governments of Europe. Soviet armies were already in Poland, Germany, the Balkans, and eastern Europe. Churchill, who had made a secret arrangement with Stalin regarding Soviet and British influence in the Balkans, joined Roosevelt in agreeing to a larger Soviet role in eastern Asia and the transfer of Poland's eastern territory to the USSR while compensating the Poles with German land. In return, Stalin promised to permit democratic elements in the postwar governments of Poland and the eastern European states.

Three days after American and Soviet soldiers met on the Elbe River on April 25, Mussolini was executed by Italian partisans. On April 30, Hitler committed suicide in a secret bunker beneath the ruined streets of Berlin. German representatives signed the surrender in Eisenhower's headquarters on May 7, 1945.

The Atomic Bomb and the Defeat of Japan

With the European conflict at an end, American strategists turned their attention to the Pacific theater, where Japanese defeat was imminent. The naval battle of Midway in June 1942 had been won mainly by American aircraft carriers, which had been on patrol when Pearl Harbor was bombed, and by use of British-developed radar. A long island-hopping campaign began in which American and Australian troops retook the fiercely defended islands of the western Pacific piecemeal. Bloody battles in the jungles of New Guinea, the Solomon Islands, and the Bismarck Archipelago were followed by a slow northward advance, with hand-to-hand fighting and heavy losses on both sides. The Allies captured Saipan, within bombing range of Japan's big cities, in June 1944, and in October the Japanese suffered a major defeat in the Philippine Sea. By early 1945 the Philippines themselves were retaken, and in June the Allies seized Okinawa, part of Japan's home territory. Fanatical Japanese defenders often fought to the last soldier. Japanese pilots began to make suicidal *kamikaze* ("divine wind") attacks in planes loaded with bombs that purposely crashed into enemy ships. American losses, though serious, were soon replaced. Japan's fleet was by now almost entirely sunk, and American submarines had destroyed the majority of its supply and merchant ships. Meanwhile, American and Chinese forces had joined British and Indian troops in the liberation of Burma, while Allied naval dominance had cut the Dutch East Indies off from Japanese supply lines.

Japan was ready to surrender by the spring of 1945 and had begun peace feelers through the still neutral Soviets. American bombers had destroyed nearly all of Japan's cities, using incendiary bombs to start giant firestorms. In one horrible night in Tokyo, fire bombing killed an estimated 120,000 people, twice the number slain throughout the war in air raids over Britain. Many of the survivors in the gutted cities starved.

Events in the United States cut short plans for the final assault against the Japanese mainland. Working in secret laboratories on the so-called Manhattan Project, American, British, and European refugee scientists developed a primitive atomic bomb. The weapon was successfully tested on July 16 at Alamogordo in the isolated desert of New Mexico. Harry S Truman (1884–1972), who became president in April on Roosevelt's death, decided to use the awesome new weapon against Japan, a decision that subsequently aroused great controversy. On the one hand, some strategists argued that an invasion of Japan would cost heavy American casualties, although Eisenhower did not believe that the atomic bomb was needed to force Japan's surrender. On the other hand, at Yalta, Stalin had agreed to attack Japan within three months after the defeat of Germany, and Truman, with a decisive weapon at hand, may have been anxious to forestall the Soviets. On August 6 an American plane dropped an atomic bomb on the medium-sized town and army base of Hiroshima, obliterating the city and killing over 100,000 civilians. Radiation fallout and other injuries eventually claimed thousands of additional victims. Truman called it "the greatest thing in history." The USSR declared war on August 8 and swept into Japanese-occupied Manchuria. The next day the Americans leveled the city of Nagasaki with a second atomic device; more than 65,000 died. On August 15, Emperor Hirohito announced the Japanese surrender.

The End of Emperor Worship

On August 15, 1945, after the atomic bombing of Japan by American planes, Emperor Hirohito spoke to his people for the first time over the radio and declared the war lost. Here is how one listener, 10 years old at the time, recalled the impact of the news.

The adults sat around their radios and cried. The children gathered outside in the dusty road and whispered their bewilderment. We were most confused and disappointed by the fact that the Emperor had spoken in a *human* voice, no different from any adult's. None of us understood what he was saying, but we had all heard his voice. One of my friends could even imitate it cleverly. Laughing, we surrounded him—a twelve year old in grimy shorts who spoke with the Emperor's voice. A minute later we felt afraid. We looked at one another; no one spoke. How could we believe that an august presence of such awful power had become an ordinary human voice on a designated summer day?

Source: O. Kenzaburo, *A Personal Matter,* trans. J. Nathan (New York: Grove Press, 1968), pp. vii–viii.

The war had cost the lives of 2.5 million Japanese soldiers and sailors, and an additional million civilians had died in air raids. The country was in ruins. But the Japanese defeat of colonial regimes in the early years of the war had destroyed the myth of Western invincibility, and Japanese brutality had further stimulated Asian nationalism. Despite the Western victory in Asia, the old Western empires were irretrievably gone.

The United Nations

Allied plans for establishing a secure peace were based on the conviction that the fascist regimes had been responsible for the war and should be destroyed. The Allies im-

posed democratic and educational reforms on Germany, Italy, and Japan and removed compromised officials from positions of influence. They also supervised the drafting of new constitutions establishing parliamentary governments and civil liberties. Furthermore, the discovery of the Nazi death camps led to the establishment of the Nuremberg military tribunal to punish prominent Nazis for "crimes against humanity." Similar trials, on different grounds and sometimes under local jurisdiction, were held in Japan and Italy.

As in 1919, the victors in World War II placed great significance on the creation of an international organization to maintain the peace. Roosevelt, a Wilsonian idealist, was an ardent advocate of a new

MAP 39.4   WORLD WAR II IN EASTERN ASIA

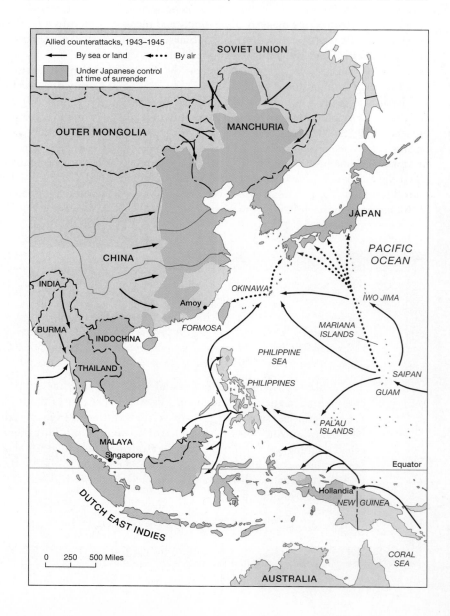

world body empowered to prevent aggression. The Allies dissolved the League of Nations, which had proved inept in dealing with fascist aggression and in its place created the United Nations, with headquarters in New York City. The formal charter, drafted at a meeting in San Francisco in April, was signed by 50 nations in June 1945.

The UN charter gave one vote to each member state in the General Assembly, which has since grown to more than triple its original size. But real power lay in the Security Council, whose permanent members were the United States, the Soviet Union, Britain, France, and China. Because each could veto council decisions, the organization was mired in controversy from the start. Subsidiary agencies, such as the World Health Organization and the Food and Agricultural Organization, however, have made important contributions in noncontroversial areas such as combating disease and starvation.

The Era of Reconstruction

The meeting of Soviet and American troops on the Elbe River in April 1945, amid the rubble of a continent, symbolized the eclipse of Europe as the dominant force in international politics. Germany had been decisively defeated and occupied. An exhausted Britain found itself the world's greatest debtor nation. France, overrun and occupied by Hitler's armies, had only de Gaulle's Free French and the internal resistance known as the Maquis to remember with any pride. The Soviet Union and the United States had been the principal architects of victory and their military strength would determine the future of the globe. For the next half century, the hegemony once exercised by western Europe would be shared by the two superpowers.

The Soviet Union

Stalin, though a brutal dictator, represented the views of most Soviet peoples when he adopted a defensive posture toward postwar geopolitics. Since coming to power in 1924, his foremost concern in foreign affairs had been Soviet national interests. From that viewpoint, he saw the spread of communism primarily as an extension of Soviet influence and only secondarily as the success of an ideology. Three times in as many decades Western powers had invaded his country, and the savage war fought on Soviet soil against the Nazis had taken an enormous toll on his nation's people

and resources. Now he was determined to strengthen the USSR against a rearmed Germany and a hostile United States.

In the postwar period Stalin's immediate concerns were to establish a Soviet presence in eastern Europe and to undertake the domestic reconstruction of the Soviet Union. These goals were linked, for he regarded eastern Europe as a region whose economic resources could be used to rebuild Soviet strength.

The Soviet Union faced an enormous task of reconstruction in the wake of a war that had destroyed much of its industry, many of its cities, and 30 percent of its national wealth. Not satisfied to restore conditions to the 1941 level, Stalin was determined to build an industrial base worthy of the USSR's new role as a world power. The Cold War increased the burden by adding massive expenditures for arms.

Stalin forced the USSR to return to the policies of the 1930s—extracting surplus capital for the development of heavy industry from the work of Soviet men and women. Although the exploitation of eastern Europe aided the work of reconstruction, most Soviets had to sacrifice their living standards again. Between 1946 and 1950 another five-year plan poured more resources into capital investment than had been spent during the 13 years after 1928, yet the economy produced only a minimum of consumer goods and began to stagnate by 1950. Housing remained so scarce that couples had to postpone marriage for years or live with in-laws in a single room.

Stalin's policies had a grimmer side. To meet the demand for workers, he deported huge numbers of people to labor camps, or gulags, across Siberia and central Asia, where thousands died from inadequate food, primitive conditions, and exhaustion. The inhuman conditions of life in the labor camps were brought to the attention of the Western world through the writings of Alexander Solzhenitsyn (born 1918), especially in his monumental work *Gulag Archipelago*. Harsh censorship policies and the repression of intellectuals remained a hallmark of Stalinist rule.

But Stalin's policies produced dramatic economic results. Tremendous increases were achieved in the production of iron, coal, steel, oil, chemicals, and electrical power, and science and technology moved ahead at an impressive rate. The USSR exploded an atomic bomb in 1949, tested a hydrogen bomb in 1953, and built high-quality fighter planes that proved themselves against American models during the Korean War (1950–1953). Most impressive, in 1957 the Soviet Union shocked the West by launching *Sputnik,* the world's first artificial satellite.

World War II had relaxed social controls, but during Stalin's final years he reimposed ideological conformity. The secret police began massive roundups of "enemies of the state" and transported them to the labor camps. There is also evidence that Stalin was planning another major purge, this time of Jews. He had already accused Soviet Jews of harboring pro-Western and anti-socialist views, and in January 1953 he ordered the arrest of nine Jewish physicians on charges that they had attempted to shorten the lives of Soviet officials. Before the alleged "doctors' plot" could unfold, however, a stroke took Stalin's life on March 5. His successors released the physicians and buried Stalin beside Lenin in the Kremlin's mausoleum.

From National Fronts to People's Democracies

Stalin's plans for eastern Europe became apparent soon after the war. Stalin did not attempt to adjust frontiers along ethnic or national lines. Instead, he forcibly relocated entire populations to fit his notions of Soviet security. This entailed the removal of 13 million ethnic Germans, including families that had resided in the Czech Sudetenland, Silesia, and areas east of the Oder and Neisse rivers for centuries. He also moved about 4.5 million Poles westward, replacing them with Russians and Ukrainians, and about 600,000 Balts from their homelands in Estonia, Latvia, and Lithuania, sending half to East Germany and half deep into Russia.

Because most eastern European states had provided troops for Hitler's legions, Stalin forced those countries to pay reparations. The Soviet Union aligned the entire region with its economic system, chiefly as a source of raw materials that satellite states were compelled to sell to the USSR at low prices.

The Soviet Union constructed new governments in states occupied by the Red Army, setting up "national front" coalitions of Communist, Social Democratic, and peasant parties. Each coalition enjoyed a degree of autonomy that varied from country to country. Where Stalin feared a serious threat to Soviet security, as in Poland and Romania, the national fronts were a sham. Bulgaria fared better, since after the arrival of Soviet troops in 1944, the Bulgarian army had joined in the war against Germany. The national front governments of Hungary and Czechoslovakia were true coalitions in which parties possessed a wide degree of freedom.

In the three years that the national front regimes lasted, they brought about fundamental changes. The Communists joined their coalition partners in breaking up the large, quasi-feudal estates that had characterized eastern European agriculture for centuries, distributing land to millions of peasant families. In addition, between 1945 and 1947 these governments nationalized the coal, steel, banking, and insurance industries.

In the late summer of 1947, Communist parties throughout the region began a concerted attack on their main rivals for popular support, the agrarian parties. Within six months all the national front regimes vanished. In their places appeared one-party Communist governments called "people's democracies." Two pressures probably led to the Soviet crackdown: the desire to use the area's wealth to support reconstruction at home and the decision to impose more direct control on the eastern European states in the face of the Marshall Plan (see below).

The people's democracies geared their economic programs to meet Soviet needs. Governments forced the collectivization of small farms, thus releasing significant numbers of peasants for work in factories under a series of five-year plans. The Soviets intensified their policy of sending high-priced exports to the region while paying low prices for imports. In essence, eastern Europe, an area containing some 90 million people, became an adjunct to the Soviet system. This policy postponed eastern European recovery, leaving the region bleak for many years.

Direct Soviet hegemony stopped at Yugoslavia. Under the leadership of the Communist leader Marshal Tito (Josip Broz, 1892–1980), the Yugoslav resistance had liberated the country from the Nazis without significant aid from the Red Army. In the postwar period Tito rejected Stalin's authority, engaging in a bitter confrontation with him over national sovereignty and Communist strategy. When Tito urged Communist leaders in the region to ignore the USSR's strategic needs, Stalin vowed to discredit him and bring Yugoslavia into the Soviet orbit. In 1948 and 1949 Stalin expelled Yugoslavia from the Cominform, placed an embargo on its economy, and isolated the country.

Within months the resourceful Tito accepted American economic assistance, simultaneously abandoning his support for world revolution while proclaiming the need for separate paths to socialism. In 1950 he initiated a policy of political decentralization that gave workers a larger voice in the management of factories than anywhere else in the world. Tito had not only maneuvered Yugoslavia into a position of nonalignment between the Soviet Union and the West but had also made his country the major model of independent Marxism.

De-Stalinization and the Rise of Khrushchev

Stalin groomed no successor. In the power struggle that erupted after his death in 1953, his closest followers lost out. A collective leadership soon emerged that abolished the office of general secretary of the Communist party, Stalin's base of power for 30 years, and established party secretaries in its place. At the top of this group was Nikita Khrushchev (1894–1971), a miner's son who as party boss had governed the Ukraine from 1939 to 1950. By 1955 he was joined by Nikolai Bulganin and Vyacheslav Molotov, Stalin's longtime foreign minister, to form a three-man troika.

Khrushchev came to personify post-Stalinist Russia. Though he would never wield the arbitrary power that Stalin had, he stood out from his rivals. Illiterate until his twenties, his bald, rotund appearance and outgoing personality belied a keen intelligence. Khrushchev solidified his position in a speech before the Twentieth Congress of the Communist party in 1956 that ranks among the most influential in Soviet history. This speech detailed Stalin's atrocities and attacked him for promoting a cult of personality. Later Khrushchev changed the name of Stalingrad to Volgograd and removed Stalin's body from the Red Square mausoleum. Official statues and portraits of Stalin also vanished.

As details of Khrushchev's speech became public, he began to take controversial action, dissolving the Cominform and meeting personally with Marshal Tito in a bid to improve relations with Yugoslavia. Stalinists on the Politburo attempted to depose Khrushchev, but the Red Army prevented the coup. In 1958 he assumed the office of premier, thus combining, as Stalin had done, the top party and state offices in his hands.

Khrushchev introduced a wide range of reforms. Downplaying Stalin's emphasis on the development of heavy industry, he increased the supply of consumer goods and housing and stimulated agricultural production with modern technology. The new policies improved the Soviet standard of living, although shortages of appliances, clothing, and food continued. The judicial system replaced police terror for all but political crimes, and intellectuals had more freedom than ever before. The party bureaucracy, however, still represented a privileged elite.

Dissent and Diversity

Ten days after Khrushchev's meeting with Tito in June 1956, anti-Soviet riots broke out in Poznan, Poland. Stalinists were quick to blame them on the liberalized policy toward eastern Europe. Actually, the first serious disorders with the people's democracies had erupted in Czechoslovakia and East Berlin shortly after Stalin's death in 1953. Khrushchev's de-Stalinization program stimulated the discontent that already existed. His speech to the Twentieth Party Congress had undermined the legitimacy of the Stalinists in Poland by reporting that Soviet agents had replaced Polish Communist leaders in 1948 with Soviet puppets. Thus in July 1956, when workers in Poznan began publicly demanding "bread and liberty," Polish police and military authorities refused to fire on them. Left with the option of calling in Soviet troops or yielding to popular demands, the Polish government promised reforms. Wladyslaw Gomulka (1905–1982), a leader who had lost favor in 1947 for seeking a Polish way to socialism, convinced the Soviet Union to permit his return to power. Gomulka accepted spontaneously formed workers' councils in the factories and began making overtures to the peasants and to the Catholic church while remaining closely linked to Soviet foreign policy.

The October 1956 Hungarian revolution challenged the USSR more directly. When Hungarian police fired

Nikita Khrushchev, who emerged as the leader of the Soviet Union after Stalin's death, initiated a new stage in domestic development and confrontation with the West.

on protesters in Budapest, sparking anti-Soviet demonstrations, the government called in Soviet soldiers. Workers' councils formed, demanding free elections, the end of the security police, and the withdrawal of Soviet troops. On October 28, when Imre Nagy (1896–1958) became premier and the Soviets began to withdraw, it appeared that the Hungarians had won. Nagy announced the reestablishment of a multiparty system and a return to the national front coalition of Communists, Social Democrats, and peasant leaders and proclaimed Hungarian neutrality between East and West. Convinced that a failure to respond would provoke further revolts throughout the Soviet bloc, Khrushchev ordered an invasion. Some 2,500 Soviet tanks moved into Hungary, shelling Budapest and other cities. When the repression was over, thousands of Hungarians were dead and more than 200,000 refugees had fled. No American intervention came.

The new Soviet-installed Hungarian premier, János Kádár (1912–1989), led the nation to a more liberal form of communism over the next three decades. Once imprisoned for nationalist activity, Kádár understood his country's desire for reform and independence. By the early 1960s he had removed Stalinists from the Hungarian Communist party and introduced programs that improved the standard of living. Although Kádár's role in the 1956 uprising undermined his leadership in the eyes of many, he remained in power until 1988.

By the early 1960s the countries of the eastern bloc had developed three different socialist systems: on the right stood the Yugoslavs, usually labeled "revisionists" because of their economic and political innovations; a number of "national Communists," such as Gomulka, straddled the middle ground, stressing solidarity with the Soviet Union in foreign policy but demanding domestic freedom to achieve communism; and the "dogmatists," including the followers of Mao Tse-tung in China and the Albanian Stalinists, vehemently opposed revisionism and resisted liberalizing tendencies. Beyond Europe the most significant example of diversity was the split between China and the Soviet Union (see Chapter 40). By the 1970s the Soviet Union remained the acknowledged leader of the Communist world, but its role was limited. The ideological unity of international communism was being eroded by diversity, internecine rivalry, and accommodation with the West.

Economic and Political Revival in Western Europe

The American people emerged from World War II with an outlook vastly different from that of the Soviets. Attacked directly only at Pearl Harbor, the United States had lost some 390,000 soldiers in the war, compared with 27 million Soviet deaths. Wartime spending had brought full employment after more than a decade of economic depression. In 1945 a wealthy America towered above its devastated allies. In the face of shattered European economies, the United States could look eagerly toward the opening of vast new markets for the products of its businesses and farms. Secure behind the world's only nuclear capability, most Americans wanted rapid demobilization, lower taxes, more consumer goods, and an end to foreign political commitments.

America's most immediate concern was Europe, to which it exported vast amounts of capital to stimulate economic reconstruction. The Marshall Plan, a massive program of economic development announced in June 1947 by U.S. Secretary of State George C. Marshall, offered economic assistance to any European nation that promised to consult with the American government to determine its needs. The plan also made possible an economic boom in the United States, for massive military outlays, together with the billions of dollars of aid sent abroad, stimulated the domestic economy. Although partly motivated by humanitarian concerns, that policy also reflected Cold War strategy: American policymakers believed that prosperity would diminish the appeal of communism and provide a basis for stable democratic governments.

Much of western Europe's prewar leadership had been discredited by the policy of appeasement or collaboration with Hitler. In the former Axis countries the purges of fascist sympathizers opened bureaucratic positions to former resistance fighters. In Allied nations the disastrous economic conditions that followed the war forced some conservatives, even wartime leaders, out of office. No less a hero than Winston Churchill was defeated at the polls, by the Labourite Clement Attlee (1883–1967), in the 1945 British elections because of his opposition to the extension of public assistance measures.

In France and Italy resistance leaders filled the power vacuum. General Charles de Gaulle, head of the exiled Free French movement, symbolized French efforts to erase the memory of Vichy collaboration with the Nazis, and in 1951 his followers emerged as the nation's largest political party. In Italy the liberal Ferruccio Parri (1890–1981) and the Christian Democrat Alcide De Gasperi (1881–1954), both former anti-Fascists, succeeded each other as prime minister. Because the Communists had been so prominent in the resistance movements, their support expanded enormously after the war. The Italian Communist party grew to some two million members by 1947, the largest in western Europe. In France the Communists were the strongest French party in 1945, and their vote rarely fell below the 25 percent level until 1958.

Despite the Marxist resurgence, western Europe did not face the prospect of social revolution, as it had in 1918 and 1919. The British Labourites and the West German Social Democrats were reformist rather than revolutionary parties. Probably at Stalin's orders, Communist resistance units stacked their arms and until 1947 participated in reformist governments. Moreover, American economic assistance encouraged the development of new center and moderate-right parties, of which the progressive Catholic parties, most often called Christian Democrats, were the most significant.

Like the Communists, many of the new Christian Democratic leaders had been in the resistance, but they supported both democratic principles and capitalism. As parties based on Catholic religious loyalties rather than social class, the Christian Democrats appealed to a wide range of voters. The partition of Germany, which placed many Protestant areas under Soviet control, gave the Christian Democrats an unexpected advantage in West Germany, where Catholics predominated.

The potential for rebuilding lay in the destruction of the war, for it cleared away antiquated factories and outdated technologies. Moreover, refugees willingly offered inexpensive labor, and a rise in the birthrate provided larger internal markets. The Marshall Plan contributed significantly to the reconstruction. The major condition for participation in the program was a willingness to join the Organization for European Economic Cooperation, which encouraged planning and free trade. The Marshall Plan stimulated Europe's economy to such a degree that by the mid-1960s production was almost triple the prewar level, and some western European nations surpassed the United States in per capita standard of living.

Toward Political Stability

The Marshall Plan weakened the extreme left and strengthened the Christian Democratic parties in Western Europe. When the USSR refused to allow eastern European participation in the plan, Communists in western Europe resigned from governing coalitions or were voted out of office. In the Federal Republic of Germany the Christian Democrats governed from 1949 to 1969, when the Social Democrats under Willy Brandt (1913–1992) came to power in coalition with a minority party, the Free Democrats. The hallmark of Brandt's tenure was his policy of *Ostpolitik,* a bold attempt to improve relations with the Communist states of eastern Europe. The results were striking: a treaty with the Soviet Union in which each country renounced the use of force to settle security issues, a treaty with Poland accepting the Oder-Neisse boundary imposed at the Potsdam

President Charles de Gaulle of France and Chancellor Konrad Adenauer of West Germany symbolized the emergence of a western European community based on cooperation and autonomy.

conference in 1945, improved relations with East Germany, and the admission of both German states to the United Nations. Brandt's spirit of reconciliation was no less dramatically manifested when he knelt on the site of the Warsaw ghetto and visited Jerusalem to express sorrow for the Holocaust. The Social Democrats pumped considerable resources into social programs and education and ran the Bonn government until the early 1980s. In 1982, a conservative reaction elected Helmut Kohl, a Christian Democrat, although the Brandt legacy continued as Kohl sought to heal the wounds of World War II and to improve relations with the Soviet Union.

In Italy, despite frequent changes of government, the Christian Democrats maintained de facto control from 1948 to 1981. Yet political and social instability was widespread. Italian students and factory workers, inspired by their French counterparts, launched crippling protest movements in 1968 and 1969, and in the latter year Communist and neofascist extremists resorted to terrorist tactics to publicize their causes. In the face of this threat to social stability, which evoked memories of the early 1920s, the Communist leader Enrico Berlinguer proposed a "historic compromise" in 1973; under its terms his party offered to cooperate with the Christian Democrats in a coalition government. In 1978 they formally voted with the parliamentary majority, the first time this had happened since 1947. Although the Communists continued to be excluded from the cabinet, largely at the insistence of the United States, the Christian Democrats yielded the premiership in 1981 to Giovanni Spadolini of the small Republican party. In 1983 the Christian Democrats supported a coalition government led by the Socialist Bettino Craxi, although by decade's end it too had given way to more cabinets headed by Christian Democrats. In the early 1990s, Italy's political institutions were shaken by the revelation of tremendous scandals that involved all political parties.

Centrist coalitions also dominated France's Fourth Republic until its collapse in 1958 and de Gaulle's return to power. Thereafter, de Gaulle established a more centralized but equally anti-Communist Fifth Republic, remaining in office until 1969. The Gaullist tradition dominated French politics for another five years under a more moderate Georges Pompidou. He dropped French opposition to British membership in the Common Market, devalued the franc to increase French exports, and cooperated with NATO. The center-right continued in power under Valéry Giscard d'Estaing, whose presidency (1974–1981) was marked by unfulfilled promises of social reform. His growing unpopularity, coupled with a rebuilding of the Socialist party, enabled its leader, François Mitterrand, to win the presidency in 1980 while his party gained control of Parliament. Although Mitterrand included Communists in his cabinet, he condemned Soviet policy and was friendlier to the United States than the Gaullists had been. In 1986 a conservative coalition gained control of the National Assembly, forcing Mitterrand to appoint the Gaullist Jacques Chirac as prime minister. Chirac returned some of the nationalized industries to private ownership. The French electorate, however, proved unwilling to move decidedly in a liberal or a conservative direction, giving neither the Socialists nor the conservatives a majority in the National Assembly.

Between 1945 and 1951 Britain's Labourite prime minister, Clement Attlee, introduced the most far-reaching reforms of the period. Attlee nationalized utilities, railroads, airlines, coal mines, the Bank of England, and the iron and steel industries. His Social Welfare Acts covered public housing, free medical care, and national insurance benefits. The Conservatives came back into power in 1951 and since then have alternated with the Labourites in heading the government. Although Conservative governments have not dismantled the British welfare state, from 1979 to 1991 Margaret Thatcher (born 1925)—the United Kingdom's first woman prime minister and the twentieth century's longest-serving one—favored private enterprise and imposed austere fiscal policies on the country. The result was a reduction of inflation, but at the price of the highest unemployment since the Great Depression and the increasing polarization of society. Although Thatcher won general elections in 1983 and 1987, her popularity plummeted in 1989 in the face of

Margaret Thatcher, longtime Conservative prime minister of Great Britain, presided over the retrenchment of domestic welfare policies and a tough foreign policy.

major economic problems. Thatcher's own party forced her to resign in 1990, but she retained enough influence to ensure the selection of her protégé, John Major, as the new prime minister. Despite a lingering recession, he led his party to victory in the 1992 election, only to see his popularity plummet in the face of a weak economy, tax increases, and deep divisions within his own party over the degree of British participation in the movement for European union.

The Cold War and the Superpowers

The conflict between Soviet and American national interests that dominated the international scene in the post–World War II period came to be known as the Cold War. As it grew in intensity after 1945, the Cold War assumed the public guise of a clash of ideologies. Many Americans saw themselves as defending capitalist democracy against communist totalitarianism, while the Soviets portrayed themselves as opponents of Western imperialism. In both instances the rhetoric obscured the reality of the Cold War as a struggle for dominance between the world's strongest nations.

Potsdam and the Origins of the Cold War

Historians disagree as to when the Cold War began and who was responsible for breaking Soviet-American wartime collaboration. Some scholars place the beginning as early as 1918, when American troops invaded northern Russia at Archangel to try to topple the Bolshevik regime. Others argue that the growing antagonism between the United States and the Soviet Union, already revealed in wartime discussions among the Allies, did not become irreversible until 1947 or 1948, when anticommunism became the guidepost of American policy. The consensus, however, is that the Cold War emerged out of the conflict between Stalin and Truman over the future of eastern Europe during the Potsdam conference in the summer of 1945.

Stalin had made it clear at Yalta that he wanted a readjustment of borders and an extension of the Soviet frontier into Polish territory. In return, he promised to allow free elections in eastern Europe after the war. Between February and July, however, the situation had changed drastically when the Red Army had overrun Poland, Romania, Hungary, Bulgaria, and most of Czechoslovakia and Yugoslavia, and Stalin installed pro-Soviet governments. The issue resurfaced at Potsdam, where Truman represented the United States and Clement Attlee, Churchill's successor, represented Great Britain.

Truman charged that Stalin had betrayed the Yalta agreement. But with eastern Europe under Red Army occupation, the Soviet leader remained adamant in the face of what some historians believe was Truman's attempt to use America's atomic monopoly to blackmail the Soviets into making concessions.

The division of Europe into Western and Soviet blocs was an accomplished fact when, in March 1946, the former prime minister Winston Churchill set the tone for Cold War rhetoric by declaring that the Soviets had lowered an "iron curtain" across the continent, an expression quickly adopted by Western cold warriors as a symbol of the division between East and West. The Soviet-American clash soon took on a more global character. The United States blocked Soviet efforts to secure a foothold in Iran, and in August, when Stalin demanded a voice in controlling the Dardenelles straits, Truman sent an aircraft carrier to the eastern Mediterranean. The future saw a pattern of repeated and dangerous confrontations.

From the Truman Doctrine to the Berlin Blockade

While relying on the nuclear deterrent to safeguard American security, Truman insisted that the United States had to counter a growing communist challenge, especially in Greece, China, and Indonesia, where com-

The Big Three at Potsdam, 1945: Churchill (soon to be replaced by Atlee), Truman, and Stalin confer on post–World War II settlements.

munist movements were attempting to overthrow local governments. Truman used the Greek case to arouse American public opinion. Since the liberation of Greece in 1944, Britain had stationed troops there in support of a corrupt monarch in order to keep Soviet influence out of the Mediterranean. A civil war, led by procommunist wartime resistance fighters, now threatened the political stability of the country. Although Stalin kept his wartime promise to recognize Greece as an Anglo-American sphere of influence, the Communist government of Yugoslavia was aiding the rebels, and the British could no longer sustain the rightist regime.

On March 12, 1947, Truman announced that America must assist nations that were "resisting attempted subjugation by armed minorities or by outside pressures. . . . The free peoples of the world look to us for support in maintaining their freedoms."[8] Urging Congress to appropriate $400 million in military aid to bolster the Greek and Turkish governments, the president inaugurated the Truman Doctrine, the cornerstone of American foreign policy for the next two decades. Soon the word *containment* came to describe the principles of the Truman Doctrine, according to which the United States should restrict communism to areas already under Soviet control. That July, Congress also passed a measure establishing the National Security Council, which was to coordinate military and diplomatic policy for the president with the assistance of the newly formed Central Intelligence Agency (CIA). Truman was especially concerned about Third World areas, where Marxists often led national anticolonial movements. Soviet propagandists answered the Truman Doctrine by accusing the United States of seeking to preserve colonialism and asserting that the Soviet Union spoke for national liberation.

Containment had its economic as well as its military side. The United States attempted to draw all European states into the American orbit through the Marshall Plan. The Soviet Union vetoed the participation of Czechoslovakia, Poland, and Hungary in the plan, fearing that Western economic penetration would weaken its hold on the eastern European states. In western Europe, however, the United States pumped $13 billion into Britain, France, Italy, Germany, and other countries. The Marshall Plan proved a huge success, inaugurating a sustained era of European prosperity that helped combat the growth of Marxist parties.

In response, the Soviet Union strengthened its hold on eastern Europe. In 1946 Stalin already controlled Poland, Romania, Bulgaria, and Albania, and over the next two years he consolidated Soviet influence over Hungary and Czechoslovakia. The Soviet counterpart to the Marshall Plan was COMECON, an economic organization that claimed to integrate the economies of the eastern European states and the Soviet Union. Under the program, some nations, such as Czechoslovakia, were assigned industrial goals, while others, such as Bulgaria, were given agricultural quotas. In place of the old Communist International (Comintern), abolished during the war, Stalin created the Communist Information Bureau (Cominform), designed to reassert Moscow's control over the world communist movement.

As the United States and the Soviet Union consolidated their positions in Europe, Germany assumed major importance. The future of Germany had been debated since Potsdam, when Stalin had insisted on moving Russia's borders westward at the expense of Poland, which in turn would receive portions of East Prussia as well as the city of Danzig, renamed Gdansk. Germany's eastern border was set at the Oder and Neisse rivers, and the country was broken into four occupation zones to be governed separately by Britain, France, the United States, and the Soviet Union. Berlin, inside the Soviet zone, was similarly divided among the four powers. Disputes between the Soviet Union and the West left Germany broken into two separate states. The Soviet Union, which had suffered such massive casualties and destruction at the hands of Germany, preferred to see it permanently divided.

After 1946 the Western powers agreed to combine the three Western occupation zones into a single economic unit as a prelude to political sovereignty for a "West German" government. In 1948 self-government was instituted on a local level, and the Germans were permitted to write a new constitution. No postwar American action antagonized the Soviet Union as much as these efforts to reestablish a German nation, which Stalin continued to fear. That June, Stalin restricted access to West Berlin. The Americans promptly closed their sector to Soviet traffic. When Stalin blockaded all land access to Berlin, Britain and the United States followed suit with a counter-blockade against goods moving from East to West Germany. Amid fear of war, the United States began to supply West Berlin by air, moving huge quantities of vital goods to the beleaguered city for almost a year until Stalin conceded defeat.

The Berlin blockade hastened the creation of a separate West German government, formally proclaimed on May 21, 1949, as the Federal Republic of Germany, with its capital at Bonn. Parliamentary elections brought to power as chancellor the Christian Democrat Konrad Adenauer (1876–1967), a former mayor of Cologne who had been imprisoned by Hitler. Adenauer represented America's Cold War position: cooperation with the West, rapprochement with France, and vigorous anti-communism. Five months after the creation of the Bonn government, the Soviet Union formed a Communist regime in the eastern sector, known as the German Democratic Republic, with its capital in East Berlin.

Cold War tensions continued to heighten. In April 1949 the United States sponsored the North Atlantic Treaty Organization (NATO), a mutual-defense pact in which most Western nations, including Greece and Turkey, pledged to treat an armed attack against one nation as an assault against all; in 1955 the Soviet Union established a similar defense system, dubbed the Warsaw Pact. But the relationship between the superpowers had already changed dramatically with news in September 1949 that the Soviet Union had detonated an atomic bomb. Several months later Communist forces under Mao Tse-tung defeated the Nationalist armies of Chiang Kai-shek and seized power in China (see Chapter 40). The end of nuclear monopoly and the Communist takeover in China replaced confidence with uncertainty in American foreign policy.

From Brinkmanship to Détente

By the early 1950s the superpowers were enmeshed in a struggle for hegemony. The pattern of conflict set in 1947 remained fairly consistent: with American influence predominant in Latin America and western Europe and the Soviet Union supreme in eastern Europe, each superpower challenged the other in peripheral regions of the globe. The danger lay in the possibility that diplomatic confrontations would lead to local military conflict, which could in turn escalate into nuclear war. The Korean War proved to be the first of several such situations (see Chapter 40).

The Cold War intensified with the election of Dwight D. Eisenhower (1953–1961) on the Republican ticket in 1953. Eisenhower delegated exceptional authority to his secretary of state, John Foster Dulles (1888–1959). A man who combined a brilliant legal mind with righteous moralism, Dulles had been part of Wilson's delegation at the Paris peace conference in 1919. He proved to be one of the most strident voices of the Cold War, denouncing Truman's containment policy and advocating an offensive program to "liberate" areas under communist control. Dulles emphasized America's nuclear strength, basing foreign policy on repeated warnings that communist aggression would lead to "massive retaliation" by the United States. The Dulles policy of

rattling nuclear missiles during international crises was dubbed "brinkmanship," but the eastern European revolts of the 1950s revealed the hollowness of these threats. America stood by in 1956 while anti-Soviet fighters in Hungary battled Soviet tanks with cobblestones and rifles.

The Eisenhower administration never abandoned containment. Using marines or covert operations directed by the CIA, the United States played a key role in overthrowing supposedly procommunist governments around the world, including those in Iran (1953), Guatemala (1954), and Chile (1973). The CIA also plotted the assassination of Congolese leader Patrice Lumumba in 1961 and, with the aid of American gangsters, made several attempts against the Cuban leader Fidel Castro.

Under President John F. Kennedy (1960–1963), American Cold War strategy shifted again, but only in emphasis. Kennedy undertook a huge buildup of conventional and nuclear weapons. In his effort to close the "missile gap" with the Soviet Union, he accelerated the nuclear arms race, to which the USSR responded in 1961 by detonating a hydrogen bomb in the atmosphere. Kennedy was fascinated with "counter-insurgency" operations, by which he meant the use of limited warfare against communist infiltration of Third World countries. One result of this was the Bay of Pigs fiasco in Cuba (see Chapter 42).

Encounters between Kennedy and Khrushchev brought the world to the edge of nuclear disaster. In the summer of 1961 Khrushchev tried to stem the flow of refugees from East Berlin to the West and threatened to sign a treaty with East Germany that would terminate Western rights in the city. Kennedy ordered reservists on military alert and urged Americans to build fallout shelters. This sharp response may have persuaded Khrushchev to back down, for on August 13 the East Germans sealed off their portion of the city by erecting a wall between the two sections of Berlin.

A year later Khrushchev intruded into the American sphere of influence in Latin America by constructing nuclear missile bases in Cuba. Khrushchev argued the need to prevent another American attempt to overthrow the Castro government, but Kennedy considered the action a direct military threat. In October 1962, when American air reconnaissance revealed Soviet missiles in Cuba, the president imposed a naval quarantine around the island and demanded the missiles' removal. For six tense days Soviet ships sailed toward Cuba and American forces went on war alert. Khrushchev finally drew back by sending Kennedy a letter deploring the horrors of nuclear war and offering a face-saving compromise. The Soviets

The Cuban Missile Crisis: Two Views

The discovery by the United States in the fall of 1962 that the Soviet Union was installing missile bases in Cuba brought the world to the edge of nuclear war. The first of the following accounts of the crisis is by special White House assistant Arthur M. Schlesinger, Jr., who described President Kennedy's speech of October 19.

Then at seven o'clock the speech: his expression grave, his voice firm and calm, the evidence set forth without emotion, the conclusion unequivocal—"The purpose of these bases can be none other than to provide a nuclear strike capability against the Western Hemisphere." He recited the Soviet assurances, now revealed as "deliberate deception," and called the Soviet action "a deliberately provocative and unjustified change in the status quo which cannot be accepted by this country. . . ." He then laid out what he called with emphasis his *initial* steps: a quarantine on all offensive military equipment under shipment to Cuba; an intensified surveillance of Cuba itself; a declaration that any missile launched from Cuba would be regarded as an attack by the Soviet Union on the United States, requiring full retaliatory response upon the Soviet Union . . . and an appeal to Chairman Khrushchev "to abandon this course of world domination, and to join in a historic effort to end the perilous arms race and to transform the history of man."

Here is Soviet Premier Khrushchev's account.

I want to make one thing absolutely clear: when we put our ballistic missiles in Cuba, we had no desire to start a war. . . . In October, President Kennedy came out with a statement warning that the United States would take whatever measures were necessary to remove what he called the "threat" of Russian missiles in Cuba. . . . In our estimation the Americans were trying to frighten us, but they were no less scared than we were of atomic war. . . .

President Kennedy issued an ultimatum, demanding that we remove our missiles and bombers from Cuba. I remember those days vividly. I remember the exchange with President Kennedy especially well because I initiated it and was at the center of the action on our end of the correspondence. I take complete responsibility for the fact that the President and I entered into direct correspondence at the most crucial and dangerous stage of the crisis. . . .

The climax came after five or six days, when our ambassador to Washington, Anatoly Dobrynin, reported that the President's brother, Robert Kennedy, had come to see him on an unofficial visit. Dobrynin's report went something like this: "Robert Kennedy looked exhausted. One could see from his eyes that he had not slept for days. He himself said that he had not been home for six days and nights. 'The President is in a grave situation,' Robert Kennedy said, 'and he does not know how to get out of it. We are under very severe stress. In fact we are under pressure from our military to use force against Cuba.'". . .

We could see that we had to reorient our position swiftly. . . . We sent the Americans a note saying that we agreed to remove our missiles and bombers on the condition that the President give us his assurance that there would be no invasion of Cuba by the forces of the United States or anybody else. Finally Kennedy gave in and agreed to make a statement giving us such an assurance.

Sources: A. M. Schlesinger, Jr., *A Thousand Days: John F. Kennedy in the White House* (Boston: Houghton Mifflin, 1965), pp. 812–813; N. Khrushchev, *Khrushchev Remembers*, trans. S. Talbott (Boston: Little, Brown, 1970), pp. 496–498.

agreed to withdraw their missiles in return for a public pledge from America not to invade Cuba; unofficially, the United States agreed to dismantle its own offensive missiles in Turkey.

American Society in Transition

For Americans, the Cold War had powerful repercussions at home. In February 1950, Senator Joseph R. McCarthy (1908–1957) of Wisconsin claimed to have a list of Communists who held important positions in the State Department and accused Secretary of State Marshall of protecting them by inaction. McCarthy never produced the name of a single Communist and repeatedly changed the number of alleged "traitors" he had discovered in the government. But his message was clear: the Truman administration had bred and coddled the communist enemy within the government.

That a senator could make such accusations against Truman appears incongruous in retrospect, for the president had shown himself to be an enthusiastic cold warrior, had imposed a loyalty program on federal employees, and had jailed most leaders of the small and nearly impotent Communist party of the United States. Yet a wave of anticommunist hysteria swept the country. McCarthy's "Red

The Cold War at home: Senator Joseph R. McCarthy of Wisconsin (seated) and his two chief aides, G. David Shine (right) and Roy Cohn (left).

scare" campaign made him a national figure. Despite the election of Eisenhower, he continued to claim conspiracy in high places. The witch-hunt spread from Communists to other groups, including homosexuals. In televised hearings that ended in mid-1954, McCarthy finally overextended himself when he charged that the army itself was riddled with Communist spies. In December the Senate censured McCarthy, ending his influence. Yet imitators perpetuated his methods, especially in monitoring schoolteachers and blacklisting actors. The anticommunist scare had lasted four years, and in some areas of American life, pools of suspicion lingered far longer.

President Eisenhower attempted to moderate the trend that Roosevelt's New Deal had set in motion toward increasing government involvement in economic and social life. Yet as large numbers of Americans were driven to leave the farms and the cities for life in the suburbs, a federal highway program improved the country's transportation system and spurred the automobile industry. The Eisenhower government, which proved more sympathetic to business than any since 1932, reduced the federal role in the marketplace wherever possible.

Despite the withdrawal of government from social policy, the movement for racial equality made important strides in this period. In 1954 a landmark ruling by the U.S. Supreme Court, *Brown* v. *Board of Education of Topeka,* held that segregated schools violated the constitution's Fourteenth Amendment, which guaranteed all citizens equal protection under the law. Correctly anticipating that the southern states would resist immediate integration, the Court ordered implementation of its ruling "with all deliberate speed." In 1957 Orville Faubus, the governor of Arkansas, summoned the National Guard to block entry of nine African-American children into Little Rock's Central High School. Eisenhower, who had not been enthusiastic about the *Brown* decision, nevertheless refused to allow such open flouting of government authority. He ordered federal troops to Little Rock, forcing Faubus to back down.

Martin Luther King, Jr., and the Struggle for Civil Rights

African-American political activism, organized for the first time on a national level, was the driving force in the civil rights struggle. Dr. Martin Luther King, Jr.

(1929–1968), a young black Baptist minister, led a mass civil rights movement. Born in Atlanta, Georgia, King was the son of a Baptist preacher. He studied sociology at Morehouse College and then entered the ministry, eventually taking a Ph.D. in theology at Boston University.

In 1954 King became pastor of the Dexter Avenue Baptist Church in Montgomery, Alabama, where he led the fight against racial segregation on public buses. His eloquent rhetoric and inspiring personality introduced a dynamic new doctrine of nonviolent protest to the nation. A year later African-Americans of Montgomery had achieved their goal.

To extend the successful Montgomery action throughout the nation, King organized the Southern Christian Leadership Conference (SCLC), which gave him a national platform. He was convinced that Ma-hatma Gandhi's tactic of nonviolent disobedience was the answer to the civil rights struggle. In 1960 King became copastor with his father at the Ebenezer Baptist Church in Atlanta but devoted his energies to the SCLC and to a concerted drive against racial injustice. While protesting segregation at a lunch counter, he was arrested and sentenced to state prison on a pretext. The case aroused the interest of Democratic presidential candidate John Kennedy.

King's influence reached its peak in the years between 1960 and 1965. The nonviolent strategy of "sit-ins" and protest marches drew an interracial following and pressured President Kennedy, who proposed a comprehensive civil rights bill in 1963 intended to end legal segregation. King's success also made him the subject of covert FBI surveillance. In the spring of 1963 his efforts

Letter from Birmingham Jail

After the arrest of Martin Luther King, Jr., in 1963, eight fellow clergymen published a statement calling his actions "unwise and untimely." In April, King wrote a lengthy response—scribbled in the margins of a newspaper and on scraps of paper—explaining "why we can't wait."

Perhaps it is easy for those who have never felt the stinging darts of segregation to say, "Wait." But when you have seen vicious mobs lynch your mothers and fathers at will and drown your sisters and brothers at whim; when you have seen hate-filled policemen curse, kick, and even kill your black brothers and sisters; when you see the vast majority of your twenty million Negro brothers smothering in an airtight cage of poverty in the midst of an affluent society; when you suddenly find your tongue twisted and your speech stammering as you seek to explain to your six-year-old daughter why she can't go to the public amusement park . . . and see ominous clouds of inferiority beginning to form in her little mental sky, and see her beginning to distort her personality by developing an unconscious bitterness toward white people; when you have to concoct an answer for a five-year-old son who is asking: "Daddy, why do white people treat colored people so mean?" . . . when you are humiliated day in and day out by nagging signs reading "white" and "colored"; when your first name becomes "nigger," your middle name becomes "boy" (however old you are) and your last name becomes "John," and your wife and mother are never given the respected title "Mrs."; when you are harried by day and haunted by night by the fact that you are a Negro, living constantly at tiptoe stance, never quite knowing what to expect next, and are plagued with inner fears and outer resentments; when you are forever fighting a degenerating sense of "nobodiness"—then you will understand why we find it difficult to wait. There comes a time when the cup of endurance runs over, and men are no longer willing to be plunged into the abyss of despair. I hope, sirs, you can understand our legitimate and unavoidable impatience.

Source: M. L. King, Jr., *Why We Can't Wait* (New York: Harper & Row, 1963), pp. 83–84.

Martin Luther King, Jr., who popularized the passive resistance strategy that led to victories in the U.S. civil rights movement, leads a march from Selma to Montgomery, Alabama, in 1965. To his left is his wife, Coretta Scott King.

to end segregation in Birmingham, Alabama, resulted in national attention as police turned dogs and fire hoses on the demonstrators and arrested King along with hundreds of schoolchildren. From jail King wrote a letter of great eloquence explaining his nonviolent philosophy. In August 1963, King and other civil rights advocates marched on Washington. Before the Lincoln Memorial, his moral passion captivated some 250,000 peaceful demonstrators as he recounted his "dream" that one day both blacks and whites would be measured by the content of their character rather than by the color of their skin.

Kennedy's legislative proposal was blocked in Congress by a coalition of Republicans and conservative southern Democrats and remained stalled in committee at the time of his assassination in 1963. His more politically astute successor, Lyndon B. Johnson (1908–1973), obtained passage of the 1964 Civil Rights Act, which prohibited discrimination in public places and in the use of federal funds. For his contributions to civil rights, King was awarded the Nobel Prize for peace in 1964.

In his final years King's leadership came under increasing pressure from more militant African-Americans, who faulted him for being too cautious. Riots in the Watts district of Los Angeles in 1965 brought attention to the enormous problems of blacks in northern and western cities, where his nonviolent tactics were questioned. King began to broaden his work to include housing discrimination in Chicago, and in 1967 he strongly opposed the war in Vietnam. In April 1968, while in Memphis, Tennessee, to support a strike of sanitation workers, he was assassinated by a white racist.

King's great contribution to civil rights had been his ability to turn regional protests into a national crusade. He had galvanized the African-American masses into action, and although complex racial problems continued to plague the nation, America would never quite be the same again.

The New Activism

The same year as the passage of the Civil Rights Act, President Johnson ran for election on a platform calling for a "Great Society" and a "war on poverty." The voters returned him to office along with 40 additional Democratic members of Congress, giving the House of Representatives a progressive majority for the first time since 1938. The triumph of liberalism reflected a new social activism that had been stimulated by the struggle for racial equality.

Since the early 1960s university students in America had been in the forefront of social and political militancy, as they were in Europe. In June 1962 about 60 young people, members of a group known as Students for a Democratic Society (SDS), met at Port Huron, Michigan, to discuss civil rights, foreign policy, education, and welfare. The declaration of principles they issued focused on the concept of "participatory democracy," the notion that people should take part in the decisions that affect their lives. SDS organized an interracial movement of the poor in northern cities, took part in sit-ins and demonstrations in the south, and became increasingly militant over the Vietnam War. By the late 1960s SDS began to split apart, one faction forming the Weathermen, an extremist group devoted to violent action. Yet the Port Huron Statement left its mark on an entire generation of Americans.

The civil rights movement and student activism transformed American society in other ways. The gay rights movement, born in 1969 when a police raid in New York's Greenwich Village sparked violent protests from men in the Stonewall Bar, raised important issues about sexual oppression and coincided with the emergence of a powerful new impetus toward women's liberation.

Many women who had left the home for the factory during World War II sought jobs traditionally closed to them. Feminists were encouraged by the controversial arguments of Betty Friedan (born 1921), whose book *The Feminine Mystique* (1963) argued that women should seek fulfillment beyond their ties to husbands and children. After the war the number of women who worked for pay outside the home rose dramatically, so that by 1960 twice as many women worked as in 1940. Equally significant was the fact that whereas only 15 percent of all wives worked in 1940, the figure exceeded 50 percent by 1980.

Two separate movements took up the challenge of feminism in the 1960s. The National Organization for Women (NOW), at first composed of older professionals and headed by Friedan, worked for women's rights through the political and legal systems and styled themselves a "militant" organization. The women's liberation movement, which attracted many younger women who had been involved in antiwar and civil rights efforts, was more confrontational. Beginning in 1968 it identified the patriarchal family and socially formed gender patterns as sources of oppression. Not only did radical feminists demand legal equality with men, but they also encouraged women to seek power through female solidarity and "gender consciousness."

Affirmative Action regulations designed to enforce equal opportunity brought about improvement in employment patterns and wage scales for minorities and women. Yet in the 1970s a woman earned only 59 cents for every dollar earned by a man. In 1972 Congress passed an equal rights amendment to the constitution, but the measure failed when a number of state legislatures did not ratify it. Racial, ethnic, and sexual prejudice remained deeply entrenched in American society.

Women and Social Change Outside the United States

Rapid modernization has marked European society since the end of World War II. Traditional class barriers have relaxed, and a salaried managerial elite has developed with the growth of public corporations and new technological industries. Social distinctions have also been blurred by a higher standard of living for many and the availability of mass-produced consumer goods. National television networks joined radio and film—which were already widely developed in the 1920s and 1930s—in reaching rural villages. Free education virtually eliminated illiteracy. The new prosperity, along with less expensive automobiles and vigorous highway construction, has made for a highly mobile society.

All European states except Liechtenstein and Switzerland gave women the vote after the war, but in other ways the status of women varied greatly from one country to another. The Scandinavian and northern European nations generally adopted legal equality for women more readily than those in the south, but everywhere traditional values have given way to greater oppor-

The new feminism began in the 1960s. Here, at a 1970s fund-raiser for the equal rights amendment, are former first lady Betty Ford (speaking), with Bella Abzug on the far right and Betty Friedan second from the left.

tunity. In 1949 the prominent French intellectual Simone de Beauvoir (1908–1986) published her highly influential book, *The Second Sex,* which demonstrated how women had been subordinated by tradition, social custom, and ideology. De Beauvoir's work provided an early theoretical basis for the women's liberation movements that developed in Britain, France, Germany, Italy, and Scandinavia in the 1960s. The revival of Socialist and Communist parties after the war gave practical reinforcement to the new feminist theory, for they combined a long tradition of female militancy with progressive social policies. Hence the representation of women is higher in Socialist and Communist parties than in capitalist ones. Feminist coalitions and left-wing parties successfully fought for legalized abortion and more liberal divorce laws, even in some Catholic societies.

Women have made up a large percentage of the workforce since the Industrial Revolution. Since 1945 they have had access to better jobs along with the growing availability of free higher education. About one out of every three workers is now female, and women have also established a strong presence in labor unions. Nevertheless, most women are still excluded from high-level managerial positions and senior government posts and, like their American counterparts, continue to struggle for full equality.

In the Soviet Union, where women made important gains after Stalin's death, more than half the workers were female. Abortion was legalized, the divorce law was liberalized, and many more child-care centers were built. In the professions, women represented 67 percent of doctors, 35 percent of lawyers, and more than 58 percent of engineers by the 1980s. (In the United States, by contrast, women make up a much lower percentage of lawyers and physicians.) Khrushchev appointed the first woman member of the Presidium of Ministers, but whereas some 29 percent of party members were women, they held only 4 percent of the high party offices. In general, women's participation in party politics in socialist and communist nations was higher at local levels than in the central governments. For example, in East Germany about 25 percent of district committee members were women in 1981, whereas only 13 percent of the posts in the Central Committee were held by women. Differences in pay and political power between males and females, as well as social inequalities among women, continued to exist, but most women in these nations enjoyed greater access to professions than women in the West.

Nevertheless, life was hard for most Soviet women, despite legal equality. They had few modern conveniences, and married women got almost no support from their husbands for the household duties they were expected to perform in addition to their paid jobs. As late as 1987, Mikhail Gorbachev, the last Soviet leader, declared that women had "inherent functions: those of mother, wife, the person who brings up children." Yet he took a greater interest in women's issues than any Soviet ruler since Lenin, supporting day-care expansion, flexible work schedules, and increases in the minimum wage for professions held mostly by women.

SUMMARY

As the world recovered from the ashes of destroyed cities and the loss of some 50 million lives, it could look back on a generation of economic depression, dictatorship, ideological strife, and the bloodiest war in history. Yet international strife did not end in 1945, for growing tensions between the former Allies resulted in the Cold War struggle between the United States and the Soviet Union. In this context, the birth of the atomic age, mirrored in the ruins of Hiroshima and Nagasaki, suggested the possibility that humans could one day destroy civilization.

As people everywhere celebrated the triumph over European fascism and Japanese militarism, the task of political and economic reconstruction presented the world with a more pressing challenge than the emerging Cold War. Moreover, out of the tragic and sobering legacy of the war, the prospect of an end to the vast colonial empires that had once held in their grip the people of Asia, Africa, and Latin America augured well for the future.

NOTES

1. L. S. Dawidowicz, *The War Against the Jews, 1933–1945* (New York: Holt, Rinehart and Winston, 1975), p. 153.
2. I. K. Leitner and I. A. Leitner, *Fragments of Isabella* (New York: Dell, 1988), pp. 18–19.
3. Ibid., p. 28.
4. Ibid., p. 31.
5. Ibid., p. 32.
6. Ibid., pp. 46–47.
7. Ibid., pp. 102–103.
8. F. Friedel, *America in the Twentieth Century* (New York: Knopf, 1960), pp. 475–476.

SUGGESTIONS FOR FURTHER READING

Boyle, J. H. *China and Japan at War, 1937–1945.* Stanford, Calif.: Stanford University Press, 1972.
Butow, R. *Japan's Decision to Surrender.* Stanford, Calif.: Stanford University Press, 1954.

Calvocoressi, P., and Wint, G. *Total War*. Harmondsworth, Eng.: Penguin Books, 1972.

Campbell, H., ed. *The Experience of World War II*. New York: Oxford University Press, 1989.

Campbell-Johnson, A. *Mission with Mountbatten*. New York: Dutton, 1953.

Conroy, H., and Wray, H., eds. *Pearl Harbor Reexamined*. Honolulu: University Press of Hawaii, 1990.

Crankshaw, E. *Khrushchev*. New York: Viking Press, 1966.

Divine, R. A. *The Reluctant Belligerent: American Entry into World War II*. New York: Wiley, 1979.

Eubank, K. *The Origins of World War II*. New York: Crowell, 1969.

Fejto, F. *A History of the People's Democracies: Eastern Europe Since Stalin*. New York: Praeger, 1971.

Fussell, P. *Wartime: Understanding and Behavior in the Second World War*. New York: Oxford University Press, 1989.

Gaddis, J. L. *The United States and the Origins of the Cold War, 1941–1947*. New York: Columbia University Press, 1972.

Gellately, R. *The Gestapo and German Society: Enforcing Racial Policy, 1933–1945*. New York: Oxford University Press, 1990.

Gilbert, M., and Gott, R. *The Appeasers*. Boston: Houghton Mifflin, 1963.

Havens, T. *The Valley of Darkness*. New York: Norton, 1978.

Herken, G. *The Winning Weapon: The Atomic Bomb in the Cold War, 1945–1950*. Princeton, N.J.: Princeton University Press, 1988.

Hilberg, R. *The Destruction of the European Jews*. 3 vols. New York: Holmes and Meier, 1985.

Hildebrand, K. *The Foreign Policy of the Third Reich*. Berkeley: University of California Press, 1973.

Hsi-sheng, C. *Nationalist China at War*. Ann Arbor: University of Michigan Press, 1982.

Ienaga, S. *The Pacific War*. New York: Pantheon Books, 1978.

Kitchen, M. *A World in Flames: A Short History of the Second World War in Europe and Asia, 1939–1945*. New York: Longman, 1990.

Kolko, G. *The Politics of War*. New York: Random House, 1969.

Langer, W. L., and Gleason, S. E. *The Undeclared War, 1940–41*. New York: Harper & Row, 1953.

Lebra, J., ed. *Japan's Greater East Asia Coprosperity Sphere in World War II*. Kuala Lumpur, Malaysia: Oxford University Press, 1975.

Marrus, M. *The Holocaust in History*. New York: New American Library, 1987.

Mastny, V. *Russia's Road to the Cold War*. New York: Columbia University Press, 1979.

Mosse, G. L. *Toward the Final Solution*. New York: Fertig, 1978.

Myers, R. H., and Peattie, M. R., eds. *The Japanese Colonial Empire, 1895–1945*. Princeton, N.J.: Princeton University Press, 1984.

Parker, R. A. C. *Struggle for Survival: The History of the Second World War*. New York: Oxford University Press, 1991.

Robertson, E. M. *Mussolini as Empire Builder*. London: Macmillan, 1977.

Spector, D. H. *Eagle Against the Sun*. New York: Free Press, 1989.

Tanaka, Y. *Hidden Horrors: Japanese War Crimes in World War II*. Boulder, Colo.: Westview Press, 1996.

Thomas, H. *The Spanish Civil War*, rev. ed. New York: Harper & Row, 1977.

Ulam, A. *Expansion and Coexistence: The History of Soviet Foreign Policy, 1917–1967*. New York: Praeger, 1974.

White, T., and Jacoby, A. *Thunder out of China*. New York: William Sloane Associates, 1946.

CHAPTER 40

Revival and Revolution in East Asia

uch of Asia was devastated by World War II, and no part of it was unaffected. There were more war casualties in Asia than in all the rest of the world. The heavy human and economic losses were, however, accompanied by the end of colonial rule and Western dominance in Asia. The Japanese conquest of Southeast Asia destroyed the image of Western superiority, while the war in Europe diminished both the ability and the desire of the European powers to resume their former positions in Asia. Japan's economy was destroyed by the war, and almost all of its cities were bombed to rubble. Japan lived under American military occupation from 1945 to 1952, but by 1950 the damage to the economy had been largely repaired and rapid new growth that would continue for decades had begun. By 1965 Japan had become the world's third industrial power, after the United States and the Soviet Union, and in the 1970s and 1980s it won a commanding position in world markets for its manufactured exports.

In China long-pent-up pressures for change resulted in civil war, from which the Communists emerged victorious over the Kuomintang (Guomindang) government in 1949. The new revolutionary government quickly repaired war damages, but in 1957 Mao Tse-tung, the Communist leader, launched the Great Leap Forward, a radical economic program that ended by plunging the country into mass starvation. It was followed in 1966 by the Cultural Revolution, a destructive effort to revive flagging revolutionary ardor, which ended only with Mao's death in 1976. China began to reopen its contacts with the West in the 1970s and to pursue economic growth rather than ideology. Korea was split by the Cold War into rival states; Vietnam, similarly divided, was unified by a successful war against the United States; and in Southeast Asia a number of new nations emerged, each following a different path.

Tradition meets modernity: a woman in traditional Japanese dress waits at a bus stop.

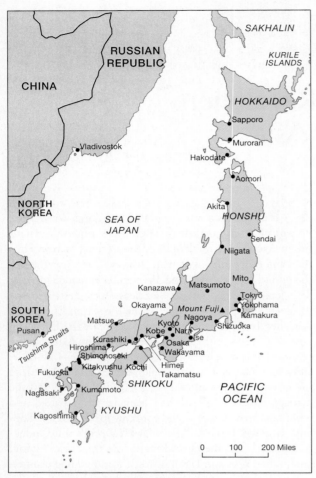

MAP 40.1   MODERN JAPAN

The Recovery of Japan

Japan had been more completely destroyed by the war than any of the other belligerents. In addition to Hiroshima and Nagasaki, which had been leveled by the atomic bombs, virtually all of Japan's cities, especially Tokyo and Yokohama, had been flattened and burned by massive conventional and incendiary bombing. A notable exception was Kyoto, the old imperial capital, which had been preserved by the intervention of American art historians. The government and what remained of the army in the home islands were still, however, in good order, and there was a smooth transfer of power to the American military government of occupation under General Douglas MacArthur. Japan had surrendered to the Allied forces, including Britain, China, Australia, Canada, New Zealand, and the Soviet Union, although the Sovi-

ets had intervened only in the last week of the war. But MacArthur permitted only token representation from each of the other allies in his SCAP (Supreme Commander Allied Powers) regime of occupation, over which he presided like a virtual emperor.

With very few exceptions, the Japanese people, including officials, officers, and troops, as well as other civilians, accepted Emperor Hirohito's pronouncement of surrender and his call to "endure the unendurable." Most felt relief that the disastrous war was over. They soon found that the occupying Americans were not the devils some had feared and vented their bitterness on the now discredited military leaders, who had so nearly destroyed the nation they were sworn to serve. In general, the occupation, which lasted from late August 1945 to late April 1952, was a period of peaceful reconstruction, with the Japanese doing most of the work of government under American supervision, except at the highest level.

The American Occupation

Relief on finding the occupying forces bent on reconstruction rather than revenge was soon joined by gratitude for American aid. Most Japanese had lived at best on an austerity diet during the last years of the war, and many were half starved, living in makeshift shelters in the bombed-out cities. The winter of 1945–1946 would have been far harder if the Americans had not flown in emergency supplies of food and gotten the main rail lines working again to transport fuel and essential building supplies. Having expected far worse from their new rulers, the Japanese were pleasantly surprised. Many were even enthusiastic about the institutional changes that SCAP began to decree to root out the remnants of militarism and implant American-style democracy.

The big prewar industrial combines were broken up, though they subsequently re-formed. Thousands of political prisoners who had been accused of "dangerous thoughts" and jailed by the military-controlled government of the 1930s and 1940s were released. Other Japanese who were identified—sometimes wrongly—as having been too closely associated with Japanese fascism or militant imperialism were removed from their posts, including a number of senior officials. Several hundred Japanese were identified as suspected war criminals, and most were tried by a special tribunal in Tokyo that included Allied representatives. Seven were executed, including the wartime prime minister, Tojo Hideki, and eighteen others were sentenced to prison terms. Nearly 1,000 minor war criminals in Japan and Southeast Asia,

MacArthur: An Assessment

Most observers described General Douglas MacArthur as a vain man, ever conscious of his public image. Here is a leading Western historian's assessment of MacArthur in his role as the head of SCAP from 1945 to 1951.

A tendency toward complacent self-dramatization was encouraged by the adulation of a devoted wartime staff that he took with him to Japan. . . . They took almost ludicrous care that only the rosiest reports of the occupation should reach the outside world. In their debased opinion the slightest criticism of S.C.A.P. amounted to something approaching sacrilege. MacArthur took up residence in the United States Embassy in Tokyo. Each day at the same hour he was driven to his office in a large building facing the palace moat; at the same hour each day he was driven home again. . . . He never toured Japan to see things for himself. . . . The irreverent were heard to say that if a man rose early in the morning he might catch a glimpse of the Supreme Commander walking on the waters of the palace moat. There is no doubt that this aloofness impressed Japanese of the conservative type. . . . But it may well be doubted whether this kind of awed respect was compatible with the healthy growth of democratic sentiment. . . . The Japanese perhaps learned more about democracy from MacArthur's dismissal than from anything he himself ever did or said.

Source: R. Storry, *A History of Modern Japan,* rev. ed. (New York: Penguin Books, 1982), pp. 240–241.

largely military men, were executed for gross cruelty to prisoners or to the inhabitants of conquered countries. This contrasted with the far more lenient treatment and in some cases even protection of all but the most major Nazi leaders by the United States and its allies in Europe and prompted charges of racism.

A victor's justice in the aftermath of a bitter war is easily criticized, especially when racially tinged, but most Japanese accepted the tribunal's verdict as inevitable and perhaps even appropriate punishment. Most blamed their failed leaders rather than their new masters. The flexibility and adaptability of the Japanese in turn impressed the Americans, who had expected resentfulness and found instead to a surprising degree both liking and admiration. Having fought ruthlessly and with immense dedication, the Japanese proved quite ready to accommodate to a relatively benign new order. Americans were admired because they had won and also because most Japanese truly appreciated their relief and reconstruction program and their efforts to democratize Japan. After all, the Japanese had suffered horribly under a militaristic police state; they were ready to follow new paths. American ways were imitated uncritically by

many, but the basic political reforms of the occupation sent down firm roots.

Most of the changes were reaffirmed after the occupation or, perhaps more accurately, were grafted onto earlier Japanese efforts to adopt Western institutions prior to the years of military government (1931–1945). In addition to a revitalization of electoral and party democracy, government was decentralized by giving more power to local organs. Public education, formerly supervised closely by the central government, was also decentralized and freed as much as possible from bureaucratic control. One of the most successful and permanent changes was the program of land reform, which compensated the large owners whose property was expropriated and sold the land to former tenants, thus ending the last surviving traces of the Tokugawa order. Japanese society began to evolve rapidly toward its present social system, in which status results from achievement rather than birth.

The new constitution drafted by SCAP officials retained the emperor as a figurehead but vested all real power in a legislature and prime minister elected by universal suffrage. There was a detailed bill of rights for the protection of individuals against arbitrary state power.

Emperor Hirohito of Japan with General MacArthur at the U.S. Embassy in Tokyo in 1945.

Article 9 of the constitution forbade Japan to have any armed forces except for police and denied it the right to go to war. To most Japanese this was not only reasonable but welcome, given the ruin that arms had brought them and the aftermath of atomic warfare, of which they were the living witnesses. Japan, many felt, should set an example of the folly of war for the rest of the world. What disillusioned the Japanese about the occupation was the shift in American policy beginning in 1948 toward rebuilding Japan's military capacity and using it as a base of American strategic operation.

The goal of making Japan a Cold War ally of the United States soon took precedence over reform and reconstruction. The Berlin blockade, the Communist victory in China in 1949, and the Korean War all further hardened the American line. Although President Harry Truman fired MacArthur in 1951 for his insubordination in the Korean War, Cold War considerations continued to dominate American policy. When the occupation ended in 1952, Japan was bound to the United States by a security treaty that permitted the buildup of a Japanese "self-defense force," the stationing of American troops, and American use of several major bases in Japan. U.S. pressures for Japanese rearmament have continued,

and the bases remain, but Article 9 of the constitution still has the support of most Japanese.

Economic and Social Development

Whatever the political shifts as the occupation wore on, economic reconstruction was almost miraculously rapid. By 1950 the shattered cities, factories, and rail lines had been largely rebuilt, and by the end of 1951 industrial production was about equal to what it had been in 1931, now from new and more efficient plants. The Korean War provided an additional economic boost as Japan became the chief base and supplier for American forces in Korea. By 1953, with reconstruction complete, personal incomes had recovered to their prewar levels, and Japan was entering a new period of rapid development. Some credit is due to American aid in the hard years immediately after the war, but the "Japanese miracle" was overwhelmingly the result of the nation's own hard work, organization, and pursuit of economic success through group effort. The growth of production and income in Japan from 1950 to 1975 was faster than has been measured in any country at any time; in those 25 years, output and incomes roughly tripled. Yet the Japanese continued to maintain a very high rate of personal savings, which as elsewhere helped fuel economic growth through investment.

At the same time, production quality also rose impressively, and in many respects Japanese goods, notably automobiles, cameras, sound reproduction equipment, optics, and many electronic items, became the best in the world market. This was a tribute to advanced Japanese technology and design, as well as to the efficiency of an industrial plant rebuilt with the latest design and equipment. Similar factors were active in the postwar recovery of Germany, while the victorious Allies, including the United States, were saddled with their older and less efficient plants. After 1953 Japan dominated world shipbuilding, although it gave ground increasingly to South Korea in the 1980s. By 1964 Japan had become the world's third largest producer of steel, and by 1980 it had overtaken both the USSR and the United States in steel output while also becoming a major producer and exporter of automotive vehicles. Japan also invaded European and American markets on a large scale with its "high-tech" and industrial goods.

Japanese democracy has retained healthy growth, although politics continued to be dominated by a conservative coalition with no effective rival parties. High school education is virtually universal, and literacy among the Japanese is the highest in the world. The press is of high quality and is avidly supported by a public that also buys and reads more books than in any other country, about ten times the figure for Americans. Over half of young Japanese continue with postsecondary education in a great variety of colleges, universities, and other institutions. Overall, the Japanese are now probably the best-educated population in the world.

Education was a major reason for Japan's spectacular economic success. Economic growth largely eliminated the nation's poverty and unemployment. With the postwar disappearance of aristocratic values, Japan became largely a nation of prosperous middle-class people in an orderly society. Despite crowded conditions—population density in its central urban corridor is the highest in the world—there are few slums, little violent crime, and few signs of social malaise. By 1980 Japan achieved the world's highest life expectancy and its lowest murder rate, less than one two-hundredth that of the United States.

Japanese disarmament, a condition at first imposed by the American occupation but now for many an ingrained social value, has also paid handsome dividends. Japan has thus been largely free of the crushing economic burden of maintaining the huge military establishment undertaken by most other large countries in the postwar world. Money was invested instead in economic growth, new technology, full employment, education, and a wide range of social services. Japan is virtually alone in the world in having escaped from most of the cankerous problems that breed in poverty, such as violence, hopelessness, and drugs. The national ethic of work, achievement, and high standards, now in the service of personal and group goals of economic advancement rather than imperial ambition, has produced a new and more constructive society.

Nevertheless, Japanese society has significant problems. The drive for achievement exacts a toll on schoolchildren as well as on adults. Pressures begin for admission to the "right" kindergarten and continue through elementary school, middle (high) school, and college or university. Each stage of schooling is accompanied by fiercely competitive examinations. Childhood, after the age of 5, is a stressful time for most Japanese. Extreme urban crowding and cramped living space add further burdens. Commuting time for people who work in downtown Tokyo averages nearly two hours each way and is only slightly less in other big Japanese cities. Parks and recreation facilities are extremely limited. Housing is fearfully expensive, and most urban Japanese, who constitute over 80 percent of the population, live in tiny apartments with minimal amenities. Yet as one of the best-informed and most widely traveled peoples in the world, most Japanese know they are generally very well off despite their cramped quarters.

Notwithstanding the newer values of social equality and status based on achievement, traditional patterns remain, especially the subordinate status of women. Deference to superiors or elders, and of all women to men, is still expected by older Japanese. New generations may well reshape their society on somewhat freer lines, but most would agree that it will be a long time before women achieve anything close to equality. In the workplace women are in subordinate or service roles, with very few exceptions. At the same time, women are often the real powers within the family and household. They usually have control of the family finances and have the preponderant role in the upbringing of children; most fathers work long hours, and their long commute usually gets them home only after the children are in bed. Nevertheless, over half of adult Japanese women work outside the house, close to the current American figure, often managing a small family business or neighborhood store. Equality in the professions remains a distant goal.

Nearly half of Japanese women get some form of post-high school education or training. Much of it is vocational, and relatively few attend the prestigious universities, which are minutely ranked; most Japanese can recite the rank order. Many women attend college or university for reasons of social status or to find a husband.

Japan's International Role

Despite their global economic stature, the Japanese have been reluctant to assume the role of a world power in political terms, a role that has brought them tragedy in the past. They have often been uncomfortably aware of this disparity between their economic power and their more hesitant political stance abroad. On a number of occasions they felt their interests ignored in the maneuverings of Cold War diplomacy. As an American client and a bulwark against neighboring communist states, Japan was dumbfounded when in 1971 Washington, reversing a 22-year policy, suddenly renewed contact with China without informing Tokyo in advance. The Japanese still refer to this event as "Nixon shock," and on many other occasions as well, U.S. actions have caused the Japanese to feel slighted or ignored.

It seems likely that in time Japan will come to play an international diplomatic role more in keeping with its economic power, and that has already begun to happen, but most Japanese continue to hope that this can be done without adding new military power. Some Japanese have

Modern Japanese women still learn traditional arts, and playing the koto is one. Koto players must wear the kimono and usually practice in a thoroughly authentic setting, kneeling on a tatami mat.

openly favored rearmament to compete in a world dominated by nations with the greatest military power, a policy that deeply concerns Japan's neighbors and former victims of its imperialism. Although the Americans have pressed for it, a rearmed Japan would no longer be their client, which is indeed why some Japanese support rearmament. More positively, by 1988 Japan had become the world's largest donor nation of foreign aid, all of it economic rather than military.

Modern Japan has been a leader in other nonmilitary directions, notably in the control of industrial pollution. Japan is small, and most of its population, cities, and industry are crowded into a narrow coastal corridor only about 400 miles long. Industrial concentration is higher there than anywhere in the world, and hence Japan was the first to notice the lethal effects of air and water pollution as one consequence of its postwar industrial growth. Many deaths and many more health casualties derived from heavy metal toxins and air pollution were traced to specific plants and their poisonous discharges into the water or the atmosphere. Once this became clear and public opinion had been mobilized, national and municipal governments quickly passed stringent legislation, beginning in 1969 with the city of Tokyo, to limit emissions and effluents from industry and vehicles. As industrial growth continues, concentration and crowding will go on generating the same problems, and pollution levels are building up again, while controls have remained incomplete. But Japanese organization, efficiency, and technology have demonstrated that the prob-

lems can be managed, given the willingness to confront them. The technology needed to control or even eliminate pollution was developed quickly, and the added expense was extremely modest, estimated at between 1 and 2 percent of total production costs.

Japan has also led the way in reducing energy use through more efficient plants and better engine design. Nearly all Japanese trains are electrified, including the heavily used high-speed line that connects Tokyo with the major cities to the south and southwest and Hokkaido to the north. Trains leave Tokyo every 15 minutes for Osaka, making the 310-mile trip in three hours, including stops at Nagoya and Kyoto, running at speeds up to 140 miles per hour.

Urbanization is higher in Japan than anywhere else in the world, and the coastal area from Tokyo to Osaka and on to northern Kyushu is rapidly becoming a single vast urban-industrial zone. Although the rural Japanese landscape, especially the mountains that cover much of the country, is very beautiful, a good deal of the remaining countryside is increasingly empty as people have flocked to the cities in search of wider economic and cultural opportunity. On weekends and holidays urbanites rush to natural beauty spots, temples or shrines, and resorts, which are often excessively crowded. Crammed onto overloaded trains or buses, most passengers must stand for hours, while many others are locked into gigantic traffic jams on the highways. Much of traditional Japanese culture has been lost or discarded in this avalanche of change. Although many Japanese regret the price they have paid for development, their sense of national identity has remained strong, bound together with many symbolic survivals of traditional culture: customary food and rituals, aesthetic sensitivity, and the commitment to order, self-discipline, and group effort in the pursuit of excellence.

Tokyo and the Modern World

By about 1965 Tokyo had become the world's largest city and a symbol of Japan's new economic leadership. The urban area had grown outward to merge with that of previously separate cities in the same lowland basin, including Kawasaki and Yokohama. By the 1980s this vast, unbroken conglomeration of dense settlement, commerce, industry, and government measured 50 miles across and included over 30 million people linked by the world's largest and most efficient subway system. Almost nothing is left of the Edo described in Chapter 30, most of which had been in any case periodically destroyed by fires. Modern Tokyo was also largely ruined by a catastrophic earthquake in 1923 and then again by American bombs and firestorms in 1944 and 1945.

The only part of the city that has survived all of these cataclysms unscathed is Tokugawa Ieyasu's massive shogunal castle, surrounded by its moats and stone walls, originally built in the early seventeenth century and since 1869 used as the imperial palace. In the middle of a huge and strikingly modern city of glass, steel, skyscrapers, and expressways, with traffic flowing around it, the palace still stands as a symbol of Japan's traditional past, both as a Tokugawa monument and as the home of a still enthroned emperor whose lineage goes back to before the dawn of Japanese history. Among Japan's many big cities, Tokyo still plays the role of the brash modernist, the focus of change, the center of everything new; but even in Tokyo the Japanese do not forget their past. The palace, though an anachronism, is nevertheless an appropriate focal point for the capital of Japan. For all its apparent emphasis on the streamlined or frantic present and future, Tokyo is also a city of the Japanese tradition.

That aspect of the city's character becomes clear beyond the immediate downtown and government areas. Except for the industrial clusters around the fringes of each originally separate municipality, Tokyo is primarily a vast collection of neighborhoods. Many are grouped around a surviving or rebuilt temple, shrine, former daimyo estate, or parklike garden. Wandering through the back streets and alleys of these neighborhoods, it is easy to imagine oneself in Tokugawa Edo. Clouds of steam escape from public bathhouses, enveloping the patrons, who include many dressed in traditional kimonos and walking in wooden clogs, especially in the evening after work. Inside countless tiny restaurants and teahouses with their *tatami* (straw mats), low tables, and wall scrolls, little seems to have changed since Ieyasu's time, including much of the food. Many inhabitants of the tiny houses or apartments maintain miniature Japanese-style gardens the size of a small tabletop or lovingly tend potted plants set out by the doorway or on small balconies to catch the sun. Street vendors, singing traditional chants, peddle roasted sweet potatoes, chestnuts, or *yakitori* (Japanese shish kebab).

Crowds of kimono-clad worshipers, or people simply on an outing, throng the courtyards of rebuilt temples and shrines, especially on festival days. Similar crowds fill the narrow streets and patronize street vendors or shops selling traditional as well as modern goods: fans both manual and electric, silks and nylons, horoscope fortunes and stock market guides, tea and beer, lacquer and plastic, scrolls and comic books. Like Japan itself, Tokyo is both very modern and very traditional, very Japanese and very Western.

China in Revolution

The cataclysmic changes that transformed twentieth-century China constitute the largest revolution in human history, measured by the numbers of people involved and the radicalness and speed of the changes. Although the events of 1911 leading to the overthrow of the Manchu dynasty are called a revolution, the pace of change was slow for many years, and the dominant political party, the Kuomintang, became in time largely a supporter of the status quo rather than a force for radical reform. The Chinese Communist party barely survived Kuomintang efforts to eliminate it, but during the anti-Japanese war from 1937 to 1945 it rapidly gained strength and support in the course of its guerrilla resistance to the invaders. The final contest between the two parties ended in Communist victory in 1949, and fundamental revolution began under a radically new set of ideals.

Postwar China and the Communist Triumph

The Japanese invasion and occupation of China from 1931 to 1945 fatally eroded the power and legitimacy of the Kuomintang government of Chiang Kai-shek. Buttressed by massive American military and economic support, it clung to a nominal authority while American representatives under General George C. Marshall tried to arrange a coalition with the Communists. When this effort predictably failed in 1947, China was torn by full-scale civil war. The Communist forces, meanwhile, had perfected a guerrilla strategy in their long struggle against the Japanese and had attracted millions of Chinese by their defense of the nation and their program of peasant-oriented reform.

Their leader, Mao Tse-tung (Mao Zedong, 1893–1976), offered a return to the simple virtues of hard work and self-sacrifice in order to build a new China, free from foreign influence and humiliation and free also from the now discredited and reactionary elitism of Confucianism and the old order it represented. The Confucian society had deteriorated sadly as China had sunk deeper into poverty, demoralization, and unwillingness to face

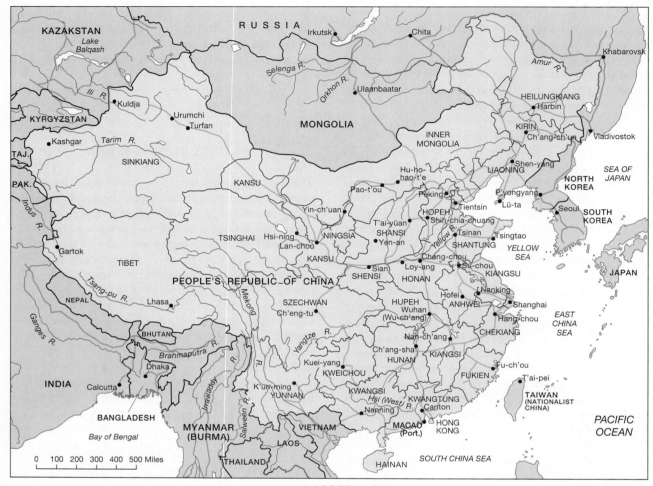

MAP 40.2   MODERN CHINA

drastically changed circumstances. People necessarily concentrated on ensuring their own survival rather than on responsibility for others or on group welfare. In their remote frontier base at Yenan (Yanan) in the northwest, where they were centered from 1934 to 1947, the Communists under Mao's direction had worked out a number of ideas for China's regeneration, while at the same time appealing broadly to the masses.

Mao himself, like several other Communist leaders, came from peasant stock, and their program emphasized peasant welfare and peasant values, as the Kuomintang had not. Landlordism and oppression of the peasantry were popular issues in the face of widespread rural poverty and mass suffering. Chinese who collaborated with foreign businessmen in the treaty ports prospered in league with a government that was prone to favor foreign influences. The cities, nearly all of which were foreign-

dominated treaty ports as well as centers of Kuomintang strength and the home of "running dogs" (collaborators with the foreigners), were obvious targets for a peasant-oriented revolutionary movement.

Success depended, however, on building a mass support base in the countryside, where most Chinese lived. The Communists initiated land reform programs in the areas they controlled—most of the north—as well as campaigns to politicize and organize the peasants. Intellectuals were also involved in an effort to create a new ideology that could appeal to peasants. Mao himself, though the son of a rich peasant turned grain merchant, was primarily an intellectual as well as a gifted poet in the tradition of the Confucian scholars and emperors. His prescriptions for art and literature that would "serve politics" and "serve the masses" attracted growing numbers of fellow intellectuals disillusioned with the corruption and spiritual bankruptcy of the

Kuomintang. As an intellectual organizing peasant rebellion, Mao consciously followed an old Chinese tradition.

The civil war that broke out in 1947 soon became a rout, despite heavy American support for the Kuomintang. The Communists had few weapons except what they could capture from their opponents or make themselves, but their strength quickly multiplied as growing numbers of Kuomintang troops and officers surrendered to them, often voluntarily, with all their equipment. The close American connection, with its connotation of foreign dominance, probably weakened rather than strengthened the Kuomintang in its fight against the Communists and left a legacy of anti-American bitterness when the civil war ended. On October 1, 1949, Mao announced the inauguration of the People's Republic of China from a rostrum in front of the Forbidden City in Peking (Beijing), conscious, as always, of the tradition of China's imperial greatness, to which he was now the heir. "China has stood up," he said, and the great majority of Chinese responded with enthusiasm.

The revolution was the culmination of a long process that began with the overthrow of the old Ch'ing (Qing) dynasty in 1911. After the failure of Sun Yat-sen and the corruption of the Kuomintang, the Communists, originally appealing largely to intellectuals, had finally succeeded in creating a mass political base, with a peasant army forged in the fires of the Japanese war. They called their program "the mass line," claiming to represent the more than 80 percent of the Chinese people who lived in the countryside.

Reconstruction and Consolidation

Chiang Kai-shek and the remnants of the Kuomintang government and army fled to the offshore island of Taiwan (Formosa), where American aid helped them in time build a prosperous economy and gain firm control of the island's population. From this tiny base, sheltered only by American power, Chiang continued to claim sole legitimate authority over China. The United States supported the Kuomintang until the desire to exploit the split between the Chinese Communists and their erstwhile Soviet allies led belatedly to official American recognition of the government in Peking in 1979. Unofficial ties with Taipei (the Taiwan capital) remained, however. On the mainland the new government moved quickly to repair the physical damage of the long years of war and to extend its land reform and political education programs into the newly conquered south and southwest. All over the country what was still called land reform became more violent as party organizers, in an effort to create "class con-

sciousness," encouraged peasants to "speak bitterness" and to identify their landlord-oppressors. Many thousands of the latter were killed by angry mobs, and their land was distributed among the poorer peasants.

Firm central government control was reestablished in all of the former empire, including Manchuria (now called simply "the northeast"), southern or "Inner" Mongolia, Sinkiang (Xinjiang), and Tibet, and a major program of industrialization was begun. War with the United States in Korea from late 1950 to mid-1953 and an American-sponsored embargo on trade with China slowed these efforts but also helped radicalize the country and strengthen dedication to the goals of self-reliance and reconstruction. By 1956 Mao judged that support for the new government was wide and deep enough to invite criticism. In a famous speech, he declared: "Let a hundred flowers bloom; let a hundred schools of thought contend." Many intellectuals and others, including many of China's ethnic minorities such as Tibetans and Muslims, responded with a torrent of criticism aimed at rigid party or government controls. Most of it was pronounced counterrevolutionary, and many of the critics were punished, jailed, or even executed.

The Great Leap Forward

Despite the evidence of dissent, Mao still felt secure enough in the support of the majority of his people that he moved swiftly to collectivize the land. By 1958 he moved beyond the Soviet model of collectivization as China's farms and fields were organized into new communes; private ownership was abolished, and all enterprises were managed collectively. The communes varied widely in area and population but averaged about 25,000 people, frequently incorporating large numbers of previously separate villages. Several villages made up a "production team," several teams a "production brigade," and several brigades a commune. Communes were supposed to include manufacturing enterprises as well, to bring industrialization to the rural areas. Communes were also set up in the cities but added little to existing factories, departments, or offices, and the experiment was short-lived.

Mao announced that 1958 would be the year of the "Great Leap Forward," in which China would overtake Britain in industrial output by united efforts within the commune structure. Communal dining halls were set up so that families need not lose work time by preparing meals. Backyard steel furnaces sprang up all over the rural landscape, using local iron ore and coal or other fuel. Communes were given quotas for production of specific agricultural and industrial goods, but too little attention was paid to the nature of local resources or to rational organization more generally.

The Great Leap was a dismal failure, and the country collapsed into economic chaos in 1959. Peasants had been driven to exhaustion in pursuit of unrealistic goals and by inefficient combinations of tasks and resources. Nearly all the iron and steel from the backyard furnaces was of unusable quality, and the same was true of much of the other commune industrial output. Crops failed as labor was shifted arbitrarily between different tasks, and for at least three years food was scarce and famine widespread. Probably about 30 million people died of starvation or malnutrition in the worst famine in world history. Mao's radical policies had brought disaster, and for several years more moderate leaders such as Chou En-lai (Zhou Enlai, 1898–1976) and Liu Hsiao-chi (Liu Xiaoqi, 1894–1971) eclipsed him, although he remained the party chairman.

The Sino-Soviet Split

The Russians were alarmed by what they saw as the radical excesses of the Great Leap and its departure from the Soviet pattern. They were annoyed also by Mao's assertion that his version of socialism was superior to theirs, his continued support of Stalinist policies after they had been discredited in the USSR, and his accusations that the Soviet Union had now become ideologically impure, or "revisionist." The Russians saw Mao's bellicose stand on the reconquest of Taiwan, for which he requested Soviet nuclear aid, as a threat to world peace, and inevitable tensions arose out of the large-scale Soviet aid program and Soviet advisers in China. In 1959 the Russians withdrew their aid and advisers and moved toward a more antagonistic relationship with China. The next 15 years saw revived territorial disputes and armed border clashes between the two former allies on the long frontier between them, especially in the Amur region of northern Manchuria and along the northern border of Sinkiang.

Each claimed to be the true heir of Marx and Lenin and hence of the correct path to socialism, and in this ideological context long-standing historical conflicts between them surfaced. These dated back to the period of early tsarist expansion into northeastern Asia and to Russia's exploitation of Manchuria and its role as one of the Western imperialist powers during China's years of political weakness. On the other side, China's billion people, bordering thinly settled Siberia and Russia's maritime provinces, were seen as an alarming threat to Soviet Asia. The rhetoric of accusation mounted on both sides; troops were stationed along the frontiers, and small clashes occurred. But China could not stand alone against the entire world, and its leaders began indirect overtures to the United States. More than a decade later, with the end of their misadventure in Vietnam in sight, the Americans finally responded. A cautious restoration of contact began when President Richard Nixon visited Peking late in 1971. This led to the establishment of diplomatic relations, with full U.S. recognition and an exchange of ambassadors with the People's Republic in 1979.

The Cultural Revolution

During the decade from 1966 to 1976, however, China passed through an unprecedented social upheaval, the so-called Cultural Revolution, in which hundreds of millions of people suffered. The failure of the Great Leap Forward had necessitated more moderate policies and a period of recovery from economic disaster. By 1966 Mao judged the recovery to be complete, and he launched a new campaign designed to renew a revolution that he saw as having slipped into bureaucratic complacency and opportunism.

Mao remarked that he felt like "an ancestor at his own funeral and at the burial of his hopes." His cure was a purge, though his message was the old one of "serve the people," with its clear echoes of Confucian responsibility. The chief targets of his purge were the members of the elite: party managers and officials, teachers, writers, and intellectuals, as well as others who were allegedly tainted by foreign influence or bourgeois lifestyles or whose class origins were not appropriately peasant or proletarian.

The results were devastating. Millions were hounded out of their jobs. Artists and musicians who showed any interest in Western styles were attacked. Many intellectuals and other "counterrevolutionaries" were beaten or killed, and others were jailed, sent to corrective labor camps, or assigned to the lowest menial tasks as a means of "reeducation." Opera stars, writers, and concert violinists were set to cleaning latrines. All foreign music, art, and literature and the expression of all ideas not approved by the state were banned. Most books disappeared or were burned, to be replaced by the ever-present works of Mao himself and the *Little Red Book* of his sayings. Chinese who had studied abroad were particular targets. People were encouraged to inform on friends, colleagues, and even family members, causing deep trauma and division in a society based on traditional family ties. The accused were often jailed or condemned to corrective labor without evidence. Few people had the courage to try to help them, for fear that they too would meet the same fate. The ensuing turmoil affected the

The leaders of Communist China in 1965: (from left) Chou En-lai, Chu Teh, Mao Tse-tung, and Liu Hsiao-chi.

lives of hundreds of millions of people and paralyzed the country. Nor were the rural communes exempt, for there, too, people were obliged to confess ideological sins and subjected to punishment and corrective labor. Many were driven to suicide.

During the height of the Cultural Revolution all universities and colleges were closed, feared as breeding grounds for a new elite. When they slowly began to reopen, it was only to the children of peasants, workers, and party loyalists still in power. The new curriculum concentrated on "political study." Most high school graduates in the decade after 1966, particularly those in the cities, were assigned to productive labor in the countryside, where, Mao felt, they would learn the value of simple toil and peasant virtues. This was partly a leveling alternative to the universities, partly a means to ease unemployment and housing shortages in the cities, and partly a way to reeducate Chinese too young to have shared the early years of hardship and sacrifice.

Some 17 million young people were sent down in this program by the time it was discontinued in the late 1970s. Most of them saw it as ruinous to their own ambitions and career plans, for which their urban origins and education had prepared them. Nor were most of them very helpful in agricultural or other development work. Their training had not in most cases been relevant, and indeed it had tended, as in China's past, to make them think of themselves as an educated elite, who looked down on peasants and manual labor. The program was understandably unpopular with peasants too, since they had to feed and house disgruntled city youth who, with

their higher level of education, were unprepared for farmwork. All white-collar workers were required to spend at least two months each year doing manual labor, mainly in the countryside, which not surprisingly met with resistance from professionals and others.

Mao called on teenagers and students to serve as shock troops for the Cultural Revolution. Like young people everywhere, they had little stake in the status quo, were filled with idealism, and were easily diverted from their studies. They welcomed their exciting new role and the opportunity to exercise authority over their elders. Mao called them Red Guards and permitted them to roam the country freely, ferreting out "rightists" and harassing everyone in responsible positions. Millions rode free or commandeered trains and buses to the cities, including Peking, where Mao addressed cheering crowds of Red Guards at mass rallies. Mao and his supporters promoted a personality cult; huge pictures and statues of the "Great Helmsman" and copies of his *Little Red Book* appeared everywhere. Rival factions quickly emerged among the Red Guards, each claiming to be followers of the true line. Many welcomed the opportunity to pay off old grudges and to denounce others, often anonymously. Uncontrolled violence broke out in many cities.

To halt the mounting chaos, Chou En-lai prevailed on Mao to call in the army in 1968. The Red Guards were suppressed, thus creating yet another embittered and dislocated group; the Guards felt they had been betrayed, a "lost generation." But the nightmare went on even after the Red Guards had been sent to the countryside. Politicians at the top, except for Mao himself, were attacked for

Revolution, Chinese Style

From the beginning of their revolutionary victory, the Chinese asserted that their principles and experience should be the guide for the rest of the world, not the Russian way. Here is Liu Hsiao-chi in 1949.

The road taken by the Chinese people in defeating imperialism and in founding the Chinese People's Republic is the road that should be taken by the peoples of many colonial and semi-colonial countries in their fight for national independence and people's democracy. . . . This is the road of Mao Tse-tung. . . . This is the inevitable road of many colonial and semi-colonial peoples in the struggle for their independence and liberation.

Lu Ting-i, director of propaganda of the Central Committee, added in July 1951:

Mao Tse-tung's theory of the Chinese revolution is a new development of Marxism-Leninism in the revolutions of the colonial and semi-colonial countries. . . . It is of universal significance for the World Communist movement. . . . The classic type of revolution in colonial and semi-colonial countries is the Chinese revolution.

Stalin's successor, Nikita Khrushchev, lectured Mao in 1958 after Mao suggested that the combined numbers of China and Russia could overcome the capitalist West.

Comrade Mao Tse-tung, nowadays that sort of thinking is out of date. You can no longer calculate the alignment of forces on the basis of who has the most men. Back in the days when a dispute was settled with fists and bayonets it made a difference who had the most men. . . . Now with the atomic bomb, the number of troops on each side makes practically no difference.

Source: I. Hsu, *The Rise of Modern China* (New York: Oxford University Press, 1975), pp. 810–813, 859.

alleged deviations from the party line, which changed unpredictably. Liu Hsiao-chi (Liu Xiaoqi), a revolutionary comrade Mao had originally picked as his successor, was purged and accused of "rightist revisionism" because of his efforts to rebuild the economy after the disaster of the Great Leap Forward. He died under arrest after public humiliation and beatings. Other high officials suffered similar fates. Professionals in all fields were scrutinized for their political views and activism. Absence from the endless daily political meetings or silence during them

Building a new irrigation dam and reservoir near Peking in 1982: mass labor and the "mass line." Note the red flags and the absence of mechanical equipment.

was evidence of "counterrevolutionary tendencies." One of the many slogans of the Cultural Revolution was "Better Red than Expert." No one at any level felt safe.

The Chinese Revolution remained primarily a peasant movement, a Chinese rather than a foreign-style answer to China's problems. This was appealing also on nationalist grounds, especially since nearly all the cities had been tainted by semicolonial foreign dominance. There was thus both a pronounced antiurban bias to the revolution and a determination to exalt the countryside, to put the peasants in charge, and to concentrate efforts on development in the rural areas, the supposed source of all revolutionary values.

This was the theme of both the Great Leap Forward and the Cultural Revolution. All movement of people was controlled, especially to the cities, where housing and ration books for food and household supplies were allocated only to those with assigned employment. Individuals could not choose jobs; they worked wherever the state sent them. In the 1970s a growing number of illegal migrants to the cities lived underground or on forged papers. Most of them are still there, their numbers apparently greatly increased; urban unemployment has become a major problem. Despite the official denigration of cities, they remained the places where most people wanted to be.

In the countryside each commune was designed to be self-sufficient as far as possible. The Cultural Revolution promoted a particularly extensive growth of small-scale rural industry, especially in what were labeled the "five smalls": iron and steel, cement, fertilizer, agricultural goods (including tools, machinery, and irrigation equipment), and electric power. There was also considerable production of light consumer goods for local use. Local manufacture did reduce the load on an already overburdened road and rail system and saved transport

Mao: The Revolutionary Vision

The Communist revolution in China was in large part a peasant-based movement against the vested power of the cities. Mao Tse-tung put it dramatically.

Since China's key cities have long been occupied by the powerful imperialists and their reactionary Chinese allies, it is imperative for the revolutionary ranks to turn the backward villages into advanced consolidated base areas, . . . bastions of the revolution from which to fight their vicious enemies.

This equally famous statement of Mao's was published in the periodical Red Flag.

China's 600 million people have two remarkable peculiarities; they are first of all poor, and secondly blank. That may seem like a bad thing, but it is really a good thing. Poor people want change, want to do things, want revolution. A clean sheet of paper has no blotches, and so the newest and most beautiful words can be written on it, the newest and most beautiful pictures painted on it.

Still driven by his revolutionary vision, Mao the poet wrote in 1963, in traditional classic verse:

> **So many deeds cry out to be done,**
> **And always urgently.**
> **The world rolls on,**
> **Time passes.**
> **Ten thousand years are too long;**
> **Seize the day, seize the hour,**
> **Our force is irresistible.**

Sources: Mao Tse-tung, *The Chinese Revolution and the Chinese Communist Party* (Peking: Foreign Language Press, 1954), p. 17 (written in 1939); *Red Flag*, June 1, 1958, pp. 3–4; "Reply to Kuo Mo-jo" (dated February 5, 1963), *China Reconstructs* 16 (March 1967): 2.

costs while providing employment and experience to the masses of rural people. But in most cases such production was considerably more expensive than that in larger-scale and better-equipped urban-based plants and of much lower quality. Decentralized industry has been considered as an alternative to the crowding, pollution, and dehumanization of industrial cities since the eighteenth century, but it has seldom proved economically practicable. Mao's utopian vision of rural development was appealing as an attempt to alleviate the real poverty of the countryside, but it was pursued at dreadful cost. China, meanwhile, lagged farther and farther behind the rest of the world, technologically and educationally.

Mao had said that the major goals of the revolution should be the elimination of the distinctions between city and countryside, between intellectuals and manual workers, and between elites and common people. In pursuit of these aims, workers or janitors became plant managers and university officials; peasants were elevated to power in the communes' "revolutionary committees"; professors, technicians, and skilled managers were humiliated or reduced to the most menial jobs. Even "rich peasants" became targets. All those with any claim to expertise were suspect and were often hounded out of their positions in angry "struggle meetings"; those who refused to join in the denunciations risked being denounced themselves. The moral virtue and practical wisdom of the peasants and the countryside were extolled.

Mao drew heavily on traditional ideas in emphasizing the duty of those in positions of power and responsibility to serve the masses, and he, like the Confucians, used moral examples and slogans to inspire and mold group behavior. He also relied on the new technique of mass campaigns to galvanize people into action. Some were constructive, like the campaigns to eliminate flies or to build new dams and irrigation canals. But most were politically inspired and were aimed at "rightists" and "counterrevolutionaries." The Chinese revolution's radical phase lasted longer and went to greater extremes than similar phases of earlier revolutions, but in time it too faded, if only because the Chinese people were exhausted by constant political campaigns and by the terror itself. Mao's death removed the chief obstacle to a return to more normal conditions, and China turned with relief from its long ordeal.

China After Mao

As Mao lay dying in 1976, a few months after his old comrade-in-arms Chou En-lai had died of overwork and exhaustion while trying to hold the country together, a radical faction led by Mao's widow, Chiang Ch'ing (Jiang Qing), tried to continue his extreme policies. But in 1978 a more moderate leadership emerged under Hua Kuofeng (Hua Guofeng), whom Mao had designated as his successor. Chiang Ch'ing and three of her associates, the so-called Gang of Four, were tried and convicted of "crimes against the people" and sentenced to jail. China began to emerge from its nightmare and to resume cautious interchange with the rest of the world after 30 years of isolation. The universities and their curricula were slowly restored, and students now had to pass entrance examinations rather than merely to demonstrate proper "class origins." Efforts were made to provide somewhat greater freedom for intellectuals, writers, teachers, and managers.

Hua was peacefully replaced by an old party pragmatist, Teng Hsiao-p'ing (Deng Xiaoping, born 1904), who returned to power in 1981 as the real head of state and chief policy maker. Most of Mao's policies were progressively dismantled. The new government acknowledged that China was still poor and technically backward, that it needed foreign technology and investment, and that to encourage production its people needed material incentives rather than political harangues and "rectification campaigns."

The communes were quietly dissolved in all but name. Agriculture, still by far the largest sector of the economy, was organized into a "responsibility system" whereby individual families grew the crops that they judged most profitable in an economy that was now market-oriented. The commune still nominally owned the land, and the state still appropriated a share of farm output, but peasants were free to sell the rest in a free market. Those who did well under this system, and urban entrepreneurs who prospered in the small private businesses now permitted, felt free once again to display their new wealth. Expensive houses with television aerials sprouted here and there in the countryside, and in the cities motor scooters, tape recorders, and refrigerators became more common. The new rich and even party officials began to indulge personal tastes in clothing, including Western-style and fashionable outfits, which replaced the drab uniforms decreed in earlier years.

Rural industry remained where it had proved practical, but renewed emphasis was placed on large-scale and urban-based industrial production and on catching up with world advances in technology to make up for the lost years. Many factory and office managers and workers were now rewarded on the basis of their productivity. Technological, managerial, and educational elites also reappeared, and with them the bourgeois lifestyles denounced by Mao as the antithesis of revolutionary social-ism. The new pragmatism was illustrated by Teng's pithy remark: "I don't care if a cat is red [socialist] or white [capitalist] as long as it catches mice." At the same time, he affirmed that China was still a socialist country under a Communist government that planned and managed the economy and aimed to provide social justice.

The Revolution Reconsidered

The decade after Mao's death saw a reappraisal of his legacy. The new leadership permitted controlled public criticism of the excesses of the Cultural Revolution and acknowledged the failures of Mao's economic policy. But much had also been accomplished. China remained poor, but there was some growth in agriculture (except for the period 1958–1964), thanks in part to irrigation, better seeds, and fertilization. Industry grew rapidly, if unevenly, from what had been a very small and limited base. In 1964 China tested a nuclear bomb and thereby joined the ranks of the major powers. Thousands of miles of new railways and roads were built. China be-came a major industrial power. One of China's greatest successes was in delivering basic health care to most of its people, including for several years the system of "barefoot doctors" who traveled even to remote villages to provide basic care and the clinics established in every commune.

As in India, this greatly reduced the death rate, while the birthrate remained high. The result was a rapid growth in population, which nearly doubled between 1949 and 1982, when the first real census was taken. This growth placed great pressure on agriculture, where gains in pro-duction barely exceeded population increase. As long as such growth continued, China could expect little progress in terms of per capita well-being, by which real economic growth must be measured. In the 1970s the government began an attempt to control population growth. Begin-ning in 1983 families were penalized for having more than a single child, a policy seen as necessary for perhaps a gen-eration if China was to escape from poverty.

Chinese socialism has also reduced gross inequities in wealth. Poverty at the bottom has not yet been elimi-nated, but increased production, better distribution, and the collective welfare system of communes and factories have benefited nearly everyone; recent inflation, however, has hurt many. Health levels, thanks in part to better nu-trition as well as improved medical care, are in general high. Literacy has more than doubled since the revolu-tion, and about half the population now gets as far as the early high school grades, although there are places for only about 3 percent in the universities.

The liberation of women, one of the goals of the revolution, is still relatively far from attainment, al-though there has been much progress. Women are less oppressed than under the old society, but they are still far from equal. The marriage law of 1950 gave them legal equality with men in marital rights, divorce, and the ownership of property, a major step forward. The tradi-tional extended family—three generations living under one roof—has largely disappeared, especially in the cities, and with it the authority of the oldest surviving grand-parent. A grandmother, and sometimes a grandfather, may live with a son's family but now serves commonly as baby-sitter, shopper, and general household help, repre-senting the family on neighborhood committees while the mother goes out to work. Nearly all adult women have full-time jobs outside the home, but they are usually not paid equally with men, and at the end of the workday it is usually they who cook the meals, clean the house, and care for the children. However, the state or employ-ers provide extensive child-care facilities for working mothers, far more than in the United States.

The top positions in government, business, industry, and education are held almost exclusively by men, with occasional token female representation on committees. At the same time, nearly all occupations and professions are open to women. There is probably a higher propor-tion of women professionals than in the United States, but most Chinese women work in lower-level or even menial jobs. Despite government efforts to persuade people that daughters are as good as sons, most families still give sons priority, since only they can continue the family name and provide some security for aged parents; daughters join their husband's family at marriage. This persistence of custom has unfortunately led, under the pressures of the "one-child policy" since 1983, to wide-spread female infanticide and abortion of female fetuses. Rural areas cling more to traditional values and often evade the one-child policy or accept the penalties in or-der to produce one or more sons. Nearly all urban and now rural women do at least keep their own names after marriage, and there is a major change from the old soci-ety in the status of and attitudes toward women. But China, like Japan and India, still has a long way to go be-fore women are truly equal members of society.

Despite Mao's efforts, living standards in the cities have risen far more rapidly and substantially than in most rural areas. The growing division between urban and rural lifestyles and levels of affluence is a particular problem for the heirs of a peasant revolution, although it is shared by the rest of the developing world. China's cities are not yet disfigured by masses of visibly homeless and unemployed

*"Women hold up half the sky," Mao said, and in China
since 1950 they have entered many occupations previously
reserved for men.*

their political system as repressive. The political grievances resulting from this, along with the effects of Western cultural influence, led to remarkable demonstrations
in Peking, Shanghai, and other major cities in the spring
of 1989 that shook the party hierarchy.

In 1987, 1988, and 1989 the government under
Teng Hsiao-p'ing became increasingly repressive in its
response to growing disaffection and protests. Meanwhile, inflation mounted, badly hurting most people, and
there was bitter resentment of the corruption of party officials and of businessmen and others who had connections to them. Student demonstrations led to a massacre
in Peking by army troops and tanks. The demonstrations
began in May 1989 in Tienanmen Square, Communist
China's chief parade ground, where Mao had once addressed a million cheering followers waving the *Little
Red Book.* The students' vague demands for democracy
were clearly inspired by the recent increase in contact
with the wider world, especially the United States, as
well as by unhappiness with censorship, controlled job
assignment by the state, inflation, corruption, and political dictatorship. Communist China's 25 million or more
officials had become a terrible burden, hated and resented by most people, and China had become the most
closely controlled society in history. The demonstrations
were never violent, but the government saw them as a
threat, and on the night of June 3–4 and the following
day the army and its tanks moved in to crush the demonstrators, killing perhaps as many as 1,000 unarmed students. They had challenged an all-powerful state, and it
responded as it had so often before. China has never had
parliamentary democracy, free expression, or the rule of
Western-style law, but the brutality of the massacre in
Peking, enacted in front of the world's television cameras, sent shock waves around the globe even as the Soviet Union and eastern Europe were entering an exciting
new phase of liberation. China stood out as isolated and
condemned, though United States support continued.

In the wake of June 4, the government imprisoned
many of the surviving demonstrators as well as thousands
of "liberals," executed many, and denounced Western influence and lifestyles. It also continued its brutal suppression of protests in Tibet against Chinese efforts to stamp
out expressions of Tibetan identity and Tibetans' requests for a more genuine role in the administration of
their supposedly autonomous area.

The death of Teng Hsiao-p'ing may well lead to a
power struggle, openly or behind the scenes, between factions urging different approaches to the country's problems. The Chinese people have suffered terribly under
successive regimes: the last decades of the deteriorating Ch'ing dynasty, the warlord years after its collapse

people, as are many elsewhere in the developing and even
the industrial world, but only because rigid controls on all
movement and employment still prevent most rural people
from migrating to the cities. Progress in other respects too
has been won at the cost of state and collective social controls and the suppression of personal choice. This is not as
disturbing to most Chinese as it might be to many westerners, since the subordination of individualism to group effort
and welfare has long been central to Chinese tradition.

China's past achievements and its revolutionary
progress were due in large part to the primacy of responsibility and the pursuit of common goals over privilege and
self-interest. Nevertheless, there have been protests and
even student demonstrations against the continuing controls on free expression and choice of employment. As
China has opened its doors to more normal interchange
with the rest of the world, more Chinese have come to see

in 1911, the reactionary and ineffective Kuomintang, and the long nightmare of Maoism, some of which was revived after 1986 when "foreign influences" were again reviled, "bourgeois" and "rightist" tendencies criticized, and, from 1989, "political study" again required of all students. But the government, though still politically repressive, vigorously pursued economic growth, especially in the private sector. In time, China may grow more open to the outside world, and more tolerant of free expression.

Taiwan and Hong Kong

Taiwan had been taken over by the Japanese in 1895 as part of their colonial empire, but with Japan's defeat in 1945 the island was returned to Chinese sovereignty. In 1949 it became the sole remaining base for the defeated Kuomintang. Some 2 million mainland Chinese, including units of the Kuomintang army and government, fled to Taiwan, where they largely excluded the Taiwanese from political power.

The island had originally been settled by Chinese from Fukien (Fujian) province, just across the narrow strait that separates it from the mainland, beginning on a significant scale in the seventeenth century. They had retained their Chinese culture while developing some regional feeling, especially when the island was under Japanese control. They welcomed the mainlanders in 1945, but after violent repressive actions in 1947, and especially after the mass influx of 1949, they tended to regard them as oppressors.

Nevertheless, Taiwan in the 1950s began a period of rapid economic growth, at first with heavy American aid and then, by the early 1960s, on its own. A land reform program gave farmers new incentives as well as increased supplies of fertilizer, new crop strains, and new irrigation. Growing rural prosperity was matched and, by the 1970s, exceeded by industrial growth as Taiwan experienced a small-scale version of the Japanese "economic miracle." Taiwanese developments followed much the same path in technological achievements and both light and heavy manufacturing. Taiwan's trade with the rest of the world quickly exceeded that of mainland China. Taipei, the capital, became a large city and was joined by other rapidly growing industrial centers and ports.

Prosperity, wider relations with the rest of the world, and an unspoken acceptance of political realities in China and East Asia began by the 1980s to soften the harsher aspects of Kuomintang control. Taiwan remained a police state, but more representation and positions were offered to the Taiwanese along with a little more freedom of expression. These trends were still increasing in 1995.

The tiny and rocky island of Hong Kong, just off the mouth of the West River, which leads to Canton, had been ceded to Britain by the Treaty of Nanking, which ended the Opium War in 1842. More land was granted on the adjacent mainland in 1860. Additional territory was later leased on the mainland peninsula to supply Hong Kong with food and water as well as to provide room for expansion. Hong Kong grew rapidly in the nineteenth and twentieth centuries. Although under British control as a crown colony, it remained an overwhelmingly Chinese city, peopled by immigrants from overcrowded southern China who brought with them their interest and skill in commerce and their capacity for hard work. With the Communist victory in China, Hong Kong was isolated from its major market, for which it had served as a leading port for foreign trade. At the same time, it was flooded by waves of refugees from the mainland. The city and its resourceful people survived the crisis by developing a highly successful array of light industries, including textiles and electronics. Although dependent on imported raw materials, they were made profitable by inexpensive labor and efficient factories.

Hong Kong became even more prosperous than it had been before World War II. As China began to resume some trade outside the Communist bloc, Hong Kong regained its former role as a major distribution, commercial, and financial center, a function it also came to perform for much of Southeast Asia. By 1995 the city and its adjacent territories had a population of about 6 million. But the Chinese government announced that when the lease on the additional territories obtained in 1898 for 99 years expired in 1997, they and all of Hong Kong would be reclaimed. To this the British agreed. It remains to be seen how this citadel of capitalism will be integrated with the socialist system of the People's Republic.

Divided Korea

Korea had suffered perhaps more than any colonial country in the world under the exceptionally harsh Japanese rule that lasted from 1910 to 1945. Living standards fell sharply during this period as Japan milked Korea of much of its raw materials and food (see Chapter 35). Virtually all nonmenial jobs were filled by Japanese. All efforts at political expression were ruthlessly suppressed, and activists were jailed, killed, or exiled. When the Pacific war ended in 1945, almost no Koreans had the educational or administrative experience to form a viable government.

EAST ASIA SINCE 1945

Japan	China	Korea
Industrial production equals 1931 level (1951)	Civil war (1947–1949) "Great Leap Forward" (1958) Sino-Soviet split (1959)	Korean war (1950–1953)
Third-largest producer of steel in the world (1964)		Military rule (1960–1963)
Tokyo becomes largest city in the world (1965)	Cultural Revolution (1966–1976)	
Largest producer of steel in the world (1980)	U.S. recognizes People's Republic (1979) Tienanmen Square demonstrations (1989)	Assassination of Chung Hee Park (1979)

In the confused weeks after the Japanese surrender, an ad hoc arrangement left Russian troops to occupy the northern half of the country above the 38th parallel while American troops occupied the southern half. The Cold

MAP 40.3   MODERN KOREA

War resulted in both a hardening of this division into a political boundary and the emergence of rival political regimes. A Russian-dominated government emerged in the north with its capital at P'yongyang, and an American client-state was formed in the south, headquartered at Seoul. The conservative, American-educated politician Syngman Rhee (1875–1965) became the first president of the Republic of South Korea, while the Communist leader Kim Il Sung (1912–1994) headed the Democratic People's Republic of North Korea. When American and Russian troops withdrew from their respective areas, they left a United Nations commission to keep the peace but also left their two client regimes heavily armed with modern weapons.

On June 25, 1950, the North Koreans, with their new Soviet equipment, launched an invasion across the 38th parallel, although the South was clearly preparing its own strike. Because the Russians were then boycotting the United Nations Security Council, the United States was able to push through a motion condemning North Korea, which the government of the North ignored. A special United Nations emergency force was raised to combat North Korea, but the United States had already committed its soldiers to action, and the United Nations force was largely American, though outnumbered by South Koreans in opposing the North. By September the North Korean forces had overrun the entire peninsula except for a small section in the southeast. General Douglas MacArthur counterattacked behind enemy lines at Inchon. Ignoring his instructions from Washington, he pushed deeply into North Korea, bombed the bridges linking it with China, and massed troops near its frontier. At this critical point, MacArthur openly advocated attacking military bases in Manchuria and using atomic weapons against the Chinese. Chinese forces entered the war in October, driving back MacArthur's troops and retaking much of the peninsula. Enraged by MacArthur's insubordination, President Truman relieved him of duty, touching off a bitter domestic debate. Dwight Eisenhower, Truman's successor, ended the hostilities. Campaigning for the presidency in 1952 on a pledge that he would bring peace, he approved an armistice signed at Panmunjom in July 1953.

Most of Korea was devastated by the fighting, as the armies of both sides surged back and forth over the country. A million Koreans and an almost equal number of Chinese (compared with 53,000 Americans) died, and 4 million Koreans were made refugees from their shattered homes and villages. Coming on top of the ruthless exploitation of Japanese rule after 1910, the war further reduced Korea to poverty. A pawn in the Cold War rivalries between the superpowers, the nation was left divided, its economy disrupted by the rift. The superpowers continued to supply the police-state regimes in both North and South with arms and economic aid, as their puppets, and the risk of another war between them remains, despite the fervent desire of most Koreans to see their country reunited.

The actions of the United States and the United Nations left most Koreans worse off. The alternative to war would have been a takeover of the entire country by the Communist government of the North, which is, of course, what prompted the American action. But the United States belatedly came to accept Communist governments in China and elsewhere, and it is not easy to argue that a Communist unified Korea would be substantially worse, especially for Koreans, than the present situation, fraught with built-in tensions. American intervention in Korea formed the background for a similar policy in Vietnam, now generally acknowledged as a tragic mistake.

Although the war devastated both halves of the country, Korean culture, language, and national consciousness nevertheless remained one. Both states continued to pour scarce resources into their military establishments. This was a greater sacrifice in the less developed North than in the South, which included most of the best agricultural land and much of the industry, which the North had earlier supplied with most of its raw materials. By the 1960s South Korea had begun to recover from the war and by the 1970s to leap ahead economically, following the same path of rapid industrial development earlier pursued by Japan.

Syngman Rhee was forced to resign as president in 1960 after his dictatorial style had alienated many of his rivals, to be succeeded by a military junta and from 1963 by equally dictatorial rulers. President Chung Hee Park took office in 1963 but was assassinated in 1979 by his own Korean Central Intelligence Agency. His policies continued under Chun Doo Hwan, while the North remained under the tight control of Kim Il Sung. In both halves of Korea free expression was savagely repressed. In 1987 a wave of student protests erupted in Seoul, and the government of Chun Doo Hwan was obliged to make a few concessions, among them the direct election of the president and somewhat more scope for political parties, including those in opposition. In the first direct presidential election in 16 years, the government's handpicked candidate, Roh Tae-woo, was chosen president in December 1987 amid charges of massive voting fraud. In 1992 Kim Young Sam was elected president.

Meanwhile, Korean economic growth continued to produce growing prosperity for most people in the South. Rising incomes were spread widely among the population, and the gap between rich and poor was smaller than in most societies. South Korea began to invade world markets in a number of advanced manufacturing sectors, including automobiles. North Korea was largely closed to non-Communist outsiders, but economic development there was substantial, including industrial growth, although less impressive than in the South. So long as Korea remains divided between two implacably hostile governments supported by the United States and Russia, respectively, the peace of this chronically troubled part of the world will continue at risk, and the welfare of its people will suffer. Kim Il Sung died in 1994 but his place was taken by his son, Kim Jong Il. As of 1995 there were some signs that the thaw in American-Russian relations might reduce tensions in Korea and also that South Korea would continue its slow liberalization.

Southeast Asia Since World War II

China's revolutionary resurgence sent shock waves through Southeast Asia, where some 15 million Chinese resided. The Japanese had helped destroy European colonialism in Asia before World War II, but the Chinese revolution now offered a new set of ideas. In neighboring Vietnam the Chinese government aided the Communist party under Ho Chi Minh (1890–1969) in its struggle first against French colonialism and then against American intervention in support of a puppet government in the South (see Chapter 43). In the Philippines the Chinese example helped inspire a peasant Communist uprising, the Hukbalahaps, whose successors still challenge the government. In Indonesia reports of an alleged coup by Indonesian Communists and Chinese led to an American-supported counterstrike in 1965. Mass killings of innocent Chinese and suspected Communists resulted, and the toll of victims

MAP 40.4   SOUTHEAST ASIA

was probably over half a million. Malaya faced an insurrection between 1943 and 1957 by a small group of native Chinese guerrillas, but most Malayan Chinese refused to join it. The rebellion was suppressed by the outgoing British colonial administration when help from China did not materialize.

Neighboring Thailand was wary, but Thai Chinese, who had been assimilated into Thai society much more completely than in any other Southeast Asian country, remained peaceful. In Burma chronic tension existed between the majority Burmans and the numerous minority groups in the mountains around the Irrawaddy plain, and the small Chinese minority in Rangoon was expelled. The military government, which came to power in 1962 under General Ne Win (born 1911), however, modeled its policy in part on the Chinese example by cutting nearly all of Burma's ties with the rest of the world and attempting to promote domestic development through state-directed socialism. Ne Win formally retired in 1989 but continued in control, changing the country's name to Myanmar. In the elections of May 1990 the opposition Socialist party won a sweeping victory, but the military government kept the winning candidate, Aung San Sun Kyi, under arrest, and savage repression continued.

The Philippines and Indonesia

The major event of the years after 1945 in Southeast Asia was the coming of independence to former colonial states. The Philippines in 1946 were the first to achieve it, as the Americans handed over the reins of government, although their continued presence was such that the country remained a virtual protectorate. The first two decades saw some token efforts at land reform, but in 1965 Ferdinand Marcos (1917–1989) became president and soon assumed dictatorial powers, which he used to favor the rich and to suppress free expression. He was finally voted out of office in 1986, and a reformist government under Corazon Aquino (born 1933) began to attempt to repair the damage he had done.

But Aquino had her own ties with rich and powerful families and came from one of them herself. Her connections with the army, the other major Philippine power broker, were uneasy, and she barely survived repeated army rebellions. Given her political base, she was unable, and perhaps unwilling, to push for the kinds of basic change that the Philippines needed if the country was to escape from poverty for most of its citizens, corrupt privilege and wealth for a few, and a political system notorious for cronyism and inefficiency. Aquino chose not to run for reelection in 1992, and a confused contest in May brought in a new government headed by a former general, Fidel Ramos.

In 1949 neighboring Indonesia won its armed struggle for freedom against the Dutch, who left the country unprepared for independence. Like the Koreans, few Indonesians had any administrative or technical experience, and the new government was unable to control inflation or corruption or to spur economic development. The outlying islands resented the dominance of Java, where the capital, Djakarta, was located, and regional rebellion became chronic. President Achmed Sukarno (1901–1970), the leader of the independence movement, suspended the ineffective parliamentary government in 1956 and gradually took personal control, together with the army, in the name of what he called "guided democracy." This too failed to deal with Indonesia's mounting problems, and in 1966 General T. N. J. Suharto (born 1921), fresh from his purge of suspected Communists and Chinese, took over, confirming his rule by stage-managed elections in 1971 and 1982. The Suharto regime has made slow progress toward more orderly development despite its repressive nature, but this vast island country of some 180 million people stretched over a

Rice fields in Sumatra, Indonesia. Rice remains the major crop of lowland Southeast Asia, and much of Indonesia resembles this scene, as do the lowland rice-growing areas of Burma, Thailand, Vietnam, Malaysia, and the Philippines.

3,000-mile-long archipelago has yet to evolve into full nationhood or to emerge from widespread poverty.

Indochina and the Vietnam War

When Japan surrendered in 1945, Ho Chi Minh, the head of Vietnam's Communist party, declared the independence of all Indochina. From the northern city of Hanoi, he began a war of liberation against French occupation. Under the leadership of General Vo Nguyen Giap, the Communists perfected guerrilla fighting techniques and conducted a war of attrition. Although the French retook southern Vietnam, Ho's forces controlled much of the north. In 1954, after the French-occupied fortress of Dien Bien Phu fell to Giap's forces, a hastily arranged summit conference in Geneva brought together French, Vietnamese, British, American, Soviet, and Chinese representatives. They agreed to break up Indochina temporarily into separate states and to hold national elections to reunify Vietnam within a year. The government under Ho Chi Minh in the north of Vietnam was balanced by an American-backed dictatorship set up in the south under Ngo Dinh Diem based in Saigon, the old French colonial capital. Laos and Cambodia became independent nations.

Diem and the Americans, fearing a Communist victory, refused to permit the national elections agreed to at Geneva. Guerrilla warfare broke out in South Vietnam in 1957, but President Eisenhower limited American involvement to matériel and military advisers. The Kennedy administration escalated the local civil struggle into a major international conflict on the basis of the "domino theory" that a Communist victory in Vietnam would threaten all governments in Southeast Asia. Some 17,000 American military personnel were assigned to Vietnam, but the Communist-led National Liberation Front (NLF) succeeded in capturing most of the countryside. In 1963 Vietnamese generals abetted by the United States killed Diem and ushered in a succession of military regimes.

Under President Lyndon Johnson the conflict became a full-scale war. He ordered air strikes against the Communist North and in August 1964, following a naval incident in the Gulf of Tongking (Tonkin), secured passage of a resolution from Congress that gave the president carte blanche to enlarge America's role in the war. By the spring of 1965 the United States was carrying out massive bombardment of North Vietnam and had committed its soldiers to offensive operations. The number of American troops grew steadily, from 184,000 in 1965 to more than 500,000 by the end of 1968.

American soldiers stop to watch as a target in a South Vietnamese village burns.

Despite this buildup, victory eluded the United States and its allies. The attempt to secure territory in the South by so-called search-and-destroy operations against the enemy proved futile, and the administration, fearing Chinese intervention as in Korea, declined to invade the North. Unable to gain victory on the ground, the United States dropped more explosives on tiny Vietnam than the Allies had dropped on all fronts during World War II, and American troops killed thousands of civilians in fruitless efforts to prevent villagers from hiding Communist guerrillas.

The turning point in the war came in February 1968, when the NLF launched a wave of attacks, known as the Tet Offensive, against towns and cities in South Vietnam. In April peace talks between the United States and North Vietnam opened in Paris, and in November, American voters elected the Republican Richard M. Nixon (1913–1994) to the presidency. Nixon began the secret bombing of Communist supply routes in Cambodia and Laos in early 1969, concealing the operation through false reports. When Congress learned of the Cambodian bombings, it repealed the Tongking Gulf Resolution. In 1971 the publication of classified war documents heightened antiwar sentiments by revealing earlier deceptions by both Johnson and Nixon. Protests mounted as the 1972 presidential elections approached, but Nixon neutralized them by removing the last American ground troops. The Paris Accords, signed in January 1973, officially ended American involvement in the war. In April 1975 the North Vietnamese captured Saigon, ousted the government of President Nguyen Van Thieu, and unified the country.

The Americans claimed that the struggle was an example of "Communist aggression." Most Vietnamese saw it as a patriotic war of "national liberation" against French colonialism and U.S. imperialism. Peasants came to fear and hate the repressive policies of the puppet government of the South and of their American supporters, as they and most Vietnamese intellectuals had hated French oppression. There were some Vietnamese anti-Communists, including Catholic converts who fled the North, and some who supported the United States–backed government, but they were mainly relatively well-to-do elites and others who benefited from the widespread corruption of the Saigon government or who profited in various ways from the American presence. The war's outcome was ultimately decided by the support of most Vietnamese, including the peasants in this predominantly rural country, for the forces of the National Liberation Front, which they saw as a national rather than a partisan effort.

In many ways the Vietnam War was a repeat of the long struggle of the Chinese Communists against the Kuomintang. In Vietnam, too, the Communist party under Ho had captured the leadership of Vietnamese nationalism by the end of World War II. Like the Chinese, Vietnamese nationalists strove to free their country from foreign domination, and like them, they drew support against a corrupt and repressive regime domestically, which was further weakened politically by its subservience to foreign interests. Between 1.5 and 2 million Vietnamese gave their lives in the struggle; perhaps as many as 4 million were wounded, and over a million were refugees. The Americans suffered 58,000 dead and some 300,000 wounded.

As in Korea but to a far greater extent, American intervention produced in the end nothing but destruction and death. Official policy was based on almost total ignorance of Vietnam, its history of repeated success in repelling vastly superior Chinese armies, and the strength of Vietnamese nationalism. The small nation's guerrilla fighters humbled the military might of the world's greatest superpower, as the Chinese Communists had earlier defeated another United States client, the Kuomintang. But Vietnam suffered terribly. Its people and its economy have not recovered from what has been called the "endless war" from 1945 to 1975, although for many Vietnamese the struggle against the French had begun in the second half of the nineteenth century. The United States merely prolonged that struggle and, far from preventing a Communist victory, had the effect of hardening the determination and the political rigidity of the government of the North. Since 1975 Vietnam has continued to suffer not only from the effects of unprecedented devastation but also from ideological tension and repression augmented by the long ordeal of conflict. If Ho had been allowed to prevail against the French in 1945 or 1946, as he clearly would have done without massive United States support for the French, most of these tragic problems would have been avoided.

Recovery from the war damage to the economy was slow. As after any civil war, bitterness remained between the victors of the north and the southerners who had opposed them. Large numbers of Vietnamese fled the country, many to the United States. But continued political and ideological tensions further slowed the recovery of Vietnam, which lagged behind much of the rest of Southeast Asia.

Vietnam's war of independence spilled over into neighboring Laos and Cambodia, with appalling human consequences. The overthrow of the neutralist ruler of Cambodia (now Kampuchea), Prince Norodom Sihanouk (born 1919), led to a civil war and subsequently to the genocidal Communist regime of Pol Pot, who was responsible for the deaths of perhaps a third of the country's people from 1976 to 1979 by forced labor, execution, or starvation. Vietnamese military intervention helped a more moderate rival government win control of most of the country in 1979, but Pol Pot's Khmer Rouge forces remain active in their northern bases, supplied by China and the United States. Vietnam was still seen as the enemy of America and now again of China, and its move to eliminate Pol Pot was therefore resisted by both countries for political reasons. Those reasons included Soviet support for Vietnam, which helped sustain it in its war with the United States and which the Chinese also

saw as a threat to themselves. Continuing Cold War rivalries in Indochina have thus prolonged its agony, but as of 1995 the United States was edging away from support for Pol Pot, and there was agreement among Russia, the United States, and China to hold elections in Cambodia supervised by the United Nations.

Malaysia, Singapore, Thailand, and Burma

Malaya's independence was delayed by the Communist insurgency, but once order was restored, the British quickly handed over power to the new state in 1957. Its major problem has been the diversity of its people. The Malays constituted a bare majority in their own homeland, thanks to massive Chinese immigration since the late nineteenth century. Most Malays were not interested in wage labor, and the booming growth of tin mining and rubber plantations brought in a wave of Chinese workers and entrepreneurs from overcrowded southern China. Many of them went on to become the dominant figures in the commercial life of Malaya and were joined by wives and families from China, as well as by immigrant laborers and merchants from India. By the time of independence Malays made up only about half the population.

This problem was eased in 1965 by the separation of the island of Singapore, overwhelmingly Chinese, as an independent city-state, and by the addition of former British colonies in northern Borneo, where Chinese were a minority. Since then the state has been called Malaysia, but there have been chronic conflicts between Malays and Chinese. The Chinese are effectively without a political voice, but Malays resent their economic power. A generally stable parliamentary system on the British model was marred in the 1980s by tendencies, like those in Singapore, toward authoritarianism and repression. The economy has remained relatively vigorous and has expanded from its colonial foundations in tin and rubber to include important palm oil production and a rapidly growing light industrial sector.

The tiny Sultanate of Brunei on the north coast of Borneo, formerly a British protectorate, was given its independence following the creation of Malaysia and then rocketed to wealth when rich oil deposits were found there. Independent Singapore continues as a high-income and high-growth center of trade for much of Southeast Asia and has become the world's fourth largest port in volume of traffic.

Thailand, just north of Malaya, was the only nation of Southeast Asia to retain independence throughout the colonial period. Since 1945 it has also enjoyed precarious political stability under democratic forms and has shared in the prosperous commercial growth of Malaya and Singapore through its port and capital of Bangkok, now a rapidly growing Western-style city. Successive military coups, including one in 1991, confirmed the army as the real power, but there was growing dissent among the rising middle class.

Burma won its freedom from Britain in 1948 in the wake of India's independence, but it has been troubled by violence between the dominant Burmans and the diverse minorities who occupy the mountain fringes of the country. Chronic guerrilla-style civil war existed between government forces and rebel groups. General Ne Win's military government was not able to resolve this problem fully, and his policy of isolation from the rest of the world had the effect of further slowing Burma's already sluggish economic growth. Burma has begun to move cautiously toward resuming some external contacts and trade. A new and more responsive government may be able to build a more equitable and consensual national partnership among Burmese and non-Burmese, but the country still has far to go to attain viable nationhood. The military government, moreover, continues to block change and in 1991 outlawed the Socialist party, which had won the May 1990 election.

For Southeast Asia as a whole, the transition from colonialism has been a hard one. Only Singapore and Thailand can be called fully successful states, and both may be regarded as special cases: Thailand never underwent colonial occupation and contains few non-Thai minorities. Singapore is in essence a creation of Western colonialism and capitalism. From the 1980s government policies in Singapore were often repressively applied and free expression was curtailed or silenced. The countries of Southeast Asia are too scattered and too different from one another to work together as a unit, even for common economic purposes. The region is a major sector of the world, but its diversity and the legacy of its colonial domination continue to retard its development.

Rewards and Problems of Modernization

East Asia as a whole had the highest economic growth rate of any part of the world in the decades following World War II, a pattern that still continues. Hong Kong, Taiwan, and South Korea rapidly developed in the wake of Japanese economic success after the mid-1950s. Much of this development was on the Japanese model, beginning in light industry and consumer goods and continuing into heavy manufacturing and precision goods. Singapore's growth paralleled that of Hong Kong;

both were tiny Chinese city-states that had originally prospered as trade centers and then moved into high-tech industrialization and processing. In China, despite the drag exerted by antiurbanism and revolutionary ideology, industrial growth was impressive, and after 1980 overall economic development was rapid. In Southeast Asia several of the major cities besides Singapore, notably Bangkok, Thailand, and Manila, the Philippine capital, grew enormously as booming commercial and light industrial centers.

Much of this growth rested on the East Asian tradition of disciplined hard work and organized group effort, but it was striking enough to attract world attention and speculation about its causes. East Asia does share, to varying degrees, an originally Chinese culture, which has for centuries stressed education, hard work, and group effort, perhaps enough to override other differences in the pursuit of advancement.

But modernization has brought new problems. These include the rapid erosion of traditional cultures (to the distress of many East Asians), the rise of huge cities inadequately supplied with basic services or housing, and fearsome pollution of urban and rural environments. Japan was only the first to suffer dramatically from industrial pollution as a result of the unprecedented concentration of cities and manufacturing in its lowlands. As a high-income and technologically developed society, Japan was also the first to deal successfully with at least some of those problems.

For the rest of East Asia, as in the developing world as a whole, largely unchecked pollution is still increasing, with deeply worrisome long-term consequences for human welfare. Other East Asian countries have passed environmental legislation too, but in most cases it is not effectively enforced. Chinese, Korean, Taiwanese, and Southeast Asian cities are dangerously polluted, their air heavy with soot and fumes, and their water supplies, often inadequate to supply their mushrooming populations and factories, are loaded with poisonous industrial residues. In rural areas heavy applications of chemical fertilizers, the use of largely unregulated chemical pesticides, and the development of factories cause additional environmental damage. Massive cutting of trees to feed the demand for new construction has exposed slopes to erosion, and silt chokes rivers and irrigation systems. In large parts of Southeast Asia the tropical rain forest that covers much of the area is rapidly being depleted to provide lumber for both domestic and world markets, with potentially serious effects on local and world climate.

Most of these countries are bent on rapid industrial and economic growth; they are reluctant to slow that growth or add to its costs, even by limiting the worst of the environmental damage. Such controls, many of them argue, are for rich countries. It may take more human disasters such as Japan experienced to persuade them that their own welfare is at stake. Japan, lacking most industrial raw materials and having to import nearly all its oil, has invested proportionately more heavily in nuclear power than any country in the world, ignoring its location in one of the world's major earthquake zones. China has huge domestic supplies of coal, most of it with a high sulfur content, which supplies about three-quarters of the nation's energy. These problems may become future disasters as East Asia continues to industrialize.

Urban growth in East Asia has taken place very rapidly and with minimal planning, especially outside China. Even in China industrial and residential areas have not been adequately separated; housing, water supply, and other urban services lag seriously behind demand; Peking has grown uncontrollably. These problems are equally pronounced in urban centers such as Seoul, Taipei, Bangkok, Manila, and Djakarta, where unchecked migration from rural areas has swollen city populations without a substantial increase in basic services.

While the problems of modernization seem especially serious in the cities, it is there also that the chief forces for economic growth are centered. The cities are the major industrial bases, educational centers, commercial and financial hubs, and centers of intellectual and cultural ferment, as they were in the history of the West. So far Asia has tended to repeat the Western experience of economic and industrial development, which in its early and middle stages was unpleasant and unhealthy for most people. As the process has gathered momentum in Asia after World War II, one may hope that the rest of the Western experience will be repeated too, as the cities become, like those in Japan, centers of improved welfare. Their advances can then spread more widely over each country.

SUMMARY

The years after 1945 were momentous for East Asia. New nations were born out of the former colonial regimes in Southeast Asia. Korea regained its independence, only to be torn by war and split by superpower tensions. China underwent the largest revolution in history, measured by the numbers of people involved, the scope of its change, and the length of both its gestation and its active course, including the convulsive struggles of the Cultural Revolution. A shattered Japan rebuilt its economy and rose to world industrial leadership. But although each of these major areas had its own internal problems, the dominant trend in all of them was eco-

nomic growth and industrialization. East Asia as a whole, led by Japan, became the world's largest and most rapidly expanding commercial and industrial network, as it had long been its most populous geographic region. It remains to be seen whether the area's new economic power will be reflected proportionately in new political power on the world scene.

SUGGESTIONS FOR FURTHER READING

Japan

Brunton, M. C. *Women and the Economic Miracle: Gender and Work in Postwar Japan.* Berkeley: University of California Press, 1993.

Cohen, T. *Remaking Japan: The American Occupation as New Deal.* New York: Free Press, 1987.

Dore, R. *City Life in Japan: A Study of a Tokyo Ward.* Berkeley: University of California Press, 1994.

Hane, M. *Modern Japan: A Historical Survey.* Boulder, Colo.: Westview Press, 1986.

Hendry, J. *Understanding Japanese Society.* London: Routledge & Kegan Paul, 1988.

Immamura, H. E. *Urban Japanese Housewives.* Honolulu: University Press of Hawaii, 1986.

Lebra, T. S. *Japanese Women: Constraint and Fulfillment.* Honolulu: University Press of Hawaii, 1984.

Minear, R. *Victor's Justice.* Princeton, N.J.: Princeton University Press, 1971.

Okata, S. *Japan in the World Economy.* Tokyo: Tokyo University Press, 1990.

Reischauer, E. O. *The Japanese.* Cambridge, Mass.: Harvard University Press, 1988.

Saso, M. *Women in the Japanese Workplace.* London: Shipman, 1990.

Sumiko, I. *The Japanese Woman.* New York: Free Press, 1993.

Vogel, E. *Japan as Number One: Lessons for America.* Cambridge, Mass.: Harvard University Press, 1979.

China

Bonavia, D. *The Chinese.* New York: Harper & Row, 1984.

Cheng, C. Y. *Behind the Tienanmen Massacre.* Boulder, Colo.: Westview Press, 1990.

Dietrich, C. *People's China: A Brief History.* New York: Oxford University Press, 1994.

Fairbank, J. K. *The Great Chinese Revolution.* Cambridge, Mass.: Harvard University Press, 1986.

Hsu, I. C. Y. *China Since Mao.* New York: Oxford University Press, 1990.

Lee, H. Y. *The Politics of the Chinese Cultural Revolution.* Berkeley: University of California Press, 1978.

Liang, H., and Shapiro, J. *Son of the Revolution.* New York: Knopf, 1984.

Murphey, R. *The Fading of the Maoist Vision.* New York: Methuen, 1980.

Nathan, A. *Chinese Democracy.* Berkeley: University of California Press, 1986.

Riskin, C. *China's Political Economy: The Quest for Development Since 1949.* New York: Oxford University Press, 1987.

Schram, S. *Mao Tse-tung: A Preliminary Reassessment.* New York: Simon & Schuster, 1984.

Schrecker, J. E. *The Chinese Revolution in Historical Perspective.* New York: Praeger, 1991.

Selden, M. *The Yenan Way in Revolutionary China.* Cambridge, Mass.: Harvard University Press, 1971.

Simon, D. F., and Kau, Y. M. *Taiwan: Beyond the Economic Miracle.* New York: Sharpe, 1992.

Sutter, R. G. *Taiwan: Entering the Twenty-first Century.* Washington, D.C.: University Press of America, 1989.

White, M. K., and Parrish, W. *Urban Life in Contemporary China.* Stanford, Calif.: Stanford University Press, 1985.

Wolf, M. *Revolution Postponed: Women in Contemporary China.* Stanford, Calif.: Stanford University Press, 1985.

Woronoff, J. *Asia's "Miracle" Economies.* New York: Sharpe, 1992.

Korea

Chandler, D. A. *The Tragedy of Cambodian History.* New Haven, Conn.: Yale University Press, 1992.

Clough, R. N. *Embattled Korea.* Boulder, Colo.: Westview Press, 1987.

Lee, K. B. *A New History of Korea,* trans. E. W. Wagner. Cambridge, Mass.: Harvard University Press, 1985.

Southeast Asia

Greene, G. *The Quiet American.* New York: Viking, 1957. (A novel about the Vietnam War.)

Karnow, S. *In Our Own Image: America's Empire in the Philippines.* New York: Random House, 1989.

Stueck, W. *The Korean War.* Princeton, N.J.: Princeton University Press, 1996.

Werner, J., and Luv, D., eds. *The Vietnam War.* Armonk, N.Y.: M. E. Sharpe, 1994.

Yahuda, M. *Hong Kong: China's Opportunity.* London: Routledge, 1996.

CHAPTER 41

Nationalism and Revolution: India, Pakistan, Iran, and the Middle East

The postwar period was a time of rapid and radical change throughout the Middle East and central Asia. Britain and France withdrew or were forced from their colonial dominions, and a host of new nations emerged, some with ancient roots, others the product of modern nationalism. Among the former, India and Egypt regained their old independence, one as a constitutional democracy, the other as a revolutionary socialist state. Among the latter, Pakistan, the world's third-largest Islamic state (after Indonesia and India), emerged from the Muslim-majority regions of pre-1949 India. Some states, such as Jordan, were created primarily as buffer zones or in acts of political compromise, while in other cases nationalist movements, such as those of the Palestinians and the Kurds, remained frustrated. The most controversial new nation to emerge was the state of Israel, where a powerful modern nationalism sought to revive the heritage of a kingdom that had flourished nearly 3,000 years before. Throughout the postwar decades, however, the region as a whole has been characterized by turmoil and instability, culminating in the 1980s in a war between Iran and Iraq that now ranks as the fourth bloodiest conflict of the twentieth century.

South Asia: Independence and Political Division

The Indian subcontinent, known since 1947 as South Asia, is composed of the separate states of Pakistan, India, Bangladesh, Nepal, and Sri Lanka and contains well over a billion people, one-fifth of the world. British colonialism died in the ashes of World War II, and the British were in any case unwilling to continue their rule

Mrs. Sirimavo Bandaranaike, widow of the assassinated Prime Minister, speaking at an election rally in Colombo. She was elected, and served two terms as Prime Minister.

of an India determined to regain its freedom. Gandhi, Nehru, and other Indian political leaders had spent most of the war years in jail after they had refused to support the war without a promise of independence. Their example inspired many new followers, and by 1945 the independence movement was clearly too strong to be denied by a Britain now both weakened and weary of colonialism. The conservative wartime leader Winston Churchill was voted out of office. Churchill had been rigidly opposed to Indian independence. During the war he had declared, "I was not made His Majesty's first minister in order to preside over the liquidation of the British Empire," and he was contemptuous of Gandhi. Lord Wavell, military commander in India and the first postwar viceroy, wrote in his diary: "Churchill hates India and everything to do with it. He knows as much of the Indian problem as George III did of the American colonies. . . . He sent me a peevish telegram to ask why Gandhi hadn't died yet."

The new Labour government under Clement Attlee moved quickly toward giving India its freedom. Elections were held in India early in 1946, but by then it had become clear that support for a separate state for Muslims had gained strength. The Muslim League, the chief vehicle for this movement, had been founded as early as 1906, but until 1945 it was supported by only a few Muslims, most of whom remained willing to work with the Congress party as the main agent of politically conscious Indians. The Muslim League's president, Mohammed Ali Jinnah (1876–1948), had earlier been a member of the Congress party and was even for a time its president. He and a few other Muslim leaders became dissatisfied with the Congress party's plans for a secular independent state that deemphasized religious identity and with the party's leaders' unwillingness to reserve what Jinnah regarded as adequate positions and representation for Muslims. Hindus and Muslims had lived together peacefully for most of nine centuries, even at the village level. Persian Muslim culture had blended in with indigenous elements to form modern Indian civilization. Both groups were long-standing parts of the Indian fabric. It was hard to see them as irreconcilable.

Jinnah, like Nehru, was British-educated. In his earlier career as a British-trained lawyer, he had paid little attention to Islam, and he knew no Urdu, the language of Islam in India. But as he saw his political ambitions threatened by the success of Gandhi and Nehru, he shifted his allegiance to the Muslim League and began to use it to persuade Muslims that a Hindu-dominated India would never, as he put it, give them "justice." He found support among some of the communal-minded (those who put separate group loyalty above national

Muslim Solidarity: Jinnah's Call

Jinnah made a number of speeches during World War II in his effort to promote Muslim solidarity and political action. Here are excerpts from a 1943 speech.

The progress that Muslims, as a nation, have made during these [past] three years is a remarkable fact. . . . Never before has a nation, miscalled a minority, asserted itself so quickly and so effectively. . . . We have created a solidarity of opinion, a union of mind and thought. . . . Let us cooperate with and give all help to our leaders to work for our collective good. Let us make our organization stronger. . . . We, the Muslims, must rely mainly upon our own inherent qualities, our own natural potentialities, our own internal solidarity, and our own united will to face the future. . . . Train yourselves, equip yourselves for the task that lies before us. The final victory depends upon you and is within our grasp. You have performed wonders in the past. You are still capable of repeating history. You are not lacking in the great qualities and virtues in comparison with other nations. Only you have to be fully conscious of that fact and act with courage, faith, and unity.

Source: W. T. de Bary, ed., *Sources of Indian Tradition,* vol. 2, 4th ed. (New York: Columbia University Press, 1964), pp. 286–287.

Mohammed Ali Jinnah in 1946. Note his totally Western clothes.

Nehru and Mountbatten in New Delhi, 1947. The two men took an immediate liking to each other, which greatly eased the transition to independence.

feeling) and also from Muslim businessmen, especially in the port city of Karachi, who saw a possible way of ridding themselves of Hindu competition. Nehru and others insisted that communalism had nothing to do with religion and that the exploitation of religious differences by a few politicians for their own ends fueled communal tensions. Hindus were often more active and more successful in business than Muslims, they were generally more educated, and as the great majority in India they also dominated politics and the professions. But they did not generally discriminate against Muslim intellectuals or professionals. Some other Muslim political figures, like Jinnah, saw greater opportunity for themselves if they could have their own state and supported the League in its campaign to convince Muslims that "Islam was in danger." When such relatively peaceful tactics did not produce enough result, Jinnah and the League began to promote terror and violence, urging Muslims to demonstrate and to attack Hindus in order to call attention to their cause.

The Congress party was slow to respond or to offer Muslims or the League a larger share in an Indian future. Gandhi and Nehru in particular were reluctant even to consider partitioning India just as it was about to win freedom. This tended to increase the League's fear of a Hindu threat to Muslims, and the League resorted to more violent tactics. In the later stages of the long nego-

tiations during 1946 and 1947 Jinnah offered to give up the demand for Pakistan (as the separate Muslim state was to be called) if he could be guaranteed the position of first prime minister of independent India. That demand was rejected, and Jinnah remained adamant in insisting on a separate state that he could head. Successive British representatives tried to work out a solution in sessions with the Congress party and the League, ending with the special mission in 1947 of Lord Louis Mountbatten (1900–1979), the wartime supreme commander in Southeast Asia. Mountbatten was appointed viceroy of India, with the sole charge of working out the terms for independence as quickly as this could be done.

If independence had been granted at any time before 1939, as most Indians and most British had wanted, the issue of partition would not have arisen. Jinnah was able to use the war years, while the Congress party leaders were in jail, to build his political base and then to spread the fear of cultural engulfment and oppression among his followers. Muslim-Hindu violence, once stirred up by the Muslim League, acquired its own dreadful momentum on both sides, especially in regions that were nearly evenly divided between the two religious communities, such as Punjab and East Bengal. Mob riots and mass killing spread widely. Although Mountbatten, like Nehru and Gandhi, hoped to avoid handing over power to a divided India, by July he as well as the party leaders recognized that partition and the creation of Pakistan were inevitable. Nehru remarked bitterly that "by cutting off the head we will get rid of the headache," while Gandhi continued to regard partition as "vivisection."

Lines were drawn to mark off the predominantly Muslim northwest and western Punjab and the eastern

India and the Sense of History

On the eve of independence, Nehru addressed the Constituent Assembly in 1946 with his characteristic eloquence, stressing the sense of history that many Indians share.

As I stand here, . . . I feel the weight of all manner of things crowding upon me. We are at the end of an era and possibly very soon we shall embark upon a new age. My mind goes back to the great past of India, to the 5000 years of India's history, from the very dawn of that history which might be considered almost the dawn of human history, until today. All that past crowds upon me and exhilarates me, and at the same time somewhat oppresses me. Am I worthy of that past? When I think also of the future, the greater future I hope, standing on this sword's edge of the present between the mighty past and the mightier future, I tremble a little and feel overwhelmed by this mighty task. We have come here at a strange moment in India's history. I do not know, but I do feel, that there is some magic in this moment of transition from the old to the new, something of that magic which one sees when the night turns into day and even though the day may be a cloudy one, it is day after all, for when the clouds move away, we can see the sun again. Because of all this I find a little difficulty in addressing this House and putting all my ideas before it, and I feel also that in this long succession of thousands of years, I see the mighty figures that have come and gone and I see also the long succession of our comrades who have labored for the freedom of India. And we stand now on the verge of this passing age, trying, laboring, to usher in the new. . . . I think also of the various constituent assemblies that have gone before and of what took place at the making of the great American nation when the fathers of that nation met and fashioned a constitution which has stood the test for so many years. . . . [He then mentions the French and Russian revolutions also.] We seek to learn from their success and to avoid their failures. Perhaps we may not be able to avoid failures, because some measure of failure is inherent in human effort. Nevertheless we shall advance, I am certain . . . and realize the dream that we have dreamed so long.

Source: W. T. de Bary, ed., *Sources of Indian Tradition*, vol. 1, 4th ed. (New York: Columbia University Press, 1964), pp. 350–352.

half of Bengal as the two unequal halves of Pakistan, separated from each other by nearly 1,000 miles. At midnight on August 14, 1947, the Republic of India and the Islamic state of Pakistan officially won their independence. Gandhi boycotted the independence day celebrations in New Delhi, going instead to Calcutta to try to quell fresh outbreaks of mass violence there as refugees streamed in from eastern Bengal.

The first months of independence were tragically overshadowed by perhaps the greatest mass refugee movement in history as over 14 million people fled from both sides in 1947 alone, about a million of whom were victims of mob massacre along the route. When it was all over, 50 million Muslims continued to live in India much as before, and India still has more Muslims than Pakistan. For those who chose to migrate to Pakistan, including further millions after 1947, life in the new state (with an initial population of 70 million) was hard in the first chaotic years as Pakistan struggled to cope with the flood of refugees. Hindus remaining in Pakistan soon found that they had little place in an Islamic state that explicitly discriminated against all non-Muslims, and within a few years most of them had migrated to India, depriving Pakistan of many of its more highly educated and experienced people. For the educated elite of both countries, including the army officers who soon faced each other across the new boundaries, partition divided former classmates, friends, and professional colleagues who had shared a common experience, training, and values.

The partition lines also split the previously integrated cultural and economic regions of densely populated Punjab and Bengal and caused immense disruption. Since the division was by agreement based solely on religion, nothing was considered except to separate areas with a Muslim majority, often by a thin margin. Many districts, villages, and towns were nearly evenly balanced between the two religions, which were deeply intertwined over many centuries of coexistence. The partition cut through major road and rail links, divided rural areas from their urban centers, and bisected otherwise uniform regions of culture and language.

The Kashmir Conflict

The still nominally independent native states, under their own Indian rulers, were technically given the choice of joining India or Pakistan, but there was really no choice for the few Muslim-ruled states or smaller Muslim-majority areas surrounded by Indian territory, which were absorbed or taken over, including the large state of

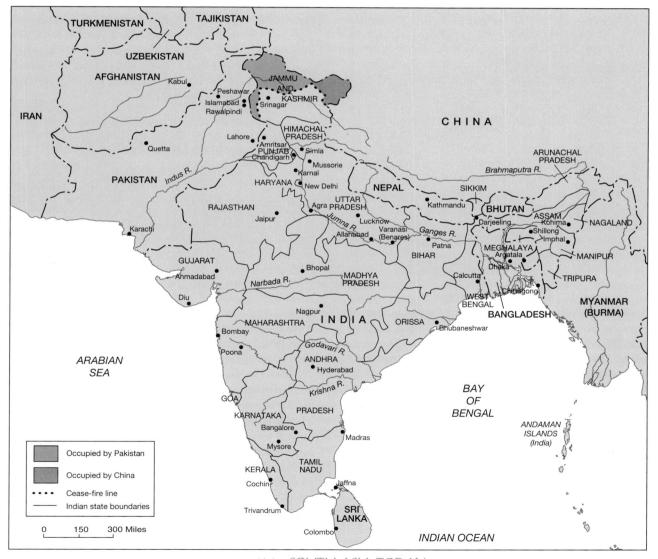

MAP 41.1 SOUTH ASIA TODAY

Hyderabad in the Deccan, Muslim-ruled but with a Hindu majority.

Kashmir, which lay geographically between the two rivals, had a Muslim majority but a Hindu ruler and its own hopes for independence. The ruler, Hari Singh, delayed his decision until his state was invaded by "volunteer" forces from Pakistan, and he agreed to join India in return for military help. Indian paratroops arrived just in time to hold Srinagar, the capital, and the central valley, the only economically important and densely settled part of the state. The cease-fire line, which still stands, gave roughly the western quarter of Kashmir to Pakistan, but the larger issue of which state Kashmir should belong to has never been resolved.

The Kashmir dispute has continued to poison relations between the two states and has sparked three inconclusive wars. Thus to the tragedy of partition and the violence following it has been added chronic Indo-Pakistani tension instead of the cooperation that would be more appropriate between two developing nations born out of the same context and sharing a common cultural tradition. Mahatma Gandhi, who had prayed and labored so hard to stop Hindu-Muslim violence, ironically became one of its victims when he was murdered on January 30, 1948, by a Hindu extremist who considered him too tolerant of Muslims. Nehru saw his death as "the loss of India's soul" and commented, "The light has gone out of our lives and there is darkness everywhere."

India After Independence

In the Republic of India, parliamentary democracy and British-style law have survived repeated tests and remain vigorous. Jawaharlal Nehru, who became prime minister at independence and served until his death in 1964, was a strong and revered leader who effectively dominated the new nation. He presided over the creation of 16 new language-based states within a federal structure. Federalism was necessary in any case given India's size and diversity, and language was the single most obvious basis of regional differences. Although Nehru and others were reluctant to acknowledge the importance of language-based regionalism, it became clear after several years of debate and negotiation that such a concession would have to be made. The states created by 1956 were the size of France, Germany, or Italy in population, and each coincided approximately with the distribution of what were officially declared to be "major" languages out of the many hundreds spoken. Each of these major languages

had its own proud history and literary tradition, older, more extensive, and with more speakers than most European languages.

Hindi, the language of the Delhi area and the upper Ganges valley, was declared the official national language, to be used in national government and taught to all Indians in every region, while leaving each state its own regional language in its schools and legislatures. English, familiar to educated people in all the states, was retained as an "associate language" at the national level and continued to be taught in nearly all schools. Indian English has more speakers than American English, and it too has diverged from its British origins. Hindi is the mother tongue of only about 30 percent of the population, and even so consists of several mutually unintelligible dialects. No other native Indian language comes close. Hindi was therefore the obvious choice for a nationwide language, but for most Indians it remains a foreign tongue. It is resented especially by Dravidian-speaking southerners as yet another example of "northern domination" and the "oppression of Delhi."

India Under Nehru

Nehru saw India well launched on the path of economic development, both agricultural and industrial, but he acknowledged the Gandhian legacy by providing special government support for handicraft production and for small-scale rural industries, especially the handweaving of cotton cloth. As in China, these were often not economically practical, but symbolically they were important because of their long association with the nationalist movement, and they also offered employment in rural areas, where most Indians still lived. Traditional village councils were revitalized and used as channels for new rural development in agriculture as well as other village enterprises.

But the most rapid growth was in the expanding cities, where industry and new economic opportunity were concentrated for the fortunate and to which streams of rural immigrants were drawn. Housing and other basic human services such as water, sewers, power, education, health care, and urban transport could not keep up with a mushrooming population, including many still unemployed, a familiar problem throughout the developing world. New immigrants took time to make a place for themselves and lived, or squatted, in slums or in the open air, but the wider opportunity that the cities potentially offered continued to attract them despite the squalor and hardships with which most of them had to contend. Cal-

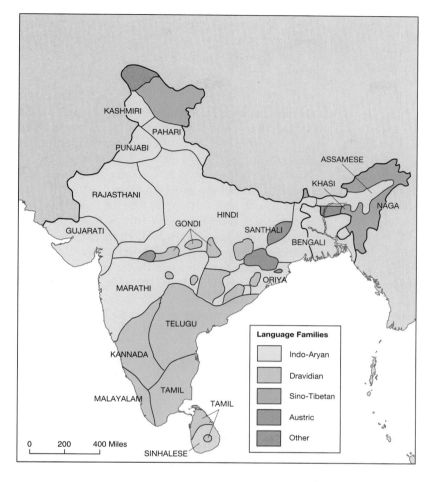

MAP 41.2 MAJOR LANGUAGES OF THE INDIAN SUBCONTINENT

cutta, Bombay, and Delhi–New Delhi, the three largest cities, are among the largest in the world, but like most, including big American cities, they combine luxurious lifestyles for a few and ragged poverty for many.

Despite government efforts to slow it down, India's population continued to grow, owing primarily to improved nutrition from agricultural gains and advances in public health that largely eliminated epidemic disease; life expectancy rose and death rates fell. But rising production, including new industrial output, more than kept pace, and per capita incomes began a slow and steady rise, which still continues. A third or more of the population, however, remained in severe poverty as the top third won new wealth.

The Nehru years were marred by a border dispute with China, in the remote Himalayas, which erupted in brief hostilities in 1962. Fresh from their armed reoccupation of Tibet, the Chinese won a quick victory. The Chinese retained control of the small border area they

had claimed, which they needed for access into western Tibet, where they were concerned with putting down rebellion against their rule. India had refused to discuss the Chinese claim and foolishly tried to eject the Chinese troops, an effort for which the Indian army was poorly prepared. Nehru had attempted, with much success until then, to build pan-Asian friendship and cooperation in partnership with China as the other major Asian power and to promote India as the leader of the nonaligned nations. His death was hastened by the failure of relations with China, which he took as a personal failure, calling it "a Himalayan blunder" (*Himalayan* is understandably used in India to mean "enormous").

With his passing, India felt it had been left leaderless and was fearful about finding an adequate successor. Nehru had been the symbol and architect of the new India and its dominant political figure for more than a generation. But the gap was filled through normal democratic processes by the old Congress party moderate Lal

Bahadur Shastri as prime minister. His promising start, including an agreement with Pakistan to reduce tensions, was cut short by his death after only a year and a half. The party then chose Nehru's daughter, Indira Gandhi (no relation to the Mahatma), who quickly established her firm leadership and vowed to continue Nehru's and Shastri's policies.

India had maintained its political stability and democratic system through successive crises, despite a still largely illiterate electorate and the multiple problems of new nationhood, wars, internal and external tensions, and poverty, a record matched by few other new nations. Illiterate voters demonstrated a surprising grasp of political issues, and a far higher proportion of those over 18 voted than in the United States. The Indian press remained freely critical of government shortcomings and offered an open forum for all opinions. India's faithfulness to the system it inherited and has continued to cultivate stands in contrast to the failure of parliamentary democracy and the rise of totalitarianism, dictatorship, censorship, and the police state in so much of the rest of Asia and the world.

Indira Gandhi

Like her famous father, Indira Gandhi (1917–1984) was British-educated and widely traveled and came to office with long experience as her father's confidant after her mother's death in 1936, acting as hostess to streams of Indian and foreign visitors who sought Nehru's counsel or favors. She had separated from her husband, Firoze Gandhi, a journalist, a few years after their marriage, and she reared her two sons in her father's house. She impressed all who knew her with her razor-sharp mental powers and her keen grasp of political affairs, but during her father's lifetime she modestly eschewed any public role. After his death in 1964, she accepted the cabinet post of information minister in Shastri's government, but only as one of many able women who had already held

India's World Role

Nehru saw India as an emerging power in the modern world and as a major Asian leader. He wrote about this and about East–West relations.

One of the major questions of the day is the readjustment of the relations between Asia and Europe. . . . India, not because of any ambition but because of geography and history . . . inevitably has to play a very important part in Asia . . . [and is] a meeting ground between the East and the West. . . . The Middle East and Southeast Asia both are connected with India. . . . You cannot consider any question concerning the Far East without India. . . . In the past the West ignored Asia, or did not give her the weight that was due her. Asia was really given a back seat . . . and even the statesmen did not recognize the changes that were taking place. There is considerable recognition of these changes now, but it is not enough. . . . I do not mean to say that we in Asia are in any way superior, ethically or morally, to the people of Europe. In some ways, I imagine that we are worse. There is however a legacy of conflict in Europe. . . . We might note that the world progressively tends to become one. . . . [We should] direct [our] policy towards avoiding conflict. . . . The emergence of India in world affairs is something of major consequence in world history. We who happen to be in the government of India . . . are men of relatively small stature. But it has been given to us to work at a time when India is growing into a great giant again.

Source: W. T. de Bary, ed., *Sources of Indian Tradition*, vol. 1, 4th ed. (New York: Columbia University Press, 1964), pp. 352–353.

Indira Gandhi in 1972, addressing a crowd at Kolhapur, India.

Grain being fed into a storage silo in New Delhi: one of the results of the green revolution.

cabinet rank and who had been prominent earlier in the long struggle for independence.

The Ministry of Information gave her new public visibility, and when Shastri suddenly died, she entered the contest for Congress party leadership, which ended in her overwhelming victory and subsequent endorsement by the national electorate. She was a consummate politician within the Congress party, and many observers accused her of becoming merely a power broker, but without her father's charisma or deft diplomacy. Indira Gandhi shared her father's commitment to Western values but drew her political strength mainly from left of center. During her years as prime minister, from 1966 to 1977 and from 1980 to her death in 1984, she was a commanding figure.

Drought in 1965 and 1966, which caused much suffering but relatively few deaths, led India to become one of the first countries to launch a major campaign in the so-called green revolution, an agricultural policy that achieved higher yields with improved seeds and expanded irrigation and fertilizer production. By the end of the 1960s there had been a real breakthrough in production, and by 1975 India was again self-sufficient in grains and had a surplus for export, a situation it has since maintained. Industrial growth also continued, but the gap between rich and poor widened. The green revolution benefited farmers with enough land and capital to use and pay for the new seeds, irrigation, and fertilizers. Small farmers and people in nonagricultural areas sank further into relative poverty, and tenancy and landlessness rose. Upwardly mobile urban workers, managers, professionals, and technicians were more than matched by rising numbers of urban and rural poor. These grow-

ing pains were typical of economic development everywhere, including the nineteenth-century West.

In part to quash charges of corruption and to weaken her political opposition, Gandhi in June 1975 proclaimed a state of national emergency in the name of "unity" and "reform." Civil rights were suspended, the press was controlled, opposition leaders and "troublemakers" were jailed, the constitution was amended to keep the courts from challenging the government, and a series of measures were announced to control inflation, inefficiency, hoarding, and tax evasion. It seemed the end of India as the world's largest parliamentary democracy, but Gandhi miscalculated her people's judgment. When she finally permitted a national election in January 1977, she and her party were defeated. The Indian democratic system and its tradition of free expression were soundly vindicated, but the coalition government of non-Congress parties that emerged under the aged Morarji Desai floundered and finally dissolved into bickering, paving the way for Gandhi's return to power in the elections of January 1980.

Although she made no effort to reestablish the "emergency," Gandhi's response to tensions and protests by disaffected regions and groups became increasingly rigid and authoritarian. Meanwhile, economic growth continued in agriculture and industry. By 1983 over a third of India's exports were manufactured goods, many of them from high-tech industries that competed successfully on the world market. India had become a major industrial power, and its pool of trained scientists and technicians, products of the British-inherited education system, was exceeded only by those of the United States and the Soviet Union. In 1974 its own scientists completed the first Indian nuclear test, though the government continued to insist it would not make nuclear weapons but would instead concentrate on the production of nuclear energy for peaceful purposes. Indian satellites joined American and Russian ones in space, and Indian-made microchips began to revolutionize industry. At the same time, many rural sectors remained in the bullock cart age, and the urban poor slept under bridges near the new luxury apartments of those who had done well in the rapidly growing economy.

The Sikhs

Of the many groups that felt disadvantaged, the most continuously and effectively organized were the Sikhs of Punjab. Ironically, Punjab had led the nation in agricultural progress under the green revolution, and although not all Sikhs were well off, as a group they had prospered more than most others. Part of their discontent was no doubt related to the rising expectations common to periods of development. Having put the green revolution to work with their traditional entrepreneurial talents and hard work, the Sikhs grew increasingly angry at government controls on agricultural prices imposed by Gandhi's fight against inflation, which severely restricted farmers' profits. A religious community founded in the fifteenth century as a reformist offshoot from Hinduism, the Sikhs also wanted greater recognition, increased political status, more control of Punjab state (where they were in fact a minority), and greater provincial autonomy.

Sikhs constituted only about 2 percent of India's population, and Gandhi was reluctant to favor them or to make concessions on provincial autonomy when she had to confront so many similar demands from other discontented groups and protest movements. But her stance on the Sikhs was rigid to a fault; she met violence with more violence, capped by the storming of the Golden Temple in Amritsar, sacred to Sikhism, which a group of extremists had fortified. Four months later, in October 1984, she was gunned down by two of her Sikh guards in the name of Indian freedom. Many others had come to see her as corrupted by power.

India After Indira Gandhi

The Congress party chose Gandhi's son Rajiv (1944–1991) to succeed her, and in January 1985 this choice was overwhelmingly confirmed in a nationwide election. Rajiv Gandhi offered peace to the Sikhs, granted many of their more reasonable demands (including new borders for Punjab that created a state with a Sikh majority), and in other ways as well showed himself to be a sensitive and responsible leader. But the reservoir of popular support for him began to decline as critics claimed that the Congress party under his leadership remained more interested in power-brokering than in serving all the needs of the people. India, in fact, has been a largely one-party democracy since independence, although the Congress party was defeated in 1977 and after Nehru's death became increasingly split into rival factions. Many Indian voters have felt that they were not offered adequate alternatives and that government was often insensitive to their needs. Rajiv Gandhi also sent Indian troops to Sri Lanka in 1987 to try to put down communal violence there. The troops were withdrawn in 1989, but many Sri Lankan Tamils remained bitter, and in May 1991 one of them assassinated Gandhi at an election rally near Madras, the main Tamil base in India. The elections were briefly postponed, and in June a new government emerged, under a former foreign minister, V. N. Rao, but India continued to be torn by communal rioting and by countermeasures that tarnished its democratic tradition.

Three basic problems stubbornly resisted solution: miserable poverty for the bottom third or more of India's people, a population still growing too rapidly (one root of poverty), and continued outbreaks of violence among many of the groups in its highly diverse population. Caste continued to weaken slowly, especially in the cities, but most Indians remained in traditional village worlds, where caste connections still served an important function. Higher, or "dominant," castes, as they were often called, resented and tried to suppress the rise of Untouchables. Hindus and Muslims fought one another in some areas. Sikh terrorism and Hindu reprisals threatened to plunge Punjab and Delhi into civil war.

Much marketing in India takes place outdoors. This scene is in Delhi but might be almost anywhere in urban South Asia.

Nationalism grew among Indian intellectuals late in the nineteenth century, but it did not stimulate a mass movement until the 1920s. Even Mahatma Gandhi did not reach all Indians, and the country since independence in 1947 has been moving toward creating a single overriding sense of Indian identity that can take precedence over regional, religious, caste, and other group loyalties. India well illustrates the dictum of the British historian Lord Acton (1834–1902): "The nation is not the cause but the result of the state. It is the state which creates the nation, not the nation the state." To many—perhaps most—Indians it remains more important that they are Bengalis or Marathas or Tamils, Hindus, Sikhs, or Muslims, Brahmins or Untouchables than that they are fellow Indians. It will take more time before such group loyalties can be merged into a common "Indianness" through common experience in a single national state. This problem is shared with most new nations, many of which have difficulties comparable to India's. The difference is partly the scale of India's problem—over 800 million people with a diversity greater than all of Europe—and partly in the recency of its modern experience as a nation-state after 5,000 years of regional and group separatism. Since 1947 the traditional world of the village and its ties has expanded to include considerable integration with the modern world of the cities and with the larger world of regional states sharing a common language and culture.

Within India's federal political structure, central economic planning and an expanding national civil service also help join people in mutual self-interest. Regular bus service on all-weather roads links every village with these wider worlds and with a national network. The sense of nationhood needs time to grow.

The war against poverty, as the government called it, is of course related to communal and intercaste tensions and is the greatest challenge of all developing countries. India has done better economically than most of the so-called Third World, perhaps overall better than China, whose record has been praised by many economists in the West. But India's new wealth has not been well distributed. The hope is that as development proceeds and as efforts to limit population growth succeed, the fight against poverty may make significant headway. This is the same path followed by the West a century earlier as the fruits of the Industrial Revolution eventually raised the economic level of most people. Life expectancy rates and living conditions for most inhabitants are in fact better for modern Calcutta and Bombay than for nineteenth-century Manchester and New York. In India, as in most of Asia, the economic trends are strongly positive, and literacy is growing fast as universal free education spreads. This oldest of world civilizations still keeps much of its ancient tradition alive and draws strength from it as it also pursues the path of modernization.

Bangladesh and Pakistan

East Bengal, which became East Pakistan in 1947, was one of the subcontinent's poorest areas and had virtually no industry of any kind. It had been heavily dependent on Calcutta as its educational, cultural, commercial, industrial, and shipping center, through which its exports and imports moved and where nearly all transport lines were focused. East Bengal contained over half of Pakistan's population and produced three-quarters of its exports, mainly jute, but much of the profit went to Karachi, the national capital in West Pakistan. Moreover, East Bengal was strikingly underrepresented in and underfunded by the national government. Even its language, Bengali, was not officially recognized.

Pakistan continued to be run by and for the small clique of Karachi and Punjabi businessmen and politicians who had pushed for its creation, although the faltering effort at parliamentary government was swept aside by a military dictatorship in 1958. When elections, finally held in late 1970, produced a victory for the East Pakistan party on a platform of greater autonomy, the military government in West Pakistan responded by arresting the party's leader, Sheikh Mujibur Rahman, and then turning its army and tanks against demonstrators in East Pakistan in a mass slaughter. About 10 million refugees poured across the nearby Indian border by the end of 1971, mainly to already overcrowded Calcutta.

Women botany students at Ludhiana Agricultural University of Punjab.

Guerrilla actions by Bengalis against the terrorism of the West Pakistani forces finally brought in the Indian army, which in ten days ended the slaughter.

With the Pakistani army defeated, East Pakistan became the new People's Republic of Bangladesh in December 1971. Sheikh Mujib, as he was called, became prime minister, and the refugees returned home, but Bangladesh proved unable to achieve political stability or even effective government. Mujib was murdered by his own army in 1974, following charges of corruption. His military successor was assassinated in 1981, and no clear or successful political order has since emerged. Bangladesh remains one of the world's poorest nations, despite the agricultural productivity of its rice lands, burdened by a still too rapidly growing population and hampered by the lack of forceful planning and leadership. Periodic flooding caused in part by deforestation has compounded Bangladesh's problems.

What remained of Pakistan, in the west, continued to be governed by a military dictatorship, although there was some respectable economic growth in both agriculture and manufacturing. Jinnah died within a year of independence, and in 1958, after a series of corrupt and ineffective prime ministers, the country came under martial law, as it has been much of the time since. The army commander in chief, General Zia-ul-Huq, seized power in a 1977 coup d'état, dissolved the politically corrupt parliamentary system, and in 1979 executed the former prime minister, Zulfikar Ali Bhutto, after he was found guilty of conspiring in the murder of a political opponent. In an effort to break the connection with the "Karachi clique," the capital had been moved in stages between 1961 and 1965 from Karachi to a new planned site called Islamabad ("City of Islam"), about 10 miles from the city of Rawalpindi in the northwest; the two cities operate as an urban unit, linked by commuting workers and civil servants, and now rival Karachi in size. Lahore, an older and larger city and the chief center of Muslim culture, was more central, but it was thought to be too close to the border with India to be safe. Pakistan lacks most industrial resources, except for some recently discovered oil, and it began in 1947 well below the all-Indian average economic level. Nevertheless, it has avoided major famine, greatly increased irrigation in Punjab and the Indus valley, and built a basic industrial structure. As in India and China, however, economic gains continue to be held back in per capita terms by a growing population. As an Islamic state, Pakistan has been reluctant to promote family planning or to limit the growth of its population. Islamic fundamentalism similar to that in Iran has also won some support in Pakistan.

The government became deeply involved in aiding and providing refuge for the Afghan guerrilla resistance to the Soviet-supported government in Kabul, the Afghan capital, only about 100 miles from the Pakistani frontier. Such activity further strengthened Pakistan's role as a Cold War client of the United States and produced a new flow of American military supplies. But such aid had little relevance to Pakistan's domestic problems and again prompted Indian complaints that the arms were being stockpiled for use against India. The two states have fought two small wars since the partition, in 1965 and 1971, in both of which Pakistan's military power came virtually exclusively from U.S. equipment. Pakistan seemed useful to the United States as a regional anticommunist bulwark against the Soviet Union and as a friend and intermediary with China, particularly during America's resumption of relations with the People's Republic in the early 1970s.

When China became a Soviet rival instead of an ally and soon thereafter came into conflict with India over a border dispute, Pakistan took the Chinese side. In 1971 Washington used the Pakistan-China connection to respond to Chinese overtures, leading to President Richard Nixon's visit to Peking. But these international power plays had little or nothing to do with Pakistan's people or their needs. Indeed, they put the Pakistanis at serious risk by exposing them to the threat of war, the suffering resulting from further conflict with India, and the massive diversion of resources from urgently needed development into military expenditures. India and Pakistan, with so much history and so many problems in common, have more recently begun to move cautiously toward a less antagonistic relationship, but only after 40 years of tragic tension and conflict. This process was helped by Soviet withdrawal from Afghanistan and by the death of General Zia in a plane crash in 1988. Bhutto's daughter, Benazir, was elected prime minister as Zia's successor in an open contest, thus becoming the first woman to govern an Islamic state, and Pakistan returned to a more democratic path. But in August 1990 she was removed from office by the president of Pakistan, with army support, and new elections in October brought in Nawaz Sharif as prime minister; he was more acceptable to Islamic fundamentalists than a woman ruler, but in 1993 Benazir again became prime minister after elections gave her party a majority.

Pakistan is a diverse state, resembling India on a smaller scale. It includes a majority whose mother tongue is not the official national language, Urdu, and many groups who feel unrepresented, neglected, or oppressed by the government. Outside the Indus valley and western

Punjab, where most of the population is concentrated, Pakistan encompasses arid mountains along its western and northern borders, inhabited by people like the Baluchis and Pathans whose cultures and histories have little in common with those of the lowlands. A truly national state that can include them as partners has not yet emerged. The partition of India has become a permanent fact of life, but Pakistan has still to develop into a nation.

Sri Lanka

The island nation of Ceylon (which changed its name officially to Sri Lanka, an old precolonial name for the country, in 1975) lies across the Palk Strait from India. It made a relatively easy transition to independence in 1948, primarily as a consequence of Indian independence rather than of any strong nationalist movement on the island itself.

Sri Lanka had been under Western domination since the first Portuguese bases there early in the sixteenth century, and its small size and population were easily overwhelmed by foreign influences. Many of the elite were more British than Sinhalese (the majority inhabitants) in language and culture, and many regretted the end of their membership in the British Empire. But in the mid–1950s Ceylon was swept by what has been called "second-wave nationalism," a belated but emotional determination to rediscover and assert its own identity. In the elections of 1956 self-serving politicians stirred up communal feelings among the dominant Sinhalese against the minority Tamils, originally immigrants from nearby South India, who form about a fifth of the population. Approximately half of them had lived there,

MAP 41.3   SRI LANKA

at the northern tip of the island, for over 2,000 years, but the other half were more recently arrived laborers recruited to work the tea plantations in the central highlands. The Tamils are Hindu and speak primarily their own language, which has heightened their distinction from the Buddhist (or for the elite, nominally Buddhist) Sinhalese. They became a convenient scapegoat to stimulate the sense of Sinhalese nationalism, like the Chinese in many Southeast Asian countries.

SOUTH ASIA SINCE 1945

India	Pakistan	Sri Lanka
Independence (1947)	Independence (1947)	
Assassination of Mahatma Gandhi (1948)	Death of Jinnah (1948)	Independence (1948)
		Assassination of S. W. R. D. Bandaranaike (1959)
War with China (1962)		First administration of Sirimavo Bandaranaike (1960–1965)
Death of Nehru (1964)	War with India (1965)	
First administration of Indira Gandhi (1966–1977)	War with India (1971)	Second administration of Sirimavo Bandaranaike (1970–1977)
Second administration of Indira Gandhi (1980–1984)	Administration of Benazir Bhutto (1988–1990)	India sends troops to quell unrest (1987–1989)
Assassination of Rajiv Gandhi (1991)		

The tragic pattern of communal violence between Sinhalese and Tamils began with the 1956 election of S. W. R. D. Bandaranaike, on a platform of Sinhalese-only nationalism. Like Jinnah, he had been educated in Britain and was thoroughly westernized; his personal ambition and his keen mind turned to communalism, until then of little interest to him, as a means of creating a new political base for himself. Once called into existence by his campaign of discrimination, it could not be laid to rest, and he was assassinated in 1959 by a Sinhalese Buddhist who felt that he had not gone far enough.

His place was taken by his widow, Sirimavo Bandaranaike (born 1916), the world's first woman prime minister. She continued most of his policies and ruled with a firm hand for two terms, 1960–1965 and 1970–1977. Like her husband, she was British-educated, sophisticated, and extremely able, showing a talent for both international and domestic diplomacy. Her authoritative rule restored order and relative stability at a time of domestic crisis. Tamils felt more and more excluded and oppressed and took to terrorism as a weapon, finally demanding a separate state. Following elections in 1994, which brought in Bandaranaike's daughter as prime minister, negotiations with Tamil leaders seemed to offer the prospect of a peaceful settlement at last.

The Sri Lankan economy was disrupted by chronic fighting, which retarded its generally healthy growth after 1948. Nevertheless, Sri Lanka became self-sufficient in rice by the late 1970s, thanks to major investments in new irrigation and agricultural technology, and at the same time maintained the profitable plantation sector in tea, rubber, and coconuts, although by 1991 the products of light manufacturing—clothing and computers and their components, mainly produced by foreign-owned companies—had become Sri Lanka's main exports. Education, literacy, and public health were improved still further from the relatively high levels established under British colonial control, and per capita incomes remained higher than in any of the other South Asian states, thanks in part to the government's success in limiting population growth. But violence and terrorism on both sides, in an atmosphere close to civil war, eroded the British-inherited system of parliamentary government and the rule of law. In 1987 Rajiv Gandhi agreed to prevent clandestine support from South India from reaching Tamil terrorists in Sri Lanka. Later that year Indian troops were invited in to help restore peace, but they were predictably resented, and were withdrawn at the end of 1989. Much bitterness and tension remained, and violence and terrorism continued unabated.

Sirimavo Bandaranaike, like her daughter, is an example of the improving status of women in South Asia.

Like China and Japan, South Asia traditionally accorded women a relatively low status, especially during the centuries of Muslim dominance in the north. There were exceptions, including even women military figures and heads of state among the Marathas and other groups and dominant figures at court such as Nur Jahan (see Chapter 20). The westernization that accompanied British control led to increasing education for women; many educated women were prominent in the independence movement and in government and the professions after 1947. In general this was a relatively small group, an intellectual and westernized elite, while most South Asian women, especially in the villages, remained uneducated and subservient to their husbands to a degree that seemed extreme to westerners. There were regional exceptions, particularly in South India and in the southern state of Kerala, where ancient matriarchal and matrilocal* social forms persisted to some degree. Husbands in this region commonly walk behind wives and defer to them, and property and family names often descend through the female line. Elsewhere in South Asia, women such as Sirimavo Bandaranaike and Indira Gandhi have achieved great prominence on the national scene since independence.

The Turbulent Middle East

When World War II ended, Britain was still the paramount power in the Middle East, directly controlling Egypt, Palestine, Transjordan, Iraq, southern Arabia, and the Persian Gulf. In the next decade, however, it withdrew almost completely from the region, leaving a vacuum of power that was filled by Arab nationalism, superpower rivalry, and the emergence of the state of Israel.

Israel and the Struggle for Palestine

Britain's first withdrawal was from Palestine, where the conflict between Palestinian Arabs and Jewish settlers, compounded by an influx of refugees and Holocaust survivors, had reached a flashpoint. That conflict, in turn, represented a clash between the traditions of two great religions and the aspirations of two nascent nationalisms.

A small number of Jews had always lived in Palestine, to which the faithful believed their people would someday return to reestablish the ancient nation of Israel and await the coming of the Messiah. In the mid-seventeenth century a messianic pretender, Sabbatai Zevi, had led an ill-

---

*In a matrilocal society, a husband joins the wife's family.

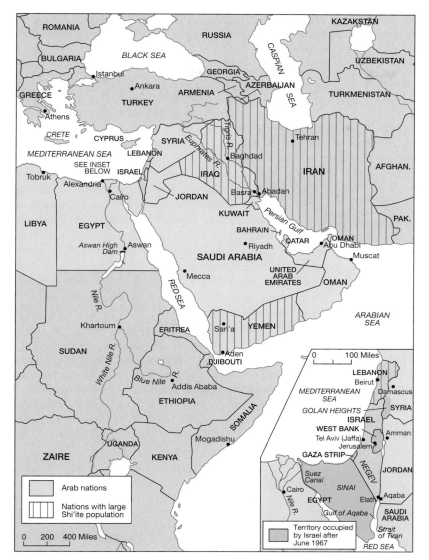

MAP 41.4   THE MIDDLE EAST TODAY

fated expedition of thousands of Jews to Palestine. The serious immigration to the region that commenced two centuries later was spurred, however, not by millennial fervor but by a secular nationalist movement, Zionism.

Zionism was a historic response to Jewish circumstances in nineteenth-century Europe. Emancipation had eliminated most of the civil restrictions that had confined Jews to the ghetto for centuries past without offering them a clear role or place in European society. Many Jews simply attempted to assimilate themselves into the larger nationalities among whom they lived, preserving their religious and cultural traditions while identifying themselves as Frenchmen, Germans, or Russians. To Zionist writers, however, as for other nineteenth-

century nationalists, political identity as a nation was the final and necessary goal of every people's development. The increasing tempo of anti-Semitic incidents in the late nineteenth century, culminating in the pogroms of Russia and, in the West, in the long, drawn-out agony of the Dreyfus affair (see Chapter 34), suggested to many that assimilation was a mirage. The result was a mass exodus of European Jews, particularly from Russia, from which 3 million emigrated between 1882 and 1914.

The great majority of Jewish emigrants went to the United States, Canada, South America, and Australia; scarcely 1 percent joined the trickle of earlier settlers in Palestine. The real impetus for creating a Jewish state in the Holy Land came from Theodor Herzl, the founder of modern Zionism. Herzl realized that the large-scale settlement necessary to provide a critical mass of population in Palestine would require both organization and capital. His solution was the Jewish National Fund, which undertook the purchase of all land to be occupied by the settlers. He envisioned a society whose growth would be rationally planned. New towns would be erected, carefully spaced and separated by belts of collective farmland and linked by express trains and superhighways. In short, the Zionist state was to be a utopian society in which mutualistic socialism was combined with technological progress and centralized planning.

Herzl's vision and Hitler's persecution combined to increase the Jewish population of Palestine tenfold between the end of World War I and the end of World War II. From less than a tenth of the total population of the territory in 1917, it had increased to a third by 1947. The Arab majority greeted the Jewish influx first with suspicion and then with alarm. The entry of Western powers into the formerly Ottoman-controlled lands of the Middle East after World War I stimulated Arab nationalists. For such nationalists, the Jews were a spearhead unit of Western colonization. Their fears were underscored by the report of an American commission Woodrow Wilson sent to the area, which concluded that the Jewish National Fund intended the eventual purchase of the entire territory of Palestine, thereby dispossessing its Arab population. From an Arab perspective, Jewish socialism was simply the handmaiden of British imperialism.

Confronted by bitter and sometimes violent Arab resistance, the British government decided in 1939 to cap Jewish population in Palestine at one-third of the whole and to limit future land purchases severely. These new controls had broader implications, as Britain, the United States, and other powers sought to restrict Jewish emigration from Nazi-held Europe in general. When the dimensions of the Holocaust were discovered at the end of World War II, there was general humanitarian pressure to establish Palestine as a refuge for the remnants of European Jewry. The British Labour party, soon to be in power, endorsed Zionist demands for the immediate creation of a Jewish commonwealth and in December 1944 called for the transfer of Palestinian Arabs to neighboring countries. Nothing came of these or more moderate postwar proposals for a federated Jewish-Arab state, which were rejected by both sides. The British, unwilling to maintain their trusteeship in the face of mounting Jewish terrorist attacks and unable to contain the flood of illegal immigrants who ran their blockade, laid the problem before the United Nations in April 1947. After

months of lobbying and debate, the General Assembly adopted in November a proposal to divide Palestine into three Jewish and three Arab sectors forming a Jewish and an Arab state, with Jerusalem as an international zone. All seven areas were to be linked in an economic union.

The General Assembly resolution was greeted with rejoicing by the Jews but unanimous rejection throughout the Arab world. The British refused to implement it on the grounds that it had not been accepted by both sides, and withdrew their troops without making provision to transfer authority to either one. When the last units departed on May 14, 1948, the Jewish communal government proclaimed the state of Israel. A general struggle immediately ensued for control of Palestine. Armies from Egypt, Syria, Lebanon, Jordan, and Iraq poured across the frontiers to assist the Palestinian Arabs, but the better-organized Jewish forces more than held their own. When a United Nations armistice halted the fighting in 1949, Israel controlled a third more territory than had been granted the Jews under the partition plan, and nearly 750,000 Palestinian Arabs had taken refuge in Lebanon, Syria, Jordan, and the Egyptian-occupied Gaza Strip in southern Palestine.

While still fighting, Israel held its first elections in January. The fiery socialist David Ben-Gurion (1886–1973), founder of the first Jewish agricultural cooperative, or kibbutz, became Israel's first prime minister and its dominant political figure until his retirement in 1966, and the veteran Zionist leader Chaim Weizmann (1874–1952) was installed in the ceremonial office of president.

David Ben-Gurion, Israel's Founder

Born David Gruen in Plonsk, Poland (then a part of the Russian empire), David Ben-Gurion was the son of a local Zionist leader. At 17 he startled the local Jewish community by calling for armed resistance against the state-backed pogroms. Three years later, in 1906, he emigrated to Palestine, where he worked as a farmer in Jewish settlements and adopted the Hebrew name Ben-Gurion ("son of the lion"). Expelled by the Ottoman Turks for his political activity at the outbreak of World War I, he eventually reached New York, where he met and married Pauline Munweis, his wife until her death in 1968.

Israel's leaders in 1955: (from left) General Moshe Dayan, Premier Moshe Sharett, President Itzhak Ben-Zvi, and Prime Minister David Ben-Gurion.

Ben-Gurion responded to the Balfour Declaration by joining the British-sponsored Jewish Legion. Returning to Palestine after its capture from the Turks, he threw himself ardently into political organization and over the next two decades forged the institutions that were to become the nucleus of the Jewish state. In 1920 he founded the Histadrut labor confederation and ten years later its political arm, the Mapai, or Israeli Workers party, which later merged into the Labour party. Besides leading both organizations, he was elected chairman of the Zionist Executive, the supreme directive body of the Zionist movement, and head of the Jewish Agency, its executive branch.

When Britain, responding to Arab pressure, abruptly pulled back on its commitment to a Jewish homeland in 1939, Ben-Gurion urged and later led armed resistance to it. In May 1942 he assembled an emergency meeting of Zionists in New York that decided on the establishment of a Jewish state as soon as the war in Europe was ended. With the proclamation of Israel six years later, Ben-Gurion became simultaneously its first prime minister and minister of defense, welding its disparate and often conflicting resistance forces into a national army.

With a single brief interval, Ben-Gurion remained Israel's prime minister from 1948 to 1963, firmly shaping Israel's identity as a modern industrial state and a bul-

wark of Western influence in the Middle East. To critics of his frank espousal of Western interests he replied characteristically, "What matters is not what Gentiles will say but what the Jews will do." Never wavering in his belief that modern Israel was the direct and legitimate heir of the ancient Jewish state, he was determined at all costs to establish it and to give no quarter to anyone who opposed it. This led him into an assault against Egypt's President Nasser in 1956 that brought about the fall of the Eden government in Britain and contributed to the demise of the Fourth Republic in France but left Ben-Gurion himself stronger than ever at home. In his last years in office he attempted, unsuccessfully, to institute peace talks with Arab leaders.

Ben-Gurion resigned abruptly in June 1963, in part because of dissension within the Labour party. He founded a new opposition party as a vehicle for his views, but it won only ten seats in the Knesset (parliament). He nonetheless remained a charismatic and controversial elder statesman, and to a world public the short, rotund man with the familiar pugnacious features and the halo of white hair was the image of Israel itself. In failing health, he retired from all political activity in 1970 to spend his last years at a kibbutz in the Negev Desert, writing his memoirs. He lived just long enough to see the twenty-fifth anniversary of the founding of Israel in 1973 and to experience the Yom Kippur War, which revealed how vulnerable the new nation still was.

Israeli Society: Challenge and Conflict

The new state chose a system of proportional representation rather than electoral districting for the Knesset, so each member represented the nation as a whole. This meant full representation for minority views but entailed coalition government as well; no single party has won a majority to date. Nevertheless, two basic coalitions have controlled the state since independence: the Labour bloc—strongly Zionist, social-democratic, and secular—and the Likud bloc, which has enjoyed the backing of Orthodox religious parties.

Despite its unity in times of crisis, Israel has been beset by contradictions from the beginning. The ideologically active left wing of the Labour bloc remained attached to the early Zionist ideal of social regeneration through physical labor and communal living exemplified in the kibbutz. The new Jewish man and woman,

Israel or Palestine?

Two rival nationalisms with ancient roots in the same land put forward their claims to modern sovereignty over it.

Declaration of the Establishment of the State of Israel (1948)

The land of Israel was the birthplace of the Jewish people. Here their spiritual, religious, and political identity was shaped. Here they first attained statehood, created cultural values of national and universal significance, and gave to the world the eternal Book of Books. . . .

On the 29th November, 1947, the United Nations General Assembly passed a resolution calling for the establishment of a Jewish state in the land of Israel; the General Assembly required the inhabitants of the land of Israel to take such steps as were necessary on their part for the implementation of that resolution. This recognition by the United Nations of the right of the Jewish people to establish their state is irrevocable. This right is the natural right of the Jewish people to be masters of their own fate, like all other nations, in their own sovereign state.

Palestinian National Charter (1968)

Article 1. Palestine is the homeland of the Arab Palestinian people; it is an indivisible part of the Arab homeland, and the Palestinian people are an integral part of the Arab nation.

Article 2. Palestine, with the boundaries it had during the British mandate, is an indivisible territorial unit.

Article 3. The Palestinian Arab people possess the legal right to their homeland and have the right to determine their destiny after achieving the liberation of their country in accordance with their wishes and entirely of their own accord and will.

Article 4. The Palestinian identity is a genuine, essential, and inherent characteristic; it is transmitted from parents to children. The Zionist occupation and the dispersal of the Palestinian Arab people . . . do not make them lose their Palestinian identity and their membership of the Palestine community, nor do they negate them.

Source: J. N. Moore, ed., *The Arab-Israeli Conflict: Readings and Documents* (Princeton, N.J.: Princeton University Press, 1977), pp. 935–936, 1086.

purged of the effects of centuries of ghettoization and bonded to the soil, would constitute the basis of a genuinely egalitarian society. What emerged instead, however, was an urbanized, consumer-oriented society that bore considerable resemblance to the social-democratic regimes of the West.

The tension between old socialist ideals and the reality of a consumer society is paralleled by that between religious fundamentalists and secular liberals. The fundamentalists, a hard core constituting 15 percent of the Jewish population, retain Orthodox diet, dress, and observance and have successfully insisted on religious controls over marriage, divorce, inheritance, and other social arrangements. Often confrontational, their influence derives not merely from their unity as a single-issue pressure group but from the unresolved debate over the nature of a "Jewish" state.

From its inception, Israel has advertised itself as the homeland of Jews the world over, and under the Law of Return, any Jew emigrating to it is automatically entitled to citizenship. Nonetheless, there is no generally accepted criterion of what defines a Jew, and a prolonged debate in the Knesset in 1960 and 1961 failed to produce one. Originally Semitic, the Jews have become racially heterogeneous through the long centuries of the Diaspora, and fair-haired Scandinavians mix today on the streets of Tel Aviv and Jerusalem with brown-skinned Indians, black Ethiopians, and even Chinese. Still more problematic is the attempt to define them as a "people," since they share few common customs, and fewer than half the population speaks the official language, Hebrew, as a native tongue. Least of all can they be distinguished on the basis of a common faith, since many secularized Jews in Israel and elsewhere no longer keep up religious observances. The fundamentalists alone have developed a clear standard, excluding anyone whose mother was not Jewish or who had not undergone Orthodox conversion. In practice, however, the authorities have simply accepted as a Jew anyone professing to be one. Even Israelis converting to Christianity have continued to be accorded the rights of citizenship.

The unresolved question of what defines a Jew goes to the heart of the central contradiction of present-day Israeli society: the situation of its Arab minority. Although enjoying formal equality, including the right to vote and to sit in the Knesset, the Arabs are clearly second-class citizens in the Jewish state, and their movements and activities are subject to state scrutiny and interference. Moreover, while Israelis can justifiably point to levels of health, literacy, and material prosperity among Arabs within their borders considerably higher than those of neighboring countries, they remain far below the national norm as a whole. The problem was compounded by Israeli occupation of the West Bank of the Jordan River as a result of the 1967 war; this doubled the number of Arabs under Israeli jurisdiction. For 20 years the occupation was relatively benign, but in 1987 popular rebellion erupted.

Whether or not the Arabs under Israeli rule would be prepared to accept integration into a multiethnic state remains part of the larger question of Palestinian self-determination and the future of Arab-Israeli relations in general. In either case, their presence poses a challenge to an Israel defined, by whatever standard, as a purely Jewish state.

The Arab-Israeli Wars

The more immediate questions in the Middle East involve the general nonrecognition of the Israeli state by the other powers in the region apart from Egypt and Jordan, and the insistence of Palestinian Arab nationalists that Palestine be restored to them. Four wars have been fought to date over this question. All have resulted in military victories by the Israelis, none in settlement. The Palestine War of 1948–1949 established Israel as an independent state while creating a major refugee problem. The Israelis refused to allow the 750,000 Palestinians who had fled their homes to return without guarantees of security from the surrounding nations, a point that became moot as the abandoned homes and lands were oc-

cupied by the almost equal number of Jewish immigrants, mostly from the other countries of the Middle East, who flocked to the new state in the first two years of its existence. In effect, the massive population transfer envisioned by Zionists had taken place. But neighboring Arab states were both unable and politically unwilling to accept the tide of Palestinian refugees who crowded at their borders. Instead, the refugees were interned in squalid camps along the narrow Gaza Strip and on the West Bank of the Jordan River, previously part of Palestine but now annexed by Jordan. The Palestinian Arabs thus became a people without a country.

Arab suspicions of Israel's imperial intentions were intensified in October 1956 when Israel joined an amphibious Franco-British force in an invasion of Egypt, whose president, Gamal Abdel Nasser (1918–1970), had nationalized the French- and British-owned Suez Canal Company in response to a cutoff of Western aid. For the British in particular, Egypt's control of the canal threatened important interests in the Far East, while Israel, alarmed at an Egyptian arms buildup, felt that a preemptive strike was essential to its security. With British air support, the Israelis swept across the Sinai peninsula to join assault troops at Port Said. But the war ended in fiasco. The United States, furious at the independent action of its allies, joined the Soviet Union in calling for an immediate cease-fire and withdrawal. Faced with the threat of ruinous economic sanctions, the British and French capitulated. Israel too withdrew, the damaging identification with colonial interests only partly compensated by the opening of the Gulf of Aqaba to Israeli shipping.

The long-term effects of the episode were profound. Nasser emerged as a hero and became the recognized leader of the Arab world until his death. The government of Sir Anthony Eden was forced from office in Britain, and with the assassination of the Iraqi king, Faisal II, and his prime minister, Nuri-es Said, in 1958 the British were forced from their last bases in the Middle East. The United States entered the breach to forestall Soviet influence, and in 1958 its own forces invaded Lebanon in support of pro-Western leadership. With Nasser and other Arab radicals looking to the Soviet Union for aid and with the crucial oil resources of the region at stake, the Middle East became an important new area of superpower rivalry.

In the meantime, a new war was brewing between the Arabs and the Israelis. In 1964 Israel began to divert water from the Jordan River to irrigate its southern Negev Desert. Jordan protested, and an Arab summit conference in Cairo set up a command force that would coordinate guerrilla activities against Israel and serve as a provisional government for the refugees, the Palestine Liberation

Arafat, Nasser, and Hussein of Jordan sign a ceasefire agreement.

Organization (PLO). Terrorist attacks and retaliatory raids increased, while Egypt, Syria, and Jordan announced plans to attack Israel. When Nasser ordered United Nations peacekeeping forces to leave the Sinai in May 1967 and closed the Gulf of Aqaba, the Israelis struck first. In a campaign lasting only six days, Israel swept again across the Sinai; seized the West Bank, including the Arab portion of the city of Jerusalem; and drove Syria off the strategic Golan Heights on the borders of eastern Galilee. Israel had occupied some 28,000 square miles, three times the size of its own territory. It was one of the swiftest and most decisive military victories in history. In November the United Nations Security Council adopted a resolution demanding Israel's withdrawal from the areas it had conquered but also calling for a settlement that would recognize its right to exist as a nation.

Humiliated by the Six Day War, Egypt rearmed with Soviet assistance and planned a new attack with Syria. This time preparations were secret. Israel was caught napping by the Yom Kippur War of 1973, so called because it began with a surprise attack on the annual Jewish day of atonement. Initially repulsed, Israeli forces quickly recovered and with American tactical assistance had regained the offensive when fighting was halted after 18 days on October 24. But they had suffered heavy losses on the ground and in the air, and the conflict brought the superpowers closer to confrontation in the Middle East than ever before.

The Yom Kippur War underlined the dangers posed by continued instability in the Middle East. It brought in its wake a cutoff of oil exports that struck at the very heart of the Western economy. Accordingly, the American secretary of state, Henry Kissinger, conducted arduous "shuttle diplomacy" between the major Arab capitals and Jerusalem in an attempt to find a basis of accommodation. These efforts bore fruit in the Camp David Accords of September 1978 between Egypt and Israel. The two parties agreed to a phased withdrawal of Israeli troops from the Sinai and a vaguely defined autonomy for the West Bank and the Gaza Strip. President Sadat had ended the humiliating occupation of Egyptian territory and gained a major American subsidy for his ailing economy. Prime Minister Menachem Begin had won diplomatic recognition for the first time from an Arab state, secured Israel's western frontier, and divided its two principal antagonists, Egypt and Syria. Both men shared a Nobel Peace Prize. But Sadat was denounced in the Arab world for having made a separate peace with Israel and for failing to secure Palestinian rights. Egypt lost the position of leadership it had enjoyed for the previous quarter century, and Sadat himself was assassinated by Muslim fundamentalists in October 1981.

Jerusalem: A City Divided

The divisions of the contemporary Middle East are nowhere more vividly symbolized than in the historic city of Jerusalem. Today, with its population of around

300,000, it reflects both a rich past and a divided present. The New City, to the west, is a modern capital, with fashionable shops, a convention center, and a Kennedy memorial. It also houses the Knesset, Israel's parliament, and the Israel Museum. The Old City, once shared by Arabs and Jews, is in the Arab quarter, a labyrinth of bazaars, market alleys, and narrow, winding streets. Administratively, the New and Old City are now one; politically, they are as far apart as ever.

After a long history as a religious center first of Judaism and then of Christianity, Jerusalem was conquered by the Muslims in 629. Unlike previous conquerors, they treated the city with great respect. It was sacred to Islam because the Jewish temple was the place to which Muhammad had been carried in his famous vision before ascending the seven heavens into the presence of the Almighty. Accordingly, the caliph Omar built a wooden mosque in the temple compound, above which rises today the gold-domed, octagonal structure known as the Haram el-Sharif (Dome of the Rock), still much as it was when completed in 691. For several centuries Christian and Jewish worship was permitted side by side with Islamic. As unrest increased in the Arab world, however, particularly after the ninth century, access to the holy sites became hazardous.

Crusader Europe recaptured Jerusalem and established Christian control of the city again for most of a century (1099–1187) and briefly from 1229 to 1244, expelling Jews and Muslims. Thereafter for nearly 700 years the city again reverted to Islam, first under the Mameluke Turks (1250–1517) and then under their Ottoman successors (1517–1917). It reached a low point in the seventeenth and eighteenth centuries as Ottoman rule decayed, but European influence began to revive it in the nineteenth century, and with the advent of Zionism it became a focus of Jewish immigration.

The British capture of Jerusalem in 1917 inaugurated its modern period. Extensive rebuilding took place, and access to the holy places was given to the three faiths, although at Muslim insistence the ban on Jews entering the Dome of the Rock on the site of the temple mount was maintained. Communal violence between Arabs and Jews erupted as early as 1929, and when the British withdrew from Palestine in 1947, the city (whose population was by now more than 60 percent Jewish) was besieged by the Arab Legion. The armistice of 1949 divided it into an Israeli and an Arab (Jordanian) sector, separated by barbed wire, sandbags, and sniper fire. The Six Day War gave Israel full control of the city, which was itself a major battlefront.

CONFLICT IN THE MIDDLE EAST SINCE WORLD WAR II

1947	United Nations partitions Palestine; Arab League rejects plan
1948	State of Israel proclaimed; defeats Arab League
1952	Revolution brings Nasser to power in Egypt
1953	Mossadegh regime overthrown in Iran
1954–1962	Algerian war of independence
1956	Nasser nationalizes Suez Canal; Anglo-French-Israeli force seizes canal; United States compels it to withdraw
1964	Palestine Liberation Organization (PLO) founded
1967	Six Day War; Israel occupies West Bank and Gaza Strip, annexes East Jerusalem
1973	Yom Kippur War
1975	Civil war in Lebanon; Syria intervenes
1979	Islamic revolution in Iran; Camp David Accords between Israel and Egypt
1980–1988	Iran-Iraq War
1982	Israel invades Lebanon
1983	241 U.S. marines killed in Beirut
1987	*Intifada* begins against Israeli rule in occupied territories
1990	Iraq occupies Kuwait; United Nations demands withdrawal
1991	Gulf War
1993	Oslo records set framework for Palestinian autonomy in the West Bank and Gaza Strip
1995	Assassination of Yitzhak Rabin

Jerusalem continues to house its three faiths. Its Christian community is particularly variegated, with Protestant, Catholic, Greek Orthodox, Armenian, Abyssinian, and Coptic churches represented. The city's shrines are once again open to all, but its future remains clouded by the Arab-Israeli controversy. As in the days of the prophet Ezekiel, it can be said of the city: "This is Jerusalem; I have set her in the midst of nations."

Arab Nationalism

Until the late nineteenth century, communal identity among the various Arab peoples of the Middle East had little to do with political self-determination or territorial units. Under the Ottoman system, members of each religious faith—Muslim, Christian, and Jewish—lived in an independent community governed according to its own law by its clerical hierarchy. Communal consciousness was therefore awareness of religious values and customs rather than ethnic differentiation. Although religious rivalries often had a territorial dimension, not until the final breakup of the Ottoman Empire and the arrival of Western imperialism did such rivalries become identified with control of political entities with discrete boundaries. The idea of nationhood in its modern meaning was, as in so many other parts of the world, a Western import that cut across religious, cultural, and tribal affiliations.

Despite a major Arab cultural revival in the nineteenth century centered in Cairo, Beirut, and Damascus, there was no serious call for Arab separation from the Ottoman Empire until Neguib Azouri, a Palestinian Arab living in Paris, published *The Awakening of the Arab Nation* in 1905, in which he envisioned a united Arab state stretching from the Persian Gulf to the Suez Canal. The revival of Turkish nationalism after the Young Turk revolution of 1908 galvanized its Arab counterpart. Moderate Arabs who had been content with the idea of greater political autonomy within the Ottoman framework rather than independence now faced a regime in Istanbul bent on more rigorous controls. When Turkey allied itself with the Central Powers in World War I, Britain, already in quest of oil for its modernized navy in the region, promised support for a united Arab state to the sharif of Mecca, Hussein ibn-Ali, in return for military assistance.

This promise was not kept. In 1920 Britain and France divided the Arab provinces of the former Ottoman Empire between them as mandates under the League of Nations, with Britain adding Palestine, Transjordan, and Mesopotamia (Iraq) to its former protectorate in Egypt and France gaining Syria and Lebanon. Although ibn-Saud united the vast interior of the Arabian peninsula as Saudi Arabia in the 1920s and proclaimed a kingdom in 1932, Britain remained in firm control of most of its coastline. At the same time, American companies began a vigorous exploitation of oil resources in Saudi Arabia and Iraq. World War II saw the Middle East turned into a major theater of operations, with Germany's failure to gain access to the oil fields a crucial factor in its defeat.

The status of some of the Arab trust territories evolved during the interwar period. Iraq had achieved at least enough of the appearance of a state to be admitted to the League of Nations in 1932, although British influence remained strong. In Transjordan a strongman who ruled with British backing, the amir Abdullah, was recognized as a king in 1946, but British control was still so transparent that not until 1955 was the renamed kingdom of Jordan, including the West Bank area seized in the Palestine War, admitted to the United Nations. The pace of change was even slower in Syria and Lebanon, where the French showed little inclination to prepare their territories for statehood. French control lapsed during the Nazi occupation, however, and in 1946 both states became independent. Although far more advanced economically than Britain's mandates, both countries faced special challenges. Lebanon had no sectarian majority, and a variety of Muslim and Christian groups vied for dominance. Syria, despite its proud heritage, was fragmented by religious and tribal divisions among both its majority Muslim and minority Christian populations. In Syria these tensions remain barely under control; in Lebanon they erupted in 1975 in a civil war that precipitated anarchy, invasion, and foreign occupation.

The end of World War II brought rapid changes. In 1945 the League of Arab States was formed under British auspices, consisting originally of Egypt, Syria, Lebanon, Iraq, Transjordan, Saudi Arabia, and Yemen. Although many of these states were as yet in no credible sense independent, they rapidly became so as British influence waned, and it was the league that coordinated the 1948 invasion of Palestine. Defeat at the hands of the tiny Jewish army provoked a military coup in Syria, an upsurge in anti-Western sentiment, and an agonizing reassessment of the wider problems of Arab development and unity.

Nasser and the Egyptian Revolution

The most significant result of this ferment came in Egypt, where in 1952 the military revolution led by Gamal Abdel Nasser drove out the corrupt, British-supported King Farouk, spelling the end of Britain's role in the Middle East and hence of the last direct Western presence in the region.

Nasser was born in 1918, the son of a postal clerk in upper Egypt. Like many young Egyptians of modest origin, he joined the army as a means of gaining educational opportunities and career advancement. His fellow graduates in the 1938 class of the military academy were mostly of similar background, the sons of minor officials, petty merchants, commercial agents, and small landowners. They shared a common sense of frustration at Egypt's continued dominance by Britain and a sense of alienation from the older and wealthier officer corps. Under Nasser's leadership they began to meet on a regular basis to discuss the nation's problems and to plan for its future. By 1942 this group had evolved into a central committee with smaller cells throughout the army. Contacts were also established with religious organizations and foreign Arab leaders. The army's humiliation in the Palestine War strengthened the resolve of the young officers to reform the nation. Now banded together as the Free Officers' Society, they staged a virtually bloodless coup on July 23, 1952, that brought a revolutionary council to power. At first the council attempted to govern the country through its civilian institutions and bureaucracy. When the latter refused to implement the council's directives on land reform, a military dictatorship was proclaimed.

The council's nominal head was a senior general, Muhammad Naguib, but Nasser remained its true leader. It was he who decided on the policy of "guided democracy." Political parties and parliamentary institutions remained the goal of the regime, he declared, but until the masses had been prepared for active political life by reform and education, these could only serve the interests of the few. The press was brought under government regulation, and political activity was exercised through a single mass party, the Arab Socialist Union. In 1954 Nasser assumed direct control of the revolution as prime minister, and two years later he unveiled a constitution guaranteeing basic rights, including racial, religious, and sexual equality.

Nasser's revolution was as much social as political. While most of Egypt's 25 million people lived on an annual per capita income of $60, an elite of 12,000 owned 37 percent of its arable land. Nasser broke up the great estates and distributed them among the peasantry, with the smaller lots subsumed into cooperative farms. The Permanent Council for National Production was established in 1953 to draft first a five- and then a ten-year plan for integrated industrial and agricultural development. Crucial to the success of these plans was the Aswan Dam, which aimed to increase cultivated land by a third by harnessing the Nile River. When the United States, alarmed at Nasser's rising popularity in the Arab world and irked by his lack of enthusiasm for an American-sponsored regional alliance, the Baghdad Pact, announced that it would not help fund the dam, Nasser responded dramatically. He nationalized the Suez Canal, with the stated purpose of using its income to build the dam, which had now become symbolic not only of his revolution but of Third World hopes in general for independent development. Launched in 1959 with a $300 million loan from the Soviet Union, the dam was completed in 1974 at a cost of more than $2 billion. Although its projected goals for irrigation and hydroelectric power were not fully met and ecological problems such as silting and stagnation continue to plague it, the dam enabled Egypt nearly to double its agricultural output.

Equally significant strides were made in the industrial sector, although much of it remained in handicraft and small-scale production. Nasser's record of accomplishment in one of the world's poorest nations, though politically and economically blemished by the disaster of the Six Day War, was impressive. Nonetheless, these gains were all but negated by unchecked population growth, running at some 3 percent a year. By the late 1970s Anwar el-Sadat had accepted a new client relationship with the United States as the price of economic survival, a policy continued since 1981 by his successor, Hosni Mubarak (born 1929). Mubarak's secular-style rule has been challenged by a powerful fundamentalist movement that has gained increasing influence among Egypt's still-impoverished masses.

The Middle East in the Postwar World

Nasser's revolution was a model for many emerging nations in the postwar period, but its influence was most direct on Egypt's North African neighbors. By 1956 the French protectorates of Morocco and Tunisia and the British-occupied Sudan had achieved full self-government, largely under the impetus of Egypt's example, and the former Italian colony of Libya was also granted independence under a feudal monarch, King Idris. However, the French refused to consider withdrawal from Algeria, where a strong settler interest prevailed. A war of national liberation ensued between 1954 and 1962, marked by savagery on both sides and resolved only when Charles de Gaulle, whom the war had brought back to power, arranged a plebiscite.

The rapid formation of new states in the immediate postwar period failed to give definitive shape or stability to Arab nationalism. Tribal groups dispersed over various borders, such as the Kurds of Turkey, Syria, Iran, and Iraq, demanded a homeland of their own. Radical nationalist parties, such as the Ba'ath movement in Syria and Iraq, remained dissatisfied with the conservative, pro-Western regimes left behind in the wake of the imperial powers. Pan-Arabic pressures for political unification between separate states also remained strong. In 1958 Syria and Egypt combined to form the United Arab Republic, with Nasser as president. Ardent Arab nationalists, particularly Syrian Ba'athists, saw this union as the precursor of a grand Islamic federation but were soon disillusioned when the Egyptians moved to take complete control of Syria's government and economy. Following a Syrian army rebellion in September 1961, the union was dissolved by mutual consent. Similar experiments with other partners have proved equally short-lived, but the dream of a single, unitary state remains deeply embedded in Arab nationalism.

OPEC and the Politics of Oil

The history of the modern Middle East has been to a large extent determined by oil. Otherwise sparing in its gifts, nature has endowed the region with 60 percent of the proven world oil reserves. Britain was already dependent on Iranian oil to power its fleet by the first decade of the twentieth century, and as the West converted rapidly from coal to oil-based energy, the strategic importance of the Middle East grew apace. The discovery of vast new reserves in the desert wastes of Arabia in the 1930s was immediately exploited by the California Arabian Standard Oil Company (later called Aramco) on concessions granted by King ibn-Saud. Almost overnight Saudi Arabia was transformed from a poverty-ridden principality of nomadic tribes to a nation with one of the highest per capita incomes in the world.

In 1960 the Saudis took the initiative in forming the Organization of Petroleum Exporting Countries (OPEC). Originally composed of Saudi Arabia, Iran, Iraq, the tiny and newly independent emirate of Kuwait, and Venezuela, it subsequently expanded to include Algeria, Ecuador, Gabon, Indonesia, Libya, Nigeria, Qatar, and the confederation of small Persian Gulf sheikhdoms known as the United Arab Emirates. At first OPEC confined its activities chiefly to gaining a larger share of the revenues produced by Western oil companies and greater control over levels of production. The persistence of the Arab-Israeli conflict, however, turned it from a simple cartel into a formidable political force. After the Six Day War the Arab members of OPEC formed a separate, overlapping group (OAPEC) for the purpose of concerting policy and exerting pressure on the West over Israel. Egypt and Syria, negligible oil producers but populous and militarily powerful, joined the latter group to underline its intentions.

The Yom Kippur War of 1973 galvanized Arab opinion. Furious at the emergency resupply effort that had enabled Israel to withstand the Egyptian and Syrian assault, the Arabs imposed an oil embargo against the United States, western Europe, and Japan. This was followed by a more than fourfold increase in the price of oil, causing sudden inflation and economic recession in the noncommunist industrial world and even greater hardship among the underdeveloped nations. At the same time, the Saudis acquired operating control of Aramco, fully nationalizing it in 1980. As other OPEC nations followed suit, the cartel's income soared. Saudi Arabia, awash in profits, undertook a series of five-year development plans, of which the most ambitious, begun in 1980, called for the expenditure of $250 billion. Other cartel members also undertook major economic programs. For the first time, Third World nations whose resources and labor had long been exploited by the industrial giants had acquired control of a vital commodity, reversing the flow of capital. Some of this income was dispensed in the form of aid to other underdeveloped nations whose economies had been caught between higher prices for oil and the lower prices for their own commodities and raw materials caused by shrinking Western demand. Much of it, however, was reinvested in the West or absorbed in massive arms purchases that exacerbated political tensions, particularly in the Middle East. When reduced demand and overproduction produced a glut on the world market in the mid-1980s, oil prices plummeted and the cartel lost its unity. Producers such as Mexico, Nigeria, and Venezuela, whose economies had expanded recklessly, were plunged into near-bankruptcy, and even Saudi Arabia felt the pinch. The enormous reserves and relative underpopulation of the leading Middle East producers guaranteed the region its continuing strategic importance, but the politics of oil had proved dangerous for all concerned.

Modernization and Revolution in Iran

Iran, though ethnologically and linguistically distinct from its Arab neighbors in the Middle East, has shared its geographic destiny. As elsewhere in the region, social and political controls on the local level were traditionally exercised by the clergy on behalf of tribal landowning elites, with civil law and custom derived directly from religious precepts, although the merchant class of the larger towns had some independent influence. Patriarchal and hierarchical in structure, Iranian society was based on the absolute control of fathers over their families, khans or leaders over their tribes, and the shah as ruler over all, subject only to the ultimate authority of Shi'ite religious principles.

Iran's modernization began with its penetration by two conflicting imperial powers, Russia and Great Britain. In the 1860s and 1870s the first telegraph lines were set up with British assistance, thus ending the country's virtual isolation from the world. Concessions were given to build railroads and develop the country's resources. By 1907 the Russians and the British had formally divided Iran into spheres of influence, but a nationalist uprising in 1921 led by Reza Shah Pahlavi produced a modernizing dictatorship that, like Kemal Atatürk's in Turkey, attempted to introduce Western cultural and industrial models and to reduce the power of the clergy by stressing the nation's pre-Islamic past. New schools and industries were begun, and a conscript army was raised. A trans-Iranian railroad from the Caspian Sea to the Persian Gulf was built from the profits of state monopolies. Wide new avenues were cut through the major towns and named for national folk heroes. Sumptuary laws mandated the wearing of Western dress, and the traditional women's veil, the chadar, was made obsolete. In 1935 Reza Shah Pahlavi changed the country's Hellenistic name of Persia to Iran, meaning "land of the Aryans."

This last change was meant to reflect Iran's Indo-European roots but had contemporary significance as well. Reza Shah Pahlavi, dictatorial and often terroristic in his methods, was an ardent admirer of Hitler, and when an Allied force occupied Iran in August 1941, he was forced to abdicate in favor of his son, Muhammad Reza Pahlavi. For the next decade the country was once again a battleground of foreign interests, with the United States replacing Britain soon after World War II and the Soviet Union trying to regain its traditional foothold in the north. A new nationalist insurrection brought Muhammad Mossadegh, a prewar opponent of Reza Shah Pahlavi, to power as prime minister in 1951. Mossadegh nationalized the British-owned Anglo-Iranian Oil Company, thereby reasserting the country's independence. The West retaliated with a boycott of Iranian oil, and a CIA-led army coup deposed him in August 1953.

The shah, who had been briefly forced to flee the country by pro-Mossadegh crowds, returned with American blessing and remained a Western client thereafter. Like his father, however, he harbored grandiose ambitions. A "white revolution" was launched in the early 1960s to complete the process of modernization begun under Reza Shah Pahlavi, although the traditional landed elite remained firmly in control of the countryside. Using the massive oil profits of the 1970s, the shah attempted to turn Iran into the major military power of the Middle East, purchasing $15 billion worth of American arms between 1972 and 1978. But by the latter part of the decade his regime was under general assault. The land hunger of the peasantry remained unsatisfied despite promised reform, while the middle classes cultivated by the shah were frustrated by their exclusion from real power. Showy industrial projects and exotic weapons could not be operated without foreign advisers and technicians, reinforcing a painful sense of dependence on the West. Even the aristocracy, which had never accepted

the Pahlavi dynasty, offered little support. The shah's most serious opposition, however, came from the Shi'ite clergy, which bitterly opposed what it took to be his promotion of corrupt Western values and mores. By raising a culturally sensitive issue that cut across class lines and evoked powerful religious and nationalist sentiment, the clergy brought to focus a general sense of grievance. Their exiled leader, the Ayatollah Ruhollah Khomeini (1900–1989), became the symbol of popular resistance.

The shah responded at first with repression and then, when crippling strikes brought the economy to the verge of bankruptcy, by desperate concessions. In January 1979 he fled into exile, and on February 1, Khomeini returned to Tehran as head of a revolutionary council, which proclaimed an Islamic republic. Real authority, however, emanated from Khomeini himself, who eliminated all political competitors and, armed with nearly absolute powers, embarked on a program of fundamentalist religious reform.

Khomeini's appeal reached far beyond the Shi'ites of Iran. His call to all Muslims to overthrow corrupt and tyrannical rulers and to return to the purity of Islamic law and ritual was particularly attractive to the migrant workers who maintained the economies of Saudi Arabia, Kuwait, and Bahrain. His order to seize 52 American

The Ayatollah Khomeini in 1979, addressing a large throng from his home.

embassy officials and workers in November 1979 was the most dramatically popular act in the Middle East since the nationalization of the Suez Canal. Depicting the United States as a "great Satan" (while at the same time firmly repressing Iran's Communist party and doing business with Israel, America's principal surrogate in the area), Khomeini skillfully combined Islamic revivalism with appeals to regional nationalism. In September 1980 Iraq's ruler Saddam Hussein (born 1937) launched an ill-judged invasion of Iran that bitterly divided the Arab world, with Syria, Libya, and South Yemen backing Khomeini and Saudi Arabia and Jordan supporting Iraq.

The war enabled Khomeini to keep revolutionary fervor high in Iran while consolidating a theocratic regime that outlasted him and to burnish his image as the leader of Islam's *jihad,* or holy war, against the corrupting influence of the West. It was militarily inconclusive, however, and hostilities were halted by a truce in the summer of 1988.

Women and the Islamic Revolution

The resurgence of Islam has not been confined to Iran. From the Atlantic coast of North Africa to the islands of the Indonesian archipelago, across the great east-west

Militant Islam

The view of Islam as historically beleaguered by alien and hostile forces from the West is put forward by the Ayatollah Khomeini in his book Islamic Government.

At its inception, the Islamic movement was afflicted by the Jews, who initiated a counter-activity by distorting the reputation of Islam, by assaulting it, and by slandering it. This has continued to our present day. Then came the role of groups which can be considered more evil than the devil and his troops. This role emerged in the colonialist activity which dates back more than three centuries ago. The colonialists found in the Muslim world their long-sought object. To achieve their colonialist ambitions, the colonists sought to create the right conditions leading to the annihilation of Islam. They did not seek to turn the Muslims into Christians after driving them away from Islam, because they do not believe in either. They wanted control and domination because during the Crusades they were constantly aware that the greatest obstacle preventing them from attaining their goals . . . was Islam with its laws and beliefs and with the influence it exerted on people through their faith. . . . Islam is the religion of the warriors who fight for right and justice, the religion of those seeking for freedom and independence, and those who do not want to allow the infidels to oppress the believers.

The role of women under revolutionary Islam is stated in the constitution adopted by the Islamic Republic of Iran on December 3, 1979.

In creating Islamic social foundations, all the human forces that had up to now been in the service of foreign exploitation will be accorded their basic identity and human rights. And in this regard it is natural that women, due to the greater oppression that they have borne under the idolatrous order, will enjoy more rights.

The family unit is the foundation of society and the main institution for the growth and advancement of mankind. . . . It is the principal duty of the Islamic government to regard women as the unifying factor of the family unit and its position. They are a factor in bringing the family out of the service of propagating consumerism and exploitation and renewing the vital and valuable duty of motherhood in raising educated human beings. . . . As a result motherhood is accepted as a most profound responsibility in the Muslim viewpoint and will, therefore, be accorded the highest value and generosity.

Source: T. Y. Ismael, *Iraq and Iran: Roots of Conflict* (Syracuse, N.Y.: Syracuse University Press, 1982), pp. 101, 147.

belt where most of the world's 1 billion Muslims live, a major reawakening of Islamic culture has occurred since 1945. In part this has been associated with the emergence of new nation-states along this belt and the consequent testing of one of the world's most important religious traditions with the essentially secular ideology of modern nationalism. In part as well it reflected a struggle for identity in a region whose people were skeptical of both Western materialism and Communist atheism and were reluctant to align themselves with either of the superpower blocs. But it also had great significance for the social position of one-fifth of the world's women.

Koranic law continues to assign women a subordinate position in society. In the more conservative Middle Eastern states the law denies them equality in the public sphere and even access to it; in Saudi Arabia women were still not permitted to drive automobiles as late as 1980. In contrast, women had made significant strides in the postwar period in countries either heavily subject to Western influence or unified by socialist revolution. Tunisia, under the presidency of the strongly pro-Western Habib Bourguiba (born 1903), became in 1956 the first Islamic nation to replace the Koranic law on marriage, divorce, and childbearing by a civil code and the first Arab state to ban polygamy. Egypt under Nasser promulgated a constitution giving women full civil equality for the first time, and the socialist governments of Algeria and Yemen have included women's groups within their ruling party organizations. Such developments, however, have tended to affect only the urban middle class, with rural, tribal, and nomadic life continuing along traditional lines. The Iranian revolution of 1979 had a dramatic effect on women; Western attire vanished almost immediately, replaced by the traditional black or gray veil and a shapeless garment covering the entire body. Elsewhere too in the Middle East the *chadar* has again become the norm, sometimes as a symbol of resistance to Western mores, but often a matter of compulsion. Thus while Arab radicalism in the 1950s was at least rhetorically receptive to women's liberation, the current fundamentalist revival has tended to consign women to their former roles, encouraging domesticity, public anonymity, and male dominance.

The Middle East Today

The hope of Camp David, that the Israeli-Egyptian accord would pave the way to a general settlement in the Middle East, has not been realized. Only Jordan among the Arab states has recognized Israel, and the Palestinian issue remains unresolved. During the 1970s the PLO was recognized as the legitimate government of the Palestinian people by many Arab, Soviet bloc, and Third World nations, and its leader, Yasir Arafat (born 1929), addressed the United Nations as a head of state. His influence declined precipitously in the early 1980s as the PLO's more militant factions fell under Syrian influence. In 1987, however, a popular uprising, the *intifada*, broke out on the West Bank against the Israeli occupation. Seizing this opportunity to reassert his leadership, Arafat began an intensive diplomatic campaign that climaxed in an address before the United Nations in 1988 and the initiation of direct bilateral talks with the United States. In the aftermath of the 1991 Gulf War, Arafat's prestige was again eclipsed by his support for Saddam Hussein, as well as by the loss of Saudi aid and Soviet support. This situation alarmed the Israelis, who feared his replacement by a more radical Palestinian leadership. The result was a U.S.-sponsored agreement in September 1993 to set up Palestinian self-rule in the Gaza Strip and the West Bank town of Jericho as a prelude to the establishment of general autonomy in the occupied territories. Progress in implementing the accord was halting, however, with militants on both sides resisting what they saw as a betrayal of fundamental interests, and in November 1995 the Israeli Prime Minister, Yitzhak Rabin, was assassinated by a Jewish fundamentalist opposed to the surrender of West Bank territories. The election of the hard-line Likud leader Benjamin Netanyahu as prime minister in May 1996 dampened hopes for an early general settlement.

The Arab-Israeli confrontation has been for 50 years a symbol of incompatible national aspirations and conflicting cultural values in a globally connected world. The Palestinian poet Mahmoud Darwish spoke perhaps best for the common feeling on both sides of the conflict when he wrote:

> *Where shall we go, after the last frontier?*
> *Where will birds be flying, after the last sky?. . .*
> *We will cut off the hand of song, so that our flesh can complete the song.*
> *Here we will die. Here in the last narrow passage. Or here our blood will plant—its olive trees.*[1]

Legacy of Violence: The Lebanese Civil War and the Gulf War

A tragic by-product of the Arab-Israeli conflict was the bloody civil war that destroyed the Middle East's only successful experiment in cultural and religious diversity, Lebanon, in the 1970s and 1980s. Lebanon's thriving commercial economy had given it one of the region's highest standards of living, and the peaceful coexistence of Christians, Muslims, and Jews had made it a model of political pluralism. Lebanon's equilibrium was, however, precarious. Urban prosperity masked rural poverty in the central valleys, a rising Muslim birthrate threatened the traditional Christian hegemony, and the country's semi-official neutrality in the Arab-Israeli conflict brought it under increasing pressure from Arab nationalists. The sudden influx of some 300,000 Palestinian refugees after the Six Day War, followed by others expelled from Jordan in 1971, greatly exacerbated these tensions. The PLO made Lebanon its main base of operations, drawing retaliatory fire from Israel. The Lebanese divided sharply over the Palestinian presence, with Christians tending to regard them as unwelcome intruders and Muslims seeing them not only as victims seeking to regain their homeland but as patriots in the common Arab cause against Israel. By 1975 the country had slid into full-scale civil war. When Syrian troops finally enforced a ceasefire 19 months later, 60,000 lives had been lost and nearly a third of the population displaced.

Syria's presence diminished the bloodshed but did nothing to restore stability. The PLO intensified its raids and attacks against Israel, while the Israelis sought to cultivate Christian allies in Lebanon. By 1980 approximately 40 armed groups were active. Two years later the Israelis invaded Lebanon, driving the PLO from Beirut and occupying the southern third of the country. This defeat marked the temporary eclipse of Arafat, but the Israelis, now a target for all forces, soon withdrew after heavy losses. An American intervention in 1983 ended even more disastrously, with the death of 241 marines in a terrorist attack. By the late 1980s Lebanon had vanished as a nation in all but name, the epitome of sectarian anarchy and of the collapse of multiethnic community in the Middle East.

Instability in the region increased further when Iraq invaded oil-rich Kuwait in August 1990. The annexation of Kuwait gave Iraq, with its own substantial oil fields, control of 20 percent of the Persian Gulf reserves. When Hussein refused to withdraw, an American-led coalition attacked Iraq in January 1991. The myth of Arab unity was shattered as numerous Arab states, including Egypt, Syria, and Saudi Arabia, joined in the assault. Although Hussein had threatened the allies with "the mother of all battles," the Gulf War lasted only six weeks, with the climactic land campaign taking a mere 100 hours. Much of Iraq's military, the fourth largest in the world, was destroyed by a coalition air assault that featured laser-guided missiles and bombs. By war's end, most of Iraq's economic infrastructure was in ruins, and the damage to the Kuwaiti oil fields, much of it deliberately inflicted by Iraqi troops, had created a formidable ecological disaster. In the aftermath of the fighting, social and ethnic unrest among Shi'ite Muslims, Kurds,

and dissident military units threatened the stability of Hussein's authoritarian regime.

The Gulf crisis pointed up the continuing instability of the Middle East. At either end of the region, in Algeria and Afghanistan, civil wars flared in the 1990s. The influence of militant Shi'ism continued to grow during the decade, particularly in countries with large Shi'ite populations, including (besides Iran) Iraq, Yemen, Bahrain, and Lebanon. In addition, economic pressures intensified on many Middle Eastern countries that had overextended themselves financially during the boom years of the 1970s, facing them with serious problems of unemployment and social unrest.

SUMMARY

The forces of religion and nationalism created powerful tides in the postwar period along the great arc stretching from the Middle East to south-central Asia. The new states of India and Pakistan were born in an agony of civil war between their Hindu and Muslim populations, and the state of Israel was created in an equally bitter confrontation between Arabs and Jews. Within Islam itself, divisions between Sunni and Shi'ite Muslims produced bloody conflict as well, most visibly in the Iran-Iraq war. At the same time, the unfulfilled national aspirations of the Palestinians and of the Kurds, the vulnerable oil economy, the problems of poverty and rapid social change, and the continuing unrest in Afghanistan, Algeria, and elsewhere all combine to make this region perhaps the most volatile in the world.

NOTES

1. M. Darwish, "Earth Scrapes Us," in *Modern Arabic Poetry: An Anthology,* ed. S. K. Jayyusi (New York: Columbia University Press, 1987), p. 208.

SUGGESTIONS FOR FURTHER READING

India, Pakistan, and Sri Lanka

Brown, J. *Modern India: The Origins of an Asian Democracy.* New York: Oxford University Press, 1994.

De Silva, K. M. *A History of Sri Lanka.* Berkeley: University of California Press, 1981.

Franda, M. *India's Rural Development.* Bloomington: Indiana University Press, 1980.

Gold, G. *Gandhi: A Pictorial Biography.* New York: Harper & Row, 1986.

Jayakar, P. *Indira Gandhi.* New York: Vantage, 1993.

Joshi, R., and Rindle, J. *Daughters of Independence: Gender, Caste, and Class in India.* London: Zed Books, 1986.

Kohli, A. *The State and Poverty in India.* Cambridge: Cambridge University Press, 1987.

Novak, J. J. *Bangladesh.* Bloomington: Indiana University Press, 1993.

Swamy, S. *Economic Growth in China and India, 1952–1970.* Chicago: University of Chicago Press, 1974.

Tomlinson, B. R. *The Economy of Modern India.* Cambridge: Cambridge University Press, 1993.

Vanderveer, P. *Religious Nationalism: Hindus and Muslims in India.* Berkeley: University of California Press, 1994.

Wolpert, S. *Jinnah of Pakistan.* New York: Oxford University Press, 1984.

Ziegler, P. *Mountbatten.* London: Collins, 1985.

The Middle East

Abdulghani, J. *Iran and Iraq.* London: Croom Helm, 1984.

Ajami, F. *The Arab Predicament: Arab Political Thought and Practice Since 1967.* Cambridge: Cambridge University Press, 1981.

Anderson, J. N. D. *Islamic Law in the Modern World.* Westport, Conn.: Greenwood Press, 1975.

al-Fassi, A. *The Independence Movements in Arab North Africa,* trans. H. Z. Nuseibeh. New York: Octagon, 1970.

Avineri, S. *The Making of Modern Zionism: Intellectual Origins of the Jewish State.* New York: Basic Books, 1981.

Bakhash, S. *The Reign of the Ayatollahs.* New York: Basic Books, 1984.

Devlin, J. *Syria: Modern State in an Ancient Land.* Boulder, Colo.: Westview Press, 1983.

Hiro, D. *Holy Wars: The Rise of Islamic Fundamentalism.* London: Routledge & Kegan Paul, 1989.

Kamrava, M. *Revolution in Iran: The Roots of Turmoil.* London: Routledge & Kegan Paul, 1990.

Kurzman, D. *Ben-Gurion: Prophet of Fire.* New York: Simon & Schuster, 1983.

Lacouture, J. *Nasser: A Biography.* New York: Knopf, 1973.

Mortimer, E. *Faith and Power: The Politics of Islam.* New York: Faber & Faber, 1982.

Peretz, D. *Intifada: The Palestinian Uprising.* Boulder, Colo.: Westview Press, 1990.

Rabinovitch, I. *The War for Lebanon, 1970–1983.* Ithaca, N.Y.: Cornell University Press, 1984.

Reich, B. *Israel: Land of Tradition and Conflict.* Boulder, Colo.: Westview Press, 1985.

Said, E. W. *The Question of Palestine.* New York: Times Books, 1979.

Salibi, K. *A History of Arabia.* Delmar, N.Y.: Caravan Books, 1980.

Sampson, A. *The Seven Sisters.* New York: Bantam Books, 1979.

Sifry, M. L., and Cerf, C., eds. *The Gulf War Reader: History, Documents, Opinions.* New York: Random House, 1991.

Taryam, A. O. *The Establishment of the United Arab Emirates, 1950–85.* London: Croom Helm, 1987.

Tessler, M. *A History of the Israeli-Palestinian Conflict.* Bloomington: Indiana University Press, 1994.

Waterbury, J. *The Egypt of Nasser and Sadat.* Princeton, N.J.: Princeton University Press, 1983.

CHAPTER 42

Decolonization and Development: Africa and Latin America

A poor woman handwashing clothes in Rio de Janeiro.

Africa and Latin America, the two largest land-masses of the Southern Hemisphere, encompass some 800 million inhabitants on 20 million square miles of territory. Each is richly varied in indigenous populations and languages, in climate and geography, and in cultures and natural resources. Each has been profoundly shaped by its contact with European imperialism. In both cases, imperialism has left a legacy of exploitation and underdevelopment, of shattered native traditions and shallowly rooted foreign ones, of resentment, resistance, and continuing dependence. The decline of colonialism after World War II compelled both regions to face similar yet distinct crises of cultural identity, political development, and economic modernization. The result in many cases was chronic instability, civil unrest, and a repeated pattern of military and authoritarian governments. Most daunting of all remain the conditions of poverty and social inequality in which the vast majority of Africans and Latin Americans continue to live.

Europeans maintained through World War II the control they had achieved over most of Africa in the nineteenth century. Few Africans held positions of influence or responsibility in their own lands, and there was little effort to educate native elites for eventual self-government as envisioned by the mandate system of the League of Nations. The Italian conquest of Ethiopia in 1935–1936 extinguished one of the last nominally independent states in Africa. Yet the colonial system disintegrated rapidly after 1945, leading to the unplanned emergence of several dozen new states, most profoundly ill-equipped for independence.

Central and South America had cast aside most direct imperial control in the early nineteenth century but remained divided by the colonial legacy and subject to Great Power influence. Latin American economies were severely affected by the Great Depression and the interruption of trade during World War II. Thus, whereas the years following World War II saw the difficult birth of political independence in Africa, Latin America experienced continuing economic decline and external political pressures, particularly from the United States.

Africa: The Seeds of Revolt

African nationalism can be traced back to the career of Edward Wilmot Blyden (1832–1912), a native of the Danish (now American) island of St. Thomas who migrated to Liberia and served in its government for four decades. Blyden, a classical scholar who had mastered Latin, Greek, Hebrew, and Arabic, among other tongues, was imbued with the thought of such European figures as Herder, Fichte, Hegel, and Mazzini. Nonetheless, he proudly affirmed his own African heritage. Each race, he asserted, was equal but distinct, with its own powers and endowments. He viewed the Western conquest of Africa as merely a stage in the continent's development and declared that "Africa may yet prove to be the spiritual conservatory of the world." Blyden was thus a forefather of the twentieth-century movement of black consciousness known as "Negritude," which asserted the distinctiveness of the African personality and the uniqueness of the African cultural heritage for black people wherever they might live. He called on Black Africa to absorb the technology of the West while rejecting its cultural imperialism and remaining true to its own traditions.

Other black intellectuals sounded a similar note. The Pan-African Conference held in London in 1900 issued a call "To the Nations of the World," written largely by the American W. E. B. Du Bois (1868–1963), which warned:

> **If now the world of culture bends itself towards giving Negroes and other dark men the largest and broadest opportunity for education and self-development, then [imperial] contact is bound to have a beneficial effect upon the world and hasten human progress. But if, by reason of carelessness, prejudice, greed and injustice, the black world is to be exploited and ravished and degraded, the results must be deplorable if not fatal—not simply to them, but to the high ideals of justice, freedom and culture which a thousand years of Christian civilization have held before Europe.[1]**

Colonial officials paid lip service to the idea of maintaining native systems of authority, but, as in India, the goal was to minimize costs rather than to preserve indigenous culture; in 1925, for example, Britain governed 20 million Nigerians with a mere 200 administrators. Here as elsewhere throughout Africa, disparate tribes were yoked together under an alien rule that ignored traditional distinctions of language, culture, and governance and erased tribal boundaries that were the result of centuries of political accommodation no less fragile and complex than those of Europe. The result was to sow the seeds of later conflict and civil war when the arbitrarily created nations of imperial convenience were suddenly thrust into independence.

The infrastructure of imperial control had been largely laid by World War I. The Gold Coast railway system was finished by 1903 and those of German East and Southwest Africa before 1914, though the French did not complete their link between Pointe-Noire and Brazzaville in the Middle Congo for another decade, at a cost of 20,000 African lives. The war curtailed virtually all investment in Africa, and little was forthcoming in the 1920s or the depression-ridden 1930s. With the slump in work projects came a rapid decline in European emigration, as most of Europe's labor surplus turned again to North America in search of opportunity. Africa found itself supporting a colonial system that had abandoned any pretext of development in favor of skimming off its natural resources and exploiting its workforce.

Resistance to colonial authority took a variety of forms. Some Africans defied it openly, like the Somba of northern Dahomey, who cried, "No more taxation, no more work on the roads, no more soldiering," as they attacked the French in 1917. Others simply migrated across colonial boundaries or disappeared into the bush. Rail strikes erupted in Sierra Leone in 1919 and 1926, in Nigeria in 1921, and in Senegal in 1926, threatening the vulnerable communication links on which imperial control depended. Apart from South Africa, however, where the African National Congress was founded in 1912 and the black Industrial and Commercial Workers Union claimed 100,000 members, there was little significant organization until the 1930s. Reflecting the effect of the Great Depression on the African proletariat, a new generation of black intellectuals, including the Jamaican-American Marcus Garvey (1887–1940), the Kenyan Jomo Kenyatta (c. 1891–1978), and the Senegalese Léopold Senghor (born 1906), combined Marxist ideology with appeals to ethnic consciousness. Although Germany's African empire had been seized after World War I, Hitler's accession to power in 1933 reinforced the militants' identification of imperialism with racism. Two

Black Power

The aspirations of African blacks to direct their own destiny was eloquently stated in 1960 by Rashidi Mfaume Kawawa, who would later succeed Julius Nyerere as prime minister of Tanganyika.

The demand for Africanization is made by the black people and means a replacement by them of those of different origin. Despite the wider meaning that the term African has acquired today, the blacks are still at the bottom of every ladder and identify themselves completely and practically with the struggle for change. To ask the indigenous Africans to forget the agony of their past is to ask them to ignore the lesson that their experience has taught them. Asians and Europeans are crying in Tanganyika today for non-racial parties, but just how practical is this? Those non-racial political parties which have been formed in Tanganyika have never succeeded, for they never aimed at emancipating the African, but only at deluding him into satisfaction with the lowest rung. It is the experience of the present that will constitute African reaction in the future; and the place that the Asian and the European will build for themselves in Africa will be governed by the degree of sacrifice they are prepared to make in the cause of a life in joint advancement and dedication with and amongst the Africans.

Source: R. Segal, *African Profiles* (Baltimore: Penguin Books, 1962), pp. 113–114.

---

years later, the brutal conquest of Ethiopia by Italy provided fascism with a toehold in Africa.

World War II brought the colonial dilemma in Africa to a head. The French mobilized 100,000 troops for combat in West Africa alone, and Africans constituted almost 9 percent of the fighting force in France itself. Both the Vichy regime in French West Africa and the Gaullist one in Equatorial Africa made heavy demands on their populations, including increased taxes, forced labor, and compulsory deliveries of crops. Similar pressures were exerted in the British colonies, where tens of thousands of natives were conscripted to work in mines and on plantations, and many hundreds died under conditions indistinguishable from slave labor. At the same time the white supremacist regime in South Africa, which had enjoyed dominion status within the British Empire since 1910, profited considerably from its strategic location and emerged from the war as a major regional power.

Neither the bitter divisions among the European powers nor their wartime reversion to the brutal practices of the colonial past were lost on African leaders, who called for postwar independence. Their position was bolstered by the American military campaign in North Africa and the determination of President Franklin Roosevelt to challenge the Anglo-French hegemony in much of Africa. Thus prodded, the British reaffirmed independence to be

the ultimate goal of their African policy, although the French continued to envision their colonies as permanently affiliated with the mother country. There was less pressure on the smaller colonial powers, Belgium and Portugal, both of which resisted change; Portugal, indeed, declared its possessions of Angola, Mozambique, and Portuguese Guinea to be overseas provinces in 1951.

The Achievement of Independence

Between 1957 and 1975 the holdings of the four major colonial powers that survived World War II—Britain, France, Belgium, and Portugal—acquired independence. As a result, 51 new nations emerged, most of them containing a variety of peoples, cultures, languages, and traditions and almost none of them adequately prepared for statehood.

The first postwar decade gave little indication of the rapid decolonization to come. Portugal, as we have seen, moved to integrate its colonies even more closely with itself; Belgium encouraged settler migration; and France, after its expulsion from Syria and Lebanon, tightened its grip on its remaining colonies around the globe. Only Britain moved to prepare its colonies for self-government within the British Commonwealth, promoting education and training African elites. British policy was complicated by the wide developmental variations among its colonies, as well as the resistance of settler populations in Kenya, Uganda, and Tanganyika. It focused at last on the Gold Coast, a prosperous colony with a cocoa-based economy on the bulge of West Africa, where a skillful nationalist leader, Kwame Nkrumah (1909–1972), playing on Western fears of communist influence, secured a commitment to independence. On March 6, 1957, the

Gold Coast, renamed Ghana, was proclaimed a sovereign state within the Commonwealth.

Ghana's independence triggered an upsurge of nationalism throughout the continent. This coincided with a change of policy in Britain and France. Britain's Suez fiasco in 1956 produced a sharp turn in favor of colonial divestiture, while Charles de Gaulle, seeking to bring matters to a head, offered France's black African colonies a choice between membership in a federal community

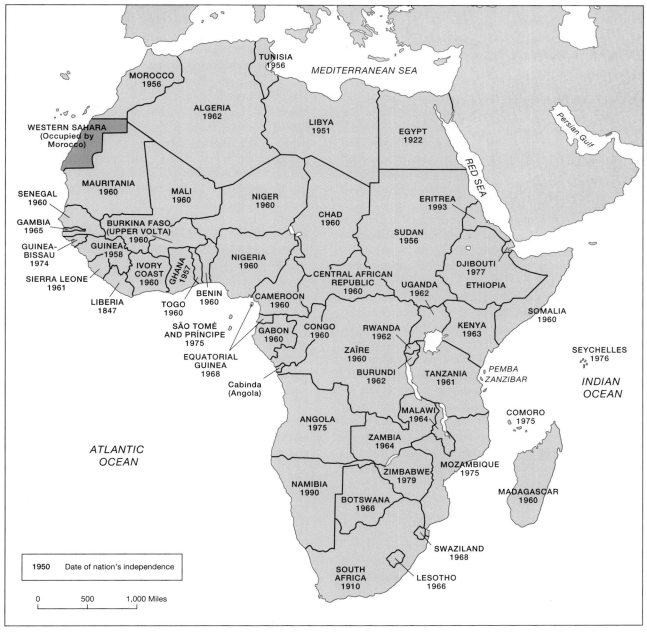

MAP 42.1   AFRICA TODAY

dominated by France or independence with an immediate cessation of aid. Taking up the challenge, the nationalist leader in French Guinea, Sékou Touré (1922–1984), called on his compatriots to opt for "freedom in poverty" rather than continuing dependence. They did so overwhelmingly, and the remaining seven French West African territories, the four of French Equatorial Africa, and the island colony of Madagascar shortly followed suit. By the end of 1960 the sub-Saharan French empire was no more, although de Gaulle, making a virtue of necessity, reversed policy and provided support for the former colonies.

Britain's empire was less easily disassembled. In colonies such as Nigeria, home to more than 200 ethnic and linguistic groups, the problem was finding a viable coalition to hand power to; in others, such as Kenya, there was fierce settler resistance and sometimes savage bloodletting. In general, in territories where either a single tribe predominated or, as in Tanganyika, where a charismatic leader was able to weld a governing consensus among many small tribes, stability could be achieved; elsewhere, most disastrously in Nigeria and Uganda, independence was followed by civil war and by regimes of sometimes appalling brutality.

Britain's most serious difficulties occurred in southern Africa, where two large settler states, Southern Rhodesia and the Union of South Africa, resolutely opposed any challenge to white minority rule. In South Africa pressures for reform were met by defiance: in March 1960, police opened fire on peaceful black demonstrators in Sharpeville township, killing 67; in October the white electorate voted for a republic, thus renouncing South Africa's dominion status; and in March 1961, South Africa withdrew from the Commonwealth. Southern Rhodesia was nominally part of a central African federation with Northern Rhodesia and Nyasaland; when in 1964 the latter two became independent as Zambia and Malawi, the white settler regime in the south, which had exercised de facto control since 1923, insisted on sovereignty without reform. Negotiations proved fruitless, and in 1965 a renegade Rhodesia declared its independence. Isolated by sanctions and faced with a determined guerrilla movement, the white regime yielded in 1980 to a popularly elected black government led by Robert Mugabe (born c. 1928), and Rhodesia became the Republic of Zimbabwe.

As might be expected, the achievement of independence was most difficult in the colonies of Belgium and Portugal. The world had paid little heed to the Congo since international opinion had forced the Belgians to take it over in 1908 from their royal entrepreneur, King Leopold II. The Belgians now fled at the first approach of insurrectionary violence, and the proclamation of an independent Congo in June 1960 under Patrice Lumumba (1925–1961) was almost immediately followed by the secession of its richest province, Katanga, backed by Western mining interests. After Lumumba's murder by CIA-supported assassins, the Congo became a hotbed of Cold War intrigue, with American, Soviet, Chinese, and residual Belgian interests competing amid virtual civil anarchy. An American-backed strongman, General Joseph Mobutu (born 1930), finally reunited the country, henceforth known as Zaïre, in 1965. The adjoining colony of Rwanda-Burundi split into two states, Rwanda and Burundi, whose rival tribes, the Hutu and the Tutsi, clashed bloodily.

Unlike Belgium, Portugal dug its heels in against the liberation movements in its major colonies, Angola, Mozambique, and Portuguese Guinea, where more than 500,000 whites had settled. After more than a decade of bloodshed the Portuguese military itself rebelled, establishing a new regime in Lisbon that recognized independence in the colonies. The long struggle had produced two black factions in Angola, each with its Great Power sponsor, and civil war raged until 1991. In Mozambique the United States backed rebels against the self-styled Marxist regime of Samora Machel.

In May 1963, representatives of 32 new African states met in Addis Ababa to establish the Organization of African Unity (OAU), which has remained an important (though not always successful) promoter of regional peace and continental interests. The OAU's charter recognized the sovereign equality of all member states and the principle of noninterference in the internal affairs of each and pledged itself to the eradication of all remnants of colonialism in Africa. A historian noted that it thereby "Africanized the European partition,"[2] legitimating the often arbitrary boundaries drawn by the colonial powers, but it is difficult to see what alternative was available. For better or worse, modern Africa, like modern Asia, had been cast in the mold of imperialism and would have to work out its destiny in the forms bequeathed by its departed conquerors.

Jomo Kenyatta: Kenya's Founding Father

Kenyan independence involved some of the most characteristic elements of the African liberation movements: tribal division, settler resistance, a wavering colonial pol-

Jomo Kenyatta, first president of independent Kenya.

icy, and a charismatic black leader, Jomo Kenyatta. The grandson of a medicine man of the Kikuyu, Kenya's dominant tribe, Kenyatta was unsure of the date and year of his birth, probably 1891. Like other modern revolutionaries, his name was an adopted one; *Jomo* means "burning spear," and *Kenyatta* refers to the beaded belt, or *kinyata*, that he habitually wore.

Kenyatta spent much of his youth traveling in Europe. He returned home in the 1920s, became secretary of the Kikuyu Central Association, and began to involve himself in his country's future. In 1929 and again in 1931 he went to London to argue his tribe's rights to the land on which it had settled. The British government refused to grant his request but allowed the Kikuyu to establish their own schools. Over the following years he attended the London School of Economics and wrote anthropological studies of his people, as well as an autobiography, *Facing Mount Kenya* (1938), that became a bible of the independence movement.

In October 1945 Kenyatta was one of the organizers of the landmark Pan-African Congress that met in Manchester, England. Seizing the postwar moment, young radicals such as Kwame Nkrumah demanded full independence for Africa. When Kenyatta returned to Kenya in September 1946 he became president of the Kenya African Union (KAU), a political party that sought to unify Kenya's tribes. While urging his follow-

ers to act with discipline and restraint, he fought for African voting rights, the elimination of racial discrimination, and the return of tribal lands.

When the British rejected these demands, Kikuyu militants organized a terrorist underground, the Mau Mau, which prompted the declaration of a state of emergency. Kenyatta was accused of masterminding the Mau Mau, a charge almost certainly false; unquestionably, however, the KAU had links to the Mau Mau, and in 1952 Kenyatta was imprisoned. But British ascendancy was on the wane, and with Ghana's independence in 1957, Kenya's drive toward nationhood accelerated. The KAU, now the dominant black party, refused any participation in a transitional government until Kenyatta was freed. In 1961 he returned home in triumph, his captivity having made him the moral leader of his people's struggle. In December 1963 he became the first president of the Republic of Kenya.

Kenyatta's firmest base of support was among the Kikuyu, who formed but 20 percent of the black population of Kenya. As president, he reached out not only to other tribes but also to white and Asian settlers, assuring them of their place in a multiracial society. Europeans continued to serve in his government, and despite his rhetorical commitment to the slogans of "African socialism," he rejected Soviet assistance and built up a wealthy black proprietor class under settlement schemes financed by the British treasury and the World Bank. This elite continued as the backbone of support for his successor, Daniel Arap Moi (born 1924).

A man of enormous vitality, Kenyatta, more than any other figure, came to represent the new Africa on the world stage. Never losing touch with his origins—he lived on a farm outside his capital, Nairobi, and regularly worked the land—he became a familiar figure at international conferences and assemblies. Wearing alternately impeccably tailored suits and resplendent tribal robes, he symbolized both the revolutionary charisma that had built modern Africa and the political pragmatism by which he hoped to forge its future. He died, still in office, in 1978.

The Quest for Unity

With independence, Africa contained more nations than any other continent in the world. They varied enormously in size, population, geography, resources, and development. The large, thinly populated states of the southern Sahara—Mauritania, Mali, Upper Volta,

Niger, Chad, and the Sudan—were uniformly impoverished, with average per capita income of less than $100 per year, few roads, and virtually no railways. West Africa was chiefly dependent on tropical agriculture and continuing French aid. Nigeria's oil and Zaïre's copper were subject to fluctuating commodity prices. East Africa's economy was based on sisal, coffee, and cotton. Only South Africa had a significant industrial capacity.

Virtually all the new nations suffered from what political scientists call *underdevelopment,* a term that implies distorted rather than just inadequate development. In colonial Kenya, for example, the demand for cheap labor to work the coffee plantations led the British to discourage the production of other crops. Such patterns of dependence on a single crop, known as monoculture, left Africans poorly prepared to face the problems of feeding a burgeoning population.

While population increased at a rate of 3 percent a year in the 1960s and 1970s, food production increased at only 2 percent; by 1980, per capita production had thus declined to four-fifths of its 1960 level. This experience contrasted markedly with that of Latin America and Asia, developing areas that achieved per capita increases during the same period. Africa entered the 1980s at the point of a subsistence crisis, which, compounded by drought and civil war, brought serious and recurring episodes of famine to the Sahel region between Mauritania and Chad and to Ethiopia, the Sudan, Somalia, and Mozambique.

Declining agricultural productivity exacerbated the social and political problems that racked sub-Saharan Africa in its first generation of independence. Civil wars that reached genocidal proportions erupted in Nigeria (1967), where a short-lived secessionist state, Biafra, was crushed, and in Burundi, where an estimated 100,000 people were massacred in 1972. Both conflicts had their origins in endemic tribal rivalries that spilled over, with statehood, into a struggle for national power sharing.

Nigeria's civil war was particularly discouraging, as its constitution, worked out over a decade of intense discussion and negotiation between the leading political parties and the dominant Yoruba and Ibo tribes, was thought to be a model of enlightened colonial devolution and native compromise. Equally disillusioning was the fall of Africa's most prominent statesman, Kwame Nkrumah. During Ghana's first decade, Nkrumah enjoyed unparalleled international stature as leader of Africa's first newly independent nation and the chief spokesman of pan-African unity. At home, however, he indulged in grandiose building projects while suppressing political opposition and moving toward one-party rule. His overthrow in 1966 by a military coup was greeted with general relief, and he died in exile in 1972.

Although several first-generation leaders, notably Kenyatta, Julius Nyerere (born 1922) in Tanzania, and Kenneth Kaunda (born 1924) in Zambia, were able to provide stability and achieve consensual if not democratic government, the typical pattern that emerged in the initial decades of African independence was of autocratic rule. The most notorious examples of this occurred in the Central African Republic, whose ruler, Jean-Bedel Bokassa (born 1921), crowned himself emperor and allegedly participated in the massacre of opponents until his removal in 1979 by a French-sponsored coup, and in Uganda, where Idi Amin (born 1925) imposed an eight-year reign of terror (1971–1979) perhaps best summed up in the chilling phrase he applied to his opponents: "I ate them before they ate me."

Such excesses, widely condemned by both the African and the world community, were the exception. Politics in most African states has often been characterized by personal and factional struggles to control or influence the national government. These struggles have been moderated by private agreements and concessions, prudential concerns, and informal alliances rather than by public laws and institutions. If they bear little resemblance to Western-style parliamentary systems, they reflect traditional power-brokering arrangements that have served African societies in the past and have for the most part provided relatively stable government.

Africa also remained subject to external pressures in the form of Cold War rivalries, economic and sometimes political dependence on former colonial masters, volatile commodity prices, and the politics of aid. The desire of many of the new states to distance themselves from their colonial governors and to redress the consequences of underdevelopment was expressed in the concept of African socialism, which, as practiced in Mali, Benin, the Congo Republic, Mozambique, Somalia, and, after the deposition of Emperor Haile Selassie in 1974, Ethiopia, aimed to promote economic growth and social equality through state control. In the absence of capital resources and technical expertise, these efforts bore little fruit; they did, however, provide an ideological focus for new regimes, as well as a pretext for superpower intervention. The Soviet Union engaged in a long and largely futile effort to extend its influence in Africa through aid to avowedly socialist states, while the United States countered with support for opposition and rebel groups, sometimes of its own invention. The result was the lengthy civil wars inflicted on Angola, Mozambique, and Ethiopia, though this last case was complicated by the rebellion of the province of Eritrea. With the waning of the Cold War, settlement was reached in these wars in the early 1990s, including Eritrean independence, and the long-withheld independence of Namibia was finally achieved. However, the bloody collapses of Samuel K. Doe's regime in Liberia and Siad Barre's in Somalia in 1991, and the appalling slaughter of hundreds of thousands of Tutsi by the Hutu majority in Rwanda in 1994, were grim reminders of the inherent instability of many African states and of the limited ability of the OAU to ensure civil peace.

South Africa

In no other region of Africa have the hopes and passions of a new continent been more intently focused than in South Africa. The withdrawal of its Afrikaner-dominated government from the British Commonwealth in 1961 signaled its determination to pursue its policy of apartheid ("separateness," a euphemism for racial segregation) in all walks of life and to deny the black majority any participation in political life. White supremacist rule was inaugurated with the constitution of 1910, which reserved virtually all political power for whites. Subsequently, blacks were driven into sparsely populated and drought-ridden reserves (which the government later called "homelands") and were prohibited from living in towns except when whites required their services. In all, the black population was barred from living in nine-tenths of South Africa.

By the end of World War II, white South Africans made up nearly a fifth of the population. Most of them were Afrikaners, but there was a large British minority along with numbers of eastern Europeans, particularly Jews, who founded a substantial community in Johannesburg. More than a million Indians had also immigrated, settling chiefly in the towns. The largest black groups were the Bantu and Khoikhoi tribes.

The Afrikaners remained politically dominant. Their conviction of racial superiority, reinforced by contact with Nazi ideology in the 1930s, was unshaken. Despite the winds of change sweeping the continent, the Afrikaners held fast to the belief, rooted in their insular Calvinist faith, that God had ordained them to rule over black South Africa in perpetuity. As the Dutch Reformed church, representing a majority of Afrikaners, stated in 1950: "God divided humanity into races, languages, and nations. Differences are not only willed by God, but perpetuated by him. . . . Those who are culturally and spiritually advanced have a mission to leadership and protection of the less advanced."[3] With the triumph of the right-wing National Party in 1948, apartheid was

proclaimed the official ideology of the government. The Population Registration Act of 1950 set up systematic race classifications among whites, blacks, Asians, and "coloreds," people of mixed European and African parentage. Marriages across these lines were prohibited, and separate facilities and inferior living areas were allocated for blacks.

In response to this, the African National Congress (ANC) and the South African Indian Congress launched a civil disobedience campaign in alliance with liberal whites. The ANC was outlawed in 1961 following the Sharpeville massacre, and seven of its most prominent leaders, including Nelson Mandela (born 1918), were arrested and sentenced to life in prison. The government ruled by emergency decrees, renewed at frequent intervals, which gave virtually unchecked powers to the police and subverted the constitutional system of justice. Renewed violence broke out after an insurrection in the black township of Soweto in 1976 and was fueled again when the black activist Steve Biko died in detention in 1977. The government of P. W. Botha, seeking to divide the resistance movement, set up separate legislatures for Indians and coloreds in 1978 and cultivated collaborationist leaders in the "homelands," notably the Zulu chieftain Mangosuthu G. Buthelezi (born 1929).

By the mid-1980s apartheid was in deep crisis. As violence and repression escalated, the Botha government found itself faced with a new right-wing opposition, the Afrikaner Resistance Movement, as well as economic sanctions from the international community. In August 1989, F. W. de Klerk succeeded the ailing Botha and

Democracy comes to South Africa. Millions of newly enfranchised black South Africans elected Nelson Mandela president of their country in April 1994, after waiting for hours in lines like this one in Soweto, southwest of Johannesburg.

Nelson Mandela takes the oath of office as South Africa's first popularly elected president. Only four years earlier, Mandela had been the prisoner of the apartheid regime.

opened direct negotiations with the ANC. Six months later the ANC was unbanned, together with 35 other political organizations; Nelson Mandela was freed to a hero's welcome around the world; and de Klerk announced his intention to dismantle apartheid and enfranchise all South Africans. By June 1991 most apartheid laws had been repealed, but the prospects for peaceful integration were darkened by the outbreak of black factional and tribal warfare, fanned by elements within the

de Klerk government. But de Klerk and Mandela, allies in their quest for a democratic and pluralistic South Africa though rivals for political power, persevered. The final obstacle was overcome when Chief Buthelezi agreed to participate in the general elections scheduled for April 1994. Those elections returned Mandela as the first majority-rule president of South Africa by an overwhelming margin. De Klerk took his place as one of two vice presidents in a government of national unity.

Nelson Mandela's Inaugural Address

Following his landslide election as the first president of a democratic South Africa in 1994, Nelson Mandela spoke at his inauguration to a huge throng that included 45 heads of state and the secretary general of the United Nations:

Today, all of us do, by our presence here, and by our celebrations in other parts of our country and the world, confer glory and hope to newborn liberty.

Out of the experience of an extraordinary human disaster that lasted too long must be born a society of which all humanity will be proud.

Our daily deeds as ordinary South Africans must produce an actual South African reality that will reinforce humanity's belief in justice, strengthen its confidence in the nobility of the human soul and sustain our hopes for a glorious life for all.

All this we owe both to ourselves and to the peoples of the world who are so well represented here today.

Nelson Mandela's Inaugural Address (continued)

To my compatriots, I have no hesitation in saying that each one of us is as intimately attached to the soil of this beautiful country as are the famous jacaranda trees of Pretoria and the mimosa trees of the bushveld.

Each time one of us touches the soil of this land, we feel a sense of personal renewal. The national mood changes as the seasons change.

We are moved by a sense of joy and exhilaration when the grass turns green and the flowers bloom.

That spiritual and physical oneness we all share with this common homeland explains the depth of pain we all carried in our hearts as we saw our country tear itself apart in territorial conflict, and as we saw it spurned, outlawed and isolated by the peoples of the world, precisely because it had become the universal base of the pernicious ideology and practice of racism and racial oppression. . . .

The time to build is upon us.

We have, at last, achieved our political emancipation. We pledge ourselves to liberate all our people from the continuing bondage of poverty, deprivation, suffering, gender and other discrimination.

We have triumphed in the effort to implant hope in the breasts of the millions of our people. We enter into a covenant that we shall build the society in which all South Africans, both black and white, will be able to walk tall, without any fear in their hearts, assured of their inalienable right to human dignity—a rainbow nation at peace with itself and the world. . . .

We dedicate this day to all the heroes and heroines in this country and the rest of the world who sacrificed in many ways and surrendered their lives so that we could be free.

Their dreams have become reality. Freedom is their reward.

We are both humbled and elevated by the honor and privilege that you, the people of South Africa, have bestowed on us, as the first President of a united, democratic, nonracial and nonsexist South Africa, to lead our country out of the valley of darkness.

We understand it still that there is no easy road to freedom.

We know it well that none of us acting alone can achieve success.

We must therefore act together as a united people, for national reconciliation, for nation building, for the birth of a new world.

Let there be justice for all.

Let there be peace for all.

Let there be work, bread, water and salt for all.

Let each know that for each the body, the mind and the soul have been freed to express themselves.

Never, never and never again shall it be that this beautiful land will again experience the oppression of one by another and suffer the indignity of being the skunk of the world.

The sun shall never set on so glorious a human achievement!

Let freedom reign. God bless Africa!

Source: The New York Times.

North Africa

North Africa has traditionally been a world apart, its culture more closely linked to the Mediterranean basin and the Middle East than to sub-Saharan Africa. The coastal plain, known as the Maghreb, was colonized successively by the Phoenicians, the Romans, and the Arabs, whose influence continues to define the region. The dominant colonial presence was that of the French, whose rule replaced the loose Ottoman suzerainty in Algeria and Tunisia in the nineteenth century and who established a protectorate over Morocco in 1912.

Algeria was the pivot of France's North African empire. First occupied in 1830, it contained a settler population of 1 million, the largest anywhere on the continent except for South Africa. The French considered Algeria a metropolitan territory, and during the Third Republic the settlers, or colons, sent six representatives to the lower house of the National Assembly in Paris and three to the upper. The native population was regarded, in the words of one historian of French colonial policy, as "partly a menace and wholly a nuisance." The settlers seized the best land and almost entirely excluded the Muslim majority from industry and commerce. Their attitude was summed up by one of their number after the suppression of a large-scale revolt in 1871: "The Arab must accept the fate of the conquered. He must either become assimilated to our civilization or disappear. European civilization can have no sympathy for the life of savages."[4]

The Nazi defeat of France in 1940 had profound repercussions in North Africa. Germany occupied Tunisia, repatriating the exiled nationalist leader, Habib Bourguiba, while in both Morocco and Algeria the overthrow of the Vichy regime by Anglo-American forces gave impetus to nationalist movements. De Gaulle offered concessions to the Muslim elite in Algeria, but these were rejected, and a rebellion broke out in May 1945 that, brutally repressed, left thousands dead. Belatedly, the Fourth Republic offered internal autonomy and majority rule, but this only stiffened the resistance of the *colons*. With a series of coordinated attacks, a full-scale war of independence was launched in November 1954 by a hitherto shadowy organization, the National Liberation Front (FLN). Thus began a seven-year struggle waged with the utmost ferocity on both sides. It ended in 1962 with the rebels victorious but much of the country in ruins and two million Algerians homeless.

The French decision to contest the rebellion despite widespread condemnation, particularly in the Arab world, was a complex one. France was smarting from its defeat in another long colonial war in Vietnam, and the very weakness of the Fourth Republic made it difficult to resist the pressure of the *colons*, strongly backed by right-wing forces in the army. Not until Charles de Gaulle was returned to power in what amounted to a coup directed from Algiers did someone wield sufficient authority to break the impasse. De Gaulle, convinced that Algeria was untenable, adroitly sidestepped his sponsors and moved to liquidate the war. He narrowly escaped assassination; France narrowly averted a civil war.

In Morocco and Tunisia the transition to independence was less traumatic, though not without violence. Tunisia gained internal autonomy in 1954 and full independence in 1957, when Bourguiba was installed as pres-

AFRICA SINCE 1945

Sub-Saharan Africa	North Africa
South Africa adopts apartheid (1948)	Independence of Libya (1951)
	Algerian war of independence (1954–1962)
	Independence of Morocco and the Sudan (1956)
Independence of Ghana (1957)	Independence of Tunisia (1957)
Independence of Guinea (1958)	
Independence of Zaïre and Nigeria (1960)	
South Africa leaves British Commonwealth (1961)	
Organization of African Unity (1963)	
Independence of Zambia (1964)	
	Haile Selassie deposed in Ethiopia (1974)
End of white rule in Zimbabwe (1980)	U.S. bombs Libya (1986)
End of civil war in Angola (1991)	Civil war in Algeria (1991)
First black government in South Africa; Nelson Mandela elected president (1994)	

ident. The Islamic monarchy of Morocco was fully restored in 1956. Both states have enjoyed relative stability since, although Morocco has experienced serious border disputes and guerilla incursions. Algeria's first years were marked by the problems of reconstruction and by dissension within the revolutionary council. Following a period of internal consolidation and relative isolation, it reemerged as an active neutralist state under the pragmatic leadership of Houari Boumediene. Social inequity persisted, however, and after Islamic fundamentalists heavily defeated the FLN at the polls in 1991, the military staged a preemptive coup. A civil war erupted in its wake that wrecked the economy of North Africa's second most populous country.

The French withdrawal from North Africa, coupled with the antagonism provoked by the creation of the state of Israel, led to the virtual disappearance of the region's flourishing Jewish community. Most of the Jews of Tunis and almost the entire Jewish population of Algeria migrated to France and Israel. The Jewish settlement in Morocco, which at 250,000 had been the largest in Africa, was reduced to a fifth of its former size. A massive Israeli airlift evacuated the Jewish population of Ethiopia, whose residence dated to biblical times, in the spring of 1991.

Much of the external support for the rebellions against French rule in the Maghreb came from Egypt, which under Gamal Abdel Nasser led the struggle against Western colonialism in the region. Nasser also played an important role in radicalizing Libya, a former Italian colony that was administered by Britain until it was granted nominal independence in 1951. Under the feudal monarchy of King Idris, Libya remained a postcolonial Western outpost in North Africa and a reliable source of oil. In September 1969 a group of young army officers, inspired by Nasser's pan-Arabism, seized power under the leadership of Colonel Muammar al-Qaddafi (born 1942). After closing Western bases and banning the teaching of English in primary schools, Qaddafi entered a short-lived political union with Egypt and then, going his own way, used the vast oil revenues generated by the OPEC monopoly in the 1970s to fund both development schemes in Africa and terrorist movements around the world. After 1980 he became embroiled in a civil war in neighboring Chad, challenging French influence in its former colony. Friction with the West climaxed in 1986 when American planes bombed Libya in retaliation for alleged Libyan involvement in terrorist incidents; Qaddafi himself was targeted but narrowly escaped.

Egyptian pressure hastened the granting of independence to the Sudan in 1956, which opted neither to join the British Commonwealth nor, as Nasser had hoped, to unite with Egypt. The Sudan was sharply divided between the Muslim north and the Christian south. The threat of an Egyptian-backed coup, together with the increasing ineffectiveness of party government, provoked a military coup in 1958. The nation veered between military and civilian rule in the years thereafter, and a secession attempt by the south in 1974 was bloodily suppressed. The deposition of the Sudan's military strongman, Gaafar Nimeiri, in 1985 failed to produce stable government, and its difficulties were compounded by a spillover of refugees from Ethiopia as well as famines in the late 1980s. Civil war resumed in the south in 1983, a struggle increasingly characterized by the attempt to forcibly impose Islam on the non-Arab population of the south.

Few other modern nations have suffered more terribly than Ethiopia. With the expulsion of the Italians by British forces in 1941, Haile Selassie was returned to power. Imperial rule did little to modernize the country; 20 years later, there was only one medical doctor for every 96,000 inhabitants, although the court and the Christian Amharic elite of the northern highlands lived in splendor and the emperor maintained a high international profile. After a period of growing chaos, characterized by student demonstrations, army mutinies, and revelations of corruption, a serious famine brought the regime to crisis. In 1974 a mixed group of moderate and radical army officers deposed Haile Selassie.

Within a short time the radicals had gained control, and under Lieutenant Colonel Mengistu Haile Mariam, Ethiopia's traditional feudal system was replaced with a repressive one-party state. The resulting disruption of food production was only partly offset by Soviet aid. Simultaneously, a rebellion broke out in Eritrea, which had been forcibly assimilated into Ethiopia after World War II, while neighboring Somalia sought to annex the province of Ogaden, largely inhabited by Somali nomads. Cuban troops shortly joined in the fighting, as in Angola. The government in Addis Ababa interdicted food relief to rebel-held areas when famine broke out in the mid-1980s, exacerbating the heavy loss of life. Mengistu was toppled in 1991 following the capture of the Eritrean capital of Asmara by the rebel Popular Liberation Front, whose arms had been scavenged largely from the Ethiopian army itself. In neighboring Somalia, meanwhile, factional fighting broke out, with heavy casualties among the civilian population and starvation among the survivors as rival chieftains fought for control. American intervention failed to stem the conflict, and the withdrawal of international forces left the country with an uncertain future.

African Perspectives and Prospects

In no other continent has change been as rapid or as traumatic as in modern Africa. Within a single generation, from 1870 to 1900, virtually the entire continent was brought under European imperial control, with shattering consequences for centuries-old native polities and traditions; with equal rapidity, the Europeans withdrew between 1945 and 1975, leaving behind a multiplicity of new states, few rooted in African history and most plagued by poverty and tribal division. It is hardly to be wondered that the first generation of African independence has been troubled and sometimes tragic; it is greatly to be admired that in the face of such a daunting challenge, so much has been achieved.

African art and music have enormously enriched the world heritage, and their influence on Western art and American jazz has been profound. In literature, too, Africans are rapidly making their mark. The novels of Chinua Achebe (born 1930) and the plays of Wole Soyinka (born 1934), both Nigerians, have reached a world audience, while the traumas of South African life have been chronicled in the novels and stories of Nadine Gordimer (born 1924) and André Brink (born 1935) and in the plays of Athol Fugard (born 1932). Three African writers have been honored as Nobel laureates in literature in recent years, including Soyinka and Gordimer.

Many problems, however, remain. The revitalization of African agriculture is a high priority as population continues its explosive growth throughout the continent. The problems of urban development must also be addressed in Africa's rapidly expanding cities, as oversimplified models of African socialism give way to a more sophisticated understanding of the importance of diversified growth, appropriate technology, and the complex interaction of town and country. Important public health problems confront most African states, most notably the AIDS epidemic, which has spread more rapidly and more devastatingly in Africa than anywhere else.

High on the agenda of social problems is the role of African women. Despite modernization, most women remain confined to traditional roles. Many of the women of sub-Saharan Africa are still subject to arranged marriages, polygamy, and, in places, sexual mutilation associated with puberty rites. Drought, starvation, forced migration, civil war, and AIDS have compounded these problems in recent years, as has the haphazard urbanization that has broken up the old communal relationships of the countryside in which men and women worked side by side. In sub-Saharan Africa a large proportion of women are involved in subsistence farming. In the cities female underemployment is particularly acute and paid jobs are the exception. Legal equality has gradually emerged, and Ghana took the unprecedented step of reserving ten seats in the national assembly for women. Women have long been active in handicraft production and trading, and when organized they have been formidable; thousands of Ibo women organized a tax strike against colonial rule in Nigeria in 1923.

The transition to democracy in South Africa, the approaches to regional cooperation in eastern and southern Africa, the end of Cold War rivalries, and the withdrawal of foreign armies from the continent were all hopeful signs for Africa's future. In November 1991 a peaceful transfer of power took place in Tanzania when the nation's founding father, Kenneth Kaunda, was defeated at the polls by a trade union leader, Frederick Chiluba (born 1943), and in May 1994 elections in Malawi ousted Africa's most venerable dictator, Hastings Kamazu Banda, while negotiated settlements brought the long-standing civil wars in Mozambique and Angola to an end.

On the debit side, the persistence of despotic rule in such nations as Cameroon, Gabon, Kenya, Nigeria, Togo, Uganda, and Zaïre, and the chronic civil wars in Algeria, Liberia, Somalia, and the Sudan, pose formidable obstacles to stability. The threat of renewed genocide in Rwanda and Burundi underscores the fragility of many African socities, and the problems of forging genuine economic independence remain. The challenges to Africa's peaceful development remain high; with ingenuity, statesmanship, and goodwill, they are not insurmountable.

South America:
Reform and Revolution

Throughout most of Latin America the mood at the beginning of the twentieth century was one of confidence and optimism. But as the century ended, the economic and political progress of the early decades of independence had been checked and, in some places, even reversed. Few Latin American governments, democratic or not, found lasting solutions to the basic social and economic problems that beset the region.

Poverty and overpopulation remain endemic. Wealth and land continue to be concentrated in the hands of a privileged elite that sometimes represents as little as 2 percent of the population and has often protected its own landed and commercial interests by supporting undemocratic regimes. The deep-rooted social ills that afflict Latin American society are revealed in

MAP 42.2   MODERN SOUTH AMERICA

THE GROWTH OF SELECTED LATIN AMERICAN CITIES

	Population (in thousands)					
	1940	1950	1960	1970	1980	Most Recent
Buenos Aires (Argentina)	2,410	5,213	7,000	9,400	9,927	11,328
Mexico City (Mexico)	1,560	2,872	4,910	8,567	12,000+	15,047
Rio de Janeiro (Brazil)	1,159	3,025	4,692	5,155	5,542	6,042
Lima-Callao (Peru)	—	947	1,519	2,500	4,601	6,414
Santiago (Chile)	952	1,275	1,907	2,600	4,309	4,750
Havana (Cuba)	936	1,081	1,549	1,700	1,935	2,096
Guayaquil (Ecuador)	—	259	450	800	1,279	1,508
Guatemala City (Guatemala)	186	294	474	770	754	N/A
La Paz (Bolivia)	—	300	400	500	635	976
San Salvador (Salvador)	103	162	239	375	400	N/A
Tegucigalpa (Honduras)	86	72	159	281	485	608
Managua (Nicaragua)	63	109	197	350	608	819

Source: Statistical Abstract of Latin America.

huge cities such as Buenos Aires and Mexico City, where millions live in overcrowded squalor. The Catholic church has maintained its influence throughout the region. Although at a local level pastoral workers have sought to improve living conditions for the poor, the official image of the church has been compromised in places by its lack of public opposition to repressive regimes.

The main force behind the maintenance of political repression has been the military. Since the mid-nineteenth century, Latin American political life has been dominated by an endless series of crises and coups provoked by the intervention of the army in civil affairs. Once in power, military leaders retained control by co-opting the support of the landed and business classes. With the notable exception of Juan Perón in Argentina, these so-called caudillo figures lacked both charisma and broad-based popular support.

In economic terms, most Latin American countries are dependent on the export of raw materials and are therefore at the mercy of world prices and demand. Continuing political instability has impeded the consistent development of natural resources and industrial production for the benefit of the population at large. The problems of financial instability have been further compounded by the inability of countries such as Mexico and Brazil to repay the vast loans made to them by international organizations and foreign banks.

Each nation in Latin America faces its own special problems, in some cases created by its history and in others by its natural environment. Yet for the most part political life has been determined by a single basic principle: revolution, or sudden changes of authority, that merely redistribute power within the old elite. Only in a few instances has the new leadership produced significant change. In Chile a military coup overthrew a left-wing government in 1973 and installed a repressive right-wing dictatorship. In Bolivia the 192 changes of government that had taken place by 1985 only worsened its problems.

Since the days of the Monroe Doctrine, the United States has assumed an important and often decisive role in Latin American affairs. In its quest for territorial expansion in the 1840s, the United States seized huge tracts of Mexican territory that later became Texas and California, and in the 1890s it stripped Cuba and Puerto Rico from Spain. Thereafter, a combination of economic and security interests led Washington not only to limit the influence of European powers in Latin America but also to intervene unilaterally in the region. Yet the role played by the United States has varied greatly from one country to another. American involvement in Central American politics increased in the 1980s, and in more repressive regimes such as Chile, the United States has sometimes encouraged their leaders to mitigate the harsher effects of military rule. Direct U.S. intervention established and supported dictatorial regimes in Nicaragua, Haiti, Guatemala, and the Dominican Republic. Successive American administrations have never accepted a left-of-center regime except in Mexico or done more than tolerate centrist governments. When Argentina became embroiled with Britain in 1982 over the Falkland Islands (Islas Malvinas), Washington secretly supported its European ally while professing neutrality. In all cases, American authorities carefully moni-

The favelas of Rio de Janeiro, slums where a quarter of the city's people live in squalid shanties without running water or sewers.

tor, influence, and often determine events throughout Latin America.

Brazil: The Unstable Giant

Brazil, which occupies almost half the South American continent—some 3 million square miles—and has a population of more than 140 million, is a far more varied nation than its neighbors. Whereas the other countries in Central and South America speak the Spanish of their conquerors, Brazil's cultural inheritance is mixed. The official language and culture derive chiefly from Brazil's Catholic Portuguese colonizers. That heritage is supplemented by the cultures of the indigenous Indian population and the Africans whose ancestors were imported as slaves in the seventeenth and eighteenth centuries.

The waves of European immigrants who came to Brazil in the nineteenth century included a sizable number of Jews. Continuing Jewish immigration was brought to a halt in 1930 by restrictive legislation, and in 1937 a secret order was circulated to all Brazilian consulates to reject visa applications submitted by Jews. In spite of official discrimination, however, small numbers of skilled workers and professionals escaped to Brazil from Nazi Germany. After World War II the Jewish population rose gradually to about 150,000, concentrating in the larger cities.

In Brazil during the 1930s and 1940s the rule of Getúlio Vargas introduced a period of relative economic and political stability. When Vargas died in 1954, the alliance between nationalism and capitalism that he had forged and maintained for a quarter of a century collapsed. The same forces that produced conflict elsewhere in South America now pitted themselves against one another in Brazil: the working class and the peasants on the one hand, the landowning elite and the military on the other. This conflict unfolded against uncontrolled economic expansion based on foreign loans, used mostly for grandiose public works projects that resulted in profiteering and disastrous inflation.

Expensive public projects took an enormous toll in foreign exchange and political stability. The consequence was growing inflation and an increase in social tension. In 1964 a military government seized power, holding it for a generation. Successive military governments held occasional elections but refused to relinquish control. Although the country has made progress toward economic stability, the gap between the prosperous business class and the poor continues to widen. Uncontrolled development and speculation have led to the spoliation of much of Brazil's land, especially in the Amazon basin. Political repression produced the familiar pattern of rigid censorship, police brutality, and human rights abuse.

By 1975 serious strains had developed in relations between Brazil and the United States. In addition to concern over Brazil's public image as a police state, Washington was alarmed at its growing involvement with nuclear technology. When the Carter administration reduced military aid, the Brazilians retaliated by canceling their military pact with the United States.

From 1979 to 1985 Brazil's military rulers slowly moved toward the reestablishment of civilian government. After parliamentary elections in 1982, a coalition of opposition groups, the Democratic Alliance, chose as its candidate for the presidency Tancredo Neves, a trusted and popular figure. His successor, José Sarney, lacked the ability to command a consensus, and the rest of 1985 was marked by a series of paralyzing strikes. Coming on top of a disastrous drought that devastated Brazil's coffee crop, a major source of exchange, the industrial unrest forced Sarney's government into action. Prices and wages were frozen, and negotiations with the International Monetary Fund and private banks rescheduled Brazil's debts. In 1994 the country finally reduced its inflation rate from 50 percent per month to 1 percent under the leadership of Fernando Henrique Cardoso, who became president in 1995.

Economically, Brazil's future seems unclear. A major steel industry has emerged; exports of goods such as chemicals, shoes, and automobiles are increasing; and minerals such as iron and bauxite are bringing in foreign currency. Nonetheless, the repayment of its foreign debts—the largest in the world—reached the breaking point in 1987, when Brazil suspended payments as inflation reached 365 percent per annum. The democratic government has yet to resolve the country's social inequities and has failed to implement land reform. Yet the spirit of optimism that led to the creation of Brasília is characteristic of Brazilian popular culture and may help the country weather its current crisis.

Brasília: The Planned City

While Brazil faced financial collapse in the 1950s, its president, Juscelino Kubitschek, inaugurated the country's most ambitious public undertaking, a new capital city, Brasília. The scheme, commissioned in 1957, was designed to give visible form to the government's faith in Brazil's future. The new capital was situated in the plains of the state of Goias, 600 miles inland. Within three years the master plan of Lucio Costa and the buildings of the architect Oscar Niemeyer had taken sufficient shape for the government to move there. As in Chandigarh, the Indian planned city designed by Le Corbusier, a major city was laid out from the beginning with an eye to its total physical and architectural design, as well as a concern for the day-to-day needs of its inhabitants.

The central part of the city, set on two main axes, north-south and east-west, is surrounded by an artificial lake that divides it from the suburbs. Most of the public buildings are set on the east-west—or "monumental"—axis. At its east end, in the Square of Three Powers, are the legislative, judicial, and executive buildings of government. Given the region's relative inaccessibility, it was necessary to construct a new highway system to connect Brasília with Rio de Janeiro, the former capital and Brazil's largest city. Brasilia boasts huge water and waste disposal systems and is entirely electrified.

Additional building projects were undertaken in the following decades. The University of Brazil is the center of the city's cultural life, with its auditorium and public library. Public services such as hospitals and clinics and fire and police departments are extensive and modern. By the late 1980s the population had reached about 1.4 million. Many of the original inhabitants came from economically depressed areas of the country to work on the construction of the city, but they have now been supplemented by those employed in local industries, which include printing, furniture, and services.

Brasília has proved both daring and controversial. The notion of moving Brazil's capital to the interior goes back to the days of Portuguese rule and had been discussed again in the 1820s. Rio de Janeiro certainly exercised a cultural and social monopoly that many Brazilians found stifling. Moreover, the new city is a prosperous one. However, the architectural plans have been criticized as an example of utopian design derived from a Bauhaus aesthetic with totalitarian overtones.

The artificial nature of the project has produced a city that is an exception to most great urban centers throughout the world, which have been almost always the result of a long period of human habitation and cultural experience. Diplomats "exiled" to Brasília complain of its arid climate and the shantytowns that have sprung up around it. Other countries that have followed Brazil's example, such as Nigeria with the construction of a new capital at Abuja, have met with mixed success. Yet the daring speed with which the scheme was executed, together with the breadth of the concept, compels admiration. Certainly the creation of Brasília has marked a commitment to urban living as the future basis of a nation that is still predominantly agrarian.

Argentina: Dictatorship and Democracy

Ever since Argentina's first struggles to win freedom from Spain in the early nineteenth century, political stability proved elusive. The second-largest country in Latin America, after Brazil, Argentina covers an area of just over 1 million square miles and is home to 30 million inhabitants.

Unlike Ecuador, which has a large Indian population, or Colombia and Paraguay, which have *mestizo* (mixed Spanish and Indian) majorities, Argentinians are overwhelmingly of European origin. The waves of immigrants, mainly Spanish and Italian, that flocked to Argentina in the nineteenth century produced conflicting interest groups that have proved difficult to reconcile. The industrialists of the capital city of Buenos Aires, the ranchers who control the great coastal estates, the farmers of the interior, and radical populists all vie for political recognition and power.

Among the European immigrants were large numbers of Jews attracted to Argentina by its relatively early industrialization. The Jewish community there, almost half a million in number, remains the largest in Latin America. The country's once liberal immigration policies changed, however, in the 1930s, when anti-Semitism made itself felt in Argentina. After World War II Argentina became a haven for escaped Nazi war criminals.

From the time of its rebellion against Spain in 1810, Argentina's history has been dominated by a series of caudillo rulers, most of whom were wealthy landowners or generals devoted to power and money. Only in 1916 were democratic radicals able to defeat the landowners and industrialists in Argentina's first open election and govern the country until 1930. But the Great Depression wrought havoc with the economy and induced the army to replace the government with a conservative coalition of bankers, landowners, and generals. This combination of interests has constituted the single most powerful force in Argentine politics ever since.

By the end of World War II the charismatic Colonel Juan Domingo Perón (1895–1974) had come to dominate the ruling clique. The archetypal caudillo, Perón's ability to mesmerize his fellow citizens owed much to the charm and brilliance of his wife Eva (1919–1952), once a

Juan and Eva Perón established a political system in Argentina that combined dictatorship with populist rhetoric and achieved wide appeal.

popular radio announcer. By the time of her death, "Evita," who sponsored much of the regime's social reform programs despite her own opulent lifestyle, had become a popular folk heroine to her people. Her memory still remains a powerful force in Argentine politics.

With Eva's encouragement, Perón realized that his personal rule could not continue without the backing of the middle classes and the poor. Gaining control of the trade unions, he was elected president in 1946 with a large majority. Through skillful propaganda and careful attention to interest groups such as the church and the army, the Peróns retained the reluctant support of the right. At the same time, they introduced health and welfare benefits for the poor and stimulated jobs for the unemployed. These measures resulted in increased taxation, which brought a drop in agricultural production and export revenues. Financial chaos and corruption, together with the death of Eva, undermined support for Perón, who was deposed by the army in 1955.

A series of military regimes followed, alternating with brief periods of civilian rule. By 1973 Perón decided to end his exile in Spain and run for the presidency again. When the army refused to allow his candidacy, he put forward Hector Campora, a Peronist party worker, as his representative. Although Campora won, the Peronist victory led to a bloody civil struggle. In less than two

months Campora was compelled to resign, Perón's opponents were forced into retirement, and new elections were called. With his new wife, Isabel, as his running mate, Perón won by a large majority.

Perón's solutions to Argentina's massive problems were contradictory and self-defeating. While courting Communist countries such as the Soviet Union and Cuba, he instituted a repressive domestic policy. Liberal government officials and teachers were dismissed, and the left-wing opposition was crushed. Perón's failures may have been the result of ill health, which prevented him from controlling the conflicting forces within his coalition.

Isabel attempted to take her husband's place after his death in 1974, but the task proved impossible. Many Argentinians resented her efforts to portray herself as Evita's successor. Occupying the highest position ever held by a woman in the Western Hemisphere, the reclusive Isabel found herself unable to control her conspiring ministers. In the 21 months that she held office, she reorganized the cabinet ten times. Nor was she able to rectify Argentina's trade deficit or maintain a policy of economic austerity. Finally, the social life of the country was paralyzed by a rash of kidnappings and assassinations carried out by terrorists of both the left and the right. In 1976 yet another military coup—the sixth in 21 years—installed an army junta.

The army restored some order to the economy, increasing agricultural and industrial production and reducing inflation. The junta raised taxes and froze wages. In the face of mounting foreign debt, however, the value of the Argentine peso fell, and the government devalued it by 70 percent. Meanwhile, thousands of political opponents were rounded up, tortured, and murdered. In protest, the United States suspended military aid to Argentina.

By 1982, with inflation and unemployment again increasing rapidly, the trade unions began a series of strikes, and the banned political parties called for a return to constitutional government. The regime, led by General Leopoldo Galtieri, sought to generate nationalist sentiment by challenging Britain for control of the Falkland Islands, a British crown colony. The Malvinas, as they are called in Latin America, are a barren, windswept chain off the southeast tip of Argentina inhabited mainly by sheepherders. In April 1982, Galtieri became an instant national hero when he ordered an invasion of the islands, but the government of British Prime Minister Margaret Thatcher, assisted by the United States, defeated Argentina.

The military government's popularity plummeted in the wake of its military defeat. The 1983 presidential

Eva Perón on Peronism

Juan Perón's dictatorship combined populism and nationalism into a political regime that in many ways resembled European fascism. Here Eva Perón, his wife and adviser and herself an important political figure, extolls Peronism with the kind of rhetoric that made the phenomenon so popular among Argentinians.

This is why we, the peronistas, may never forget the people; our heart must always be with the humble, the comrades, the poor, the dispossessed, for this is how to carry out best the doctrine of General Perón; and so that the poor, the humble, the working forces, and we ourselves, do not forget, we have pledged to be missionaries of Perón; to do this is to expand his doctrine, not only within our own country, but to offer it to the world as well, as a hope of the rewards always wished for by the working classes. . . .

General Perón has defeated internal capitalism, through social economy, putting capital at the service of the economy, and not vice versa, which only gave the workers the right to die of hunger: the law of the funnel, as it is called, the wide part for the capitalists and the narrow part for the people.

Perón has suppressed imperialist action. Now we have economic independence. He knows well all the insults he will receive for committing the "crime" of defending the country. Some Argentines allied themselves with foreigners in order to slander him, because General Perón was the first to make foreign powers respect Argentina, and treat it as an equal.

Source: E. Perón, *Historia del Peronismo* (Buenos Aires: Presidencia de la Nacion, 1951), trans. in R. Cameron, *Civilization Since Waterloo* (Itasca, Ill.: Peacock, 1971), pp. 529–531.

campaign was won by a political moderate, Raúl Alfonsín. Despite his efforts to prosecute Galtieri and his associates for human rights violations, pressure from the army frustrated the process. Nevertheless, Alfonsín's election helped restore international confidence in his country, and in 1986 he succeeded in negotiating loans from private banks in the United States and from the International Monetary Fund. Under his successor Carlos Saul Menem, the country began to face its troubled past. But lasting democratic solutions to the problems facing Argentina still remain an unrealized goal.

Chile and Peru: Socialism and the Military

Peru and Chile form much of South America's west coast. Both contain wide variations in climate and geography and have a population that is overwhelmingly *mestizo*. In Peru a left-wing military regime has given way to an unstable democracy, while in Chile a democratically elected socialist leader was replaced by a right-wing military dictatorship whose legacy persists.

Throughout the nineteenth and early twentieth centuries Chilean politics was marked by continual struggles between the Liberal party, which first came to power in 1861, and the Conservatives, who represented the army and wealthy landowners. In 1920 the middle classes joined with the workers to bring the populist Arturo Alessandri Palma to power. While his government was ousted and reestablished, left-wing political parties continued to develop. In the 1930s the Radical party replaced the Liberals, and the Socialists and Communists grew in importance. Indeed, by the end of World War II the Communists were the focus of parliamentary opposition.

From 1946 to 1964, as coalitions formed by smaller parties replaced one another, public support for the left increased as a result of a well-organized labor movement. In 1970 Salvador Allende (1908–1973), a Marxist, came to power with a left-wing coalition government. Continuing support for Allende was demonstrated by large victories for his supporters in local elections the next year.

In his three years of power, Allende sought to redress many of Chile's social and economic inequities.

Farms were distributed to peasants, who were provided with a wide range of social benefits. But Allende lacked the resources to pay for his programs, and deficit spending finally produced uncontrolled inflation.

Allende's government was isolated from abroad. His nationalization of American copper mines, together with other industries, led to the suspension of U.S. aid and trade. The United States even refused to sell food to Chile. The Soviets and the Chinese provided some help but not enough to offset a general boycott by noncommunist countries. Finally the army, with assistance from the American CIA, seized control in September 1973 and has remained in power ever since. Allende was slain during the coup. A prolonged period of military rule followed under General Augusto Pinochet. Political parties and unions were banned, and, as in Argentina, thousands of suspected opponents "disappeared." Civilian administration returned in 1989, but Pinochet remained as commander of the army.

Pinochet, who proclaimed himself president, established a repressive dictatorship in Chile, one of South America's most established democracies. His well-documented policies of arbitrary arrests, torture, and executions led to a temporary suspension of American aid in 1979, although President Reagan restored it in 1981. Pinochet's constitution provided for his continued rule until 1997. Demonstrations of public opposition in 1985 and 1986 provoked brutal reprisals. Pinochet's presidential rule was repudiated in the elections of 1988, but as head of the armed forces he remained the effective head of the country, even after ceding power to a civilian government in 1990.

Like Chile, Peru was the scene of an experimental socialism, but under the unlikely direction of the army. A liberal reformist movement developed among the Peruvian educated classes in the early twentieth century. In 1924 this progressive coalition crystallized in the creation of the American Popular Revolutionary Alliance (APRA). Although anticommunist, the APRA borrowed socialist ideas from the Soviet Union and western Europe and became the focus of an Indian rights movement. Most of Peru's history from the appearance of the APRA to 1968 consisted of periods of liberal government interrupted by army coups and military regimes.

The 1968 coup was unusual. The military leaders proclaimed a policy of "social democracy," intending to follow a middle way between capitalism and communism on the basis of a mixed economy. Banks, mines—some of them U.S.-owned—and other key industries were nationalized, and many large estates were distributed to peasants. Educational programs were expanded and social benefits introduced. The regime suppressed political opposition movements and censored the press.

The international effects of these policies were predictable. The Soviets sent money, weapons, and advisers, while in 1974 the Peruvian government expelled U.S. officials on charges of spying for the CIA. Peru became one of the leading advocates of Third World causes and an outspoken critic of American policies. As a result, foreign investment declined and Peru's economy began to collapse. Some industries were returned to their owners after 1975, but the damage had been done. By 1978 the regime had returned the country to civilian rule.

Both of Peru's subsequently elected presidents have been drawn from the APRA. Their problems—a declining economy, massive debt, drug trafficking, and industrial unrest—were compounded after 1983 by bands of guerrilla fighters in the countryside of southern Peru. Calling themselves *Sendero Luminoso* ("shining path," a quotation from Lenin), they represented a splinter group of the Peruvian Communist party. In 1984 they were joined by another revolutionary movement, the *Tupac Amaru,* named after an eighteenth-century Indian who revolted against the Spaniards. The former group was active in rural areas; the latter operated primarily in the cities, including Lima, the capital. The guerrilla groups continue to present problems, together with the terrorist activities of cocaine traders. In 1987 President Alan García survived mutinies and public outrage against police and army brutality, partly stemming from attempts to suppress the guerrillas, but his successor, Alberto Fujimori, suddenly suspended the constitution after his election in 1991. Propped up by the military he won reelection, but Peru faces an uncertain future.

Bolivia: Land of Revolutions

Although the history of Bolivia, with its succession of military coups, superficially resembles that of Argentina, fundamental social differences prevail. The overwhelming majority of Bolivia's population is either of pure Indian or of mixed European and Indian descent. In the early days of independence after 1825 no educated middle class existed to run the state bureaucracy. Wealthy landowners were interested only in protecting their own interests. The military filled the vacuum with 50 years of misrule.

By the end of the nineteenth century, political parties led by Bolivia's landed aristocracy had developed. The Liberal party exploited Bolivia's major resource, tin, and constructed road and rail networks throughout the country. The proceeds from these modernization programs further enriched the wealthy, who became known as the "tin barons," instead of improving living conditions for the poor.

Ten Peruvian farmers buried themselves in a lettuce field to protest their eviction. The farmers claimed they owned abandoned land near Lima.

By the 1930s most of Bolivia's mineral wealth had been sold to American investors, and the Great Depression devastated the economy. In 1932 conflict broke out between Bolivia and its southern neighbor, Paraguay, complicating an already difficult situation. The so-called Gran Chaco War ended in 1935 with Bolivia losing a sizable chunk of its territory.

Military governments continued into the postwar period. In 1941 a reformer, Victor Paz Estenssoro, managed to unify various urban protest groups into the National Revolutionary Movement (MNR). A decade later the MNR won the national elections, but the army refused to allow Estenssoro to take power. Their action finally prompted a revolution that put Estenssoro in office as president.

In 1952 the new government took over the tin mines and raised workers' wages and benefits. Unfortunately, these moves coincided with a fall in tin prices on the world market, pointing up the danger of dependence on a single export. Not until 1966 did the mines return to their former profitability. Estenssoro also tried to redress the grievances of the Indians, most of whom lived in a condition of servitude that had changed little since the sixteenth century. The urban rebellion of the MNR had been accompanied by widespread uprisings and Indian land seizures in the countryside. The government recognized the claims of the Indians in 1953 and distributed land to the farmers.

The democratic government brought genuine social and economic improvement to Bolivia, but it failed to reduce the domination of the military, which seized power once more in 1964. Estenssoro returned to office in 1985 after 20 years marked by a succession of military coups. Most of the regimes were repressive and reactionary, although the pattern was briefly broken by General Juan José Torres, who seized power in 1970. Known for his left-wing sentiments, Torres relied on peasant, worker, and student support and convened a "people's parliament" to represent their views.

In 1972 Torres was deposed by Colonel Hugo Banzer, who remained in office for six years, a record in Bolivia's political history. Banzer attempted to introduce a coherent economic policy but also sold off the country's natural resources, including oil and natural gas, to foreign business interests. Although these measures stimulated economic growth, the rich gained most of the benefits. Another bewildering succession of coups marked the post-Banzer period. As unfavorable international reaction to drug trafficking and human rights violations grew, the United States broke diplomatic relations with Bolivia, forcing elections in 1982.

The new moderate government of Hernan Siles Zuazo appealed to foreign banks and the International Monetary Fund for help. The aid did little, however, to reduce inflation or satisfy worker demands. In the ensuing chaos, Estenssoro emerged once again, at the age of 77, as president. Despite sporadic efforts at reform, Bolivia's history, already witness to nearly 200 changes of government, offered gloomy expectations.

Central America and the Caribbean

Private American businesses, especially the United Fruit Company and sugar, coffee, and tobacco firms, had entered Central America and the Caribbean in the late nineteenth century. The United States maintained a more direct presence in the region since the Spanish-American War. In the wake of its victory over Spain in 1898, the United States declared a protectorate over Cuba and annexed Puerto Rico.

Five years later, when Panamanian rebels revolted against Colombia, which claimed the territory of Panama, the United States supported the rebels and quickly imposed its control over the newly formed republic. Americans then built the Panama Canal on land leased from its new dependency. The strategic impor-

MAP 42.3   MEXICO, CENTRAL AMERICA, AND THE CARIBBEAN

tance of the canal for the United States, together with extensive economic interests, has maintained the U.S. presence in the area ever since.

In September 1977, President Jimmy Carter concluded a treaty with Panama whereby the United States would withdraw its military forces from the Canal Zone and transfer control to the Panamanians by the end of the century. The subsequent administration of Ronald Reagan, however, turned against Panama's dictator, General Manuel Noriega, when he ceased to support efforts to overthrow the Sandinista government in Nicaragua. In December 1989, President George Bush ordered an invasion of Panama that resulted in the seizure of Noriega and the installation of a new government. Anti-U.S. feelings were high in the wake of the widespread devastation caused by the attack.

The Cuban Revolution

Cuba has been one of the most prominent nations in Latin America since 1959, when the country experienced a dramatic political upheaval that challenged America's sway over the Central American region.

Fidel Castro (born 1927), a charismatic leader and brilliant propagandist, united forces opposed to the corrupt dictator Fulgencio Batista, who had ruled the island since 1936. Yet when Castro's guerrilla campaign overthrew Batista in 1959, his goals were unclear. Although he had plans to hold elections, he quickly suspended them. By 1961 he had begun introducing state economic and social controls and declared himself a Marxist-Leninist.

Castro's revolution aimed at a radical transformation of Cuba's social and economic structure. His socialist programs drove much of the middle class—some 750,000 people—from the island, and many opponents who stayed were silenced by means of firing squads or imprisonment. Collective farms replaced the estates once owned by large landowners, and the government nationalized the sugar and tobacco industries. Moreover, significant social and educational reforms improved the lives of Cuba's citizens, and today Cuba's infant mortality and illiteracy rates are the lowest in Latin America. Castro's reforms also gave women equality before the law and open access to education and the professions.

Ernesto "Che" Guevara and Fidel Castro
greet Soviet leader Anastas Mikoyan in 1961.

In many ways Cuba's history embodies the dilemma created by America's dealings with its southern neighbors. Batista's rule collapsed only after the withdrawal of American support in 1958. Yet Castro anticipated that his radical economic and social policies might bring American intervention. He therefore turned to the Soviet Union, which he hoped would serve as a counterweight to the United States. The Soviets proved powerful and willing patrons in return for a base of operations only 90 miles from the coast of Florida.

In April 1961 the United States sponsored a badly organized invasion by Cuban exiles at the Bay of Pigs on the southern coast of Cuba. The United States, reluctant to engage Cuban forces directly, refused air cover at the last moment, and the invaders were routed. The fiasco confirmed Castro's belief that American imperialism was poised to undermine him and encouraged the Soviets to exploit their foothold in Cuba. Weapons, including intercontinental missiles, were deployed on the island, only to be withdrawn in 1962 when an alarmed American government confronted the Soviet Union.

In the 1960s Castro's Cuba served as a center for revolutionary aspirations throughout Latin America. Castro's chief aide in seizing power and organizing the new state had been Ernesto ("Che") Guevara (1928–1967). Guevara now became the principal theorist of guerrilla insurgency as a technique for bringing revolution to the rest of the Americas, personally encouraging rebel forces there and elsewhere. He was killed in Bolivia in October 1967 by U.S.-trained counterinsurgency forces, and Castro pursued a more pragmatic course thereafter.

In the face of an American trade boycott, the stability of the Cuban economy was maintained largely by Soviet aid. In the 1970s Cuba began to involve itself in revolutions beyond Latin America, including those in Angola and Ethiopia. An apparent easing in relations with the United States in 1984 was reversed the following year when a private American-based radio station, Radio Martí, began to transmit anti-Castro propaganda to Cuba. Castro himself has been elected president three times, and in 1986 he proclaimed a new emphasis on women, blacks, and young people and appointed his sister-in-law as the first female member of the party council.

The collapse of the Soviet Union in 1991 removed Castro's patron from the scene, and with the continuing U.S. trade boycott Cuba faced increased shortages and hardship. Despite marginal concessions, however, Castro continued to affirm his brand of socialism and to resist calls for political and economic reform.

Patterns of Violence

Military dictatorships have dominated Central American politics since the turn of the century. In the 1970s elections in Guatemala, Salvador, and Nicaragua were subverted by military intervention. In Guatemala, where half the arable land is owned by 2 percent of the population, each military regime tried to outdo its predecessor in violently repressing popular discontent. The result was some of the bitterest guerrilla warfare in Latin America.

Haiti, which achieved independence from France in 1804 following a slave revolt, has been racked by violence ever since. In 1957 François Duvalier established a police state, which his family maintained for two generations by a combination of brutality and superstition. After Jean-Claude Duvalier succeeded his father, his wife exhausted the country's treasury with extravagant shopping trips to Paris while the people suffered the worst social conditions in the Caribbean. When rioting broke out in 1986, the Duvaliers fled the country, taking millions of dollars with them. American military invention in 1994 restored only a semblance of order under the populist government of Jean-Bertrand Aristide, a former priest. Family rule proved equally unstable in the Dominican Republic, where with American support General Rafael Trujillo maintained a harsh but effective dictatorship from 1930 until his assassination in 1961. His son failed to retain power and, together with his family, fled the island. United States troops occupied the country between April 1965 and September 1966, thwarting the reformist candidacy of Juan Bosch and installing a rightist regime whose successors governed the country. In Salvador, a coffee-producing country in which a tiny oligarchy controls three-fifths of the land, civil war claimed thousands of civilian casualties in the 1980s. A brokered agreement brought peace in the early 1990s, but few promised reforms have materialized.

The Nicaraguan Revolution

If fear of Castro's Cuba had earlier dominated American policy in Central America, the Nicaraguan revolution of 1979 set the tone for the 1980s. Like prerevolutionary Cuba, Nicaragua was ruled harshly for more than 30 years by a corrupt and stubborn dictator under American protection. When Anastasio Somoza García was finally ousted, the new revolutionary government and the United States confronted each other with mutual suspicion.

The ruling revolutionary party, the *Sandinistas* (named for César Augusto Sandino, a guerrilla leader of the late 1920s and early 1930s), created a "national reconstruction government" under the presidency of Daniel Ortega. It improved public health, education, and food production through land reform. Sandinista economic policy contained a mix of capitalist and socialist elements. Nevertheless, much government spending was devoted to fighting the U.S.-sponsored *contra* rebels

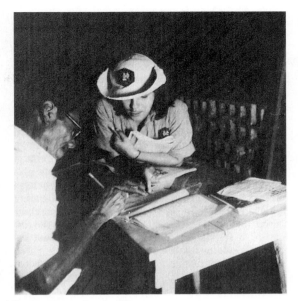

A literacy campaign in Nicaragua.

in a war that claimed over 30,000 lives. Much to the displeasure of Washington, the Ortega regime did not implement Western-style democracy or guarantee a free press. While America provided aid to the *contras,* Nicaragua accepted Cuban, Soviet, and Swedish assistance. Fears of intervention in the region were heightened by the American invasion of the Caribbean island of Grenada in 1983 and the installation of a pro-American government there.

At the beginning of that year, representatives of four Latin American countries—Venezuela, Colombia, Panama, and Mexico—met on the island of Contadora off the coast of Panama to develop a peace plan for Central America. The revelation late in 1986 that arms sales to Iran had secretly been used to fund *contra* forces caused a major scandal in the Reagan administration and undermined America's credibility as an opponent of international terrorism.

The war in Nicaragua ended as a result of peace initiatives from other Central American states and Mexico. In 1987 Oscar Arias Sanchez, president of Costa Rica, proposed a plan for the withdrawal of foreign troops, the disarming of the *contras,* and the restoration of democracy in Nicaragua. The Arias plan, monitored by international observers, resulted in a Sandinista agreement to hold free elections in 1990. The victors were an anti-Sandinista coalition party led by Violeta Barrios de Chamorro, widow of a newspaper editor whose murder in 1978 had sparked the Sandinista revolution.

Daniel Ortega, the outgoing president of Nicaragua, assists Violeta Barrios de Chamorro at her inauguration in April 1990.

Mexico in the Twentieth Century

Although 300 years of Spanish control over Mexico ended in 1821, the modern republic was not inaugurated until a century later. When Porfirio Díaz resigned the presidency and left Mexico in 1911 (see Chapter 33), the liberal opposition united peasants, workers, and intellectuals behind Francisco Madero (1873–1913), supported by bandit revolutionaries such as Pancho Villa and Emiliano Zapata. Madero assumed the presidency but was murdered in a military uprising openly encouraged by the United States' ambassador to Mexico. After a period of misrule, Madero's last successor, who had held power with American backing, was overthrown in 1920. Mexico was now a republic, with a democratic constitution based on universal male suffrage.

Although since 1920 Mexico has had a parliamentary government, in practice the chief political force, the Institutional Revolutionary Party (PRI), dominated the country, winning every election since 1929 and providing all of Mexico's presidents. Virtually every aspect of Mexican life is under PRI control, including political patronage, education, the economy, and cultural activities. Lázaro Cárdenas, who served as president from 1934 to 1940, introduced ambitious plans for the redistribution of land, causing confrontation with the Catholic church, and expropriated foreign-owned oil properties in 1938.

Mexico's population, currently 90 million, has more than doubled since 1960. Initial attempts to improve the lives of its vast and underprivileged peasant population gave way after World War II to a drive to industrialize. The result was the creation of large modern cities and an incipient middle class. Yet there has been little change in the lot of the urban or rural poor, whose numbers continue to swell. By the late 1960s the postwar economic boom had begun to decline, and inflation mounted. Following the killing of some 300 university students during a demonstration in 1968, unrest beset the country. In the 1970s the political leadership did little to arrest the erosion of public confidence, borrowing heavily from foreign investors attracted to Mexico's huge oil reserves, the fourth largest in the world.

With the fall of oil prices in 1981, Mexico's economy collapsed. The currency was drastically devalued, and the prices of electricity and gasoline were increased. In the 1982 elections—which featured the candidacy of Rosaria Ibarra de Piedra, the first woman to run for president in the nation's history—the PRI presidential candidate, Miguel de la Madrid, won 74 percent of the vote, a small victory by Mexican standards. The challenge to PRI control was confirmed by bitterly contested elections in 1988 and 1994, the latter marked by the assassination of the PRI's candidate. As president, the reformer Ernesto Zedillo faced an immediate fiscal crisis resolved only by U.S. assistance.

Mexican society is beset by a wide range of natural and human problems. In 1985 a massive earthquake rocked the capital, Mexico City, leaving thousands dead or homeless. Even with international aid, the damage left irreparable wounds in a city already on the verge of collapse. The plight of Mexico City was, in fact, already one of the country's most serious problems. With more than 17 million people, many living in hovels, and plagued by pollution, it embodies the worst aspects of urbanization, with day-to-day difficulties in energy and public services. Like other Third World urban centers such as Calcutta, Mexico City symbolized the crisis of city life in the late twentieth century.

Mexico's relations with the United States, always strained, deteriorated in the 1970s. Illegal immigration into America, formerly tolerated by both nations, was more tightly checked. Mexican drug trafficking, a national industry in which the PRI was heavily involved, added to these tensions, along with a rash of kidnappings and murders of Americans by Mexican bandits posing as policemen. Rural unrest sparked a rebellion among the poverty-stricken Indian population of the south in 1993.

Mexico negotiated a free trade agreement with the United States and Canada in 1992, but sharp economic reverses caused a plunge in the peso and only American intervention stabilized the economy. Sustainable growth and the elimination of the harsher inequities that pervade Mexican society represent major challenges to one of Latin America's most populous countries.

Society and Culture in Latin America

It is difficult to generalize about so vast and varied a region as Latin America, but certain broad observations applied during the twentieth century. The first is that democratic participation in the political process was the exception rather than the rule. Paradoxically, because most citizens were excluded from an active role in government, they turned to direct political action far more than North Americans or Europeans. The abuses of the secret police in Chile or Guatemala and the massive protests of the "mothers of the disappeared" (missing political prisoners) in Argentina demonstrated how political realities affected the daily lives of Latin Americans in a direct and often violent manner.

The Catholic church played an important, if inconsistent, role in Latin American society. Catholicism was deeply rooted in virtually every country of the region, al-

though its external manifestations were often affected by indigenous Indian traditions and its influence varied from country to country. Hence, whereas the church occupied an important position as a force for national unity in Argentina, Bolivian Catholicism represented only a thin veneer of European culture on an Indian civilization that goes back to pre-Columbian times. In Mexico the church had almost no influence in public affairs. In the 1970s Latin America saw the growth of so-called liberation theology, a philosophy of social activism that condones the use of violence to promote change in extreme circumstances. Generally developed by worker-priests closely involved in social reform in local communities, this philosophy met with a mixed reception from Catholic religious leaders, both in Latin America and in the church hierarchy. It was condemned by Pope John Paul II, most notably in his 1987 visit to Chile and Argentina.

The reactions of individual national clergy were determined in part by local conditions. Whereas the archbishop of Salvador played an important part in negotiations there before his assassination in 1979, the confiscation of church property by Nicaragua's Sandinista regime generated official Catholic protests. Yet even though Catholic influence varied throughout Latin America, the phenomenon of secularization that has swept Europe and North America has yet to make serious inroads there.

A third characteristic common to many Latin American countries has been the vitality and persistence of their popular cultures. With the possible exception of Mexico, more directly influenced by its powerful northern neighbor, Latin America shows less cultural conformity than Europe, where American influence has produced a degree of uniformity in popular music, television entertainment, and fast food. The folk songs and dances of Brazil's Carnival, the *reggae* music of Jamaica, and the traditional pottery and weaving of Peru, are all manifestations of living and thriving cultural traditions.

Latin American achievements in the arts have also maintained a sense of national character. The Argentinian novelist Jorge Luis Borges (1899–1986) captured the blend of Spanish and Indian mysticism that pervades the life of his country while constructing parables of universal significance. Pablo Neruda (1904–1973), the Chilean writer and diplomat, is probably Latin America's best-known poet and one of four of the region's writers to win the Nobel Prize for literature—the others being his compatriot Gabriela Mistral, the Guatemalan novelist Miguel Angel Asturias, and the Colombian novelist Gabriel García Márquez (born 1928). If there is a feature

Liberation Theology

Liberation theology is the name given to the gospel of social reform preached by some Catholic priests and bishops in Latin America since the 1960s. The church hierarchy has continued to insist on sharply distinguishing between pastoral duty and impermissible activism. The following excerpts indicate the basis of liberation theology as defined by a Peruvian priest, Gustavo Gutierrez, and the far more cautionary attitudes of popes Paul VI and John Paul II. First, Gustavo Gutierrez:

Love for one's neighbor is an essential component of Christian existence. But as long as I consider as my neighbor the man "near me," the one I meet on *my* way, the one who comes to me seeking aid ("Who is *my* neighbor?"), my world remains the same. All individual gestures of aid, all superficial reform of society is a love that stays comfortably at home ("If they love those who love them, what reward will they have?"). If, on the other hand, I consider my neighbor as the man in *whose* path I deliberately place myself, the man "distant" from me, the one whom I approach ("Which of these three was neighbor *to this man*?"), if I make myself the neighbor of the man I seek out in streets and squares, in factories and marginal *barrios,* in the fields and the mines, my world changes.

That is what happens when an authentic and effective "option for the poor" is made, because for the Gospel, the poor man is the neighbor *par excellence.* This option is the axle on which turns a new way of being a man and being a Christian in Latin America. But the "poor" do not exist as an act of destiny; their existence is not politically neutral or ethically innocent. The poor are a by-product of the system in which we live and for which we are responsible. The poor are marginalized in our social cultural world. They are the oppressed, the exploited, the workers cheated of the fruits of their work, stripped of their being as men. The poverty of the poor is not therefore an appeal for generous action, but a demand for the construction of a different social order.

Pope Paul VI:

We must not ignore the fact that many, even generous Christians who are sensitive to the dramatic questions involved in the problem of liberation, in this wish to commit the church to the liberation effort are frequently tempted to reduce its mission to the dimensions of a simply temporal project. They would reduce its aims to a human-centered goal; the salvation of which it is the messenger would be reduced to material well-being. Its activity, forgetful of all spiritual and religious preoccupation, would become initiatives of the political or social order. But if this were so, the church would lose its fundamental meaning. Its message of liberation would no longer have any originality and would easily be open to monopolization and manipulation by ideological systems and political parties. It would have no more authority to proclaim freedom as in the name of God.

Pope John Paul II:

The church does not have technical solutions to offer for the problem of underdevelopment as such, as Pope Paul VI already affirmed. . . .

The church's social doctrine is not a "third way" between liberal capitalism and Marxist collectivism, nor even a possible alternative to other solutions less radically opposed to one another; rather, it constitutes a category of its own. Nor is it an ideology, but rather the accurate formulation of the results of a careful reflection on the complex realities of human existence, in society

Liberation Theology (continued)

and in the international order, in the light of faith and of the church's tradition. Its main aim is to interpret these realities, determining their conformity with or divergence from the lines of the gospel teaching on human nature and the human vocation, a vocation at once earthly and transcendent; its aim is thus to guide Christian behavior. It therefore belongs to the field, not of ideology, but of theology.

Sources: Gustavo Gutierrez, "Liberty, Theology, and Proclamation," in *Liberation Theology: A Documentary History,* ed. Alfred T. Hennelly, S.J. (Maryknoll, N.Y.: Orbis Books); Pope Paul VI, "On Evangelization in the Modern World," in *The Pope and Revolution: John Paul II Confronts Liberation Theology,* ed. Quentin L. Quade (Washington, D.C.: Ethics and Public Policy Center), p. 187; Pope John Paul II, "On Social Concern," ibid., pp. 521, 522.

common to the work of these writers, it is the use of fantasy and magic that provides an escape from reality: Marquez' novel *One Hundred Years of Solitude* describes life in an imaginary town in a remote region of Colombia, where extraordinary events are the order of the day.

Mexico has produced a number of major painters, including Diego Rivera (1886–1957), whose communist sympathies influenced much of his work. Rivera's murals in Rockefeller Center, New York City, were removed after fierce controversy. Among his associates was José Clemente Orozco (1883–1949), famous for the bold realism of his frescoes. By contrast, Rufino Tamayo (1899–1991) created a more cosmopolitan style that invokes a magical world comparable in painting to that of Borges' and Marquez' novels. On the whole, realistic depictions of the lives of workers and peasants have dominated Latin American painting, as in the moving frescoes of Rivera and the Brazilian Cândido Portinari (1903–1962), whose work can be seen at the United Nations building in New York.

Latin American composers have frequently been inspired by the folk music of their homelands. The Brazilian musician Heitor Villa-Lobos (1887–1959) wrote a series of works titled *Bachianas Brasileiras,* in which he treated Brazilian folk motifs in a style reminiscent of Johann Sebastian Bach. Among the works of the Mexican Carlos Chávez (1899–1978), who founded the Mexican Symphony Orchestra, is the *Sinfonia India,* which uses folk motifs to evoke the country's Amerindian past. The generally underdeveloped state of musical conservatories in Latin America has forced most performing artists, including the famous Chilean pianist Claudio Arrau

(1904–1991), to study abroad. Yet many capital cities in the region have a thriving operatic tradition that goes back to the nineteenth century. The most famous and most beautiful opera house in South America is the Teatro Colón in Buenos Aires, where performances meet international standards.

The best film production unit in Latin America is the Cuban Film Institute, where young directors and performers are encouraged to develop their skills at government expense. Elsewhere, filmmakers have used their works to document their country's history. The Argentinian film *The Official Story,* which describes events in Argentina after the fall of the military dictatorship in 1983, won an Academy Award as the best foreign film of 1985.

The thriving arts and popular culture of Latin America represent both a reminder of and an escape from the grim realities of everyday life. Unlike much of the rest of the world, the twentieth century has seen little change in age-old social patterns in the region anywhere but in Cuba and Nicaragua. Apart from Mexico, and to a lesser extent Argentina and Brazil, the population remains split into the wealthy few and the many poor, with little sign of a developing middle class. For example, in Brazil, Colombia, and Peru half or more of the households live in absolute poverty, defined as the inability to purchase the barest necessities for subsistence. Yet Latin America has the fastest-growing population in the world, increasing about 3 percent each year. In these same countries approximately one out of five adults is illiterate, and infant mortality remains high. Despite huge potential resources, most of the region is still

LATIN AMERICA SINCE 1945

South America	Mexico and Central America
Perón administration in Argentina (1946–1955)	
	Beginning of police state in Haiti (1957)
	Castro overthrows Batista in Cuba (1959)
	Bay of Pigs invasion (1961)
Military rule in Brazil (1964–1979)	
Allende administration in Chile (1970–1973); Pinochet dictatorship (1973–1989)	
Military rule in Argentina (1976–1983)	Panama Canal Treaty (1977)
	Sandinista rule in Nicaragua (1979–1990)
Falklands War (1982)	
	Mexico City earthquake (1985)
	Haitian revolution (1986)
	U.S. invasion of Panama (1989)
	Violeta Chamorro elected president of Nicaragua (1990)
	North American Free Trade Agreement (Canada, U.S., Mexico) (1993)

predominantly agricultural. Industrial production is unequally distributed: as late as 1970 three nations—Argentina, Brazil, and Mexico—accounted for 80 percent of all industrial production in Latin America, and a third of that was confined to the cities of Buenos Aires, São Paulo, and Mexico City.

Women and the Culture of Machismo

Women in Central and South American society have only recently begun to regain the position they held in most communities before the Spanish conquest. Among the Aztecs, for example, women came close to legal equality with men. They could possess property, enter into contracts, testify before tribunals, seek divorce, and remarry freely. At the age of 50 they were accorded full equality and enjoyed equal status with men as elders.

Under the colonial regime, women lost most of their rights. The law presumed them to be mentally inferior, and the style of male bravado and presumption known as *machismo* that produced such laws became deeply ingrained in the culture. Yet in colonial times women were allowed to own property and to sign for mortgages in their own names. Independence brought little but lip service to the idea of greater equality for Latin American women. Not until the Mexican revolution in the early twentieth century was legal equality recognized. Argentina, Uruguay, and Chile followed suit in the 1920s and 1930s. Yet women in Argentina did not get the vote until 1947 and in Mexico until 1953; only with the passage of a female suffrage law in Paraguay in 1961 did all women in the Americas win the right to vote.

Despite progress, the goal of full equality remains elusive. Men are still recognized as head of the household in many Latin American countries, with the legal right to choose the place of domicile, direct the education of children, administer family property, and retain custody in case of divorce. *Machismo* enforces a double standard of sexual morality, with men permitted and even encouraged to form extramarital liaisons as proof of their virility. The result is a very high incidence of rape and illegitimacy, particularly marked in Brazil.

As elsewhere, the position of women is greatly affected by the variables of class, status, and income, by residence in town or country, and by skin color. The women of the elite are in many respects indistinguishable from their counterparts in the industrial West; for those trapped in rural poverty or urban squalor, the still-halting steps toward equality have had little effect. Eva and Isabel Perón notwithstanding, until recent years few women have played a visible part in public life. Beginning in the 1970s, however, more and more women have held appointed or elected positions in government. In Venezuela and Mexico women have served in presidential cabinets, and Violeta Chamorro became president of Nicaragua in 1990.

Differences in education and training have generally relegated women to lower-paying jobs in the workforce, and men usually displace women as a result of

A Latin American Feminist Speaks Out

Magaly Pineda, a prominent feminist in the Dominican Republic, offers her perspective in 1994 on the progress of women in Latin America.

Although the economists insist that the decade of the '80s was a time of loss for Latin America, I believe that for women, especially Latin American women, it was a time of great gain. . . . In almost all our countries women have made extraordinary strides in education. And I think this has been important in terms of our recognizing our own dependency, recognizing the need to fight for our rights, to fight for equality. Women have also moved massively into the labor force during this period of time. And though this hasn't always signaled the kind of independence we're looking for, or the political involvement we might like, I think it's introduced a different sort of logic into women's way of thinking. It's changed the nature of our relationships.

The immense growth of our women's movements has also been important. It's phenomenal how, from the tip of Chile to a tiny island in the Caribbean . . . we see women rising up. Indigenous women are beginning to make known their demands, like the *mestizas* (mixed bloods) have made ours known, and the professional women. We're seeing movement after movement with women in the forefront. And we've moved from a time of denunciation to a time of action— without giving up denunciation because there's certainly a lot to denounce. . . .

The feminist movements in Latin America possess an originality, a creativity, and a force that allow them to speak with authority in the struggle with the North. We've acquired a confidence in ourselves, so that in spite of the terrible disasters, in spite of the corruption of our governments, in spite of our material situation, the debt, the natural disasters we've suffered . . . in spite of all that constitutes our lives and would seem to rob us of our hope, we women have managed to feel confident.

Source: Margaret Randall, ed., *Our Voices, Our Lives: Stories of Women from Central America and the Caribbean* (Monroe, Maine: Common Courage Press, 1995), pp. 117–118.

technological and unemployment cycles. Thus although women have been part of agricultural labor in Latin America for centuries, mechanization has made it difficult for them to obtain work in that sector. Similarly, ever-larger numbers of Latin American women have moved into factory work, but they are generally paid less than men and hold less skilled jobs. Nevertheless, some exceptions hold out the promise of future change. In Brazil, for example, where the proportion of economically active women is lower than that of men, more women actually hold professional positions. Moreover, the number of working women doubled in the decade after 1970.

Experience has shown that when organized, women can exert a powerful force for change, as in the case of the Argentinian mothers of the disappeared. More re-vealing still, it has been estimated that women constituted as much as a third of the Sandinista People's Army in Nicaragua. In Cuba legislation passed in 1976 actually provided a legal basis for the sharing of housework and child care. Despite such transformation, however, the pattern of custom and prejudice dies slowly, and *machismo* continues to exert a powerful influence on male attitudes toward women.

SUMMARY

Chief among the myriad problems facing the global community as the second half of the twentieth century draws to a close is the need to secure economic, social, and political well-being for the bulk of the world's inhabitants—an issue symbolized by the status of Africa and Latin America.

Both regions have undergone significant political change since the end of World War II as their peoples struggled against colonialism and continue to work to free themselves from dependence on the more advanced industrialized states. Yet the political systems under which many African and Latin American nations operate have been fraught with instability and a marked tendency toward authoritarianism. In part this political experience has been the result of the massive problems of development that each faces. The economic potential of the regions is vast, but immediate financial resources are limited. In most cases the small, privileged elites that control much of the wealth of these countries have neither directed resources toward the people nor been willing to extend democracy to them. In many areas racial and ethnic tensions contribute to political and social instability. Inefficiency, corruption, and lack of infrastructure have combined to retard development, and despite productive agricultural soils, many states cannot feed their rapidly growing populations. Africa and Latin America are burdened with the fastest-growing populations in the world, high illiteracy, daunting health problems, and widespread poverty. Only far-reaching changes in the social and political structures of these regions can, in the long run, resolve such dilemmas.

Though these and other challenges appear at times insurmountable, the future holds substantial promise. Africa and Latin America possess not only extensive natural resources and rich cultural heritages but also populations that have repeatedly proved their creativity and resilience.

NOTES

1. G. M. Carter and P. O'Meara, eds., *African Independence: The First Twenty-five Years* (Bloomington: Indiana University Press, 1985), p. 4.
2. J. D. Hargreaves, *Decolonization in Africa* (New York: Longman, 1988), p. 203.
3. J. Hayward, *South Africa Since 1948* (New York: Bookwright Press, 1989), p. 14.
4. Robin Hallett, *Africa Since 1875: A Modern History* (Ann Arbor: University of Michigan Press, 1974), p. 197.

SUGGESTIONS FOR FURTHER READING

Africa

Amin, S. *Neo-colonialism in West Africa.* New York: Monthly Review Press, 1973.

Beinart, W. *Twentieth-Century South Africa.* New York: Oxford University Press, 1994.

Bretton, H. *The Rise and Fall of Kwame Nkrumah: A Study of Personal Rule in Africa.* New York: Praeger, 1966.

Carter, G. M., and O'Meara, P., eds. *African Independence: The First Twenty-five Years.* Bloomington: Indiana University Press, 1985.

Davidson, B. *Modern Africa: A Social and Political History,* 3rd ed. London: Longman, 1994.

Decalo, S. *Coups and Army Rule in Africa,* 2nd ed. New Haven, Conn.: Yale University Press, 1990.

Gifford, P., and Louis, W. R., eds. *The Transfer of Power in Africa: Decolonization, 1940–1960.* New Haven, Conn.: Yale University Press, 1982.

Gordon, D. F. *Decolonization and the State in Kenya.* Boulder, Colo.: Westview Press, 1986.

Hargreaves, J. D. *Decolonization in Africa.* New York: Longman, 1988.

Horne, A. *A Savage War of Peace: Algeria, 1954–1962.* Harmondsworth, Eng.: Penguin Books, 1985.

Jackson, R. H., and Rosberg, C. G. *Personal Rule in Black Africa.* Berkeley: University of California Press, 1982.

Leys, C. *Underdevelopment in Kenya: The Political Economy of Neocolonialism.* Berkeley: University of California Press, 1974.

Mandela, N. *Long Walk to Freedom: The Autobiography of Nelson Mandela.* Boston: Little Brown, 1994.

Meredith, M. *The First Dance of Freedom: Black Africa in the Postwar Era.* London: Abacus, 1984.

Murray-Brown, J. *Kenyatta.* New York: Dutton, 1973.

Ottaway, M., and Ottaway, D. *Ethiopia: Empire in Revolution.* New York: Africana Publications, 1978.

Verrier, A. *The Road to Zimbabwe.* London: Cape, 1986.

Welch, C. E. *Dream of Unity: Pan-Africanism and Political Unification in West Africa.* Ithaca, N.Y.: Cornell University Press, 1966.

Young, C. *Ideology and Development in Africa.* New Haven, Conn.: Yale University Press, 1982.

———. *Politics in the Congo: Decolonization and Independence.* Princeton, N.J.: Princeton University Press, 1965.

Latin America

Aguilar Camin, H., and Meyer, L. *In the Shadow of the Mexican Revolution: Contemporary Mexican History, 1910–1989,* trans. L. A. Fierro. Austin: University of Texas Press, 1993.

Bergmann, E., et al. *Women, Culture, and Politics in Latin America.* Berkeley: University of California Press, 1990.

Blasier, C. *The Hovering Giant: U.S. Responses to Revolutionary Change in Latin America.* Pittsburgh: University of Pittsburgh Press, 1985.

Burns, E. B. *A History of Brazil,* 3rd ed. New York: Columbia University Press, 1993.

———. *Latin America: A Concise Interpretive History,* 4th ed. Englewood Cliffs, N.J.: Prentice-Hall, 1986.

Calvert, P., and Calvert, S. *Latin America in the Twentieth Century.* New York: St. Martin's Press, 1990.

Cottam, M. L. *Images and Intervention: U.S. Policies in Latin America.* Pittsburgh: University of Pittsburgh Press, 1994.

Grugel, J. *Politics and Development in the Caribbean Basin: Central America and the Caribbean in the New World Order.* Bloomington: Indiana University Press, 1995.

Landau, S. *The Guerilla Wars of Latin America: Nicaragua, El Salvador, and Guatemala.* New York: St. Martin's Press, 1993.

Lewis, P. H. *The Crisis of Argentine Capitalism.* Chapel Hill: University of North Carolina Press, 1990.

Meyer, M. C., and Sherman, W. L. *The Course of Mexican History.* New York: Oxford University Press, 1979.

Paterson, T. G. *Contesting Castro: The U.S. and the Triumph of the Cuban Revolution.* New York: Oxford University Press, 1994.

Rock, D. *Argentina, 1516–1982.* Berkeley: University of California Press, 1985.

Skidmore, T. E., and Smith, Peter H. *Modern Latin America,* 3rd ed. New York: Oxford University Press, 1992.

Skidmore, T. L. *The Politics of Military Rule in Brazil, 1964–1985.* New York: Oxford University Press, 1988.

Spooner, M. H. *Soldiers in a Narrow Land: The Pinochet Regime in Chile.* Berkeley: University of California Press, 1993.

Thomas, H. *The Cuban Revolution.* New York: Harper & Row, 1977.

GLOBAL ESSAY

Maps and Their Makers (II)

The attempt to map the environment began with the earliest human societies. By the middle of the first millennium B.C., the first world map had been produced in Babylonia. Maps of considerable sophistication were drawn in the ancient West and China, but not until the discovery of the Americas and of the Pacific by Columbus and his successors in the late fifteenth and sixteenth centuries were the true dimensions of the earth known with any accuracy.

The discovery of the New World coincided with the development of movable type in the West. Printed maps circulated rapidly, facilitating trade and exploration. In 1570 Abraham Ortelius, a Flemish contemporary of Gerardus Mercator, published his *Theater of the World,* a collection of 70 maps covering the entire globe and incorporating the latest discoveries. It became a traveler's bible, going through 40 editions; a French reader enthused that it was the greatest work in the world after the Holy Scriptures.

Globes came into fashion too, and as Aristophanes had unfolded a map of the world on the ancient Greek stage, so William Shakespeare referred to the first English globe in *The Comedy of Errors.* Shakespeare remarked that "all the world's a stage," and it was no accident that the most important theater of his time was called the Globe. The European imagination of the late sixteenth century was as fascinated with the idea of a knowable world as it was soon to be with its conquest.

The discovery of a new earth stimulated speculation about a new heaven as well. In 1595 the great Mercator's final work was published, called *Atlas*—the first collection of maps to bear this title—and subtitled *Cosmographical Meditations upon the Creation of the Universe, and the Universe as Created.* As this subtitle made clear, Mercator envisioned the mapping of the earth as only a first step toward a new understanding of the cosmos. Fourteen years later, in 1609, Galileo Galilei trained his telescope on the heavens and saw the four largest moons of Jupiter, the first new objects, apart from comets, to be observed in the heavens in thousands of years.

The discovery of these new celestial objects had a very different import from Columbus' discovery of the New World. Although pre-Columbian maps, based on Ptolemy, had underestimated the size of the globe, it was known and accepted that there were places on it where no humans lived and perhaps none had ever gone. The Ptolemaic heavens, however, for all their greater size, were believed to be fully mapped; nor had the Copernican system, in transposing the earth and the sun, enlarged them. Galileo's four moons changed all that. The

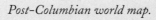

Post–Columbian world map.

cosmos had begun to be explored; as much might be hidden as was known.

If the real exploration of the heavens had to await the development of radio astronomy in the twentieth century, the telescopes of the seventeenth were able to bring at least one celestial body within reach of the cartographers: the moon. Although only one side of it was visible from earth, some 48 craters had been located and named (mostly after ancient philosophers and modern scientists), as well as 8 so-called seas. Celestial globes, depicting the sun, the earth, the planets, and the stars, became almost as popular as terrestrial ones. Such representations suggested an attempt to domesticate the cosmos. Europeans began to speculate whether beings like themselves might not inhabit other celestial bodies, and in 1639 the Italian friar Thomas Campanella published one of the earliest works of science fiction, *The City of the Sun*. With the publication of Sir Isaac Newton's *Mathematical Principles of Natural Philosophy* in 1687 (see Chapter 25), the distinction between celestial and terrestrial mechanics that had been maintained since the time of Aristotle collapsed, and it was soon generally accepted that the same physical laws governed both the earth and the heavens.

At the same time, cartography became a weapon in the struggle for commercial advantage and empire. As the imperial initiative passed in the seventeenth and eighteenth centuries from Iberia to England and France, both nations realized the crucial importance of reliable maps. Under Louis XIV mapmaking became a state enterprise. Astronomers were sent to Egypt, South America, and the West Indies to make the celestial observations essential for accurate mapping. The explorer La Salle was commissioned to survey the newly established colony of New France in North America, and a team under Jean-Dominique Cassini, director of the Royal Observatory, set out to produce a true map of France itself. Using the moons of Jupiter as a point of reference for sighting latitude, they discovered that previous maps had placed the port of Brest too far west, in what was actually open sea, and Marseilles too far south. When Louis XIV was shown these results, he exclaimed, "Your work has cost me a good part of my state!"

What France itself lost, however, its colonies regained in Guillaume Delisle's maps of Canada (1703) and Louisiana (1718), which extended French claims in the New World at the expense of England's. The British were not slow to respond, and a veritable war of maps ensued in fixing the boundaries of Nova Scotia, ceded by the French at the end of the War of the Austrian Succession (1748), with Britain ironically citing French maps to

substantiate its claims to more of the coastline with its rich fisheries and the French citing British maps to limit them.

Despite these conflicts, however, the two nations were able to cooperate occasionally in a common scientific interest. In the 1730s French expeditions to Lapland and Peru confirmed Newton's hypothesis that the earth was not a perfect sphere but, because of its variable motion, a prolate one, bulging at the equator and flattened at the poles. This was important to navigation, because it meant that degrees of latitude and longitude were not uniform but lengthened as they approached the equator and shortened as they receded. Fifty years later a joint team of British and French geographers measured the precise distance between Greenwich, England, and Paris, using French techniques of triangulation and a new British instrument, the theodolite, a 200-pound device consisting of telescopes, reflectors, and angle registers. One hundred years later, in 1884, an international conference established Greenwich as the prime meridian, the point of 0 degrees of longitude from which all divisions of east and west would thenceforth be measured. Among other things, this made it possible to divide the earth into its present 24 time zones, each 15 degrees of longitude apart. Greenwich thus became, as Babylon, Jerusalem, and Ch'ang An had once been, the center of the earth.

Magellan had crossed the Pacific, but for the next 250 years little was reliably known about its western expanses. It found its geographer at last, however, in James Cook (1728–1779), the son of a Yorkshire laborer who worked himself up to a naval commission, driven by a passion for discovery that, as he confessed, "leads me not only farther than any man has been before me, but as far as I think it possible for man to go." Cook's three voyages set out in search of those will-o'-the-wisps of cartographers, a navigable shortcut to Asia through the Americas called the Northwest Passage and a great southern continent called Terra Australis, hypothesized by the ancient Greeks, popularized by Marco Polo, and still a standard feature of eighteenth-century maps. Cook found neither, but he did map thousands of miles of northwestern American coastline and virtually every island in the Pacific, and he did go farther than any man had been, sailing to within a few hundred miles of both the north pole and Antarctica.

Cook's voyages put a third of the world on the map, although it remained for others to complete his work. The Norwegian Roald Amundsen (1872–1928) finally traversed the chain of bays, straits, and sounds across northern Canada to the Beaufort Sea in 1903–1906.

Antarctica, the true southern continent, was first sighted in 1820; the name Australia was given to the great landmass that the British explorer Matthew Flinders was the first to realize in 1801 was not an archipelago but a continent in its own right. Cook himself was tragically murdered in Hawaii, another of his discoveries, while preparing to make a fourth voyage.

The efforts of Cook, Flinders, and two other Englishmen, George Vancouver and Francis Beaufort, had given a tolerably good idea of the coastal contours of the six habitable continents by the mid-nineteenth century. It remained to map the equally challenging interiors of the Americas, Africa, and central Asia.

One of the first native surveyors of North America was George Washington, who as a young man charted the region between the Potomac River and Lake Erie and, failing to persuade Congress of the urgency of a full geographic survey of the young American republic, left his countrymen at his death a full set of surveying instruments, including parallel rules, compasses, and a theodolite. The acquisition of the Louisiana Territory from France in 1803, however, provided the needed incentive. No one knew exactly what the country had bought. Some people speculated that the Missouri and Columbia rivers might provide a passage to the Pacific. Others imagined the West, as the Greeks had once imagined Terra Australis, as a land of milk and honey. The actual barrier of the Rocky Mountains was barely guessed at.

In 1804 the government dispatched a party of 45 men under Meriwether Lewis and William Clark that two years later, guided by Indian maps, reached the Pacific, laying claim to the western territories beyond Louisiana. They were followed by settlers, adventurers, and, after 1838, the systematic surveys of the Army Corps of Topographical Engineers. In the 1870s John Wesley Powell rafted down the Colorado River, mapping much of the plateau and desert west, and in 1879 the United States Geological Survey was instituted. Its work continues today.

The British mapped India rapidly after its final conquest in 1818, proceeding northward to the Himalayas, where a Bengali clerk surmised that the mountain known as Peak XV and called in Tibetan Chomolungma, or "Goddess Mother of the World," was the tallest in the world. The British renamed it after an Englishman, George Everest. Similarly, the mapping of Africa awaited its intensive colonization after 1870. In contrast, the Jesuits who reached China and Japan in the sixteenth century found an ancient and sophisticated cartographic tradition in both countries. When Matteo Ricci presented a world map to the Chinese emperor in 1602, he tactfully placed China in the center. The Italian Jesuit Martino Martini published the first European atlas of China in 1655, based on Chinese sources. But the Chinese, with their proud isolation, were slow to adopt Western mapping techniques or to accept the results of Western discoveries. The consequence was to place them at a considerable disadvantage in dealing with European imperialism in the nineteenth century.

While the true dimensions and contours of the earth were slowly yielding to exploration and measurement, a similar process was taking place with regard to the heavens. One of the stumbling blocks to the acceptance of the Copernican theory in the seventeenth century was that it suggested a far greater distance to the fixed stars than that of Ptolemy. By the latter part of the century, however, Copernicus had won the day, and French astronomers had calculated the distance between the earth and the sun with better than 90 percent accuracy.

A better appreciation of the scale of the cosmos, however, awaited one of the most important conceptual breakthroughs in history: the realization that the sun itself was a star. Only by means of this could even a rudimentary notion of the immensity of interstellar space be achieved. If any single individual may be credited with it, it was perhaps the martyred Giordano Bruno, who had argued—at the cost of his life—for the idea of an infinity of worlds and hence of an infinite space. A century later the great Dutch astronomer and mathematician Christian Huygens (1629–1695), hypothesizing that the star Sirius was a body as bright as the sun, calculated its distance as 27,664 times that of the earth from the sun. Sirius was in reality nearly 20 times farther away, but Huygens' estimate was at least a beginning. William Herschel

A sketch of Herschel's 20-inch telescope. Later the astronomer built a giant reflecting telescope with funds provided by Britain's King George III.

(1738–1822) took a quantum leap by suggesting that the universe was a sea composed of great galactic islands, of which the sun's island, the Milky Way, was but one. Since Herschel had calculated the equatorial plane of the Milky Way at 7,000 light-years and since the distance between galaxies must necessarily be far larger than their internal dimensions, he was faced with a universe that was, if not infinite, then perhaps ultimately incalculable.

Herschel was the first to realize that the light from the stars he gazed at had traveled so far—for millions of years, he thought—that the bodies which had emitted them might no longer exist. At the same time, his slightly older contemporary James Hutton (c. 1726–1797) was suggesting, on the basis of his observation of geologic strata, that the earth itself was not (as had been thought only a century before) only a few thousand years old but many millions. The universe was receding in time as it was expanding in space.

These twin conceptions may have led to a fresh attempt to humanize space by populating it with intelligent life. In 1877 the Italian astronomer Giovanni Schiaparelli observed a network of fine symmetrical lines on the surface of Mars. An American, Percival Lowell, argued that these were elaborate canals built by a race of technologically advanced beings. This theory had wide credence in scientific circles and entered popular culture as well; in 1938 millions of Americans were panicked by a radio hoax that announced that Martians had landed in New Jersey. Not until the *Mariner 9* space probe orbited Mars in 1971 and the unmanned *Viking* spacecraft landed on the planet in 1976 were these fantasies laid to rest.

If the period from Columbus' discoveries and Copernican astronomy to Newtonian physics had seen an enormous advance in human knowledge of the earth and the heavens, and that from Newtonian to Einsteinian physics a similar one, the twentieth century marked the beginning of an era of unprecedented exploration and discovery. In 1909 Robert Peary reached the north pole, and in 1911 Roald Amundsen arrived at the south pole. Aerial photography of the Antarctic began in 1928, but not until the postwar period, particularly as a result of the International Geophysical Year of 1957–1958 and the U.S. Geologic Survey of 1961–1962, did the continent's true outlines begin to emerge.

At the same time, the oceans and their depths were at last surveyed. Magellan, having probed the depth of the Pacific to about 2,300 feet in 1521, pronounced it immeasurable, and many sailors indeed believed the seas to be bottomless. Not until 1856 was the Pacific's depth roughly ascertained (using tidal wave measurements), and only in the 1950s was the first map of the ocean floors produced. It revealed a planet beneath the planet, with mountain ranges greater than the Himalayas, chasms deeper than the Grand Canyon, and plains broader than the Russian steppe.

The discovery of the ocean's great topographic diversity, particularly of the earth's largest single feature, the Midocean Ridge in the Atlantic, led to the realization that the earth was dynamic and the continents themselves in motion. A theory of "continental drift" had been proposed 50 years earlier, to wide ridicule, by the German meteorologist Alfred Wegener. As the discovery of deep space had opened up the geographic dimension of time—as Herschel and his successors had realized that the image of the heavens was a record of past events—so the present generation of cartographers has begun to work backward to reconfigure the continents of past geologic ages. As Wegener had hypothesized, there may have been a single landmass or supercontinent, Pangaea, from which the present seven continents have emerged over the past 200 million years. Such projections may ultimately read forward too, enabling us literally to ascertain the shape of things to come.

At the beginning of the twentieth century the size of the universe was still estimated at no more than 10,000 light-years, and the existence of other galaxies was still an unproven hypothesis. The picture was rapidly transformed by the development of powerful new telescopes, the analysis of light spectra, and the discovery of stars whose variable luminosity enabled astronomers to use

Kingdoms of space: the great spiral galaxy Andromeda, known as M 31, is similar to our own Milky Way in shape but larger in size, with a diameter of some 180,000 light-years. About 4 billion galaxies, each consisting of billions of stars, lie within reach of modern telescopes.

them as cosmic yardsticks, like beacons at sea. By 1930 Edwin Hubble (1889–1953) had demonstrated not only that other galaxies existed but also that they were receding at a velocity proportional to their distance from our own. Hubble's law, as this discovery was called, suggested both that cosmic magnitudes were far greater than had been hitherto supposed and that those magnitudes were indefinitely expanding. Estimates of the present size of the universe have been extended continuously since then. Hubble calculated the edge of the universe as 500 million light-years away, but by midcentury that estimate had doubled, and with the introduction of radio telescopes after World War II and the consequent discovery of quasars (quasi-stellar discrete radio sources), it was soon revised tenfold upward again. In the farthest reaches of space, stars may be beaming their light toward us while simultaneously receding from us at a speed nearly equal to that of light itself, and it appears certain that light has reached the earth that was propagated before our planet existed.

It has been only some thousands of years since humans first attempted to mark the distance between here and there on stone, skin, and sand, but our maps have now led us billions of years back in time and billions of light-years outward in space. As astronomers and geologists pursue their visions, the variety, utility, complexity, and sophistication of the mapmakers' art continues to increase. Maps are now indispensable for such diverse projects as weather prediction, flood control, agricultural and urban planning, mining, and—a sad commentary on the human adventure—arms control. At the same time, satellite photography, electronic data processing, and computer simulation have greatly increased the range and precision of mapping. The hand-drawn map, in use for scientific purposes until only a few years ago, may soon go the way of the hand-lettered book. Yet the caution of a nineteenth-century British surveyor remains valid: "All observations are liable to error; no telescope is perfect; no leveling instrument is entirely trustworthy; no instrumental gradations are exact; no observer is infallible."

SUGGESTIONS FOR FURTHER READING

Bagrow, L. *A History of Cartography.* London: Watts, 1964.

Bricker, C., and Tooley, R. V. *A History of Cartography: 2500 Years of Maps and Mapmakers.* London: Thames & Hudson, 1969.

Brown, L. A. *The Story of Maps.* Boston: Little, Brown, 1980.

Harley, J. B., and Woodward, D., eds. *The History of Cartography.* Chicago: University of Chicago Press, 1987—.

Kopal, Z. *Widening Horizons: Man's Quest to Understand the Structure of the Universe.* New York: Taplinger, 1970.

Schlee, S. *The Edge of an Unfamiliar World: A History of Oceanography.* New York: Dutton, 1973.

Sullivan, W. *Continents in Motion.* New York: McGraw-Hill, 1974.

Thrower, N. J. W. *Maps and Man.* Englewood Cliffs, N.J.: Prentice-Hall, 1972.

Wilford, J. N. *The Mapmakers.* New York: Knopf, 1981.

CHAPTER 43

The Contemporary Age

Apollo 11 liftoff, July 16, 1969. Aboard the spacecraft were Neil Armstrong, Michael Collins, and Edwin Aldrin. Apollo 11 is the United States' first lunar landing mission.

For the first 20 years of the postwar era, the two superpowers had been locked in a Cold War struggle for global hegemony. Yet far-reaching changes in both societies, along with the recognition of the larger common peril of nuclear disaster, brought the superpowers into a new, more optimistic age of understanding and cooperation.

But as the superpower rivalry unfolded, other, more subtle forces had begun to emerge that offered less powerful countries opportunities to exercise leadership. Movements for nonalignment and for the creation of a united Europe provided alternative strategies for a new international order, while regional and resource-based economic organizations began to exercise a growing influence in world affairs.

The economic reconstruction of Europe restored political stability in the West and created a mass consumer society characterized by unprecedented prosperity and social justice. In the East, almost half a century of repression ended in the late 1980s as the Soviet Union underwent a profound domestic transformation and the peoples of eastern Europe overthrew their own Communist regimes. In 1991 Communist control there collapsed, followed by the dissolution of the Soviet Union itself.

Coexistence and Détente

The turbulent Kennedy-Khrushchev era, climaxed by the dramatic confrontation over Cuba, came to an end in 1963. Kennedy was assassinated in Dallas, Texas, on November 22 of that year. The following summer, while Khrushchev was vacationing in the Crimea, the Communist party's Central Committee stripped him of his power, charging him with a host of errors that included the Cuban crisis, the rift with China, and setbacks in Russia's agricultural and industrial growth. After a brief period of collective leadership, a veteran bureaucrat, Leonid Brezhnev (1906–1982), took Khrushchev's place. Brezhnev served as both Soviet president and Communist party secretary.

In the 25 years following the clash over Cuba, American-Soviet disagreements remained sharp. Yet from the mid-1960s on, superpower relations became clearer, as both sides came to realize that nuclear confrontation would be a mutual disaster. Summit meetings and disarmament talks formed the backdrop to a mitigation of tension and a turning away from ideological rhetoric. If, in the 1960s, Cold War propaganda gave way to a public discussion of peaceful coexistence, so in the 1970s the United States and the Soviet Union began to define their relationship in terms of détente, literally a "relaxation of tensions."

American involvement in Vietnamese affairs (see Chapter 40) sparked a political and social crisis at home.

The escalation of the war under President Johnson resulted in the sending of more than 500,000 American troops to Vietnam by the end of 1968. A vigorous antiwar movement emerged in America. The protests started on college campuses, but outspoken opponents soon emerged in Congress and in the press. In 1967 demonstrations spread throughout the country while thousands of young Americans declared themselves conscientious objectors or fled the United States to avoid the draft. Senator Eugene McCarthy, campaigning on an antiwar platform, challenged President Johnson for the Democratic nomination. In March 1968, following McCarthy's strong showing in an early primary, the president announced that he would not seek another term.

After the Tet Offensive in February 1968, peace talks with North Vietnam opened in Paris, and in November voters elected the Republican Richard M. Nixon (1913–1994) to the presidency. Nixon began the secret bombing of Communist supply routes in Cambodia in early 1969, concealing the operation through false

"Doomed to Coexistence": Reflections on Détente

In January 1980 U.S. Secretary of State Henry Kissinger warned that the traditional division of the postwar period into the Cold War and the age of détente was too simplistic, and offered guidelines for future relations with the USSR.

First, I do not like the distinction of the postwar period into a period of Cold War and a period of détente. The Cold War was not so terrible and détente was not so exalted. In the Cold War, we had a certain amount of ideological hostility and a number of Berlin crises. In the détente period, we had a number of summit meetings and Soviet rearmament and expansionism. So we should not treat international relations as if there had been a clearly defined period in which we lived with a consciousness of harmony. Indeed, the tendency to deal with East-West relations as if they were like relations among individuals, the tendency to attempt to solve the problem of war and peace psychiatrically, as it were, by creating an atmosphere without substance, is in itself a problem of contemporary policy.

Relations between the West and the Soviet Union must be based on two fundamental principles. The first is: We must be strong enough and determined enough to resist expansionism, whatever form it takes. Second, possessing, as we do, weapons of untold destructiveness, we are also doomed to coexistence, and we must seek means by which this coexistence can be made more tolerable and, in time, less dangerous and perhaps even constructive. The desire for peace must not be permitted to turn into a form of blackmail, but the willingness and necessity to resist expansion must not seek confrontation for its own sake.

Source: Henry Kissinger, *For the Record: Selected Statements, 1977–1980* (Boston: Little, Brown, 1981), p. 262.

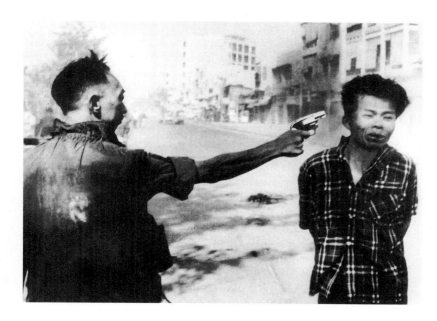

South Vietnam's national police chief executes a Viet Cong officer on a Saigon street. Such scenes aroused opposition to the war in the United States and abroad.

reports. In 1971 the publication of classified war documents heightened antiwar sentiments by revealing earlier deceptions by both Johnson and Nixon. Protests mounted as the 1972 presidential elections approached, but Nixon neutralized them by removing the last American ground troops. The Paris Accords, signed in January 1973, officially ended American involvement in the war.

The 1962 Cuban crisis and the Vietnam War provided the superpowers with unstated but important lessons in international relations. In withdrawing Soviet missiles from Cuba, Khrushchev had tacitly recognized America's predominance in Latin America.* Vietnam had forced the United States to accept the limitations of its military strength. The leaders who followed Johnson and Khrushchev spoke increasingly of tempering Soviet-American relations with détente. Détente actually defined the process by which the superpowers agreed to formalize the dominance that the postwar settlements had given them.

This rapprochement was the work of an unlikely pair: Richard Nixon, a lifelong anticommunist, and Leonid Brezhnev, who had opposed Khrushchev's revisionist policies. Nixon repudiated the Dulles doctrine, which had demanded a rollback of Soviet communism, while Brezhnev fell back on Lenin's notion that direct confrontation with the West was unnecessary in light of

the inevitable decay of capitalism and the overthrow of colonialism by wars of national liberation.

The scandal known as Watergate ended Nixon's presidency but not the era of détente. It was revealed that Nixon and his aides had illegally manipulated the 1972 presidential election campaign and had authorized surveillance and espionage against his political opponents. The crisis, which climaxed in 1974, exposed Nixon's efforts to cover up illegal White House operations. In August, faced with the possibility of impeachment, the president resigned in disgrace. Nixon's successor, Gerald R. Ford (born 1913), continued the policy of détente.

Détente contributed to the Helsinki Accords. In 1973 the United States and the Soviet Union joined Canada and almost all the European nations at the Conference on Security and Cooperation in Europe, held in Helsinki, Finland. In the final treaty, signed two years later, the Soviets endorsed political and human rights statements and agreed to encourage closer relations with the West. In return, the signatories guaranteed Europe's political boundaries, including the division of Germany into two states. The Soviet Union thus obtained formal recognition of the territorial adjustments in eastern Europe that had been arranged at Yalta and Potsdam. In effect, détente had served to achieve permanent agreement on the postwar settlements that had established the Soviet—and, by implication, the American—sphere of influence in Europe.

American foreign policy remained basically unaltered under Ford's successor, Jimmy Carter (born 1924). Carter denounced repressive governments that violated

---

*Mexico, though geographically part of North America, is usually grouped, for linguistic and historical reasons, with the other nations of Latin America.

basic human rights and decried the plight of political dissidents in the Soviet Union, but he continued to support dictatorships in Chile and Iran. He also cited the Soviet military buildup to justify an increase in American arms spending.

The Superpowers Challenged

In the decades since 1950, a number of factors limited or prevented the superpowers from acting with a free hand in international affairs. For one thing, the delicate balance of nuclear terror acted as a check on the actions of the superpowers, whose relationship with each other was determined in part by the potential disaster of accidental and unwanted nuclear holocaust. In order both to maintain their own nuclear monopolies and to limit the possibility of nuclear war, the United States and the Soviet Union also sought to limit the extension of nuclear capability to other nations. In the competition for world hegemony between the two great powers, smaller nations saw opportunity not only to avoid entanglement but to develop a degree of autonomy and exercize influence through a deliberate policy of nonalignment. Furthermore, the new realities of the postwar era meant that countries that formerly had little or no influence in international politics, but who now controlled valuable raw materials, such as oil, could challenge the economic well-being of the superpowers. Europe's move toward unity signaled the emergence of still another form of regional autonomy that could act to curb the ambitions of the superpowers.

The Nuclear Peril and the Quest for Disarmament

Despite a history of ideological conflict and Cold War confrontations since the end of World War II, the United States and the Soviet Union remained at peace. Indeed, relations between the superpowers grew less tense in the 1980s, and efforts at political cooperation and disarmament held out the promise of a more peaceful world.

Nuclear arms limitations talks have been a feature of diplomatic relations for more than 40 years. Some progress was made; the superpowers were forced to be sensitive to the demands of the international community, and their monopoly over nuclear arms had in any case ended.

In 1946, when it still had the world's only atomic weapons, the United States suggested the creation of an international atomic development authority with the power to inspect all countries to prevent the manufacture of nuclear weapons. America proposed turning its research data and facilities over to the agency. The Soviet Union, in the midst of developing its own atomic capability, vetoed the proposal and in 1949 detonated an atomic device. Thereafter, the United States and the Soviet Union engaged in a costly and dangerous nuclear arms race. Each ultimately possessed enough nuclear weapons to exterminate most of the life on the planet.

During the height of the Cold War the superpowers developed their nuclear arsenals and delivery systems and conducted unrestrained testing of atomic weapons that threatened to destroy the environment. In 1952 the United States exploded a hydrogen bomb, an even more destructive weapon. The following year the Soviets announced their own hydrogen device, and in 1961 they tested a 50-megaton bomb, the equivalent of 50 million tons of TNT.

The first important step in nuclear disarmament came in 1963 with the signing of a test ban treaty that permitted only underground explosions. Although more than 100 nations signed the treaty, some states, hoping to achieve their own nuclear capability, refused. In 1968 the United States and the Soviet Union jointly sponsored a nonproliferation treaty that sought to restrict nuclear weapons to the five nations already in possession of them—the United States, the Soviet Union, Britain, France, and China. The pact called for international inspections to ensure that nuclear energy facilities would be used only for peaceful purposes. Eight countries (Argentina, Brazil, Egypt, India, Israel, Pakistan, South Africa, and Spain) did not sign the agreement. A similar pact in 1977 secured the agreement of 90 nations, but again those approaching nuclear capability refused. The limited success of the nonproliferation effort not only made disarmament more difficult but also reflected the sobering failure of the superpowers to reach their own accord.

Little progress was made in American-Soviet disarmament until the 1972 SALT I treaty, which froze the number of offensive "strategic" intercontinental missile launchers for five years. The antiballistic missile (ABM) provisions of SALT I limited the number of ABM sites. In theory, ABMs could provide a nuclear defense by intercepting attacking missiles, although the cost would be prohibitive and decoys could make the system ineffective; in a nuclear exchange, even a small margin of error could result in tens of millions of fatalities. The ABM accord was based on the notion of deterrence, which argues that each side would not attack the other because it feared counterattack. By contrast, an unrestricted ABM race might tempt the nation that acquired an effective defense to consider a first strike against the other if nuclear war seemed "winnable."

The SALT I pact was imperfect. The United States possessed a manned nuclear bomber fleet that the Soviets could not match. Moreover, nothing prevented either side from equipping its missiles with multiple warheads (MIRVs), and no restrictions were placed on technical improvements in either missiles or warheads. The 1979 SALT II treaty limited each superpower to 2,400 nuclear launchers, of which only 1,320 could have MIRVs. But the U.S. Senate refused to ratify SALT II because of conservative opposition and the difficulty of maintaining true parity in the face of continued weapon research. The treaty was observed informally until President Reagan exceeded SALT II limits in 1986. Both the United States and the Soviet Union continued to test nuclear weapons, as did France and China.

Changing Realities

Despite a stagnant economy, the United States continued to fund and in some cases to expand welfare programs in the 1970s. Dissatisfaction with the costs of government, combined with record levels of peacetime inflation, high interest rates, and the perception that America had lost power and prestige (as exemplified in part by the Carter administration's failure to secure the release of American hostages seized in Iran), resulted in the election of Ronald Reagan (born 1911), the first ideological conservative to win the presidency since the 1920s.

Reagan passed large tax cuts, ostensibly to stimulate investment, while instituting a major military buildup. After a severe economic contraction in 1982–1983 that curbed inflation but left the highest levels of unemployment since the Great Depression, a boom period set in for much of the decade, fueled by real estate speculation and corporate mergers. The end of this period was signaled by a stock market crash in October 1987, and by 1990 the economy was in recession. Reagan's government left a $150 billion annual budget deficit, which by 1992, under Reagan's successor, George Bush (born 1924), had ballooned to nearly $400 billion, partly because of massive bank failures. At the same time, mounting poverty was evidenced by the largest homeless population in the United States since the 1930s.

For all its bellicose rhetoric, the Reagan and Bush administrations were generally cautious in foreign affairs. The chief exception to this was in Latin America, where the United States invaded Grenada; fought proxy wars in Nicaragua and Salvador; and invaded Panana in December

ber 1989, overthrowing its military strongman, Manuel Noriega. An ill-fated attempt to garrison war-torn Beirut in 1983 left 241 marines dead. Reagan and Bush provided assistance to the Iraqi dictator Saddam Hussein (born 1937) in his war with Iran, but with Iraq's seizure of the oil-rich emirate of Kuwait in August of 1990 the United States led a United Nations coalition that drove Saddam from Kuwait in February 1991.

The Iran hostage crisis had demonstrated that the postwar world hegemony jointly exercised by the United States and the Soviet Union had not gone unchallenged. Smaller states continually sought to mitigate superpower dominance and exert autonomy. In Europe and the non-Western world, national leaders employed a variety of techniques to maneuver between America and the Soviet Union. Within the Communist world, ideological nonconformity proved a powerful means of asserting independence, while in both western and eastern Europe, nationalism was used as a lever against Washington and Moscow.

Outside the immediate areas of superpower hegemony, states often exploited Cold War rivalries to extract economic and political concessions from each side. Neutralism and ideological nonalignment, especially among former colonies, achieved the same results. The balance of nuclear terror actually enhanced such possibilities, for to avoid mutual destruction over issues that did not threaten their vital interests, the superpowers were forced to act with restraint. Regional and economic organizations exercised a moderating influence through the control of vital natural resources and markets. The revival of religious fundamentalism among Islamic states, so dramatically demonstrated in the United States–Iran crisis, suggested the availability of still other alternatives.

The Nonaligned World

The colonial territories that gained nationhood after World War II found themselves economically dependent on the industrialized, wealthier Western states. Much-needed developmental resources came through assistance programs sponsored by the United States and the Soviet Union, which vied with each other to capture the political support of the newly independent countries. Yet, rather than becoming pawns in the East-West competition, underdeveloped states devised a strategy that turned the Cold War into what they called "creative confrontation"—playing off the superpowers to their own advantage while maintaining nonaligned status. India's Jawaharlal Nehru saw neutralism as a means of forging a "third force" among nonaligned nations, much as de

Gaulle would attempt to do in Europe in the 1960s. The Egyptian leader Gamal Abdel Nasser maneuvered skillfully between the superpowers in pursuit of his goals.

In 1955 a large number of neutralist states convened the Afro-Asian Conference in Bandung, Indonesia, to discuss mutual interests and strategy. The United Nations soon became a focus of Third World nonalignment. The ranks of the General Assembly swelled rapidly as former colonies won independence, thus forming a substantial voting bloc with members from Latin America. Anticolonial sentiment, reinforced by the Soviets, often translated into anti-Western positions, but the primary agenda among nonaligned countries was to secure passage of social and economic assistance measures. Superpower refusal to fund such programs often undermined the effectiveness of the neutralist coalition.

The Bandung conference symbolized continuing efforts to establish regional organizations designed to forge unity of policy and economic cooperation among Third World nations. The Organization of African Unity (OAU) was established because African leaders believed that disunity played into the hands of the superpowers. Founded in 1963, the OAU required a policy of nonalignment from each of its 30 member states and spawned a number of subregional economic groups similar in concept to the European Common Market. The OAU also pursued a policy of political cooperation with other Third World regional coalitions, especially with Arab countries.

Much of the frustration expressed by nonaligned nations stemmed from the vastly unequal relationship separating rich and poor states. The resentment, strongest where key resources and local economies have been exploited by multinational Western corporations, had a major impact on world events. The formation of the Organization of Petroleum Exporting Countries (OPEC) in 1960 reflected these concerns. OPEC devised the strategy of counterpenetration, whereby it hoped to make industrial economies that relied heavily on oil imports vulnerable to Third World pressures. Initially, the strategy had resounding success. Dwindling foreign aid from the United States and its allies, coupled with the West's pro-Israeli policy in the Middle East, angered the Arab nations in OPEC. In 1973 the group quadrupled the price of crude oil. The sudden rise in fuel costs intensified inflation and recession in the West and underscored the interdependence of world societies. The next year the nonaligned bloc in the United Nations passed a resolution demanding the creation of a "new international economic order" in which resources, trade, and markets would be distributed equally.

Nonaligned states forged still other forms of economic cooperation as leverage against the superpowers.

OPEC, the OAU, and the Arab League had overlapping members, and in the 1970s the Arabs began extending huge financial assistance to African nations in an effort to reduce African economic dependence on the United States and the Soviet Union. At a 1977 Afro-Arab summit conference in Cairo, oil producers pledged $1.5 billion in aid to Africa. Later divisions within OPEC made concerted action more difficult. Nevertheless, the 1973 oil crisis provided dramatic evidence of the potential power of resource suppliers in dealing with the developed world.

The Growth of European Autonomy

European efforts toward economic unity led to a subtle undermining of American influence. In 1950, against the background of the Marshall Plan, French foreign minister Robert Schuman (1886–1963) proposed a plan for cooperating in the production of steel and coal. Belgium, Luxembourg, and the Netherlands joined France, West Germany, and Italy in forming the European Coal and Steel Community (ECSC), which quickly tripled iron and steel output and increased coal production almost 25 percent. By 1957 the ECSC concluded that further cooperation could strengthen Europe's economies and enable its members jointly to influence the superpowers. As a result, ECSC members created the European Economic Community (EEC), better known as the Common Market. Through the elimination of tariff barriers and the free exchange of labor and capital, the Common Market achieved remarkable success in economic integration. After years of French objection, Britain, Ireland, and Denmark became members in 1973. Although the United States still exercises a major influence in European economic life, Europe has escaped the direct dependence it once had on America. Indeed, while the Common Market brought an increase in American business in Europe, in the 1980s the flow of capital began to move in both directions as European products and investments entered the United States.

Charles de Gaulle, president of France from 1958 to 1969, led a more direct challenge to American hegemony. Proud and intensely nationalistic, he wanted to put France at the center of a Europe that would reassert its autonomy from the United States and the Soviet Union. For that reason, de Gaulle pulled French forces out of NATO, twice vetoed the entry of America's closest ally, Great Britain, into the Common Market, and condemned America's escalating role in Vietnam. More grating still to Washington, the French leader tried to weaken the American economy by demanding gold for the large quantity of U.S. dollars held in Paris.

Claude Monet's painting IMPRESSION: SUNRISE (1872), which gave the Impressionist movement its name, reveals the techniques of Impressionism in its early phase. The Impressionists concentrated on the visual effects of light and color rather than on realistic forms.

Among the Postimpressionist painters, Vincent van Gogh gave powerful expression to his tormented emotional vision through the swirling movement of form and color, as in his painting THE STARRY NIGHT.

In MONT SAINTE-VICTOIRE and other works, Paul Cézanne reduced landscape elements to flat planes of pure color to emphasize the three essential shapes that he believed made up all of nature—the cylinder, the sphere, and the cone.

The prostitutes of Avignon Street in Barcelona provided the subject of Pablo Picasso's DEMOISELLES D'AVIGNON, which reveals the influence of African culture on artists of the period and presages the development of Cubism. Picasso moves from poses reminiscent of classical sculpture on the left to distorted, broken shapes on the right.

The leading member of the Fauvist movement, Henri Matisse, used flat surfaces of strong color and undulating lines to give his work a primitive flavor. In HARMONY IN RED (also known as RED ROOM), by carrying the blue-on-red pattern of the tablecloth over to the wall and the red of the room over to the pink of the house seen through the window, Matisse reduces the number of tints to a minimum, making color an important structural element in the painting.

The most talented of the Futurists, Umberto Boccioni combined innovative formal artistic elements with a social and political conscience. In RIOT IN THE GALLERY, the surging demonstrators reveal his concern for the dynamic interaction of motion and space in time. "Everything is in movement," the manifesto of Futurist Painting proclaimed; "everything rushes forward, everything is in constant swift change."

Wassily Kandinsky, PANEL (3), 1914. Of his work, Kandinsky said: "Painting is a thundering collision of different worlds, destined to create a new world."

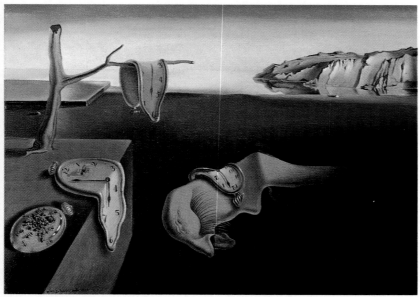

Surrealism was based on Freud's theory of the dream world of the unconscious. In THE PERSISTENCE OF MEMORY, one of the key works of the movement, Salvador Dalí used an almost photographic realism to create an infinite, silent space in which objects cease to comply with the laws of physics. As the watches melt, they suggest the theories of Einstein about the relativity of time and raise questions about what is real and what is not real.

Legend:
- Original members of European Economic Community, 1965; merged into European Union, 1992
- Later members with dates of admission
- European Free Trade Association, 1961
- Nations formed since 1990

ICELAND
Reykjavik

SWEDEN
1995

FINLAND
1995

NORWAY
Oslo
Stockholm
Helsinki

NORTH
SEA

DENMARK
1973
Copenhagen

BALTIC SEA

Tallinn
ESTONIA

RUSSIA

LATVIA
Riga

Moscow

IRELAND
1973
Dublin

GREAT
BRITAIN
1973

LITHUANIA
Vilnius

THE FORMER
SOVIET UNION

RUSSIA

London

English Channel

NETHERLANDS
Amsterdam

Berlin

Minsk

BELARUS

Brussels
BELGIUM

GERMANY
(East admitted
to EEC in 1990)

Warsaw

POLAND

Kiev

ATLANTIC
OCEAN

Paris

LUXEMBOURG

Bonn

Prague
CZECH
REPUBLIC

UKRAINE

SLOVAKIA
Bratislava

MOLDOVA

FRANCE

SWITZERLAND
Bern

AUSTRIA
1995

Vienna

Budapest

HUNGARY

Chisinău

ROMANIA

SLOVENIA
Ljubljana

Zagreb

Bucharest

BLACK
SEA

PORTUGAL
1986

Madrid

CROATIA

BOSNIA AND
HERZEGOVINA
Sarajevo

Belgrade

SERBIA

BULGARIA
Sofia
MACEDONIA

Lisbon

SPAIN
1986

BALEARIC
ISLANDS

CORSICA

ITALY

Rome

ADRIATIC
SEA

MONTENEGRO
ALBANIA

YUGOSLAVIA
Skopje

Istanbul

TURKEY

SARDINIA

Tiranë

Strait of
Gibraltar

Gibraltar (British)
Ceuta (Spanish)
Melilla (Spanish)

MEDITERRANEAN SEA

Algiers

Tunis

GREECE
1981

Athens

CRETE

MOROCCO

ALGERIA

TUNISIA

Valletta
MALTA

0   150   300 Miles

MAP 43.1   EUROPE, 1945–1995

West Germany also demonstrated more autonomy. When the socialist Willy Brandt became chancellor in 1969, he embarked on a policy of reconciliation with the Communist bloc countries of eastern Europe. In exchange for guarantees of West Berlin's freedom and a mutual renunciation of force, Brandt concluded treaties with the Soviet Union, Czechoslovakia, and Poland that formally recognized existing frontiers. Of equal importance, he also began the normalization of relations with East Germany.

The desire for ideological autonomy was linked to the growing identification of Communist parties with the idea of an independent Europe free from the influence of both superpowers. This trend gave rise to the phenomenon known as Eurocommunism, which found its first example in Italy, whose Communist party was inspired by the theoretical writings of Antonio Gramsci (1891–1937). Italian Communists adopted considerable tactical flexibility based on Gramsci's notion that the history of a nation should guide the development of its Communist movement. Not unlike the European Popular Front policies of the 1930s, Italian Communist leaders accepted both democratic principles and the possibility of sharing power in a coalition with bourgeois parties. The Communists of France, Spain, and most other Western countries moved in the same direction, at times breaking with Moscow over international issues. In 1968 the Italian Communist party, together with its French counterpart, criticized the Soviet Union's invasion of Czechoslovakia. In 1990, as a symbol of the new emphasis on democracy, the Italian party changed its name to the Democratic Party of the Left.

The success of the Common Market, together with the experiences of de Gaulle and Brandt, led to Europe's increasing political independence from Washington. Although some Europeans expressed anxiety at the prospect of an American missile withdrawal, powerful grassroots peace movements challenged American nuclear policy. Moreover, most European states refused to follow the American lead in applying sanctions against the Soviet Union in 1979 after that nation's invasion of Afghanistan. A similar request was rejected in 1981 following the suppression of the Polish trade union movement, and in 1986 many European states refused an American request for overflight permission during the bombing raid against Libya. With the end of the Cold War and the pledge by the United States and the USSR of drastic arms reduction, European dependence on American military power was greatly reduced, although the civil war among the former republics of Yugoslavia demonstrated that regional security in Europe was by no means assured.

Toward Unity

In 1986 Europe moved closer to economic union when members of the EEC adopted the Single European Act, which called for a unified European internal market and the end of trade barriers by the end of 1992. Moreover, all border formalities would disappear for citizens of the EEC, now known simply as the European Community

MAP 43.2 THE BREAKUP OF YUGOSLAVIA

(EC), and labor and capital would circulate freely. Member states also committed to cooperate in improving the environment and adopting a general plan of social legislation. Some states, especially Britain, opposed the environmental and social aspects of the Single European Act as interference in domestic affairs.

In the late 1980s member nations began to prepare for 1992. Under the plan, the end of all restrictions would place each private corporation in direct competition with others throughout Europe, including service industries such as banking and insurance, which in many cases had been protected by government regulations. Financiers from one country would be free to invest their money in another, and drivers in nations with high insurance rates would be able to insure their automobiles with foreign companies. As a result, insurance firms and other service companies began to diversify their operations throughout the continent, and American and Japanese investors, once discouraged by European protectionism, began to make plans to participate in the vast new market.

European economic unity promised to create a bloc powerful enough to compete successfully with Japan and the United States. By 1987 western Europe had become the world's largest commercial unit, dealing with 37 percent of the world's trade and holding a third of the world's monetary reserves, despite the fact that the region possessed only 6 percent of the world's population. In the spring of 1992 Danish voters dealt hopes for Europe's political unity an unexpected blow by refusing to ratify the enabling treaty signed by European Community members the previous year at Maastricht. In part this reflected Danish fears of being swallowed up by an entity 340 million strong, but in part as well the resurgence of ethnic divisions in eastern Europe and the flight of foreign refugees from that region to western Europe.

More widespread economic changes also affected the movement for unity. The collapse of the "Socialist bloc" and the rapid transformation in China accelerated the process of global capitalism. The Communist era, in fact, might be seen as a temporary and partial diversion of that process. The movement toward regional federation—visible in North America, the Middle East, and the Pacific Rim as well as in Europe—is a response to the displacement of nationally (or imperially) defined economies by a common world labor pool controlled by giant transnational corporations, themselves shifting and often ill-defined entities. At the same time a new international elite of bankers, businessmen, and stockholders seeks to organize and profit from this emerging system, leaving political leaders to police the ever-more restless populations of the new world economy and to negotiate broad frameworks to facilitate the movement of trade and capital. The North American Free Trade Agreement (NAFTA) and the 1948 General Agreement on Tariffs and Trade (GATT), both of which were designed to lower trade barriers, are key examples of such frameworks. The result can be catastrophic for poor nations, though developed ones too are not immune, as reflected in the high levels of unemployment in Western Europe, particularly in Spain. Such considerations shape the pace and design of European union, and the national political story will become progressively less relevant to understanding the present world. Despite the countermovement of ethnic nationalism, the modern nation-state is giving way to new forms of organization. Ethnic backlash, though of continuing importance in both advanced and underdeveloped states, is essentially a reactive, rearguard phenomenon in a world whose political configurations are in a state of unparalleled flux.

The Revolution in Eastern Europe

The trend toward autonomy in eastern Europe had been slower until the late 1980s, when domestic reforms in the Soviet Union released the iron grip that Stalin had imposed on the region. Although the open revolts against Soviet authority in East Germany (1953) and Hungary (1956) were swiftly crushed, cautious ideological divergence from orthodox Communist policy drew many

eastern European regimes away from Moscow. Combining Yugoslav nationalism with doctrinal innovation, Marshal Tito steered his country into a quasi-neutral position even during the Stalinist period. Tito's example no doubt contributed to the harsh Soviet reaction against similar efforts in Czechoslovakia. In January 1968, reformists within the Czech Communist party installed Alexander Dubček in office. Dubček lifted censorship and permitted local decision making in factories, unions, and the Communist party itself. The Czech example aroused demands for similar reforms elsewhere in eastern Europe. In August 500,000 Soviet and Warsaw Pact troops poured into Czechoslovakia and arrested Dubček and his reformist supporters. Brezhnev subsequently asserted the Soviet Union's right to intervene in the affairs of any socialist nation whenever necessary—the so-called Brezhnev Doctrine. By the 1970s a subtle shift in Soviet policy was introduced as Moscow sought to reduce the need for military intervention by stimulating economic integration with the eastern European region.

Efforts to achieve autonomy within the Communist world accelerated in Poland. In 1980 a rash of illegal strikes led to a massive work stoppage at the Gdansk shipyards and inspired the formation of the noncommunist Solidarity movement, headed by Lech Walesa (born 1944), a tough union organizer. With support from almost 10 million workers and the Catholic church, Solidarity won major concessions from the government before party leader General Wojciech Jaruzelski imposed martial law and arrested union leaders. Walesa was eventually freed and Solidarity recognized. In the midst of a deepening economic crisis, partially free elections were held in 1989, leading to the formation of a coalition government headed by Tadeusz Mazowiecki, a Solidarity member whose cabinet included both Solidarity representatives and communists. In the spring of 1990 Walesa was elected president of Poland.

In the last months of 1989, decades of Soviet and communist domination in eastern Europe finally ended as the long-suffering peoples of the region, inspired by developments in Poland, drove their governments from power. In late summer East Germans, frustrated by the refusal of Communist party leader Erich Honecker to institute reforms, began leaving their country for the West. As East Germany celebrated its fortieth anniversary in October, mass demonstrations were organized and the number of refugees reached tens of thousands. By the end of the month, Honecker had been forced to resign as party chief.

Thanks in part to financial subsidies from West Germany, Communist East Germany enjoyed the highest

Leading Polish workers in Solidarity, a union movement of great political importance, Lech Walesa speaks to a crowd of strikers outside the Lenin shipyard in Gdansk in 1988.

standard of living and the strongest industrial base in eastern Europe. Nevertheless East Germans experienced shortages of consumer goods, massive environmental damage, and a decaying infrastructure. As the spirit of reform swept eastern Europe in 1989, East Germany's leader, Erich Honecker, was ousted with the acquiescence of the Soviet Union. In an attempt to deter its people from abandoning the country, the East German authorities opened the borders to the West and began to tear down the Berlin Wall, which became the site of huge celebrations. As information about party corruption and government repression became public, the Communists were discredited and new political parties emerged. In March 1990 the first free elections in East German history were held. The Christian Democrats, campaigning on a platform of German unification, won almost half the vote. The process was speeded when the Soviet Union agreed that the reunified Germany could join NATO and that Soviet troops would be withdrawn from East Germany within three to four years. The four powers that had occupied Germany since 1945—the United States, the Soviet Union, Britain, and France—joined with West and East Germany in signing the Treaty on the Final Settlement with Respect to Germany, effectively ending the Cold War and the policy of containing Germany by keeping it politically divided. In the treaty Germany pledged to respect its existing border with Poland and renounced the manufacture or possession of nuclear, biological, and chemical weapons. That July, the economies of the two Germanies were united, and on October 3 political unification was implemented.

Children at play in the rubble from the dismantled Berlin Wall.

Despite the costs of integration, including the restructuring of East German industry, united Germany is one of the world's major economic powers, ranking first in exports ($354.1 billion at the time of unification, compared with $321.6 billion for the United States) and second in favorable balance of trade ($73.9 billion, compared with $77.5 billion for Japan and a deficit of $138 billion for the United States). Germany held its first free nationwide election since 1932; with the victory of the Christian Democrats, Helmut Kohl became the first chancellor of the reunited country and won re-election in 1995. The cost of rebuilding the east (which reached $330 billion in 1995) coupled with growing numbers of immigrants subjected the country to mounting civil unrest, however. Much of it was sparked by neo-Nazi "skinheads," disgruntled youth groups opposed to immigrant workers in Germany and manipulated by ultraright nationalists.

Inspired by success in Poland and Germany, the people of Hungary and Czechoslovakia moved cautiously toward liberation. In Hungary, despite reforms that permitted small private enterprises, economic setbacks resulted in the fall of János Kádár in 1988. Deep-seated dissatisfaction led to the emergence of new political parties, a change of name in the Hungarian Communist party, and free elections, in which the Communists were repudiated. In Czechoslovakia the government responded harshly to dissident demonstrations, but by late 1989 Prague was awash with rallies of more than 500,000, and the Communist government finally collapsed. The playwright Vaclav Havel (born 1936), one of the leaders of the opposition, became president and began to preside over the democratization of his country. In 1992 long-standing ethnic differences led to discussions that culminated in the division of Czechoslovakia into two separate states.

In Romania, which had remained unaffected by the upheaval in eastern Europe, Nicolae Ceauşescu (1918–1989) and his wife Elena had created their own form of Communist dictatorship that had strained relations with the Soviet Union. Although Romania experienced food shortages and economic collapse, Ceauşescu had wasted limited resources on sumptuous palaces. In the countryside he destroyed villages and forced their inhabitants into collectives. A vicious secret police kept the population in a state of constant fear.

In December 1989, when demonstrators protested the repressive regime, the police shot and killed some 200 people. The bloodshed sparked a sharp reaction from the people, who raged through the streets of Bucharest, and resulted in battles between anti-Ceauşescu army units and the secret police. Ceauşescu and his wife attempted to flee but were captured by army rebels and, after a military trial, executed. Despite the end of the dictatorship, however, the prospects for Romanian democracy remained uncertain. Even Bulgaria, a country with virtually no democratic experience, deposed its aging Stalinist dictator, Todor Zhivkov (born 1911), and changed the name of its Communist party to the Bulgarian Socialist party.

In Yugoslavia, where Marshal Tito's death in 1980 had been followed by a collective presidency, the collapse of Soviet hegemony led to radical destabilization. A postwar federation forged of six republics and two semiautonomous provinces with five languages, two alphabets, and three major religious groups, Yugoslavia experienced turmoil as economic woes fanned national rivalries. In January 1990 the Communist leadership called for an end to authoritarian government and held multiparty elections. The most prominent Yugoslav political leader since Tito, Slobodan Miloseviĉ, aggravated tensions by championing greater power for the Serbs, who formed the largest ethnic group (36 percent) in the country.

The republics of Slovenia and Croatia elected noncommunist governments in 1990, and both voted overwhelmingly the following year to become independent. In the summer of 1991, a fierce civil war erupted between these districts and the Serbs, who championed unity. The war was characterized in part by the revival of concentration camps and the relentless shelling of urban centers. In March of 1992 the war spread to Bosnia-Herzegovina, which had also asserted its independence but failed to stem intercommunal violence that led to the heaviest fighting on European soil since World War II. The European Community recognized Croatian and Slovenian independence. In 1992 Serbia and Croatia seized large portions of Bosnia-Herzegovina, and by the end of the year a much smaller Yugoslav state appeared to be an accomplished fact. The fighting left much of Bosnia in ruins, and the inability of the European powers and the United States to stop the worst fighting on the European continent since World War II called into question the viability of NATO and other European security organizations. By 1996 an uneasy peace had been imposed with UN and NATO assistance.

The Collapse of the Soviet Union

During the almost two decades that Brezhnev ruled, the Soviet Union underwent a return to government repression, although not to the extremes of the Stalin era.

Party officials agreed on the need for stability and re-trenchment after the changes wrought by Khrushchev. Restraints were reimposed on Soviet intellectuals, symbolized by the expulsion of Alexander Solzhenitsyn in 1974. Despite Moscow's acceptance of the human rights provisions of the Helsinki Accords, criticism of government policy by prominent dissidents such as Andrei Sakharov (1921–1989), an internationally acclaimed physicist, brought persecution and long periods of Siberian exile. Recalling Russia's wartime sacrifices, Soviet leaders stressed nationalist traditions and the unity of the Soviet Union, crushing regionalism in the Ukraine and elsewhere.

The new wave of repression also affected the Soviet Union's 1.8 million Jews, who suffered from a long tradition of repression. In the Soviet system, state atheism discouraged Judaism along with all other religions, but the government also claimed that Jewish cultural identity and Zionism undermined the unity of the nation. Khrushchev's liberalization program had hardly affected the Soviet Union's Jews. In the 1960s they formed underground networks to keep Jewish tradition alive, circulating typewritten translations of books such as Leon Uris' novel *Exodus* (1958), which traced the emigration of the Jewish people to Palestine and the founding of the state of Israel. The Brezhnev regime, preoccupied with nationality problems within the Soviet Union and political dissidence, stepped up persecution of the Jews. Emigration to Israel, which had been virtually impossible before, was loosened as a result of international pressure in the 1970s. The exit rate reached a peak in 1979, when over 51,000 Jews left the Soviet Union, but declined steadily thereafter. Only in 1987, under Mikhail Gorbachev's more liberal policies, did the number begin to increase again. Since then, an estimated 600,000 Jews from the former Soviet Union emigrated to Israel, with others settling elsewhere.

Leonid Brezhnev died in November 1982, bequeathing a legacy of political and economic stagnation that was compounded under the brief regimes of his successors, the former secret police chief Yuri Andropov (1904–1984) and the Politburo veteran Konstantin Chernenko (1912–1985), both of whom were preoccupied by the Afghan war and the bellicose tone of the Reagan administration. Using Afghanistan as a pretext, Reagan had begun a massive arms buildup early in his administration. He increased the level of military spending from one-quarter to one-third of the federal budget, aiming at both the achievement of a first-strike nuclear capability and the development of a defensive shield against missile attack, the so-called Strategic Defense Initiative (SDI). Dubbed "Star Wars" by the media, the SDI plan called for the development of satellite-mounted lasers capable of destroying enemy missiles in flight. The Kremlin claimed that such satellites were actually intended for purposes of attack, a charge made credible by attempts to develop space-based offensive systems under the cloak of SDI. The Soviet Union took expensive countermeasures, further burdening its strained economy.

In March 1985, Mikhail Gorbachev (born 1931) succeeded Chernenko as first secretary of the Communist party. The son of a peasant, Gorbachev had risen through the party's ranks. He had become convinced, however, that only radical reform could arrest the Soviet Union's decline. Moving boldly on both the domestic and foreign fronts, he announced a general program of economic "restructuring," or *perestroika*, while pressing the United States to negotiate major cuts in nuclear weapons.

Gorbachev's initiatives were interrelated. Faced with a declining GDP barely half the size of that of the United States, he knew that he could not match the Reagan military buildup without straining the Soviet economy to the breaking point. Beginning at Geneva in 1985, he pressed negotiations that culminated in 1988 with an agreement to eliminate Soviet and American medium- and short-range land-based missiles. At the same time he withdrew Soviet troops from Afghanistan and ended three decades of frozen relations with China by visiting Peking.

Gorbachev's urbanity and charm disarmed many, as did those of his attractive wife, Raisa. His evocation of Europe as a "common home" spoke tellingly to those who yearned for an end to the division that had beset the continent since 1945. At home he instituted a policy of "openness" (*glasnost*) that included the release of prominent dissidents, most notably the physicist Andrei Sakharov, and the publication of such long-banned works as the novel *Dr. Zhivago*, by Boris Pasternak (1890–1960), and *Requiem*, a memorial to the victims of Stalinism by Anna Akhmatova (1889–1966).

But Gorbachev's essential goals, though broad, were limited. In a speech at Prague in 1987 he spoke of *perestroika* as reconstructing rather than dismantling socialism. At home he remained committed to the Communist party's monopoly of power and to state control of the economy. *Glasnost*, too, revealed its limits.

Gorbachev's initial economic reforms were embodied in the Law on State Enterprise (1987). Individual managers, freed from the control of the all-powerful State Planning Commission, could now buy supplies directly from one another and sell a portion of their output on the market. Prices, however, remained controlled, preventing the formation of wholesale markets and leav-

Perestroika: Reform in Gorbachev's USSR

In April 1985, Mikhail Gorbachev announced a policy of far-reaching reform that he called perestroika *("restructuring"). Gorbachev claimed that this policy of delegating more responsibility to the people, of encouraging initiative and openness, was a natural next stage in the development of the Soviet system. Here he describes his goals as a phase in the continuing revolution.*

We have come to the conclusion that unless we activate the human factor, that is, unless we take into consideration the diverse interests of people, work collectives, public bodies, and various social groups, unless we rely on them, and draw them into active, constructive endeavor, it will be impossible for us to accomplish any of the tasks set, or to change the situation in the country. . . .

It is wrong, and even harmful, to see socialist society as something rigid and unchangeable, to perceive its improvement as an effort to adapt complicated reality to concepts and formulas that have been established once and for all. The concepts of socialism keep on developing. . . .

Perestroika is a word with many meanings. But if we are to choose from its many possible synonyms the key one which expresses its essence most accurately, then we can say thus: *perestroika* is a revolution. A decisive acceleration of the socioeconomic and cultural development of Soviet society which involves radical changes on the way to a qualitatively new state is undoubtedly a revolutionary task. . . .

In accordance with our theory, revolution means construction, but it also always implies demolition. Revolution requires the demolition of all that is obsolete, stagnant and hinders fast progress. . . . *Perestroika* also means a resolute and radical elimination of obstacles hindering social and economic development, of outdated methods of managing the economy and of dogmatic stereotype mentality. . . .

And like a revolution, our day-to-day activities must be unparalleled, revolutionary. *Perestroika* requires Party leaders who are very close to Lenin's ideal of a revolutionary Bolshevik. Officialdom, red tape, patronizing attitudes, and careerism are incompatible with this ideal. On the other hand, courage, initiative, high ideological standards and moral purity, a constant urge to discuss things with people, and an ability to firmly uphold the humane values of socialism are greatly honored. . . . We still have a long way to go to achieve this ideal. Too many people are still "in the state of evolution," or, to put it plainly, have adopted a wait-and-see attitude.

Source: M. Gorbachev, *Perestroika: New Thinking for Our Country and the World* (New York: Harper & Row, 1987), pp. 29–55 passim.

ing managers dependent on the ministries in Moscow, themselves in disarray. The result was erratic supply, uncertain production, and inefficient distribution. Shortages cropped up everywhere, putting further pressure on official prices and shunting even basic commodities onto the black market.

While party conservatives stubbornly resisted the erosion of their power, free market advocates demanded the complete abandonment of centralized planning. *Glasnost* also produced unexpected results. A loose coali-tion of youth groups, intellectuals, and academics condemned the abuses of the Soviet system and appealed directly to the public with such tactics as impromptu street polls. Their ranks were swollen by returning veterans from Afghanistan. By 1987 more than 1,000 independent political clubs and study groups had sprung up in Moscow alone.

These new groups were embraced by Boris Yeltsin (born 1931), a maverick politician who broke with Gorbachev and, after being expelled from the Central

Committee, dramatically resigned from the Communist party. Gorbachev, assailed from the left and the right, sought to consolidate power on an ever-narrowing base. He created the new executive post of president for himself but clung to his position as general secretary.

Refusing to submit his presidency to a popular election, Gorbachev replaced the Supreme Soviet in 1989 with a new body, the Congress of People's Deputies. Although a portion of its seats were reserved for party nominees alone, non-Communists were permitted to contest the remainder in the first free elections held in the Soviet Union since 1917. At the same time, reformers swept to power in civic elections in Moscow and Leningrad, and Boris Yeltsin, elected president of the Russian Republic, promptly challenged Gorbachev's right to issue decrees binding on this government.

Sensing weakness at the center, Lithuania, forcibly incorporated into the USSR in 1940, declared its independence, and secession movements arose in the other Baltic republics of Latvia and Estonia as well as in the Ukraine and the Transcaucasus. Communist rule meanwhile collapsed throughout eastern Europe in 1989. The secession of Lithuania posed a threat to the Soviet Union itself. Aligning himself with conservative forces, Gorbachev imposed an economic blockade on the region and in January 1991 seized public buildings in Vilnius as 14 died. Ethnic strife broke out between Armenia and Azerbaijan and elsewhere as Moscow's power waned and other republics defied the center. Embracing the left again, Gorbachev staked the remainder of his prestige on a new Union Treaty, which devolved extensive powers on the republics, leaving Moscow with control over foreign policy, the military, the currency, and other vaguely defined powers of coordination. At the same time, he renounced Marxism-Leninism as the official ideology of the Soviet Union.

The most difficult component of Gorbachev's program was *perestroika,* an ambitious restructuring of the Soviet economy. At the heart of this policy in its early stages was the 1987 Law on State Enterprise, intended to make Soviet factories profitable by requiring them to purchase raw materials from suppliers, sell what they manufactured, and share any profits. The government dropped production quotas for the factories but replaced them with state orders substantial enough to monopolize most of their output. The net effect was to introduce some freedom into the industrial sector without sacrificing government planning. In the agricultural realm *perestroika* enabled families to obtain long-term inheritable leases on land with the right to earn profits on what they raised. By moving toward a mixed agricultural economy

(collectives continued to exist), Gorbachev hoped to reduce the Soviet Union's need to import food, which in the late 1980s consumed approximately 15 percent of the country's annual budget. At the same time, he implemented unilateral cuts in Soviet forces to reduce the pressure of military spending on the budget and the economy. Gorbachev also actively courted foreign investors, particularly West Germans and Americans, to pursue joint ventures in the Soviet Union. In 1990 and 1991 the government authorized the transition to a market economy, which led to increased shortages of consumer goods and food, sparking considerable disaffection.

On the eve of the treaty's signing in August, hardline ministers and military chiefs sequestered Gorbachev in his vacation home in the Crimea and announced the seizure of power. The coup collapsed overnight as thousands of citizens poured into the streets of Moscow in protest. A defiant Boris Yeltsin barricaded himself in the Russian parliament building, and most military units withheld their support from the disorganized plotters. Despite its brevity, the coup's effect was decisive. When the shaken Gorbachev returned to Moscow, he found that many were suspicious of his own role, and most held him responsible for the treason of his cabinet.

Although Gorbachev dramatically dissolved the Communist party and offered other new concessions, the republics now balked at the treaty, and as the sovereignty of the Baltic republics was recognized and the Ukraine voted overwhelmingly for independence as well, the Soviet Union collapsed. Effective power passed to Yeltsin as leader of the largest of the republics, and in late December Gorbachev resigned as president of a country that had already ceased to exist. Of the 12 non-Baltic republics, 11 adhered to a loose federation brokered by Yeltsin and the presidents of Ukraine and Belarus (Byelorussia), the Commonwealth of Independent States (CIS).

The CIS was little more than a fig leaf over the dissolution of the Soviet empire. From the beginning it was hamstrung by the rivalry between the two most populous republics, Russia and Ukraine, which vied for control of the Red Army and the Black Sea fleet. Ethnic violence broke out in Georgia and Moldova and continued between Armenia and Azerbaijan. Unable to secure the cooperation of the other republics, Yeltsin freed prices in Russia on January 2, 1992, effectively severing it economically from the rest of the CIS. The immediate result for Russia itself was unchecked inflation and crippling shortages of food, fuel, medicine, and other commodities. A $24 billion aid package was offered by the Western powers, but staggering problems remained.

Demonstrators in Moscow swarm over a tank as they protest the attempted coup against Gorbachev in August 1991.

The collapse of the Soviet Union allowed for a real breakthrough in nuclear disarmament. In June of 1992 Yeltsin and U.S. president George Bush agreed to cut their missile arsenals by two-thirds by the year 2003, restricting each nation to 3500 missiles apiece. The problem of nuclear proliferation remained, however, as four new nuclear powers emerged from the former Soviet Union, one of which, Ukraine, possessed a significant nuclear capability.

The swift collapse of the Soviet Union was the result of two principal factors. First, from the Stalinist era it had felt compelled to build a military machine, buttressed by heavy industry, capable not only of defending itself but ultimately of extending its influence abroad. To achieve these ends the USSR imposed rigid economic and social controls, overburdening its people and channeling vast sums to the military and the arms race with the United States. Ultimately the Soviet economy proved unable to sustain such demands. Gorbachev's efforts to move to a market economy in stages failed, bringing down the Soviet Union. Second, the Soviet Union succumbed to the pressures of nationalist rivalries which it had more or less kept in check for seven decades.

The collapse of the Soviet Union did not solve most of Russia's problems. The transition to a market economy and the sharp reduction in military expenditures led to mounting unemployment and soaring inflation (more than 1000 percent in 1993). Fearing riots by unemployed workers, the Russian Parliament continued to subsidize state factories, contributing thereby to both inflation and the continued production of substandard goods. In 1993 a mere 20 percent of the workforce was employed in the private sector. Taking advantage of the economic disruption and the government's preoccupation with economic and political concerns, a Russian Mafia made organized crime a serious problem. Disenchanted with these conditions, former Vice President Alexander Rutskoi led a rebellion against Yeltsin's government in 1993 that was designed to restore the Soviet Union. The revolt collapsed only after the army shelled Rutskoi and his principal supporters, who had barricaded themselves in the Parliament Building. Yeltsin faced another crisis in late 1994 and early 1995, when he ordered Russian troops to quash rebellious nationalists in the tiny province of Chechnya in southwestern Russia. Having already lost 14 former republics as well as Eastern Europe, the Russian government had obviously decided to

Mikhail Gorbachev and Boris Yeltsin at the Russian parliament following the abortive coup of August 1991.

Following the coup, angry Russians topple a statue of the founder of the KGB (secret police).

stop the hemorrhaging regardless of the cost in lives, money, or international opinion.

Moscow: From Communist Hub to Capitalist Metropolis

The dramatic changes that occurred in Russia in the 1990s were especially evident in Moscow, long a mirror of Russia's rich history. The soaring golden domes of the fifteenth-century Cathedrals of the Assumption and the Annunciation that rise from behind the imposing walls of the Kremlin testify to a Russian past in which Moscow, the "Mother City," was both capital and the spiritual center of the Orthodox faith. Although the site has been inhabited since Neolithic times, the origins of the city began in the twelfth century when a Russian prince constructed a wooden citadel, the Kremlin. Two centuries later the Kremlin received its first stone walls, which enclosed palaces, churches, monasteries, and government buildings. The rulers of Moscow took the lead in driving the Mongols out of Russia and creating a unified state, but in the eighteenth century Peter the Great, whose eyes were on the west, moved the capital to his new city of St. Petersburg. There it remained until Lenin transferred the center of government back to the Mother City in 1918.

Much of historic Moscow was destroyed during the Napoleonic invasion of 1812, but the city recovered dramatically. From a population of less than 300,000 in 1812, it mushroomed to nearly 2 million a century later,

doubled to more than 4 million by 1939, and more than doubled again in the next 50 years to a population of 9 million in 1989. The city has expanded in a series of concentric rings, at the heart of which is the Kremlin and the adjacent "Red Square," as it was known during the Communist regime. Like the spokes of a wheel, major roads radiate from the center of Moscow, reaching eventually to the towering white apartment complexes that dominate the outer rings and house much of the population in small flats. The middle and outer rings contain industrial plants, many of them built in the 1960s and in need of major renovation in the 1990s.

Moscow has been called a museum of Russian civilization and is in fact home to more than 60 museums, one of which is housed in the majestic sixteenth-century Cathedral of St. Basil. The Bolshoi theater, completed in 1780 and twice reconstructed after fires in the nineteenth century, is the home of both opera and one of the world's greatest ballet companies. Lenin once addressed party meetings amid its splendor, but political gatherings now occur in the Palace of Congresses, built within the Kremlin's walls in 1961. Stalin had begun construction of a mammoth Palace of the Soviets shaped like a wedding cake and with a planned height of 1,161 feet, above which a 200-foot chromium-plated statue of Lenin would have stood; the unfinished building was dismantled in 1941 when its materials were needed for defense. "Stalin-Gothic" architecture can be seen in the buildings of Moscow University, constructed after World War II in the hills above the city; its central tower soars to a height of 994 feet. Fittingly, given the size of the country and its once extensive empire, much of the dominant architecture in Moscow conveys the impression of great size.

Following the collapse of the Soviet Union, Moscow reverted to its earlier role as the capital of Russia. With the transition to capitalism came inflation, mounting unemployment, major shortages of food and consumer goods, a decrease in social services, a decay in the city's infrastructure, and the introduction of organized crime. For many Muscovites, the cost of political freedom was at least a temporary decline in their standard of living.

The Soviet Union in Retrospect

History offers no parallel to the breakup of the Soviet empire. Itself the heir of a tsarist state that had gained control of the major part of the Eurasian landmass over half a millennium, it extended in an unbroken territorial

MAP 43.3   THE INDEPENDENT REPUBLICS OF THE FORMER SOVIET UNION

arc from Germany to the Pacific Ocean, and its allies and dependencies had stretched around the globe. For 40 years its rivalry with the United States had structured world politics. With a monolithic bureaucracy, a centrally administered economy, and the world's largest military, it seemed profoundly resistant to change. Yet in only six years, without natural calamity or external conquest, it had ceased to exist. Its demise left a score of new states, most ill-prepared for independence and with no tradition of self-rule, in its wake.

THE AGE OF THE SUPERPOWERS

Détente: 1963–1979

1963	Partial Nuclear Test Ban Treaty
1965–1975	Vietnam War
1968	Soviets crush "Prague Spring" reform movement
1972	SALT I treaty
1975	Helsinki Accords

Containment and Collapse: 1979–1991

1979–1989	Afghan War
1980	Solidarity movement in Poland
1988	Gorbachev announces unilateral withdrawal of 500,000 Soviet troops from eastern Europe by 1991
1989	Communist ruling parties fall in Poland, East Germany, Czechoslovakia, Romania; Berlin Wall dismantled
1990	Rebellions in the Soviet republics; Germany reunited
1991	Dissolution of the Soviet Union

Vaclav Havel on the End of the Modern Era

Vaclav Havel, playwright, former dissident, and former president of Czechoslovakia, comments on the significance of the collapse of communism in the Soviet Union and Eastern Europe.

The end of Communism is, first and foremost, a message to the human race. It is a message we have not yet fully deciphered and comprehended. In its deepest sense, the end of Communism has brought a major era in human history to an end. It has brought an end not just to the 19th and 20th centuries, but to the modern age as a whole.

The modern era has been dominated by the culminating belief, expressed in different forms, that the world—and Being as such—is a wholly knowable system governed by a finite number of universal laws that man can grasp and rationally direct for his own benefit. This era, beginning in the Renaissance and developing from the Enlightenment to socialism, from positivism to scientism, from the Industrial Revolution to the information revolution, was characterized by rapid advances in rational, cognitive thinking.

This, in turn, gave rise to the proud belief that man, as the pinnacle of everything that exists, was capable of objectively describing, explaining and controlling everything that exists, and of possessing the one and only truth about the world. It was an era in which there was a cult of depersonalized objectivity, an era in which objective knowledge was amassed and technologically exploited, an era of belief in automatic progress brokered by the scientific method. It was an era of systems, institutions, mechanisms and statistical averages. It was an era of ideologies, doctrines, interpretations of reality, an era in which the goal was to find a universal theory of the world, and thus a universal key to unlock its prosperity.

Communism was the perverse extreme of this trend. It was an attempt, on the basis of a few propositions masquerading as the only scientific truth, to organize all of life according to a single model, and to subject it to central planning and control regardless of whether or not that was what life wanted.

The fall of Communism can be regarded as a sign that modern thought—based on the premise that the world is objectively knowable, and that the knowledge so obtained can be absolutely generalized—has come to a final crisis. This era has created the first global, or planetary, technical civilization, but it has reached the limit of its potential, the point beyond which the abyss begins. . . .

What is needed is something different, something larger. Man's attitude to the world must be radically changed. We have to abandon the arrogant belief that the world is merely a puzzle to be solved, a machine with instructions for use waiting to be discovered, a body of information to be fed into a computer in the hope that, sooner or later, it will spit out a universal solution. . . .

We must try harder to understand than to explain. The way forward is not in the mere construction of universal systemic solutions, to be applied to reality from the outside; it is also in seeking to get to the heart of reality through personal experience. Such an approach promotes an atmosphere of tolerant solidarity and unity in diversity based on mutual respect, genuine pluralism and parallelism. In a word, human uniqueness, human action and the human spirit must be rehabilitated.

Scholars will long debate the reasons for this stunning denouement, as the world will long live with its consequences. The Soviet system was, in retrospect, the last of the great empires that had characterized the world of the nineteenth and early twentieth centuries. As the Turkish, Austrian, British, and French empires, weakened by war, collapsed in turn under the pressure of nationalist revolts, so ultimately did that of the Soviets. Yet the Soviet Union was also unique as a political entity, being predicated on the idea of a state whose function, as the dictatorship of the proletariat, was the supersession of all states, including itself. The power and privilege of the Communist party was based on this notion of a temporary stewardship and on its historic role as the solvent of class society. When Mikhail Gorbachev admitted that it had failed in this task and permitted the party to be openly criticized as an entrenched elite, he undermined whatever pretense of legitimacy it retained, and when in his last days of rule he formally jettisoned Marxism-Leninism and dissolved the party itself, he left no ideology around which his state could cohere.

SUMMARY

*T*he Cold War had begun to run down in the 1970s, at the same time that serious nuclear disarmament agreements were being explored. Even before the Soviet system had disintegrated, however, the Cold War was virtually over as a result of the policies of Mikhail Gorbachev. The collapse of the Soviet Union also effectively ended the age of the superpowers.

These dramatic events also had severe secondary consequences. The transition to market economies wreaked havoc in eastern Europe, where fledgling democracies struggled, as after World War I, to overcome a legacy of dependence and autocracy. In Romania, the more or less open sale of children from state orphanages provided a source of hard currency, while in Albania, the last European state to renounce communism, prisoners refused their freedom for fear of going unfed. Yugoslavia disintegrated as its constituent republics renounced their union and savage wars among them claimed tens of thousands of lives.

As the twentieth century approached its end, two distinct political trends became apparent. On the one hand,

ethnic particularism seemed triumphant in the former Soviet empire, where a score of new states emerged and the potential for still further secession remained. On the other, the lessons of nonalignment and the European Community furnished models for supranational associations around the globe, suggesting a future of blocs grouped around dominant regional powers. Thus economic integration and political separatism, both growing apace but pulling in different directions, contested the future of the late-twentieth-century world.

SUGGESTIONS FOR FURTHER READING

Ash, T. G. *The Uses of Adversity: Essays on the Fate of Central Europe.* New York: Random House, 1990.

Brown, J. F. *Surge to Freedom: The End of Communist Rule in Eastern Europe.* Durham, N.C.: Duke University Press, 1991.

Daltrop, A. *Politics and the European Community,* 2nd ed. New York: Longman, 1986.

Dawisha, K. *Eastern Europe, Gorbachev and Reform: The Great Challenge.* Cambridge: Cambridge University Press, 1988.

De Porte, A. W. *Europe Between the Superpowers.* New Haven, Conn.: Yale University Press, 1979.

Epstein, W. *The Last Chance: Nuclear Proliferation and Arms Control.* New York: Free Press, 1976.

Freedman, L. *The Evolution of Nuclear Strategy.* New York: St. Martin's Press, 1982.

Kriegel, A. *Eurocommunism.* Stanford, Calif.: Stanford University Press, 1978.

Laqueur, W. *Europe Since Hitler.* London: Weidenfeld & Nicolson, 1972.

Lovenduski, J. *Women and European Politics.* Amherst: University of Massachusetts Press, 1986.

Mazrui, A. A. *Africa's International Relations: The Diplomacy of Dependency and Change.* Boulder, Colo.: Westview Press, 1977.

Milward, A. S. *The Reconstruction of Western Europe, 1945–51.* Berkeley: University of California Press, 1984.

Mowat, R. C. *Creating the European Community.* London: Blandford, 1973.

Pinkus, B. *The Jews of the Soviet Union: A History of a National Minority.* Cambridge: Cambridge University Press, 1988.

Rothschild, J. *Return to Diversity: A Political History of East Central Europe.* New York: Oxford University Press, 1989.

Sheehy, G. *Gorbachev: The Man Who Changed the World.* New York: Harper & Row, 1990.

Van der Wee, H. *Prosperity and Upheaval: The World Economy, 1945–1980.* Berkeley: University of California Press, 1988.

Von Laue, T. *The World Revolution of Westernization: The Twentieth Century in Global Perspective.* New York: Oxford University Press, 1987.

EPILOGUE

Civilization and the Dilemma of Progress

In the modern era the prevailing view of the historical process has been defined by the concept of progress, which sees history as a steady advance toward a better world. A century ago one proponent of progress, the American writer Edward Bellamy (1850–1898), wrote a popular novel that embodied this belief. In *Looking Backward*, Bellamy imagined a man who fell into a hypnotic sleep in 1887 and awoke in the year 2000. The man discovered a perfect world of universal peace and happiness in which all people shared equally in the wealth and benefits of a society freed from conflict, greed, and even the need for laws. Repelled by the social evils of his own day, Bellamy believed that the future had to be better than the past and that it would inevitably lead to an ideal civilization.

History, Time, and Progress

Looking Backward belongs to a long utopian tradition that stretches back to Plato's fourth-century B.C. *Republic*. Bellamy's optimism for the future stemmed from a prejudice against the past, for his vision of progress did not permit him to see the mixture of good and bad that is present in every period of history. Like many others then and now, he assumed that the passage of time automatically brought with it improvement over what had been before. Those who embrace this view generally assume that the closer in time to our own day, the better human

The structure of DNA, the substance that allows for the transfer of hereditary information in genes, was discovered in 1953 by American scientist James Watson and British scientist Francis Crick, shown here with their DNA model. The greatest achievement in biology in the twentieth century has been the development of the field of molecular genetics, although some scientists worry about the wisdom of manipulating human genes.

1166

life has been, that the present is superior to the past because it is now rather than then. Yet in his letter from Birmingham Jail, written in 1963, the American civil rights leader Martin Luther King, Jr., pointedly rejected the "strangely irrational notion that there is something in the very flow of time that will inevitably cure all ills."[1] The notion of progress has often obscured the fact that even at moments of relative peace and prosperity, certain groups without power or status—such as workers, racial minorities, and women—have not shared in the broad advances made by society at large.

Bellamy's understanding of progress reflects a relatively modern, peculiarly Western world view that broke with older Western and non-Western traditions alike. Earlier civilizations had viewed progress chiefly in spiritual or theological terms and tended to see history as cyclical rather than progressive. The ancient Greeks of the Classical Age believed that their ancestors had been more "heroic" and thus better. Confucius, whose ethical philosophy dominated Chinese thought, accepted the notion of social improvement through education and good example, but he also inculcated a respect for the knowledge and wisdom of the past and a measured view of the present and future. The Judeo-Christian and Islamic religions prophesied salvation and the attainment of a heavenly paradise through spiritual rectitude but had no place for a secular conception of progress. The Hindu and Buddhist concept of reincarnation, which stressed "progress" from lower to higher states of being, aspired to the ultimate spiritual state of nirvana that would transcend the material world. Indian conceptions of history were decidedly cyclical; the period since about 900 B.C., in which we still live, the *kali-yuga*, was conceived as one of decline and chaos.

Nineteenth-century Western thinkers were thus a minority in viewing progress in secular terms, based on belief in the material perfectibility of society. In this sense the human adventure is measured in terms of our ability to master the physical environment through scientific and technological advances and to improve the level of material well-being and comfort through the ever-increasing accumulation of wealth. Advocates of this conception of progress claimed that improvement would come through the application of knowledge to political, social, and economic problems. History, according to this view, would unfold as the natural laws that governed the universe were discovered and manipulated in the interest of human improvement. The ethos of liberal capitalism sought to unfetter the laws of economics in order to achieve the greatest material good for the greatest number of people.

Even while this conception gained ascendancy in the West, a variety of reform-minded thinkers recoiled against the effects of industrialism by experimenting with socialist utopias in which private ownership of capital was replaced by communal property in rural egalitarian societies. Some utopian socialists even conceived of a technocratic society in which scientists and industrialists governed on behalf of the general populace. Then, in the mid-nineteenth century, "scientific" socialists explained history as the product of class conflict: categories of human beings—classes—competed for ascendancy by seeking control over the means of production and distribution. The Marxist utopia looked forward to the inevitable triumph of the working class over the capitalists and the ultimate creation of a classless society.

Bellamy's utopia was a combination of these visions. It imagined a highly organized industrial society in which a secular state exercised complete authority and evoked voluntary compliance from its citizens because it provided them with material comfort and well-being. Though repelled by the poverty and exploitation that characterized the expanding industrialization of his time, Bellamy remained a believer in the ability of technology to resolve the ills of modern society.

More than a century after the publication of *Looking Backward*, modern writers have become less sanguine about the benefits of a technological society. In 1932, in the midst of the Great Depression, the British author Aldous Huxley published *Brave New World*, a novel that depicted a totalitarian society in which people lacked no bodily comfort but were without freedom or creativity. In 1949, following World War II, George Orwell portrayed a dehumanized totalitarian society of the future in his book *Nineteen Eighty-four*. The appalling nature of such totalitarian regimes as those of Hitler and Stalin and the specter of the atomic bomb provided the impetus for Orwell's novel and its bleak vision of the future. Orwell's message, in the words of the psychologist Erich Fromm, was intended to awaken us to the common "danger of a society of automatons who will have lost every trace of individuality, of love, of critical thought, and yet who will not be aware of it."[2]

Global Implications of Progress

The materialist theory of progress provided a powerful rationale for the imperialism that conquered much of the non-Western world in the late nineteenth century. Many Europeans believed that they were bringing the benefits of their technologically superior civilization to unfortunate primitive peoples. Western science and industry, on which the theory of progress was based, in turn made possible imperialist domination over much of the rest of the world.

As we have seen, the reaction of the non-Western world to the Western intrusion has been mixed. The Chinese effort to keep all Western influences out of their country was by no means the norm, for the Japanese aggressively adopted Western-style industrialization and technology, both to resist Western domination and to extend their own hegemony over East Asia. Similarly, some southern African states conquered their neighbors with European firearms, and Arab traders used Western weapons to capture Africans for the slave market. In the early twentieth century Turkish and Iranian admirers of Western technology attempted to "modernize" their countries along the Western model, but more recently Islamic fundamentalists, particularly in Iran, have strenuously repudiated Western influences.

The Western idea of progress continues to influence both Western policies toward the nonindustrialized nations and Third World thinking about how to solve the immense social, economic, and cultural problems endemic to their own countries. Since World War II, industrialized nations have systematically exported their notion of progress to underdeveloped states as they emerged from colonial status to independence. In 1961 President John F. Kennedy announced a massive program of economic assistance for Latin America that he called the Alliance for Progress.

As Western developmental strategies for "modernization" replaced imperialism as the basis of the global dynamic, new forms of dependence have been substituted for older forms of subjugation. During the struggle for India's independence from the British, Mahatma Gandhi—who recognized the relationship between imperialism and the materialist notion of progress—rejected the Western model of development by urging his fellow Indians to adopt the traditional spinning wheel as the symbol of freedom and national regeneration.

Despite Gandhi's rejection of modern technology, his successors embraced Western-style industrialization, making India one of the first Third World countries to develop not only conventional electrical energy sources but a nuclear capability as well. Most other underdeveloped nations followed suit, generally adopting an enthusiastic attitude toward technology, with its capacity to enhance health as well as material comforts. Thus agricultural societies often seek to build huge dams, hydroelectric plants, and nuclear energy stations in order to electrify and industrialize their economies, but sometimes at the expense of destroying millions of acres of irreplaceable forests in the process of extracting raw materials and constructing factories. The problem is clearly one of balance; industrialization and conservation need not be mutually antagonistic.

Reliance on Western technology has at times been seriously disruptive to the Third World. The technology of advanced industrial nations and the accompanying infrastructures of such technology are not necessarily ideal or suited for developing countries. Historically, modern technology has been marked by its complex and large-scale character, and its success has depended on extensive national markets, skilled labor, and substantial investment capital. Because developing countries generally lack these resources, simple and inexpensive machinery that does not require extensive education and training may be more appropriate to agrarian societies. Moreover, since 1945 most technological development in the Third World has been undertaken with extensive loans borrowed from Western nations; the resultant economic dependence has crippled the debtor nations, most of which are unable to repay their huge obligations.

In recent years a rethinking of the Western notion of material progress has been unfolding. Not only has the idea of "appropriate technology" gained currency, but it is now increasingly recognized that Third World nations need not necessarily undergo the same stressful stages of development experienced by earlier industrial societies. It is probable, nonetheless, that the rapid transformation of the globe and of its human societies will continue, driven by technological change and its political ramifications.

Science, Technology, and the Environment

As the twentieth century draws to a close, civilization appears to be beset with a host of unparalleled problems. There is irony in the fact that science and technology have made the lives of millions of people more comfortable, yet they have also been the source of unanticipated dilemmas, not the least of which is the ultimate challenge of avoiding nuclear war.

Advances in health care have been startling, especially in the prevention and cure of human diseases. Foremost among them has been the discovery in 1930 of penicillin, which led to the development of numerous other antibiotics to combat bacteria. Equally important was the discovery of microscopic organisms called viruses, which can reproduce inside living cells and cause such diseases as poliomyelitis and measles. These achievements eventually enabled scientists to explain the

The poverty and social despair that plague the Third World are vividly reflected in this photograph of two children rendered homeless by a hurricane that struck Bangladesh in the spring of 1991.

cause of a host of dangerous diseases and to develop vaccines against them.

Yet such medical breakthroughs have resulted in lower mortality rates and longer lives, so that a global population explosion threatens to engulf the poorer societies of the Third World in a relentless cycle of poverty and social despair. Although new agricultural methods have increased food productivity, natural disasters and political upheavals periodically create crises of starvation and malnutrition for millions. Nor has medical science shown itself to hold all the answers to health problems. The human race, for example, is now faced with a medical challenge of immense scope that offers no immediate hope of resolution: AIDS (acquired immune deficiency syndrome). First recognized in 1981, AIDS is a viral disorder, spread through blood or body fluids, that affects the body's disease-fighting mechanisms. Although perhaps as many as 20 million people are currently infected by the AIDS virus

throughout the world, especially in Africa, there is as yet no known cure.

Despite the Western reliance on the vision of unrestricted progress, one of the most serious problems facing the global community is the challenge of improving and protecting the environment. The earth's ecological balance is maintained by a complex series of biological and chemical subsystems, all of which are kept in balance by delicate interaction with one another. The danger lies in the fact that the demands of industrialization and other forms of economic development, which have despoiled much of the globe's forests, rivers, seas, and air, may push environmental destruction beyond the point of salvation.

Factories and automobiles have already polluted the air over large American and European cities with dangerous levels of carbon monoxide, nitrogen oxides, and sulfur dioxide. One result has been that as chemicals fill the air above the planet, the normal composition of the atmosphere has begun to change. Some scientists believe that these chemicals trap infrared rays within the atmosphere, producing the so-called greenhouse effect, whereby the earth's temperatures are increasing. No less critical is the fact that the coastal waters of the Mediterranean are so damaged by chemical pollutants that much of the seafood caught there is now inedible. Industrial plants pour millions of gallons of chemical waste into rivers and oceans, while synthetic products that are not biodegradable—that is, that cannot be broken down by biological processes—accumulate in ever-greater amounts. In this connection, the disposal of nuclear waste from energy production has become an especially critical issue, for such waste products become nonradioactive only after thousands of years. Government and private attempts to bury nuclear waste deep in the deserts of the United States have met with stiff resistance from local inhabitants and environmentalists.

However serious its impact, the pollution of the environment is only one side of the ecological damage wrought by humans. The other is represented by the wasteful destruction of limited natural resources. Serious efforts to conserve fossil fuels, for example, have been resisted by both private industry and government policy. Now that the depletion of finite energy resources looms as a distinct possibility, the harnessing of atomic power as an energy alternative is fraught with other dangers, as dramatized by the 1979 meltdown at the Three Mile Island nuclear power plant in Pennsylvania and the 1986 disaster at the plant in Chernobyl, Ukraine.

In the United States and elsewhere, lumber interests and developers have pressed for ever-greater access to forest lands, and in the state of Washington ancient forests have fallen to the timber saw. More startling, however, has been the deliberate destruction of the rain forests in the Amazon region of South America as well as in Costa Rica, Indonesia, and Malaysia. Every day, millions of acres of these dense tropical forests are destroyed, mainly by burning, as enormous population pressures prompt governments to clear land for agricultural purposes. Yet the tragic irony of this process is that rain forest soil is unsuited to crop production and much of the land is quickly abandoned, although it cannot easily return to its original state. If the destruction continues at the present rate, most of the immense rain forests of the globe will be gone in 20 years.

These and similar problems are international in scope. Industrial fumes from factories in the United States, for example, have caused environmental problems in Canada through acid rain, in which atmospheric pollution is brought back down to earth in rainfall. Similarly, the fallout from Chernobyl reached western European nations. The need to combat all forms of ecological damage grows more pressing every day. Concerted efforts in this direction may yet reverse the harm already done, but the urgency is critical. Today, material "progress" is more than ever a two-edged sword as the human race faces the prospect of self-destruction.

Facing the Future: History as Freedom

Despite advances achieved in the struggle for human rights by racial minorities, women, and other oppressed groups, vast inequities in economic justice and political freedom continue to exist—in Third World countries, in ex-Communist nations, and in the Western world.

These and other issues are compelling and dangerous, but the problems of our age are unique only in the particular forms they now assume. If nothing else, history provides us with perspective: war and conflict, disease and hunger, prejudice and exploitation, torture and state repression are some of the less pleasant features of history that our age has in common with all civilizations of the past. Over the course of 5,000 years, all societies have at times perceived the challenges facing them as insurmountable. Yet history also suggests that even though the problems recur relentlessly, determined people continue to seek durable solutions to them.

Change, often rapid and unpredictable, has been the hallmark of history. Even the most conservative of cultures, as in ancient Egypt or medieval China, underwent sudden and dramatic shifts in social and religious beliefs and political structure. Later generations do, of course, inherit traditions and values from the past, but they sometimes choose to discard them in the light of new circumstances. Those moments when people have overcome adversity represent recurrent evidence of the open-endedness of history. Perhaps the only constraint under which our own age operates is the fact that as the world develops into a truly global community, we increasingly share the same human experience and thus equal responsibility for the world we make.

NOTES

1. M. L. King, Jr., *Why We Can't Wait* (New York: Harper & Row, 1963), p. 89.
2. E. Fromm, "Afterword," in G. Orwell, *Nineteen Eighty-four* (New York: New American Library, 1961), p. 267.

Credits

*Positions of the photographs are indicated in abbreviated form as follows: top **T**, bottom **B**, center **C**, left **L**, right **R**. Unless otherwise acknowledged, all photographs are the property of Scott, Foresman and Company.*

VISUAL EXPERIENCE

Color Insert 1 (following page 64): 1T Eisei-Bunko Foundation; **1B** SuperStock; **2T** Chinese Overseas Archaeological Exhibition Corporation; **2B** Courtesy of the Trustees of the British Museum; **3** Wim Swaan; **4T** SEF/Art Resource, New York; **4B** C. M. Dixon

Color Insert 2 (following page 224): 1T Scala/Art Resource, New York; **1B** Scala/Art Resource, NewYork; **2T** Scala/Art Resource, New York; **2B** Erich Lessing from Art Resource, New York; **3T** Edinburgh University Library; **3B** Edinburgh University Library; **4T** Francis Bartlett Donation of 1912 and Picture Fund. Courtesy, Museum of Fine Arts, Boston; **4B** Arxiu MAS, Barcelona

Color Insert 3 (following page 256): 1T The British Library; **1BR** Lee Boltin; **1BL** Kimbell Art Museum, Fort Worth, TX; **2T** Photograph by Hillel Burger. Peabody Museum, Harvard University; **2B** Library of Congress; **3T** Field Museum of Natural History, Chicago; **3B** Tony Linck; **4L** Photograph by Frank Khoury. Gift of Milton F. and Frieda Rosenthal, National Museum of African Art, Eliot Elisofon Photographic Archives, Smithsonian Institution; **4R** Phoebe Hearst Museum of Anthropology, University of California, Berkeley

Color Insert 4 (following page 416): 1T Art Resource, New York; **1B** Scala/Art Resource, New York; **2T** Scala/Art Resource, New York; **2B** Scala/Art Resource, New York; **3T** Scala/Art Resource, New York; **3B** National Museum, Poznan, Poland; **4R** Erich Lessing from Art Resource, New York

Color Insert 5 (following page 768): 1T The British Library; **1B** Spinks & Sons Ltd., London; **2T** John L. Severance Fund, 79.27b, the Cleveland Museum of Art; **2B** National Palace Museum, Taipei, Taiwan, Republic of China; **3T** The Metropolitan Museum of Art, Fletcher Fund, 1947 (47.18.116); **3B** Fujita Art Museum, Osaka; **4T** Fenollosa-Weld Collection. Courtesy, Museum of Fine Arts, Boston; **4B** Nezu Institute of Fine Arts, Tokyo

Color Insert 6 (following page 832): 1T Giraudon/Art Resource, New York; **1B** Erich Lessing from Art Resource, New York; **2T** Hamburg Kunsthalle; **2BL** Musée Carnavalet, Paris/Collection Viollet; **2BR** Erich Lessing from Art Resource, New York; **3** Bridgeman Art Library/Art Resource, New York; **4T** Cliché des Musées Nationaux, Paris; **4B** By permission of Birmingham Museums and Art Gallery

Color Insert 7 (following page 896): 1T Musée Royale de l'Afrique Centrale, Tervuren/Werner Forman Archive; **1B** Courtesy of the Freer Gallery of Art, Smithsonian Institution, Washington, DC; **1C** Asian Art Museum of San Francisco, the Avery Brundage Collection, Gift of Mr. Richard Gump (# B81 D6a,b,c); **2TL** Rijksmuseum, Amsterdam; **2BL** Van Gogh Museum, Amsterdam/Collection Vincent van Gogh Foundation; **2TR** Rijksmuseum, Amsterdam; **2BR** Van Gogh Museum, Amsterdam/Collection Vincent van Gogh Foundation; **3T** The Granger Collection, New York; **3BR** Courtesy of the Freer Gallery of Art, Smithsonian Institution, Washington, DC; **3BL** Gift of Mrs.

Walter F. Dillingham in Memory of Alice Perry Grew, 1960, Honolulu Academy of Arts (2732.1); **4** The Metropolitan Museum of Art, Bequest of Sam A. Lewisohn, 1951 (51.112.2)

Color Insert 8 (following page 1152): 1T Erich Lessing from Art Resource, New York; **1B** Vincent van Gogh. *The Starry Night.* (1889.) Oil on canvas, $29 \times 36^1/_4$ " (73.7 × 92.1 cm), The Museum of Modern Art, New York. Acquired through the Lillie P. Bliss Bequest. Photograph © 1995 The Museum of Modern Art, New York; **2T** Giraudon/Art Resource, New York; **2B** Pablo Picasso. *Les Demoiselles d'Avignon.* Paris (June–July 1907). Oil on canvas, $8' \times 7' \times 8''$ (243.9 × 233.7 cm), The Museum of Modern Art, New York. Acquired through the Lillie P. Bliss Bequest. Photograph © 1995 The Museum of Modern Art, New York; **3T** George Roos/Art Resource, New York; **3B** Scala/Art Resource, New York; **4T** The Granger Collection, New York; **4B** Salvador Dali. *The Persistence of Memory (Persistance de la Mémoire).* 1931. Oil on canvas, $9^1/_2 \times 13''$ (24.1 × 33 cm). The Museum of Modern Art, New York. Given anonymously. Photograph © 1995 The Museum of Modern Art, New York

TITLE PAGES

Single Volume Edition SuperStock; **Volumes I and A** Brown Brothers; **Volumes II and B** Sonia Halliday Photographs; **Volume C** Robert Frerck/Odyssey Productions

PROLOGUE

1 Peter Kain, © Richard Leakey. From *The Making of Mankind* by Richard E. Leakey, E. P. Dutton, New York, 1981; **6L** From *The Story of Art*, 11th edition, by E. H. Gombrich, Phaidon Press Ltd., London, 1966; **6R** Neg. No. 329853. Courtesy Department of Library Services, American Museum of Natural History; **7L** Conservé au Museé d'Aquitaine, Bordeaux, France, tous droit réservés; **7R** Itar-Tass/Sovfoto; **10** Jane Taylor/Sonia Halliday Photographs; **11** Arxiu MAS, Barcelona; **12** From *The Gods and Goddesses of Old Europe* by Marija Gimbutas, University of California Press, 1974

CHAPTER 1

17 Harvard Museum of Fine Arts, Boston Expedition. Courtesy, Museum of Fine Arts, Boston; **19B** Hirmir Fotoarchiv, Munich; **19T** University of Pennsylvania Museum, Philadelphia; **23** Hirmir Fotoarchiv, Munich; **25** George Holton/Photo Researchers; **26** The Metropolitan Museum of Art, Rogers Fund, 1925 (25.3.182); **28** SuperStock; **31** Alinari/Art Resource, New York; **36** Drawing from *In the Shadow of the Temple* by Meir Ben-Dov, translation by Ina Friedman. Copyright © 1982 by Keter Publishing House Jerusalem Ltd.; English translation © 1985 by Keter Publishing House Jerusalem Ltd. Reprinted by permission of HarperCollins Publishers; **40** Courtesy of the Trustees of the British Museum; **42** Bildarchiv Preussischer Kulturbesitz; **44** Courtesy of The Oriental Institute of the University of Chicago

CHAPTER 2

46 Courtesy Indian Museum, Calcutta; **48** Borromeo/Art Resource, New York; **49** Archeological Museum, Mohenjo-Daro; **51L** Stella Snead/Archaeological Survey of India; **51R** National Museum of India, New Delhi/Art Resouce, New York; **55** Art Resource, New York; **60** Dinodia Picture Agency

CHAPTER 3

68 Ronald Sheridan/Ancient Art & Architecture Collection; 72 Courtesy of the Freer Gallery of Art, Smithsonian Institution, Washington, DC; 73 Courtesy of the Freer Gallery of Art, Smithsonian Institution, Washington, DC; 77 Neg. No. 219658/American Museum of Natural History; 83 Innervision/Overseas Archaeological Corporation; 84 The Granger Collection, New York; 86 Innervision/Sichaun Provincial Museum, China

CHAPTER 4

89 Ronald Sheridan/Ancient Art & Architecture Collection; 91 Hirmir Fotoarchiv, Munich; 92 Hirmir Fotoarchiv, Munich; 95 Scala/Art Resource, New York; 96L Hirmir Fotoarchiv, Munich; 96R Caroline Buckler; 98 *World Book* illustration by Richard Hook, Linden Artists Ltd., from *The World Encyclopedia.* Copyright ©1996, World Book, Inc. By permission of the publisher; 103 Alinari/Art Resource, New York; 104 American School of Classical Studies at Athens; Agora excavations; 106 Alinari/Art Resource, New York; 111 Deutsches Museen, Munich

CHAPTER 5

113 Marburg/Art Resource, New York; 114L UPI/Corbis-Bettmann; 114R Alinari/Art Resource, New York; 115 Ronald Sheridan/Ancient Art & Architecture; 116T Hirmer Fotoarchiv, Munich; 116B Ronald Sheridan/Ancient Art & Architecture; 117 Wim Swaan; 129L Bildarchiv Preussischer Kulturbesitz; 129R Victoria and Albert Museum, Scala/Art Resource, New York; 135 Bildarchiv Preussischer Kulturbesitz

CHAPTER 6

139 Giraudon/Art Resource, New York; 141 Alinari/Art Resource, New York; 145 Rheinischeslandesmuseen, Bonn/e.t. archive; 149 Bildarchiv Preussischer Kulturbesitz; 151 Steve Vidler/Leo de Wys Inc.; 154 Marburg/Art Resource, New York; 156 Alinari/Art Resource, New York; 164 Werner Forman Archive

CHAPTER 7

168 Cameramann International, Inc.; 172 Dinodia/N. G. Sharma from Dinodia Picture Agency; 174 Brown Brothers; 175 Neg. 35933/Field Museum of Natural History, Chicago; 181 Courtesy of the Union of American Hebrew Congregations; 184 Alinari/Art Resource, New York; 188 Alinari/Art Resource, New York; 191 Fitzwilliam Museum, Cambridge

CHAPTER 8

197 Museo Cristiano, Brescia; 198 Scala/Art Resource, New York; 200 Ronald Sheridan/Ancient Art & Architecture Collection; 206 G. E. Kidder Smith, New York; 207 Giraudon/Art Resource, New York; 209 Giraudon/Art Resource, New York; 210 Courtesy of the Freer Gallery of Art, Smithsonian Institution, Washington, DC; 212 Ronald Sheridan/Ancient Art & Architecture Collection; 218R The Granger Collection, New York; 218L The Metropolitan Museum of Art, Rogers Fund, 1913 (13.152.6); 222 University of Pennsylvania Museum, Philadelphia; 223 Fred J. Maroon/Photo Researchers; 225 Palestine Exploration Fund; 226 Ronald Sheridan/Ancient Art & Architecture Collection

CHAPTER 9

227 © 1995, The Detroit Institute of Arts. Founders Society Purchase, Eleanor Clay Ford Fund for African Art; 231 Courtesy Federal Department of Antiquities, Nigeria; 233 Sudan Museum, Khartoum/Werner Forman Archive; 234 Werner Forman Archive; 236 Victor Englebert/Photo Researchers; 241 Photograph by Franko Khoury, National Museum of African Art, Eliot Elisofon Photographic Archives, Smithsonian Institution; 243T C./J. Lenars/Explorer/Photo Researchers; 243B The British Library; 244L Ife Museum, Nigeria; 244R Photograph of Franko Khoury, National Museum of African Art, Eliot Elisofon Photographic Archives, Smithsonian Institution; 245 Photograph by Michael Cavanagh, Kevin Moniague, Indiana University Art Museum, Bloomington; 247 Jason Laure/Woodfin Camp & Associates

CHAPTER 10

249 North America, New Mexico, Cliff Valley Area, Mimbres Culture, Large Standing Figure, wood, stone, cotton, feathers, fiber, black, blue, yellow, red and white earth pigments, carbon black from vegetable source, c. 1150–1400, 63.5 × 17.1 cm, Major Acquisitions Centennial Fund, 1979.17.1 overall: front. Photograph © 1995, the Art Institute of Chicago. All Rights Reserved; 251L Central America, Mexico, Teotihuacán Culture, Mask from incense burner depicting the old deity of fire, ceramic, 450–750 A.D., 36.8 × 33.5 cm, Gift of Joseph Antonow, 1962.1073 overall: front. Photograph by Robert Hashimoto. Photograph © 1995, the Art Institute of Chicago. All Rights Reserved; 251R The Metropolitan Museum of Art, the Michael C. Rockefeller Memorial Collection, Bequest of Nelson A. Rockefeller, 1979; 252 Steve Vidler/Leo de Wys Inc.; 254 Doug Bryant/D. Donne Bryant Stock; 256T The Metropolitan Museum of Art, the Michael C. Rockefeller Memorial Collection, Bequest of Nelson A. Rockefeller, 1979 (1979.206.1063); 256B Photograph by Hillel Burger. Peabody Museum, Harvard University; 257 Werner Forman Archive/Art Resource, New York; 258 Werner Forman Archive/Art Resource, New York; 259L Musée de l'Homme, Paris; 259R Bodleian Library, University of Oxford; 260 Scala/Art Resource, New York; 263 The Metropolitan Museum of Art, Harris Brisbane Dick Fund and Fletcher Fund, 1967 (67.239.1); 265 George Holton/Photo Researchers; 267 Ohio Historical Society; 269 Werner Forman Archive/Art Resource, New York; 270 From the Smithsonian Institution Exhibition *Crossroads of Continents: Cultures of Siberia and Alaska.* From the collections of the Museum of Anthropology and Ethnography in St. Petersburg, FL

CHAPTER 11

273 Dinodia Picture Agency; 274 Roland Michaud/Woodfin Camp & Associates; 283 Dinodia Picture Agency; 284L Jehangir Gazdar/Woodfin Camp & Associates; 284R *Nataraja: Siva as King of Dance.* Bronze, h. 111.5 cm. South India, Chola Period, 11th c. © 1995, the Cleveland Museum of Art. Purchase from the J. H. Wade Fund, 30.331; 289 Wim Swaan; 291 Brian Brake/Photo Researchers

CHAPTER 12

295 The Granger Collection, New York; 300 Tokyo National Museum; 307 Courtesy of the Freer Gallery of Art, Smithsonian Institution, Washington, DC; 310L Werner Forman Archive; 310R Werner Forman Archive; 311 National Museum of Korea, Seoul; 314 Tony Stone Worldwide

CHAPTER 13

320 Mansell Collection; 331 Giraudon/Art Resource, New York; 332 The Walters Art Gallery, Baltimore; 337 Scala/Art Resouce, New York; 341 Bibliothèque Nationale, Paris; 344 Arxiu MAS, Barcelona

CHAPTER 14

348 Otto Müller Verlag; 350 Peter Paul Rubens, Flemish, 1577–1640. *Saint Francis,* oil on panel, c. 1615, 99.0 × 78.8 cm. George F. Harding Collection, 1983.372, the Art Institute of Chicago; 359 Scala/Art Resource, New York; 361 Marburg/Art Resource, New York; 362 Marburg/Art Resource, New York; 363 Marburg/Art Resource, New York; 364L Marburg/Art Resource, New York; 364R Bildarchiv Preussischer Kulturbesitz; 366 Marburg/Art Resource, New York; 372 Musée de l'Homme, Paris; 373 Deutsches Archäologisches